D0582592

Footprint

Andalucía

The travel guide

Handbook

Rowland Mead

with additional contributions by Josephine Hodgson,
Guy Hunter-Watts, Jo Williams and Sarah Thorowgood

Dale limosna mujer,
que no hay en la vida nada
Como la pena de ser ciego y
en Granada.

Give him alms, woman, for there is nothing
in life so cruel as being blind in Granada.

Francisco de Icaza

Andalucía Handbook
Third edition
© Footprint Handbooks Ltd 2002

Published by Footprint Handbooks
6 Riverside Court
Lower Bristol Road
Bath BA2 3DZ. England
T +44 (0)1225 469141
F +44 (0)1225 469461
Email discover@footprintbooks.com
Web www.footprintbooks.com

ISBN 1 900949 83 0
CIP DATA: A catalogue record for this
book is available from the British Library

Distributed in the USA by
Publishers Group West

Credits

Series editors
Patrick Dawson and Rachel Fielding

Editorial
Editor: Jo Williams
Maps: Sarah Sorensen

Production
Typesetting: Mark Thomas and
Davina Rungasamy
Maps: Robert Lunn, Claire Benison
Colour maps: Kevin Feeney
Cover: Camilla Ford

Design
Mytton Williams

Photography
Front cover: Art Directors
& Trip (R Belbin)
Back cover: Impact Photo Library
(Carlo Chinca)
Inside colour section: Carlo Chinca;
gettyone Stone; Impact Photo Library;
Robert Harding Picture Library

Print
Manufactured in Italy by LEGOPRINT

Every effort has been made to ensure
that the facts in this Handbook are
accurate. However, travellers should still
obtain advice from consulates, airlines
etc about current travel and visa
requirements before travelling. The
authors and publishers cannot accept
responsibility for any loss, injury or
inconvenience however caused.

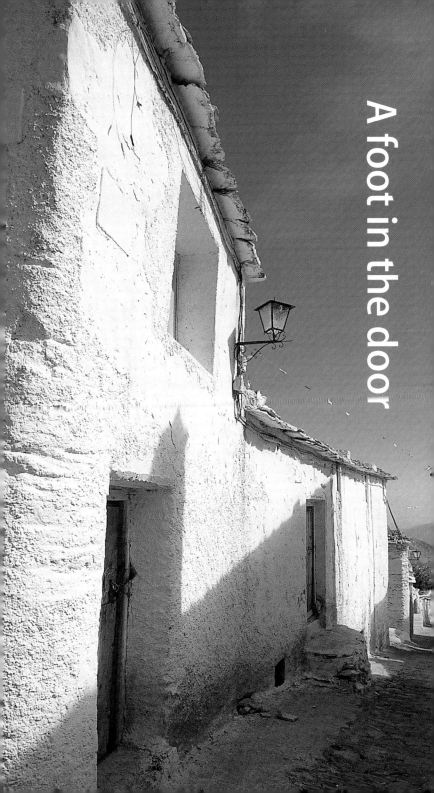

A foot in the door

2

Ftont cover *Alcazaba framed by oranges*
Previous page *A village in the Alpujarras.*
The name comes from alp meaning high
place, and Ujar, the goddess of clear light
Right *The snowy peaks of the*
Sierra Nevada
Below *Best seen in the triangle of land*
between Málaga, Sevilla and Algeciras
– the pueblos blancos of Andalucía

Above *The picador weakening the*
bull before the matador enters the ring –
bullfighting, Spain's national pastime
Right *Another pastime,*
sunbathing on the costa
Next page *Seville's highly*
acclaimed Puente de la Barqueta

Highlights

More than anything else, the word 'Andalucía' conjures up images of colourful flamenco and ghosts of the region's Moorish past. Given this, it is hard to come to terms with the fact that many visitors to this extraordinarily diverse region of Spain never penetrate through the coastal strip of resorts, golf courses and marinas to catch a glimpse of the underlying spirit of the place. As one Europe's sunniest areas, however, the attractions of the coast can be alluring, but it's worth bearing in mind that this is only one of many other highlights of Andalucía.

It would be a mistake to visit Andalucía and not venture inland. The ancient cities of Granada, Sevilla and Córdoba, with their wealth of historic monuments, cannot fail to leave a lasting impression of a splendid Moorish past. The other provincial capitals of Jaén, Cádiz, Málaga, Almería and Huelva also have much to offer in the way of history, as do smaller towns such as Ronda and Antequera, which can be reached within an hour's drive from the coast.

Moor or less

For many visitors, however, the most potent image of the essence of Andalucía is the countryside. The towering mountains of the Sierra Nevada, pine-clad slopes and flower-rich meadows form the backdrop for the *pueblos blancos* – the white villages, which nestle among the hill slopes straddling Cádiz and Málaga provinces. While some are content simply to drive around and soak up the atmosphere of these inland areas, there is also scope for a great deal of outdoor activity, from hill walking and mountain biking to pot holing and rock climbing.

Whiter shade of pale

With the best climate on the mainland of Europe, the Costa is the perfect place for an all-the-year-round beach holiday. Resorts such as Torremolinos, Benalmádena, Fuengirola and Marbella have all the trappings that one would expect and luxury hotels, international restaurants, nightclubs and casinos proliferate. Numerous marinas, such as those at Cabopino, Benalmádena, Estepona and Sotogrande, offer all manner of opportunities for sailing, water skiing, sail boarding and jet skiing. For those who prefer less aquatic, or energetic, sporting activities, the Costa del Sol also has over 30 golf courses and even quite modest hotels have tennis courts and swimming pools.

Coast with the most

Andalucía's impressive variety of land supports an abundance of birds, butterflies, flowers and reptiles, plus some of the continent's rarest mammals, including the Lynx, Genet and Mongoose. Over 350 species of birds are recorded annually and the Straits of Gibraltar form a major migration route for raptors during the spring and autumn. Fortunately the Andalucíans have a much more enlightened attitude towards wildlife now – the bad old days of bird liming and indiscriminate shooting have largely gone – and Andalucía is rapidly becoming one of the prime eco-tourist destinations in Europe.

Close encounters of the bird kind

It was in the Andalucían town of Ronda that the rules of modern bullfighting were drawn up. Every year Ronda holds its magnificent *goyesca*, in what is claimed to be the oldest bullring in Spain, where matadors strut their stuff in costumes inspired by Goya's 18th-century engravings. But there are bullfights in every town worth its salt during the bullfighting season from April to October. More a set piece drama than a sport, bullfighting is an event that no visitor can feel neutral about, yet it is the essence of this hot, harsh area of southern Spain.

Toro, toro, toro

It is thought that this flamboyant music and dance was brought to the area by gypsies or *gitanos* in the 15th century. Accompanied by guitarists, the dancers use foot stamping and finger cymbals to create percussion. The singing follows two basic styles and is generally speaking either in the form of an evocative lament, or *jondo*, expressing centuries of gypsy suffering, or it is playful and lighthearted in the case of the *chico*. Either way, to experience a *tablao* or Flamenco show is to begin to get near the very heart of Andalucían existence.

Strictly flamenco

Frederico Garcia Lorca once described flamenco as one of the most gigantic inventions of the Spanish people and certainly there is nothing that evokes the spirit of Andalucía more. Throughout the summer months there are countless flamenco festivals in towns and cities all over Andalucía, ranging from the full-on tourist spectacle at the Sacromonte caves in Granada to the more intimate flamenco circles or *peñas* of the *pueblos blancos*.

Late plate

The Spanish are famous for eating at what to some, in this age of weight-consciousness, seems like a ludicrously late hour. Who in most countries would think of sitting down to a full meal at ten o'clock in the evening, as a matter of course? Indeed, it is often difficult to book a meal in a restaurant in Andalucía before this time. This late night carousing is all to do with the Andalucíans' siesta-adjusted body clock - most people do not finish work until half past seven or eight o'clock. Fortunately, for starving North Europeans, whose stomachs are not adjusted to eating this late, there is a godsend in the form of tapas. This is a much more civilized alternative to the crisps that the British are used to having to put up with in pubs – drinking without eating is virtually unheard of in Spain.

A tapas treat

Tapas come in all sorts of delicious forms and are readily available in most bars across the region. When you order a drink at any time of day, you will usually be offered a small bowl of complimentary olives or nibbles to go with it, but for a little more than a couple of euros per dish, you can pick your own selection of tapas. Depending upon the region, these dishes vary in style and content. *Calamares*, or squid, deep fried in rings are very popular as is *chorizo*, a spicy, cured sausage. For the more adventurous, there are the delights of *callos*, or tripe, to be tried, and for those unfortunate vegetarians that find themselves in Spain, there are several animal friendly tapas such as aubergine and bean salads or delicious olives marinaded in chillis and olive oil.

Eat, drink & be sherry

The drink of British grandmothers enjoys a far more upbeat image in Spain. Go in to any bar in Andalucía and you will come across people of all ages washing down their tapas with a glass of fino sherry. Whilst this fortified wine could hardly be considered the height of chic in most other countries (despite the fact that 70% of exported sherry goes to Britain), it still enjoys a loyal and strong following in Andalucía. True sherry is produced within a triangle formed by the towns of Jerez de la Frontera, El Puerto de Santa María and Sanlúcar de Barrameda, covering some 20,000 hectares of agricultural land and any fortified wine not produced within this region cannot officially be termed sherry.

The essential factor that gives sherry its inimitable flavour is the combination of the chalky *albariza* soil and the *palomino* grape variety which is ideally suited to it. The soil soaks up water during the winter and then releases it slowly during the long, hot summer to replenish the vines. Visit a bodega and witness the process while sampling some of this top tipple.

Left Grape baskets at harvest time
Below Ronda, a town set in the hills, in the province of Málaga

Above The Alhambra in Granada
Right A few of the 27 million joints of ham consumed in Spain each year
Next page The Mezquita in Córdoba – building began in 785 with the intention of creating Islam's most grandiose mosque

Blast into the past

Ever since Neanderthal Man lived in a cave in Gibraltar, Andalucía has been subjected to wave after wave of invaders, including some of the most warlike people in the Mediterranean and beyond. Yet the response has always been the same – not to fight back, but to conquer the invaders by beguiling and assimilating them with Andalucía's special brand of atmosphere (a process which continues today as foreigners from many parts of the world relocate to the Costa del Sol).

Remains of the day

Successive groups of Iberians, Phoenicians, Carthaginians, Romans and Visigoths made their mark on the area, before the long occupation of the Moors, which ended with the Christian Reconquest by Los Reyes Católicos, Ferdinand and Isabel. The result is that Andalucía is rich in history, archaeology and architecture. From the pre-historic times, there are burial chambers or dolmens at Antequera. The Romans left the huge amphitheatre at Italica on the outskirts of Sevilla and the settlement at Baelo Claudia near Tarifa, which includes the remains of a factory. The Moors left remnants of baths and irrigation systems, while old minarets are often incorporated into modern day church towers.

Undoubtedly the most cherished Moorish remains, however, are the mosque or *Mesquita* in Córdoba and the incomparable Alhambra in Granada. They should head the list of sights to see for any visitor to Andalucía.

The Mesquita

Abd ar Rahman I laid the first stones of the Mesquita, or Great Mosque of Córdoba, in 756 and it was then enlarged by four of his successors. Its size is breathtaking, it has nearly 3,000 arches and pillars at two levels, plus some beautifully preserved stonework and mosaics. After the Reconquest, the building was 'christianised' by constructing a Renaissance cathedral within the interior of the mosque. A quite stunning piece of vandalism, but at least the mosque survives.

The Alhambra

The Alhambra is the name given to a group of buildings on a hill overlooking Granada. They consist of the Royal Palace, the Alcazaba or fortress and the Palace gardens known as the Generalife. The Royal Palace represents the finest example of Moorish architecture in Europe and has some extraordinary patios and carved plaster work. Also a victim of vandalism, this time at the hands Napoleon's forces during the Peninsula War, the Alhambra's restoration was given impetus by the American writer Washington Irving, who wrote *Tales of the Alhambra* in one of the empty rooms of the Royal Palace.

Cathedrals & churches

Andalucía's cathedrals are predominantly Gothic in style, but for some superb examples of Renaissance architecture, head northeast to Jaén province. Many of the churches in this area are impressive monuments to the genius of Andrés de Vandelvira. For Baroque architecture, head for the small hill town of Priego de Córdoba, where there is a collection of remarkable churches, built on the proceeds of the lucrative 18th-century silk industry.

Next page *Life on a finca*

A life less ordinary

Holiday of a lifetime It is said that Andalucíans have more holidays than anyone else in Europe. Certainly, scarcely a day goes by without a fiesta happening somewhere in the region and travellers often find themselves caught up in the festivities. If a fiesta is on a Thursday or a Tuesday, an extra day is taken to make a *puente* or bridge, resulting in a very long weekend. Andalucíans know how to enjoy themselves and holidays are often a riot of singing, dancing and drinking, regardless of whether the fiesta has religious, pagan, secular or historic origins. Many festivals were banned during Franco's time because he regarded them as subversive, but they have been taken up again with admirable tenacity and enthusiasm!

Ecclesiastical excess Undoubtedly the most impressive religious festivals are the *Semana Santa* (Easter Week) processions. Religious images are placed on floats and carried by brotherhoods through the streets, proceeded by hooded penitents and accompanied by the sinister beat of drums and the blare of brass bands. At intervals a *saeta* – a sort of emotional flamenco lament – is sung from balconies.

    Romerías are pilgrimages to small chapels or shrines, often headed by decorated ox carts. The most impressive, an explosive mixture of the devout, the violent and the bucolic, because of the sheer numbers of participants, is that in El Rocío, to the Shrine of La Paloma Blanca, the White Dove of the Marshes. Rivalling El Rocío as a spectacle is the gypsy romería at Cabra in Córdoba province to the Sanctuary of *La Virgen de la Sierra*. When the flamenco mass is being performed, it is often difficult to distinguish the religious from the pagan. Another impressive religious festival takes place in coastal towns in July, when local fishermen pay homage to their saint, the Virgen del Carmen, with a procession which ends with her being taken out on the sea.

Lost in time The background of other fiestas may be lost in the history of time. In Baza, in Granada province, the annual fair begins with the arrival of *El Cascomorras*, a man 'chosen' by the neighbouring town of Guadix to try to recover a disputed virgin. He always fails, getting covered in black paint for his pains, but later Baza relents and he is given a special place in the main processions. Mock battles between Moors and Christians take place all over Andalucía, as do *encierros* or bull runs, when youths try to prove their manhood by running through the streets in front of the bulls.

Vanity fair Many towns have *ferias* which began as markets or horse fairs, but now they are week-long festivities with flamenco, bullfighting, singing and dancing. Larger towns have their own showgrounds, with permanent brick buildings for private clubs. It is necessary to have *enchufes*, or 'connections', to gain admittance to the clubs and not to do so will mean certain loss of face. The Sevilla *feria*, which comes soon after Holy Week, is famous as a time when the great and good of the city display themselves in their finery on horseback or in carriages.

Livin' la vida loca The most exuberant fiesta in Andalucía is without doubt the February *Carnaval* in Cádiz. This mother of all Andalucían parties is said to rival that in Río de Janeiro, Brazil, as a spectacle and few people come away from it with the same perspective of life, or the same liver. Extravagantly dressed groups are judged for their originality, wit, political satire and general outrageousness, as well as for their musical ability.

    As with so much in Andalucía, often the religious, the pagan and the political mix without apparent reason in celebrations. Above all, it is an opportunity to let off steam and have a good time – something at which the Andalucían is a past master.

Left Old traditions die
hard, a cart for fiesta
Below Pilgrims follow
the piper and his drum

Above Dancing, singing and little sleep aren't
the preserve of the young in southern Spain
Left Holy processions in Semana Santa,
Easter Week
Next page Sunset from one
of Andalucía's many churches

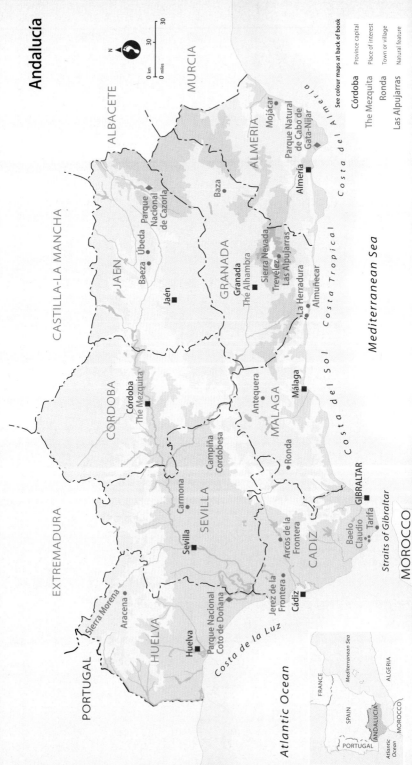

Andalucía

See colour maps at back of book

Córdoba Province capital
The Mezquita Place of interest
Ronda Town or village
Las Alpujarras Natural feature

PORTUGAL

EXTREMADURA

CASTILLA-LA MANCHA

ALBACETE

MURCIA

Sierra Morena
Aracena

HUELVA

Parque Nacional
Coto de Doñana

Huelva

Costa de la Luz

Sevilla

SEVILLA

Carmona

Campiña
Cordobesa

CÓRDOBA

Córdoba
The Mezquita

JAÉN

Jaén

Baeza Úbeda

Parque
Nacional
de Cazorla

GRANADA

Antequera

Ronda

MÁLAGA

Málaga

Jerez de la
Frontera

Arcos de la
Frontera

Cádiz

CÁDIZ

Baelo
Claudio

Tarifa

GIBRALTAR

Gibraltar

Straits of Gibraltar

Costa del Sol

Granada
The Alhambra

Sierra Nevada
Trevélez
Las Alpujarras

La Herradura
Almuñécar

Costa Tropical

Baza

ALMERÍA

Almería

Parque Natural
de Cabo de
Gata-Níjar

Mojácar

Costa del Almería

Mediterranean Sea

Atlantic Ocean

MOROCCO

N

0 km   30
0 miles   30

FRANCE

SPAIN

Mediterranean Sea

PORTUGAL

ANDALUCÍA

Atlantic
Ocean

MOROCCO   ALGERIA

Contents

Essentials

2

Essentials

Planning your trip

Where to go

Andalucía is relatively small and with your own transport, you can feasibly dip into each area within several weeks. However, this would be something of a whistle-stop tour and wouldn't allow you to soak up the distinctive atmosphere of each area. Also, if you're relying on public transport, you will have allow extra time to visit any out-of-the-way places, which have less frequent services. The airport you fly into can affect the travelling time you have. If you want to concentrate on Sevilla, Granada and Córdoba, you could fly directly into Sevilla. If you want to see western Andalucía, you can fly into Sevilla or Jerez de la Frontera, or Almería for eastern Andalucía. Gibraltar is handy for the south and coastal resorts like Tarifa. The following suggested itineraries use Málaga, since this is the airport used by the majority of travellers.

Two weeks Within this time, you could visit the main three cities: Sevilla, Granada and Córdoba, allowing at least two or three days in each and taking in a few short trips outside one or more cities to the mountains and beach. From Málaga, you can get to Sevilla in a few hours. Visit the nearby Sierra de Aracena for a bit of bucolic peace. After a detour north to Córdoba to see the renowned Moorish mezquita, go to Grananda for a few more days of Moorishness before heading southeast to Trevélez in the Alpujarras. As the highest village in Spain, it's a good place to trek to the peaks of the Sierra Nevada. To complete your round trip, go south to the coast and Málaga, leaving enough time for a paddle in the sea in Almuñeca or a quick jetski in nearby La Herradura.

Three & four weeks This time is long enough to allow a little variation on the Sevilla, Granada and Córdoba theme; you could choose one or more of these cities and then explore the hinterland around. From Granada you can easily visit eastern Andalucía, from the snowcapped mountains of the Sierra Nevada to the lunar landscapes and beaches of Almería. From Málaga to Granada, stop at Alhama de Granada and baptise yourself in the spa town's thermal baths. If you're in Granada in winter, go snowboarding or skiing in the Sierra Nevada or hike either here or in the neighbouring Alpujarras. Between Granada and Almería is the spa town of Los Millares, where you can dip into the local thermal baths or visit the impressive Copper Age archaeological site. Then you could explore the windswept and deserted Cabo de Gata coastline, a good spot for birdwatching or scubadiving. Inland is the desert and so-called Mini Hollywood, the location of spaghetti westerns.

With an extra week, from Granada you could slot in a visit northeast to Jaén, taking in the Renaissance architectural splendours of the hilltop towns Baeza and Úbeda. If you've got time, don't miss the Parque Natural de Cazorla, Spain's largest, which has outstanding wildlife. From here, to avoid going back on yourself, you could head south to the Moorish town of Baza and then down to Almería.

For western Andalucía, skip the Costa del Sol resorts of Torremolinos to Estepona and head straight for Tarifa, with a possible quick detour to Gibraltar. In Tarifa, you can windsurf or, if you're there in April or September, watch the famous bird migration. Afterwards, go along the coast towards Cádiz where you can pick your spot from a number of tiny fishing villages and beach resorts. Also along here are the Roman remains at the Baelo Claudio archaeological site. Make sure you visit Cádiz cathedral; another must is the sampling of the city's famed fish. Sherry tasting is available in nearby Jerez and you can also catch an 'equestrian ballet' here at the renowned equestrian school. After a sample of sights and nightlife in Sevilla, go to the Costa de la Luz in Huelva, for a bit of Colombus history or relaxing on the beach. With an extra week,

Essentials

you'll probably have time for some birdwatching in the Parque Nacional Coto de Doñana, one of Europe's most important wetland areas, or a visit to the Río Tinto mines north of Huelva, or a leisurely hike in the Sierra de Aracena.

Alternatively, after Sevilla you could head northeast up to Córdoba through the gently rolling landscape of La Campiña, stopping off at the historic town of Carmona, with its Moorish monuments and a Roman archaeological site. South to the coast is the Campiña Cordobesa, where you can go on winetasting tours in the many vineyards, particularly in Montilla.

When heading back to Málaga from either of these detours from Sevilla, leave enough time to take in some of the so-called white towns, including Arcos de la Frontera and Ronda.

When to go

You'll find the cheapest flights out of season – any time apart from the summer months (especially July and August), Easter and Christmas

Andalucía has one of the most agreeable climates on mainland Europe. Winters are mild with some rain, but plenty of sunshine. Coastal temperatures in January average 15-17°C, but it is colder inland, particularly in the mountains, where snow lies on the Sierra Nevada for much of the year. Summers are hot, especially inland, but the coasts have the benefit of sea breezes, particularly in the area from Gibraltar to Cádiz, where the strong *levante* can last for days on end, to the joy of windsurfers. Midday temperatures in July are usually 25-30°C and many areas receive no rain at all from May to October, although thunderstorms are always a possibility in late summer. The height of summer, however, is not the best time to explore the interior of Andalucía, as the heat in places like Sevilla can be searing, with temperatures topping 40°C. Almería rarely gets more than one or two days rain a year and the countryside around is classed as semi-desert. July and August, as well as being the hottest months, are also the most crowded.

Tours and tour operators

All the major travel and tour companies arrange package tours to Andalucía, generally located at resorts on the Costa del Sol. Although the hotels are often noisy and crowded, you can find exceptional bargains and they can make a good base for exploring the interior of Andalucía.

IB Tours, Level 1, 47 New Canterbury Rd, Petersham, Sydney, T612-9560 6722, **Australia** www.ib-tours.com.au Variety of city tours. *Spanish Tourism Promotions*, Level 1, 178 Collins St, Melbourne, T03-9750 7377. Four-day Andalucían tours.

Abercrombie and Kent, 1520 Kensington Rd, Oak Brook, IL 60521, T1-800-323 7308, **North America** www.abercrombiekent.com Packages include walking holidays. *Discover Spain Vaca-* **& Canada** *tions*, 120 Sylvan Ave, Englewood Cliffs, NJ 07632, T1-800-227 5858. Programme includes parador tours. *Heritage Tours*, 121 West 27th Street, Suite 1201, New York City, T1-800-3784555, www.heritagetoursONLINE.com Custom designed in-depth itineraries. *MI Travel*, T1-800-8482314, www.mitravel-melia.com For historic city tours and parador accommodation. *Sarah Tours*, 1803 Bellview Blvd, No A-1, Alexandria, VA22307, T1-800-2670036, www.sarahtours.com City tours, study trips, activity breaks, culinary courses, etc. *Sun Holidays*, 1650 Avenue Rd, Toronto, ON M5M 3Yl, T1-800-3870571, www.sunholidays.ca Programme includes parador tours and city packages.

Walking and trekking *Andalucía Tours*, T958-610261. Horse trekking around **Spain** Granada. *Benamorda*, F952-152336. Rambling, horse riding, mountain biking, nature tours. Based in Málaga. *Burro-Adventure*, Camping de Pitres, Granada, T958-766112. Donkey treks in the Alpujarras. *Finca El Moro*, Fuenteheridos 21292, Huelva,

T/F959-501079, www.fincaelmoro.com Highly recommended walking and riding holidays in the Sierra de Aracena with accommodation and food provided on the farm Finca El Moro. *Rustic Blue*, Barrio La Ermita, 18412 Bubión, Granada, T958-763381, F958-763134, www.rusticblue.com Walking in the Sierra Nevada and Alpujarras, also arranges a range of accommodation throughout Andalucía. *Taste of Spain*, T952-886590. Specialized tours of Andalucía by jeep, horse or on foot. Based in Málaga.

UK & Ireland *Andalucian Adventures*, Washpool, Horsley, Gloucester, GL6 0PP, T01453-832583, T01453-834137, F01453-835984, info@andalucian-adventures.co.uk *Exodus*, 9 Weir Rd, London, SW12 0LT, www.exodus.co.uk, T0208-7723822. Well-established world wide tour operator. You can find other accommodation with *Magic of Spain*, 227 Shepherd's Bush Rd, London, W6 7AS, T020-82415135, www.magicofspain .co.uk Unusual and quality accommodation. *Mundi Color*, 276 Vauxhall Bridge Rd, London SW1, T020-7828 6021, www.mundicolor.co.uk. Wide range offered, including paradores, villas and cottages. *Travellers Way*, Hewell Way, Tradebigge, Bromsgrove, Worcs, B60 1LP, T01527-836791, www.travellersway .co.uk For self-catering accommodation on the coast, the Alpujarras and Sevilla. *USIT*, 19-21 Aston Quay, Dublin, T01-6021600, www.usit.ie Student discounts and cards.

City breaks *Time Off*, 1 Elmfield Park, Bromley, Kent, BR1 1LUT, T0845-7336622. For holidays in Granada, Córdoba and Sevilla.

Cooking *Pata Negra*, 29 Parsons Green, London SW6 4UH, T020-7736 1959, F7736 1925, www.patanegra.net Spanish cooking holidays at three venues in Andalucía, including guided tours to sherry and vineyards, organic farms and food markets.

Drawing and painting *Andalucían Adventures*, Washpool, Horsley, Gloucester GL6 0PP, T/F01453-834137, www.andalucian-adventures.co.uk Small group walking and painting holidays in the Alpujarras, the Parque Natural Subbética in Córdoba and the Sierra de Aracena, Huelva. *Spain at Heart*, Watley Farm, Watley, Frome, Somerset, BA11 3LA, T01373-814222, www.spainatheart.co.uk Drawing and painting holidays in the Axarquia region.

Historical tours *Ace Study Tours (UK)*, Babraham, Cambridge, CB2 4AP, T01223-835055, F837394, www.acestudytours.com

Horse riding, walking and mountain biking *Adventura*, T01784-459018. Mule trekking and horse riding in the Sierra Nevada. *Discover Adventure*, 5 Netherhampton Cottages, Netherhampton Rd, Salisbury, Wiltshire, SP2 8PX, T01722-741123, www.discoveradventure.com Mountain bike and walking tours in the Sierra Nevada, Las Alpujarras and Sierra de Cazorla. *Explore Worldwide (UK)*, 1 Frederick St, Aldershot, Hants, GU11 1LQ, T01252-760100, www.exploreworldwide.com Walking in the Sierra Nevada and the Ronda area. *Spanish Steps*, 60 Great Brington, Northamptonshire, NN7 4JB, T01604-770012, www.spanish-steps.com Walking holidays based around Compéta including hikes around Ronda and the white villages.

Naturist *Peng*, T01402-471832. Naturist holidays based at Costa Natura, near Estepona.

Wine tours *Blackheath Wine Trails*, 13 Blackheath Village, London SE3 9LA. Bodega tours based at Jerez de la Frontera. *Wine Trails*, Greenways, Vann Lake, Ockley, Dorking, T01306-712111.

Birdwatching All of the following run birdwatching holidays in southwest Andalucía. *Bird Watching Breaks*, 9 Little Britain, Dorchester, DT1 1NN, T01305-267994. *Gullivers*, Oak Farm, Stoke Hammond, Milton Keynes, MK17 9DB, T01525-270100. RSPB leaders used. *Ornitholidays*, 1/3 Victoria Drive, Bognor Regis, Sussex, PO21 2PW, T01243-821240, F829574.

Finding out more

The Spanish National Tourist office produces a mass of information which you can obtain before you leave from one of their offices abroad. **Australia**, 203 Castlereagh St, Suite 21, Sydney, NSW 2000, T02-2647966. **Canada**, 102 Bloor St West, Suite 3402, Toronto, Ontario, M4W 3E2, T416-9613131, www.tourspain.toronto.n.ca **UK**, 22-23 Manchester Square, London, W1M 5AP, T020-7486 8077, www.tourspain.co.uk **US**, 666 Fifth avenue, 35th floor, New York, NY 10103, T212-2658822, oetny@tourspain.es; 8383 Wilshire Blvd, Suite 956, Beverley Hills, CA 90211, T323-6587188, losangeles@tourspain.es; 845 North Michigan Ave, Suite 915-E, Chicago, IL 60611, T312-6421992, chicago@tourspain.es

Useful websites

www.okspain.org Spanish tourist office site aimed at the US packed with practical information with an extensive list of useful web links.

www.tourspain.es Another useful Spanish tourist office website.

www.cma.junta-andalucia.es/parques/ Andalucían government site with details of protected areas, including facilities and maps.

www.aena.es Details of Spain's airports including facilities available.

All sites listed here have an English version unless indicated

www.cetursa.es and **www.sierranevadaski.com** Two sites covering the Sierra Nevada ski resort, including ski run details, summer activities, accommodation and transport.

www.inturjoven.com Details of youth hostel locations, facilities and prices in Andalucía.

www.raar.es Site of Andalucían rural accommdation network with details of mainly self-catering accommodation to rent, including cottages and farmhouses.

www.parador.es Parador information, including, locations, prices and photos.

www.dgt.es Useful motoring tips, with up-to-date traffic news, as well as suggested itineraries, when to travel and toll roads.

www.renfe.es Site of RENFE, Spain's national rail company, with timetables, types of ticket available and fares.

www.spainnet.co.uk.com and **www.typicallyspanish.com** Useful search engines on all things Spanish.

www.red2000.com/spain/index.html All About Spain website with loads on cities, provinces and a database of accommodation and tour operators. English.

www.andalucia.org The official site of the Andalucían government, with information on even the smallest villages, accommodation and tourist office locations.

www.andalucia.com Excellent site for a whole range of both practical and background facts and features.

www.spaindata.com Interesting selection of Spain-related subjects, from online versions of the Spanish constitution and Don Quijote (only available in Spanish), to a Costa de Sol property index and links with online newspapers.

www.cyberspain.com Good background on culture and fiestas.

www.plazamayor.net Specific information on individual provinces.

www.elpais.es Online version of the daily newspaper *El País*.

www.surinenglish.com News articles from the weekly English edition of the Málaga newspaper.

www.expedia.com For online maps and itineraries.

www.inm.es Site of the national metereological institute, with the day's weather and next-day forecasts. In Spanish only, but relatively easy to find information.

Language

In Andalucía Spanish is the main language spoken, with some English used on the Costa del Sol and in other areas popular with tourists like Córdoba, Granada and Sevilla. Elsewhere English may be spoken very little or not at all and so you'll have to be prepared to at least attempt some communication in Spanish, particularly in shops, bars and restaurants. Language schools are listed in the directories of towns and cities throughout the book.

See page 431 for lists of useful words and phrases

Essentials

Disabled travellers

It has to be said that Spain in general and Andalucía in particular are not noted for the excellence of their provision for travellers with disabilities. Things are improving however, and most areas will have at least one hotel that is wheelchair friendly. All new hotels and public buildings are now required by law to be fully accessible. Facilities on public transport remain generally poor. The best advice is to check with tour operators and the specialist agencies for the disabled before booking a holiday.

Some travel companies are beginning to specialize in exciting holidays, tailor-made for individuals depending on their level of disability. For those with access to the

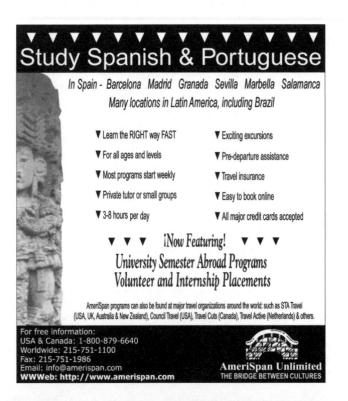

internet, a Global Access – Disabled Travel Network Site is www.geocities .com/ Paris/1502 It is dedicated to providing information for 'disabled adventurers' and includes a number of reviews and tips from members of the public. You might want to read *Nothing Ventured* edited by Alison Walsh (Harper Collins), which gives personal accounts of worldwide journeys by disabled travellers, plus advice and listings.

Gay and lesbian travellers

The main urban centres and resorts of Andalucía have a fairly relaxed attitude towards gays and gay life. Cádiz and Torremolinos have sizeable gay communities, with a lively club and beach scene. Attitudes towards gays in the more rural parts of Andalucía can be less tolerant. Useful websites include: http://aleph.pangea.org/org/cgl/ with information on Spanish gay and lesbian campaigns (in English).

Student travellers

Students can get discounted flights to Spain through *Usit Campus* 52 Grosvenor Gardens, London SW1, T0870-2401010, www.usitcampus.co.uk with 49 branches in the UK including many university campuses and YHA shops. Andalucía has a network of Youth Hostels, 19 of which stay open throughout the year (see page 39), but many of the hostels are in out of town locations. It is often cheaper and more convenient to find a city centre *pensión*.If travelling around Andalucía by rail, there are a number of passes students can use, such as the Eurail Youthpass, allowing a bargain 15 days or three month's second class travel. Hitchiking is not recommended in Andalucía, but as the buses and coaches are so cheap, travel need not be a major expense. Don't expect any concessions on the buses, however. Museums, cathedrals and theme parks, on the other hand, nearly always offer concessions to students, particularly those from EU countries.

Travelling with children

Spanish people of all ages are very receptive to babies and children and you'll find that bars, hotels and restaurants are often more child-friendly than those in your own country. Spanish parents often take their babies and children out with them in the evenings to bars and restaurants, which if your children can stay up late, solves the potential babysitting problem. Many parents also take their children to the *paseo*, or square, in the evenings, which could be a good place for your children to make some friends. It's not unusual to see babies and children with their parents at fiestas until well past midnight, although unless you're lucky enough to persuade your children to siesta at length, they may not have the same stamina. Nevertheless, with so many children out in the evening as well, your children may able to keep up.

In terms of basic necessities, nappies, baby wipes, ready-made baby food and formula milk are all widely available. Facilities like baby changing rooms or changing tables in toilets are virtually non-existent in Andalucía. If you're breastfeeding, don't be put off by the fact that you'll rarely see a Spanish mother breastfeeding (although this is common practice until the babies are around six months' old); as long as you're reasonably discreet you won't encounter any negative responses.

Take extra care with the sun, especially during the summer months. Use a high-factor sun protector cream, make sure your children wear sunhats, keep them out of the sun altogether during the hottest time of day and give them lots of fluids to drink. Bear in mind that Andalucía can get unbearably hot in the summer for some children, and babies especially, particularly in certain hotspots like Seville. Try and stay in accommodation with air conditioning, or better still, avoid the hotter parts altogether in July and August.

Spanish embassies and consulates abroad

Australia 15 Arkana St, Yarralumba, ACT 2600, Canberra T02-62733555.
Canada 74 Stanley Av, Ottawa, Ontario, K1M 1P4, T613-7472252.
Ireland 17A Merlyn Park, Ballsbridge, Dublin 4, T01-2691640.

UK, 39 Chesham Pl, London, SW1X 8SB, T020-72355555.
USA 2375 Pennysylvania Ave, Washington DC 20037, T202-452 0100; 150 E 58th St, New York, NY 10155, T212-3554080.

Essentials

Children under four get free rail travel on RENFE, as well as free or discount entry to museums and other sights. For comprehensive tips on travelling with babies and children, see the useful site www.babygoes2.com

Women travellers

Although the age of machismo is far from dead in Andalucía, the area is generally a safe place for women to travel. Women are unlikely to suffer any harassment.

Working in Andalucía

As Andalucía has the highest unemployment rate in Spain, the chances of getting official long term work is both remote and shrouded in red tape and bureaucracy. If you have a TEFL (Teaching English as a Foreign Language) certificate there may be possibilities at language schools or by giving private lessons. Short-term seasonal work is often available in bars and restaurants, but for EU nationals a temporary residence permit (permiso de residencia) is officially required after three months, see below. Wages will be a pittance. The backpackers standby of fruit picking is non-existent for foreigners in Andalucía.

Before you travel

Getting in

British citizens need a valid passport. Other EU citizens need only their national identity cards, providing their stay is no longer than 90 days. US citizens need a passport and can stay for up to six months, but the 90-day rule applies for citizens of Canada and New Zealand. Australians do not need a visa for stays up to 30 days. Visitors wishing to stay for longer periods should officially apply for a temporary residence permit (permiso de residencia), valid for up to one year, although this is widely ignored. Nationalities not mentioned above should consult their nearest Spanish embassy or consulate, as should any visitor wishing to stay for a longer period of time.

Visas & immigration
See box for Spanish embassies and consulates abroad. For embassies in Andalucía see individual town and city directories

Duty free goods and Allowances Duty free allowances throughout the EU were abolished in 1999. There are restriction on entry for non-EU travellers, but in practice customs controls are very slack in the tourist areas You are most likely to encounter difficulties when crossing from Gibraltar back into Spain, when clearance can be very slow on some days. It is also important to bring with you receipts for any valuables you are bringing into the country to avoid any problems when you leave or return to your own country.

Duty free

When leaving Spain, remember that there are no restrictions for EU citizens on the amount of wine, spirits and tobacco that can be taken home, and all of these goods can be bought cheaply at supermarkets and tobacconists.

Health
insurance &
vaccinations
See also page 59

Spain has reciprocal health arrangements with other EU member countries, so British visitors are entitled to emergency care from the Spanish health service, providing that they can show form E111, which you can get from main post offices. If you want more comprehensive cover for every medical eventuality, as well as luggage, cancellation, theft and personal accident, you should take out an insurance policy. No inoculations are required for Spain, but you should ensure that your tetanus injections are up-to-date. The usual precautions should be taken against HIV, AIDS and other sexually transmitted diseases.

What to take

Always take less clothes and more money than you think you may need

Try and keep your luggage to a minimum particularly if you are planning to be on the move. The most convenient way to carry your things is in an internal frame rucksack, with a small rucksack for carrying valuables and for use as a daypack. Hybrid backpacks that can be converted into a more conventional suitcase are also good.

A lightweight cotton shirt and trousers are ideal during the summer with a pair of sandals on your feet. This will also give you protection from the sun and against the mosquitoes which plague parts of the country. In the winter Andalucía can be chilly, so don't forget a sweatshirt or a lightweight fleece.

During the summer a good sun hat and sunscreen are essential. If you intend to do some walking a pair of lightweight trekking boots is recommended and an umbrella helps keep the sun off. Insulated bottle-carriers are excellent for keeping your trusty bottle of mineral water cool.

Any medication you use regularly should be brought from home although it's probably available without prescription from one of the ubiquitous pharmacies. Insect repellent, tampons and contraceptives are easily found but you may prefer to bring your own from home.

If you're staying in budget accommodation it's useful to carry a rubber plug for using in washbasins and bathtubs. A 100-watt light bulb will brighten the dingiest of rooms and help avoid eye strain if you are reading at night. A cotton sheet sleeping bag is also a bonus when the sheets provided are not the cleanest.

Money

Currency

Spain entered the Economic and Monetary Union, or EMU, on 1 January 1999, along with Austria, Belgium, Finland, France, Germany, Ireland, Italy, Luxembourg, The Netherlands and Portugal. Greece joined on 1 January 2001. The euro's (€) value against the peseta (pta) is fixed at 166.386 ptas until the peseta is completely phased out, on 1 July 2002.

Until 31 December 2001, the euro was used only for non-cash transactions such as inter-bank transfers, but bills and receipts were quoting the euro equivalent for many months before this. Euro notes and coins were introduced on 1 January 2002 for cash transactions and the two currencies operated side by side for two months. Pesetas are no longer legal tender (as of 1 March 2002).

One euro is worth 100 cents, or *centímos*. Euro notes – in denominations of 5, 10, 20, 50, 100, 200 and 500 – show the seven main architectural styles in Europe while the coins have one European image common to all countries and the other a Spanish image. Despite the distinct appearance of each country's coins, they will be legal tender in all 12 countries using the euro.

Major credit cards, such as *Mastercard, Visa* and *American Express* are widely accepted, although smaller establishments may only deal with cash. Check restaurants before you eat. They can also be used at cashpoint machines (ATMs), although you should find out how much commission your bank/card company charges for this service. ATM's are now found in all towns and cities and some villages. They offer a choice of European languages (look for the *telebanco* sign). ATMs will accept most common cards in circulation; check with your bank at home before leaving. There is often a minimum charge for each cash withdrawal transaction abroad. Keep a record of your credit card numbers and make a note of emergency telephone numbers to be contacted should a card be lost or stolen.

You should have no difficulty in cashing travellers' cheques, or foreign notes, in any bank. Hotels and change shops will also cash traveller's cheques, but may charge a hefty commission. In addition to banks, there are *Cajas de ahorros* (building societies), but some of the smaller branches may be unwilling to cash traveller's cheques. Banking hours are Monday to Friday 0830 to 1400, Saturday 0830 to 1300, except June to September when they are closed on Saturdays.

Credit & debit cards & travellers' cheques
Eurocheques and Eurocards were phased out in 2000

Variable rates of IVA (the Spanish equivalent of VAT – sales tax) are applied from a basic 6% to 12% or 33% for luxury goods. Major department stores, such as *El Corte Inglés* (in Granada, Málaga and Sevilla) or *Galerias Preciados* (Granada) operate IVA exemption schemes for non-residents, and this is well worth the trouble for large purchases. Consult their multi-lingual staff for details.

Taxes
IVA is normally included in the stated prices

Spain is no longer the cheap destination that it was 20 years ago and visitors will find that the prices on balance are much the same as they are at home. A holiday here need not be expensive, however, and budget travellers are well catered for, if you are prepared to shop around for meals, buy fruit and vegetables in season and search out cheap accommodation. Whilst petrol prices are similar to northern Europe, buses are cheap to use and car hire is reasonable, so that travelling within Andalucía should not be a major expense. Drinks of all kinds are ridiculously low-priced, as are cigarettes – particularly in Gibraltar, where there is no purchase tax.

Cost of living

The minimum you could get by on in Andalucía is around €18-30 a day, by sharing a double room in the cheapest accommodation, eating picnic lunches and, if eating in restaurants at all, choosing the set *menú*. This wouldn't cover public transport, entrance fees to sights or nightlife. You could probably get by on less than this if you stayed on campsites or in self-catering accommodation, although for both of these options you may need your own transport. A budget of around €72 would mean you could stay at a more comfortable hotel for around €48 a night and eat out for €12 day, with a bit left over for transport and nightlife. If you want to splash out, then budget for around €120 to 150 a day, which would mean you could stay in the more expensive hotels costing around €90 a night for a double room (but this will probably include breakfast), and eat out at pricier restaurants, which can charge €15 for a set *menú*, drink wine with your meals, as well as experiencing a bit of nightlife and seeing the sights.

Public transport is inexpensive although if you plan to see a lot of places, these costs could mount up. Drink is cheap, especially if you stick to beer, but wine in all but the most expensive restaurants is reasonably priced. Remember that if travelling alone you'll invariably pay more for a single room than the price of a double divided between two people.

Cost of travelling

Essentials

Airlines flying from the UK

British Airways, T0845-7733377, www.britishairways.com Direct flights from Gatwick and Heathrow to Málaga, Sevilla and Gibraltar.

Buzz, T0870-2407070, www.buzz away.com Low-cost airline flying from Stansted to Jerez 10 times Monday to Friday, twice on Saturday in the summer and twice a week (Thursday and Saturday) in winter. £2.50 discount for online bookings.

Easyjet, reservations T0870-6000000 (24 hr), www.easyjet.com Low-cost airline flying from Liverpool and Luton to Málaga twice a day Monday to Friday, five times a

day on Saturday and three times a day on Sunday. £5 discount for online bookings. **Go**, T0870-6076543, www.go-fly. com Low-cost subsidiary of British Airways, flies Stansted and Bristol to Málaga 22 times a week, daily. £10 discount for online bookings.

Iberia, T0870-5341341, www.iberia.com Flights from Heathrow to Málaga and Sevilla, with onward connections to Jerez, Almería and Granada.

Monarch, T08700-405040, www.monarch-airlines.com Flies daily from Luton to Málaga and Gibraltar and Manchester to Málaga.

Discount flight agents in the UK and Ireland

Council Travel, 28a Poland St, London, W1V 3DB, T020-74377767, www.destinations-group.com

STA Travel, T08701-600599, www. statravel.co.uk Branches in London, Brighton, Bristol, Cambridge, Leeds, Manchester, Newcastle-Upon-Tyne and Oxford and on many university

campuses. Specialists in low-cost student/youth flights and tours, also good for student IDs and insurance.

Trailfinders, 194 Kensington High St, London, W8 7RG, T020-79383939, www.trailfinders.co.uk Cheap flights and discounts on car hire, accommodation and tours.

Accommodation, restaurants and bars usually charge more during fiestas and in major tourist areas, while during the high season (July, August, Holy Week and Christmas) hotels can be more expensive. If you're hiring a car, Málaga is the cheapest place in Andalucía. Bear in mind that petrol is not much cheaper than northern Europe.

In some places, particularly in tourist areas, you may be charged up to 20% more to sit outside a restaurant. It's also worth checking if the IVA (sales tax) is included in menu prices, especially in the more expensive restaurants; ask *está incluido el IVA?* (is IVA included?).

Getting there

Air

From the UK
Málaga and Sevilla are the main destinations of the scheduled flights

You've got a choice of charter or scheduled flights. Charter flights are cheaper and are run by package holiday firms, who sell off un-used seats to 'flights only' passengers. You can find very good bargains by taking last-minute bookings through the so-called 'bucket shops', which advertise mainly in Sunday newspapers and magazines such as *Time Out*. The disadvantage of charter flights is that they usually have a fixed return flight, which is often no more than four weeks, and they often leave at antisocial hours. It may, nevertheless, be cheaper to take two separate charter journeys than one return scheduled flight. Charter flights also leave from a number of British regional airports. Useful websites for cheap tickets are: www.cheaptickets.com, www.cheapflights. co.uk, www.ebookers.com and www.ryanair.com

Airlines flying from North America and Canada

American Airlines, T1-800-4337300, www.aa.com Flies from Miami to Madrid.
British Airways, T1-800-2479297, www.britishairways.com Flights to Málaga, Sevilla and Gibraltar via London from many US cities.
Continental, T1-800-2310856, www.flycontinental.com Flights from Newark to Madrid.
Delta, T1-800-2414141, www.delta-air.

com Flights from Atlanta to Madrid.
Iberia, T1-800-7724642, www.iberia.com Flights to Madrid from New York, Chicago, Miami, Los Angeles and Toronto.
KLM, T1-800-4474747, www.klm.com Flights to Málaga via Amsterdam.
Spanair, T1-888-5455757, www.spanair.com Flies from New York, Washington, Toronto and many other North American cities to Malaga via Copenhagen or Frankfurt.

Discount flight agents in North America and Canada

Air Brokers International, T01-800-883 3273, www.airbrokers.com Consolidator and specialist on round-the-world and Circle Pacific tickets.
Council Travel, T1-800-2COUNCIL, www.counciltravel.com Student/budget agency with branches in many US cities.
Discount Airfares Worldwide On-Line, www.etn.nl/discount.htm A hub of consolidator and discount agent links.
International Travel Network/Airlines of the Web, www.itn.net/airlines Online air

travel information and reservations.
STA Travel, 5900 Wilshire Blvd, Suite 2110, Los Angeles, CA 90036, T1-800-7770112, www.sta-travel.com Also branches in New York, San Francisco, Boston, Miami, Chicago, Seattle and Washington DC.
Travel CUTS, T1-866-2469762, www.travelcuts.com Specialist in Canadian student discount fares, IDs and other travel services. Branches in many Canadian cities.
Travelocity, www.travelocity.com Online consolidator.

American and Canadian visitors to Andalucía will need to arrange flights to major European cities and then take connecting flights to Málaga or Sevilla. On the other hand some APEX flights to Madrid throw in a free connecting flight to Málaga, Sevilla or Almería, so it is worth doing some research. Travellers from Canada will find it cheaper to fly via London. Canadian students should contact: *Travel CUTS*, 187 College Street, Toronto, Ontario, M5T 1P7. **From North America & Canada**

There are no direct flights from Australia and New Zealand to Spain. Most European destinations are 'common rated', so it is possible to have stopovers in a variety of European cities before going on to Andalucía. There are more than 10 airlines working this route, so it is worth shopping around for bargains, such as free car rental, on-going flights or accommodation. Fares will vary according to the season – what is high season in the Antipodes may be low season in Spain. Round the World tickets can be a cheap option, especially the *BA/Qantas* 'Explorer Plus', which offers a number of free stopovers, and the *Thai airways/Air NZ* 'Star Alliance', which offers up to 15 stopovers, but not in the USA or Canada. **From Australia & New Zealand**

Road

The most popular but expensive route to Andalucía by car is via the ferry services from England to Santander or Bilbao in Northern Spain. Scenic routes can be chosen through Spain with hotel stops so that this can be an enjoyable part of a holiday.The Plymouth to Santander is run by *Brittany Ferries* twice weekly and takes 24 hours. **Car & ferry**

☞ Airlines flying from Australia and New Zealand

British Airways, Sydney T02-8904 8800, Auckland T093568690, www.britishairways.com Flights from many Australian cities to Madrid via London and from Auckland to Madrid via London, Los Angeles and/or Hong Kong. **KLM**, www.klm.com Flights from Sydney to Madrid via Amsterdam.

Singapore Airlines, Singapore Airlines House, 17-19 Bridge St, Sydney, NSW 2000, T61-131011, www.singaporeair.com Flies to Madrid via Singapore. **Thai Airways**, www.thaiair.com Flies from Auckland, Melbourne and Sydney to Madrid via Bangkok.

Discount flight agents in Australia and New Zealand

Flight Centres, 82 Elizabeth St, Sydney, T13-1600; 205 Queen St, Auckland, T09-309 6171. Also branches in other towns and cities. **STA Travel**, T1300-360960 (Australia), T0800-874773 (New Zealand; toll free), www.statravel.com.au. In major towns and university campuses.

Trailfinders, 8 Spring St, Sydney, T02-9247 7666, www.trailfinders.com.au Cheap flights and discounts on accommodation, car hire and tours. Branches also in Brisbane, Cairns, Melbourne and Perth. **Travel.com.au**, 72 Clarence St, Sydney, T02-9249 5232, www.travel.com.au

---

Some form of accommodation must be booked and this varies from four-berth cabins to pullman reclining seats. For information contact Brittany Ferries, T0870-5360360, www.brittany-ferries.com An alternative is the P&O service from Portsmouth to Bilbao, which takes 33 hours and runs twice weekly. A cabin is included in the price. For information contact P&O, T0870-2424999, www.poportsmouth.com

If you want to drive through France, there are cross-channel routes from Dover, Folkestone, Portsmouth, Weymouth and Plymouth. In addition to the conventional ferries, there is the Hovercraft service from Dover and le Shuttle through the Channel Tunnel.

For details of pricing and timetables on cross-channel routes, contact: **Hoverspeed**, T0870-5240241, www.hoverspeed.co.uk; **Stena Line**, T0870-6000600; **Seafrance**, T0870-5711711, www.seafrance.com

Coach Buses run from London to Málaga, Córdoba, Granada and Sevilla twice a week, a journey which takes in the Dover-Calais ferry and lasts 33 hours. Another route runs via Paris and Madrid to Algeciras, taking 39 hours. On these marathon journeys, there are toilet/refreshment stops every four to five hours, but they remain tests of stamina. Tickets cost £79 if booked seven days in advance and are valid for one-month fixed return; an open return valid for six months costs £139. For more information, contact **Eurolines**, National Express, 164 Buckingham Palace Road, London SW1, T0870-5143219, www.gobycoach.com

Train

From London to Málaga by train used to be a 35-hour journey and involved changing trains (and stations) at Paris, and later at Barcelona. The opening of the Channel Tunnel and the use of the Eurostar service has speeded up this journey considerably, but it will still take over 20 hours and will probably only appeal to railway buffs. The cost is more expensive than an average charter flight, although cheaper than most scheduled flights. For students, the *InterRail* pass is an attractive and cheap possibility, which can be obtained from travel agents, but note that the pass is not valid on the high speed

Touching down

Emergencies: *Police: 091; Ambulance: 061; Fire service: 085*
Business hours: *0930-1330 Mon-Sat, 1630-2000 Mon-Fri. In high season along the coast shops stay open until at least 2200.*

IDD code for Spain: *34*
Official language: *Spanish*
Official time: *GMT+1*
Electricity: *110/220 volts; plug socket: 2-pin*
Weights and measures: *Metric*
Directory enquiries: *1003*

AVE or EuroMed trains. Travelling by Eurostar London-Paris cost from £120 in low season if booked 14 days in advance. Check the website www.eurostar.com or T020-79285163 for more details.

Contact **Rail Europe**, Victoria Station, London SE1, T0870-5848848, www.raileurope.co.uk for more information on Eurostar tickets, travel on Eurorail networks and French motorail. For information on transporting your car and passengers through France, contact **Rail Europe** or see the **SNCF** website, www.sncf.com

Also recommended is the *Thomas Cook European Timetable* which contains schedules for over 50,000 trains in Europe, as well as timings of over 200 ferry routes and rail connecting bus services. It is updated and published monthly.

The Spanish national rail company, **RENFE,** has details of discount railcards like Eurodomino and Europass, as well as Spain Flexipass for route information (eg night trains from European capitals to Madrid), (34)902-240202 or see their website, www.renfe.es

Touching down

Airport information

There are two major international airports in Andalucía, at **Málaga** and **Sevilla**. The airports at **Almería, Jerez** and **Gibraltar** also handle a small amount of international traffic, while **Granada** airport has only internal flights.

By far the greatest number of visitors to Andalucía will land at Málaga Airport. Officially known as the Pablo Picasso airport, it handles nearly eight million passengers a year and is located, some 7 km west of the city centre. A new terminal was completed in 1991, with the old building now dealing with internal flights. The international terminal has two levels, with arrivals on the ground floor and departures on the first floor. On arrival, be prepared for a long walk from the plane to the luggage reclaim area, despite a few moving walkways. Those with mobility problems should use the buggies provided. There are usually plenty of luggage trolleys available. **Taxis** can be hired immediately outside the arrivals hall. It will cost about €75 to the centre of Málaga. **Buses** also leave from the same area, departing at 30-minute intervals. The **car hire** offices can be found by proceeding down the ramp from the baggage reclaim area to the floor below. All the main international firms are represented here, plus a few local firms. Cars are collected from the underground parking area next to the terminal. Some other firms have their offices along the airport approach road and transfer their clients by minibus. Hire cars are returned to an open car parking area that is clearly signposted.

The cheapest way of getting into Málaga and westward to the resorts of the Costa del Sol is by the electric **train**. The station is right opposite the airport. It can be reached from the arrivals hall by going up to the departures level and on leaving the building turn right to the end of the terminal where there is a pedestrian footbridge to the

Málaga airport
T952-048844

station. The nearest platform is for the resorts to the west. The far platform, reached by underpass, is for Málaga. Tickets may be bought on the train. The train runs at 30-minute intervals from 0711 to 2345, costing about €1. The journey takes 15 minutes. There are two Málaga stations; the main RENFE station for connections to elsewhere in Andalucía and Guadalmedina stop at the end of the line and most convenient for the town centre. There is a **tourist information office** in the arrivals hall. Note that there are **no hotels** or other accommodation in the immediate vicinity of the airport. The nearest are in Torremolinos.

Airport tax   There is no tax payable on departure.

Tourist information

The regional government, the Junta de Andalucía, prints a good range of information. Particularly recommended are the *guías practicas*, informative leaflets on all the main towns of Andalucía, and currently costing under €1. There are also free leaflets on the region's main natural parks. See also Useful websites, page 25.

Tourist offices   Local government tourist offices are (*oficinas de turismo*) in all the major towns, providing more specific local information. In addition, many towns run a municipal *turismo*, offering locally produced material. The tourist offices are generally open during normal office hours, but will usually be closed at fiesta and holiday times. The offices in the main holiday areas normally have enthusiastic, multi-lingual staff, but the same service can often be found lacking in the more remote areas. The tourist offices will be able to provide local maps and town plans, but be warned that even in the *guías practices*, they can be unreliable. In smaller places with no turismo you could try asking for local information in the Ayuntamiento.

Local customs and laws

Tipping   A service charge may be included in restaurant and hotel bills, but tipping is not widely practiced in Andalucía. It is more common to round up your bill to the nearest convenient figure. Small tips may be expected by guides and car park 'attendants', see Parking, page 41.

Opening hours   In Andalucía, more than in any other part of Spain, the afternoon *siesta* is rigidly adhered to, and is an essential part of the rather quirky business hours. The usual working hours are 0930-1330 and 1700-1930; few Andalucíans take lunch before 1400 or eat dinner before 2100. Some tourist shops on the coast may open all day, as will large department stores such as *El Corte Inglés*, but this is unusual in the interior of Andalucía.

Nearly all museums, galleries and monuments close on Monday. Usual opening hours for the sights are 0900-1900 Tuesday to Saturday and 0900-1400 Sundays and holidays, but check with local tourist offices. Tourist offices close on Saturday afternoons and Sunday. Cathedrals and larger churches follow the same hours as museums (and often charge an entrance fee), while small churches are usually locked up and the search for a key can often be a challenge. Otherwise, visit cathedrals and churches during services.

Toilets   Public lavatories are hard to find, but this is not usually a problem as there are plenty of facilities in bars, hotels and restaurants and other tourist places, which tend to be used by customers and non-customers alike. Ask for the *servicios, baños, sanitarios* or *aseos*. Women's toilets are labelled *damas* or *señoras*, men's toilets labelled *caballeros* or *señores*. If this is confusing, be reassured by the fact that most toilet doors have the easily recognizable international logos. It's worth bringing your own supply of paper.

Last resort

Spain in general, and Andalucía in particular, has been anxious to dispel the image that the area is attractive only to the beach-goer and the lager lout and this has helped to develop the concept of green/rural tourism. The idea is to encourage tourists away from the coasts to inland areas, without ruining the rural environment. If successful, rural tourism provides jobs for local people and helps to prevent depopulation, particularly of younger people. The pueblo blanco of Grazalema, Cádiz province, for example, has less than 2,000 inhabitants, which is half the number it had at the turn of the century, while in the village of Cartajima there were only two weddings between 1990 and 1995, which does not make the future birth rate look encouraging.

The government of Andalucía has provided money for rural hotels, villas turísticas (self-catering apartment complexes in keeping with the local architecture) and campsites and given grants for private enterprise schemes. Local handicrafts have been encouraged, including woollen goods at Grazalema and leather making at Ubrique, Cádiz province. Local festivals, such as the bull running Lunes de Toro at Grazalema have been widely publicized.

A recent development has been the negotiations between RENFE, the Spanish railway company, the regional government and private companies to purchase a number of rural railway stations to increase tourist potential.

Another initiative is the development of spas and health baths. There are estimated to be over 300 spas in Spain. Many go back to Roman times, but the majority have fallen into disuse. In Andalucía, there are well-known privately run spas such as those at Carratraca and Alhama de Almería, in the provinces of Málaga and Almería respectively, but there are many others which could be rehabilitated and the regional government is actively collaborating with private investors.

All these developments are dependant on rural accommodation so the Andalucían government has set up the Red Andaluza de Alojamientos Rurales (RAAR) – the Andalucían Network of Rural Accommodation. It offers a range of possibilities including rustic cottages, rooms in large haciendas, private rooms in modern family homes, hostels, basic campsites and even old converted cork workers' huts. The majority are privately run and the owner provides local information such things as local swimming pools, hiking trails and riding opportunities. The scheme has proved extremely popular and all accommodation can be fully booked at peak holiday periods. To obtain the detailed RAAR brochure and make a booking through the Central Reservation Service, telephone in Spain T34-950265018, F950270431, info@raar.es In UK, contact Atlantida Travel, T020-72402888.

Safety

Crime In Andalucía, crime is largely an urban phenomena fuelled by unemployment, drug dependence and easy pickings from tourists. Both Málaga and Sevilla have bad reputations for street crime. The most common forms are bag snatching, pickpocketing, mugging and theft from cars. Sevilla is well-known for its semaforazos who smash car windows at traffic lights, steal whatever is available and make off down side streets on mopeds. Pickpockets often work in pairs, so beware of anyone standing close to you in a crowded place and demanding your attention, as the accomplice will be nearby.

Some simple precautions will reduce the risk of becoming a victim and having a holiday ruined: If staying in a city, try to choose a hotel with a lock-up garage for cars. Remove all luggage, the radio and valuables from cars at night. If it is a private car remove the radio also. Do not have cameras and other valuables on display in a car when travelling through a city and make sure that the doors are locked while driving. Leave valuables in hotel safety deposit boxes. Don't carry handbags unless absolutely necessary or keep wallets in rear pockets. Avoid poorly lit and less salubrious areas of cities, especially, late at night. Take a taxi, rather than public transport late at night.

If, however,you are unfortunate enough to be robbed, you should report the theft immediately at the nearest police station, as insurance companies will require a police statement. Be prepared to spend at least half a day there while you queue and complete the interminable paper work.

However most visitors will not experience crime of any sort. Northern Europeans and North Americans will feel safer on the streets at night than in their own countries. The Spanish authorities are very conscious of the 'Costa del Crime' description and have made considerable efforts in recent years to clean up the image, with extra officers drafted in from other parts of the country for the summer season.

Police   There are three separate police organizations in Andalucía, so the situation may initially be confusing. The **Guardia Civil** wear green uniforms and are less important today than they were in the time of Franco, although they are still a reactionary organization. Even today they seem specially selected for their lack of humour. They mainly operate in rural areas or on motor bike traffic control. The **Policía Municipal** are local police who wear blue and white uniforms and spend much of their time directing urban traffic. The **Policía Nacional** wear a brown military-style uniform and can be heavily armed as their duties include guarding public buildings. They deal with most crime investigation so you should go to them to report a crime or theft. They will issue the documents which insurance companies need. All three branches of the police are armed and should not be treated frivolously. Be prepared to have some form of identification available and always carry your driving licence when in a car.

Where to stay

Hotels &
pensiones
See inside front cover
for a quick reference
guide to hotel
categories

There is a wide variety of state-registered accomodation in Andalucía. All establishments are shown by blue plaques with white letters – Hotels (H), Residential Hotels (HR), Hostales (Hs), Pensiones (P) and Casa de Huéspedes (CH). Hotels are graded by 1-5 stars and hostels by 1-3 stars, but the distinctions are blurred and a good hostel may be better than a low grade hotel. The term *hostal* is officially being phased out and establishments have to decide whether they are a hotel or a pensión. In addition there are *fondas* (F), which may be inns or simply rooms above a bar. Travellers on a budget should look out for signs saying *camas* (beds) or *habitaciones* (rooms). Be prepared to bargain for this type of accommodation; owners may provide meals as well. This type of accommodation is usually in the historic centre of a town. Curiously, you do not pay more for accommodation in a city centre location in Andalucía.

Many of the hotels in the inland cities are often old, traditional and with a certain gloomy grandeur, which is in direct contrast with the coastal hotels, which tend to be new and in well-landscaped grounds and have facilities such as pools, laundries and nightclubs. The disadvantages of coastal hotels are noise from discos and package tour parties. Should you be dissatisfied with the services provided, ask for the *libro de reclamaciones* (complaints' book) which, by law, all establishments should display.

Paradores   At the top end of the scale are the paradores, which are expensive state-run luxury hotels, often located in historic buildings. They tend to be furnished with antiques, while their restaurants concentrate on local specialities. Bedrooms are spacious and well fitted, as are public rooms and bars. Even if you cannot afford to stay in a parador, they are worth wandering around and having a drink in their bars. Booking is essential

Hotel prices and facilities

Essentials

AL *(over €91)   International class luxury hotel. These offer unrivalled personal service, sumptuous extras, luxury rooms and bathrooms, and just about every amenity that you can think of. Most of the top hotels now provide two in-room phone lines (for modems and calls), 24-hour business facilities, several pools, jacuzzis, health spas, tennis courts, numerous restaurants, and much else besides.*

A *(€73-90) and **B** (€61-72)*
Hotels in this category will range from very comfortable to functional. Rooms in the 'A' category will have most extras like daily clean linen, minibar, TV, and tea and coffee making facilities. They will also have a choice of restaurants (including a coffee shop), swimming pool, sports

facilities, bank and travel agent. Rooms in the 'B' category may be lacking some, or most, of these amenities (fewer shops and sports facilities for instance).

C *(€49-60)   The best rooms should have air-conditioning with a hot water shower attached; there might also be a coffee shop. These are no-frills, functional affairs. They are comfortable and may provide money changing facilities, pool and shop.*

D *(€25-48) and **E** (€ 24 and under)*
Best rooms in the D category will have air conditioning or a fan. Expect to share bathrooms and toilets in the poorer rooms and always in the E category. Eating facilities are limited in the choice of menus and are often just room service. Hot water is not always available in the E category.

(there used to be a strongly held rumour that rooms were kept open until 1800 for cabinet ministers, after which time visitors might be able to take them without booking!). They can be booked in advance from the Madrid head office at Requena 3, 28013 Madrid, T915-166666, F166657, and in UK through **Keytel International**, 402 Edgware Rd, London W2N 1ED, T020-74028182. For more information see www.parador.es Do not be deterred if you arrive at your pre-booked parador and they try to persuade you they have no record of your reservation. Polite, firm insistence should secure your room.

Particularly recommended paradores in Andalucía are those at Arcos de la Frontera, Carmona, Granada, Jaen, Málaga and Úbeda, which are in superb, historic buildings in spectacular locations. There are other paradores at Antequera, Ayamonte, Bailén, Cádiz, Cazorla, and Córdoba. Those at Mazagón, Mojácar, Nerja and Torremolinos are in modern buildings and less attractive, although the standard of service, remains high.

There are 147 youth hostels, or *albergues juveniles*, in Andalucía plus one in Gibraltar. **Youth hostels** For a list, contact the English Youth Hostel Association (YHA), Trevelyan House, 8 St Stephen's Hill, St Albans, Herts AL1 2DY, T01727-854047, www.yha.org.uk or Spanish tourist offices worldwide (see page 25). Andalucía's youth hostel association, **Inturjoven**, has details of its affiliated hostels, T902-510000, www.interjoven.com Prices range from €8 (low season) to €16 (high season) per person for bed and breakfast. Hostels in Córdoba, Granada and Sevilla are the most popular (and therefore the most expensive), while those in coastal resorts are in high demand in July and August. Many hostels have facilities on par with hotels, including pools, ensuite double rooms and wheelchair access.

However, block booking by Spanish school groups is common (which may mean a sleepless night) and the cost of staying in a hostel can be more than that in a *casa de huéspedes*. Hostels are mainly located in towns and cities, often in inconvenient out-of-town locations.

Apartments & villas On the Costa del Sol, residential tourism is far more important than hotel tourism and consequently there are literally thousands of apartments and villas available for hire, often on a long-term basis. Out of season, reduced rates can be negotiated, but check carefully what is included in the rental agreement. Some expatriates are happy for 'caretakers' to stay in their properties while they are away. Be prepared to provide references. Look for advertisements in the free newspapers, in the windows of *inmobilarios* (estate agents) or simply look for signs saying *Se alquila* (to rent).

Rural tourism The Andalucían government has made strenuous efforts in recent year to encourage rural tourism in order to prevent depopulation in the inland areas. As a result there has been an upsurge in rural accommodation available in some of the most attractive scenic parts of Andalucía. There are a number of guides that detail farmhouses and village properties offering accommodation, including *Anuario de Turismo Rural* (Ediciones Susaeta, Madrid) and the *Guía de Alojomiento Rural* (ElPaís/Aguilar). The Andalucían government organisation *Red Andaluza de Alojomientos Rurales* T950-26518, F270431, www.raar.es will take bookings. **Villas turísticas** are rural complexes run by the regional government, with self-catering apartments and all the facilities of an upmarket hotel. Full details are to be found by contacting the Centro Internacional de Turismo de Andalucía, 29600, Marbella, T952-920210, F920216, www.andalucia.org **Casa rurales** are restored cootages in the countryside, sometimes on farms. Full details can be obtained from local tourist offices, RAAR (see above) or look for adverts that say '*se alquila casa de campo*'.

Camping There are 130 official campsites in Andalucía plus a number of unofficial ones. Many have excellent facilities, particularly those on the coast. They are rated in categories 1-3, depending on their facilities, and many sites have swimming pools, restaurants, sport grounds and supermarkets. They are relatively cheap by European standards – €2.50 to 3.50 a night, with additional similar charges for cars and caravans. The more popular sites may need to be booked during the summer months and on fiesta weekends, while in the winter months the coastal sites attract large numbers of caravans. Official campsites are listed in the regional government's leaflet *Guía de Camping*, available from tourist offices and from Spanish National Tourist Offices overseas, see page 25). This also includes a decent regional map. For those staying on the coastal strip, *Campings en la Costa del Sol* is a brochure produced in four languages. Reservations may be made through the *Federación Española de Empresarios de Camping*, General Oraa 52-2°D, 28006, Madrid, T956-29994. Note that inland campsites can be few and far between away from the natural parks. An International Camping Carnet, available from the motoring organizations, is strongly advised if a lengthy camping holiday is planned. Camping away from official sites, whilst not illegal, should be approached with care. Avoid beaches, urban areas and private land unless you have permission from the owner. Spanish campsites can be quite noisy; if you want a quieter spot avoid camping next to people who have radios and TV's blaring.

Getting around

Andalucía is well-served by public transport and buses are generally the most convenient way of travelling. The main centres are well-connected by bus and train but for more remote areas, buses may be your only choice. Given the exceptionally good deals in Andalucía, car hire may be your best bet if you can afford it.

Air

Iberia and its subsidiaries operate services between the national airports, but this is an expensive way of travelling around Andalucía and there are more attractive alternatives. Note that there are no services from any of the regional Andalucían capitals to Gibraltar. *Iberia* have special rates available for unlimited travel within Spain, although this is probably not worthwhile if you are only visiting Andalucía.

Road

The main cities of Andalucía are all linked by long distance coach services generally run on time and are cheap and comfortable. However, the services are run by a number of private bus companies, whose offices may not be at the main bus station, while the *estación de autobuses* itself may be remote from the town centre. *Horarios* (timetables) are rarely printed, but each separate company will usually display theirs on the wall of the bus station. It is worth getting an overall picture of the bus services from the local tourist office, which will advise you of any cheap period tickets. Long distance coaches have air conditioning in summer and often show videos. Book your ticket well before departure, as ticket offices have erratic hours and those who turn up at departure time are likely to encounter a full bus, especially in summer or at weekends. Note also that only minuscule services run on Sunday and fiesta days, particularly in rural areas.

Bus

If you bring your own right-hand-drive vehicle from the UK, remember that driving is on the right in Andalucía and that overtaking can be hazardous. All foreign drivers are advised to take an International Driving Permit (or EU driving licence), plus insurance and vehicle documentation. Non-EU citizens will also require a Green Card and it is advisable to obtain a Bail Bond in order to avoid imprisonment in the event of a serious accident. You should carry the required documentation whenever you are in the car.

Car

Andalucían roads have improved out of all recognition in the last decade, with the help of EU grants and money to improve the infrastructure for EXPO'92 at Sevilla. Most cities are now linked by *autovía* (motorway) or dual carriageway roads (except Málaga-Córdoba). Some motorways, such as the A4 from Sevilla, have tolls (costing around €2.50 Sevilla-Cádiz), although there is a free, slower, alternative road that runs parallel. Safety on the notorious N340 between Málaga and Marbella is much improved, although being both a motorway and a local road, it is still highly dangerous. A new parallel toll road was completed in 1999, but is under-used. Speed limits are clearly shown, with a maximum of 40 kph in urban areas, motorways 120 kph and other roads 100 kph. Radar speed traps are becoming increasingly common and fines upwards of €90 can be expected. Foreigners have to pay fines on-the-spot. Failure to pay will lead to the car being impounded by the Guardia Civil. For more information see the transport department website, www.dgt.es, which is also in English. It has suggested itineraries, travel recommendations (eg warnings of heavy traffic during holidays) and information on licences and vehicle documentation.

Spanish road accidents are among the highest in Europe, classic traits are tailgating and dangerous over-taking. Be particularly careful near motorway junctions – Spanish drivers come from the fast lane into the slip roads within the space of a few metres, cutting up anyone in the way. Particular care should be taken in the summer months when convoys of tired, Moroccan workers in over-laden cars and vans head through Andalucía to the ferry ports. The first and last weekends in August, when large numbers are on the move, are also times when many accidents occur. Road signs are similar to those in the rest of Europe. When turning left on a main road, look out for a loop to the right marked *cambio de sentido* as turning directly left is often illegal.

Essentials

Petrol in Spain is slightly more expensive than in the UK, and considerably more so than in North America. Since the deregulation of filling stations and the growth of foreign petrol companies, the acceptance of credit cards is now normal, but attendant service rather than self service is still common. The different fuel types are *súper* (96 octane); *gasóleo* (diesel) and *sin plomo* (lead free). Confusingly, super lead free is sometimes called *Euro-súper*.

Parking is a horrendous problem in all Spanish cities. The newly affluent Andalucíans all wish to have cars, but unfortunately, as they are largely apartment-dwellers, few have garages. The result is on-street parking. Few Andalucían cities (with the notable exception of Cádiz) have invested to any great extent in underground or multi-storey car parks. This situation has spawned a thriving *grua* (tow-crane) business. Blue curb markings indicate a pay-and-display area. Do not park where there are yellow markings on the curb. If you park illegally (or at fiesta times in the path of a procession), your car will be towed away. Getting it back from the local pound will be both expensive and stressful.

In bigger cities, like Sevilla, you may see unofficial parking 'attendants' who will attempt to guide you through into a parking spot and then expect a minimum of a euro. If you fail to pay, it's likely that your car will be scratched or damaged upon your return. One solution is to avoid them and park elsewhere. Occasionally, you may see official attendants, employed by the government and uniformed, who will issue you with a ticket for around the same price.

RENFE rail network

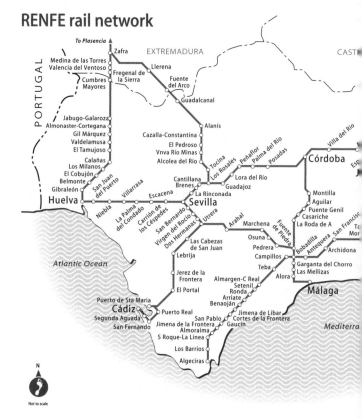

Car hire Small cars are inexpensive to hire in Andalucía and are the cheapest in Málaga. The large international companies, such as *Hertz* and *Avis*, are at the main airports and cities, as are smaller local companies who may be able to offer a cheaper deal (although their back-up services may not be so comprehensive). **ATESA**, a government-owned Spanish firm, is reliable, has air-conditioned cars and offices in all the regional capitals.In Spain, T902-100101 or see www.atesa.es *Holiday Autos* (UK T020-74911111/US T800-4427737) is a worldwide organization and because of its volume of bookings can undercut its rivals and still use reliable local firms. Prices for a Fiesta-sized car at Málaga airport are from €100 in the winter to €130 in the summer (one week's rental with unlimited mileage and all taxes). There are also some excellent fly-drive deals available from the airlines and tour operators.

Mopeds and cycles can be hired, particularly on the coast. Helmets for moped and motor cyclists are now compulsory (although widely disregarded). Headlights must be on at all times. Cycling is a major sport in Spain (Spaniards have won the Tour de France many times in recent years) and racing cyclists are common on the roads of Andalucía, mainly at weekends. Leisure cyclists are less obvious and mountain bikes have not penetrated the Spanish market to any extent, despite the suitable terrain. Motorists are obliged by law to give cyclists 2 m clearance when overtaking, a manoeuvre which many Spaniards take seriously, often to the detriment of other road users. Cycle helmets are rarely seen. Taking your own bike to Andalucía is well worth the effort as most airlines are happy to accept them, providing they come within your baggage allowance. Bikes can be taken on RENFE, but have to travel in the guard's van and must be registered. Remember to take a strong lock or chain. **Cycling & motorcycling**

Away from the tourist areas, hitching will involve some long, hot waits. Spanish drivers are reluctant to pick up strangers, especially backpackers, and are likely to regard women hitchhikers without rucksacks as prostitutes. Foreign cars are the best bet, but considering the cheapness of buses, this is not a recommended way of travelling and is frowned on by the police. **Hitchhiking**

Taxis are reasonably cheap, but not always metered. Since there are supplements (eg at night, from airports, for baggage) it is best to clarify the price in advance. Official rates should be displayed at airports and inside any licensed taxi. There are usually taxi ranks in city centres and it is possible to hail a taxi in the street; look for the *libre* notice on the windscreen or the green light on the roof at night. If you have an address to go to, it is a good idea to write it down on paper to show the driver. Tourist information material will usually quote a local radio taxi number. Taxis are excellent value **Taxis**

Essentials

.A MANCHA

MURCIA

drid

Linares-Baeza

Jodar-Úbeda
Los Propios y Cazorla
Larva
Huesa
Cabra Santo Cristo
Alamedilla

Iznalloz   Moreda
Benalúa
Fiñana
Guadix
Gérgal
Gador

Granada
Almería

Sea

within cities and, particularly at night, they are a safe way of travelling. Spanish taxi drivers, however, are notorious for their flamboyant driving and passengers will often need to keep their eyes shut – images of St Christopher on the dashboard are not just for decoration!

Maps **Road maps** can be bought in petrol stations and bookshops (*librerías*). Undoubtedly the best road map is the *Michelin Andalucía* (1:400,000), which also includes some town plans. A good alternative is the Marco Polo *Andalusien* (1:200,000). If you are not intending to stray far from the main roads you could buy the *Linea Contínua Andalucía*, which can be bought in many petrol stations. This also has some town plans, plus some basic tourist information. The Spanish government tourist department produce an excellent city map guide. This comes free, but only if you buy the expensive Official Hotel Guide that covers the whole of Spain. The regional government also print an Accommodation Guide, detailing Andalucía's hotels, pensions, apartments and campsites. It is, however, frustratingly difficult to obtain. The *turismos* normally have a copy and will usually be willing to photocopy the relevant local pages. For **topographical maps** go to the Centro Nacional Información Geografíca (CNIG), which are found in most of the provincial capitals. They stock maps produced by a couple of government agencies in various scales. The best ones are by the Instituto Geográfico Nacional (IGN) or the army. Remember, however, that hiking is not a popular activity amongst Andalucíans and that the maps available will not be as accurate as those found in North America or Britain. London's *Stanfords*, 12-14 Long Acre, Convent Garden, T020-78361321, F78360189, www.stanfords.co.uk sells a wide variety of maps and guides.

Train

Contact RENFE on T902-240202 or see www.renfe.es

Train stations are not always in the villages they serve and may not be linked with it by a regular bus service, so beware of being stranded

Train buffs recognize that RENFE is Europe's most eccentric railway. It has improved its timetabling and rolling stock considerably over the past decade, but suffers from having an incomplete rail network and a huge length of single-track line, leading to much frustrating time spent in stations and sidings waiting for another train to pass. There are, in fact, over a dozen types of train service, varying from the *AVE* high speed train connecting Madrid to Sevilla and Córdoba (expect to pay twice the cost of the basic fare, but you get your money back if the train is more than five minutes late), down to regional trains which stop at every hamlet. In between there is the *TALGO* which is fast but costly and the *TER* which is much the same. The *expreso* and the *rápido*, which are neither quick nor fast. If you are travelling to Andalucía from Madrid, you might be advised to book an inexpensive *litera* (bed) on an overnight train, rather than losing a

The luxury of Al Andalus

Train journeys in Andalucía tend to be rather spartan affairs, but for railway buffs who enjoy the refinement and touches of a bygone era, then a holiday on the Al Andalus Expreso is an experience to remember. Al Andalus is really a luxury hotel on wheels. There are twelve carriages. Five are sleeping cars, were built in France in 1929 and used to take the King of England between Calais and the Cote d'Azur. The recreation car was built in Bilbao in 1930 as a restaurant car and rebuilt in 1985. There are two restaurant cars. One known as Alhambra was constructed in France in 1929 and the other, Gibralfaro, was built in Britain and was used in Spain for many years. Giralda is a bar car and was built in France in 1928 for a luxury train. Finally there are two cars devoted entirely to showers. Here passengers are pampered with cotton robes, slippers, shampoos and soaps. Meals are taken on boards or in some of the best restaurants in Andalucía.

There are two main tours available. One starts and finished in Madrid and uses the high speed AVE to Sevilla where Al Andaluz is boarded. The train then visits Granada, Antequera, Ronda, Carmona and Jerez before returning to Sevilla. A second tour starts and finishes in Sevilla, giving more time for sightseeing in this city. Prices vary from £1046 to £1544 (€1570-2320) on the Madrid-round trip and from £889 to £1386 (€1335-2080) on the Sevilla-round trip. There is also a golf tour by Al Andaluz, with an opportunity to play on some of the most prestigious courses in Andalucía and a programme of tours for non-playing companions.

For bookings from UK, contact Cox and King, T020-78735010, F76306038. In Spain, You can book through travel agents. See also www.iber-rail.es

whole day travelling. Between Madrid and Málaga there are six trains a day 0710-2010 on TALGO, which takes four hours and 10 minutes and costs around €40-48. The AVE from Madrid to Sevilla runs frequently, at least every hour, takes 2½ hours and costs €60, while the AVE from Madrid to Córdoba costs €45. RENFE has cut a number of smaller lines in recent years and made arrangements with local bus companies to complete these routes.

Buying a ticket can be extremely complicated as there is a wide range of discounts and concessions, such as the reductions of between 12% and 50% on 'blue days'. RENFE offers a tourist card that allows travellers to use all lines and all scheduled trains in Spain for periods of eight, 15 or 22 days. The card is also valid on international trains, except the Madrid-Paris *TALGO*. The card is only available to travellers who normally live outside Spain. Details from RENFE's General Agency for Europe in Paris, T47-235201. The site has an English version. A *Spain Flexipass* is available for visitors from North America, allowing three, five or 10 days cheap travel, but the pass must be bought from travel agents in North America before departure. As lengthy negotiations about discounts and fares can go on at a ticket office, early booking is strongly advisable. Look for the window marked *Venta anticipada*, where tickets can be bought up to 60 days ahead. For last minute bookings, go to the *Venta immediata*. Remember that if you get on to the train without a ticket hoping to buy one from the conductor, you may be charged twice the normal fare. Visitors travelling extensively by rail should obtain the Thomas Cook European Timetable.

Essentials

Keeping in touch

Communications

Internet Internet cafés are increasingly common in many ports of Andalucía, particularly in Granada, Sevilla and on the Costa de Sol. Prices range from €1.50-3.50 an hour, with the cheapest ones in Sevilla and the most expensive on the Costa del Sol. For a list of many internet cafés in the region, see www.netcafeguide.com

Post The Correos is famous (or infamous) for its unreliability and slow service. Many letters still fail to reach their destinations at busy times, while a letter can take months to travel between neighbouring towns. The service within large cities is usually least satisfactory. Post offices are usually open from 0900 to 1400, but times vary from one city to another and the correos may also be open again in the afternoon, but not on Saturday. *Poste restante* letters can be collected at the post office. They should be addressed Lista de Correos, followed by the post code, town and province (emphasizing the surname, as letters are often filed under the first name). Be prepared to show some form of identification when collecting mail. When posting a letter look for a yellow box or *buzon*. Post boxes at main post offices may have different destinations – note the local, national and international sections. Be prepared for long queues at the correos. For this reason, stamps (*sellos*) are also available at tobacconists (*estancos*). Many hotels and gift shops also sell stamps. Allow at least five days for a postcard to arrive in UK, longer to North America.

Telephone
Cheap rates for calls to other countries are between 0800 and 2000; charges vary depending on individual countries

Public telephones take the following coins: euro 1, 2, 50 cents, 20 cents, 10 cents, 5 cents and 2 cents pieces. The minimum charges are €0.15 for local calls, €0.30 for national, €0.60 for international and €0.75 for mobiles. The main telephone company, *Telefónica* is efficient and its booths are clean and rarely vandalized. Instructions are in both Spanish and English, some booths accept phone cards, which can be bought at tobacconists. If you need to reverse charges, make a lengthy call or phone abroad, try to find a *locutorio* – a large cabin with several booths and an exit desk where you settle your bill. Credit cards are usually accepted. Special low level booths are available for disabled travellers in some towns. Many bars and restaurants also have public telephones. When phoning abroad from Spain, dial 00 and wait for the constant high pitched tone, then continue with the country code and the rest of the number. Country codes include US 1; Australia 61; Canada 1; NZ 64; UK 44 and Ireland 353. Call T1003 for directory enquiries (T025 for international enquiries): you're only allowed one number per call. When calling Spain from elsewhere, use the appropriate international number, then 34 for Spain.

From April 1998, all Andalucían telephone numbers changed to include nine digits to bring the area in line with the rest of the EU. This largely involved adding the provincial code to the local number. In this guide, therefore, the complete nine figure numbers are given and no STDs quoted. Most numbers in Andalucía begin with 95. Those beginning with 900 are freephone numbers; 901 are charged at a local rate; 902 are national rate; and 906 are premium rate (eg chatlines). *Telefónica* special services have four digits beginning with 1; call the emergency numbers for police (091), ambulance (061) and fire service (085).

If you have a GMS digital **mobile phone** you should be able to use it in Andalucía. Although the service is patchy inland, there is no problem along the coast when making local or international calls, but the latter are expensive. There are two efficient local service providers – AIRTEL and MOVISTAR. All mobile phone numbers begin with a six. Check with your own service providers before departure and if necessary have the international bar removed. Don't forget the battery charger and plug adapter.

Media

Of the Spanish national newspapers, *El País* (www.elpais.es), is generally regarded as the best and produces an Andalucían edition. Others worth reading are *ABC* (www.abc.es) and *Diario 16*. For local information see Andalucía provincial newspapers; one of the best city papers is Sevilla's *El Correo*. Also good for what's on is the monthly *El Giradillo* (www.elgiradillo.es) for Sevilla and Andalucía. Outside Sevilla, where it's widely available, you can find it in tourist offices and museums.

The main Andalucían newspaper, produced in Málaga, is *Sur*, which publishes an excellent free weekly edition in English (www.surinenglish.com). In addition, there are a number of other free English-language news sheets, which can be picked up in bars, supermarkets and other outlets. Don't expect any serious international news, but they can be useful for finding accommodation for rent or recommended restaurants. British daily newspapers are on sale by the early evening of the day of publication in the main tourist areas. Inland, if they can be found, they will be a day or two old. Other European newspapers, plus the *New York Herald Tribune*, are also widely available. English newspapers and magazines are easily obtainable in Gibraltar.

Spanish magazines, of which there are a vast number, are typified by their glossiness and their obsession with royalty and gossip. The best English language magazine is the well produced *Lookout*. Once a modest publication based on the Costa del Sol, it is now available widely throughout Spain.

Football fans are well catered for, with four daily newspapers and a weekly magazine, *Don Balón*. Until recently, *El Marca* (www.elmarca.com) dominated the market but in the last few years three more daily papers have become widely available: *El As*, *El Sport* and *El Mundo Deportivo* (www.elmundodeportivo.es). *El Marca* and *El As* are biased in favour of Real Madrid while the other two are pro-Barça. *Don Balon* is largely unbiased. Despite beings 'sports' papers, about three-quarters of the coverage is devoted to football.

Newspapers & magazines

Essentials

You cannot escape Spanish TV, as it is invariably switched on in bars and restaurants (usually at the same time as the radio) whether anyone is watching or not. There are two state-run channels – TVE-1 and 2 – plus *Canal Sur*, which is sponsored by the Andalucían government. In addition, there are three private subscription channels. Whatever the channel, the offerings are uninspiring, being dominated by game shows, soap operas (telenovelas) and sport, particularly basketball, football and bullfighting. Gibraltar TV can often be received in southwest Andalucía, showing a good variety of BBC and ITV programmes. Sky TV can also be obtained with a satellite dish and subscription.

Short wave radio will pick up the *BBC World Service*. Gibraltar Radio uses the World Service news, while there are numerous foreign language stations in the resort areas.

TV & radio

Food and drink

Food

Whilst not having the finesse or reputation of French or Italian cooking, Spanish cuisine has the benefit of simplicity and healthy ingredients. In Andalucía, there is the added advantage of having a wide variety of fruit, vegetables and fresh fish, plus the distinctive Moorish inheritance. One of the best ways to sample as many different Andalucían dishes as possible is to graze your way through the tapas menu at bars and restaurants.

Cuisine
See page 434 for the food glossary

Although cooked **breakfasts** may be available in the coastal resort areas, The Spanish have a light continental-type breakfast (*desayuno*) with rolls or toast (*tostada*) and coffee (*café*). Many Andalucíans prefer a hot chocolate drink into which they dip thin tube-like doughnuts (*churros*). Workmen often spread *zurrapa* or *manteca* on their rolls, which might best be described as an orange-coloured dripping containing left-over pieces of meat and sausage – definitely an acquired taste. Other additions to *tostada* include a clove of garlic (*ajo*) rubbed on dry toast before adding olive oil (*aceite*) and tomato (*tomate*). Or you could have just plain butter (*mantequilla*) and jam (*mermelada*). In some places you can also ask for *paté de higado*, or live paté.

Main meals in restaurants usually consist of three courses. Starters are many and varied. In the winter, thick country soups (*cocidos*) are popular, while in the summer light mixed salads (*ensalada mixta*) are widely eaten. *Gazpacho*, an Andalucian speciality, is a cold soup containing finely chopped garlic, onions, tomatoes and peppers. *Tortilla española*, a Spanish potato omelette, also makes a filling starter. Main courses will feature fish, meat or game, but don't expect sophisticated sauces or exotic vegetables. The main item will usually be fried or grilled, smothered in garlic and accompanied by a few fried potatoes.

Fresh fish and shellfish are the main joys of Andalucían cooking. With both the Atlantic and Mediterranean to call upon, the variety is enormous. Common fish on menus are *merluza* (hake), *sardinas* (sardines), *calamares* (squid) and *pez espada* (swordfish). Amongst the shellfish, *gambas* (prawns) and *mejillones* (mussels) are the most popular and both figure prominently in *paella*, a rice dish which originated in Valencia. The Andalucían version contains less meat, but is equally good. Fish can be expensive inland and here it is worth trying the game dishes, which include rabbit, partridge, venison, wild boar and hare. *Jamon serrano* (cured ham) is also superb, particularly in the north of the region, and will be found hanging from the ceilings in many bars and restaurants. But, beware, some varieties are extremely expensive. *Carne* (meat) is generally good and usually served grilled. *Cerdo* (pork) and *cordero* (lamb) are normally reliable, but beef is often disappointing and steak should only be tried at the specialist steak houses which are beginning to appear on the coast. *Estafada*, a meat stew flavoured with cloves, is a typical country dish.

Desserts in the cheaper restaurants tend to be limited to *flan* (cream caramel), ice cream and *fruta del tiempo* (fruit in season). It is worth searching for some of the regional specialities, which are usually very sweet and a throwback to the Moorish occupation. You are more likely to find these in the north of the area (see regional escriptions). Cheese is not offered at the end of a meal and is more likely to be found as a *tapa*. Cheese is not, in fact, produced to any great extent in Andalucía. Supermarket shelves, however, are full of interesting Spanish regional cheeses, many of which are worth trying.

Vegetarians and vegans will find life difficult in Andalucía, as despite the abundance of vegetables produced in the area, particularly under plastic in Almería, little finds its way onto the menu. Some tapas dishes are vegetarian like *ensaladilla* (diced vegetables in mayonnaise), *pimientos* (peppers) *garbanzoz con espinaca* (chickpeas and spinach) and *patatas alioli* (potatoes in garlic mayonnaise), as well as the ubiquitous *tortilla española* (potato omelette).

Eating out

Traditional Spanish bars and restaurants are found throughout the region, and the latter are graded in a fashion. The classification, however, tends to depend on the facilities and prices, rather than the excellence of the cooking, so it is probably best ignored. The more pretentious establishments call themselves *mesónes*, while the larger hotels will have expensive dining rooms or *comedores*. In the coastal resorts, look out for beach bars (*merenderos* or *chiringuitos*) which serve fresh fish and stay open late (see box, page 232). In the fishing ports in western Andalucía are *freidurías* and *marisquerías*, specializing in fish and shellfish. Sandwich bars, cafeterias and milk bars often aim at an up-market clientele. Inland, the roadside *ventas*, often offer excellent regional game dishes. Over the last decade the coastal resorts have seen the introduction of numerous international restaurants, such as Chinese, Indian and Italian, plus a whole range of American fast food outlets and take-aways. Restaurants often offer a *menú del dia* (set menu), typically a three-course meal with bread and a drink, generally costing anything from €5 and 15. There are confusing terms for the amount of food on offer. Free *tapa* food provided with a drink is known as a *pincho*. The larger sized tapa dish which is paid for is known as a *ración*. In some parts of the region, particularly in the east and inland, the menu may also include several *platos combinadas*, or combined plate, involving meat or fish, plus potatoes and a vegetable or salad; sometimes with bread and a drink.

Spanish mealtimes reflect the unusual working day. Breakfast (*desayuno*) is often taken out in a café or bar usually around 1000. Lunch (*almuerzo*) is usually the main meal of the day and will rarely start before 1400, allowing a siesta before returning to work. The evening meal (*cena*) is lighter and is eaten about 2100 or 2200. Many Andalucíans will prefer some *tapas* instead of a full meal in the evening. Away from the tourist areas, restaurants stick to these times, but on the coast they adapt to the requirements of visitors.

Drink

Alcoholic drinks are plentiful and the supermarket shelves are lined with a huge variety of wines, beers and spirits, all at prices which seem remarkably cheap to visitors from the UK and North America. *Vino* (wine) is widely drunk with meals, but it is usually *tinto* (red). *Rosada* (rosé) and *blanco* (white) are less popular, probably because their quality in Spain is generally poor. Indeed, in the summer, red wine is frequently produced from the fridge as an alternative to white. At this time of the year, *tinto de verano* (summer wine) is a combination of red wine, ice and lemonade. A stronger version is *sangría*, with the addition of fruit and sherry, brandy or fruit liqueur. Few table wines are produced in Andalucía, with the exception of the white wines of the Condado region of Huelva province and the strong rosés of the Alpujarras. The main offerings in restaurants come from the Rioja, Valdepeñas and Navarra areas. A drinkable wine can be bought from supermarkets for as little as €1.5, but the same bottle can cost two or three times as much in a restaurant. Foreign wines are a rarity, although you may find some Portuguese varieties, like *Vinho Verde*. Most restaurants will have a *vino de la casa* (house wine), but the quality varies. Try it first, before ordering a bottle.

It is with the fortified wines, such as sherry, that Andalucía excels. It is produced in the 'sherry triangle' between Jerez, Sanlúcar and El Puerto de Santa María and comes in a bewildering variety of forms. The most popular is *fino* (dry), which is served cold and is the usual accompaniment to *tapas*. Then there is *amontilado* (medium) and *oloroso* (sweet). Similar to sherry is the *montilla*, produced south of Córdoba.

Cerveza (beer) is of the lager type and is usually served chilled. It is available in bottles, but the cheapest way to drink beer is in draught form. Ask for *una caña*, which will cost you the equivalent of half a pint for around 70 *centímos* to €1. The two local brands are *San Miguel*, which is brewed next to the airport at Málaga, and *Cruz Campo*, which is made in Sevilla. Other commonly found varieties are *Victoria* and *Majón*. All are good. A bottle with *sin alcohol* on the label will be low, or totally lacking, in alcohol.

A wide variety of spirits are also available. Undoubtedly the most popular with the Spanish is *coñac* (brandy). Made in the sherry producing area, its slightly spicy taste makes it instantly distinguishable from the French variety. Some of the more expensive brands are *Carlos 1* and *Gran Duque de Alba*; at the other end of the scale are *Soberano* and *Fundador*. Many Andalucíans start the day with a large *coñac* with their

Essentials

Alcoholic drinks

Optics are unknown in Spanish bars and measures of spirits are often alarmingly large

☞ Barrels of beer

Spain is a well-known wine-producing country, but you may be surprised by the quality of the beer on offer. It is Europe's third largest producer of beer, after Germany and the UK.

There are two main factors for this enthusiasm for beer in Spain. The first is climate. The Andalucían weather is hot and during the summer with searing temperatures, it is a cold lager-type beer that is the most refreshing drink. Spaniards like to order a caña, a small glass of beer, which they drink quickly standing at a bar and then go about their business. The second factor is the ubiquitous tapas. Many of the dishes on offer are fairly acidic and beer combines better with them than wine.

There are four main brands of Spanish beer available in Andalucía and all have an interesting background and history. Arriving at Málaga airport you can immediately see and smell the **San Miguel** factory. Few people realize, however, that the beer originated in the San Miguel area of Manilla in the Phillipines, where it was brewed by monks. Their small factory was taken over by a Spanish entrepreneur named Andrés Soriano, who, in the 1950s extended the operations to Spain. The firm

was taken over by the multinational company Danone in 1994. San Miguel's main rival is CruzCampo, which was founded by the sherry making Osborne family from Puerto de Santa María. Two members of the family went to Germany to study beer making and on their return in 1904 set up a brewery on the outskirts of Sevilla. It was built near a shrine with a stone cross known as the Cruz del Campo – hence the name of the beer. Cruz Campo has also been taken over by multinationals, with Guinness the major shareholders.

The first **Mahou** beer was brewed in Madrid in a building that now houses the city's archives. It was here that the first pressure barrels in Spain made their appearance. The name Mahou comes from mid-19th century immigrant from Lorraine. Two-thirds of the company is still family owned with the remaining third owned by Danone.

The final member of the big four is **Damm**, founded by August Damm, an immigrant from Alsace who settled in Barcelona. The original brewery dates from 1876 and Damm remained essentially a Catalan beer until the 1950s. It is still 80% Spanish-owned.

breakfast coffee. The other locally produced spirit is gin, made by the *Larios* family in the eastern part of Málaga province. For a change from *coñac*, try some Pacharán, which is a pink drink made from sloes and anis. It can be drunk with ice as an apéritif or neat as a liqueur.

Non-alcoholic drinks Tap water is safe to drink in Andalucía but also try the pure spring water from village and town *fuentes* or fountains. It's worth asking first if the water is *agua potable*. Or drinking water. Of the soft drinks and mixers, *limon* (lemon), *naranja* (orange) and *tónica* (tonic water) are the most common. A delightful thirst-quencher on a hot day is *horchata*, a non-alcoholic drink made from ground almonds or the *chufa*, or tiger nut.

An integral part of Spanish life is coffee, which is served in a variety of ways. First thing in the morning people drink *café con leche*, which is half-coffee, half-milk, while a *café solo*, or espresso, may end the day. Also available are a *café cortado*, coffee with a drop of milk, or a *café sombra*, coffee with lots of milk. In the summer, try a *café con leche* served in a glass of ice. Té or tea is also sold in bars, although it is not nearly as popular as coffee.

Shopping

Andalucía has a wealth of handicrafts (*artesanía*) including pottery, leather goods, textiles and wickerwork, which are relatively cheap and widely available in craft shops (look out for the sign *Artesanía*) and markets. Traditional crafts seen today in Andalucía are a legacy from those who have lived in the region over centuries, like the Phoenicians, Romans and Moors. The best places to buy *artesanía* is where it is produced. For example, you can buy handmade classical guitars in Granda and, if you could find a way of transporting them home, barrels from the wine-producing areas of Cádiz, Córdoba and Jerez. You can also find antiques and interesting artefacts at flea markets (*mercadillos*), car boot sales (*rastros*) and in antique shops.

Furniture & woodwork

Huelva province is a good place to buy traditionally crafted furniture, particularly in Valverde del Camino, Galaroza and Zalamea. Brightly handpainted Sevillian chairs, with a rush-woven seat, are made in Galaroza and can be bought throughout the Sierra de Aracena. If you find these too bulky to take home, you could buy the tiny children's version. Another good place to buy woodwork is Grazalema, Málaga. In Granada, you can marquetry boxes, trays and chess sets. Lucena in Córdoba province is the most famous place in Andalucía for furniture, but more modern showrooms have replaced many traditional workshops.

Gold & silver jewellery

Córdoba is by far the most important centre for this, producing two-thirds of Spain's jewellery. Granada also has a number of workshops.

Leather goods

These are available throughout Andalucía, but one of the best-known places for traditional leatherwork is Ubrique in Cadiz, where you can buy excellent purses and bags. Saddle making workshops can be found in Ronda, but the province of Huelva has the highest concentration of these, which also produce related goods like bridles and riding boots. You can find harness-making workshops in Sevilla, which also make saddles to order. Particularly good footwear are made in Valverde del Camino, while Aroche, Huelva and Zalamea produce excellent saddles. Handmade shoes are produced in Antequera, Málaga province; Montoro, Córdoba; and the provinces of Almería and Huelva.

Pottery

The main centres that have been famous for pottery production, often for centuries, are Triana in Sevilla; the Alpujarras, Fajalauza and Guadix in Granada; Lucena and La Rambla in Córdoba province; Bailén, Andújar and Úbeda in Jaén province; and Jimena, Níjar and Sorbas in Almería province. Some of the most common pottery products are colourful painted flower pots, decorative plates and bowls and terracotta ovenware. Moorish techniques and designs are still widespread; look out for Moorish-style tiles and, in Sevilla, copies of tiles with 16th-century designs. In Almería, centuries-old Moorish kilns are still in use, especially in the pottery centres of Níjar and Sorbas. In Córdoba, potters use distinctive Caliphate Moorish designs. In Málaga you can buy barros Malaguenos, small clay figuerines. Potters in La Rambla, Córdoba, specialise in drinking vessels with spouts known as botijos.

Sherry

For fino and brandy, visit bodegas in Jerez de la Frontera, also El Puerto de Santa María, and you can buy manzanilla sherry from Sanlúcar de Barrameda, all in Cádiz province.

Textiles

Grazalema, Málaga, produces handwoven wool blankets and ponchos. Also made on hand-operated looms are jarapas, rugs and blankets woven from scraps fabric and wool, which you can buy in Almería province, in places like Níjar. The Alpujarras is famed for its Moorish rugs and alpujarreño cloth. Look out for intricately hand-embroidered shawls, tablecloths and flamenco dresses, as well as lace products. Holy Week in Sevilla has greatly influenced the city's tradition of embroidery, with some workshops often located near churches and convents producing hand-embroidered cloth used for religious processions. In Málaga and Macharaviaya you can find hand-embroidered tablecloths.

Entertainment and nightlife

Buy a local newspaper (or a national one like El País with an Andalucía supplement) for list of what's on or contact the local tourist office

Throughout Andalucía, nightlife gets going during the summer months. When in more northern climates most people wind down a bit. The major cities are geared up to all-night drinking, clubs, live music, cinema, theatre or just evening strolling. On the coast you can drink at *chiringuitos*, or beach bars, that often stay open all night during the summer months (see box, page 232). In smaller towns and villages, nightlife revolves around the *paseo* or main plaza, where there is usually a smattering of bars and *kioscos* where children congregate to stock up on sweets. Even the smallest village will be lively on summer evenings at weekends, while larger villages and towns will be buzzing every evening. Not much happens until after 10pm, when families sit down to dinner at home. Pubs, late-night bars (*bares de copas*) and discotecas open until at least 0300-0400, especially Thursday to Sunday. However, during the winter – apart from Christmas and New Year's Eve – nightlife is much more low-key and in the smaller places may be virtually non-existent beyond hanging out in local bars until midnight.

One major feature of nightlife are the seemingly endless round of fiestas from May to September. So numerous are village and town fiestas, ferias and romerías that it is hard to miss them even during the shortest visit. This is also due to the fact that they often last for at least three days, sometimes a week. During this time, many stay up all night and daytime activities are at a minimum. The liveliest time to be at a fiesta is usually from around 1am to 3am, when it's common to see whole families out enjoying themselves; if you turn up before 10pm, you may be among the first arrivals. There is usually an array of religious processions and invariably a bullfight in all but the smallest villages.

Cinema & theatre
Unfortunately most foreign films are dubbed in Spanish so unless you're watching Charlie Chaplin, your Spanish has to be up to scratch if you want to appreciate the cinema experience. Most towns have a cinema, or a venue to screen films, as do some villages who may show films periodically. In the summer, watch out for cine de verano, where films may screened at an outdoor venue, so at least if you don't understand the Spanish, you can enjoy the night sky pricked with stars. Films are generally inexpensive, with tickets costing around €2.50, rising to around €6 in multi-screen venues in cities. Cities and towns have theatres, where plays are usually staged in Spanish. Some villages will put on plays from time to time; look out for posters. For details of films and plays in larger places, see local newspapers or ring venues directly; see listings under individual towns in the guide for contact details.

Flamenco
See also page 416
Pure flamenco is an essentially private phenomenon and often difficult to find. Some shows or *tablaos* with live musicians can be very entertaining, but they will not be the real thing. The best bet is to head for some of the following flamenco clubs or *peñas* for something more spontaneous: *El Tablao*, C Santa María de la Cabeza 4, Cádiz; *Mesón de la Luna*, Calleja de la Luna s/n, Córdoba; Barrio Santiago, Jerez; *Jardines de Neptuno*, *Camino de Ronda* and *Reina Mora*, Mirador de San Cristóbal, Albaicín, Granada; *Tablao El Arenal*, C Rodó 7, Los Gallos, Plaza de Santa Cruz and *Palacio del Embrujo*, C María Auxiliadora 18, Sevilla.

Alternatively, ask the local tourist office for details for any flamenco festivals being held. The following are the biggest and most popular. In Jerez, the *Flamenco Festival* held in February/March is one of the most important flamenco festivals. One of Andalucía´s biggest cultural events is Granada´s *International Festival of Music and Dance* in June/July, held in the Alhambra´s Carlos V Palace, with classical music and ballet shows as well as flamenco. At the end of August is *Almería's Flamenco Festival*, which mainly concentrates on *el cante* and *el toque*, although it includes some dance too. The *Flamenco Biennial* in Sevilla takes place every two years in September/October of even numbered years and offers the chance to catch the most respected names in flamenco, with more than 600 artists taking part. In December is *Encuentros Flamencos* in Granada, where the city brings together the biggest flamenco names, taking a different theme each year.

Holidays and festivals

It is believed the Spanish take more holidays than any other Europeans. There are 14 national holidays, when everything closes down, plus Andalucían holidays and local fiestas. If the fiesta is on a Thursday, many people make a *puente* or bridge by adding a day on to a holiday, thereby creating a very long weekend.

Most people take their main holiday in August. During this period, plus *Semana Santa* (Holy Week) hotels are usually full and you'll need to book in advance. Prices for accommodation, as well as food and drink in bars and restaurants, are often higher than usual. To find out more on what's on where and when, contact tourist offices, see www.andalucia.org or check out the *ferias y fiestas de Andalucía* guide published annually by the Andalucían government.

National holidays 1 January **Año Nuevo** New Year's Day; *6 January* **Epifanía** Epiphany; *March/April* **Semana Santa** Holy Week; *1 May* **Fiesta del Trabajo** Labour Day; *June* (movable) **Corpus Cristi**; *24 June* **Día de San Juan** The King's Saint Day; *25 July* **Día de Santiago** Spain's patron saint; *15 August* **La Asunción de la Virgen** The Assumption of the Virgin; *12 October* **Día de la Hispanidad** Columbus Day; *1 November* **Todos los Santos** All Saints' Day; *6 December* **Día de la Constitución** Constitution Day; *8 December* **Día de la Inmaculada Concepción** Immaculate Conception; *25 December* **Navidad** Christmas Day.

Ferias Every town and village has a yearly fair during the summer, Spain's largest and most famous being Sevilla (see page 66); Málaga's is also worth seeing. Typically, the whole village or town virtually shuts down, the main street is closed to traffic, decorated and a fair is set up. Tables and chairs outside makeshift bars line the street, with a stage set up in the main square for bands. In larger ferias there may be *casetas*, or marquees, which are funded by groups of friends or families, who club together to buy food and drink and invite people in to join them. A bullfight is usually held some time duing the week; look out for posters. Ferias last from midweek to the following Sunday (Monday may also be a holiday for the larger ferias).

Romerías These pilgrimages, known as *romerías* because pilgrims traditionally went to Rome and were thus known as *romeros*, are to local shrines and have become increasingly popular in post-Franco times. Many travel on horseback and are colourfully dressed, the women in flamenco dresses and the men in wide-brimmed hats, tight trousers and pin-striped waistcoats, with children elaborately attired in smaller replica costumes. Casetas, are usually set up on the pilgrimage site. Spain's largest (with around a million pilgrims) is held at Whitsun in El Rocío, Huelva province, see box, page 133. The second most important one is the Virgen de la Cabeza, in Andújar, Jaén, where thousands of pilgrims from throughout Spain converge at the end of April.

Grape harvests Vendimia, or grape harvests, are held in August and September, often with a fiesta. The most famous ones are celebrated in Montilla, Córdoba; Jerez, Cádiz and La Palma del Condado, Huelva.

Año Nuevo On New Year's Eve, people congregate in village squares and eat 12 grapes, which correspond to the 12 strokes of midnight from the church bells, amid the deafening sound of firecrackers.

Epifanía Otherwise known as *Día de los Reyes*, this is the day that the 'three kings' appear on horseback in the streets to distribute children's Christmas presents and sweets.

Carnaval Carnival is a riotous week-long celebration held throughout Andalucía with parades in most towns the weekend before or after Shrove Tuesday (12 February 2002 and 4 March 2003). Spain's best carnival is in Cádiz, which takes place for 10 days and is renowned for its satirical songsters and the flamboyant gay contingent. See www.carnavaldecadiz.com for pictures and more information. Also good is carnival elsewhere in Cádiz province, particularly in Algeciras, Chiclana, Medina Sidonia, El Puerto de Santa María and Rota. In Huelva province, Ayamonte and Isla Cristina are the most popular.

Semana Santa Holy Week processions take place in the week before Easter Sunday (31 March 2002 and 20 April 2003), with a passion play enacted on Good Friday. The best ones to see are in Córdoba, Granada, Málaga and Sevilla. Figures of Christ on the cross, the Virgin Mary and other holy images mounted on *pasos*, or floats, are carried by eerily hooded figures accompanied by other penitents, or *nazarenos,* slowly and solemnly through the streets. Religious brotherhoods who take part in the processions are usually made up of important local inhabitants and tradesmen's guilds.

Other dates Corpus Cristi starts on the Thursday after Trinity Sunday in May/June (30 May 2002). The most renowned processions are held in Granada.

Día de San Juan A national holiday in honour of the King Juan Carlos I's saint day, this is celebrated on the evening of 23 June, with bonfires and fireworks. Those on the beach dip their feet in the sea just after midnight for good luck.

Other events **Día de Santiago** is the celebration of Spain's patron saint. Most places have religious services on **La Asunción** to celebrate Spain's patron saint. **Día de la Hispanidad** marks the so-called 'discovery' of the Americas by Columbus. **Todos los Santos** is the day for remembering the dead. **Navidad** is the time when families celebrate with a large dinner at midnight on Christmas Eve, so you'll find the streets deserted at this time, although people do go out afterwards.

Sport and special interest travel

Birdwatching
See also page 424 Andalucía is rich in birdlife, partly because it has 80 protected areas covering 17% of the region. One of the most spectacular aspects of birdwatching here is the twice-yearly migration, which you can observe in spring and autumn at locations around Tarifa and Algeciras in Cádiz province and the Upper Rock Nature Reserve, Gibraltar (see box, page 204). Other good spots for birdlife include the Coto Doñana National Park, one of Europe's most important wetland sites, the nearby Marismas de Odiel, both in Huelva province; Las Salinas on the Cabo de Gata coastline, Almería; Laguna de Medina, Cádiz; Campiña Cordobesa, Córdoba for winter wildfowl on

semi-saline lakes; Spain's largest protected area, the Parque Natural de Cazorla, Jaén and the Sierra Nevada, Granada. Also in Granada province is one of the best places to see steppe birds, the Hoya de Guadix. For tour operators see page 23.

Climbing

Spain is not generally thought of as a mecca for climbing, or *escalada*, but it is, nevertheless, a popular sport and Málaga province in particular offers some superb climbs. Indeed, some of Spain's foremost rock climbers come from Málaga. The place where most aficionados head for is the El Chorro Gorge, where there are 300 m cliffs cut by the Río Guadalhorce that can be glimpsed from the train as it spasmodically emerges from the tunnels which line the gorge. The main meeting place in El Chorro is *Isabel's Bar*. There are other challenging equipped climbs in Málaga at Benaoján, Benhavís, Casares, El Torcal, Mijas and Puerto del Viento at Ronda. For further details, contact: **Sociedad Excursionista de Málaga**, Calle República Argentina 9, 29016, Málaga, T952-650258. Outside of Málaga province, there is good climbing at Guëjar-Sierra in the Sierra de Nevada; Cerro del Hierro, a Roman iron mine, outside Sevilla; and Cerro San Bartolo near Bolonia, Cádiz province.

Unlike climbing routes in Britain which are generally unassisted, climbs in Andalucía are sport climbs, that is they are 'equipped' already with bolts and rings, thereby removing much of the danger involved in case of equipment failure. If you become detached from the rock face, you will not fall completely to the ground. Although this does not entirely eliminate accidents, serious casualties are rare.

Fishing

You should bring your own tackle as it is almost impossible to hire equipment

It is a common sight in Andalucía to see people sea fishing from beaches and rocks, but what is not generally known is that there are also good opportunities for freshwater fishing. All the major towns and provincial capitals have nearby reservoirs to ensure their water supply and these are often well-stocked with fish, as are the rivers which feed them. The main type of fish found are: carp (*carpa*), mirror carp (*ciprinidos*), golden carp (*carpa de oro*), barbel (*barbo*), black bass (*perca negra*), eel (*anguila*), brown trout (*trucha comun*) and rainbow trout (*trucha arco iris*).

Just a few kilometres north of Málaga, close to the N331, is the Pantano del Agujero, which has good numbers of carp, black bass and golden carp. Further north are the Guadalhorce reservoirs, where good catches of carp have been recorded. Running through the village of El Burgo (between Coin and Ronda) is the Río Turo, which, though small, is well-stocked with barbel and brown and rainbow trout. In Cádiz province, the prime location is the Bornos Reservoir, near Arcos de la Frontera, which has enormous numbers of carp. Fly fishing is good at Río Frio, halfway between Málaga and Granada, where there are several kilometres of fast-flowing river with large numbers of rainbow trout weighing up to 6 lbs. There is fly fishing in the rivers of the Parque Natural de Cazorla, Jaén province. For fishing in natural parks, contact the individual park offices.

A fishing license is required for all freshwater fishing in Andalucía and this may be obtained from branches of the *Caja Rural* savings bank. There is a simple license for coarse fishing and a small surcharge for game fishing. Expect to pay a bank fee for all trout waters, but fishing in major rivers and reservoirs is usually free. There is no 'close season' as such, but there are often rest days along heavily fished trout waters.

Reservoirs have considerable seasonal changes of water level. During the summer months, the beds are exposed and shrubs and reeds grow rapidly. When the water levels rise after the autumn rains, this vegetation is submerged, but remains as an underwater hazard for coarse fishing.

Essentials

Essentials

☞ Striding out

As a general rule the very best time to walk in Andalusia is from late April through to early June and from mid-September to the end of October. You are almost guaranteed mild, sunny weather, it is warm enough to picnic and the chances of rain are slight. The wild flowers tend to be at their very best in late April/early May and this is the time when most walking companies tend to plan their walks. The months that most people avoid are July and August: temperatures are generally just too high to make walking easy or pleasant. If you limit yourself to shorter circuits, get going really early and take plenty of water you can still enjoy walking in summer. But you should be in good physical shape.

If you are prepared to risk rain then the winter months can be a wonderful time to be out walking, especially from December to February when rainfall is generally less than in November, March and April. 'Generally' means exactly that: rainfall statistics for the past century confirm all of the above but the past decade, with the prolonged drought of the 1990s, followed by some unusually wet winters, provide no steady yardstick against which to base your predictions. The exception is the Parque Natural de Cazorla which is further north than any of the other parks included in this book. Here the Mediterranean influence is less marked and there may well be snow and ice on the higher routes from November onwards. On the other hand the Alpujarras, although higher than Cazorla, rarely have snow settling beneath 1,200m and to walk with the snowy Sierra Nevada as a backdrop makes for truly memorable experience. But you will need to be well-equipped and ready for brusque changes in temperature.

Golf

Peak times are in spring, when booking is essential

There are nearly 100 golf courses in Andalucía, over a third of all the courses in Spain. The majority are in Málaga and Cádiz provinces and close to the coast, with more than 30 of the courses along the Costa del Sol. The better courses are of championship standard and have been designed by the well-known names of the golfing world, such as Las Brisas, Marbella (T952-810875); Sotogrande (T956-795050); Los Naranjos, Marbella (T952-815206); San Roque (T956-613030); and Valderrama, Sotogrande (T956-795750).

Golf courses mushroomed in the 1980s, when golfers were not deterred by prohibitive green fees. By the late 1980s the recession was beginning to bite and golfers went elsewhere, to Portugal and Florida. Nowadays, golf in Andalucía has regained its popularity with much-reduced green fees and improved facilities. Valdarrama was chosen as the venue for the 1997 Ryder Cup between the European and American teams, the first time in the 70-year history of the tournament that the home match has not been played in the UK.

The courses in the west of the region have high green fees – at euros 120, a round at Valdarrama does not come cheap – but for courses designed by top golfers, there is no lack of takers. East of Marbella, the green fees become more reasonable and there are bargains to be had at courses such as those around Mijas. There is also a great variety of courses to play, from the semi-links course at Alcaidesa overlooking Gibraltar (T956-791040) to the floodlit course that you can play at night at Dama de Noche near Marbella (T952-818150). For more information, contact *Vacation Golf*, T952-837272, who can arrange reservations, competition entries and lessons.

Horse riding

This is extremely popular in Andalucía daily life, as seen in the renowned equestrian school at Jerez and in romerías where people participate in the procession on horseback (and donkeys). Horses can be hired at numerous stables and equestrian centres; contact local tourist offices for more information. Some of the best areas for horse riding are the Alpujarras and the Sierra Nevada. For tour operators see page 23.

As the one of the highest and the most southerly ski resort on mainland Europe, **Skiing**
Solynieve in the Sierra Nevada has a long season, until May. Solynieve hosted the 1995
World Championships here and as a result the facilities are excellent . For more infor-
mation, see the resort's website www.cetursa.es and page 336.

Andalucía is the second most mountainous country in Europe (after Switzerland) and **Walking**
has a plethora of deep gorges, forests and picturesque lakes. The Andalucían govern- **& hiking**
ment is keen to encourage rural tourism and has been actively opening up overgrown *There are walking*
footpaths and old drovers' trails, as well as improving waymarked paths, especially in *routes throughout*
protected areas. Local organisations and individual ex-pats, such as Elma Watson at *the book*
Nerja and David Lanfear at Grazalema, are also helping to establish and maintain walking routes. Walking routes are often classified as GR or PR, which mean *gran recorrida*
(long distance) or *pequeño recorrida* (short distance). Long distance walks may be part
of a route that crosses much of Spain, while shorter routes can be walked in a few days
or a few hours.

Some of the best walking, or *senderismo*, in Andalucía can be found in the Alpujarras
on the southern flanks of the Sierra Nevada – the information centre in Pampaniera has
a good supply of maps and can arrange guided walks. Neighbouring Trévelez is the
starting point for tackling Mulhacén, which at 3,482 m is the highest mountain on
mainland Spain. Gentler walking can be found in Parque Natural de la Sierra de
Aracena in Huelva province. There are few marked footpaths in the Cazorla Natural
Park, but those that do exist, such as the walk up the Barrossa Valley, are exceptionally
good. Another popular area for walking can be found amongst the White Villages
southwest of Ronda, based around Gaucín and Grazalema. In the La Axarquía area,
there is good hiking country around the villages of Cómpeta and Frigiliana.

The best time to take a walking holiday in Andalucía is undoubtedly late spring.
The weather is good, the birds in full song and the wild flowers prolific. Late September and early October is cooler too and the autumn colours can be spectacular, especially in areas such as the Sierra de Aracena. Although winter is officially the rainy
season, there can be some superb weather for walking – although it cannot be guaranteed. The higher paths, however, are likely to be snow-covered, particularly in the
Cazorla region. Avoid July and August, when the heat is searing and walking is an
endurance test.

Make sure that you are well-equipped, with strong footwear, plenty of water and
a good map (see page 44). For tour operators see page 23. An excellent book is the
informative *Walking in Andalucía*, by Guy Hunter-Watts, published in 2000 by
Santana, which describes in detail a number of walks with background information
and suggested accommodation. The regional tourist department produce a booklet
entitled *Hiking – Andalucía Walking Tours*. It lists 25 walks in each province, produced
in quaint English with picturesque maps. Unfortunately, many of the routes simply
follow roads.

Diving, sailing, parasailing, waterskiing and windsurfing are well catered for along the **Watersports**
whole coast of Andalucía. Tarifa in Cádiz province is the Europe's Mecca for
windsurfers, while the Cabo de Gata, Almería, is a good spot for diving. There is a string
of marinas along both the Atlantic and Mediterranean coastlines, where you can hire
boats or have lessons.

Wine cellars or *bodegas*, in wine and sherry producing areas in Andalucía, offer **Wine & sherry**
tastings; it's best to ring first. Sherry is produced mainly within the triangle formed **tasting**
by the towns of Jerez de la Frontera, El Puerto de Santa María and Sanlúcar de
Barrameda in Cádiz province. The main wine-producing area is Montilla in
Córdoba province.

Essentials

Spectator sports

Bullfighting Like it or not, bullfighting is an unavoidable aspect of daily life in Andalucía during the sport's season. This kicks off with a bullfight in Sevilla's Real Maetranza ring on Easter Sunday and ends with a fight in the same place on 12 October. With around 70 bull-rings in Andalucía, it's easy to see a *corrida*, or bullfight, wherever you are and many smaller ones are held during annual fíestas of towns and villages. Look out for posters advertising bullfights, which will appear two weeks before a fight. There's even bullfighting magazines available, like *6toros6*. Sevilla's bullring is the most important where a week-long series of fights are held during the Feria in April. Ronda has one of the oldest bullrings in Spain, dating from 1785, and holds a Pedro Romero festival with so-called *corridas Goyescas*, in September when bullfights take place with the *matadores*, or bullfighters, attired in dress from the painter Goya's time. If you want to know more, visit one of the region's bullfighting museums at Córdoba, Estepona, La Linea, Ronda or Sevilla.

The bullfight begins with a procession including the three matadores, who will fight two bulls each, their teams and the *alguacilillos*, or 'bailiffs'. The bailiffs open the gate to let the bull in the ring and the first stage consists of the matador's team assessing the bull by flourishing pink and gold capes. Then mounted *picadores* pro-voke the bull and one of them drives a lance into the bull's neck, which weakens the bull and makes it lower its neck for the matador's performance. The next stage involves a *banderillero*, brandishing two *banderillas* (barbed darts with colourful rib-bons), charging at the bull and putting banderillas in its neck; another technique aimed at slowing down the bull. At the beginning of the last stage the matador enters the ring and salutes the 'president', an important figure who is in charge of the fight. The matador has a red cape that he or she uses to draw the bull closer, with each pass of the cape marked by a shout of 'óle' from the audience. When the mata-dor thinks the bull is sufficiently tired, he or she plunges a sword between the bull's shoulders and to its heart. A successful matador will be applauded, showered with flowers and given a show of hankerschiefs. Rather gruesomely, if the bull has per-formed particularly well, its carcass is dragged out for a lap of 'honour'. But the kill can also be a messy and drawn out affair, with the matador having many attempts and calling on one of his team to help.

You can buy tickets (*billetes*) from the bullring ticket office (*taquilla*). Tickets often start at less than €6 for a *novillada*, which is not technically a bullfight since it involves a novice bullfighter, or *novillero*, and a young bull, *novillo*. Bullfights start at €8, costing up to €90 for those held at major rings like Sevilla's Maestranza. You pay according to where you sit around the bullring. Seats in the sun (*sol*) are cheaper than those in the shade (*sombra*). Inbetween are *sol y sombra* seats, which are in the shade after a while. Seats closest to the bullring itself cost more, with ringside ones (*barrera*) being the most expensive; *contrabarrera* are those in the next row back . Beyond these are the cheaper seats, *tendidos*, which are *alto* or *bajo*. The cheapest seats are *gradas*, which are at the top at the back. As the seating is often on stone steps, it's worth renting a cushion. On your ticket will be the area (eg *barrera*), num-ber, row (*fila*) and seat (*asiento*). Don't listen to ticket touts who tell you that the bull-fight is sold out, since this is rarely the case, especially if you arrive early to buy a ticket from the *taquilla*. Children are not allowed to see bullfights. For more information, check out the following websites: , for Sevilla's bullring (in English); and for the latest news on events and bullfighters.

Although most Spanish people unquestionably accept bullfighting as an integral part of their lives, there is some organized anti-bullfight protest. The Spanish animal rights group, ADDA, has joined forces with the international Anti-Bullfighting Cam-paign (ABC) and launched a letter-writing protest urging the Catholic Church to stop bulls being killed during Catholic fiestas. Elsewhere in Europe, the London-based World Society for the Protection of Animals (WSPA) encourages tourists to boycott bullfights and is calling for a government ban of fights. Contact ADDA in Spain at: C/ Bailén 164, Local 2 interior, 08037 Barcelona, T954-591601, and WSPA at: 89 Albert Embankment, London SE1 7TP, T020-7793 0540, www.wspa.org.uk

Football

Andalucía boasts the first football team in the country, Recreativo de Huelva, which was founded by English miners working in Rio Tinto in 1889. The two biggest stadiums are Sánchez Pizjuán (Sevilla FC) and Ruiz de Lopera (Real Betis, also in Sevilla), with a capacity of 45,000 and 52,000 respectively. There are four ligas, or divisions, the Primera Liga being equivalent to the Premiership in the UK. Of these 20 teams, only three are Andaluz: Sevilla FC, Real Betis and Málaga (liga 2001-2002), with five more in the second division: Recreativo de Huelva, Jaén, Xerez, Córdoba and Ejído (Almería). Due to the lack of success of the Andalucían teams (at least in recent years), support from the local population tends to focus on the big two: Real Madrid and Barça, with many bars blatantly supporting one or the other, by hanging up football posters and other paraphernalia and only screening games on TV featuring their team. However, this isn't always the case and true fans will stick with their teams. Real Betis is a favourite in western Andalucía (also boasting 260 *peñas* or fan clubs dotted around the country) thanks to its working class fan base. This is in contrast to Sevilla FC which has to hold a more middle-class following.

Tickets start cost from €8 to 60 for first division matches,with more expensive tickets at games with more popular teams. Failing the real thing, you can catch major matches at local bars, which invariably have a great atmosphere. The daily sports newspapers have information of these and general fixtures; see page 47. The Monday editions have details of what games are on the following weekend, as well as results from the last weekend.

Health

Most visitors will have no medical problems travelling in Andalucía. However, during the summer months it's worth taking precautions against the sun by applying high-factor sun protection, wearing a hat, keeping in the shade or indoors around the hottest time of the day and drinking lots of water. Tap water is generally OK to drink, as is water from drinking fountains. If in doubt, ask *es potable el agua?*

If you need a doctor (*médico*), expect to pay around €8 to 30. Keep the receipt for insurance purposes. You can often find a multilingual doctor in tourist areas. You can find chemists or *farmacias* in most towns and villages; look for a green cross sign. These provide most medicines, often without a prescription, and will give advice (although not in English away from tourist areas) about ailments and suggest remedies. They open from 0930-1330, 1630-2000; some *farmacias* in bigger cities are open 24 hours. For details of those chemists on a rota system (*farmacias de guardia*) that are open all night and at weekends, see *farmacia* windows and local newspapers.

Medical facilities

Dial T061 for emergencies, including ambulance services

The Andalucían health service runs a variety of medical facilities: *consultorios* (doctors' surgeries), can be found in many villages, while *centros de salud* (health centres), which can give some emergency treatment, are in towns and cities. The Cruz Roja (Red Cross) is situated on beaches, along main roads and in towns. There are a number of excellent hospitals throughout Andalucía with emergency departments (*urgencias*), plus some private clinics. For contact details and addresses, see the directories of individual towns in this guide or the Yellow Pages (*Páginas Amarillas*). For vaccination and health insurance information, see page 24.

What to take   It's not necessary to take medical supplies from home since you can buy most items in Andalucía. However, if you need medication, make sure you bring a copy of your prescription as well as a letter from your doctor in case you need additional supplies.

Sevilla Province

3

Sevilla Province

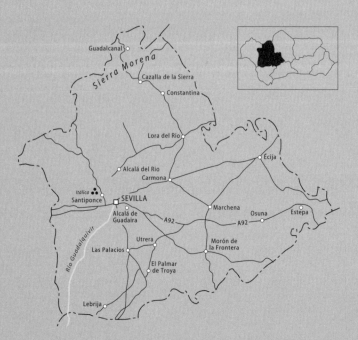

The province of Sevilla is landlocked, with Huelva to the west, Cádiz to the south and Málaga and Córdoba provinces to the east. Sevilla, the provincial capital, is on most itineraries, due to its wealth of monuments and vibrant atmosphere. As well as a wealth of tapas bars and a zinging nightlife, Sevilla boasts two of Spain's most famous festivals, its Semana Santa celebrations and its Feria de Abril. The remainder of the province is little visited, which is a pity, because towns such as Carmona, Osuna, Écija and Estepa have much of interest.

For centuries the province's main artery has been Andalucía's largest river, the **Guadalquivir***. Running through the centre of the area, the river's flood plain provides fertile farmland for the production of cereals, vines, sunflowers and olives. But the same silt that fertilizes the soil has also clogged up the river, which is kept navigable to Sevilla only with extensive dredging.*

To the north are the wooded hills of the **Sierra Morena** *rising to a little over 900 m. In the Sierra Morena, is the* **Parque Natural de Sierra Norte***, which makes a welcome change from the heat of Sevilla. To the south of the capital, there are reserves based on the marshlands on either side of the Guadalquivir.*

Sevilla

Population: 701,927
Colour map 1, grid C5

Capital of Andalucía and its largest city, Sevilla is located at the head of naviga-tion on the Río Guadalquivir. The home of Carmen, Sevilla is an essentially romantic and exuberant city. There are monuments in profusion, from a Roman amphitheatre at Itálica to the modern remains of EXPO '92. In between are a Moorish Giralda tower, a Mudéjar Alcázar and the huge Gothic Catedral, plus a host of other historic attractions. Furthermore, there are some outstanding works of art on show at the many museums. The sombre Holy Week processions are arguably the most impressive in Spain and are quickly followed by the deter-mined gaiety of the Feria de Abril. Much of its charm, however, is found in wan-dering through its barrios, each with its own distinct character, stopping for tapas at any one of its hundreds of bars and watching the Sevillano world buzz by.

A largely misplaced reputation for street crime should not deter the visitor – spend at least two days here, preferably a week! Remember, though, that accom-modation costs more than elsewhere in Andalucía – particularly during Easter and Feria. Also, it gets unbearably hot in July and August, when it is wise to follow the example of the Sevillanos – and leave town.

Ins and outs

Getting there
See page 99
for further details

The **airport** is at San Pablo, 12 km east of the city for both internal and international flights. For information, T954449023. An *Amarillos* bus runs to the city centre at Puerta de Jerez, via the train station, costing €2 and taking 30 mins. Taxis are available, but watch out for fiddled fares. The set fares can be seen in the airport and are currently €15. The main **bus** station is Prado de San Sebastián in C Manuel Vásquez Sagastizábal, T954417111, and is within walking distance of the city centre. Cross C Menéndez Pelayo and at Plaza Don Juan de Austria turn down C San Fernando to Puerta de Jerez, where a right turn takes you down Av de la Constitución past the tourist office and the cathedral. The other bus station is at Plaza de Armas, T954907737, next to the Puente del Cachorro on the river. You can walk to the centre from here, or take the C4 to the Puerta de Jerez and beyond. If arriving by car, **parking** can be horrendous, although new underground car parks have been built. If staying overnight, try to find a hotel with a garage or secure parking. Santa Justa **train** station is on Av de Kansas City, T954414111 (information), T954421562 (reservations). Bus 32 runs to Plaza Encarnación in the centre, while C1 and C2 buses go to the Prado de San Sebastián station.

Getting around
Useful buses are C1,
C2, C3, and C4 which
go around the
inner ring road

Sevilla is a large city and the monuments are scattered around the inner area, so there is a limit to the amount of foot-slogging which can be done in the city's notorious heat, particularly in the summer months. Fortunately there are plenty of **taxis** available, with ranks at the Parque de María Luisa, Plaza de la Legión, C Reyes Católicos and Plaza de Cuba on the other side of the river. Sevilla has a cheap and efficient **bus** system.

Tourist offices

The main **regional turismo** is at Av de la Constitución 21, T954221404, open Mon-Fri 0900-1900, Sat 1000-1400, 1500-1900, Sun and holidays 1000-1400. They can provide maps of the city and copies of the monthly free what's-on guide *El Giraldillo*. Perhaps not surprisingly, the *turismo* can be swamped with tourists during the height of the season. There is also a smaller *turismo* close to the Parque de María Luisa, open Mon-Fri 0830-1830. Small kiosks operate at the terminal building at the airport and at Santa Justa train station, T954541952. Useful websites include www.sol.com7sevilla; www.sevilla.org/tur.html; www.turismosevilla.org; and www.spa.es/turismo/spain/sevilla

24 hours in Sevilla ★

- **9am** Breakfast in Barrio Santa Cruz and visit the Alcázar before the heat and crowds get too much
- **11am** Have a *merienda* in *Casa Roman*, Plaza Venerables, Barrio Santa Cruz
- **12pm** Laze about in the Parque de María Luisa and the Plaza de España
- **2pm** When the heat gets too much, head for *Kiosko de las Flores* on Calle Betís, Triana, for a fried fish lunch extravaganza by the Río Guadalquivir
- **4pm** Saunter along the river and Calle Betís to *Café de la Prensa* for coffee and cake
- **5pm** Siesta in hotel room
- **7pm** Bar hop around Plaza Alfalfa, taking your pick from *Sopa Ganso*, *Casa Los Caracoles* and *Bodega Extremadura* tapas bars, and have a 'Blood of Christ' cocktail in *Bar Garlochi*
- **10pm** Go to the *Carbonería* bar for some free flamenco
- **12pm** Head to the Alameda to the *Fun Club* and then sample a few more *bares de copas* like *Café del Mar* and *El Bosque Animado*. If you're still up for more action, check out *Antigua*, on Calle Marqués de Paradas, which is open until 8.30am
- **8am** Breakfast and a game of pool in *Café Marigalante*, Calle Baños

Sevilla Province

History

Both the Iberians and the Phoenicians occupied the site of what is now Sevilla, attracted by the minerals such as silver and copper which were found in the mountains to the north. The Carthaginians arrived around 500 BC and named the place Hispalis. Later the Romans arrived and under Julius Caesar they captured the settlement, renaming it Julia Romula or little Rome. This became capital of the Roman province of Baetica, while just to the north the city of Itálica was growing quickly, eventually providing two Roman emperors in Trajan and Hadrian. After a brief period of occupation by the Visigoths, Sevilla was taken by the Moors under Musa in 712. They changed the name to Ishbiliyya and also renamed the river Wadi El Kabir (which remains as the present Guadalquivir). The town, despite its own great wealth and status, became subject to the Caliphate of Córdoba, but in 1023 following the disintegration of the Caliphate, Sevilla took the opportunity to declare itself an independent *taifa*. The town was successively ruled by the Abbasids, the Almoravides and the Almohades. It was under the Almohad Emirs that the city achieved its greatest prosperity, especially between 1068 and 1095 under Al-Mutamid, when the silk trade was at its peak.

Sevilla eventually fell in the Reconquest in 1248 to Ferdinand III and thereafter became a favourite residence of the Spanish monarchs. By the 15th century, with the discovery of the New World, Sevilla entered a new age of splendour. The gold from the Indies poured in and by the 1500s it had an estimated population of 150,000, making it one of the most important cities in Europe and a magnet for painters and writers. It is during this period that many of the city's monuments were constructed.

Then followed a period of decline, which began with the silting up of the river, so that the port activities and trade with the Americas moved downstream to Cádiz. Sevilla was later affected by plagues, earthquakes and floods, to say nothing of decadence, while it was unaffected by the Industrial Revolution.

☞ April contrasts in Sevilla

To be in Sevilla in April is a memorable experience, with two of the most extraordinary festivals in the whole of Spain, let alone Andalucía. The month begins with Semana Santa *or Holy Week, when each of the parish churches of the city celebrate Easter. There are over 100* cofradias *or brotherhoods who organize processions in which there are normally two* pasos *or floats, one of the Virgin Mary and the other of Christ, each carried by scores of* costaleros *or bearers. They are accompanied by bands that play deeply disturbing funereal tunes and march to the beat of drums, followed by members of the brotherhoods in their somewhat sinister, slit-eyed conical hats and accompanied by penitents, known as* Nazarenes, *who might be walking barefoot. Occasionally an onlooker, often from a balcony, will launch into an impromptu* saeta, *an eerie form of* cante hondo *or deep song in praise of the Virgin. Each procession eventually reaches the official route which leads along the pedestrianized Calle Sierpes and through the cathedral, accompanied throughout by the thunder of drums. The complete journey from and back to their own parishes can take as long as 12 hours, so it is hardly surprising that there are informal moments when the float is set down and a bearer takes the opportunity to nip into the nearest bar to use the toilet or to have a quick beer. The whole thing makes excellent street theatre.*

The most popular procession is without doubt that of La Macarena, the goddess of the city, who incites an almost pagan adulation and whose paso is attributed to Luis Roldán. Indeed, many of the floats are considerable works of art in their own right and the brotherhoods (which include members from across the whole social range) spend much of the year in their preparation.

After the tense human emotion of Holy Week, it is almost inevitable that the Sevillanos will let off steam. Two weeks later the Feria de Abril *takes place. Dating back to 1293, when Alfonso the Wise granted the city a charter to celebrate Pentecost, the feria is undoubtedly the largest and most vibrant in Andalucía. Since 1973 it has taken place at a permanent fairground in the barrio of Los Remedios. Here, large marquees or* casetas *are set up, many belonging to the more wealthy Seville families, while others are run by companies or political parties. The important thing is to have* enchufes *or the right connections – not to have access to the hospitality of a* caseta *means certain loss of face. The majority wear traditional costume, with the women in their colourful flamenco dresses and the whole city resounding to the wail of flamenco, the sound of guitars and the percussion of feet and hands. The climax comes when the great and good of Sevilla parade around in carriages or on horseback, while in late afternoon there are the traditional bullfights at the Maestranza bullring. The continual drinking, dancing, merry making and sheer exuberance of the* feria, *make it unique in Andalucía.*

For more on Semana Santa, *see* www.semanasanta.andal.es *and* www.hermandades-de-sevilla.org

The 20th century was marked by two exhibitions. In 1929, the Latin America exhibition never achieved the success desired because of the Wall Street crash, but the Plaza de España and the María Luisa Park plus a number of pavilions remain and add to the appearance of Sevilla today. 1992 was marked by the Fifth Centenary of the Discovery of the Americas and by Expo 92, giving the city a year of wonderful publicity along with vast improvements in its infrastructure, including the AVE high speed train link with Madrid.

The post-Franco era saw a number of developments in Sevilla, helped by the fact that both the long standing premier, Felipe González, and his deputy

Processions of a different kind

You may get used to processions of all types in Andalucía, but one kind which occurs in spring is to be avoided like the plague. This is the line of hundreds of furry caterpillars which can be seen in a nose to tail convoy crossing roads and tracks and climbing walls. These are the caterpillars of the processionary caterpillar moth, and known in Spain as orugas. The moths lay their eggs in grey, pendulous cotton wool-like 'nests' high in pine trees and on hatching, the gregarious caterpillars make their way to the ground in a nose-to-tail chain in their search to find a place to pupate, which is the next stage in their life cycle.

Don't touch or go near these caterpillars, fascinating though they may be. If their hairs (and each caterpillar has 600,000 of them) come into contact with the skin they will cause a painful rash and if disturbed their hairs give off a fine dust which can cause respiratory problems. Children can become quite ill and there have been cases of cats and dogs dying after coming into contact with the Orugas.

If you go into a farmacia and ask for a remedy, be careful how you pronounce 'oruga'. The similar sounding 'arruga' is a wrinkle and crema para arrugas will not cure a rash caused by a caterpillar!

Sevilla Province

were both Sevillanos. Whether Andalucía in general, and Sevilla in particular, will receive similar benefits from the new right-wing government and its regional allies is doubtful. Despite increasing industrial development in the city (the factories stretching out of Sevilla on the Málaga road are particularly hideous), the unemployment rate remains higher than any other Andalucían city. Probably as a result, petty crime in the city is rife. Much is made of the activity of the *semaforazos*, whose speciality is to break car windows at traffic lights and make off with anything they can reach. Bag snatching and pickpocketing are also common. But the situation should not be over exaggerated. The vast majority of visitors to Sevilla will encounter no problems, provided that they take the usual precautions which are detailed elsewhere in this handbook.

Sights

After Sevilla fell to the Christians in 1248, the existing mosque was retained for a while for Christian worship. In 1401, however, a decision was made to build a new cathedral on the site, designed by Alonso Martínez and on such a scale that people in the future would 'think its architects mad'. It was always thought to be the third largest cathedral in the world after St Pauls in London and St Peters in Rome, but latest calculations based on volume put it in first position – if you don't believe it, look in the *Guinness Book of Records*. Based on the rectangular plan of the mosque (116 m long and 76 m wide), extra height has been added, with the central nave rising to 42 m and even the side chapels looking like small churches. It is late Gothic in style and took four centuries to complete. The mosque's minaret, known today as the Giralda, was retained as the bell tower, while the Patio de los Naranjos, the Moorish ablutions area, has also survived.

Catedral
The largest cathedral in the world

The exterior of the cathedral probably has more merit than the rest of the Andalucían cathedrals put together, with some superb stonework and crocketing on its doorways and windows, sturdy flying buttresses and even some stained glass of interest. There are, in fact, seven exterior doors, varying in age, from the Moorish Puerta del Perdón leading into the Patio de los Naranjos to the Puerta Principal, built in the 19th century. The interior is magnificent, combining grandeur, space and solemnity. The five naves based on the Moorish ground plan give a rather box-like feeling. In the central area of the main nave, the *coro* or choir leads to the Capilla Mayor, notable for its huge *retablo*, which must be the most impressive altarpiece in Europe, if not the world. It was the life work of the Flemish carver Pieter Dancart, although many others contributed before its completion in 1526. Depicting the life of Christ, the screen contains a vast number of figures and scenes, all dripping with gold leaf, but look particularly for the Virgin of the Sea and the scale model of Sevilla as it would have been in the 15th century.

There are no fewer than 20 chapels located around the naves, of which the most important is the Capilla Real or Royal Chapel. Here are the remains of Ferdinand III in an urn, while his sword is kept in the chapel treasury. On either side of the domed chapel are tombs containing the remains of Ferdinand's wife, Beatrice, his son Alfonso the Wise, Pedro the Cruel and Pedro's mistress María de Padilla. Other chapels worth looking at, mainly because of their artwork, are the Capilla de San Antonio, which contains Murillo's *Vision of St Anthony* and the Capilla de San Pedro, with a clutch of

Catedral

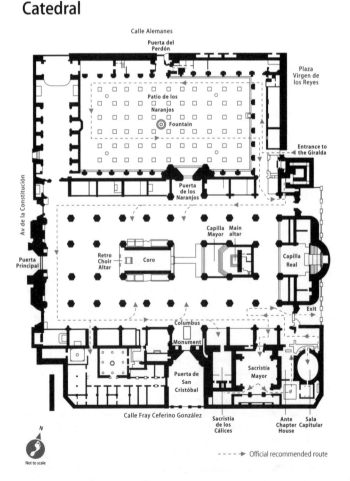

Calle Alemanes

Puerta del Perdón

Plaza Virgen de los Reyes

Patio de los Naranjos

Fountain

Entrance to the Giralda

Av de la Constitución

Puerta de los Naranjos

Capilla Mayor   Main altar

Retro Choir Altar   Coro

Capilla Real

Puerta Principal

Exit

Columbus Monument

Puerta de San Cristóbal

Sacristía Mayor

Calle Fray Ceferino González   Sacristía de los Cálices   Ante Chapter House   Sala Capitular

N

Not to scale

- - - - → Official recommended route

paintings by Zurburán showing the life of St Peter, part of a 17th-century *retablo* by Diego Lopéz Bueno.

In the southeast corner of the cathedral is a fascinating complex of rooms. A delightful antechamber leads into the oval-shaped Sala Capitular or Chapter House, with a superb white and gold domed ceiling. At the far end is the Bishop's Throne, inlaid with mahogany, and above this more Murillo's, including probably his best *Inmaculada* and a circle of eight saints, all considered to be from Sevilla. Nearby is the Sacristía Mayor or Main Sacristy (try to locate this building from the top of the Giralda – it is identified by its domed roof with tiled and buttressed cupola). It is also the cathedral's treasury and contains a vast array of art works, books and silver work, including in the centre a huge four-tier monstrance, said to be nearly 4 m high and weighing 475 kg.

Finally, don't miss the Monument to Christopher Columbus (Cristóbal Colón in Spanish), on the south side of the cathedral. The monument was completed in the late 19th century by the local Sevillan sculptor Arturo Mélida and displays the figures of four kings representing Aragon, Castile, León and Navarra carrying the navigator's coffin. The remains of Columbus are supposed to be in the crypt below, but the tomb may or may not contain his body – it could be his son Diego or even his grandson Luis. On the other hand the tomb may contain the remains of all three. The truth may never be known.

The bell tower of the cathedral, La Giralda is elegantly constructed of patterned brick and stone. It dates from the 12th century, a few decades before the Almohads lost control of the city. It was the main minaret on Sevilla's mosque, Islam's second largest mosque at that time. The Emir who ordered its construction in 1184 (12 years after work had begun on the mosque itself) instructed the Maghribian architect, Ahmad Ibn Baso, that it should be more beautiful than any other in existence. It is 100 m high and built on a Visigothic base. In Renaissance times balconies were added and a belfry of four diminishing storeys. The tower was originally surmounted by four globes, but these were destroyed by an earthquake in 1568. They were replaced by a *giraldilla* or weather vane, representing Faith, from which the tower's present name has been derived. Unusually, access to the summit is via 35 (seemingly endless) ramps, rather than steps, apparently designed to be sufficiently wide to allow two mounted horsemen to pass. The view from the top is well worth the toil, giving superb views over the pinnacles, buttresses and domes of the cathedral itself, as well as rooftop vistas of the city, which is useful for future orientation for ground level sightseeing. It is also hard to miss the noisy colony of lesser kestrels which wheel around the tower in summer.

La Giralda
Sevilla's most famous landmark

■ *A combined ticket secures entry to both the Cathedral and the Giralda. Mon-Sat, 1030-1700; Sun 1000-1330 for Giralda only, 1400-1600 for Giralda and cathedral. €4.20, students and pensioners €1.20; free on Sun. T954214971.*

The Alcázar is one of the best surviving examples of Mudéjar architecture in Spain and has always been a popular place of residence for Spanish royalty when visiting the area. Work on a Moorish fortress in the Plaza del Triunfo originally began in 712 following the capture of Sevilla. In the ninth century it was transformed into a palace for Abd-Al-Rahman II. The wall which still runs between the Plaza del Triunfo and the Barrio de Santa Cruz dates from this period. During the prosperous rule of the Almohads, the palace was extended further. The Patio del Crucio and Patio del Yeso are remnants of this period, but the fortress was vast, stretching right down to the Guadalquivir. However, much of the existing Alcázar was built in the 14th century for Pedro

Alcázar
Numbers in brackets refer to the plan, page 72

Sevilla Province

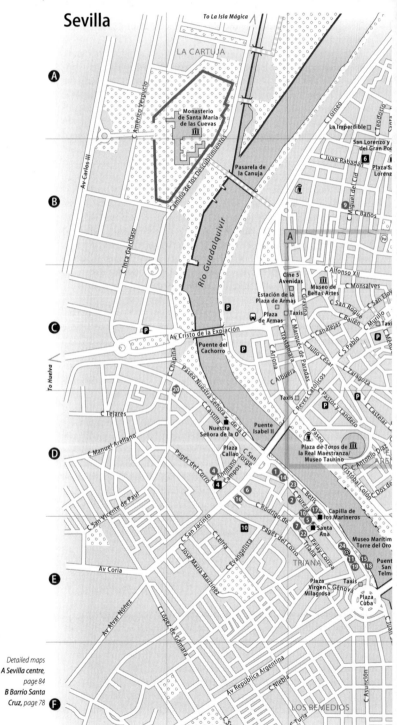

Sevilla

To La Isla Mágica

LA CARTUJA

Monasterio
de Santa María
de las Cuevas

Pasarela de
la Canuja

Río Guadalquivir

C Américo Vespucio

Av Carlos III

C Juan Sebastián Elcano

Cinta Garciaso

C Chipiona

To Huelva

C Tejares

C Manuel Arellano

C Vicente de Paul

Av Coria

Av Alvar Núñez

C López de Gomara

Camino de los Descubrimientos

Paseo Nuestra Señora de la O

Nuestra
Señora de la O

C Castilla

C San Jorge

C Arellano
Campos

Pagés del Corro

Plaza
Callao

C San Jacinto

José María Martínez

C Evangelista

C Lerria

Pagés del Corro

C Rodrigo de

TRIANA

Plaza
Virgen
Milagrosa

Taxis

C Génova

Plaza
Cuba

Av República Argentina

C Niebla

LOS REMEDIOS

C Turia

C Asunción

La Imperdible

San Lorenzo y
del Gran Po

C Juan Rabadán

6

Plaza
Loren

C Miguel de Cid

C Baños

9

Av Cristo de la Expiación

Puente del
Cachorro

Cine 5
Avenidas

Estación de la
Plaza de Armas

Plaza
de Armas

Taxis

C Gravina

C Marqués de Paradas

C Alfonso XII

Museo de
Bellas Artes

C Monsalves

C San Roque

C San Eloy

C San Pablo

C Bailén

C Canalejas

C Murillo

Taxi

Julio César

C Zaragoza

C S Pablo

C Reyes Católicos

Pastor y Landero

C Castelar

Puente
Isabel II

Taxis

Plaza de Toros de
la Real Maestranza/
Museo Taurino

Cristóbal Colón

C Antonio Díaz

ARE

C Dos de

Puente del
Cachorro

C Betis

C Pureza

Capilla de
los Marineros

Santa
Ana

C Pelay Correa

Plaza
Santa
Ana

Museo Marítim
Torre del Oro

Puent
San
Telmo

20

4

4

6

16

10

1

14

23

2

10

5

7

22

17

24

11

19

15

18

@

Detailed maps
A Sevilla centre,
page 84
**B Barrio Santa
Cruz,** page 78

Sevilla Province

N

| 0 metres | 200 |
| 0 yards | 200 |

■ **Sleeping**

1 Alfonso XIII *E4*
2 Corregidor *B5*
3 Hostal Alameda *A4*
4 Hostal Guadalquivir *D2*
5 Hostal Hércules *B5*
6 Hostal La Francesa *B3*
7 Hostal La Muralla *A5*
8 Hostal Macarena *A5*
9 Hostal Picasso *D4*
10 Husa Sevilla *E2*
11 Patios de la Cartuja *A4*
12 Pensión Alcázar *E4*
13 San Gil *A4*

● **Eating**

1 Ali Baba *D2*
2 Antigua Abacería de San Lorenzo *D3*
3 Bar El Sardinero *B3*
4 Bar Los Golondrinas *D2*
5 Bar Santa Ana *E3*
6 Bodega Miami *D2*
7 Bodega Siglo XVIII *E3*
8 Café Hércules *A4*
9 Café Marigalante *B3*
10 Calle Larga *D3*
11 Casa Nostra *E3*
12 El Pucherito *A4*
13 Il Ilustre Víctima *B4*
14 La Albariza *D2*
15 La Primera del Puente *E3*
16 Mariscos Emilio *D2*
17 Molino Pintado *D3*
18 Río Grande *E3*
19 San Marco *E3*
20 Sol y Sombra *C2*
21 Taberna del Pájaro *B4*
22 Taberna La Plazuela *E3*
23 Taberna Ruta de la Plata *D3*
24 Tex Mex *E3*

the Cruel, who employed Moorish architects to undertake the work, many of them from the neighbouring Moorish Kingdom of Granada under Yussef I. Many fragments from earlier Moorish buildings, such as those from Medina Azahara near Córdoba, were incorporated in its construction. Successive centuries saw various additions and restorations.

Entry to the Alcázar is from the Plaza del Triunfo through the splendidly Moorish, red coloured, **Puerta del León** (**1**), the Gate of the Lion – named after a tiled heraldic lion over the main arch. This leads into the **Patio del León** (**2**) – a caged lion once guarded the entrance – and then into the **Patio de la Montería** (**3**), or Royal Guard, which has 14th-century buildings at each end with galleries and marble and brick columns. This is pure Mudéjar and sets the scene for the interiors to come. At the side of the patio is the Sala del Justicia, where Pedro dispensed his summary rulings. Firstly, however, the route goes through the **Salón del Almirante** (**4**), built by Isabel to administer the expeditions to the Americas. These gloomy rooms have little of architectural merit, but it is interesting to muse that the biggest empire in the world at that time was ruled from these quarters. The best part of Isabel's complex is undoubtedly the Sala de Audencia, or **Capilla de los Navegantes** (**5**), with a fine *artesonado* ceiling. Above the altar

Alcázar

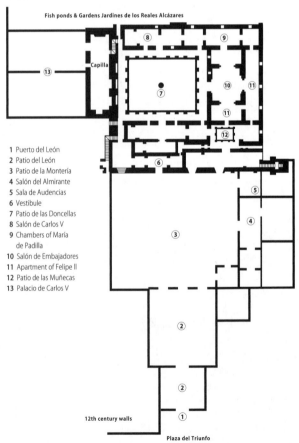

1 Puerto del León
2 Patio del León
3 Patio de la Montería
4 Salón del Almirante
5 Sala de Audencias
6 Vestibule
7 Patio de las Doncellas
8 Salón de Carlos V
9 Chambers of María
  de Padilla
10 Salón de Embajadores
11 Apartment of Felipe II
12 Patio de las Muñecas
13 Palacio de Carlos V

is a large painting, *La Virgen de los Mareantes*, by the Sevillano artist Alejo Fernández, which is thought to be the oldest representation of the Virgin as protectress of sailors. In the painting, the Virgin spreads her protective mantle over, on her left, Columbus and the Pinzón brothers, while on her right is Carlos I and his retinue. In the foreground is a collection of boats, while in the background a selection of native people lurk, no doubt blessing their good fortune in having new-found Christian guardians. All very symbolic.

The tour of the Alcázar now moves into the main palace and from even the small entrance **vestibule (6)**, the combination of carved stucco work, horseshoe arches and *azulejos* so typical of Moorish and Mudéjar architecture is immediately evident. A narrow passage now leads into the **Patio de las Doncellas (7)** – the Patio of the Maidens – and here one immediately recognizes that the Mudéjar workmen from Granada had certainly seen the Alhambra. This was the main courtyard of the palace and was named after the maidens who would line the upper gallery when visiting ambassadors trooped in. The patio has double columned arches which, with the upper storey, were added by Carlos V and these seem to merge agreeably with the original Mudéjar work. The route passes through the **Salon of Carlos V (8)** – it appears that when the monarchs came to Sevilla in the summer, they preferred to sleep on the ground floor because the rooms were cooler, which in fact was a continuation of a Moorish habit. We now pass into the **chambers of María de Padilla (9)**, the mistress of Pedro the Cruel and who was believed to have some magical hold over him – just as well because he has been described as "tall, handsome with a lisping speech and an insatiable pursuer of beautiful women".

The route then leads to the **Salon de Embajadores (10)** – Salon of the Ambassadors – which has more echoes of the Alhambra in Granada. It was named because this was where the ambassadors were received, but is also sometimes known as 'de la media naranja' after the half orange domed roof. Its arcades of horseshoe arches were inspired by the palace of Medina Azahara, near Córdoba. Unfortunately, Carlos V, in his usual way, made 'improvements' by adding balconies and panels of royal pictures to mark his marriage on this spot, to Isabel of Portugal. Nevertheless, the room is the highlight of the Alcázar.

Leading off is a small dining room which then brings us to a modest **apartment built for Felipe II (11)**. After this is the last of the classic rooms of the Alcázar, the **Patio de la Muñecas (12)** – Patio of the Dolls – named after two tiny faces carved in one of the arches and reputed to have been built as a playroom for King Pedro's daughter and her maids. But it was also the scene of some dirty deeds. It is probable that it was here that Pedro murdered his brother Fadrique in 1358. It was also the place where the visiting Abu Said of Granada was murdered for his jewels. One, an enormous ruby, was given by Pedro to the Black Prince and it is now in the collection of British Crown Jewels. Before the gardens is the Palacio of Carlos V.

The Alcázar gardens are a somewhat rambling area, the result of several centuries of alterations and additions, which also provide welcome coolness and shade. The gardens were often used for balls. One, in 1350, was in honour of the Black Prince, who was greatly impressed by the Moorish dances performed by the Sevillan ladies. When he returned home, the dance became fashionable in England, giving rise, it is claimed, to the Morris Dance. Features of the garden include an unusual myrtle maze, a small pavilion built by Carlos V and some vaulted baths where María de Padilla was said to have bathed (and courtiers subsequently drank the water).

Sevilla Province

■ 1 Apr-30 Sep, Tue-Sat 0930-2000, Sun and holidays 0930-1800; 1 Oct-31 Mar Tue-Sat 0930-1800, Sun and holidays 0930-1430. €4.20, children under 16, OAPs and registered disabled free; Cuarto Real Alto (Upper Palace) €2.40. Ticket office shuts 1 hr before closing time. T954560040. Owing to the pressure of visitors during the summer months, when satisfactory photography is impossible, a flow control system operates allowing in a certain number of people every 30 mins. You are advised to visit early in the morning or late afternoon or, preferably, out of season.

The Lonja The Lonja, one of Sevilla's numerous palaces, on Avenida de la Constitución next to the cathedral, was designed for Felipe II by Juan de Herrera and completed in 1598 in pure Renaissance style. Today it houses the **Archivo General de Indias**, comprising some 38,000 files, documents, letters and manuscripts concerning the discovery and colonization of the Americas. Here you can see Columbus's diary and the Mapa Mundi by Juan de la Cosa. *■ At the time of writing the Archivo was closed temporarily for building work. T954211234 for current information, or contact the tourist office.*

Torre del Oro This 12-sided tower on Paseo Colón was built in the early 13th century by the Almohades, under Yussef II, to protect the city from the Christians when the latter had become a threat following their victory at the Battle of Las Navas de Tolosa. It is located on the east bank of the Guadalquivir and used to be linked by chain to a similar tower on the west bank, being part of the city's fortifications, which once included 166 towers and 12 gates. It gained its name from the gilded tiles that originally decorated it and its Arabic name, Bury Al Dahab means Golden Tower. Today the main part of the tower is made of stone, while the upper section, which is made of brick, was added in the 18th century. It houses a small Maritime museum. *■ Tue-Fri 1000-1400, Sat-Sun 1100-1400. €0.60, Tue free. T954222419.*

Hospital de la Caridad Located in a back street, close to the Torre del Oro and parallel with the river, the 'charity hospital' was built in Baroque style in 1676 by Miguel de Manera, a reformed local 'Jack the Lad', to help the destitute – a function which it still fulfils today. The main reason for paying a visit, apart from admiring the colonnaded, plant-filled patio with its two fountains, is to view the paintings in the chapel.

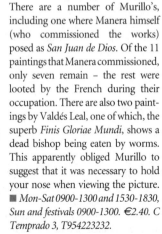

There are a number of Murillo's, including one where Manera himself (who commissioned the works) posed as *San Juan de Dios*. Of the 11 paintings that Manera commissioned, only seven remain – the rest were looted by the French during their occupation. There are also two paintings by Valdés Leal, one of which, the superb *Finis Gloriae Mundi*, shows a dead bishop being eaten by worms. This apparently obliged Murillo to suggest that it was necessary to hold your nose when viewing the picture. *■ Mon-Sat 0900-1300 and 1530-1830, Sun and festivals 0900-1300. €2.40. C Temprado 3, T954223232.*

The 12 sided tower of Torre del Oro SEVILLA.

Sevilla has a number of parks and open spaces, but the best, without doubt, is the Parque María Luisa, which was founded in 1893 by the widowed Duchess of Monpensier, who donated to the city half of the gardens of the Palacio de San Telmo. (The palace itself, once a nautical college, is now a seminary.) The gardens were turned into a park as part of the 1929 Exhibition. Many of the exhibition buildings have survived (in contrast to the Expo 92 pavilions), and some now function as museums. The Spanish exhibitions were housed in the specially built Plaza de España, a semi-circular complex located on the spot where the Inquisition burned the last witch in 1781. In front of the building is a vast square, with a canal and computer-controlled fountains. Unusual blue and white balustraded bridges cross the canal at intervals and lead to tiled seats with *azulejos* depicting the main features of each of the Spanish regions. If it's not too hot, this is a delightful place to spend the afternoon when most places are closed.

Plaza de España & Parque María Luisa

Between the Plaza de España and the cathedral are two other buildings of interest. Alongside the Puerta de Jerez is the **Hotel Alfonso XIII**, built in Baroque style in 1929 for some of the more prestigious guests at the exhibition. Prices are still outrageous, but the interior patio, which is something special, is open to non residents and worth a look. Next door to the hotel is one of the main **University** buildings based in the old **Tobacco Factory**, which was made famous by Bizet's opera *Carmen*. Cigarette production continued here until 1965, when the building was taken over by the university. It remains the second largest building in Spain (after El Escorial) and budget travellers might be interested in trying the students' cafeteria.

Located on the far northwest side of the Barrio Santa Cruz, the Casa de Pilatos is sufficiently far from the main sites to deter coach parties and you won't be crowded out by loads of visitors. It was built by the Marquis of Tarifa on his return from the Holy Land and was wrongly thought to be modelled on the house of Pontius Pilate. It is in fact a combination of Mudéjar and Renaissance styles, Moorish and Italianate in flavour, with wonderful patios and probably the best display of *azulejos* anywhere in Andalucía. The house is owned by the Medinaceli family (some of whom live in part of the upper floor) and the various Dukes have meticulously restored the building over the last 50 years.

Casa de Pilatos
Sevilla's most impressive mansion

An entry gate leads into a courtyard where the *apeadero* (or mounting stone) marks the spot where carriages were boarded. The Patio Principal, one of the great patios of Andalucía, has a combination of Mudéjar arches and stucco work, traditional tiles, Gothic balconies, Italianate fountains and Roman statuary which merge in harmony. The route leads into the Salón Pretorio, with a coffered ceiling incorporating the family coat of arms. The tour continues into the Jardín Chico or small garden, past a Chapel of Flagellation and into the shade of the formal Jardín Grande. From here, a four-flighted, domed stairway, covered with the most superb *azulejos*, leads to the family quarters. Following the Moorish tradition, they slept on the upper floor in the winter and the ground floor in the summer. ■ *Daily 0900-1900. €3, with a further €3 for a guided tour of the upper floor. Free on Tue 1300-1700 with EU passport. T954225298.*

This 215 ha site on the west bank of the Río Guadalquivir was once notable only for its old monastery, the **Santa María de las Cuevas**, where Columbus frequently visited and where he lay buried for 37 years. After the monastery was closed, it became a barracks for the French forces under Marshal Soult for

La Isla de la Cartuja

Sevilla Province

two years during the Peninsular War, before being used as a pottery. The five huge kilns can still be seen towering over the old monastery. Today, one of the monastery's buildings houses the **Centro Andaluz de Arte Contemporáneo,** showing the works of modern Andalucían artists, along with the occasional exhibition of international works. ■ *Tue-Fri 1000-2300, Sat 1000-1500, €1.80, free Tue with EU passport. T954480611.* The Cartuja site was then chosen as the location for Expo 92 and the monastery restored at great cost, becoming the Royal Pavilion. Following the closure of Expo 92, the Isla de la Cartuja was initially developed as a a theme park, El Parque de los Descubrimientos. This never really took off and soon closed. Much of the Expo site has now been taken over by the university and hi-tech industry. The area around Expo's artificial lake is now known as **Isla Mágica,** an amusement park. Its theme is claimed to be the 16th-century Spanish Empire, although this is tenuous. Isla Mágica is, however, highly popular with children. ■ *Apr-Sep daily 1100-2400, €20; evening only tickets €14 (children €15, 10 eves). T902161716.* Also on the site is the new Estadio Olímpico – part of Sevilla's push to host the Olympics in 2012.

Museums

Museo Arqueológico

Entrance to all public museums is free for EU citizens with proof of identity. Also see www.sevillacultural.com/museos/sevilla

Located in one of the pavilions which has survived from the 1929 Exhibition, this museum is the most important of its type in Andalucía. The collection runs from prehistoric times to the end of the Moorish occupation. Outstanding are the Carambalo Treasures, a hoard of gold coins and jewellery discovered in a Sevilla suburb in 1958. The Roman section is very thorough, with a comprehensive collection of mosaics, kitchen utensils, statuary and tombs, much from the nearby site of Itálica. The star exhibit here is the statue of Venus, dating from the second century. ■ *Tue 1430-2000, Wed-Sat 0900-2000, Sun 0900-1430. Free with EU passport. Plaza de América, Parque María Luisa, T954232401.*

Museo de Arte y Costumbres Populares

Provides a fascinating insight into the traditional crafts, customs and domestic life over the last 300 years in Andalucía. The sections devoted to Sevilla's Semana Santa and the April Feria are particularly good. ■ *Tue 1500-2000, Wed-Sat 0900-2000, Sun 0900-1430. Free with EU passport otherwise €1.50. Plaza de América, Parque María Luisa (opposite the Museo Arqueológico), T954232576.*

Museo Marítimo

Located in the Torre de Oro is this small exhibition on the naval history of Sevilla. ■ *Tue-Fri 1000-1400. Closed on festivals and in Aug. €0.60.*

Museo de Bellas Artes

Claimed to be second only in importance to the Prado in Madrid, this museum is located in a renovated former convent in an attractive square, where the scene is set with a statue of Murillo. The museum concentrates on the rather heavy religious art of its local Sevillan stalwarts, Zurburán, Murillo and Valdés Leal. Certainly, the small 19th and 20th century collection is uninspiring. The highlight, however, is Room 5, which is the convent's former church, where the light is exceptionally good. Here the vaulting and dome have been restored showing the 18th-century work of local artist Domingo Martínez. In the apse of the church are some of Murillo's best paintings, superbly set off by the surroundings. The museum also has some outstanding sculptures, including works by Montañes and Pedro Millan. ■ *Tue 1500-2000, Wed-Sat 0900-2000, Sun 0900-1500, Mon and holidays closed. Free with EU passport, otherwise €1.50. Plaza de Museo 9, T954221829.*

Located in an old building between the cathedral and the tourist office, this Modern Art Museum is something of a disappointment, with many of the works little better than scribbles in felt and ball point pen. The upper floors, however, will reward the climb. ■ *Tue-Sat 1000-2100, Sun 1000-1500, closed Mon. Free with EU passport otherwise €2. T954480611.*

Museo de Arte Contemporáneo

Located within the famous Real Maestranza bullring, one of the oldest bullrings in Spain, is this fascinating museum for bullfighting fans, complete with antique posters, costumes and even heads of famous bulls. ■ *0930-1400, 1500-1900 daily. On bullfighting days, 0930-1500. €3. Paseo Colón 12, T954210315, www.realmaestranza.com*

Museo Taurino

This 16th-century *casa-palacio* was once the seat of the Renaissance-Mudéjar court and later, in the early 20th century, the home of the Countess of Lebrija. It's worth a visit for its magnificent Roman mosaics, which the *Condesa* brought from the site of Itálica, elaborate carvings and profusion of Moorish tiles dating from the 16th and 17th centuries. It is also full of Roman and Greek statues, antiques and paintings. ■ *1100-1300, 1700-2000 Mon-Fri; 1000-1300 Sat. €3.65. C Cuna 8, T954227802.*

Palacio Lebrija

Barrios of central Sevilla

Around the central monumental area of Sevilla are a number of districts or barrios, each with their own distinct character. Close to the cathedral and much visited is the Barrio Santa Cruz, a maze of narrow streets (many of which are pedestrianized), whitewashed houses, small squares and flower festooned patios. A stroll around this atmospheric barrio with frequent stops at its plethora of bars is one of the delights of a visit to Sevilla. One its highlights is the Hospital de los Venerables, Plaza de los Venerables 8. This magnificent 17th-century Baroque building is full of fine religious mural paintings, sculptures and altarpieces by artists like Juan de Oviedo in its church. ■ *1000-1400, 1600-2000 daily. Guided visits in Spanish only, €3.60. T954562696, www.focus.abengoa.es* Amongst other locations of interest are the Palacio Arzobispal, the Convento de San José with some marvellous Mudéjar plasterwork, Plaza Santa Cruz and a gateway marking the former entrance to a synagogue - the only surviving evidence of what was once a busy Jewish Quarter. This gateway now forms part of the Iglesia Santa María La Blanca, located down a street of the same name. The church has an exquisitely ornate interior with a sculpted ceiling and paintings by Murillo. ■ *Mass 1030 and 1930 Mon-Sat, 1000, 1130, 1300 and 1900 Sun and holidays.* The Casa de Murillo, Calle Santa Teresa 8, is also worth a visit, which contains audiovisual displays and photos about the painter. ■ *1000-1300, 1600-1900 Mon-Fri, 1100-1400 Sat-Sun. Free. T954217535.*

Barrio Santa Cruz

Santa Cruz's only drawback is that during Sevilla's busiest months, you'll have to share the streets, sights and bars with the multitude of tourists who inevitably make a beeline for this barrio.

Sevilla Province

Barrio Macarena To the north of the centre of Sevilla is this barrio. Always solidly working class and rarely visited by tourists, the district is now undergoing a certain amount of gentrification. Running parallel with the inner ring road is the finest remaining section of the old city walls, including the Puerta de Córdoba with its horseshoe arch. Just across the road is the Hospital de las Cinco Llagas (Hospital of the Five Wounds), the restored building of which now operates as the Andalucían Parliament. At some time in the future the public will be allowed into the debating chamber, which is sited in the Hospital's old church. There are some fine churches in the barrio, but the most famous is in fact quite modern. This is the Basílica of Macarena, home of La Macarena, the star of the Easter processions. This 17th-century image of the Virgin is normally located on the *retablo* behind the main altar. Inside the church is a museum. ■ *Daily 0930-1300, 1700-2000. €2.40.* Other churches of interest are San Marcos, with some interior horseshoe arches still intact despite Civil War damage, San Julián dating back to the 14th century and San Gil, boasting a Mudéjar tower and ceiling.

Triana Located across the river to the southwest, this was the centre of the city's *gitano* community until they were relocated throughout the city. It was the

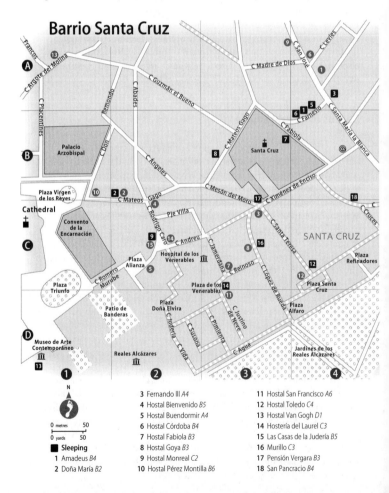

Barrio Santa Cruz

Sleeping
1 Amadeus *B4*
2 Doña María *B2*
3 Fernando III *A4*
4 Hostal Bienvenido *B5*
5 Hostal Buendormir *A4*
6 Hostal Córdoba *B4*
7 Hostal Fabiola *B3*
8 Hostal Goya *B3*
9 Hostal Monreal *C2*
10 Hostal Pérez Montilla *B6*
11 Hostal San Francisco *A6*
12 Hostal Toledo *C4*
13 Hostal Van Gogh *D1*
14 Hostería del Laurel *C3*
15 Las Casas de la Judería *B5*
16 Murillo *C3*
17 Pensión Vergara *B3*
18 San Pancracio *B4*

same gypsies who made Sevilla the home of flamenco. Triana is still the traditional starting point for the annual *romería* to El Rocío in the marshlands of the Coto Doñana (see page 133). The district has a long standing ceramics industry based on local supplies of clay, which back in Roman times made the amphorae used for the transportation of wheat, olive oil and other agricultural products. Bricks were also produced, but today decorative tiles or *azulejos* are the chief product. If you wish to buy straight from the producer, go to *Cerámica Santa Ana* on Plaza Callao – you can't miss the amazing tiled façade. Calle Antillano Campos and the surrounding area is also packed with ceramic shops.

Triana was, naturally enough, thought to be the home of Roger de Triana, the sailor on Columbus's *Santa María* who first sighted land on the other side of the Atlantic. Research has shown, however, that he came from Lepe, near Huelva. But this has not stopped the residents of Triana erecting a modern statue to his memory – presumably their contribution to the Fifth Centenary celebrations.

Triana today is well worth a wander to see its striking architecture, including famous *azulejos* covering house façades and its wrought iron balconies, as well as numerous great tapas bars. These are within easy walking distance of the centre if you stick to Calle Betís along the river and the streets immediately parallel. Calle Betís has wonderful views across the river to famous landmarks like the Real Maestranza bullring and the Torre del Oro, as well as some impressive 18th-century architecture and a mooring quay, a relic of its dockland days. However, these are becoming increasingly popular with tourists and Sevillanos from across the river; for more of Triana itself, you could venture further into the barrio. Also worth a visit is the Capilla de los Marineros, Calle Pureza 53, dating from the 18th century, and containing a statue of the famed Virgen Esperanza de Triana, who vies with La Macarena for Sevillano adoration and is carried with equal pride through the streets for the Semana Santa processions.

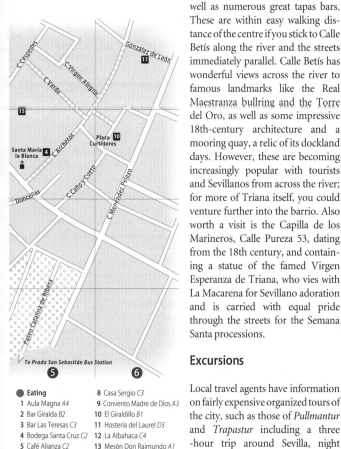

Sevilla Province

Excursions

Eating
1 Aula Magna *A4*
2 Bar Giralda *B2*
3 Bar Las Teresas *C3*
4 Bodega Santa Cruz *C2*
5 Café Alianza *C2*
6 Café Levíes *A4*
7 Casa Roman *C3*
8 Casa Sergio *C3*
9 Convento Madre de Dios *A3*
10 El Giraldillo *B1*
11 Hostería del Laurel *D3*
12 La Albahaca *C4*
13 Mesón Don Raimundo *A1*
14 Mesón Don Rodrigo *C2*
15 Monreal *C2*

Local travel agents have information on fairly expensive organized tours of the city, such as those of *Pullmantur* and *Trapastur* including a three-hour trip around Sevilla, night cruises, flamenco evenings and excursions to nearby towns.

City tours

Information and departures from Calle Almirante Lobo 13. *Sevirama*, Calle General Sanjurjo 2, T954560693, run a hop-on/hop-off multi-lingual city tour in open-topped buses, lasting one hour. Departures from the Torre del Oro. Tours start at 1000 and claim to cover over 50 historic monuments. Adults €10. *Sevilla Tour* runs a similar tour for €9, T954502099.

River cruises In summer nine *Cruceros Panorámicos* depart from the Torre del Oro daily, 1130-2215. €6.02, children free. There is a new boat service which takes visitors to the Parwue Nacional Coto Doñana, leaving the Torre del Oro at 0900 and reaching Sanlúcar at 1300. Then follows an itinerary which is basically the same as that from Sanlúcar (see page 170). Return is by coach, getting back to Sevilla at 2100. The trip can also be done in reverse. €20, tickets from the office next to the Torre del Oro.

Sevilla Province (side margin)

Alcalá de Guadaira
Population: 56,244

Located 10 km southeast of Sevilla on the N334, this small town is well worth a visit. The spectacular fortress after which the town was named was built by the Almohads on the river Guadaira as part of their defence system for Sevilla itself. It is one of the best remaining examples of Almohad military architecture and the largest of their fortresses to have survived. Following its capture in 1246 by Fernando III, it was modified for use as a prison by Pedro the Cruel. Also of interest is the Iglesia de San Miguel, which was originally built as a mosque. Alcalá has now increasingly become a dormitory town for Sevilla, and as in Sevilla, cars and their contents are vulnerable. For accommodation, try **B** *Silos*, Calle Silos s/n, T955680059, F955684457, a modern hotel built round a Moorish style patio, with 54 rooms, restaurant, parking. Recommended. Just outside Alcalá is *Camping Oromana*, Camino de Maestre s/n, T955683257, oromana@eresmas.com, an excellent campsite with pool, bar and bungalows for rent.

Itálica The Roman ruins of Itálica are some 9 km north of Sevilla next to the village of Santiponce. The original city was founded in 206 BC by General Publius Cornelius Scipius as a convalescent area for his soldiers wounded in the Battle of Ilipa. The men called the place Itálica presumably to remind them of home. Trajan, the first Emperor to hail from a Roman province, was born in Itálica. His successor, Hadrian, whilst born in Rome, received much of his education here and whilst he was Emperor he richly endowed the city, building a large new section.

Itálica is actually divided into two parts. Firstly, there is the *vitus urbs* or old city, much of which now lies under the town of Santiponce. Hadrian built the *nova urbs* or new city, which is the part forming the archaeological site which can be visited today. At its peak, Itálica had a population of over 500,000, but declined under the Visigoths and the Moors, who finally deserted the site after the Guadalquivir changed its course following some flooding. In the succeeding centuries the site was looted initially for its building stone and later for its artefacts. Serious excavation began as early as the late 18th century and has gathered apace during recent years.

What has been uncovered from the farmland is quite remarkable. Most astonishing of all is the huge amphitheatre. Composed of a crumbling conglomerate, it consists of three rows of seats, of which only the lower two rows remain intact. It is estimated that it could hold some 25,000 people – believed to be the third largest in the Roman Empire. Beneath the arena with its central pit, you can wander along the corridors where the gladiators would have strode and look into the pits where the wild animals were kept. An eerie experience. To the west of the amphitheatre is the city, which is laid out on a rough grid plan. Between the well-marked roads, which were wide and colonnaded, public buildings would have occupied a whole block. It is believed that the site contained six public buildings and around 50 houses, with probably two in each block. Most of the houses have yet to be excavated, but those that have been uncovered have revealed an amazing collection of mosaics. The houses have been named according to the subjects of the mosaics; for example, the bird mosaic in the Casa de los Pájaros, the Neptune mosaic and the Casa del Planetario, where the mosaic shows planetary divinities, which gave their name to the seven days of the week in the Roman calendar. Also of interest is the Exedra House, with baths for men and women and a number of cement blocks that are thought to be the remains of a dome which covered the exedra.

If visiting in the summer, beware of the heat, as there is little shade. Easter is the most popular time for coachloads of Spanish school children, who make more noise in the echoing amphitheatre than the original wild animals probably did. There is a string of restaurants along the road opposite the entrance to the site, ranging from the sordid to the reasonably presentable. ■ *Tue-Sat 0900-2000, Sun 0900-1500 (summer); Tue-Sat 0900-1700, Sun 1000-1600 (winter). Closed festivals. Free with EU passport, otherwise €1.50. T955996583. Frequent buses run from the Plaza de Armas station (20 mins).*

Sevilla Province

Itálica

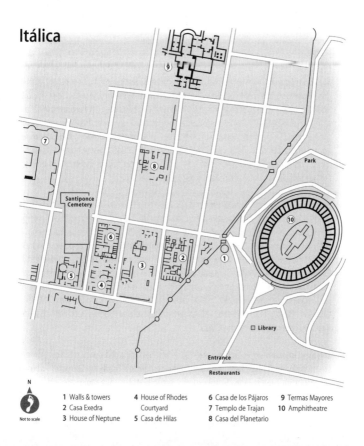

N
Not to scale

1 Walls & towers	4 House of Rhodes	6 Casa de los Pájaros	9 Termas Mayores
2 Casa Exedra	Courtyard	7 Templo de Trajan	10 Amphitheatre
3 House of Neptune	5 Casa de Hilas	8 Casa del Planetario	

Essentials

Sleeping

■ *on maps, pages 70, 78 and 84 See inside front cover for price codes*

The price of accommodation in Sevilla and the surrounding area still remains ridiculously high in the aftermath of Expo 92, particularly when one considers the glut of available rooms. Hopefully, prices will eventually fall to more reasonable levels. The hotel classifications below are for *temporada alta*, which varies from hotel to hotel but most commonly is Mar-Jun, Sep-Oct (for certain hotels Sep-Dec); it's worth checking if you book in advance. *Temporada baja* is usually Jan-Feb, Jul-Aug and can be Nov-Dec. *Temporada extra* or *especial* is *Semana Santa* and *Fería de Abril*, when prices are typically double those shown here. Booking is essential at these times and is also advisable during holidays and *temporada alta*. In the low season it's worth bargaining, especially in the cheaper hotels. If you're driving it's worth staying somewhere with a garage, but bear in mind that you may well have to pay for it. With some 50 hotels and over 100 *pensiones*, there is certainly no lack of choice. See also www.sol.com/hotel/index.html

Barrio Santa Cruz **AL** *Las Casas de la Judería*, Callejón de Dos Hermanos 7, Plaza Santa María La Blanca, T954415150, F954422170, www.ibernet.net/lascasas This 17th-century mansion has 95 luxurious rooms around a series of patios full of orange and banana trees and pot plants. If you want to splash out and can't quite afford the *Alfonso XIII*, then this is the place to come. Piano-bar. A/c, TV, garage (€12.5 a night). **AL** *Doña María*, C Don Remondo 19, T954224990, F954219546. Near Giralda is this luxury hotel with 61 rooms, garage, a/c, restaurant, pool. **A** *Amadeus*, C Farnesio 6, T954501443, F954500019, www.hotelamadeussevilla.com As its name suggests, this hotel in a beautifully restored 18th-century building with antique furnishings was designed with musicians in mind. Some rooms have stereos with classical music or a piano. With a grand piano in the main reception area, impromptu evening concerts are common. Rooftop terrace with superb views. A/c, TV, lift, wheelchair access. **A** *Fernando III*, C San José 21, T954217301, F954220246. Large hotel in relatively quiet area, convenient for monuments, a/c, some rooms with balconies, pool, garage, garden. **A** *Hostería del Laurel*, Plaza de los Venerables 5, T954220295, F954210450, www.hosteriadellaurel .com Smart, comfortable rooms with TV, a/c. Excellent restaurant (see Eating below). For Semana Santa, prices increase by €15 per room.

B *Murillo*, C Lope de Rueda 9, T954216095, F954219616, www.hotelmurillo.com Traditional hotel featuring a pseudo-medieval décor theme and stuffed with elaborately carved antique furniture, suits of armour and coats of arms. Comfortable rooms have bath, a/c. Quiet street. For self-catering **B** *Apartamentos Murillo*, C Lope de Rueda 7, T954210959, F954219616, www.sol.com/apartamentos/murillo **C** *Hostal Córdoba*, C Farnesio 12, T954227498. On same quiet street as *Hotel Amadeus* and *Hostal Buen Dormir*. Attractive rooms, some with balconies, a/c, with central fern-draped central patio. One of the better hotels in this category. 0300 curfew. **C** *Hostal Goya*, Mateos Gago 31, T954211170, F954562988. Smartly decorated a/c rooms with bath. Easy to find; near the Iglesia de Santa Cruz.

D *Hostal Bienvenido*, C Archeros 14, T954413655. Basic rooms with shared bath in a street with similar *hostales*. One of the cheapest in this category. **D** *Hostal Fabiola*, C Fabiola 16, T954218346. Simple rooms, some with bath, arranged around a light, plant-filled patio. Expensive for what it is. **D** *Hostal Monreal*, C Rodrigo Caro 8, T954214166. Moorish-style hostal with flower-bedecked balconies close to the Giralda. Restaurant (see Eating below). **D** *Hostal Pérez Montilla*, Plaza de Curtidores 13,

Sevilla Province

T954421854, amadel2000@hotmail.com Better value than its neighbours but like nearby *Hostal San Francisco*, noisy from nearby C Menéndez Pelayo. **D** *Hostal San Francisco*, C González de León 4, T954536876. Plain but adequate rooms with TV. **D** *Hostal San Pancracio*, Plaza de las Cruces 9, T954413104. Popular *hostal* with basic rooms and shared bath. **D** *Hostal Toledo*, C Santa Teresa 15, T954215335. Small, friendly *hostal* on Plaza Santa Cruz with simple rooms, all with bath. **D** *Pensión Vergara*, C Ximenez de Enciso 11, T954215668, www.es.geocities.com/pension vergara/vergara.html Restored 15th-century building with individually decorated rooms around a pretty central patio with exposed beams, Moorish-style arches and plants. Most original décor of the cheaper hotels, but in a busy part of the barrio over-run with tourists in high season. **D-E** *Hostal Buen Dormir*, C Farnesio 8, T954217492. Family run *hostal* with plain rooms, some with bath, around a tiled patio with caged birds. Rooftop terrace. A/c costs slightly more, or fans; laundry service.

AL *Alfonso XIII*, C San Fernando 2, T954222850, F954216033. One of the priciest in Spain, this famous hotel close to the monumental quarter has 149 rooms in a luxurious 1920s building. Garage, pool, a/c, wheelchair access, restaurant. **AL** *Husa Sevilla*, C Pagés de Corro 90, T954342412, F954342707. Located in a quiet part of Triana barrio within walking distance of the monumental area, with 128 a/c rooms. Garage. **A** *Europa*, Jimios 5, T954214305, F954210016, www.hoteleuropasevilla.com Classy, traditional hotel in 18th-century building near the Cathedral. Excellent value; ask for room with balcony. A/c, TV, bath. Garage, lift. **A** *Hostal Picasso*, C San Gregorio 1, T954210864, www.ventalia/hpicasso.com Under same management and just round the corner from *Hostal Van Gogh* (see below). Refurbished house dating from the early 20th century, colourfully decorated with an attractive patio filled with plants trailing from inner balconies above. Rooms with bath, a/c, TV. Excellent spot to view the Semana Santa processions, but remember that prices rise accordingly. **A** *San Francisco*, C Alvarez Quintero 38, T/F954501541. Good location between Cathedral and Plaza Salvador. Smart comfortable rooms with TV, bath, a/c. **A** *Hostal Van Gogh*, C Miguel de Mañara 1, T954563727, www.ventalia/hvangogh.com In the shadow of the Alcázar, restored Sevillian house with similar décor to *Hostal Picasso*. Rooms have bath, a/c, TV. Ask for a room with a balcony, from where you can see the Giralda and surrounding area. Like *Hostal Picasso*, this is a prime spot for the Semana Santa processions.

Catedral, El Arenal & Triana

Sevilla Province

B *Maestranza*, C Gamazo 12, T954561070, F954214404, www.andalunet.com/maestranza Near Plaza Nueva, immaculate rooms, some with view of Giralda (just), best ones at front of hotel. All have bath, TV, a/c, safe. Lift. **B** *Simón*, C García de Vinuesa 19, T954226660, T954562241. This grand 18th-century mansion is a stone's throw from the Cathedral; all rooms with a/c, bath. **C** *Hostal Atenas*, C Caballerizas 1, T954218047, F954227690, atenas@jet.es On a quiet street near the Casa de Pilatos, entry down a plant-filled passageway to a beautiful old patio with a tiled staircase. Attractive rooms with bath, a/c. **C** *Hostal Sierpes*, C Corral del Rey 22, T954224948, F954212107, sierpes@infonegocio.com Restored 17th-century mansión near Cathedral, with bar, restaurant and garage. A/c rooms with bath. **C-D** *Hostal Sánchez Sabariego*, C Corral del Rey 23, T954214470. Small *hostal* on same quiet street as *Hostal Sierpes* north of Cathedral with individually furnished rooms. **D** *Pensión Alcázar*, C Deán Miranda 12, near Plaza Contratación, T954228457. As it's names suggests, located near Alcázar down a quiet street. Simple but comfortable rooms; you pay for the location. 2 superb roof terraces with good views. **D** *Hostal Central*, C Zaragoza 18, T954217660. A few mins walk west of Plaza Nueva, a/c rooms around a small, attractive Moorish patio. Discount of 25% for nearby parking. Same management as *Hostal Londres* (see below). **D** *Hostal Guadalquivir*, C Pagés del Corro 53, T954332100. Only cheap hostal in Triana. Beautifully tiled foyer. Some rooms with bath.

Sevilla centre

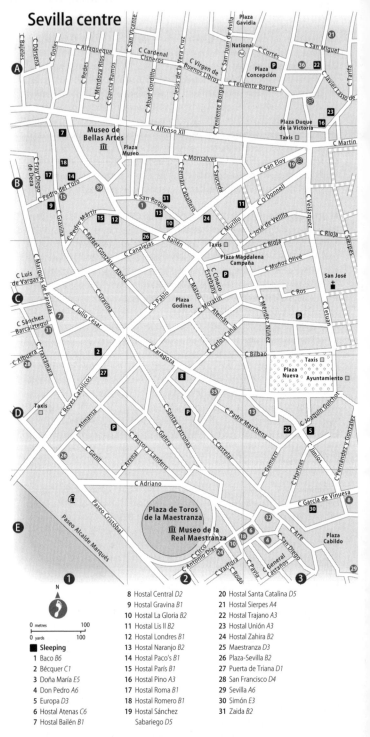

Sleeping

1 Baco *B6*
2 Bécquer *C1*
3 Doña María *E5*
4 Don Pedro *A6*
5 Europa *D3*
6 Hostal Atenas *C6*
7 Hostal Bailén *B1*
8 Hostal Central *D2*
9 Hostal Gravina *B1*
10 Hostal La Gloria *B2*
11 Hostal Lis II *B2*
12 Hostal Londres *B1*
13 Hostal Naranjo *B2*
14 Hostal Paco's *B1*
15 Hostal París *B1*
16 Hostal Pino *A3*
17 Hostal Roma *B1*
18 Hostal Romero *B1*
19 Hostal Sánchez
   Sabariego *D5*
20 Hostal Santa Catalina *D5*
21 Hostal Sierpes *A4*
22 Hostal Trajano *A3*
23 Hostal Unión *A3*
24 Hostal Zahira *B2*
25 Maestranza *D3*
26 Plaza-Sevilla *B2*
27 Puerta de Triana *D1*
28 San Francisco *D4*
29 Sevilla *A6*
30 Simón *E3*
31 Zaida *B2*

Sevilla Province

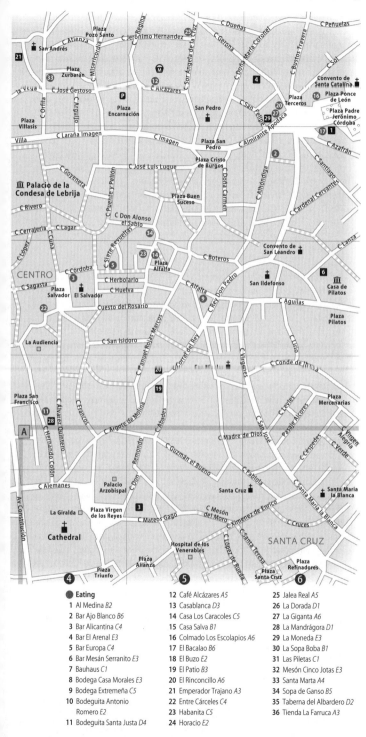

Eating

1 Al Medina *B2*
2 Bar Ajo Blanco *B6*
3 Bar Alicantina *C4*
4 Bar El Arenal *E3*
5 Bar Europa *C4*
6 Bar Mesán Serranito *E3*
7 Bauhaus *C1*
8 Bodega Casa Morales *E3*
9 Bodega Extremeña *C5*
10 Bodeguita Antonio Romero *E2*
11 Bodeguita Santa Justa *D4*
12 Café Alcázares *A5*
13 Casablanca *D3*
14 Casa Los Caracoles *C5*
15 Casa Salva *B1*
16 Colmado Los Escolapios *A6*
17 El Bacalao *B6*
18 El Buzo *E2*
19 El Patio *B3*
20 El Rinconcillo *A6*
21 Emperador Trajano *A3*
22 Entre Cárceles *C4*
23 Habanita *C5*
24 Horacio *E2*
25 Jalea Real *A5*
26 La Dorada *D1*
27 La Giganta *A6*
28 La Mandrágora *D1*
29 La Moneda *E3*
30 La Sopa Boba *B1*
31 Las Piletas *C1*
32 Mesón Cinco Jotas *E3*
33 Santa Marta *A4*
34 Sopa de Ganso *B5*
35 Taberna del Albardero *D2*
36 Tienda La Farruca *A3*

Centro & **AL** *Bécquer*, C Reyes Católicos 4, T954222172, F954214400, www.hotelbecquer.com
Santa Justa Sumptiously furnished upmarket hotel with excellent service and facilities. All 139
rooms with a/c, TV, minibar, internet access. Central location, garage, lift. **A** *Baco*,
Plaza Ponce de León 15, T954565050, F954563654. Traditional mansion away from
main tourist area with impressive 19th-century façade and superb ceramic decoration. The well-appointed rooms have TV, a/c, minibar, bath. Lift. On busy street so
can be noisy. Below is hotel's own supermarket and restaurant *El Bacalao* (see Eating
below). **A** *Corregidor*, C Morgado 17, near the Alameda, T954385111, F954384238,
www.sol.com Traditional hotel with Sevillian tiling, a pretty flower-filled patio and
rooms with a/c, bath, TV. Bar. Down a quiet street; parking 200m from hotel (€12 a
night). **A** *Don Pedro*, C Gerona 24, T954293333, F954211166, www.hoteldonpedro
.net Beautifully restored Sevilliano *palacio* with a superb patio containing a fountain
and plants. Some rooms with terrace; all with bath, a/c, TV. Under same management as *Hostal Santa Catalina* (see below). **A** *Puerta de Triana*, C Reyes Católicos 5,
T954215404, T954215401, www.puertadetriana.com Tastefully modernized luxurious hotel. A/c, TV, bath in all 65 rooms. Located opposite *Hotel Bécquer* (see above);
25% discount for nearby public parking. Price includes breakfast. Superb value for
this category.

B-C *Hostal Santa Catalina*, C Alhóndiga 10-12, T954214688, F954563442. Located
near *Hotel Baco*, plain but comfortable rooms with bath. Can be noisy. Under same
management as *Hotel Don Pedro* (see above). **C** *Hostal Doña Pepa*, C Juan de Vera 20,
T/F954413628, hostal-d-pepa@airtel.net Only 300m from Santa Justa train station,
with pleasant rooms, a/c, some with bath. Parking. Plans to double room capacity by
late 2002, so check first to see if building work is underway. **C** *Hostal Londres*, C San
Pedro Mártir 1, T/F954212896, www.sol.com/hostal-londres Recently decorated
attractive rooms with a/c, TV, bath; under same management as *Hostal Central* (see
section above). Between *Hotel Colón* and Museo de Bellas Artes. **C** *Hostal Paris*, C San
Pedro Mártir 14, T954229861, F954219645, www.sol.com/hostal/paris Modernized,
functional *hostal* that feels somewhat like a motel with TV, a/c in all rooms, but not as
good value as others in this category. Under same management as *Hostal Gravina*
(see below). **C** *Plaza-Sevilla*, C Canalejas 2, T954217149, F954210773. You can't miss
this hotel because it has a wonderfully grand 19th-century façade designed by
Aníbal González. A/c, bath, TV; parking nearby at *El Corte Inglés* department store.
Lift. **C** *Hostal Roma*, C Gravina 34, T954501300, F954501301, www.sol.com/
hostales-sp Opened in 2001 after extensive and tasteful refurbishment of Sevillian
mansion. Well-appointed rooms with bath, TV, a/c. Lift. Handy for Plaza de Armas
bus station. **C** *Sevilla*, C Daóiz 5, T954384161, F954902160. Charming, traditional
hotel with beautiful plant-bedecked patio situated on tranquil, pretty square in front
of San Andrés church; ask for a room overlooking the plaza. All 36 rooms have bath,
a/c. Top-floor rooms have own terrace. Lift. **C** *Zaida*, C San Roque 26, T954211138,
F954218810, www.andalunet.com/zaida 18th-century mansion located in quiet
street near Museo de Bellas Artes with patio entrance area comprehensively refurbished in Moorish style. Compared with patio, rooms are rather plain; bath, TV, a/c.
Lift. Cheaper end of category. Recommended. **C-D** *Hostal Unión*, C Tarifa 4,
T954211790. Small *hostal* in central location near Plaza Duque de la Victoria. Bath, TV
and a/c in all rooms but not as good value as others in this category. **C-D** *Hostal
Zahira*, C San Eloy 43, T954221061, F954213048. Well-furnished rooms with a/c and
bath around a typical plant-filled patio. Central location.

D *Hostal Bailén*, C Bailén 75, T954221635. Small, friendly *hostal* with basic rooms,
some with bath, near Museo de Bellas Artes. The best room is on the top floor at the
front. Cheapest end of category. **D** *Hostal La Gloria* , C San Eloy 58, T954222673.

Central location, but can be noisy, including the antiquated plumbing. **D** *Hostal Gravina*, C Gravina 46, T954216414. Rather characterless *hostal* with simple rooms. Additional similar *hostales* down this street, which is close to the Plaza de Armas bus station. Same management as *Paris*, *Paco's* and *Roma*. **D** *Hostal Lis II*, C Olavide 5, off C San Eloy, T954560228, www.sol.com/hostal-lisii Typical 1920s Sevillian house with Moorish-style interior, pretty patio and plants trailing from balconies inside and out. Good value, friendly; rooms have fans, some with bath. Great location, in centre but down a quiet street. Internet available, €2.50 per hr. **D** *Hostal Naranjo*, C San Roque 11, T954225840, F954216943. Wonderfully kitsch reception area that makes rooms seem tame in comparison; all with bath, TV, a/c. Quiet street near Museo de Bellas Artes. **D** *Hostal Paco's*, C Pedro del Toro 7, T954217183, www.sol.com/hostales-sp Under same management as *Hostal Gravina* (see above), basic rooms with best ones at front on top floor. **D** *Hostal Pino*, C Tarifa 6, T954212810. Next door to *Hostal Unión* (see above) and slightly better value, with funky patio surrounded by red-and-blue stained glass. Bright blue-and-yellow décor in rooms, with a/c or fan. Central location. **D** *Hostal Romero*, C Gravina 21, T954211353. Mid-19th century building with simple rooms around a light patio, opposite *Hostal Roma*. **D** *Hostal Trajano*, C Trajano 3, T954382421. Central location near Plaza Duque de la Victoria, simple rooms with newly added baths.

AL *San Gil*, C Parras 28, T954906811, F954906939, hsangil@arrakis.es Magnificently restored former *palacio* dating from 1901, with elegant tiled reception area and tranquil leafy patio. All rooms with TV, minibar, safe, a/c, bath. Hotel upgraded in 2001. Pool, solarium, bar, restaurant. Only drawback is no garage; parking nearby (€10 a night). **A** *Patios de la Cartuja*, C Lumbreras 8-10, T954900200, F954902056, www.patiosdesevilla. Superb value apart-hotel in a restored Sevillian building around a long plant-filled patio, in a quiet location. Smartly decorated apartments have bedroom, living room, fully equipped kitchen, bath, a/c, TV. Garage (€8.41 a night). Under same management is the similar *Patio de la Alameda*, located nearby at Alameda de Hércules 56, T954904999, F954900226. **D** *Hostal Alameda*, Alameda de Hércules 31, T954900191, F954902248. Modern hostal lacking in character but good value. Comfortable rooms with TV, a/c, bath. Bar. Can be noisy. **D** *Hostal La Francesa*, C Juan Rabadán 28, T954383107. Small hostal with basic rooms located in Barrio San Lorenzo between the Alameda and river. **D** *Hostal Hércules*, C Conde de Baraja 2, T954908856. Small hostal near Alameda with all-white comfortable rooms, but can be noisy. All with shared bath. **D** *Hostal Macarena*, C San Luis 91, T954370141. Tastefully refurbished family run *hostal* on Plaza Pumarejo, in heart of La Macarena barrio and near the Alameda. A/c, some with bath, TV. Excellent value for this category. Recommended. **D** *Hostal La Muralla*, C Fray Diego de Cádiz 39, T954371049, F954379411, hmuralla@teleline.es Comfortable rooms with bath, a/c, TV near the Almohad wall on the edge of the barrio.

Alameda & La Macarena

Albergue Juvenil Sevilla, C Issac Peral 2, off Av de la Palmera, T954613150. Out of the centre but accessible from Plaza Nueva on bus no 34. Usually crowded, 198 beds with shared bathrooms, TV lounge, meals available, wheelchair access, airport 14 km, train 7 km.

Youth hostels

Sevilla, Ctra Madrid-Cádiz, Km 534, T954514379, 12 km from city, near airport, hot showers, pool, restaurant, bar. *Villsom*, Ctra Sevilla-Cádiz, Km 554.8, Dos Hermanas, T954720828. 14 km from the city, pool, showers, open Feb-Nov only. *Club de Campo*, Av de la Libertad 13, Dos Hermanas, T954720250. 12 km from the city, pool, restaurant. A *Los Amarillos* bus runs to Dos Hermanas every 45 mins.

Camping
Because of the heat, camping in high summer can be uncomfortable

Sevilla Province

Eating

● on map, pages 70,
78 and 84
See inside front cover
for restaurant price
codes

Remember that outside of the most tourist areas, where restaurants may stay open 1200-2400, places typically open for lunch around 1300-1400 and for dinner around 2000-2100. Many restaurant menus, particularly those at the mid to upper end, do not include tax, or IVA, and will say so on the menu.

Barrio Santa Cruz Despite being the most touristy areas in Sevilla, this area has loads of restaurants offering a good-value *menú del día* for around €6-9. Several restaurants in Santa María La Blanca have economical *menús*; also here are shops and a bakery selling food for packed lunches, although this costs a bit more than the nearest supermarket, *Mas*, on nearby C Menéndez Pelayo.

Expensive *La Albahaca*, Plaza Santa Cruz, T954220714. This is the place to come if you can afford a splurge. Sumptuous food served in a choice of exclusive *salones*, with lavish furnishings to match the food. With delights like o*stras gratinadas al aroma el eneldo y cava*, gratin of oysters in dill and Cava, on the menu you can't go wrong – but don't forget your credit card. The *menú del día* is a whopping €27. *El Giradillo*, Plaza Virgen de los Reyes, T954214525. You couldn't get a better view of the Giralda, but you pay for the privilige; *menú del día* for €18 served in grand and pampered surroundings. *Hostería del Laurel*, Plaza de los Venerables 5, T954220295. This traditional restaurant located in the hotel of the same name looks like an old gaming lodge, with stags' heads and antlers on the walls and ironwork chandeliers and hams suspended from the ceiling. The food matches, with *cochinillo lechal asado* (roast suckling pig) among the specials. *Mesón Don Raimundo*, Argote de Molina 26, T954223355. Splendid restaurant in a restored 11th-century building with a rich and colourful history, reflected in its cornucopia of antiques, religious artefacts and other curiosities like suits of armour and a stuffed bull's head. Extravagant prices match the luxurious surroundings, but the *menú del día* is only €12. House specials include *costillitas de jabali al horno de leña* (roasted wild boar ribs) and *sopa de perdiz al Jerez* (partridge soup with sherry). **Mid-range** *Mesón Don Rodrigo*, C Rodrigo Caro 8, T954563672. Original menu with a definite fruity note - *salmón a la parrilla con vinagreta de frambuesa* (grilled salmon with raspberry dressing) and *salmorejo de fresas* (chilled strawberry soup). Stylish décor of the usual Moorish tiles, with handpainted furniture, ornate mirrors and old bullfighting photos. **Cheap** *Monreal*, C Rodrigo Caro 8. Inexpensive lunches in restaurant under hotel of same name, with an airy plant-filled patio. But breakfast costs more than you'd pay in a bar.

Centro & the Alameda Parts of this area have the advantage of being a bit less touristy than Barrio Santa Cruz, so you can get a more authentic glimpse of Sevillano life. The area around the Alameda is currently undergoing a spot of urban regeneration. This formerly seedy redlight area has been a hive of building activity since 2001, with the Alameda itself due for completion in late 2002. The bad news is that the Alameda is to lose its leafy charm, as virtually all the trees are due for the chop to allow for the construction of an underground car park. Changes in this area have been underway since the late 1990s, when the opening of alternative and trendy bars mushroomed. Today, the Alameda is one of Sevilla's most vibrant areas to visit at night with loads of *bares de copas* and several *discotecas*, as well as cinema and theatre (see Bars and nightlife below).

Expensive *Taberna del Albardero*, C Zaragoza 20, T954502721. This must be one of Sevilla's best offerings for dining out in sheer opulence, with prices to match. If you can't afford dinner upstairs, try the better value *menú del día* served downstairs, €10.

El Buzo, Antonio Díaz 5, T954210231. Smart restaurant near the bullring full of barrels of manzanilla and sherry and bullfighting paintings. Wide range of Andalucían cuisine and seafood; *menú del día* €21. **Mesón Cinco Jotas**, C Castelar 1, T954215862. One of many *Cinco Jotas* in Spain selling the famed Jabugo top-grade *jamón Ibérico* and other pork products. Surprisingly, the menu also features several vegetarian options. Prices can vary considerably; tapas also available in the bar, starting at a reasonable €1.50. *La Dorada*, Paseo Colón 3, T954227828. Fish restaurant featuring Andalucían catches appropriately situated across the road from the river. Try the *sopa marinera de rape, almejas y gambas con azafrán* (seafood soup with monkfish, clams, prawns and saffron). *Media raciones* also available. Closed Mon. **La Moneda**, C Almirantazgo 4, T954223642. Superb seafood restaurant by the main post office, specializing in fried fish and *guisos* (stews). Excellent tapas (€1.80) also available.

Mid-range *El Bacalao*, Plaza Ponce de León 15, T954216670. As the name suggests, this is the place for *bacalao* aficionados, with practically every way of cooking salt codfish on offer in a stylish Sevillian-tiled bar-restaurant. Also at *Victoria Eugenia*, Plaza Villasís, near the Campana end of C Cuna, T954227459, and *Las Columnas de Baco*, Santa María de Gracia 2, T954215151. **Casablanca**, C Zaragoza 50, T954224698. Small seafood restaurant with specialities like *dorada rellena de bacalao* (bream stuffed with cod). Closed Sun. **Hellas**, C Gonzalo de Bilbao 26, T954534844. Opposite Santa Justa train station is this popular Greek restaurant, with taverna-style décor and great moussaka. Closed Mon. **Horacio**, C Antonio Díaz 9, T954225385. Situated on a street next to the Real Maestranza bullring with loads of bar and restaurant choice, this place is worth a stop for specialities like *pimientos de pico con bacalao* (spicy red peppers with cod) and *codillo de pato al oporto* (duck wings in port wine sauce). Tapas also available. *Al-Medina*, C San Roque 13, near the Museo de Bellas Artes, T954215451. Classic Moroccan dishes, like harira, tadjines and couscous. Closed Sun evening and Mon. *La Mandrágora*, C Albuera 11, T954220184. Many return to this small, friendly vegetarian restaurant because of its intimate atmosphere and imaginative and constantly changing menu of excellent dishes. A bit out of the centre, but worth the effort. Closed Sun and Mon. *Las Piletas*, Marquéz de Paradas 28, near C Reyes Católicos, T954220404. Andalucían décor and food with *corrida* paraphernalia festooning the walls, including bulls' heads watching over you as you eat, which may put you off your *cola de toro a la Real Maestranza* (Maestranza oxtail). Opens at 0700 for breakfast. *La Sopa Boba*, C Bailén 34, T954564884. Well-presented and unusual dishes like *magret de pato con mango y salsa de frambuesas al Oporto* served in a brightly decorated restaurant near the Museo de Bellas Artes. Closed Mon evening and Sun.

Cheap *Bauhaus*, Marquéz de Paradas 53. Innovative and stylish DJ-bar/restaurant specializing in international dishes like crêpes, quiche and couscous. Also limited tapas (€1.80) and a *menú del día*, €7.85. DJs from 1600 onwards, playing mainly house music. *Casa Salva*, C Pedro de Toro 12, T954214115. Good-value and cheerful place near the Museo de Bellas Artes with abstract paintings on walls and a Mediterranean menu that changes regularly. Open Mon-Fri lunchtimes only. *Il Ilustre Víctima*, Doctor Letamendi 31. International bar-restaurant near the Alameda serving anything from shawarma kebabs to enchiladas in colourful surroundings. *Jalea Real*, C Sor Angela de la Cruz 37, east of Plaza Encarnación, T954216103. Small, busy vegetarian restaurant with salads, pancakes, crêpes and tapas available. Excellent value *menú del día*, €8. Closed Sun.

In the last decade Triana has undergone a transformation with the opening of many **Triana** new bars and restaurants, particularly along C Betís and the area near the river, attracting an increasingly upmarket clientele and more tourists. The further into Triana you go, away from the river, the more bars you'll find full of Triana residents only, like the bars along C López de Gómara.

Expensive *Río Grande*, C Betís s/n, T954278371. Boasting the best views across the Río Guadalquivir to the Torre del Oro, this famous riverside restaurant specializes in fried fish and many other seafood dishes. **Mid-range** *Casa Nostra*, C Betís 52, T954270752. Delicious freshly made Italian pizzas and pasta. Closed Mon. *Kiosco de las Flores*, C Betís s/n, between Plaza Cuba and the C Duarte, T954274576. This legendary fried fish emporium has a superb new position right on the riverside with irresistible seafood smells emanating before you even step in the door. *Raciones* served only on the attractive tree-lined terrace, tapas and *media raciones* at the bar. Try their plate of *fritura variada* (€16). *La Primera del Puente*, C Betís 66, T954276918. Cheaper than its neighbour, the *Río Grande*, but serving the similar ubiquitous fried fish dishes, this restaurant has excellent river views from its terraza. *San Marco*, C Betís 68, T954280310. Italian pizzería chain with a reputation for fine food served in original surroundings; in this case, a marvellously restored 18th-century Sevillian house. **Cheap** *Ali Baba*, C Betís 5. Wonderful new Lebanese café-restaurante with specialities like shawarma kebabs, hommous and falafel. *Tex Mex*, C Betís 41-A, T954284012. Mexican bar-restaurant with some riverside seating serving the usual eponymous fare of nachos, burritos and enchiladas.

Tapas bars As Sevilla is the place which claims to have originated the tapa, it is no surprise to find tapas bars in profusion throughout the city. Many are bedecked with sherry barrels and hanging hams and are full of atmosphere. Locals generally drink *fino* with their tapas.

Barrio Santa Cruz This area has a plethora of bars offering tapas at reasonable, but sometimes slightly higher, prices than other areas in Sevilla. They are generally still surprisingly excellent value, given the touristy nature of the area, but don't give a true picture of the Sevillano tapas bar. *Café Alianza*, C Rodrigo Caro 9. Wonderful position in a small cobbled square shaded by orange trees and the Alcázar walls, with a glimpse of the Giralda. *Casa Roman*, Plaza de los Venerables 1. Former grocer's shop beautifully decorated with antique lamps, oil paintings and the ubiquitous hanging *jamones*, the latter being the bar's speciality. Try the tapas of *jamón Ibérico bellota* (€1.80) or *estofado Ibérico*, pork stew (€2), but watch out for *raciones* of Iberian pork products – they can be quite expensive (€20 for a selection, or *surtido*). *Casa Sergio*, C López de Rueda, opposite *Hotel Murillo*. This small bar does excellent cheap tapas (€1.50); the best value for this area. Try the *espinacas con garbanzos* (spinach and chickpeas). *Flaherty*, C Alemanes 7, T954210451. Large, traditional Irish pub, with a pretty patio shaded by grapevines. Its location in the shadow of the Cathedral means it's often crammed with tourists, but worth it for a Guinness and Irish-influenced tapas or even a full Irish breakfast. Live music Thu, big screen for sports events. *Bar Giralda*, C Mateos Gago. Long established bar in an attractive restored Moorish bathhouse just down from the Giralda with a good range of tapas – including *langostinos*, or king prawns. *Bar Las Teresas*, C Las Teresas. Popular tourist haunt but don't let that put you off – atmospheric bar decorated with old posters of Sevilla, hanging *jamones* and bottles of vintage sherry. Good for a mid-morning coffee or early evening beer. *Bodega Santa Cruz*, C Rodrigo Caro. On the corner with C Mateos Gago near the Giralda, this busy and cheerful bar seems more Spanish than its neighbours, although it's equally packed with tourists. Perhaps something to do with its nicotine-stained walls and cheaper prices. Good choice of *montaditos*. *La Bodeguita de Santa Justa*, Hernando Colón 1-3. Lots of fish choice (try the *albóndigas de chocos y langostinos*, squid and king prawn fish balls) and cheaper than bars closer to the Cathedral, only a few mins' walk away. Mediocre *menú del día* for €7.

Centro Plaza Alfalfa and the streets around it are bursting with excellent and cheap tapas bars; it's only 5 mins' walk from Barrio Santa Cruz (if you don't get lost), but Sevillanos outnumber tourists. Another fertile area is along C San Eloy and Plaza Duque de la Victoria. *Bar Ajo Blanco*, C Alhóndigas 19, near Plaza Ponce de León. Closed Mon evenings and Sun. Small bar adorned with old jazz posters serving delicious Latin American tapas (€1.80) like enchiladas, tacos and quesadillas, as well as couscous and *empanadas*. *Menú del día* €6. *Café Alcazares*, Plaza Encarnación 13. Tucked away in the corner near the market, this light and airy bar serves all the usual tapas (€1.70). *Bar Alicantina*, Plaza Salvador 2-3. Great spot in a bustling square by the Iglesia del Salvador to people-watch and enjoy some of the best (and most expensive) seafood tapas in town. *Bodeguita Antonio Romero*, C Antonio Díaz 19. Pleasant bar near the Maestranza Plaza de Toros with a good range of tapas (€1.50), available only at the bar; *raciones* are served at tables. Also on C Gamazo round the corner. *Bar El Arenal*, corner of Antonio Díaz and C Adriano. No-frills bar in contrast to the rest along this street. Basic tapas served only in the day, but worth a visit for its old photos of the Maestranza and general unaffected ambience of bygone days. *Bodega Casa Morales*, C García Vinuesa 11. Wonderful famous bodega whose décor looks untouched since it opened in 1850, including an antique cash till. Standing only at tatty wooden bar or huge wine barrels. Limited tapas, closed Sun. *Casa Los Caracoles*, C Pérez Galdós, just off Plaza Alfalfa. Cheap and varied tapas including lots of fried fish choice and the eponymous snails. Busy with a young crowd mid-evening at weekends. *Colmado Los Escolapios*, Plaza Ponce de León 5. Tiny bar located on leafy square offering delicious tapas of *jamón*, *chorizo* and cheese from all over Andalucía; try the *queso fresco con miel y frutas secas* (fresh cheese with honey and dried fruit). *Entre Cárceles*, near Plaza Salavador. Tiny atmospheric bar lined with bottles of sherry, with a tapas menu including goodies like *calamar relleno en salsa oporto* (stuffed squid in port sauce) and *habas con choco* (beans with squid). *Bar Europa*, C Siete Revueltas 35, near Plaza Salvador. Innovative tapas like *pollo al curry con puré de manzana* (curried chicken kebab with apple puree) served in classy but minimalist blue-and-white tiled bar. Charging 20% extra for largely indifferent service at tables makes this a slightly pricier place than its neighbours. Opens 0800 for breakfast. *Bodega Extremeña*, just off Plaza Alfalfa. Small, busy bar displaying bottles of wine and hams from Extremadura province; specialities are olives, cheese and *jamón* from the same region. *Emperador Trajano*, C Trajano 10. Located near Plaza Duque de la Victoria, this split-level bar with bare-brick walls serves original tapas including delicious homemade *pasteles*, or patés, and *tapitas de la Abuela*. Also excellent breakfasts from 0800. *Tienda La Farruca*, C Aponte 10, off Plaza Duque de la Victoria. Tiny, original bar on 2 levels hung with old photos of Sevilla, which offers excellent cheese and ham specialities, like *queso cabrales con datiles* (goat's cheese with dates). Closed Sun evenings. *La Giganta*, C Alhóndigas 6. Typical Andalucian tapas (€1.50) served in minimalist but cheerful bar near Plaza Terceros; specials (€2) include *bacalao con ajetes* (salt codfish with garlic) and *solomillo a la pimienta verde* (pork loin with green peppercorns). *Habanita*, C Golfo 3, off C Pérez Galdós, near Plaza Alfalfa, T606716456. Great little Latin café-bar dishing up a mix of Spanish and Cuban flavours, with lots of vegetarian and even some vegan options. Tapas start at a very reasonable €1.20 and include *arepas* and empanadas. Open 1230-1630, 2000-2400 Mon-Sat and Sun lunchtime. *Bar Marigalante*, C Baños 60. Opened in 2001, this great bar has internet access (€2.50 per hr), a pool table and art exhibitions. It serves *montaditos*, quesadillas and tapas, as well as an array of special coffees. *Mediterráneo*, Pasaje Amor de Dios 2, between Plaza Duque de la Victoria and the Alameda. Wonderful tapas (like the *berejenas rellenas*, or stuffed aubergines), as well as good-value *menú del día* (€6) and breakfasts (try the *churros y chocolate*). Located down a quiet alleyway, with outdoor seating. Opens 0830. *El Patio*, C San

Sevilla Province

Eloy 9. Sandwich emporium stuffed with almost every format you could dream of, featuring unusual tiled stepped seating. *El Rinconcillo*, C Gerona 40. Established in 1670, this is probably the oldest bar in Sevilla, which is oozing character and seemingly untouched in a decorative sense for years. Ceiling-high shelves of bottles line the walls, while the flagstone floor, beautiful tiles and chunky wooden bar make this the most atmospheric bar in town for a drink and some no-frills tapas (€1.20). *Santa Marta*, C Angostillo 2-4. Typical Andalucían tapas (€1.50) served outdoors in a quiet, pretty square in front of the Iglesia de San Andrés. *Menú del día* €9. Also open early for good-value breakfasts. *Taberna del Pájaro*, C Santa Bárbara 7, near the Alameda. Creative homemade tapas and an excellent wine selection, including the bar's own Rioja and Ribera del Duero. *Bar Mesón Serranito*, C Antonio Díaz, near *Bodeguita Antonio Romero* (see above). In keeping with its location near the bullring, bulls' heads and pictures of the Maestranza line the walls. Usual tapas, as well as the eponymous *serranito* (a huge sandwich of pork loin, ham and grilled pepper). *Sopa de Ganso*, C Pérez Galdós 8, just off Plaza Alfalfa, T954212526. Extensive menu of great-value tapas (from €1.50), many of which are a meal in themselves - although with delicacies like the *croquetas de cabrales y nueces* (goat's cheese and walnut croquettes) and *flamenquines de espinaca y beicon* (bacon croquettes stuffed with spinach) it can be hard to stop eating your way down the menu. Wider than usual choice of vegetarian dishes, also salads and pizzas.

Alameda and La Macarena *Café Hércules*, C Pérez Mencheta, esquina C Guadiana. Lively mixed-gay bar near the busy C Feria with limited tapas but great atmosphere. Opens 0900 for breakfast. *El Pucherito*, C Relator 37. Friendly, arty bar-café near the Alameda with a choice of excellent tapas that are changed daily and a wide range of teas. *Bar El Sardinero*, Plaza de San Lorenzo, between the Alameda and the river. Busy bar on a leafy square in front of the Iglesia de San Lorenzo. Specialities include *cabrillas* (snails), fried fish and *guisos* (stews). Cheap *menú del día* (€5) and *platos combinados* (€3.60). Open 0800 for cheap breakfasts. Other good bars around this square, in a lively part of the Barrio San Lorenzo, including *Bodega San Lorenzo*, an atmospheric bar with cheap, typical Andaluz tapas, and *Bar Esclavas*.

Triana *La Albariza*, C Betís 6. Like most places along the river, this typical bodega charges higher prices than the rest of Triana. Seafood specials include *coquinas al Jerez* (cockles in sherry) and *almejas natural al vapor* (steamed clams). *Antigua Abacería de San Lorenzo*, C Pureza 12. Charming wooden-floored *quesería* exuding mouthwatering cheese aromas, bursting with jamones, cheeses and bottles of wine. Homemade patés including *castaña* (chestnut) and *setas* (wild mushroom) and *montaditos* also available. Closed Mon. Also at C Marquéz de la Mina 2, Barrio San Lorenzo, between the Alameda and the river. *Calle Larga*, C Pureza 72. Busy, friendly bar lined with bullfighting photos; try the *cabrillas en salsa* (snails cooked in a sauce). *Bar Los Golondrinas*, C Antillano Campos 26. Located down a quiet, pretty street near C San Jacinto, this small bar is worth a visit for its *azulejos* and cheap tapas, *raciones* served in upstairs dining area with hand-painted furniture. *Mariscos Emilio*, C San Jacinto 39. Excellent seafood bar serving delights such as *ostras* (oysters) (€1.50 each) and sizzling *gambas al ajillo* (prawns with garlic). Also at Génova 1 in Triana. *Bodega Miami*, San Jacinto 21. Long-established watering hole with excellent tapas (€1.50), walls covered with the usual Triana *azulejos* and wonderful photos of the *romería* at El Rocío, bullfighting and Sevilla. *Molino Pintado*, C Betís 20. Pleasant bar with serving *tarteletas* (mini pizzas) of various kinds and lots of cheese and *chacina* tapas choice (€1.50). *Taberna La Plazuela*, Plaza de Santa Ana. One of 2 bars on this pretty square, which is a peaceful spot for a *montadito* in front of the Iglesia de Santa Ana. *Taberna Ruta de la Plata*, C Betís 10. Opened in 2001, this small bar with riverside seating (*raciones* only) specializes in

Nibbles – Spanish style

The custom of taking tapas is not, historically speaking, a long standing habit. Tapas are thought to have appeared in Sevilla in the 19th century, when legend has it that drinkers protected their glass of fino from flies, dust and dripping hams by putting over them a cover or tapa. The cover was often a slice of bread and before long enterprising bartenders were putting some food on the bread. The rest, as they say, is history.

'Grazing' - nibbling at small amounts of food - is nowadays a popular way of eating throughout Europe, but nowhere is it more common than in Spain. This may be due to the quirky mealtimes in Spain, with lunch rarely starting before 1400 and dinner beginning at 2200 in the evening, with long gaps to fill the rumbling tummy. Of equal importance, however, is the fact that the tapas bar or tasca is an essential part of Spanish life, a place where people meet to eat and drink, gossip, carry out business and generally pass the time. A tapas crawl, hopping from bar to bar and sampling a nibble of food at each one, is one of the delights of Andalucía.

So what should the uninitiated visitor expect and what etiquette is involved? Firstly, tapas are usually taken standing at the bar. Expect to pay more if you sit at a table or on a terrace, sometimes larger portions, called raciones or media raciones, may only be available here. Sometimes cold tapas are laid out on the bar, so you can point to the ones you want. The food may be served in a small dish called a concha or in tiny earthenware casserole dishes, accompanied by bread (good for mopping up sauces) or dry breadsticks and possibly a small fork. Tapas have always traditionally been served cold, but many are now popped into a microwave before serving. In some of the more remote parts of Andalucía you may still be lucky enough to be given a free tapa with your drink, most commonly just olives, but normally expect to pay between €1.20 and €1.80.

The food provided varies enormously from simple olives and chunks of cheese or tortilla to quite elaborate dishes. Some bars have their own specialities, which are well known in the area, such as jamón or a seafood dish. But in the majority of bars, as in the Spanish home, the type of tapas may depend on what was left over yesterday, what is in season (like setas, or wild mushrooms in autumn) or whether there has been a glut of sardinas at the local fish market. If a tapa looks particularly good, ask for a ración, which can be shared with more than one person. For translation of specific tapas, see box on page 436.

When choosing a drink to accompany tapas, bear in mind that the traditional slurp is a cold fino sherry, often drawn from a barrel, but in reality anything goes. A beer, red wine or even carbonated water is quite acceptable. Most Spanish people would draw the line at a gin and tonic, however, while a coffee with a tapa is definitely NOT on.

Other essential points to remember in tapas etiquette is that it is a social activity, so bring a friend or two; order a variety of tapas; try and sit outside (weather permitting) in a picturesque spot.

cheese from all over Spain and pork products, as well as a great *empanada de la casa*, a tuna pastry. **Bar Santa Ana**, C Pureza 82. Good location opposite the Iglesia de Santa Ana for a beer-and-tapas stop to see its photos of the Virgen del Rocío, as well as its neo-Moorish tiled arches. **Bodega Siglo XVIII**, C Pelay Correa 32. One of Triana's most stunning bars, this 18th-century bodega has splendid antique furnishings, Moorish tiles, an electic mix of paintings and a magnificently carved wooden bar and ceiling. Apart from its excellent tapas, the *bodgea's* most memorable feature is its somewhat incongrous Moorish patio. Closed all day Mon and Tue morning. **Sol y Sombra**, C Castilla 151. Characterful bar with lots of old bullfighting posters and typical Andaluz dishes, like *solomillo al ajo* (pork loin with garlic) and seafood choice.

Cafés & breakfast bars

Barrio Santa Cruz *Aula Magna*, C San José 21, outside San José church. Good spot for breakfast with wide range of *tostadas* and all the daily papers; opens 7am. Also does baguettes and *montaditos*. On the same square is *Café Levíes*, an excellent place for breakfast and sandwiches, opens 8am.

Centro and Alameda C San Eloy and Plaza Duque de la Victoria has loads of places serving up excellent value breakfasts; try *Jugopan*, C San Eloy 42 , while at nearby *Don Julián* you can choose from Mexican, French, German, English or Spanish breakfasts, all for around €3. Choices on Plaza Duque include *Horno del Duque* or *Bar de la Victoria*. Just off the square, at C Trajano 10, is *Emperador Trajano*; nearby is *Mediterráneo*, Pasaje Amor de Dios 2 (see under Tapas bars above). Further away, but worth the walk, is *Café Marigalante*, C Baños 60, which has a great range of breakfasts and internet access to have with coffee. Opens 0730. *Café Picalagartos*, C Hernando Colón 7, is a popular café-bar which is good for a late-afternoon coffee-and-cake stop. Opens 1630. *Alamo*, Alameda de Hércules 57, near C Relator. Internet café-bar open 1200-0600. Internet €1.80 per hr. *Planet Internet*, C San Hermenegildo, local 16C, next to the Iglesia de la Hiniesta. Stylish cyber café open 1100-2400, internet €1.80 per hr. **Triana** *Tequila Connection*, C Betís 41. Internet café with mock-Maya/Mexican décor serving a wide variety of coffee, ice cream and *batidos*, or milkshakes. Also does breakfast. Internet €2.40 per hr.

Dulces del Convento, pastelerías & heladerías

Barrio Santa Cruz *Convento de Madre de Dios*, San José 4. Dulces available 0930-1300, 1630-1830; while you're here, the *convento* itself is worth a look. *Il Garibaldi*, Santa María La Blanca. Ice-creams, pastries and cakes, also cheap breakfasts, served in bright and cheerful café. *El Horno de San Buenaventura*, Av Constitución, opposite the Cathedral. A good place for a caffeine-and-sugar fix after a hard morning's sightseeing; choose from a tempting show of handmade chocolates, pastries and cakes. One of a chain; other locations include Plaza Alfalfa and near Plaza Ponce de León in the centre. **Centro** *La Campaña*, C Sierpes 1. Long-established *confitería* with a tantalizing display of pastries, cakes and confectionery to recharge your shopping batteries. *Convento de Santa Paula*, C Santa Paula. *Dulces* available 1000-1300, 1630-1830. *Heladería La Fiorentina*, C Zaragoza 16. Italian ice-cream parlour. *Mamá Goye*, Maese Rodrigo 8, at the end of Av Constitución near *Hotel Alfonso XIII*. Delicious array of ice creams.

Bars and nightlife

As elsewhere in Andalucía, Sevilla's nightlife doesn't get going until past midnight, and once it does, there is loads of choice – particularly for flamenco, jazz and blues and dance music. If you want to sample Sevillano bars, you could head for an area where there is a concentration of late-night bars, or *bares de copas*, like between Plaza Alfalfa and Plaza Salvador in the centre (including the lively C Pérez Galdós); C Betís, C Castillo and Plaza Chapina near the river in Triana; or around the Alameda de Hércules in the centre. Another popular area is the streets around Plaza Ponce de León. C Adriano in El Arenal and C Pastor y Landero near the Plaza de Toros are both lined with good bars.

Many bars have live music or late-night DJs and some have dancefloors. Later on the action gyrates from bars to *discotecas*, of which Sevilla has many (see below). A popular Spanish pre-clubbing pastime is *la movida botellona*, where hordes of young people congregate in one area with bottles of beer, wine and spirits. In Sevilla, the main places for this *movida,* or action, in summer are along the river in Triana and in C Torneo opposite Isla La Cartuja. People also get together in Plaza Cristo de Burgos in the centre, east of Plaza Encarnación, popularly known as Plaza San Pedro, as well as Plaza Salvador and the nearby C Cuesta del Rosario, all year round.

Also see the excellent monthly free what's-on publication, *El Giraldillo*, available from bars, restaurants, hotel and *turismo*, or see www.elgiraldillo.es Other sources are *Tu Guía*, *Welcome & Olé* and *The Tourist*, also free and found in hotels and bars. The latter two are bilingual, as they are specifically aimed at tourists and despite the rather offputting titles have lots of useful information. The newspapers *El Correo* and *El Diario de Sevilla* have daily what's on sections and *ABC* has a Thu supplement on going out in Sevilla. You can also get information from the tourist offices (see page 64 or see www.turismosevilla.org)

Flamenco

Due to the spontaneous nature of this art form, it can be remarkably difficult to find. Many visitors only see a *tablao*, which are overpriced shows put on for tourists. *Los Gallos*, Plaza de Santa Cruz 11, T954216981, 2130-0130, is probably the best of these. *El Arenal*, C Rocío 7, T954216492, www.tablaoelarenal, can have a more spontaneous performance. 2 shows, 2100-2230 and 2300-0030; dinner available. €25 for show only. Also contact *Teatro Central* (see under Theatres below) for details of flamenco shows.

The following are recommended for their mainly more impromptu nature: *La Abacería*, Rosario Vega 3-4. Lively flamenco in informal, young Triana bar with drinks served in bottles only and tapas on paper plates. *La Anselma*, C Pagés del Corro esquina C Covadonga. Triana bar where the owner sings flamenco, with occasional group performances. *Carbonería*, Levíes 18, T954214460. Long-established, popular sprawling bar with 3 areas. The first is the most atmospheric, a former coal yard where flamenco is performed at 2230 every night. In the second area is a counter selling tapas (try the *chorizo infierno*, that you cook yourself over a flaming dish at your table), with an outdoor, tree-filled large patio. Also other live performances, like folk or Arabic music, and art exhibitions. Free, open until 0330. *Casa de la Memoria*, C Ximénez de Enciso 28, T954560670. Cultural centre located in a typical Sevillian restored mansion, with Moorish tiles and a plant-draped 16th-century patio. Flamenco at around 2100 (from €9) every night except Wed when there's Sephardic live music. Exhibitions and course in traditional Andalucían culture, including flamenco. *La Espiga*, C Virgen de Begoña. Cosy atmophere with the owner, Pepín, and his wife singing flamenco and encouragement for everyone to join in. *Taberna Flamenca y Rincón Rociero*, C Adriano 5, El Arenal. With a slightly older crowd, flamenco bar with tapas available open from 2200 for impromptu performances nearly every night, 2400 weekends. Free entry. *Lamadrugá*, C Salado. Lively flamenco bar attracting the younger Triana inhabitants. Also along the same street is a similar bar, *La Campana*. *Lola de los Reyes*, C Blás Infante. The eponymous Lola is the soul and sometime singer of this bar. *Las Niñas*, Plaza Chapina s/n. Popular flamenco bar in Triana with a younger crowd. *Bar Quita Pesares*, Plaza Jerónimo de Córdoba, near Plaza Ponce de León. Often live flamenco at weekends, but hard to predict exactly when it takes place. *El Rejoneo*, C Betís, Triana. Flamenco singers perform in front of youngish audience. Also on same street is *Lo Nuestro*. *Sevillanas*, C Canalejas 1, opposite *Hotel Colón*. Centrally located bar with an older crowd and performances by flamenco groups, occasionally featuring famous singers. *Taberna Sonanta*, C San Jacinto 31. Triana bar with flamenco on Thu at 2230 and some Fri evenings. Situated between two dance academies, one of flamenco, you can sometime see spontaneous flamenco shows by students at lunchtime. Occasional theatre performances on Fri evenings. Also has internet (€2.40 per hr). Its sister bar in Plaza Chapina 22 also has flamenco on Thu evenings (2200), free. Open 0800-0300; tapas and dinner menu available. *El Tejar*, San Jacinto 68, Triana. Great bar with a slightly older crowd with flamenco on Fri, art exhibitions and good tapas. Open 2030-0200. Closed Sun.

Sevilla Province

Bars **Centro** *Alcaicería*, C Empecinados s/n. Long established bar playing jazz from the 1960s-1980s. *Almacén*, Plaza San Antonio de Padua 9, off C Santa Ana, T954900434. Bar of *La Imperdible* theatre (see below), which has its own events, like poetry night on Wed and live music on Fri and Sat. Free. Open 1900 onwards; closed Mon. *Antigua*, C Marqués de Paradas 30. Dance bar with theme nights Fri and Sat. Open 2200-0800. Closed Jun-Sep. *Antigüedades*, C Argote de Molina 10. Larger-than-life figures hang from the ceiling and walls and the original décor gets a regular makeover. Cocktails and good selection of malt whiskies. Open 2100 until late. *El Barón Rampante*, C Arias Montano 3, next to the Centro Cívico in the Alameda de Hércules. Buzzing bar with a great atmosphere and a mixed-gay crowd. Open 1600-0400. *Bauhaus*, Marqués de Paradas 53. Stylish dance music bar with DJs from 1600 onwards, with occasional video DJ performances and exhibitions. Food served until 2400 (see Tapas bars above); open until 0400. *Blue Moon*, C Antonio Cavestany 10. One of the best places to see live jazz Tue-Sat at 2400. *El Bosque Animado*, C Arias Montano 3. Situated next to *El Barón Rampante* (see above) attracting a similar crowd. Original bar design with a forest theme in keeping with its name. Mellow music on week nights and early evening, anything from African to Arabic, with more upbeat sounds at the weekend. Open 1600 until early morning. *La Buena Estrella*, Trajano 51. Mellow atmosphere in this small café-bar that specializes in original herbal tea concoctions. Livelier later, with DJs and occasional live music. Open 0900-0300. *Capote*, El Barranco, off C Arjona. Friendly bar under Puente Isabel with theatre on Thu and a cocktail bar. Great outdoor terraza with good river views. Open 1100-0200. *Café Central*, Alameda de Hércules 64. Trendy bar similar to the neighbouring *Habanilla* (see below) with art exhibitions. Try their Caipiriña cocktail. Tapas available 2100-0200. *Carbonería*, Levíes 18, T954214460. Flamenco nightly, live blues and swing every Wed and Sat 2230; free. See under Flamenco above. *Envidia*, J Antonio Cavestany, esquina Gonzalo Bilbao. Lively bar opposite the Santa Justa station. Live music on Thu, Fri and Sat comedy; also art exhibitions. Open 1600-0100. *Garlochi*, C Boteros 26. Unusual and long-established cocktail bar with the most original décor in Sevilla – stuffed with religious paraphernalia, pariculary from Semana Santa, and gilt mirrors. Music - classical or religious - and drinks - *Sangre de Cristo*, or Blood of Christ – to match the surroundings. Closes 2 weeks in Jul or Aug. *Habanilla*, Alameda de Hércules 63. Located next door to *Café Central*, this is a popular hangout with young and trendy Sevillanos. Art exhibitions, theatre and live music. Tapas available. *Café del Mar*, C Jesús del Gran Poder 83, near Alameda de Hércules. Stylish bar playing mainly house music, with DJs from midnight onwards. Thu-Sat. Open 1600-0300, until 0500 Fri-Sat. *Naima Café Jazz*, Trajano 47. Cosy bar lined with jazz pictures that plays jazz music, but no live bands. Open 1200-0300. *Noveccentro*, C Julio Cesar 10. Gay-mixed bar with art exhibitions and live music – anything from jazz to flamenco. Free entry to performances on Sun 2030-2400. *The Scottish Pub*, C Adriano 3, El Arenal. Formerly called *A3*, this bar has a mellow atmosphere during the week, until Thu night when there's live music (with flamenco every 2 weeks) and dancing at weekends. *Café La Sirena*, Alameda de Hércules 34. Funkily painted lively bar with outdoor seating. Open 1700-0200. *Summertime Café*, Plaza del Museo 1, next to the Museo de Bellas Artes. Live jazz on Fri and Sat. *Zapata*, C Álvarez Quintero esquina Rodríguez Zapata, near the Cathedral. Tiny Mexican long-established bar painted in bright Latin colours with art exhibitions. Cocktail specialities are margaritas and tequila sunrises – good for warming you up on chilly nights when you can't squeeze in the bar. Open Thu-Sat 2200-0300. *Trinity Irish Pub*, C Madrid s/n. Busy, large bar near Plaza Nueva decorated as a 19th-century Irish watering hotel. *Urbano Comix*, C Matahacas 5. Alternative bar east of Plaza Ponce de León featuring live jazz and blues on Thu. Opens 2100 until late.

Bar Betís 29, C Betís 29. Laid back atmosphere with good music, open 2100-0330 **Triana**
Mon-Thu (opens 1600 at weekends). *Big Ben*, C Betís 54. Live jazz and blues in summer. Open 2130-0430. *Fundición*, C Betís 49-50. *Bar-discoteca* with mixed music,
beer €2.40. Sangría and tequila night on Tue. *Mu d'aqui*, C Betís 55. Lively Triana
bar, but a bit of a pick-up joint, particularly for single men. Closed Aug. Opens
2130-0300. *Las Niñas*, Plaza Chapina 7. Typical Triana bar with wide range of music
and occasional impromptu flamenco performances. *Café de la Prensa*, C Betís 8.
Relaxed ambience in this cosy bar by the river in Triana. Sometimes stages art exhibitions. Open 1500-0300. *La Otra Orilla*, Paseo de la O s/n. Behind *Bar Las Niñas* next to
the river, this great bar with summer terraza has live jazz and blues. Open every night
in summer, Thu-Sat in winter, until 0600. *Puerta Triana*, Plaza Chapina. Triana lively
bar popular with younger local crowd. *Si Rocco*, C Betís 57. Music bar that gets more
alternative after 0300, more a mixture of foreigners and Spanish than other bars
along C Betís. Open 2200-0630.

An area with several popular clubs, like *Antique*, is between the Puente de la **Nightclubs**
Barqueta and Palenque, in front of Isla Mágica. *Boss*, C Betís 67. Upmarket *discoteca*
with events like Spanish pop concerts and record launches. Expensive drinks. Open
Thu-Sat only 2200-0800. *Catedral*, C Cuesta del Rosario 12. Club playing mainly
house music, featuring video DJs. Open Wed-Sat only 2400-0700. €9 (some nights
free for women), drinks €6. Closed Aug. *Circus*, Pabellón de los Descubrimientos, Isla
de la Cartuja. Large *discoteca* featuring variety of dance music and some live music.
Open Thu, Fri, Sat from 2400. Entry fee varies, but can be quite expensive. *Collage*, C
Julio Cesar 13. Club playing mainly house music open from 2400 Wed-Sat, with occasional theatre performances, on a street with several good late-night bars, like
Novoccentro and *Coliseum* (see above). €6; if it's very busy there are certain door
restrictions, like no trainers. Before midnight it's a cyber cafe with a more laid back
atmosphere. *Fun Club*, Alameda de Hércules 86. *Discoteca* with DJs and live music
Thu-Sat 2230. Closed Jul-Aug. *Itaca*, Amor de Dios 25. Mainly gay club between the
Alameda and Plaza Duque de la Victoria. *Weekend*, C Torneo 43. Formerly the
Salamandra, this club is somewhat with a Sevillano institution, staging a wide range
of music concerts and DJ nights. Open Thu-Sat. Closed 1 week in Aug.

Entertainment

These are held Apr-Oct in the Plaza de Toros de la Real Maestranza, Paseo de Cristóbel **Bullfights**
Colón, T954210315 , www.realmaestranza.com, one of the largest bullrings in Spain.
Tickets are bought directly from the bullring and also from a kiosk in C Sierpes.

For details of the many other cinemas in Sevilla, see the newspapers *El Correo* or *El* **Cinema**
Diario de Sevilla; the free monthly what's-on guide, *El Giraldillo*; www.cineciudad.com
or ring T954380157. *Cine Club UGT*, Salón de Actos de UGT, Av Blas Infante 4,
T954273003, union@sevilla.ugt.org. Art house cinema. Buses 6,42, C1 and C2. *Avenida
5 Cines*, Marquéz de Paradas 15, near the Marquéz de Paradas bus station,
T954293025. Unlike most cinemas which dub foreign films in Spanish, this place shows
foreign films in the original language, with Spanish subtitles. Buses C1, C2, C3. *Cine
Universitario*, Universidad de Sevilla, Pabellón Uruguay 2, T954551048.

Sevilla has two teams in the First Division of one of the most competitive leagues in **Football**
Europe. Real Betis play at the Benito Villamarín Stadium in the south of the town, Av
Heliópolis, T954610340. Sevilla FC are at the Sánchez Pizjuan stadium in the eastern
suburbs, Av Eduardo Dato, T954489400.

Sevilla Province

Theatre *Teatro Central*, C José Gálvez s/n, T902400222, www.teatrocentral.com Located in Isla de la Cartuja with a varied programme of dance, drama, jazz and flamenco. *La Imperdible*, Plaza San Antonio de Padua 9, off C Santa Ana, T954388219, www.imperdible.org Small theatre staging diverse productions, including comedy, dance and children's theatre. Also has a new exhibition space, La Herrería. Tickets cost €7, Thu are *día de la pareja*, or two for one. *Teatro Imperial*, C Sierpes 25, T954226868. *Teatro Lope de Vega*, Av María Luisa s/n, T954590856. *Teatro de la Maestranza*, Paseo Colón 22, T954226573, www.maestranza.com Impressive building near the bullring on the river, staging mainly opera, dance and classical music. *Sala Coro*, C Miguel Cid 67, T954902736. Stages fringe theatre and dance productions.

Fiestas and festivals

Jan 6 The *Labalyata de los Reyes* (Cavalade of the Magi) has the 'kings' throwing sweets from their floats. **Mar-Apr** The *Semana Santa* celebrations in the week leading up to Easter are arguably the best in Spain, with effigies of Christ and the Virgin Mary being paraded through the streets by the brotherhoods; solemnity is replaced 2 weeks later by the riotous *Feria de Abril*, marked by bullfights, fireworks, dancing and general merrymaking lasting for a week (see also box, page 66).**Jun** *Corpus Cristi* is celebrated by a procession through the streets which are decorated by flowers and herbs, while choirboys dance according to a 14th-century tradition. Triana holds its own smaller version of the event, the *Corpus Chico*, the following day.**15 Aug** *Virgen de los Reyes* celebrates the patron saint of Sevilla. **Sep** *Bienal de Flamenco* takes place in even years. **Nov** *International Jazz Festival.*

Shopping

The main shopping street is the pedestrianized C Sierpes, Sevilla's famed heart of the commercial area and packed with stylish shops. The parallel C Cuna has similar shops, particularly clothes at the end near C S Eloy. A large branch of the department store, *El Corte Inglés*, is to be found in Plaza Duque de la Victoria. There is also a *Marks and Spencer* on C San Eloy/Plaza Duque de la Victoria. Local handicrafts include leatherware, flamenco costumes, ceramics, fans, gold and silver jewellery and shops selling these items can be found in the area around C Sierpes. Alternatively, try the handicraft markets held on Thu, Fri and Sat on Plaza Duque and nearby Plaza Magdalena. For *azulejos* and other *cerámica*, go to C Antillano Campos in Triana. The main fruit and vegetable markets include Plaza Encarnación in the centre, C Feria in La Macarena and Plaza Altozano in Triana. A flea market is held on Thu in C Feria, La Macarena. On Sun there is a pet market in Plaza Alfalfa and a collectors' market in Plaza Cabildo (stamps and coins). Branches of Librería Beta (Av Constitución between the Cathedral and Plaza Nueva and off C Sierpes) have a good selection of maps and guidebooks on Sevilla and Andalucía, as well as books in English. One of the best maps of Sevilla is the laminated and widely available *Walk Map*, published by RACC Club (1:8,500, with enlarged central area, 1:5,500), €6.

Sport

Golf There are two local courses: *Club Pineda*, Av de Jerez s/n, T954613399 and *Sevilla Golf*, Ctra Isla Mayor, T955750414. **Horse riding** *Hípica Puerta Principe*, Ctra de Sevilla-Utrera, Km 11.5, T954860815. **Parachuting** *Parachuting Sports Club*, C Rodrigo de Triana 62, T954451267. **Shooting** *Club el Carambolo*, T954390401. **Swimming** There are 2 swimming pools, *Piscinas Sevilla*, Av Ciudad Jardín, and *Piscina Municipal Virgen de los Reyes*, Av Doctor Fedriani s/n. Both pools also offer tennis. There is **canoeing** and **rowing** on the Río Guadalquivir. A variety of sports are offered at the *Municipal Sports Centre* at the Polígono de San Pablo.

Tour operators

With over 80 travel agents in Sevilla, this is a very small selection: *Viajes Barceló*, C Reyes Católicos 4, T954226131. *Viajes Iberia*, C Tetuán 24, T954224160. *Julia Tours*, C Bilbao 22, T954224910. *Viajes Meliá*, Av de la Constitución 30, T954218700. *Torre de Oro*, Av de la Miraflores, T954358984. *Universal*, Av de la Constitución 26, T954227819. *Usit Unlimited*, Av de la Constitución (opposite the Cathedral) and C Mateos Gago 2, T902252575, www.usitunlimited.es   Specialists in youth and student travel.

Transport

Road Bus: Sevilla has a cheap and efficient bus system. A map of routes covered by the city bus company, Tussam, is available from a kiosk (0900-1345, 1700-1900 Mon-Fri) on Plaza Nueva, €0.30. Also available are special tourist tickets, *tarjeta turística*, €6.50 for 3 days, €9.60 for 7 days. A *bonobús* for 10 bus trips costs €4.70 (€4.20 for a *transbordo*, if you want to change buses in the same journey) and is available from kiosks and tobacconists. A single ticket costs €0.90. Useful buses are C1, C2, C3, and C4 which go around the inner ring road. **Cycle hire**: *Quiquecicle*, Parque de María Luisa, opposite Plaza España, T954921781. Daily. **Parking**: This can be horrendous, although some new underground car parks have been built (typically €0.75 per hr). A cheap, but more risky place to park – in terms of theft – is between the Torre del Oro and river, €0.60 for as long as you want. Theft from cars is widespread, so don't leave any possessions visible inside the car. If staying overnight, try to find a hotel with a garage or secure parking. **Taxi**: *Radiotaxi*, T954580000; *Teletaxi*, T954622222.

Local
The city's infrastructure, particularly its communication system, underwent many improvements for EXPO '92

Air A new airport has been built beside the old one at San Pablo, 12 km east of the city for both internal and international flights. For information T954449023. An *Amarillos* bus, T902210317 (24 hr), runs every 30 mins (less frequently on Sat, Sun and holidays) between the airport and the city centre at Puerta de Jerez, via the train station, costing €2 and taking 30 mins. Taxis are available, but watch out for fiddled fares. The set fares can be seen in the airport and are currently €15.

Long distance

Bus The main bus station is Prado de San Sebastián in C Manuel Vásquez Sagastizábal, T954417111. From here there are frequent services to Granada, Córdoba and Málaga, among other destinations. Many companies operate from here including *Alsina Graells*, T954418811, to: **Córdoba** (12 daily, 2-3 hrs, €8); **Granada** (9 daily, 4-5 hr, €14.95); **Jaén** (3-4 daily, 4 hr, €14.25); and **Málaga** (6 daily, 2hr, €12.25). *Linesur*, T954988222: **Jerez** (5-6 daily, 1¼ hr, €4.80); **Algeciras** (5 daily, 3-3½ hr, €12.50). *Comes*, T954416858: **Algeciras** (4 daily, €13.25); **Cádiz** (9 daily, 3 hr, €8.70); **Jerez** (9 daily, €5.60); and **Tarifa** (4 daily, €13.05). *Los Amarillos*, T954989184: **Ronda** (5 daily, 2½ hr, €8.40), also stopping at Arcos de la Frontera. Nearby, on the corner of C Carlos de Borbón and C Diego de Raño, the *Casal* company operate an hourly service from Carmona (€1.90). The other station is at Plaza de Armas, T954907737, next to the Puente del Cachorro. Buses leave from here to Madrid, destinations in northern Sevilla province, as well as the provinces of Huelva – including Aracena (2 daily, 1½ hr, €5.20) – and Extremadura. For Lisbon connections, take the *Casal* bus to Rosal del la Frontera on the Portuguese border. The C4 bus runs between the 2, or it's a 30-min walk. Both bus stations have luggage lockers (€2.40).

Bus company telephone numbers are published in the Cartelera section of El Correo daily newspaper

Sevilla Province

Train The new Santa Justa train station (with exchange facilities) is on Av de Kansas City, T954414111 (information), T954421562 (reservations). There are 2 trains a day from **Algeciras**, 13 from **Cádiz**, 12 from **Córdoba**, 3 from **Granada**, 7 from **Huelva**, and 3 from **Málaga**. The 9 daily trains from **Madrid** include the new AVE high speed service which makes the 340 mile trip in just under 2½ hrs. There is a RENFE ticket office at C Zaragoza 29, in the centre, T954211455, which can also provide timetables. For AVE timetables also see the free magazine *The Tourist* or www.renfe.es

Directory

Banks Banks open Mon-Fri 0830-1400, Sat 0830-1300. Closed Sat May-Oct. Banks cluster around Av de la Constitución, Plaza Nueva and C Tetuán. There are change facilities outside banking hrs at the Santa Justa station and in many of the more central hotels. The department store, *El Corte Inglés*, in Plaza Duque de la Victoria, also provides change facilities at convenient hrs.

Communications **Internet** Sevilla has loads of internet places, particularly in the central areas. Many sell cheaper time in *bonos*, which are cards allowing a fixed number of hrs on the internet for use at different times if required. See also Tapas bars and Cafés above. The following is a selection: *Amazonas Cyber*, Conde de Barajas 6A, esquina Potro, near the Alameda. €1.50 per hour. Mon-Fri 1000-1400, 1700-2230; Sun 1700-2230. *Ciber Boston*, C San Fernando 27, opposite the university, €1.80 per hr, with *bono* of 10 hours, €1.50 per hour. Mon-Fri 0900-0100, Sat-Sun 1200-2400. *Ciber Sevilla*, C Pérez Caldo 1, near Plaza Alfalfa, €1.80 per hr, daily 1200-0200. *Cyber@lameda*, C Doctor Letamendi 46, near the Alameda. Only €0.90 per hr 1030-1800 Mon-Fri, 1600-1800 Sat-Sun. 1800-2330 Mon-Fri and 1800-2400 Sat-Sun, €1.80 per hr. *You2go*, Av Constitución 34, opposite the Cathedral, T954215622, €2.40 per hr, with 5 hr *bono* €1.20 per hr. Mon-Sat 0900-2230, Sun 0930-2230. **Post office** Correos, Av de la Constitución 32, Mon-Fri 0830-2030, Sat 0900-1300. **Telephones** *Locutorio* in Plaza de Gavidia, open 1000-1400 and 1730-2200.

Embassies & consulates **Austria**, C Marqués de Paradas 26, T954222162. **Belgium**, Av San Francisco Javier 20, 3A, T954647061. **Canada**, Av de la Constitución 30, T954229413. **Denmark**, Av Reina Mercedes 25, 1B, T954611489. **Finland**, C Adriano 45, 2B, T954225079. **France**, Plaza Santa Cruz 1, T954222896. **Germany**, Av Ramón de Carranza 22, T954457811. **Greece**, Ctra de Carmona 30, T954419000. **Italy**, C Luis Montoto 107, T954577102. **Netherlands**, C Gravina 55, T954228750. **Portugal**, Pabellón de Portugal, Av del Cid, T954231150. **Sweden**, Av Reina Mercedes 25, T954611489. **Switzerland**, C Luis Montoto 112A, T954575355. **UK**, Plaza Nueva 8, T954228874/5. **USA**, Pabellón de los EEUU, Paseo de las Delicias 7, T954231883.

Medical services **Hospitals** *Cruz Roja*, Av de la Cruz Roja, T954351400. *Hospital Universitario*, Av Doctor Fedriano s/n, T954378400. *Hospital General*, Av Manuel Siurot, T954558100, emergencies T954558195. *San Lázaro*, Av Fedriani s/n, T954378737. **First aid** *Casa de Socorro*, T954411712. The local web site is www.sevilla.org

Useful addresses **Car repairs** *Citroën*, Polígono Industrial Ctra Amarilla, T954554500; *Ford*, Av de Andalucía 1, T954576880; *Renault*, Autopista San Pablo s/n, T954360100; *Peugeot*, Autopista de San Pablo, Km 537, T954350450; *Seat/VAG*, Ctra de su Eminencia 2, T954644766.

East from Sevilla

*Two main routeways lead east from Sevilla across the rich undulating farming landscape known as **La Campiña**. After 35 km the NIV, an autovía to Córdoba, bypasses the ancient towns of **Carmona** and **Écija**. A more southeasterly route, the A92, leads to Antequera and Málaga, bypassing **Osuna** and **Estepa**, while diversions from this road lead to **Utrera** to the south and **Marchena** to the north. All of these ancient towns are worth a visit if you have time.*

Carmona

Situated 33 km east of Sevilla in a commanding position on a promontory of the Alcores Hills, Carmona overlooks the Guadalquivir basin, with its fertile farmland devoted to olives and cereals. Bypassed by the *autovía*, it is well worth a diversion or better still an overnight stay, for the town is full of historic interest. There are two Moorish *alcázares* (one now a parador), a unique Roman necropolis and a string of interesting churches and palaces. Most sites can be reached on foot, apart perhaps from the Roman Necropolis, which, as was the custom, was located outside the city walls. The *turismo* is located inside the ancient gateway of the Puerta de Sevilla at the Casa de Cultura, T954190955. ■ *Mon-Sat 1000-1800, Sun 1000-1500.* The Casa de Cultura itself is open during the afternoons, so it may be possible to obtain information when the tourist office is closed.

*Colour map 1, grid C6
Population: 25,326*

Sevilla Province

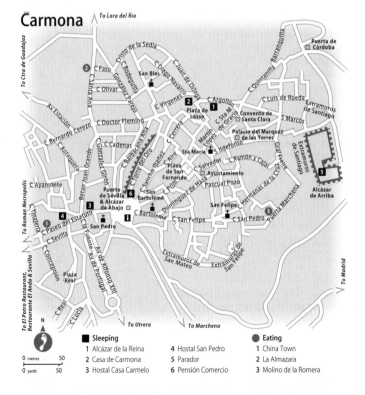

	Sleeping		
1	Alcázar de la Reina	4	Hostal San Pedro
2	Casa de Carmona	5	Parador
3	Hostal Casa Carmelo	6	Pensión Comercio

	Eating	
1	China Town	
2	La Almazara	
3	Molino de la Romera	

History Archaeological remains show that settlement goes back to Palaeolithic times, but the most important of the early settlers were the Carthaginians during the third century. The Romans then conquered the town in 206 BC, naming it Carmo. It became one of the major fortified towns of the Baetica province of the Roman Empire, when most of Carmona's ancient walls were built. The town achieved its greatest splendour under the Moors, who led by Muza Ben Nosair, laid siege to Carmona, taking over after negotiations allowing the Jewish community to remain. (The Jewish presence continued until the 16th century, greatly aiding the town's prosperity.) The Moors rebuilt the Roman walls and gateways and constructed two *alcázares* and several mosques. After the collapse of the Córdoba Caliphate, Carmona became capital of its own *taifa* (or small kingdom), until its capture by Ferdinand III during the Reconquest in 1247.

It was later a favourite residence of Pedro the Cruel, who built a country palace within the castle. In 1630 Felipe IV awarded it city status, on the payment of 40,000 ducats. Two centuries later, horsemen from Carmona played a prominent part in defeating Napoleon's elite Dragoons in the crucial Battle of Bailén.

Sights The **Alcázar de Arriba** (Upper Palace-Fortress) was extended by both the Almoravids and the Almohads before the building of Pedro's palace. A large part of the structure was destroyed in the earthquakes of 1504 and 1755, leaving only the entrance gate and three towers. In 1976 it was tastefully rebuilt as a parador in the style of a Moorish palace. Entry is through an impressive Moorish horseshoe arch. Just to the north of the parador is the **Puerta de Córdoba**, with two octagonal towers of largely Roman origin and marking a sudden end to the town, the old road to Córdoba now being little more than a rough track. The **Alcázar de Abajo** (Lower Palace-Fortress) includes the **Puerta de Sevilla**, a double archway with both Roman and Moorish elements. Although probably started by the Carthaginians, much of the early work on this Alcázar was constructed in Roman times and the temple and moat date from this time. The Moors added significantly to the building during the 12th and 13th century, when cisterns, barbicans and gates appeared. The building was renovated in 1975. Today there is an audio-visual room, after which visitors can make self-guided tours with the aid of brochures. There is a small museum in the

Roman Necropolis

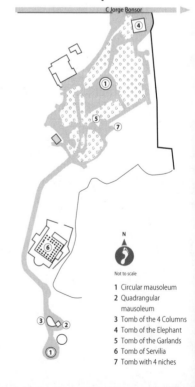

N

Not to scale

1 Circular mausoleum
2 Quadrangular mausoleum
3 Tomb of the 4 Columns
4 Tomb of the Elephant
5 Tomb of the Garlands
6 Tomb of Servilia
7 Tomb with 4 niches

Alcázar. ■ *Mon-Sat 1000-1800, Sun 0930-1500. €1.50, EU residents free.*
T954190955, www.andal.es/carmona Running north from here is a sizeable
stretch of the old walls of Carmona.

On the corner of Calle Santa María and Calle San José is the Gothic 15th-cen-   **Churches**
tury **Iglesia de Santa María de Mayor.** Built over the Moor's Great or Friday
Mosque, which itself is believed to have been built over a Roman Temple of
Hercules, it retains the Patio de los Naranjos, with some fine horseshoe
arches. The Mudéjar tower, with its pyramidal capping of tiles, may well contain some elements of the original minaret. The church has a rectangular floor
plan with three naves and some intricate stellar vaulting. Note also the superb
16th-century high altar and the Visigoth calendar marked on a pillar.
■ *Mon-Fri 1000-1400, 1700-1900. €1.20.* Other churches of note include the
Iglesia de San Pedro, with a 16th-century Giralda lookalike tower dominating the main square. ■ *Mon, Thu-Fri 1100-1400, 1600-1800. €1.20.* The
Iglesia de San Felipe, which retains some of its original 14th-century lancet
arches and has a fine coffered ceiling, can only be visited at service times.

Located to the west of the town outside the walls (as was the custom in   **Roman**
Roman times) is a Roman burial ground which is unique in Spain and com-   **necropolis**
parable only with some examples in Italy. Excavation of the site, which
began in 1881, has revealed over 1,000 tombs dating from the second to the
fourth centuries. Some 250 remain in their subterranean chambers and are
often decorated with such motifs as birds and flowers. The larger tombs are
massive. The most impressive is the Tumba de Servilia, named after the separate spaces for servants of the family. The Tumba del Elefante is named
after a stone-carved elephant and has a number of ante rooms which may
well have been kitchens among others, for use at funeral banquets. There is
also a small museum with statues, urns and mosaics. On the opposite side of
the road is a modest **amphitheatre** which is still being excavated and not yet
part of the guided tour. ■ *Tue-Fri 1000-1400 (opens 1 hr earlier Jun-Sep)*
and 1600-1800, Sat and Sun 1000-1400. Free with EU passport, otherwise
€1.50. T954140811. Getting there: Take C San Pedro from the Puerta de
Sevilla and proceed along C Enmedio for some 500 m. The necropolis is on the
lefthand side of the road.

Carmona also has a small zoo to the west of the town, just off Carretera El Viso   **Zoo**
del Alcor. It specializes in education and the return of threatened species to
the wild. ■ *Summer 1100-1900 daily, winter 1100-1700 Sat-Sun only. €3,*
children €2.40. T954191696.

AL *Alcázar de la Reina*, Plaza de Lasso 2, T954190064, F954142889. Garage, a/c, pool.   **Sleeping**
AL *Casa de Carmona*, Plaza de Lasso 1, T954143300, F954143752. Restored   *See inside front cover*
casa-palacio with antique furnishings, 30 luxurious rooms, garage, wheelchair access,   *for price codes*
a/c, pool. **AL** *Parador Nacional del Rey Don Pedro*, C Los Alcázares, T954141712,   *Most of Carmona's*
F954141010. Stunning views from most of the 30 rooms at this historic site. Garage,   *hotels are in the luxury*
wheelchair access, a/c, pool. If you can't afford to stay here, you can still experience a   *range, while the*
bit of its sumptuous interior with a drink in the bar – although prices are hardly in the   *pensiones are*
budget range here, either. **D** *Hostal Casa Carmelo*, C San Pedro 15, T954140572. 6   *expensive for what*
rooms. Located near the Puerta de Sevilla in newer part of town, formerly a casino.   *they offer. Budget*
D *Pensión Comercio*, C Torre del Oro 56, T954140018. 14 rooms, restaurant, clean,   *accommodation is*
noisy cockerel next door. **D** *Hostal San Pedro,* C San Pedro 3, T954141606.   *almost nonexistent*
Well-appointed, a/c rooms.

Sevilla Province

If you have your own transport there are a number of possibilities along the autovía

Outside Carmona **B** *Cortijo El Triguero*, Crta El Viso del Alcor, T955953626. Country house 5 km out of Carmona, surrounded by orange groves. Pool. Stables and bull ranch adjacent. **B** *Palmero*, Ctra N IV, Km 523.7, T954254945, F954524946. 27 rooms, a/c, pool. **D** *El Aguila*, Ctra Madrid-Cádiz, Km 520, T954140014. 17 rooms.

Eating

All the hotels listed above have good international restaurants though they tend to be on the pricey side. The parador serves, in addition, some local specialities such as marinaded partridge and spinach *a la Carmona*. **Expensive** Another upmarket possibility is *El Ancla*, C Bonifacio IV s/n, which serves excellent seafood. **Mid-range** *La Almazara,* C Santa Ana 33. Traditional local game dishes in an old olive mill setting. *Molino de la Romera*, Puerta de Marchena, T954190084. Halfway between San Pedro Church and the Alcázar. Local dishes served in this old olive oil mill. Superb views from its terrace. **Cheap** At the other end of the spectrum, some of the *pensión* restaurants could be tried, along with some of the tapas bars, particularly those around Plaza San Pedro. The local tourist office have produced a guide describing the town's best bars – ideal for those fancying a tapas crawl. For a change from Spanish food, try the cheap and cheerful *China Town,* Paseo del Estatuto 4. *El Potro,* C Sevilla 78. Bargain *hostal* restaurant. There are 2 *ventas* on roads out of town which also offer cheap regional food: *Venta El Recreo*, Ctra El Viso, Km 13, and *Venta El Tentaero*, Ctra Madrid-Cádiz, Km 506.

Fiestas & festivals

Late Feb-early Mar *Carnaval.* Dating back to the 18th century, *Carnaval* is celebrated with children's fancy dress parades, dances and competitions. **Easter** *Semana Santa* Celebrated along the lines of that in Sevilla with 8 *cofradías*, or brotherhoods, involved in the processions. **Mid-May** *Feria de Mayo*, 4-day fiesta. **Sep** *Romería de la Virgen de Gracia*. Pilgrimage held on the first Sun in the month to the shrine of the same name. Another pilgrimage, the *Romería de San Mateo*, is held at the Ermita San Mateo to mark the reconquest of Carmona by Ferdinand III in Sep 1247.

Tour operators

Triana Viajes, Paseo de Estatuto 6, T954190745.

Transport

Road Car: If you arrive by car be warned that parking is impossible – if you are staying overnight, book into accommodation with parking facilities. **Bus:** *Casal* bus company runs an hourly service from Sevilla, stopping outside the rather dingy *Bar La Parada* on Carmona's main street. Timetables are available at the bar and nearby ice-cream kiosk.

Directory

Banks On C San Pedro in the newer part of town. **Communications** Post office: Correos, C Prim 29, open 0900-1400. **Telephones**: no *locutorios*, but cabins may be found on Plaza San Fernando in the old town and C San Fernando in the new town. **Medical services** Emergencies: *Paseo de la Feria*, T954140997, T954140761. **Hospitals**: *Cruz Roja*, Ctra de Madrid, T954140751.

Écija

Colour map 2, grid C2
Population: 37,113

Located some 52 km west of Córdoba and 54 km east of Carmona, Écija is a tempting halfway stop. Sandwiched between the Río Genil and a range of hills, it is known as the 'City of Sun and Towers'. Records show that it is the hottest spot in the region, earning the description *La Sentenilla de Andalucía* – the frying pan of Andalucía. Sightseeing on a summer afternoon is definitely not recommended. There are some 11 towers, 15 bell towers, plus churches, palaces and belvederes which thrust up above the general level of white houses.

There has been a settlement here since Iberian times and it was later an important Roman town known as Astigi, which was basically an agricultural centre dealing with olive oil. In Moorish times it was part of the Caliphate of

Córdoba, until overrun by Ferdinand III in 1240. Its main period of prosperity came in the 17th and 18th centuries, based on the *latifundia* or agricultural estates. The wealth produced did not filter down to the landless labourers, but poured into the hands of the landed nobility, who built magnificent mansions and *palacios* in Écija. The Lisbon earthquake in 1755 destroyed most of the churches in the town, which were then assiduously rebuilt, which explains the large number of Baroque towers in Écija.

All the major churches and palaces can be reached within minutes from the central, shady **Plaza de España**. The Ayuntamiento is also located here with the tourist office inside, as well as a fine Roman mosaic. Worth a look is the **Iglesia de San Juan Bautista**, which has an ornate belfry in white stone – one of the few towers not capped with coloured tiles. Amongst the palaces, the most impressive is the huge **Palacio de Peñaflor**, with a pink marble portal and a curving balcony running the full length of the façade.

There is a limited but varied choice of accommodation. More comfortable options include: **D** *Platería*, C Garcilópez 1A, T/F954835010. Best hotel in town tucked away in a small quiet side road, with 18 rooms, a/c, wheelchair access, restaurant. At the cheaper end of the range, there are a couple of *pensiones* close to the *autovía*. **E** *Santa Cruz*, C Practicante Romero Gordillo 8, T954830222. The only budget option in the town centre which can be recommended is this attractive, but spartan *pensión* with 18 rooms, near the Plaza de España. **Outside Écija** **C** *Astigi*, Ctra Madrid-Cádiz, Km 450, T954830162, F954835701. 18 rooms, a/c, restaurant, disco.

Sleeping & eating

This small town is surrounded by olive groves and ranches rearing fighting bulls. Archaeological finds suggest that there was a settlement here in Chalcolithic times, while there are also Roman remains and a ruined Moorish fort. The parish **Iglesia de Santiago El Mayor** was built in the late 13th century and its impressive west doorway, the Puerta del Perdón, has some imposing 'barley sugar' columns. Another church of significance is the 15th-century **Iglesia de Santa María de la Mesa**, in largely Gothic style, with a Plateresque entrance which served as a model for many of the first churches built in the New World. This rather staid town comes alive during June when the *Potaje Gitano* flamenco festival is held in the open space near the Moorish castle.

Utrera
Colour map 4, grid A3
Population: 46,017

South of Utera at **El Palmar de Troya** is the Mount of Christ the King, the headquarters of Clemente, the bizarre, self-styled alternative Pope, Gregorio XVII. For those who are intrigued, there are tours of the building, which is reputed to have over 50 altars.

East of Utrera and some 15 km south of the A92 is this ancient town which has had continuous settlement from Palaeolithic times to the present. Its Roman name was Arunci, but it has been known as Morón since the third century. The ruined Moorish castle is, in fact, largely medieval. Although destroyed by French troops in 1812, the surviving sections include a rampart walk linking 12 towers and two of the original five gates, plus a Moorish cistern. Near the castle is the Paseo del Gallo, from where there are superb views over the town. Before leaving, take a look at the Church of San Miguel, dating from 1503 in Gothic and Renaissance style, with a Giralda-type tower.

Morón de la Frontera
Colour map 4, grid A4
Population: 28,232

North of Morón and some 7 km north of the A92 is another ancient town, Marchena. Although going back to prehistoric times, it was the Moors who built its great walls and four gates, including the Puerta de Sevilla, the Arch of

Marchena
Population: 18,018

Sevilla Province

the Rose. After the Reconquest, the town was distinguished by the family of the dukes of Arcos (which included the *conquistador* Ponce de León) who made Marchena a centre for artistic patronage. Don't miss the Iglesia de San Juan Bautista, which dates from 1490. The remarkable *retablo* contains 14 panels by Alejo Fernández and an alabaster head of St John the Baptist dating from 1593. The church's museum has no fewer than nine paintings by Zurburán, plus the usual books, gold and silver.

Osuna

Colour map 4, grid A5
Population: 17,306

The charming town of Osuna is located a further 35 km along the A92. As with the neighbouring towns, it has an Iberian past, when it was known as Urso. An artefact, the 'Bull of Urso', dates from this time. It was also important in Roman times, when Caesar gave it the status of a colony. Although occupied by the Moors, it was of little importance, falling to the Christians in 1239. Three hundred years later it came into the hands of the Dukes of Osuna, particularly the Téllez Girón family, who founded many of the buildings still to be seen in the town today, including churches, mansions, the university and the Ducal Palace.

The hilltop above the town is dominated by two buildings, the old university and the collegiate church. The **university**, which was founded in 1548 by Juan Téllez Girón, is a rather austere, rectangular building in Italian Renaissance style with towers at its four corners and a central atrium. Its chapel displays a good collection of paintings and the main hall has a Mudéjar coffered ceiling. The **Collegiate Church of Santa María de la Asunción** was founded by the same man, who used some of the finest craftsmen in Sevilla for its construction. The cream stone building has five naves with round Renaissance arches. The main Plateresque door of the church, the Puerta del Sol, was damaged by French troops during the Peninsular War, but remains impressive. The church also has some fine sculptures and paintings, including a Crucifixion by Ribera. Next to the church is the gloomy Plateresque-style pantheon which contains the tombs of the various dukes of Osuna and their families. ■ *Guided tours only, Tue-Sun 1000-1330 and 1530-1830.*

Down in the town are a clutch of other churches and convents worth a visit, including the **Iglesia de la Merced**, with a barrel vaulted ceiling, the **Iglesia de Santo Domingo** and the **Convento de Santa Catalina**. There is also a small **Museo Arqueológico**, based in the Torre del Agua, part of the original Almohad fortress, and containing largely local finds. ■ *Tue-Sun 1130-1330 and 1600-1800. Free with EU passport, otherwise €0.60.*

Sleeping & eating

There is a shortage of decent accommodation in Osuna, particularly in the old part of the town, although there are some possibilities close to the A92. **C** *Villa Ducal*, Ctra 334 Sevilla-Málaga, Km 88, T955820256. The best hotel in the area with 23 rooms, a/c, restaurant. Within the old town there is **D** *Caballo Blanco*, C Granada 1, T954810184. 14 en-suite rooms, a/c, wheelchair access, recently renovated, good restaurant. **E** *Las Cinco Puertas*, C Carrear 79, T954811243. The best of the cheaper places, with 15 rooms and a restaurant.

Estepa

Colour map 4, grid A5
Population: 11,654

This is a historic town in the east part of Sevilla province. Once a Carthaginian settlement known as Astapa, it was involved in the Punic Wars with the Romans, who captured the city in 208 BC. It was later occupied by the Moors, but there is little which remains from this early history, the town being essentially Baroque in character, with a number of churches and convents in this style, including the Iglesia del Carmen, the Iglesia de Santa María and the Iglesia de San Sebastián. Also of interest is the slim 18th-century Torre de la Victoría, with some elegant and ornate stonework. Sadly this is all that remains of a once resplendent convent of the same name.

Sierra Morena

*The road leading north from Sevilla quickly leaves the Guadalquivir valley behind and climbs gently into the foothills of the **Sierra Morena**, where in the Sevilla province they are at their lowest, being little more than rounded hills. There are in fact three distinct ranges of hills, the Sierra Padrona, the Sierra del Viento and the Sierra Bajosa, none of which rises much above 750 m. This area is rarely on the tourist trail, but is popular with Sevillanos at the weekends.*

Ins & outs For more information on the Sierra, including details of accommodation and transport, see www.sierranortesevilla.com   There are *Linesur* buses between Constantina (four a day) and Cazalla (three a day) and the Plaza de Armas bus station in Sevilla, T954988221, www.linesur.com   Frequent trains run between Sevilla and the stations at Constantina-Cazalla and El Pedroso; for timetables T902240202 or see www.renfe.es

Parque Natural Sierra Norte

Much of the hilly area of the northern part of Sevilla province lies within the boundary of the Parque Natural Sierra Norte, which covers some 165,000 ha of the Sierra Morena. Its rounded hills are well wooded with stone pines, holm oaks and cork oaks, while the river valleys have sweet chestnuts and poplars. Although not ornithologically outstanding, a good range of raptors can be expected in the summer, including black and Griffon vultures, golden and booted eagles and red kite. Both black and white storks breed. Among those widely hunted are wild boar, fallow deer, rabbits, while other mammals include otters and wild cats. The park has some excellent walks, three of which are described below. There is a visitors' centre for the park at **Constantina** (see below), which has details of walking trails, trout fishing, hire of bikes and horses, and non-motorized watersports on the **El Pintado reservoir**.

Constantina
Population: 7,246
Altitude: 556 m

There are in fact two or three small towns well worth a visit, particularly if you have your own transport. The small town of Constantina goes back to Roman times and is said to have been named after the Emperor Constantine. There is a fascinating old quarter, the Barrio de la Moreria, with a number of distinguished mansions. The parish church of Santa María de la Encarnación has a Mudéjar tower and a Plateresque doorway, while high above the town is a Medieval castle, the Castillo de la Armada. The Centro de Visitantes for the Parque Natural Sierra Norte is 1 km along the El Pedroso road south of the village, T955881597. There are several accommodation possibilities, including the *Albergue Juvenil*, Calle Cuesta Blanca s/n, T955881589. In Pedroso further west is **C** *Casa Montehueznar*, T954889000, is a restored town house in the centre of the village. It can be noisy at the weekends when local youth cruise the streets on their mopeds.

Sleeping and eating A *Villas Turística de Cazalla*, Ctra de Constantina, Km 3, T954883308, F954883312. 39 self-catering apartments built in a complex in traditional style, hotel services including restaurant, indoor and outdoor pool, tennis, bikes and horses for hire. **B** *Monasterio Cartuja*, Ctra de Constantina, T954884516. Restored Carthusian monastery where pilgrims to Santiago de Compostela once stayed, with a family atmosphere; 8 rooms. The monastery's hostel is now the restaurant; monthly concerts. **B** *Posada El Moro*, Paseo El Moro s/n, T954884326. 15 rooms, pool. **E** *La Milagrosa*, C Llana 29, T954884260. 10 rooms.

Guadalcanal
Population: 3,067
Altitude: 662 m

Guadalcanal, a further 35 km north from Constantina, is another historic town situated in the irrigated valley of the Río Sotillo. There is a ruined castle and a fair stretch of the medieval walls which still remain. The nearby Hermitage of Guaditoca is the venue of a popular local *romería*. A number of churches in the town have Mudéjar elements. **B-C** *Hostal los Diezmos*, T954886190, is a grand old village house which is by far the best place to stay in the village. There are also self-catering apartments here.

Cazalla de la Sierra
Population: 5,242
Altitude: 590 m

The main centre of the area is the small town of Cazalla de la Sierra. Occupied in turn by Iberians, Romans and the Moors (who called it Kazalla, meaning fortified town), it has a number of historic buildings, including the massive parish church of **Nuestra Señora de la Consolación**. Today, Cazalla makes its living as a minor centre for agriculture and tourism and as one of the principal locations for the production of aguardiente, a type of brandy made in the area since Roman times. A number of surprisingly ornate churches and mansions bear witness to the wealth that was once accrued from this industry. As this book goes to press one of these grand old mansion houses was in the throes of being converted into a luxury hotel; call the tourist office for further information. With a few accommodation possibilities, Cazalla makes a good centre for exploring the Sierra Norte Natural Park. There are some good walking trails in the vicinity (see below) and the local tourist office at Paseo del Moro 2, T954883562, has a small booklet describing these.

In the Middle Ages rich Sevillians – including King Pedro 'el Cruel' – came to hunt in the thick forests which surrounded the town. The forests were later partially cleared in order to create the *dehesas* which are so characteristic of the area. The *dehesa* system, by thinning out the trees and clearing away the thick undergrowth, provided both grazing ground, shade and fodder for animals in the form of acorns. The *dehesas* have a unique beauty and nowadays are home to the much-prized black-trottered pigs as well as fighting bulls or *ganado bravo*. But don't worry – the walks described below avoid areas of *ganado bravo*.

Sleeping and eating B-C *Posada del Moro*, T954884858. On the south side of town this rather kitzchly decorated place has very comfortable rooms with all mod cons. The staff are friendly and the food is excellent. **B** *Las Navezuelas*, T954884764. A beautiful farm B&B just to the south of Cazalla run by a friendly Italian and his Spanish wife. By far the nicest place to stay in the area. **C** *Riscos Altos*, T669861636. A beautiful old farm just outside of Cazalla run by a friendly young Spaniard, Enrique. Lots of organic, home-grown fruit and veg. Rooms are 200 m from the main house in a modern annex. Good value.

Walking in the Sierra Norte

The park is easily accessible from Sevilla yet it receives relatively few visitors. This is bound to change: a number of new 'agroturismos' have recently been opened, routes through the park are being waymarked and northern European walking agencies are just beginning to set up tours in the area. Cazalla de la Sierra, almost plum at the centre of the park, makes an ideal base from which to plan your walks. The walking in the Sierra Norte, because of the number of large estates or *latifundia*, is often by way of the dirt tracks which divide them (eg the Guadalcanal circuit described below). There are also wonderful stretches of ancient footpaths like the one leading down to the Huesnar from Cazalla. And the paths which follow the park's tree-lined river valleys; in particular, those of the Huesnar and the Viar rivers are particularly memorable. For places to stay, see Sleeping sections above in Cazalla, Guadalcanal and El Pedroso.

There is still no single **map** available of the park. If you're planning to do the walks listed here you'll need the 1:50000 Military Map, Constantina:13-37. You won't find the maps in Cazalla or other villages in the park; the nearest place to get hold of them is in Sevilla, where the best map shop by far is *LTC*, Avenida Menéndez Pelayo 42-44, T954425964. It also stocks the more detailed 1:25000 maps of the area as well as a wonderful selection of guide-books on Andalucía.

Sevilla Province

This beautiful circular walk leads out from Guadalcanal, a pretty village northwest of Cazalla. The first section of the walk is nearly all uphill to the summit of La Capitana, the highest point in the Sierra Norte (959 m). The views from here on a clear day are exceptional: south to the foothills of the Sierra Morena and northwards to Extremadura. After leaving the summit of La Capitana the walk continues westwards before dropping down once again to the valley between the Sierra del Viento and the Sierra de San Miguel which you follow back to Guadalcanal. Map 1:50000 Military Map: Constantina:13-37.

Guadalcanal Circuit: La Capitana & the Sierra del Viento
Time: 5 hours with rests/picnic
Distance: 16½ km
Difficulty: medium

The start To being from Cazalla de la Sierra follow signs for Alanis. When you reach Alanis turn left to Guadalcanal. At the entrance to Guadalcanal ignore a right turn to Llerena and carry straight on into the town centre. You pass a cross, then the Colegio público. Continue straight on and then take the second turning on the right after the Michelin garage. You arrive in the town square where you can normally find somewhere to park.

The walk begins in the main square of Guadalcanal. With your back to the town hall climb northwards, up through the village to the chapel of El Espíritu Sanctu. Just past the chapel (15 minutes) turn left at a sign 'Mirador de la Sierra del Viento: 5 km' and climb up a dirt track that runs between olive groves. When you reach a fork keep left on the main track. You pass through a gate (55 minutes) and the track again divides: keep right here, following marker posts, up towards a television mast. You pass by a ruined farm (beneath you, to the left) with an unusual stone igloo-style shelter. Soon the track swings hard to the right (one hour 15 minutes) towards a gate. Don't go through this gate: continue straight until you reach a sign 'Vía Pecuaría: Cordel de los Molinos de la Sierra del Viento'. Here you go through a gate. On the other side a sign marks the way up to La Capitana at 959 m. Remember you will later need to return to this sign. Marker posts lead you up through the broom and wild olive trees to the summit (one hour 20 minutes). The views are wonderful and a ceramic tiled map helps you to identify the surrounding villages.

From here retrace your steps back down to the sign by the gate (one hour 30 minutes). Here turn left (unless you want to return to Guadalcanal by the same route by which you arrived earlier). Soon the track bears right, descends, then swings left again towards Fuente del Arco. The track descends, swings left then right and continues on the same course. You reach a point where to the left of the track there is a large pile of stones and an empty steel drum just to right (one hour 45 minutes). Here, turn left. The track drops steeply down through olive groves towards a farmhouse. Follow the track past a thick stand of trees and just before the farm bear sharply right along a good track (a black nylon pipe runs along beside it). You pass a ruined building then go through a gate (two hours). Here turn left: you will soon reach another farm. Careful! Just past the main house turn right through the farm gates and pass between the farm and its swimming pool. Soon the track bears left and winds on through the olive groves. Eventually the track meets with a much broader one (two hours 35 minutes) which you follow back towards Guadalcanal. Careful! Just past a red gate with round concrete posts on the left of the track (three hours) branch left on a narrower track. After 200 m you pass by a small house to your right. At the next major fork head straight on into the village and retrace your footsteps back to the main square (three hours).

El Pedroso Circuit

Time: 3½ hours
Distance: 11½ km
Difficulty: easy

This circular walk from El Pedroso is an easy excursion which could easily be undertaken en route to Cazalla where much better accommodation is available. The first part of the walk takes you through an unusual area of granite outcrops: look carefully and you'll spot areas where the rock was once quarried. The middle section of the walk follows a narrow path that hugs the left bank of the Arroyo La Peña through an area of beautiful dehesa or woodland. The final leg back to El Pedroso is via a broad farm track. Leave time for a drink in the village at the end of your walk, perhaps in one of the bars close to the church of Nuestra Señora de la Consolación. Map: 1:50000 Military Map: Constantina:13-37.

The start The walk begins at *Bar La Triana* on the west side of El Pedroso. Cross the road to a sign 'Sierra del Norte: Arroyo Las Cañas'. From here follow a short section of tarmac that leads away from the village past an olive oil factory. The tarmac soon gives way to a broad, stony track. To either side of the track are enormous granite boulders, weathered into fantastic shapes: spot the Henry Moore! Soon you pass through an area where granite has been quarried. Just past an abandoned rubbish tip the track ends at a fork (20 minutes). Here branch left on a prettier, sandier track. You pass a dilapidated farm, the track narrows and you go through a gate bearing the sign 'Coto privado de caza' (private hunting area). Here bear right and continue on through a stand of evergreen oaks. The track meets with a broader one (35 minutes). Go right: you'll see a sign explaining that this is a 'Vía Pecuaría' or drover's route. Descend on this broad, sandy track. You pass a number of huge eucalyptus. At the next fork bear left. You cross a cattle grid then pass by a plantation of pines. A large house comes into view, up to your right. At the far side of a huge plantation of baby olives, just past an enormous cork oak (50 minutes), turn right and head north along the edge of the field. The track bears left, close to the bank of the stream Arroyo Las Cañas. Where it divides (one hour) turn left, go through a gate marked 'J del C' and cross the stream. The track adopts a northerly course, through an area of cork and evergreen oaks. The track leads on through a gate (one hour 10 minutes). Ignore a marker post on the right after just 20 m. Go straight on to a point where another track crosses yours. Turn right here and after another 150 m – careful! – bear right beneath the oaks on a track which descends towards the stream. Don't cross it. Instead, swing left, and pick up an indistinct path, marked by white posts. This is a pretty, if overgrown, section of the walk: a good place to picnic. The path meanders along the left bank of the stream which now has a stone wall just above its left bank. You cross a (dry) stream, a tributary of Las Cañas, then bear left and you reach another marker post which leads through a fence via a wire-and-post gate (one hour 25 minutes). Beyond the fence, go straight ahead, cross a (dry) stream and continue along its right bank. A wall runs to your right and soon you pass by a gate to Cortijo Narcisso. Soon the wall drops into the river bed. You continue parallel to stream's left bank: a fence now runs on the same side of the stream as your path. This fence cuts left, climbs slightly, then again swings right. When you meet with a broad track (one hour 50 minutes) bear right and after 50 m go through a green gate. Continue for 50 m then turn right, cross a bridge over a tributary of the Arroyo Las Cañas then after 100 m go through another gate and again swing right. A sign tells that this is the 'Cordel de Cazalla a Cantillana', the old livestock route. Follow this broad track eastwards back towards El Pedroso until (two hours 20 minutes) you reach a 'Stop' sign on the A433. Turn right and follow the road back to Bar La Triana (two hours 30 minutes). Better still, turn left at the sign 'Bienvenido al Pedroso' and wind your way back through the attractive village centre.

This long, varied itinerary is one of the Sierra's most beautiful walks. From Cazalla you drop steeply down to the river along a lovely old path. Reaching the Huesna river, you cross back and forth between its left and right banks, later following the course of the old railway line that runs more or less parallel to the river. The walk is beautiful at any time of year but is particularly memorable in autumn. Map   1:50000 Military Map: Constantina:13-37. You twice ford the river so be prepared to remove boots and socks.

Cazalla to San Nicolás del Puerto along the Huesna Valley
Time: 6 hours with rests/picnic
Distance: 17 km
Difficulty: Medium

The start The walk begins at *Restaurante Julía y Lucía* on the south side of Cazalla. From here head up the hill past an aguardiente factory: there were once a dozen in the village but now just two remain. Continue up the hill then turn right at a sign for 'Alanis/Guadalcanal' into Calle del Peso. You reach a small square. Pass to the left of the church and 50m past Bar Taburete go left at a ceramic picture of the Virgin into Calle de Mañuel Cabrera which becomes La Cuesta del Pozuelo. At the top of this street turn right to reach Plaza del Pozuelo. The concrete road ends (10 minutes) and you pick up a track heading eastwards: the Camino de la Estación, or the station path. It leads past several houses and farms then descends. Ignore tracks branching left and right to the farmhouses. Just before you reach a gate (35 minutes) - careful!- bear right following a sign for 'camino de la estación'. The track becomes a path. Soon you go through a gate then drop down through stands of oaks and at a ruined farm (55 minutes) the path bears left. It soon swings right, leads through a green gate then passes beneath the righthand arch of a railway bridge. Just beyond you cross a bridge, pass by a barrier and continue past the 'Descansadero de Castillejos'. After passing El Molino del Corcho, the track meets with a tarmac road. Here turn right, descend and cross the Huesna (one hour 20 minutes) following signs for Constantina. After 200 m, just past Villa Monte, turn left at a sign for 'Area Recreativa', which you soon pass by to your left. The track runs between a pines and a large expanse of grazing land. Eventually you reach a fork (one hour 50 minutes) by a sign 'Cañada Real de la Ribera de Huesna'. Turn left, pass the Descansadero del Río de Huesna then continue past the gate to the El Acebuche farm. The track bears left and runs past an enormous walled enclosure. After passing a white cottage and a second gate to El Acebuche the enclosure ends and the track crosses the Huesna (two hours 10 minutes). You may need to take your boots off here. On the far side, just before a tunnel, bear right and pick up the abandoned railway line which soon crosses the Cazalla-San Nicolás road (two hours 25 minutes). It passes through a deep cutting then, just past a ruined farm (2 hours 40 minutes), meets with the road. Bear left, follow the road for 600-700 m to a sign 'Ribera del Huesna'. Here turn right, descend, and cross the Huesna again. Again, you may need to remove your boots.

The track runs along the river's right bank passing Camping-Cortijo Batán de las Monjas (three hours five minutes) before climbing away from the river. Where the railway line (three hours 20 minutes) crosses your track by a ruined hut turn left and pass through a deep cutting. When you reach the track again, bear left: don't head along the railway line which leads into a long, dark tunnel. Soon the track bears right and again the old railway line cuts bisects your track. Go left following a sign for 'Vías Verdes' and after crossing the second of two cattle grids (three hours 50 minutes) turn left, cross the Huesna and head up into San Nicolás. Here head for Plaza de España, the square next to the Church, where *Bar Plaza Alta* is a good place for a beer and a tapas.

Other walks The Penthalon guide *Andar por la Sierra Norte de Sevilla* by Jorge Blanco Cano lists (in Spanish) several routes in the park but most require a lengthy drive to their starting points. There are good walks close to Almaden de la Plata at the western end of the park; the route along Arroyo de los Molinos is particularly attractive and easy to follow. Another good walk begins on the southern side of the El Pintado reservoir and leads south along the valley of the Viar river which quickly narrows to become a spectacular gorge. Also highly recommended is the walk leading south along the Huesnar valley to the hamlet of Fábrica de El Pedroso. You could also follow the valley south then cut eastwards via Cortijo Campoallá to Constantina; it is a long, lovely and varied excursion and especially so if you enter Constantina from the northwest.

South from Sevilla

There is a choice of parallel roads heading south from Sevilla towards Cádiz – the A4 *autovía*, which is a toll road and therefore used less than the dual carriageway NIV. As the rolling agricultural landscape is generally as dull as the towns of **Dos Hermanas**, **Los Palacios y Villafranca** and **Las Cabezas de San Juan** (which are thankfully bypassed), there is little reason to stop.

Birdwatchers, however, could be tempted by the **Brazo del Este Natural Park**, located between the town of Los Palacios y Villafranca and the Río Guadalquivir. This small site of little over 1,000 ha is located along a former course of the Guadalquivir, which is now a winding reed-fringed lagoon, surrounded by rice fields and drainage ditches. Although little visited, this is a superb spot for water birds and probably the best reserve in Andalucía for observing purple gallinules. There is a wide range of breeding herons and bitterns, along with rarities such as little and spotted crakes and collared pratincole. The reed beds hold Savi's warblers and great reed warblers. Access is from Exit 3 on the Sevilla-Cádiz A4.

Huelva Province

4

Huelva is the most westerly and one of the least visited of the provinces of Andalucía. The tidal Atlantic coastline, known as the Costa de la Luz, consists largely of lagoons and dunes, often pine covered, with a string of minor holiday resorts such as Ayamonte, Punta Umbría, Mazagón and Matascalañas. On this shoreline is **Huelva**, the provincial capital, industrial city and port. East of the capital are a number of locations associated with the voyages of Columbus to the New World, including the monastery of La Rábida and the villages of Palos and Moguer. Further east is the nature reserve of **Coto Doñana**, one of the top three wetlands in Europe. Bird watchers also flock to the **Odiel Marshes** to the west of Huelva.

The province of Huelva has some 425,000 inhabitants, of which a quarter live in the capital. To the west, the Río Guadiana forms the boundary with Portugal, while to the east the Río Guadalquivir is the border with the Cádiz and Sevilla provinces. Across the centre of the province runs an undulating area of farmland, specializing in cereals, fruit and sunflowers. The land rises gently to the north in the rolling hills of the **Sierra Morena**, subdivided into a number of ranges of which the Sierra de Aracena is the most attractive. The main centre here is the town of **Aracena**, with its remarkable caves, the **Gruta de las Maravillas,** while neighbouring **Jabugo** is an important centre for the production of Serrano ham. In the southeast of the Sierra Morena are the **Río Tinto Mines**, worked for centuries and worth a visit if only to appreciate the scale of the desecration of the landscape.

Huelva

Colour map 1, grid 1
Population: 139,991

There is a saying in Spain which, roughly translated, means that once you have been to Huelva there is no need ever to return. An understandable sentiment, particularly if the city is approached from the southeast through the stench of interminable oil refineries and chemical works alongside the lifeless **Río Tinto**, *polluted by centuries of mining in the area to the north. But penetrate this desolation, however, and you will find a surprisingly pleasant city, but don't expect any outstanding monuments. If there were any, they have been flattened by numerous earthquakes over the ages. The real charm of Huelva lies in its surrounding area, with nature reserves such as the incomparable* **Coto Doñana** *and the* **Marismas del Río Odiel**, *as well as a shoreline of high dunes topped with pines, and a clutch of sites associated with the voyages of Christopher Columbus.*

Ins & outs
See page 120
for further details

Getting there **Damas buses** arrive at Av de Portugal. There are also small bus stations in Av de Italia, Av Alemania and Av Federico Molina. As usual with most provincial capitals, **parking** can be difficult. Try the multistorey car park at the rear of *El Corte Inglés* department store. **Trains** arrive at the station on Av de Italia on the southwest side of the town. **Getting around** There are **taxi** ranks in Av Federico Molina, Av Portugal next to the bus station and by the Plaza 12 de Octubre. **Tourist offices** The **provincial tourist office** is located at Av de Alemania 14, T/F959257403. Open Mon-Fri 0900-1900, Sat 1000-1400. There is also a **municipal tourist office** at Plaza de las Monjas, open 1000-1400 and 1700-2000 Mon-Fri; 1000-1400 Sat.

History

Huelva is a port of some antiquity, having been founded by Phoenician traders over 3,000 years ago, when it was known as Onuba (its citizens are still known as *onubenses*). The Romans used it as a port for minerals, which they extracted from the Río Tinto mines to the north, as did the Moors who knew it as Guelbah. Alfonso X El Sabio (The Wise) recaptured it from the Moors in 1257. Huelva's status as a port was enhanced when Columbus, using crews from the local area, set out from here for his voyages to the New World. It also prospered when it was used as a trading base by the *conquistadores*, although it later lost ground to Cádiz and Sevilla. Unfortunately, little of this rich historical heritage is evident today, largely due to the 1755 earthquake (the same one which destroyed Lisbon). There has recently been a resurgence of prosperity stimulated by the petrochemical industry (set up by Franco in the 1950s), the continuing exports of Río Tinto minerals and spin-offs from tourism.

Sights

The attractive Plaza de las Monjas, the main square, is replete with palm trees. Some of the streets leading off the square are pedestrianized and decorated with the occasional modern sculpture.

★

Things to do

- Take some binoculars to El Rocío bridge and go birdspotting in one of Europe's best wetland sites, the Coto Doñana National Park
- Walk through the woodland of sweet chestnuts from Castaño del Robledo to Galaroza in the Sierra de Aracena
- Go 'tapeando' in Jabugo and sample some of Spain's finest *jamón serrano*
- Follow in the footsteps of Christopher Colombus around the city
- Don your best flamenco dress or suit and join the Romería del Rocío
- Paddle in the sea in Punta Umbría before enjoying some of the local *mariscos* and other fine fishy fare

Museo Provincial

Some would say that the museum is the only thing worth looking at in Huelva and it is certainly not to be missed

Housed in a pleasant modern building on Alameda Sundheim, the museum's ground floor consists of sections on archaeology and mining while the upper floor has a fine arts collection. The huge Roman water wheel in the entrance hall was found at the Río Tinto mines, one of a series used by slaves to raise water from flooded parts of the underground works. From here coloured lines on the floor take you on different tours. The archaeological section is excellent, with artefacts from the Bronze Age through to Moorish times. The displays devoted to mining are also outstanding, particularly the items of Roman origin. The fine arts collection on the upper floor is not distinguished. If you've had a surfeit of heavy religious art at other provincial Andalucían galleries, you will probably be relieved that there is not a Murillo in sight, but the alternatives are hardly worth displaying. An exception is the work of the local 20th-century artist Daniel Vásquez Díaz, responsible for the murals at La Rábida monastery, who has a number of competent paintings, including one stunning nude and portraits of the poets Ruben Dario and Juan Ramon Jimenez. ■ *Tue-Sat 0900-2000, Sun 0900-1500. Free. Alameda Sundheim 13, T959259300.*

Barrio Reina Victoria

An architectural curiosity in Huelva is the Barrio Reina Victoria, along the Avenida de Guatemala, which is an estate built by the Río Tinto company to house its British workers around the turn of the century. Much on the lines of those built by the industrial philanthropists in England, it is now decaying badly, despite its designation as being of 'historico-artistic interest'. The wrought iron Río Tinto pier at the mouth of the estuary dates from the same period.

Churches & convents

There are one or two churches and convents of interest in Huelva. The **Catedral de la Merced** dates from 1605 and was once a convent. It was designated a cathedral in 1953, largely, it would seem, on the grounds that it was the largest church to survive the 1755 earthquake. Located just north of the Plaza de la Merced, it has a refreshingly white marble interior, but frankly is hardly worth a visit. Two other churches are of more interest. The **Iglesia de la Concepción** in Calle Concepción is believed to be the first church in Spain to be consecrated in the name of the Immaculate Conception. First constructed in the 14th century, it was rebuilt after the 1755 earthquake, retaining the richly decorated choir stalls. It also has paintings by Francisco de Zurburán. The **Iglesia de San Pedro** in the plaza of the same name was built in the 15th century over a mosque. The oldest church in the city, it has numerous Baroque modifications including the tower. Of most interest, however, is the **Santuario de Nuestra Señora de la Cinta**. Standing at the end of the tree-lined Paseo del Conquero just off the road to Portugal, the sanctuary is a

Huelva Province

simple white walled affair where Columbus is said to have prayed before setting out on his first voyage. The event is portrayed in traditional *azulejo* tiles by Daniel Zuloaga. There is also an impressive altar grille. ■ *Take bus no 6 from the Plaza de las Monjas.* The **Columbus Monument** is located on the point between the rivers Tinto and Odiel; see page 122.

Essentials

Sleeping
See inside front cover for price codes

There are half a dozen hotels and 9 *pensiones* in Huelva and booking is not normally a problem. For a more attractive location, try Punta Umbría to the south and Mazagón to the southeast. The nearest paradores are at Ayamonte, close to the Portuguese border, and Mazagón. Most of the *pensiones* are located in the area to the southeast of the Plaza de Monjas.

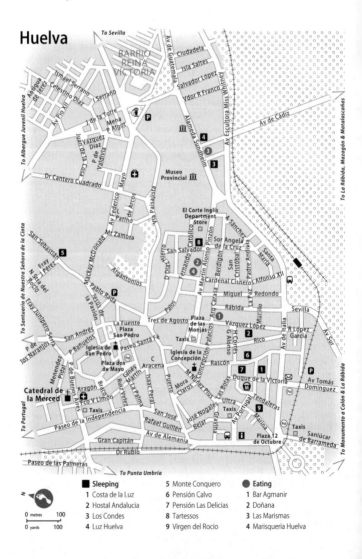

Huelva

■ Sleeping	5 Monte Conquero	● Eating
1 Costa de la Luz	6 Pensión Calvo	1 Bar Agmanir
2 Hostal Andalucia	7 Pensión Las Delicias	2 Doñana
3 Los Condes	8 Tartessos	3 Las Marismas
4 Luz Huelva	9 Virgen del Rocio	4 Marisqueria Huelva

AL *Luz Huelva*, Alameda Sundheim 26, T959250011, F959258110. The most upmarket option in Huelva with 106 rooms (views over the river and Columbus statue – but also the petro-chemical works). Garage, wheelchair access, a/c, tennis, golf. Also recommended are: **A** *Tartessos*, Av Martín Alonzo Pinzón 13, T959282711, F959250617. 112 rooms. Garage, a/c, centrally placed. **A** *Monte Conquero*, C Pablo Rada 10, T959285500, F959283912. 168 rooms. Garage, a/c, wheelchair access, to the west of the town. **C** *Los Condes*, Av Sundheim 14, T959282400. 93 rooms. Garage, wheelchair access, centrally placed. **D** *Costa de la Luz*, C José María Amo 8, T959256422. Central location. Rooms with balcony and TV. **D** *Santa Ursula*, Ctra Huelva-Ayamonte (Peguerillas), T959285211, F959256212. 134 rooms. Garage, wheelchair access, a/c, pool tennis, golf, northern outskirts of Huelva. **D** *San Miguel*, C Santa María 6, T959245203. 25 rooms. **D** *Virgen del Rocío*, C Tendaleras 14, T959281716. Centrally placed, all rooms en-suite, some with a/c. **E** *Hostal Andalucía*, C Vázquez López 22, T959245667. 17 rooms. Located in the main shopping area, some rooms with a/c. **E** *Pensión Las Delicias*, C Rascón 42, T959248392. Pleasant patio. **E** *Calvo*, C Rascón 33, T959249016. Currently the cheapest place in town.

Youth hostels *Albergue Juvenil Huelva*, C Marchena Colombo 14, T959253793. Located in the northern suburbs with 130 beds, meals available, wheelchair access. *Mazagón*, Cuesta de Barca s/n, T959536262. Situated 25 km southeast from Huelva on the coast, with 100 beds, meals available, free use of kitchen, wheelchair access. **Camping** There are 11 campsites within 30 km of Huelva mainly at coastal locations. The only first category site is *Camping Doñana Playa*, Ctra Huelva-Matascalañas, Km 29, T959376281. Beach, pool, restaurant.

Eating
See inside front cover for price codes

For eating, head for the Plaza de las Monjas and the streets around. As Huelva is a fishing port it is no surprise that some good seafood is available. **Mid-range** *Doñana*, Av Martín Alonso Pinzón 13, T959242773. Local seafood specialities include sardines with peppers, skate in paprika and clams in saffron sauce. *Las Marismas*, C Padre Laraña 2, T959245272. Another good seafood spot with an economical menu. **Cheap** *Pizzería Napoli*, appropriately located in Av de Italia 79, T959252396 or *Pizzería Don Camillo e Peppone*, C Issac Peral s/n, with good pizzas. **Tapas bars** Try *Bar Berdigón* in C Berdigón, *Bar Agmanir* in C Carasa or *Marisquería Huelva* in C Cisneros – all have good seafood possibilities and local specialities.

Bars & nightclubs

Discos The liveliest scene is at Puerto Umbría in the summer, but in Huelva itself the best spot is *Alameda*, Alameda Sundheim.

Entertainment

Huelva is definitely not the entertainment capital of Andalucía and much of the nightlife that there is migrates to the nearby coastal resort of Puerto Umbría in the summer. **Bullfights** The Plaza de Toros is located in the west of the city on the Paseo de Independencia. *Aficionados* claim that the best *corridas* take place during the Fiestas Colombinas in Aug. **Cinemas** Apart from films at the Gran Teatro, there are 2 multi-screen cinemas: *Emperador Multicines*, C Berdigón 6, T959248100 and *Multicines La Rábida*, C Rábida 17, T959281403. **Flamenco** Supposedly famed for its flamenco, the genuine article is hard to find in Huelva. The best bet is *Peña Flamenca de Huelva*, Av de Andalucía. Otherwise, try *Mesón Tablao Solera*, C Conde 9, or *Pub Bodegones*, Av Federico Molina 4. Failing these, check with the tourist office. **Theatre** *Gran Teatro*, C Vázquez López 13, T959245703. There is a 'Pueblos de España' theatre display for 1 week during May or Jun, an International Festival of Dance usually in Jul and a 'Classical Theatre Campaign' in the Autumn. There are also occasional theatre performances at the Escuela de Magisterio, C Cantero Cuadrado.

Huelva Province

Fiestas & festivals	**6 Jan** *Día de los Reyes* There is the traditional cavalcade of the Three Wise Kings through the streets of the city. **Late Jul-early Aug** *Fiestas Colombinas* The Columbus Festivals (it's significant that the anglicized word is now used) commemorate the departure of the caravels and is marked by bullfights, sports events and regattas. **8 Sep** *Virgen de la Cinta* The feast day of Huelva's patron saint.

Shopping The main shopping area is around the Plaza de las Monjas and includes some pedestrianized streets such as C Concepción. A branch of the department store *El Corte Inglés* has opened fairly recently at the rear of the museum and provides convenient multi-storey parking as well as a good restaurant. You can also buy local craft items including basketwork, wrought iron goods, ceramics and leather work. There is a street market on Fri in El Recinto Colombino.

Sport **Football** The local football stadium is located in the north of the city, on Ctra de Sevilla. Football was introduced to the area by English workers of the Río Tinto company – which may explain why the local team habitually languishes at the lower end of the Spanish football league system. **Golf** *Bellavista*, Ctra de Huelva-Aljaraque, T959318083. **Tennis** Available at the club at C José Avila s/n, Huelva, T959248978. **Watersports** *Club Marítimo*, Av Montenegro, T959247627.

Tour operators *Bonanza*, Av Martín Alonso Pinzón 8, T959261100. *El Corte Inglés*, Av Federico Molina, T959280008. *Melia*, Av Martín Alonso Pinzón 20, T959245811. *Ultratur*, C Puerto 49, T959252811.

Transport **Long distance** **Air**: The nearest airport is at Sevilla. **Bus**: The main company serving Huelva is *Damas*, Av de Portugal, T959256900. There are also small bus stations in Av de Italia, Av Alemania and Av Federico Molina. Daily bus services come from Aracena (2), Ayamonte (6), Granada (1), Málaga (1), Matalascañas (1) and Sevilla (12). **Train**: The Moorish-style train station is in Av de Italia on the southwest side of the town, T959266666; also T902240202, www.renfe.es There are daily express trains from Sevilla, linking with the Madrid high speed AVE and other Andalucían regional centres. There are also 2 daily trains north to Almonaster and Zufre. **Boat**: There is a boat service between Huelva and the resort of Punta Umbría operating Jul-Sep between 0930 and 2130.

Directory **Banks** Banks are mainly located in the streets leading off the Plaza de las Monjas. **Communications** Post office: Correos, Av Tomás Domínguez 1, T959249184. **Telephones**: no *locutorios*, but plenty of cabins. **Embassies and consulates** *Denmark*, C Lazo Real 4, 5°, T959240127; *Finland*, Av Martín Alonso Pinzón 4, T959249583; *France*, C Rico 53, 1°, T959257700; *Greece*, C Marina 19, T959251706; *Netherlands*, C Marina 19, 1°, T959251706; *Portugal*, C Vázquez López 15, T959245569; *Sweden*, C Rico 53, 1°, T959257700. The nearest British, Canadian and American consulates are in Sevilla. **Medical services** First aid: *Casa de Socorro*, Via Paisajística s/n, T959253800. **Hospitals**: *Hospital del SAS Huelva*, Av Federico Mayo s/n, T959242222; *Hospital del SAS Infanta Elena*, Autovía Huelva-Sevilla s/n, T959232100. *Cruz Roja*, Paseo Buenos Aires s/n, T959261211. **Useful addresses** Garages/repair workshops: *Citroën*, Ctra de Sevilla, Km 637, T959229609. *Ford*, Pol San Diego s/n, T959228512. *Peugeot*, Ctra de Sevilla, Km 638, T959221988. *Renault*, C Legión España 2, T959254964. *Seat/VAG*, Ctra N431, Km 637.5, T959234051.

West from Huelva

The west boundary of the city of Huelva is the Río Odiel, which in comparison with the Río Tinto to the east, suffers little from pollution. The estuary to the west and its accompanying marshland is a protected area, covering some 7,000 ha of varied habitat, with a wide range of bird species, whatever the season. The reserve can be viewed from a number of sites, but undoubtedly the best is the causeway, which runs right down the centre of the area ending in a 10 km jetty to the lighthouse. A car is absolutely necessary and makes an excellent mobile hide, being easy to pull off the road in a number of places. The north of the area is not too promising with commercial salt pans. Then follows stretches of freshwater marsh with occasional clumps of trees. Finally there are saltwater marshes and intertidal sands and lagoons. The range of species is enormous, but the stars are undoubtedly the colonies of spoonbills. There are estimated to be 400 pairs, which if precise, would amount to around a third of the total European population. Grey and purple herons also breed along with little egrets, black winged stilts and some 300 pairs of little terns. Marsh harriers can usually be seen and there are thousands of waders on the lower part of the river during the migration seasons. Salt marsh flowers form an incredible carpet of blue and yellow in the spring and early summer.

The newly built **Centro de Visitantes** has a rather uninspiring display area, with biological and archaeological specimens. Tours can be arranged, which include visits to observation hides away from the main causeway. Literature is available, but only in Spanish. There is a newly opened restaurant next door. Located in a white octagonal building, it serves fresh seafood and local Condado white wines.

■ *Getting there: On arriving at Huelva, cross the Río Tinto bridge, turning left at the Columbus statue and follow the road through the docks to the north of the city. Cross the new Río Odiel bridge and at the end don't take the left fork, (which is the logical route) but carry straight on towards Portugal and then turn immediately left as though heading back into Huelva. Take the first right down the road marked rather grandly 'Carretera de las Islas Dique Juan Carlos I, Rey de España'. The road runs down the centre of the reserve for nearly 20 km. On the left after 2 km is the Centro de Vistantes (see above).*

Paraje Natural de las Marismas de Odiel
Colour map 1, grid C2

Huelva Province

From the Río Odiel mouth westwards to the Portuguese border is a string of minor resorts. Due south 19 km from Huelva is the first and most important of these, **Punta Umbría** (*population*: 11,523). Reached via a new road bridge and ferries in the summer from Huelva, it is not a particularly inspiring resort. It does, however, have a fine sandy beach and with fresh sea breezes it can be a relief from the heat of Huelva. There are half a dozen small hotels (none in the luxury class) and a similar number of *pensiones*, so accommodation is not a problem except in July and August, when the place can get quite lively. There is also an *Albergue Juvenil*, Av Océano 13, T959311650, with meals available and wheelchair access. With a small port and a fishing fleet, good seafood restaurants are not hard to find. 4 km west is **El Rompido**, a former fishing village now expanding with tourism. Between the two is the village of El Portil, where there is a small freshwater lagoon, **La Laguna de el Portil**. This 15 ha lake is now a protected area and amongst its breeding birds are black necked grebes.

West of El Rompido is the mouth of the Río Piedras, which, due to the growth of a spit known as the Flecha del Rompido, has extensive salt marshes alongside its banks. With the coastal pinewoods, tidal creeks and dunes, there

West to the border

is a variety of habitats and some 2,500 ha of the area, known as the **Marismas del Río Piedras**, now has Paraje Natural status. Its unspoilt nature makes it a delightful reserve to visit and a good variety of birds and plants can be expected, particularly in spring. The best viewing is from the fishing village of Puerto de El Terrón on the west bank of the river.

To the west of the Río Piedras is the long sandy beach of Playa de las Antillas, part of which is reserved for naturists. This area comes under the administration of **Lepe**, a few kilometres inland. Lepe, which is in the centre of a fruit growing area, is best known in Spain as the butt of the nation's jokes of the 'How many men from Lepe does it take to change a light bulb?' variety. The inhabitants of Lepe are not that dim, however, as they now host an annual jokes festival in late May, which attracts not only a host of visitors, but most of the better comedians in Spain.

The next resort is **Isla Cristina**, which, as its name implies, was once an island. It is still the second most important fishing port along the Huelva coast, with an important canning factory. Tourism is now becoming increasingly significant, with the population of 18,000 trebling during the summer months. There is an excellent sandy beach, backed by some good fish restaurants. There are a few accommodation possibilities. At the top of the range is the large **AL** *Riu Canela*, Ctra La Antilla-Isla Cristina, 3 km, T959477124, F959470460, with wheelchair access, pool, tennis, air conditioning and gardens. There is little in the budget range. Book well in advance for everything in Isla Cristina during July and August.

The rather scruffy border town of **Ayamonte** (population: 16,891) is the only resort with anything in the way of monuments. It is located on the Río Gaudiana opposite the Portuguese village of Villareal de San Antonio, with which it is now linked with a modern suspension bridge – replacing a 15-minute ferry journey. The 15th-century Iglesia de San Salvador is worth a visit and if you can find the place open, the tower repays the slog to the top with marvellous views over the river and marshes. Also of interest are the Iglesia de Nuestra Señora de las Agustias dating from the 16th century and the convents of San Francisco and Santa Clara. The castle has only its foundations remaining, but these appear to have Roman origins.

Marismas de Isla Cristina The area between Ayamonte and Isla Cristina forms yet another nature reserve, the Marismas de Isla Cristina. Tidal activity has led to the formation of sand spits protecting areas of salt marsh, tidal creeks and abandoned salt pans. The dunes have extensive vegetation, including stone pine and juniper, while there is a wide variety of salt marsh plants dominated by glasswort. Breeding birds include white stork, black winged stilt, collared pratincole and Montagu's harrier. There is a good variety of waders and gulls during the winter months. Access is best from the road/causeway south from Ayamonte towards the beach at Playa de Moral.

East from Huelva

In the footsteps of Columbus

The area immediately east of Huelva has rich connections with **Christopher Columbus** (Cristóbal Colón in Spanish) and his quest to find the New World. At the narrow tip of land between the mouths of the Río Tinto and the Río Odiel, the **Punta del Sebo**, is the imposing monument to Columbus

*Columbus
Monument, Huelva*

Huelva Province

known as the *Spirit of Exploration*, completed by the American sculptress, Gertrude Whitney, in 1929. The caped figure stares resolutely out to sea, ignoring the towers of the petrochemical plant that provide a backdrop for the most commonly used photographic view.

Across the river, on a small hill and built on the site of what was probably an Almohad mosque, this Franciscan monastery was dedicated soon after the Reconquest. The gatehouse dates from this time, while the cloister was rebuilt after the 1755 earthquake. The monastery's church survived the earthquake and is in Gothic-Mudéjar style. Columbus came here in 1491, after failing to gain royal approval for his plans. He met two friars, Antonio de Marchena and Juan Pérez (the latter having formerly been the Queen's confessor) and they took his case to court gaining permission for his venture. The monastery today receives visitors from all over the world who see it as an important symbol of the Hispanic world.

**Monastery of
La Rábida**
Colour map 1, grid C2

Visiting is by guided tour only (in Spanish) by one of the Franciscan friars. At most stops there are small unobtrusive plaques with brief comments in English. The tour begins in a small anteroom where there are frescoes, painted in 1930, by Daniel Vásquez Díaz, a local artist from Huelva. There is also a plaque commemorating the Quincentenery of Columbus's voyages. The next stop is in the cloisters, known as the Patio de las Flores. The cloisters contain an Almohad arch, which may have been the original entrance door. Just off the courtyard is the monks' refectory, where no doubt Columbus would have eaten. The tour now moves into the 14th-century church, which is dominated by the 15th-century Image of the Crucifixion. There are frescoes from the same period on the walls and in the apse. Also of interest is the 14th-century Alabaster image of the Virgen de los Milagros, before which Columbus and his crew prayed before setting sail. Martín Alonzo Pinzón, the right hand man of Columbus, is buried in the church, beneath the Shrine of Santa María as he had requested. On the first floor is the Chapter House, where Columbus, the Pinzón brothers and the friars met to discuss the plans for the voyages. The same room was used on 3 August 1992 by the King of Spain and the whole government to commemorate the 500th anniversary of the event. In the nearby rooms are models of the three caravels, the *Niña*, the *Pinta* and the *Santa María*, plus other artefacts connected with the voyages. The Sala de Banderas or Flag Room contains the standards of the South American countries along with boxes of soil from each – now covered with glass to keep out cigarette ends and other forms of vandalism.

The monastery is surrounded by pleasant tree-lined gardens, in which there is a Latin American University and monument celebrating the 400th anniversary of the Discovery of the Americas. This is a stout column with a simple cross on the top. ■ *Guided tours every 45 mins 1000-1300 and 1600-1815. Free; donation appreciated. T959350411.*

Muelle de las Carabelas Lying between the river and the bluff on which the monastery stands is the Muelle de las Carabelas. At this point, close to where Columbus's flotilla sailed in 1492, are accurate replicas of the *Niña*, the *Pinta* and the *Santa María* caravels, which were built for the 500th anniversary celebrations in 1992. The replicas give a realistic idea of the shipboard discomforts of the time. Lying along the jetty are artefacts from the age of Columbus, such as anchors and capstans, while at craft stalls artisans make rope and tar to the background noises of birds and animals from the Americas. There is an audio display room and, on the upper level, a restaurant with fine views out over the estuary. ■ *Winter Tue-Sat 1000-1700; summer Mon-Fri 1000-1400 and 1700-2100, Sun 1100-2000. €3, children €1.20. T959530597.* Opposite the Muelle is the **Foro Iberoamerica**, a modern Roman-style brick and concrete outdoor theatre used for summer performances.

Palos de la Frontera
Population: 7,009
Just 5 km north of La Rábida is this town of little attraction, where few people would bother to stop if it were not for the Columbus connection. This was the port from where Columbus set sail in 1492 on his first voyage and was the home of many of his sailors, such as the Pinzón brothers. In those days Palos was a prosperous port, its river location sheltering it from the Atlantic winds. Because the people of Palos had offended Portugal, they were forced to serve the Spanish crown with caravels that had been built and fitted out in the town's shipyards. In 1492, the Catholic monarchs ordered them to supply Columbus and so in this way the cost of the voyage was greatly reduced. Today the river has silted up the bay and a stretch of marshland separates Palos from the water. The inhabitants of Palos tend to revere the Pinzón brothers more than Columbus and there are a number of commemorative monuments and reminders of the past. The 15th-century orphanage that took in the Pinzón brothers still stands, while there is a statue of Martín Alonso Pinzón in the main square. His home, at Calle Colón 24, is now a museum. ■ *1030-1330, 1730-1930 Mon-Sat; 1030-1330 Sun. Free.* La Fontanilla – the fountain with Roman origins where the caravels took on water before setting sail, is now dry, but had a facelift for the quincentenary in 1992. The jetty from where the caravels left was rebuilt for the 400th anniversary, but as this is now a collapsed heap of rotting timber it is hardly worth the effort of finding it. Better, instead, to take a look at the 15th-century Church of San Jorge, with a mixture of styles from Mudéjar to Gothic. The 18th-century bell tower is pyramid shaped, while the nave has a coffered ceiling and some fine two-tone brickwork. Columbus and the Pinzón brothers attended mass here before setting sail. ■ *Open at service times only.* Today Palos no longer has a maritime role, its inhabitants largely making a living from agriculture, specializing in strawberry growing.

Seven kilometres up river is the altogether more attractive town of Moguer, with its delightful square, Baroque mansions and a handful of convents. Moguer provided many of the crew members of the caravels and Columbus frequently visited the town. A tour of Moguer should certainly include the **Convento de Santa Clara**, which was founded in the 14th century by Alonso Jofre Tenorio, who surrounded it with high walls and battlements. The convent's church is in Gothic-Mudéjar style and has a number of interesting features. The altars, dating from the 17th century, have glazed tiling from Sevilla, while the impressive Mudéjar choir stalls are 15th century. The three sets of cloisters are similar in style to those that were later built in American missions. Columbus often came to the convent and was in correspondence with the abbess, Doña Inés Enriquez. When he returned from his first voyage he spent a night in prayer at the convent, fulfilling a vow he made on surviving a fearsome storm off the Azores. The nuns left the convent around the turn of the century and it is now a museum. ■ *Guided tour only, every 30 mins, Tue-Sat 1100-1400 and 1700-2000; Sun 1700-2000. €1.50.*

Also of interest in Moguer is the **Iglesia de Nuestra Señora de la Granada**, surrounded by whitewashed houses and mainly constructed of rather severe brick, but having a tower which is remarkably similar to the Giralda in Sevilla. Moguer was also the birthplace of **Juan Ramón Jiménez** (1881-1958), the poet and winner of the Nobel Prize for Literature in 1956. During Franco's times, the poet spent 20 years of exile in Puerto Rico, but his body was returned to Moguer in 1958 for burial. The house in which he was born, Calle Jiménez 5, is now a museum to his memory. ■ *Daily 1000-1400 and 1630-2000. €0.60.* There is also a statue of Jiménez in the main square, the Plaza de Cabildo.

Finally in Moguer, take a look at the 18th-century Ayuntamiento. Its cream coloured, double-arched neoclassical frontage is topped by a clock (usually stopped), which used to feature on the 2,000-peseta banknote.

Moguer
Population: 13,749

Huelva Province

Niebla

Twenty-nine kilometres east of Huelva on the old road to Sevilla, the N472, is the fortified walled town of Niebla. It is located where the main road crosses the Río Tinto and its strategic position warranted protection, as the Romans, who called it Ilipla, moved their silver by barge downstream. It was the Romans who built the bridge to the southeast of the town and which has carried traffic for 2,000 years since. It was blown up during the Civil War, but has since been carefully restored. Niebla is, in fact, the archetypal walled city. The pink sandstone walls stretch for 2 km, completely encircling the town, and are in places 15 m wide. They were largely built during Moorish times, when Niebla was Medina Labla, capital of a caliphal district and later an independent *taifa*. During the Reconquest, it fell to Alfonso X in 1257 after a nine-month siege in which gunpowder was used for the first time in Spain. Niebla then gradually declined in importance.

Colour map 1, grid C3
Population: 3,814

Today, the Río Tinto's bed is red and yellow and the water totally lifeless, but the Roman bridge and the Moorish walls of Niebla are intact. There are four horseshoe Arab gates, named Sevilla, Socorro, Buey and Agua. The gate to the east of the town is the most convenient as it is closest to the monuments and has ample parking nearby. Close to the main gate is the ruined **Iglesia de San Martín**, dating from the 15th century and possibly built on the site of a synagogue. The road separates the bell tower from the apse and the chapel, which is all that survives. Storks nest on the roof and there is a lesser kestrel

☞ Columbus - man of mystery

Although Spain has always regarded **Christopher Columbus** as one of its national heroes, it is now generally agreed that he was born in Genoa in Italy. Columbus was the son of a weaver and began his maritime career at the age of 13, eventually becoming a trading agent. In 1476 he travelled to England, being shipwrecked on the way and swimming ashore near Cape St Vincent. He took refuge for a while in Lisbon, before eventually arriving in London in December 1476. He spent the winter and spring there before embarking on a ship at Bristol for Iceland.

Columbus then settled in Lisbon, where his brother Bartholomew was working as a cartographer. In 1479 he married Felipa, the daughter of the governor of Porto Santo, and their son Diego was born 2 years later. By now he was beginning to formulate his ideas, by reading maps and charts, that the world was 25% smaller than previously thought and that the East Indies could be reached much more quickly by sailing westwards. These erroneous beliefs remained with him until he died. In 1484 he put forward his ideas to King John II of Portugal with the suggestion that he finance a westward crossing. A Royal Maritime Commission rejected his proposals because of his miscalculations and that Portuguese vessels were already rounding the southern point of Africa on their way eastwards.

Disappointed, Columbus moved to Spain with his son (his wife having died), and stayed at La Rábida Monastery, near Huelva (see page 123). In 1486 he presented his plans to the Catholic Monarchs, Ferdinand and Isabel. While waiting for their decision he stayed in Córdoba and developed a liaison with a wealthy widow, Beatrice Enríquez de Harana, who eventually produced his illegitimate son Ferdinand. The plans were rejected and Columbus again retreated to La Rábida to lick his wounds. Here he found an ally in the abbot, Juan Pérez, who had formerly been the confessor to Isabel. The Catholic Monarchs had now completed the Reconquest with the fall of

Granada, but as a result were short of funds. The thought of riches from the New World led them the to change their minds and sponsor an expedition. The persistence of Columbus had eventually paid off.

The **First Voyage**, which left Palos on 3 August 1492, was a modest affair with three ships, the 30 m decked Santa María and two small 15 m caravels, the Pinta and the Niña, captained by the Pinzón brothers, Martín and Vicente. The total of the crews was probably no more than 90. After a brief stop for repairs in the Canary Islands (where Columbus had a continuing love affair with Beatrice Bobadilla) the fleet resumed the voyage westwards. With his crews almost on the point of mutiny, land was sighted on 12 October and landfall was made on the island of Guanahani in the Bahamas group. Columbus continued to Cuba, which he named after Juana, one of the Spanish princesses, and Española (later corrupted to Hispaniola and now the Dominican Republic and Haiti). In December 1492, the Santa María was shipwrecked. A fort, La Navidad, was built with salvaged wood from the wreck and left with a garrison of 35 men, while the Niña and the Pinta returned home, Columbus arriving back in Palos in March 1493 to receive a noble title.

Columbus began planning almost immediately for his **Second Voyage**. This was an altogether grander affair, with 17 vessels and around 1,500 men. The fleet left Cádiz in September 1493 and the voyage was to last for almost three years. Countless islands were discovered, including Dominica, Guadalupe and Antigua. When he returned to La Navidad, he found that the fort had been destroyed and the men killed by the natives. Columbus abandoned the site and set up the colony of Isabella, which was effectively the first settlement of Europeans in the New World. The natives, however, were becoming increasingly rebellious and Columbus defeated them in a battle in March 1495 and sent five shiploads of them back to Spain, which could be claimed to be the start of the slave trade.

He then established a new capital, Santa Domingo, and set sail for Spain, leaving his brother Bartholomew in command.

Columbus left Cádiz on his **Third Voyage** on 30 May 1498. He made his first landing on a 3-peaked island which he called Trinidad after the Holy Trinity. Next day he sighted the mainland of South America (now Venezuela). He continued along the coast looking for a strait which he was convinced would lead westward. He eventually returned to Española to find the colony in revolt against his brother Bartholomew. Meanwhile, his enemies in Spain had convinced the Catholic Monarchs that the colony should have a new governor, who duly arrived and sent the Columbus brothers back to Spain shackled in irons. Columbus insisted in retaining his irons until personally pardoned by the Queen.

Columbus began campaigning for his **Fourth Voyage**. He had now become something of a nuisance and the only ships he could obtain were four worm-eaten caravels. These left Cádiz in May 1502 and after 21 days anchored off Santo Domingo. Here Columbus sensed the onset of a hurricane and made for shelter. A large homeward-bound fleet, with many of his enemies on board, ignored his warnings and were drowned. Columbus then explored the coast of Central America, still searching for a westward passage. The last two caravels of his small fleet finally foundered off Jamaica in June 1503. The remains of his party were shipped back to Spain, arriving in Sanlúcar in November 1503. He was never to sail again. Christopher Columbus died three years later in Valladolid, a wealthy but bitter man.

So how does history rate Christopher Columbus, 500 years after his first voyage? On the debit side he was clearly hopeless at administration, particularly at managing people. He was also somewhat greedy and self-righteous, which in his old age developed into a paranoia about the way it appeared to him that he had been cheated and slighted. On the other hand, he was a brilliant navigator and never lost a boat through his own faulty seamanship and obviously had a natural instinct for the sky, the stars and the wind. He also had an obsessive perseverance to prove that his ideas and concepts about a westward passage were correct. The fact that they were erroneous does not lessen his achievements. The US has always celebrated the idea of Columbus discovering America and the 400th centenary was held in Chicago. Yet the nearest he got to discovering what is now US territory was the island of Puerto Rico and the US Virgin Islands, which are part of the commonwealth of the US.

The Columbus story ends, as it begins, with a mystery. Where are his remains? Initially laid to rest in the Franciscan monastery in Valladolid, his body was taken to the Carthusian monastery in Sevilla. About 20 years later, his daughter-in-law María de Toledo, arranged for the remains of Columbus and her husband Diego to be sent to the cathedral at Santo Domingo where they were buried in the vaults. By 1795, the whole of Hispaniola had been taken over by France and the remains were removed to Spanish soil – in this case to the cathedral at Havana in Cuba. Just over a century later Cuba gained independence and in 1899 the coffin was taken to the cathedral in Sevilla where today it lies in a crypt beneath an impressive monument. However, in 1877, back in Santo Domingo, another coffin was discovered in the cathedral's crypt in which was a silver plate claiming that the remains were those of Christopher Columbus. American examination in the 1960s suggested that the remains were of two bodies, presumably those of Columbus and his son Diego. But the mystery does not end there. Gianni Granzotto, whose biography of Columbus, published in 1986, claims that his remains were never taken from the Franciscan monastery in Valladolid. The monastery no longer exists and above its site is a bar. If the remains are still there then Columbus' body will lie under its billiards room!

colony in the tower. The main church is the **Iglesia de Santa María de Granada** in the Plaza Santa María in the town centre. The church site was occupied by a Visigoth cathedral and a Moorish mosque before the Reconquest. Bits and pieces of masonry from such times seem to be scattered about the entrance area with its 11-lobed doorway. Inside there is a well preserved *mihrab*, some Roman altars and the throne of the Visigoth bishops. The tower is the original Arab minaret. Niebla's **castle** was first Moorish, but later modified by the Christians (it is usually known as the Castillo de Guzmán today). It was badly knocked about by French troops in the War of Independence and today, with a modicum of restoration, it is mainly used as a cultural centre. Most visitors will be happy to wander around and enjoy the ambience of Niebla. ■ *For details of the town's monuments (and the key to the church) visit the Casa de Cultura, (an old 15th-century hospital), on the next side of the square. Open Mon-Fri 1000-1400. There is a permanent exhibition in the foyer.* Food outlets are hard to find, but there is a good bar-restaurant in Plaza San Martín. Accommodation is also scarce; try **E** *Pensión Los Cazadores*, Calle Quepo de Llano 4, T959363071.

Villages of the Condado
Colour map 1, grid C3

East of Niebla is an area known as the Condado, reflected in the place names of its main town and villages, **La Palma del Condado**, **Rociana del Condado** and **Bollullos Par del Condado**. The name has its origins in the administrative district of Niebla, set up by Henry II of Castile. The area is notable today for its wine production, with over 16,500 ha under cultivation. Palomino and Garrido are the main grapes used, with the white table wine having its own Denominación de Origen – one of the few decent white wines coming from Andalucía. Some powerful 'sherries' are also produced. The Condado is also famous for the Huelva's regional dish of *migas*, breadcrumbs fried in olive oil and garlic and an accompaniment to almost any meat or seafood meal of the province. **Bollullos** is the main centre of the area, with its principal street like an elongated square with numerous bars and outdoor tables. There are also a number of bodegas – some of which sell shellfish and strawberries – along the main road in town.

Parque Nacional Coto Doñana

Colour map 4, grid A1

One of Europe's best wetland reserves, rivalled only by the Camargue and the Danube Delta

This national park, the only one in Andalucía, covers some 50,270 ha and there is a protective zone around it of similar size. It forms the western edge of the Guadalquivir estuary and consists of a variety of habitats; being above all a wetland, its largest habitats are the *marismas*, marshland which is inundated each winter and spring by the flood waters of the Río Guadalquivir. The fresh water marshes are surrounded by salt pans and rice paddies. These various wetland habitats attract birds in huge numbers and more than 250 species have been recorded.

Despite being one of only five national parks on mainland Spain and being designated a Unesco Biosphere Reserve, the Coto Doñana has been under threat in recent years. Firstly, there have been plans put forward for further development at Matalascañas, including a golf course, which will put extra demands on water supply that threatens the water table levels on the reserve. Farmers wish to reclaim more land for agriculture, which will then need more irrigation water, which will also affect water levels. Local people, who through economic necessity see jobs as more important than wildlife, have organized a number of demonstrations and some of the park property and vehicles have been vandalized. Environmentalists throughout Europe have sprung to the

Saving the Iberian lynx

Europe's worst toxic spill in April 1998, which threatened the fragile ecology of the Parque Nacional Coto Doñana, brought to the world's attention the plight of the Iberian lynx. This is now the most endangered feline species, with around 600 left in Spain and Portugal. About 50 of these are believed to live in the Coto Doñana, making it the animal's last real stronghold.

The lynx is a beautiful animal with a spotted coat, tufted ears and a distinct beard around the face. It is bigger than a wildcat and much more savage. There are a number of factors for its near extinction. Its finely marked pelt is widely sought by fashion houses, so many have been shot. Probably more important is its loss of habitat. The lynx prefers dense woodland and scrub, but in recent years many cork oak forests have been felled as the demand for natural corks has fallen with their replacement by plastic stoppers. The cork oak woodland has been replaced by arable crops or by the planting of fast-growing timber such as eucalyptus, which has little in the way of undergrowth. The loss of food supply has also been a contributory factor. Rabbits have always been the main diet of the Iberian lynx, but the outbreak of myxomatosis in the 1960s reduced the rabbit population dramatically. Lacking rabbits, the lynx often turns to farm animals such as sheep and goats, leading to persecution by farmers. The lynx is highly territorial and once the cubs are a year old, they have to find their own territory and a mate, but this is impossible with small relic populations.

Ironically, it is the toxic disaster that may save the lynx, which needs an ecological corridor to link the Doñana population with the Sierra Morena lynx population in the north of Andalucía. It has recently been announced that the decommissioned land along the toxic spill will be a green corridor which could allow the expansion of the lynx population. If it saves the lynx from extinction, then the toxic spill may not have been a total ecological disaster after all.

Huelva Province

rescue of the Coto Donaña with petitions and pressure through the EU and at the moment an uneasy peace prevails. A further threat to the Coto Doñana came in 1998 when a mining dam burst its banks releasing a flood of toxic chemicals into the Guadiamar River, which runs through part of the park. Considerable numbers of wildlife were killed, but the long-term damage is still difficult to assess (see box, page 131).

Flora & fauna

The beach, with its inter-tidal sands, stretches for over 30 km and is largely deserted. Inland there is an extensive system of sand dunes, initially mobile dunes, but further back are older dunes fixed with marram grass and occasional stone pines. These pass into open woodland with cork oaks and pines, with clearances covered with scrub *(mator-rales)* dominated by rock roses, lavender and cistus. The woodland clearings are the best places to see the herds of fallow and roe deer along with small parties of wild boar. Other mammals include some 25 pairs of the rare pardel lynx, which are, however, nocturnal and elusive. The Egyptian mongoose is more readily seen as are the polecat and otter, while there are also three varieties of bat. The camels which used to splash around the wetter areas have now died out due to poaching and old age.

Winter wildfowl from Northern Europe include some 60,000 grey lag geese and over 250,000 ducks and coots. Spring and autumn passage migrants are dominated by waders such as both types of godwit, ruffs, stints and purple sandpiper. It is the breeding birds in the spring and early summer that are the most spectacular. There are a number of large heronries containing cattle egrets, little egrets, grey herons, night herons, purple herons and squacco herons (one, in fact, is right opposite a hide at the park headquarters). Spoonbills and white storks are always around, while whiskered terns and collared pratincoles hawk over the water. Glossy ibis have appeared regularly in recent years. The reed beds and scrub are alive with the calls of nightingales, cettis warblers, great reed warblers and savis warblers. The reeds are also the home of the purple gallinule –, the emblem of the Coto Doñana. The sky is full of raptors, including red kites, booted eagles, short toed eagles and hundreds of black kites. There are an estimated 15 pairs of the rare Spanish imperial eagle nesting within the reserve. Azure-winged magpies commonly scavenge around the car parks and picnic site.

When to visit the Coto Doñana Late February and mid May is the most rewarding time in terms of the maximum number of bird species, but this will depend entirely on the water level. After a dry winter, breeding conditions can be disappointing. In summer, the *marismas* dry out, the heat is intense and the mosquitoes are out in force. Avoid the Whitsun *romería* at El Rocío (see below).

Park essentials
See also www.mma.es
Large areas of the Coto Doñana have restricted access, but the official locations around the fringe of the reserve will satisfy all but the most fanatical birdwatchers.

The **Centro de Visitantes** or park's main visitors' centre (and the Coto Doñana headquarters) are at **El Acebuche**, 3 km north of Matalascañas and 12 km south of El Rocío on the A483, T959448711. Open 0800-1900 /2000/2100, depending on the time of year. The centre has an audio visual room, an exhibition room, a restaurant and shop, which sells maps. There is a 5-km trail from the centre. On the roof is probably the most photographed storks' nest in Andalucía. There are a series of nine hides overlooking a large lake of 33 ha, surrounded by trees and marsh. From late April, the trees on the far side support a busy heronry. The last three hides overlook a fenced-in area where there are wildfowl no longer able to fly, but which seem to attract truly wild birds to the location.

Parque Nacional del Coto de Doñana

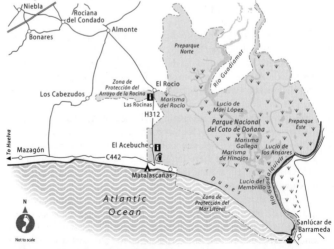

Yet another threat to the Coto Doñana

Europe's premier wetland site has been threatened for years by developers and farmers, whose demands for water seem insatiable. In April 1998 more serious and lethal danger occurred, when a dam burst at a Swedish-Canadian owned mine at Aznalcóllar, northwest of Sevilla, releasing some 158,000 tonnes of toxic waste into the Río Guadiamar. The river runs through the park – the 'buffer zone' around the Coto Doñana National Park – and empties into the estuary of the Rio Guadalquivir. The toxic waste took the form of a liquid sludge, made up of a lethal cocktail of zinc, copper, sulphur, lead, cadmium and arsenic, which in volume was almost four times as great as that released from the Exxon Váldez tanker disaster of 1989. It ruined a considerable amount of land in the park which was farmed for rice, oranges, olives and cotton, before being diverted by hurriedly constructed earth banks. Only 3% of the Coto Doñana was covered with the sludge, but the poison will soon get into the food chain and effect every aspect of wildlife in the area. Frantic attempts were made to remove the sludge during the summer of 1998, before the autumn rains washed the poison into the water table, but a spokesperson for Britain's Royal Society for the Protection of

Birds commented that it would take as much as 25 years for the area to fully recover and it might turn out to be the worst environmental disaster of its kind in Europe this century.

Who is to blame for this disaster? Predictably, everyone involved blamed someone else. The park comes under the jurisdiction of central government, while the park's buffer zone is the responsibility of the Andalucían government. Local officials had, in fact, passed the dam as safe only a few days before the disaster, despite local complaints from ecological groups that it had been leaking. One local politician made the classic comment that 'mines aren't normally dangerous until an accident like this one happens'. Clearly the mining company were culpable and helped to fund the clean-up operation but did not compensate farmers until legally obliged to do so. Meanwhile, it was impossible to compensate the already dead wildlife.

By 2002, however, it was clear that the effects of the disaster were not as bad as everyone feared and that nature itself has seemed to have overcome the problem. Astoundingly, however, the mining company involved has resumed operations without penalty and is even using the repaired dam!

La Rocina sub centre is located 500 m from El Rocío on the road to Matalascañas, T959442340. It's open 0900-2100 and has rooms for exhibitions and audio visual presentations. There is a 3½ km trail with a series of hides overlooking a fresh water lake and marsh known as the Charco de la Boca (the second hide is particularly good for purple gallinules). There are also areas of pinewood and scrub, plus a large reed bed where savis warblers breed. Some 7 km from La Rocina along a minor road through the scrubland is the **Palacio de Acebrón**, an old mansion with exhibitions and audio visual presentations. It's open the same hours as La Rocina. The grounds have mature woodland and a delightful shady walk of 1½ km around a small lake.

There is a further visitors' centre called José Antonio Valverde, T955959096, open 1000-1830, but get directions from La Rocina or El Acebuche, since it can be difficult to find.

The bridge and promenade at El Rocío (see below) give excellent views of a range of water birds (a telescope is useful here). The SEO (Spanish Ornithological Association) run a small, delightful observation centre looking over the water, with telescope, information and English speaking staff. Near Plaza del Azebuchal, T959506093.

It is possible to book a **bus tour** of the reserve from El Acebuche, run by *Cooperativa Marismas del Rocío*, T959430432. These trips of 3½ hours leave twice a day at 0800 and 1500 or 1700, depending on the time of year, and cost €18.03. It's advisable to book well in advance. These tours start by driving along the beach and then hurtle up the dunes and into the woodland. Groups of serious birdwatchers may prefer to hire the buses for the day. It is also possible to visit the southern edge of the reserve by boat from Sanlúcar (see page 170) and Sevilla (see page 80).

El Rocío
See also
http//:rocio.andal.es

The centre of the Parque Nacional Coto Doñana is the remarkable town of El Rocío, which, with its sand-covered streets and houses with verandas, looks like a set from a Wild West film. The town is the venue of the famous Whitsun *romería* to the sanctuary of the image of the Virgen del Rocío, held in the Iglesia de Nuestra Señora del Rocío. Dominating the town, the church belies its elderly appearance, having only been built in the 1960s to replace one flattened in the 1755 earthquake. El Rocío is also a Mecca for birdwatchers, who can be seen in the spring lining up along the bridge and the paseo with their telescopes trained on the *marismas*. There is an information centre at Avenida Canaliega s/n T/F959443808, elrocio@infodonana.es

Sleeping and eating Accommodation in El Rocío is scarce and impossible to find during the *romería*, when rooms are booked sometimes years in advance. **AL** *Puente del Rey*, Av de la Canaliega s/n, T959442575, F959442070. Elegant, large new hotel close to the bridge, with pool and restaurant. Excursions arranged. **D** *Doñana Tour*, Plaza Real 29, T959442468. 44 rooms. **D** *Isidro*, Av los Ansares 59. 14 rooms. a/c. **D** *Vélez*, C Algaida 2, T959442117. **E** *Las Marismas*, C Baltasar III 4. 23 rooms. Camping: The nearest **campsite** is *Rocío Playa*, Ctra Huelva-Matalascañas, Km 45, beachside, second category site.

Matalascañas

This is a purpose-built resort located on the coastal dunes, which have been flattened to make way for the featureless hotels, apartment blocks and villas that line the beach. There is a newly opened golf course, which consumes vast amounts of water from the wetlands. Matalascañas is not a pretty sight, but it makes an excellent base for exploring the area and its beach is wide, sandy and safe. The road back to Huelva runs for nearly 50 km between the massive tree clad dunes and the marshes, until the provincial capital's petrochemical industry hoves into sight.

Sleeping and eating There are loads of beach hotels to choose from. *La Carabela*, Sector L parc 59, T959448001, F959448125. 275 rooms. A/c, wheelchair access, pool, restaurant. **A** *El Cortijo*, Sector E parc 15, T959430259, F959448570. A/c, wheelchair access, restaurant, pool, tennis. **A** *El Flamero*, C Ronda Maestro Alonso, T959448020, F959448008. 484 rooms. A/c, pool, disco, closed Oct to Easter. Beachside location. **A** *Gran Hotel del Coto*, Sector D, T959440017. 467 rooms. Wheelchair access, pool restaurant, tennis. **A** *Tierra Mar*, Parcela 120, sector M, T959440375, F959440720. 253 rooms. A/c, pool, tennis, disco, restaurant, beachside location. There are also half a dozen *pensiones*, the best of which is **D** *Los Tamarindos*, Av Adelfas 31, T959430119.

Mazagón

Mazagón, 35 km along the coast towards to Huelva, is a more pleasant and low-key coastal resort than Matalascañas. It has several *hostales*, campsites and a parador (T959536300, mazagon@parador.es), as well as many excellent fish restaurants and tapas bars.

Viva La Paloma Blanca!

Follow a car in Andalucía and you may see a sticker in the rear window proclaiming 'Soy Rociero' indicating that the driver is proud of the fact that he or she has been on the annual Whitsun pilgrimage to El Rocío. This romería is unique not only in Andalucía, but is one of the most amazing spectacles anywhere in the world. A mixture of the religious, the profane, the violent and the bucolic, it could perhaps only happen in Andalucía.

It all started in the 13th century when a shepherd found a carved image of the Virgin in a hollow tree. While carrying her home, he stopped for a sleep and when he awoke he found the statue missing. Retracing his steps he found that the Virgin had miraculously returned to her tree. Villagers from Almonte came to his aid and took the statue away, but again she returned, resisting all attempts to move her. Eventually a shrine was built on the spot, where healing and other miracles were often reported.

Today, in Whitsun week, thousands of pilgrims, many in brotherhoods from all over Andalucía, converge on El Rocío to pay their respects to Nuestra Señora del Rocío, La Paloma Blanca (the White Dove) and Queen of the Marshes. The object of their devotion is a white, carved, life-sized statue with a gold head dress and six white petticoats, kept in a sanctuary in El

Rocío Church. The traditional way for the brotherhoods to travel to El Rocío is by horseback or ornately decorated ox carts, a journey which takes several days, but which is well fortified by alcohol and paella. Each brotherhood carries a simpecado, a mini shrine with a portrait of the Virgin. Thousands more arrive by coach, car and four-wheel drive vehicles, many of which have been ferried across the Guadalquivir by the army. During the last few years the number of Rocieros has risen to over 500,000, providing a serious headache for the local authorities.

On the Saturday evening, each brotherhood files past the shrine to pay their respects to the Virgin. On the Sunday there is an outdoor mass in the square, followed by more drinking and dancing. Monday morning is the highlight of the pilgrimage, when the Virgin is taken from her shrine by the senior brotherhood, the Hermanedad de Almonte to visit the simpecados of the various brotherhoods, greeted by cries of 'Guapa!' or 'Viva la Paloma Blanca!'. Any pilgrim wishing to help carry the Virgin, or even touch her, must literally fight for the honour and will be thuggishly repelled by the Almonteños. Eventually La Paloma Blanca is returned to her sanctuary and the ox carts, coaches and their inhabitants return home to dry out.

North from Huelva

*The main route north from Huelva to the Sierra Morena is the N435 which leaves the Sevilla-Huelva A49 at San Juan del Puerto. Initially it passes through pleasant farmland dominated by cereal growing, bypassing the unremarkable villages of **Trigueros** and **Valverde del Camino**, famous for its leather industry. After the latter the route becomes hillier, with more woodland, much of it eucalyptus groves.*

Minas de Río Tinto

Coming from either Huelva or the western part of the Sierra de Aracena on the N435 is the turning for the C421 near Zalamea la Real, which leads to the Minas de Río Tinto. Huge open-cast copper mines may not be everyone's cup

Colour map 1 grid B3

Huelva Province

of tea, but the sheer scale of the operations and the way the landscape has been desecrated has a certain horrific fascination and most people find the detour well worthwhile.

Minerals have been extracted here from the Devonian and Carboniferous rocks since the time of the Phoenicians. It is the iron content of the rock that has stained the waters and bed of the Río Tinto red and yellow and given it its name. The Romans deepened the mines in an effort to find silver, but this led to flooding problems, which were resolved by the use of a complicated system of slave-driven wheels to bring the water to the surface. A number of these wooden wheels have survived and may be seen in Río Tinto's Museo Minero (see below) and in the Museo Provincial, Huelva (see page 117). The mines were less important during the Moorish occupation and when the New World was discovered and cheap minerals were brought back to Spain, the mines all but closed down.

In 1873, the mines were sold to an Anglo-German consortium and the *Río Tinto Mining Company* was formed. Large numbers of British workers and managers came to the area and there are a number of quaint reminders of their influence today. It was the British who brought their sports of cricket, football and golf to the area. Football immediately became popular with the Spanish workers and it is a little known fact that Spain's very first football club was founded here in 1889. The team, known as *Real Club Recreativo de Huelva*, played its first match in 1890 against a club formed by British ex-pats in Sevilla. The mines were sold back to the Spanish government in 1954.

Driving into Río Tinto (population 6,013), one can appreciate the paternal nature of the company, which has provided many facilities for the community. Look out for the Barrio de Bella Vista, a Victorian estate built specifically for the English workers, complete with church, tennis courts and swimming pool. There are remnants of the high perimeter wall built to deter fraternization with the 'natives'. It's hard to believe that the tranquil Barrio, with its pretty English gardens, lawns and trees, is a mere stone's throw from the devastated landscape of Cerro Colorado.

Museo Minero

This museum is an absolute gem and has already established itself as one of the major theme museums in Andalucía

An absolute must on a visit to this area is this outstanding mining museum, which is housed in the former hospital built by the English for the miners in 1927. Unfortunately, virtually all the information on display in the museum is in Spanish, as are the tours around the Roman mines and Corta Atalaya (see below). There is still enough to see, however, to make a visit worthwhile for non-Spanish speakers.

A superb geological section has display of fossils, rocks and minerals in abundance. In the same room are local flora and fauna, although one wonders how any wildlife at all survives in the lunar landscape outside. The latest addition to the museum, opened in mid-2001, is a reproduction of a Roman mine. This consists of a tunnel running underneath the museum, complete with two huge water wheels and the sights and sounds of Roman slaves working the rock. To get an idea of the sheer scale of devastation and the gradual relocation of the village caused by mining operations, see the four mini-relief maps showing the stages of expansion from 1892 to 1987. One of the most engrossing parts of the museum is the railway section. On taking over the mines, the Anglo-German company built a railway line to the coast at Huelva to export the minerals. The most delightful exhibit is the Maharajah's Carriage, which was built in Birmingham in 1892 for Queen Victoria's visit to India. She never went (despite being Empress) and the carriage was sold to Río Tinto, who used it for the visit to the mines by King Alfonso XIII.

It is nowadays considered to be the most luxurious narrow gauge passenger carriage in the world. There is also a cafetería at the museum selling drinks and sandwiches. ■ *Daily 1030-1500 and 1600-1900 (closed 1 Jan, 6 Jan and 25 Dec). €2.50, children €1.80. Tours around the whole complex, including the museum, Corta Atalaya mine and the railway, can be booked at the museum, €13.25, children €10.95; museum and Corta Atalaya, €6, children €4.95. T959590025, www.aventuraminaparque.org Getting there: follow the signs from the village; coming from the C461 or Aracena, take a right at the first roundabout (where the large Ayuntamiento is being restored) and left at the second. If on foot, take the path up hill on the second roundabout.*

There is also a 22-km round trip taking two to three hours in a restored train dating from the early 20th century. The train travels along a refurbished line that follows the course of the Río Tinto towards Huelva. On the first Sunday of every month, October to May, trips are available on a steam train. ■ *Sat, Sun and holidays, 1400, 1600 or 1700, depending on the time of year (daily – including holidays – Jul-Sep). €8.50, children €7.25. Steam train trips, adults €12, children €10.95.*

There are five open-cast mines around Río Tinto, the largest being Corta Atalaya. It is also one of the oldest, having been worked since Phoenician times. Standing on the edge of the mine is like peering down into a huge man-made volcano, although instead of spitting hot lava there is a lake – as big as two football pitches – full of bright orange acid. Since the fall in copper prices in the mid-1980s the mine has been virtually closed, with only five workers employed to do basic maintenance. Rather bizarrely, a golf course has been created next to the mine. Like the construction of the top-notch *Hotel Santa Bárbara* (see Sleeping below), this is probably to attract more tourists to the area. It is also an attempt to landscape the area around Corta Atalaya – although given the unbelievable scale of destruction, it will take more than a golf course and pine and eucalyptus trees to rejuvenate the area. ■ *Excellent guided tours in Spanish only are available from the Museo Minero (see above), 1200, 1300, 1400 and 1700 (also 1800 Apr-Oct). €4.25, children €3.50.*

Corta Atalaya & Cerro Colorado
At 1,200 m long, 900 m wide and 335 m deep, Corta Atalaya is Europe's largest open-cast copper mines

The other main open-cast mine, Corta Cerro Colorado, is located on the road to Aracena, which passes right through it. There is a viewing platform from where you can see the mining operations with the enormous earth-moving equipment dwarfed by the precipitous side of the quarry. Next to the main mining offices at La Dehesa village just past the mine is a recently unearthed Roman graveyard. Entry is, unfortunately, only for guided tour groups organized through the Museo Minero (see above), but from the roadside a number of stone coffins can be seen lying around under the trees.

On the Aracena road heading north, 5 km out of Río Tinto, are several small reservoirs with strangely coloured turquoise water. However, with the pungent smell of sulphur, dead vegetation and a notice stating 'Danger, do not bathe. Acid Water', you won't be tempted to swim.

C *Santa Bárbara*, Cerro de los Embusteros, T959591852, F959590627, sta.barb @teleline.es Situated on the top of a hill with great panoramic views of Río Tinto and environs is this newish upmarket hotel. For some strange reason the hotel's ostriches are made a feature, even figuring in its promotional leaflet. Maybe this is part of the village's attempts to breathe (wild)life into an area made barren by mining. Comfortable rooms with balcony, TV, a/c. Restaurant, pool; price includes breakfast. **D** *Hostal Los Cantos*, Nucleo Residencial Los Cantos, left just after *Hostal Galan*, T959591689.

Sleeping & eating

Huelva Province

20 basic and rather characterless a/c rooms with bath, above a restaurant and bar serving cheap and varied tapas, pizzas and set meals. **D** *Hostal Galan*, Grupo Romero Villa, 200 m from the Centro de Salud next to the museum, T959590840. Similar to *Hostal Cantos*; clean rooms have a/c and bath. The restaurant below serves slightly pricier food than *Los Cantos*.

Sierra de Aracena

The Sierra Morena, which forms the north boundary of Huelva province, consists of wooded gently rolling hills, subdivided into a number of lesser sierras. The most scenic is the Sierra de Aracena. The Parque Natural de Sierra de Aracena and Picos de Aroche covers some 184,000 ha and boasts 90% woodland cover, as well as an impressive rollcall of wildlife, like black and white storks, the rare black vulture, red and black kites, stone martens, polecats, genets and even the odd lynx.

The area is bisected by the N433, which runs from north of Sevilla to the Portuguese border. The improvement of this road as part of the Expo 92 celebrations has, to some minds, irrevocably transformed the area. Before, a journey from Sevilla took twice its present 1½ hours, meandering its laconic way through the pretty whitewashed villages and extensive groves of sweet chestnuts, indigenous oaks and cork trees characteristic of the Sierra. Now, Sevillanos flock to the Sierra at weekends and holidays, but despite its relative accessibility, few foreign visitors venture here.

Although seemingly hot in summer by North European standards, the Sierra is positively air-conditioned compared with the furnace-like heat of Sevilla in July and August. The summer is a good time to join in with the exuberent fiestas in the villages, who's inhabitants know how to party with week-long celebrations, bullfights and processions. The best time to visit, however, is in spring, when an incredible profusion of wild flowers colonize a still-verdant Sierra. Or in autumn, when the sweet chestnut trees are ablaze and orchards are laden with fruit.

With a myriad of mule tracks linking the villages, this is also excellent walking country. Several guides are available, unfortunately only produced in Spanish. *Andar por la Sierra de Aracena*, by Pablo José Romero Gomez (Penthalon, 1991: Madrid), is a good starting point. Most hotels have the book for reference and may let you photocopy relevant sections. Another useful book is *Sierra de Aracena y Picos de Aroche*, by Luis Fernando García Barrón and María Márquez Rodríguez (Ananya Touring Club, 1998: Madrid) which describes six routes by road and 15 by foot. The Natural Park of the Sierra de Aracena can provide free maps – one covering 64 walks – at its information centres in Aracena and Cortegana, in the Cabildo Viejo and the Castillo, respectively (see below). The best guidebook of the area is the *Sierra de Aracena y Picos de Aroche: Recorrido Natural and Cultural*, by Antonio Fajardo de la Fuente and Amalia Tarín Alcalá-Zamora (1999). This has in-depth coverage on all aspects of life in the Sierra, past and present, and is well illustrated with many photos and maps. Also see the useful website www.sierradearacena.net, in English and Spanish, which details history, fiestas, walks, hotels, restaurants and much more in the area.

Five of the best: views in the Sierra

- Castle, Aracena
- Viewpoint on the Aracena-Castañuelo road
- Peña de Arias Montano, Alájar
- Castle, Cortegana

Aracena

An attractive market town set in the heart of the Sierra, Aracena makes a good base to explore the area. Dominating the town is the hill to the south capped with a church and a ruined castle. The view from the castle hill over the town is spectacular. The church, the **Iglesia de Nuestra Señora de los Dolores**, was built by the Knights Templar in the 13th century. The Mudéjar tower is decorated with brickwork reminiscent of Sevilla's Giralda. Inside are some elaborately carved altarpieces and fine ironwork doors. Dating from Moorish times, the **castle** was built by the Portuguese on the remains of an Andalucían fortification. It is possible to drive up, passing through a striking 16th-century brick gateway, which also acts as a belfry.

Below the hill is the Plaza Alta, a large cobbled sloping square around which most of Aracena's oldest buildings are located. The square is dominated by the Gothic Mudéjar **Iglesia de Nuestra Señora de la Asunción**, complete with stork nests on its towerless roof. The church was begun in the early 16th century and was left unfinished in 1603. In 1970 work recommenced but the building is still not complete and a peep through the cracks in the door will show builders and masons still at work. Opposite the church is the **Cabildo Viejo**, which houses the excellent **visitors' centre** for the Parque Natural de la Sierra de Aracena. It sells books and maps of the area and has excellent permanent displays on all aspects of *serrano* life, from food and fiestas to flora and fauna. Unfortunately much of the information is in Spanish, but there are enough maps and pictures to compensate. The helpful staff speak some English. ■ *Daily, 1000-1400, 1600-1800 (winter), 1800-2000 (summer). Plaza Alta, T/F959128825.*

Nearby is the beautifully restored 16th-century **ayuntamiento**, the oldest in the province. In the more modern part of the town life revolves around the elegant Plaza de Aracena, where there are a number of tapas possibilities.

Most people come to Aracena to see the Gruta de las Maravillas (the Cave of the Marvels), an impressive maze of 12 caves of over 2 km (half of which are open to the public) and six incredibly beautiful lakes that lie deep below the castle on the hill. In terms of limestone redeposition structures it is probably the best in Spain. Its stalactites, stalagmites, pillars, organ pipes and tufa screens are lit with low orange lighting giving them a somewhat surreal glow. This atmosphere of unreality is compounded by the occasional background music (said to be specially written for the cave) and the natural glittery quality of the formations. The caves were discovered by a boy looking for a lost pig (amazing how many Spanish caves are discovered by small boys), and were opened in 1914. The last of the caverns, known as the 'Chamber of the Nudes', has some extraordinary rounded redeposition features resembling various parts of the human anatomy, leaving little to the imagination and ensuring that everyone leaves the caves having had a good laugh. ■ *1030-1500 and 1430-1800. €6. Obligatory guided tours in Spanish only; the time of the tour is given when buying a ticket. Plaza San Pedro, T959128355.*

Also here is the local **tourist office**, which has some maps and information – most of which you have to pay for – and details of accommodation in the Sierra (including *casas rurales*), but is not nearly as helpful and informative as the visitors' centre in the Cabildo Viejo (see above). ■ *Opening times as the Gruta booking office (see above), T959128206.* Near the booking office is an interesting geological museum, with over 1,000 specimens from all over the world (but none from the cave). In the streets and squares around the cave is a

Colour map 1, grid B3
Population: 6,800
Altitude: 730 m

Gruta de las Maravillas

Huelva Province

permanent **Outdoor Museum of Modern Sculpture**. Although none of the sculptors are internationally known and the standard varies from brilliant to ridiculous, the idea is a good one.

A good way to cool off after a hard day's sightseeing is to visit the municipal **swimming pool**, about five minutes' walk from the Gruta (follow the signposts). There is a decent-sized pool and a children's pool with some shaded areas, a children's play area and a good bar/restaurant. ■ *Mon-Fri 1100-1900, Sat, Sun and holidays 1200-2000. €2.50 (except Sat and holidays, €1.80).*

Alternatively, you could head out of town for a dip in the **Embalse de Aracena**, a huge reservoir surrounded by trees. During the driest months, this can shrink considerably to reveal the former bridges, buildings and even trees submerged when the reservoir was created. ■ *Getting there: Take the road from the centre of town signposted Finca Valbono on C de la Infante del Real – the first left after the market coming from the main plaza – until you reach the Ermita de Nuestra Señora los Angeles. Take the road to the left under the bridge. Go through Carboneras towards Cañaveral de León. Alternatively, take the N433 towards Sevilla and turn left after 3 km to Corteconcepción, and then head towards Cañaveral de León.*

Sleeping
See inside front cover for price codes

C *Los Castaños*, Av de Huelva 5, T959126300, F959126287. A similar hotel to the *Sierra de Aracena*, reasonable but nothing special, with 33 comfortable rooms, garage, restaurant, a stone's throw from the caves. Not the quietest hotel; disco across the road can get a bit noisy late at night, as can the construction site next door (for a new theatre due to open in 2002) during the day. **D** *Sierra de Aracena*, Gran Vía 21, T959126175,

Aracena

Not to scale

Sleeping
1 Casa Manolo
2 Los Castaños
3 Sierra de Aracena

Eating
1 Bar Casa Sirlache
2 Bar Manzano
3 José Vicente
4 Mesón Camino Real
5 Rincón de Juan
6 Sierpes

F959126218. A central hotel with 50 a/c rooms, TV, bath, wheelchair access, restaurant. Also runs *Finca Valbono* (see below). **E** *Casa Manolo*, C Barbero 6, T959128014. The only budget hotel in town. Central, some shared bath.

Outside Aracena AL *Finca Buen Vino*, Km 95 on the N433, Los Marines, T/F959124034, buenvino@facilnet.es. English-run farmhouse converted into an elegant and beautifully furnished guesthouse with 4 rooms, set in woodland 6 km west of Aracena. Fabulous views and outstanding food (Jeannie also runs cookery courses; see www.patanegra.net). Price includes breakfast and dinner. Cottages (each with pool) cost €965 per week. Booking essential. Recommended. **C** *Finca Valbono*, Ctra de Carboneras, Km 1, T959127711, F959127576. Located 2 km from Aracena; take the road from the town centre signposted to the finca on C de la Infante del Real – the first left after the market coming from the main plaza – until you reach the Ermita de Nuestra Señora Los Angeles. Take the road to the left under the bridge for Carboneras. Under the same ownership as *Hotel Sierra de Aracena* (see above), Finca Valbono is a 20 ha farm with a luxurious 6-room hotel and 20 cottages to rent in a beautiful setting. Each cottage sleeps 3-5 and has a/c and TV. Horseriding, cycle hire, swimming pool, restaurant and volleyball court. **E** *Granja Escuela El Barrial*, 9 km from Aracena on the Corterrangel road, T959-501001. This so-called 'farm school' – with 8 cabañas, campsite, pool, bar/restaurant – is situated in a spectacular position on top of a hill with fantastic views. It's worth stopping at the viewpoint 3 km along the road from Aracena. The road passes through 2 tiny villages, Castañuelo and Corterrangel, the latter with the second oldest church in the Sierra. Turn right at the plaza in Corterrangel and follow the road around the square. Up the hill 200 m is a gate for El Barrial. From there, it's another 750 m up a steep gravel track. A 30-min walk along the remains of a Roman road brings you to neighbouring Cortelazor. Since El Barrial may have school parties staying, ring first to see if there is space.

Since the accommodation options are rather limited within Aracena, it's worth looking outside the town for something a bit different

Camping *Camping Aracena Sierra*, Ctra Sevilla-Lisboa Km 83, T959501004. Just off the N433, 3 km from Aracena towards Sevilla, is this campsite, with some shaded areas, a pool and bar/restaurant. Next to it is a picnic and barbecue area.

Expensive *José Vicente*, Av Andalucía, 200 m from the bus station away from the centre. If you're feeling extravagant, head here to enjoy locally produced pork and ham at its best (try the succulent *solomillo*). Huge portions served in a/c and pampered comfort, but no fish or vegetarian options. A *menú* will set you back €15, but you won't need to eat for a week. *Venta de Aracena*, on the N433 to Sevilla. Slightly cheaper than *Jose Vicente*, this restaurant also serves excellent local pork specialities, in an attractive rustic restaurant, furnished with beautifully hand-painted *serrano* furniture. Opens every lunchtime and Fri and Sat evenings.

Eating
On map opposite
See inside front cover for price classifications

To Finca Valbono (2 km), Carboneras & Embalse de Aracena
Ermita de Nuestra Señora Los Angeles
Av de Andalucía
N433
Parque de Arias Montano
To Venta de Aracena Restaurant, Camping Aracena Sierra (3 km) & Sevilla

Huelva Province

Mid-range *Sierpes*, C Mesones 13, just to the left of the Convento del Carmen, T959128746. Good value *menu del día*; opens evenings.

Cheap There are a number of restaurants around the caves, but most close evenings; the best bet for food in the evening is to sample the tapas in the many excellent bars in and around the main plaza, such as *Bar Manzano* and *Bar Gran Vía*. *Bar Casa Sirlache*, a few doors' down from *Jose Vicente* restaurant, T959128888. Extensive menu of cheap tapas (also in English), open evenings, closed Wed. *Mesón Camino Real*, Av Reina de los Angeles 10, on the road to the Piscina Municipal a few mins' walk from the Gruta, T959127292. This cheerful bar serves a wide range of the best (and slightly pricier) tapas in town, including mushrooms and asparagus (in season), as well as great breakfasts – try the *jamón Ibérico de bellota* on *tostada* with coffee for €4.25. Closed Mon; seating outside costs an extra 20%. *Rincón de Juan*, up from *Almacenes Carmen* near the Convento del Carmen, is a great little bar serving good cheap tapas. Opens for breakfast at 0700. *Panadería Rafalito*, C Rosal, sells the best bread in the Sierra. You can either visit the bakery itself (take the first left off the Gran Vía from the plaza; turn right at the end and look out for the Panadería sign on the right) or buy it from many shops throughout the Sierra; ask for *pan Rafalito*. *Confitería Rufino*, C Constitución, just off the plaza, sells a variety of delicious cakes and sweets.

Entertainment & nightlife The main evening activity centres on the plaza, where people hang out on the plaza itself, or go for a *paseo* – or stroll – stopping for beers and tapas at one of the many bars. There are a few **discotecas** where the younger inhabitants of Aracena hang out, like *Malhaman* and *Jumping*, on the road left at the end of Gran Vía. There is no **cinema** or theatre building as such, although a new municipal theatre – designed by the same architect as Cortegana's theatre; a somewhat worrying prospect – is under construction next to the *Castaños* hotel and is due to be completed in 2002. However, there is a thriving **cultural scene** in Aracena, with many films, plays, exhibitions and concerts on regularly at various locations in the town, including the Instituto San Blas at the end of the Gran Vía. To find out what's on where, check out the noticeboard in the plaza opposite *Bar Manzano*. During the summer months,

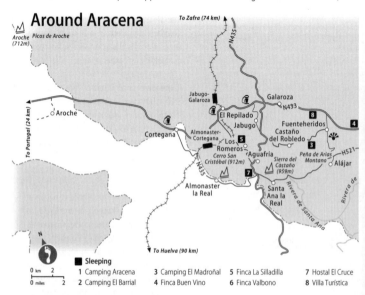

Around Aracena

To Zafra (74 km)

Aroche Picos de Aroche
(712m)

To Portugal (24 km)

Aroche

Cortegana

Jabugo-Galaroza

Galaroza

N433

El Repilado

Jabugo

Almonaster-Cortegana

Los Romeros

Aguafria

Cerro San Cristóbal (912m)

Fuenteheridos

Castaño del Robledo

Sierra del Castaño (959m)

Peña de Arias Montano

Alájar

H521

Rivera de Santa Ana

Almonaster la Real

Santa Ana la Real

To Huelva (90 km)

N

0 km 2
0 miles 2

■ **Sleeping**
1 Camping Aracena
2 Camping El Barrial
3 Camping El Madroñal
4 Finca Buen Vino
5 Finca La Silladilla
6 Finca Valbono
7 Hostal El Cruce
8 Villa Turística

films are screened outdoors on Fri and Sat evenings at the municipal pool (see under Sights above), where there is also a bar/restaurant.

Bus Many villages in the Sierra are accessible by public transport, but because bus services are not always frequent, travelling by bus requires a certain amount of pre-planning. 2 companies serve Aracena, *Damas* (for Huelva) and *Casal* (for Seville and Aroche). To **Huelva**, 0700 and 0800 Mon-Sat. To **Sevilla**, 0745 and 1700 Mon-Sat, 1030 and 1700 Sun and holidays. To **Cortegana** and **Aroche** (calling at intermediate villages along N433), 0730, 1030, 1315, 1730 Mon-Sat; 1030, 1730 Sun and holidays (from Cortegana to Aracena: 0625, 0900, 1400, 1555 Mon-Sat; 0940, 1610 Sun and holidays). To Cortegana via Linares, Alájar, Santa Ana and Almonaster: 1300 and 1730 Mon-Sat, returning from Cortegana 0635 and 1530. Bus office in Aracena , T959128196 (open 0900-1030, 1130-1315, 1600-1730).

Transport
104 km N of Huelva
89 km NW of Sevilla

Train From El Repilado to **Zafra**, daily 2111; to **Fregenal de la Sierra**, 1502 (1137 holidays). To **Huelva**, daily 0719 and 1704. For more information, contact the RENFE station at El Repilado, T959122674.

Communications Internet: *Ar@net*, Plaza de Abastos (in the market), T629118254. Friendly internet café/bar serving drinks and sandwiches, some outside seating, internet €2.75 per hour, open daily 1000-1500 (Sun 1200-1500), 1730-2400. **Medical services** *Centro de Salud*, T959126053.

Directory

Huelva Province

Fuenteheridos

This pretty village just off the N433 8 km from Aracena is named after its magnificent fountain, the Fuente de Doce Caños, or 12-piped fountain, situated in the plaza. The sheer volume of water that passes through the fountain is astounding – an estimated two million litres a day. A good time to visit Fuenteheridos is on a warm evening, when you can enjoy a cool beer and some tasty tapas outside one of the bars clustered around two tiny plazas.

Colour map 1, grid B3
Population: 677
Altitude: 717 m

As with all serrano villages, this is a prime spot to watch the world go by – which, in the case of Fuenteheridos, can seem rather busy for such a small place. The central plaza has an 18th-century marble cross in its centre, a tribute to the nearby marble quarries that used to generate much of the village's income. Around the plaza are some of the village's oldest houses – including the one housing *Mesón La Posá* (see below) – many with pots of geraniums suspended from balconies. Up a cobbled street by *Bar El Niño* is the grand 18th-century **Iglesia de Espíritu Santo**, with a typical *serrano* spire of blue-and- white tiles. ■ *Open 30 mins before a service.*

Sights

One kilometre outside Fuenteheridos on the N433 towards

Cortegana are the Sierra's only botanical gardens, **Villa Onuba**. Created over a century ago by the German engineer Guillermo Sundheim, who was in charge of the Huelva-Zafra railway, the gardens are today the residence of the Hermanos Maristas. The paths through the gardens, shaded by over 120 different species of trees, shrubs and plants, provide a cool respite from the heat of the summer months. ■ *0900-1330, 1500-1800, closed to the public during the spiritual retreats of the Maristas. Free. T/F959125135.*

Sleeping **B** *Villa Turística*, signposted just off the N433 outside Fuenteheridos, T959125202, F959125199, villatfh@arrakis.es This purpose-built hotel complex – or 'tourist village' – is one of 8 in Andalucía. An upmarket mini-Andalucian hamlet with all the obligatory whitewashed walls, exposed beams, terracotta-tiled floors and open fireplaces with all mod cons (but little charm). Luxuries include a/c, swimming pool, laundry, restaurant and babysitting service. Its 41 self-catering villas each have a bedroom, living room and courtyard. **E** *Hostal Carballo*, C La Fuente, T/F959125108, hostalcarballo@latinmail .com This friendly hotel has 7 rooms; the front ones have a balcony overlooking a quiet cobbled street while the back ones – along with an upstairs terrace – have great views over the village rooftops and surrounding countryside. It's worth booking ahead during the summer.

Camping *El Madroñal*, 3 km from the N433 just before Fuenteheridos from Aracena and 1 km from the village plaza, T959501201/669434637 (mob). Located on the road to Castaño del Robledo, this lovely shaded campsite is set in a 6 ha wood of sweet chestnuts and oaks. It has 2 pools, a bar/restaurant, barbecue area and bicycles for hire, as well as wooden cabañas (€39.75 a weekend, €105.50 a week).

Eating There are several good restaurants serving fine local specialities at reasonable prices, including the small *Mesón La Posá* on the plaza, T959125178 and the *Restaurante Biarritz* and its sister across the road, *Mesón Biarritz*, T959125088 and T959125152, respectively. As well as the usual choice of pork and ham dishes, the *Biarritz* has a good selection of fish dishes (try the *pez espada*), great homemade *albondigas* and *croquetas*.

Festivals **30 May** Fiesta for the village patron saint, Espíritu Santo. **15 Aug** Procession to the fountain in honour of the Virgen de la Fuente. **Sep** The village also takes part in the *Romería* at the Peña de Arias Montano (see page 144). **Dec** *Fiesta de la Castaña*, to celebrate the harvest of sweet chestnuts, which are a major source of income for many *serrano* villages.

Castaño del Robledo

Population: less than 300
Altitude: 738 m

Four kilometres from Fuenteheridos – along a beautiful road lined with the sweet chestnut trees that give Castaño del Robledo its name – is this tiny village. The *castaños*, which cover more hectares here than anywhere else in the Sierra, were planted by the newly arrived Galicians and Castilians in the 16th century to replace the ancient groves of indigenous oaks. Sweet chestnuts were – and still are – prized for their use as food for both animals and humans and have been an important source of income for serrano villages for many years (see also box). Castaño del Robledo, like the sweet chestnuts around it, seems as if it's remained unchanged for centuries; indeed, many houses date from the 16th and 18th centuries and the centre itself was completed in the late 1700s. In the heart of the village is the Baroque church, the Iglesia de Santiago, where Arias Montano (see page 144) was the parish priest in the 16th century when the church was built. Inside is the province's oldest organ, dating from

Five of the best: tapas bars in the Sierra

- *Biarritz,* Fuenteheridos
- *La Bodeguita,* Castaño del Robledo
- *El Molino,* Jabugo
- *Mesón Camino Real,* Aracena
- *Las Palmitas,* Alájar

1750. It is interesting that the main – but tiny – square with its Ayuntamiento are situated behind the church. Shaded by elm trees, the plaza is a good place to stop on a sunny day. Two bars provide seating most of the year; one of them, the lively, small *Bar La Bodeguita,* has some interesting old photos on its walls and serves limited, but delicious, tapas. There are also a few small shops; *Rincón de Pepe* sells *serrano* ham products, as well as chestnuts in autumn. Castaño's other, larger church – the Iglesia Inacabada del Cementerio, or Iglesia Nueva – is on the left as you enter the village from Fuenteheridos. Started in 1788, it was supposed to supersede the smaller Iglesia de Santiago. Like elsewhere in the Sierra, there was a population boom in the 18th century. But whereas most villages doubled in size, the population of Castaño (and Jabugo) increased six-fold. By 1793, money ran out for the new church and it remains unfinished today. ■ *Ask for the key in the* ayuntamiento. Behind the church is an 18th-century fountain with a water trough.

There are several good **walks** from the village. On the right of the road towards Fuenteheridos is a footpath leading, after a 30-minute-walk, to the Sierra's highest point at 962 m, the Sierra del Castaño (known locally as Los Riscos Altos). One of the most beautiful walks in the Sierra is from Castaño to Jabugo. Leaving Castaño on the Fuenteheridos road, you go past a bar on your left and 100 m later is a track leading to a picnic area and a whitewashed shrine. The path starts to the right of the shrine, where there is post marked with two red arrows; take the wider track, to the left of the post. The trail goes through a shaded area, past a few fields of Iberian pigs snuffling around for acorns, before opening out with wonderful views across the Sierra towards Jabugo. South of the village is a signposted path to Santa Ana starting from the cemetery and passing near the Ollarancos waterfall, known locally as the Chorros de Santa Ana.

Santa Ana la Real

The narrow, winding road from Castaño to Santa Ana passes through woodland of mainly cork trees, until it reaches the N435. Turn left here towards Zalamea; about 200 m later is an excellent viewpoint and picnic area on the right. Just past the tiny village of Aguafría at the N435-A470 crossroads is the **D** *Hostal-Restaurante El Cruce,* T/F959122333. It has seven rooms with bath, good views from the rooms at the back and a pretty shaded terrace bordered by roses and bougainvillaea. This is the closest restaurant and hotel to Santa Ana, which has neither. Santa Ana is 1½ km away on the A470.

One of the smallest villages in the Sierra, Santa Ana is perched on top of a hill with glorious views over the Sierra. Just down from the plaza is a great place to watch the sun set, as the village drops away to the west. The tiny leafy plaza with its Neoclassical parish church has some beautifully tiled benches. There are a few bars here serving limited tapas. Tucked away on the right by the entrance to Santa Ana is the whitewashed Ermita de San Bartolomé.

Around the village are some excellent walks to Santa Ana's surrounding areas, such as La Presa 1½ km away, with its enormous oak and cork trees. To get there, take Calle Fuente from the plaza and follow it to the end, then turn

Colour map 1, grid B3
Population: 505
Altitude: 680 m

Huelva Province

right passing the Fuente de los Tres Caños, next to a large walnut tree; this fountain also provides water for the adjoining washhouse. Continue down the cobbled track, which passes vegetable gardens and cork trees, to La Presa. Another good walk is to the waterfall at Los Chorros de Ollarancos; with a 50 m drop, this is the highest waterfall in the Sierra. To get there, walk out of Santa Ana on the Alájar road for 1 km and around the Km 17 sign, next to a bend in the road and a bridge, is a track to the Chorros. Alternatively, you can go via a path marked PRA-38 towards Alájar or Castaño, starting at the Fuente de los Tres Caños and passing through La Presa, a walk of four to five kilometres.

Alájar

Colour map 1, grid B3
Population: 864

It's not hard to see why this beautiful village, surrounded by olive and pine trees, has become increasingly popular over the last decade, with its narrow cobbled streets radiating from two small attractive plazas, perfect places to stop for a beer and tapas. However, the village can also get very crowded on summer weekends, so much so that it is impossible to park in the centre. The **Iglesia de San Marcos**, a surprisingly big church for less than 900 villagers, was extended in the late 17th century to accommodate Alájar's swelling population, which at its peak reached 2,000. Inside the church, the 18th-century figure of San Marcos was the church's sole survivor of the civil war's destruction of religious objects. ■ *Open during services, 2000 Mon-Fri, 2100 Sat, 1100 Sun; outside of these times ask for the key at the flower-bedecked house to the right of the Ayuntamiento.*

Sleeping
See inside front cover
for price codes

AL *Molino Río Alájar*, Finca Cabeza del Molino s/n, 1 km from Alájar signposted off the road to Santa Ana, T959501282. In a beautiful wooded spot by a mill pond are these delightful stone *casas rurales*, individually furnished with antiques. TV, heating, pool. Good walks in surrounding countryside; mule rides also available. Produce of organic garden included in price. **D** *La Posada*, C Médico Emilio González 2, T/F959125712, hotel.laposada@navegalia.com This pretty hotel, the only place to stay in the village itself, has 6 comfortable en-suite rooms, some with balcony. Horse riding, walking trips and mountain bike hire available. Restaurant; price includes breakfast.

Eating
Alájar has an excellent
choice of restaurants
and tapas bars

Mesón Restaurante El Corcho, T959125779 (closed Tue, except holidays). On the Plaza de España, opposite the Ayuntamiento, is this excellent but slightly pricey bar and restaurant. It lives up to its name; there is a profusion of *corcho*, or cork – an elaborately sculptured ceiling as well as shelves and stools in the bar – with the cork theme continuing in the restaurant. The bar serves some great tapas, including the *langostino a la plancha* (grilled king prawns). *El Molino*, up the hill by *Bar La Parra*, is in a beautifully restored rustic building of a former water mill. If you find the restaurant too expensive, you can admire the water wheel while having a drink and some tapas instead. Open at weekends only, apart Jul-Sep, when it's open daily except Mon. Another fine restaurant with a great outdoor terrace is *El Padrino*, by the church. Cheaper food is available at the a/c *Las Palmitas*, on the right as you enter the village. If you're really ravenous, try their *serranito*.

Peña de Arias Montano

Altitude: 900 m

AOne reason many come to Alájar is to visit the Peña de Arias Montano, situated 1 km out of the village on the road to Fuenteheridos. Here is a shrine sitting on top of a rocky outcrop, the Peña itself, which protrudes dramatically from the near-vertical hillside giving a perfect bird's eye view of Alájar and the hills towards the south. It's a view that, apart from the odd car and swimming pool, seems as if it's been unchanged for centuries. Understandably, the Peña is a popular tourist spot; its car park has been expanded in recent years to accommodate the coachloads of visitors who descend, particularly in summer months. It's worth visiting when the place is more deserted; early in the morning is a good time to avoid the crowds and the heat in summer. Then you can appreciate why the theologian and poet Arias Montano (1527-98), who gave the Peña his name, chose this place for his retreat. Born in Fregenal de la Sierra 40 km to the north, Arias Montano was the royal chaplain, confessor and political adviser to Felipe II, whose visit to the Peña in 1578 is celebrated with a monolith by the belfry. Parish priest in nearby Castaño del Robledo, Montano restored the hermitage, the Ermita de Nuestra Señora de los Angeles, which is still here today; a somewhat plain whitewashed building which is nonetheless elaborately decorated inside. Next to the hermitage is the impressive belfry.

Hidden deep inside the Peña is a warren of limestone caves, which according to the letters of Arias Montano, contain stalagmites, stalactites and underground lakes similar to those in the Gruta de las Maravillas in Aracena (see page 137). From these caverns comes the abundant water that feeds the profusion of springs at the Peña. Several of these can be seen just above the car park. On the level below the belfry, if you take the steps down to the right, you can peer through a locked gate at the entrance to the caves. Also here is a restaurant (with a cheap *menú del día,* €4.80), above some mediocre ceramic and souvenir shops, as well as a small garden and picnic-barbecue area next to the car park.

The Peña is host to the famous annual **Romería de los Angeles**, in honour of the patron saint of the Sierra. Held during the first weekend of September, many surrounding villages participate. Processions leave villages early in the morning, converging on the Peña around midday for an afternoon of eating and drinking. It was created in 1924 by the wealthy Francisco Sánchez Dalp, the Marquéz of Aracena and Aracena's Conservative parliamentary member for 30 years. He was also responsible for opening the Gruta de las Maravillas in 1914 and an ambitious building programme in Aracena – including the Casino in the main square – using the architect Aníbal González, famous for his designs in Sevilla's 1929 Exhibition.

Almonaster la Real

The name Almonaster comes from the Arabic *al-Munastyr*, taken from the Latin *Monasterium*, and the village is still dominated today by the 10th-century *mezquita*, or **mosque**, on the hill to the south of the town. Unlike most Andalucían mosques, it was not destroyed or altered after the Reconquest (although it was consequently used as the Ermita de Nuestra Señora de la Concepción). This means that today you can see a perfectly preserved minaret, a *mihrab*, reputedly the oldest in Spain, and an interior with five naves showing some superb brick horseshoe arches. The columns appear to have come from the original Roman buildings on the site. Next to the mosque is the 19th-century bullring, which seats 1,200 and is used for a bullfight in the village's fiesta in August. The mosque is usually open during the day, but if it's not, ask for the key in the Ayuntamiento in the pretty Plaza de la Constitución, bordered by orange trees. In this plaza is the whitewashed 18th-century Ermita de la Trinidad, a bar and a few shops. Also worth a look is the parish church, the 14th-century **Iglesia de San Martín**, with bushes and a massive stork's nest sprouting out of the belfry beneath its tiled spire. It has an

Colour map 1, grid B3
Population: 2,418
Altitude: 610 m

Huelva Province

interesting façade in the Portuguese-influenced Manuelino style, which was added in the early 16th century. If possible, time your visit to coincide with the **Fiesta de las Cruces de Mayo**, held during the first weekend in May and one of the best in Andalucía. Other cultural events in Almonaster include Medieval music concerts and Muslim religious services held in the mosque.

Just outside the village on the road to the N435 and Jabugo is a signpost for the road up to the Cerro San Cristóbal, which at 917 m is the second highest point of the Sierra de Aracena. It has spectacular panoramic views of the Sierra and, on a clear day, far beyond. You can either drive up a signposted 4 km road to the summit or, if you're feeling fit, follow a scenic track lined with stone walls, up past fruit orchards and through oak and cork woodland. The start of the trail can be found opposite a mirador marked by some fine palm trees (with great views of the mosque and village below), on the same road to the N435 and Jabugo; look out for an information board on your left.

Sleeping
& eating

D *Casa García*, Av San Martín 2 (on the right as you enter the village), T959143109, F959143143. Recently upgraded hotel, with 22 comfortable rooms; bath, a/c, TV, heating. A pool is planned for 2002. Upmarket restaurant serves the usual local specialities and has an outside terrace. **E** *Hostal La Cruz*, Plaza del Llano 8 (down some steps from the Iglesia de San Martín), T959143135. 6 simple rooms with bath. Good bar/restaurant downstairs. Apart from the 2 hotel restaurants, options for eating out are rather limited. With by far the best setting is the **mid-range** *Restaurant Las Palmeras*, T959143105, which has a wonderful outside terrace shaded by an incredible profusion of pot plants, vines and the eponymous palm trees. Situated on the main road into Almonaster from the N435, it is a handy place to stop for a drink and some good typical *serrano* food (try the *cocido serrano* in winter, homemade *croquetas*, ham and chorizo).

Cortegana

Colour map 1, grid B3
Population: 5,483
Altitude: 690 m

A less attractive town than Aracena, Cortegana is nevertheless worth a visit for its dramatic hilltop setting and restored **castle**. A good time to climb the 745 m castle hill (although the castle itself will be closed) is early morning, when the hills of the Sierra may be shrouded in mist, or at sunset. In fact, the magnificent panoramic view is one of the best in the Sierra at any time of day. It's not hard to see why Sancho IV ordered a castle to be built here in 1293, as part of the so-called Banda de Gallega. This was a series of fortresses used to prevent a Portuguese invasion during an era of border disputes between the two countries and included the castles of Aracena and Aroche. The castle, built over Moorish remains and showing Romanesque and Gothic influences, has two sections: the Plaza de Armas, a courtyard shaded in summer months, and the Alcázar, on two levels, as well as six towers with superb views. Underneath the courtyard is the *aljibe*, or underground reservoir that still provides water for the castle. The Alcázar houses a small but excellent tourist office and a museum with reproduction suits of armour and Medieval furniture. ■ *Tue-Sun 1100-1400, 1730-1930, €1.20 (voluntary donation), T649265126. Useful websites in Spanish on the castle include: www.terra.es/personal/fructos/cortegana/castillo.htm and http://alcazaba.unex.es/~msorlob* Next to the castle is the Ermita de Nuestra Señora de la Piedad, Cortegana's patron saint. Built during the repopulation period in the 14th-15th centuries, the Ermita's more recent additions include some funky looking angels, verging on caricature, painted on its inside walls. ■ *Daily 0900-1400, 1800-2100*.

Unlike the wide and elegant streets of Aracena, Cortegana's layout is like that of a village, with narrow streets and small plazas. The pretty Plaza del

Divino Salvador with its orange trees, somewhat dilapidated Casino and other several other bars, is named after the imposing **Iglesia del Divino Salvador**. This listed building was built on the site of an ancient Mudéjar church in the 14th century, with Gothic elements added in the late 16th century. It has Baroque pulpits and an impressive collection of gold and silver religious objects dating from the 15th century. Nearby is the equally small Plaza de la Constitución, with an Ayuntamiento and Cortegana's second Casino. This grand building is beautifully decorated inside with Andalucían-Moorish tiles and has comfy sofas, all the daily newspapers and a pool table upstairs.

For short walks around Cortegana, see the leaflet *Senderos de pequeña recorrida en el entorno de Cortegana*, available from the castle's information office.

Sleeping
See inside front cover for price codes

D *Villa Cinta*, Av de las Minas 61, T959131522, http://cintatoscanotripod.com With great views over Cortegana and the surrounding countryside, this *casa rural* has 4 rooms with bath, all beautifully decorated and furnished. Pool and several attractive sun terraces. Price includes breakfast. **E** *Posada Cervantes*, Cervantes 27, signposted from Plaza de la Constitución, T959131592. The only place to stay in the centre, with 10 basic rooms.

Eating

Mid-range *Casa Jaime*, C Eritas B 6, take the turning opposite the petrol station on the N433 as you come into Cortegana, T959131192. Lively restaurant and bar serving good breakfasts and all the usual tapas. *La Peñalta*, C Santa Bárbara, just out of the centre past the Plaza de Toros, T959132240. Small attractive restaurant serving good range of tapas and raciones. *Los Peroles*, C Eritas B 32, T959131352. On the same road as *Casa Jaime*, is this large, rather characterless restaurant, which specializes in *jamón serrano*. Just out of the centre past *La Peñalta* restaurant on the Almonaster road, Av de las Minas, is the bar *El Nogal*, T600270295. This is a great place to enjoy a cheap beer (especially if you buy it in a litre bottle) and tapas, with a spectacular view of the castle and town from a terrace bedecked with grapevines and pots of geraniums.

Entertainment

Opened in 1999 and adjoining an ugly square on C Esperanza, Cortegana's theatre/cinema has a wide range of films (dubbed in Spanish), plays and concerts in its 515-seat auditorium, as well as regular exhibitions. See the notice board outside the theatre for what's on. Tickets cost between €2.50 (for films) and €6 and are sold 1 hr before performances in the ticket office.

Fiestas

Feb *Carnival:* This was revived again in the late 1970s and is great fun; one highlight is the universal throwing of flour and eggs. **Late Jun** *Romería de San Antonio*, La Corte village. This is one of the best *romerías* in Huelva province, with its parade of men in wide-brimmed hats, tight pinstriped trousers and waistcoats on horseback, women flamboyantly dressed in colourful gypsy clothes, some sitting sidesaddle, and flamenco dancing. Families and friends club together for a *caseta*, or marquee, where they eat and drink. But like most *romerías*, this is most fun if you know people who will invite you into the *casetas*. **First weekend of Aug** Excellent *Medieval fair* held in a stupendous and atmospheric setting at the castle and the streets leading up to it, with Medieval music concerts, plays, food stalls, market, children's workshops and exhibitions.

Jabugo

Eighteen kilometres west of Aracena, just south of the N433/N435 crossroads, is the village of Jabugo, the famous centre of the production of cured ham, or *jamón serrano*. Since the early 1980s, this has brought increasing

Colour map 1, grid B3
Population: 2,618
Altitude: 642 m

Huelva Province

prosperity to an area previously suffering from a decline in its income and population. With its large ugly curing factories and abattoirs such as that of *Sánchez Romero Carvajal* (the main employer in this area) littering the outskirts of Jabugo, this isn't one of the Sierra's most attractive villages. But if you're keen to sample Jabugo's famed delicacy, then head for Calle San Juan del Puerto (turn right at the T-junction as you enter Jabugo). This street is lined with excellent shops and restaurants selling ham, including one of the best (and most expensive), the *Mesón Cinco Jotas*, run by the *Sánchez Romero* company (T959121515). Check the prices carefully, however, as *jamón serrano* can be very expensive, particularly the *jamón Ibérico de bellota*. This is the best ham, otherwise known as *pata negra*, which comes from black Iberian pigs fed on acorns only. Also along Calle San Juan are several bars serving good breakfasts.

Alternatively, you could meander down one of the pretty narrow cobbled streets that lead to the small plaza. From Calle San Juan is Calle Barco, where there is a good restaurant, *Mesón Los Romeros*, T959121611. Here you can sample a wide range of *jamón* delicacies, amid the ubiquitous *jamones* hanging from the ceiling and pictures of *jamón* on the walls (like much of Jabugo, this is not the place to come if you're vegetarian). At the end of this street is a rather dilapidated Baroque church, the **Iglesia de San Miguel**. ■ *Open during services (midday on holidays) and in the evening, daily except Mon.* Another good restaurant is located a few minutes' walk from the plaza, down Calle La Fuente. On terraced Plaza de la Constitución (used in summer for outdoor films) is *El Molino* restaurant (T959121059), housed in a converted water mill. It serves excellent pork dishes; especially good are the *secreto* and *lomo*. As elsewhere in Jabugo, options are limited if you don't eat pork or ham, although they could rustle up a fish dish. A good value *menu del día* is available Monday to Friday lunchtimes, otherwise restaurant prices are expensive. There is also a good selection of reasonably priced tapas. During July and August, it's worth cooling down at the local **municipal pool**, which also has a tapas bar. The pool is located on the road out of Jabugo towards the N435.

If you're a bullfight aficionado then visit Jabugo during the second weekend in July for the Fiesta de Nuestra Señora los Remedios. At both this and the Fiesta de San Miguel Arcangel in the last weekend in September bullfights are staged in the local bullring. During both fiestas there are also religious processions, concerts and general partying until the early hours over the whole weekend.

Sleeping & eating With many other more attractive villages around, Jabugo is not an obvious choice for somewhere to stay. **E** *Pensión* Aurora, C Barco 9, T959121146. 11 rooms with bath. **A** *Finca La Silladilla*, just outside Jabugo, 4 km from the N433 in El Repilado towards Los Romeros, T959501350. This 130-ha farm has 4 farm buildings converted to sumptuous cottages. All have beautiful handmade furniture, Portuguese tiles and own design features (the most memorable being a tree growing out of a bathroom ceiling). Cottages have all mod cons, including jacuzzi, TV, CD player. Cured ham served for breakfast is from pigs raised on the farm; an excellent small shop serving other delicious (and expensive) local delicacies, as well as an extensive selection of Spanish wines. There are several pools and one cottage has wheelchair access. T959-501350, www.visionrent.com

El Repilado A religious curiosity is to be found at the nearby train station of El Repilado. Here a small obelisk marks the spot where, near to a Chinese banana tree, an apparition of the Holy Virgin of Fátima revealed itself to a local girl. The occasional pilgrim can still be spotted.

Galaroza

From the N433 road, this attractive village is half-hidden in the small valley it occupies, which winds around the hill of the Ermita de Santa Brígida. Legend has it that the name Galaroza comes from Arabic, meaning the 'promised valley', and with its abundant springs and fountains (40 and 15, respectively), it's not hard to see why. These, and the nearby River Múrtigas, provide water for the village and its plentiful fruit orchards and vegetable plots surrounding it. Until recent decades, Galaroza boasted a bountiful harvest of apples, mainly of the small and sweet Cachón variety, and today the villagers are still known as *cachoneros*. Galaroza's most remarkable celebration of its water is its annual Fiesta de los Jarritos on 6 September, when the entire village – and any casual passers-by – get a thorough soaking. As to its origins, the story goes that sometime around the mid-19th century a group of young *cachoneros* on their way to the *romería* at the Peña de Arias Montano (see page 144) stopped by the Fuente de los Doce Caños, the fountain by the village's main plaza. They started throwing water at each other using *jarritos,* the clay water jugs with a spout used to transport water from the fountains and keep it cool. Today, the more modern plastic bucket is used and the action spills over (literally) from the fountain into the whole village.

Colour map 1, grid B3
Population: 1,657
Altitude: 566 m

During the rest of the year, Galaroza is equally lively, especially during summer evenings around the elegant plaza, where there are many bars with seating in the street. Coming from Aracena, you enter the village by a plaza with the bar and ham shop, *El Rincón de Pepe* on the corner. The track up to the **Ermita de Santa Brígida** is towards the village centre, signposted to the left about 100 m from the plaza. Built in the late 13th century, the building had fallen into disrepair by the 19th century and was being used as a stable before it was restored. From here are superb views over the roofs of Galaroza, with its cluster of houses around the beautiful **Iglesia de la Purísima Concepción**. This fine Neo-classical church, with its typical serrano blue-and-white tiled spire, was completed in 1614 and has some interesting doors. ■ *The church can be visited during Mass: Sat 1930 and 2030, Sun 1230; 1 hr earlier in winter. Or see the parish priest, C Martínez Chaparro.* The area around the church is the oldest in the village and there are some beautiful cobbled steps and small winding roads to wander up here. Also worth a look is the 17th-century whitewashed **Iglesia de Nuestra Señora del Carmen** on the main square. Apart from the Ermita de Santa Brígida, another good view of the village is from the well-preserved Era Comunal, at the end of Calle Nuestra Señora del Carmen. This was used for separating wheat husk from the grain, by a mule pulling a board – embedded with sharp stones – over the wheat.

The second entrance to Galaroza is past a square with huge palm trees, off the N433. Just above the square is a bar, *La Fuente,* famed for its *patatas bravas* (although if you're feeling brave, it also serves pigs'ears, or *orejas*).

Apart from its water, Galaroza is also famed for its flourishing carpentry industry, which produces superb traditional windows and doors, as well as pretty hand-painted furniture. Many use the locally produced, but expensive, wood from the area's sweet chestnut trees. It's also worth checking out the various ceramic shops, most of which are situated on the N433 around Galaroza. These are also good places to buy local products such as honey, chestnuts, walnuts and lemons when in season. Horse riding in the surrounding countryside and accommodation is available at *Picadero La Suerte*, Km 102 on the N433, on the outskirts of Galaroza, T959123010.

Sleeping **C** *Galaroza Sierra*, Ctra N433 Km 69, on the right on the way out of Galaroza from Aracena, T959123215, F959123236. A few mins' walk from the centre, attractive hotel with 22 comfortable rooms (7 of which are located at the poolside), TV. Restaurant. **E** *Hostal Toribio*, C Iglesia, just below the Iglesia de la Purísima Concepción. 10 basic rooms, some with bath and balcony. **E** *Hostal Venecia*, Ctra N433, before *Hotel Galaroza Sierra*. 12 rooms, some with bath. Restaurant has a cheap *menu del día* of €5.50 and serves breakfast.

Eating Try the tapas in any of the numerous bars scattered around Galaroza. Particularly good in the evening is *Bar El Paso*, try the *chocos fritos* and *pescado a la plancha*. One of the newer bars is *Las Salinas*, with a *discoteca* of the same name next door, just up from the main plaza. Despite being on the site of a former abattoir, this popular bar is housed in a large, pretty whitewashed courtyard, and opens later than most other bars. Another late-night bar with great table football, where the younger *cachoneros* (and Sevillanos at weekends and holidays) hang out, is *Bar de Julio*, located in a basement just past the Iglesia del Carmen.

Fiestas Apart from *Fiesta de los Jarritos* (see above), Galaroza's main festivals include Easter. **Easter Sunday** is called *día del huevo y el bollo*, or day of the egg and bread roll. Villagers hold a picnic up at the Ermita de Santa Brígida to eat rolls made specially for that day and on Mon, everyone heads out to the countryside with their family and friends for another picnic. Of greater interest to outsiders, however, is the *Fiesta de la Virgen del Carmen*, held over the **last weekend of Jul**. This is an exuberant 4-day fiesta for Galaroza's patron saint, with a fair, stalls selling local handicrafts and food, live music in the main square until the early hours, sports tournaments and a huge makeshift bar stretching down the main street by the plaza.

Zufre In the east of the region is the wonderfully sited village of Zufre, sitting along the top of a ridge. The Paseo de los Alcades (often called the Balcony of the Sierra) gives superb views over the terraced farmland of the surrounding countryside. The village itself has a strong Moorish influence, with its narrow winding streets, whitewashed houses and small squares. The largely brickbuilt parish church, with Renaissance and Gothic elements, was constructed by Hernán Ruiz, who was responsible for the Renaissance part of the Giralda tower in Sevilla. There was some damage from the 1755 earthquake and a new tower was completed in 1758. In the same square as the church is the arcaded *ayuntmiento*, built in the 16th century. Nearby is a large reservoir, the Embalse de Zufre, which offers possibilities for fishing. Enquire about permits at the town hall.

Aroche

Colour map 1, grid B2
Population: 3,599
Out on a limb in the west of the area and only 24 km from the Portuguese border, is the hilltop town of Aroche sitting snugly around its Moorish castle. The town has a long history being first fortified by the Romans, who called it Arruci Vetus. Built by the Almoravids in the 12th century, the **castle** was one of the so-called Banda Gallega created by Sancho IV in the late 13th century, to help defend the border against Portuguese invasion. The most bizarre of the Christian reconstructions was to include within its walls the local bullring in 1802. This is now rather overgrown, but is spruced up once a year for the annual bullfight on August 15.

The guide Manuel Amigo García has the keys to all the main sights in Aroche, which are otherwise closed due to lack of funding (unfortunately, the information centre for the Parque Natural de la Sierra, in the restored Cilla de los Jerónimos just up past the Ayuntamiento in the plaza, is also closed). Ask for him at *Bar Lalo* in the main square. He gives guided tours in Spanish for a voluntary contribution.

With its beautiful, vaulted Gothic ceiling, the **Iglesia de la Asunción** is one of the Sierra's most impressive churches. Taking 140 years to complete, the church has elements of Mudéjar, Gothic and Renaissance styles, as well as work of the architect Hernán Ruiz, famed for designing Seville's Giralda. Also here are some exquisitely ornate altarpieces dating from the 17th and 18th centuries.

There are two small museums in the village. Housed in the Cilla de los Jerónimos (see above) is the **Museo Arqueológico**. It has a fascinating display of artefacts from Aroche and the surrounding area; particularly interesting is its collection of well-preserved Roman remains from a nearby excavation site. An oddity is the **Museo del Santo Rosario** (Museum of Rosaries), which contains a collection of over 1,200 rosaries from all over the world, including donations from Mother Teresa, various Popes, royalty and politicians.

If you're interested in heraldry you'll find plenty to see in Aroche. A number of aristocratic families built mansions in the village and their coats of arms are displayed in marble on the house fronts.

Just outside Aroche on the N433 towards Portugal is the **Ermita de San Mamés**, venue of a *romería* at Whitsun. The building is in Mudéjar style and contains the statue of San Mamés, which, when it was brought here in the 18th century, was the subject of a long and expensive lawsuit, documented in the cashbook of the hermitage.

Sleeping & eating

Accommodation options are limited. The best bet is **D** *Hostal Picos de Aroche*, Ctra Aracena 12, on the right as you come into Aroche from the N433, T959140473. Comfortable rooms with TV, bath and some a/c. **E** *Pensión Romero*, Ctra Aracena, T959140022. On the same road as *Hostal Picos de Aroche*, this hotel is unmarked and hard to find. On a sharp bend just after the *Hostal*, take a walk up a driveway and some steps to the left of the road; the hotel is the last door to the left of the terraza, the site of the hotel's former restaurant. Basic, functional rooms with bath but not much else.

A handy place to stop for a morning coffee is the *Centro Cultural las Peñas*, otherwise known as *Casa de los Socios*, between the Cathedral and the plaza. Like all working men's clubs, or casinos, it serves cheap beer and tapas (€0.90). On the square is *Cafetería Las Peñas*, which serves good tapas. Upstairs, *Bar Lalo* – a lively bar, especially in the evenings – is a good place to have a drink and watch the world go by from one of its small balconies with seating.

Huelva Province

Huelva Province

Cádiz Province

5

Cádiz Province

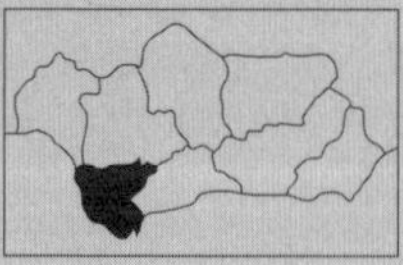

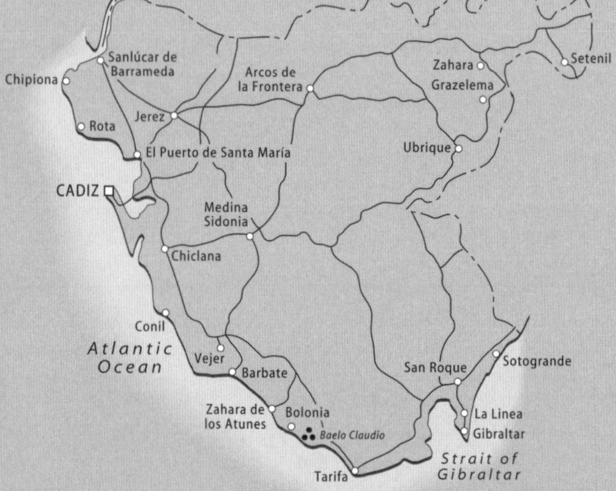

Cádiz is the most westerly and southerly of the provinces of Andalucía. Its two main cities are the port of **Cádiz**, home of Spain's most vibrant carnival, and **Jerez**, the centre of the country's sherry production. Cádiz's laid-back grace has as much to do with its crumbling plazas, shady parks and barrio backstreets as its special sights such as the Catedral Nueva and the Gran Teatro Falla. Here the sea is never far away and getting lost seems like an adventure rather than a threat.

East of Jerez are the so-called **Pueblos Blancos**, or White Towns, which are becoming increasingly popular. Yet despite an expanding tourist industry, it is fair to say that the pueblos retain much of their early Moorish flavour and later impressive Christian architecture, and in the **Parque Natural Sierra de Grazalema** you will find one of the best places in Andalucia to get away from everyone if you want to go walking.

Back by the sea, the Atlantic coastline, known as the **Costa de la Luz** because of the clarity of light, has the best, and least developed, beaches in Andalucía. In the south, the strong levante wind gives some of the finest windsurfing conditions in the world, while the narrow Straits of Gibraltar provide a routeway for thousands of migrating storks, eagles and other raptors during spring and autumn. Perched impressively on a huge outcrop of rock, the British colony of **Gibraltar** is one of the best places to observe the migration. It is, however, becoming increasingly swamped by hordes of Costa del Sol - mainly English - tourists, who come here to take advantage of the colony's tax-free shopping.

Cádiz

Colour map 4, grid B1
Population: 143,129

'Unique' is undoubtedly an overused word in travel guides, but Cádiz is certainly a one-off as far as Andalucían cities are concerned. Surprisingly, despite a long history going back to Phoenician times, it is a little short on monuments (apart from its famous **cathedral**), largely owing to the effects of earthquakes and buccaneers, but it is nevertheless a sophisticated seaport that has been open to outside influences for centuries. As a result, its people seem untypically Andalucían, more cosmopolitan, tolerant and fun-loving to the extreme – characteristics that come to the fore during the riotous February **Carnaval**, which even Franco was unable to suppress. The joy of Cádiz is to wander around its narrow streets full of tall 18th-century houses and elegant squares. You will almost certainly get lost, but not for long, for there seems to be a view of the sea at the end of every road. During the middle of the day, the squares make for welcome, tranquil resting places when the heat gets too much; at night they begin to come alive, first with the sound of the nesting starlings, then with the gabble of Gaditanos out for an evening paseo or promenade. The all-encompassing presence of the Atlantic in this part of the city has an oddly calming effect – and indeed the sea has always been the city's provider and protector.

Ins and outs

Getting there
See page 165 for further details
The 2 main **bus** companies are *Comes* and *Los Amarillos*, both of whose stations are conveniently centred in the old part of the city: *Los Amarillos*, Paseo de Canalejas (near Plaza San Juan de Dios), T956285852, and *Comes*, Plaza de Hispanidad, north of Plaza de España, T956807059. Street parking is difficult, but fortunately there are several large underground car parks, which usually have plenty of free places; the one on Paseo de Canalejas is probably your best best. The **train** station is close to the entrance of the old part of the town.

Getting around
Fortunately, all the worthwhile features of Cádiz are contained within a very small area of the old part of the city and most can easily be covered on foot in a day. The streets are on a grid pattern and therefore it's easy to find your way around, although looking for the name of a street can often be frustrating. The map shows a route which will cover all the main sights (see page 160). If you're feeling lazy, there's an open top hop-on/hop-off bus tour of the city, starting at Plaza de la Constitución. Tickets, €7.25, are valid all day.

Tourist offices
The tourist office is on Plaza San Juan de Dios 11, next to the Ayuntamiento, T956241001, F956241005, www.infocadiz.com Open Mon-Fri 0900-1400 and 1700-2000. At weekends the office is shut but there is a kiosk in the plaza just opposite the office, open Sat-Sun 1000-1330 and 1600-1830. The website is a useful source of current events information. The office provides useful city maps. However, the other 2 previously helpful tourist offices have now closed, suggesting a cutback in resources, so don't expect too much. There is also a further temporary municipal office in the summer at Victoria beach.

History

The capital of the province, but not its largest city, Cádiz has a long and fascinating history, claiming to be the oldest continuously occupied urban settlement in Western Europe. In Phoenician times it was known as Gadir, the port

Things to do ★

· Dress up as outrageously as possible for Cadiz's carnival in February
· Take the *vapor* from Cádiz to El Puerto de Santa María and sample some of Andalucía's finest seafood at a seafront *marisquería*
· Visit Morocco in a day: take a boat from Tarifa to Tangier
· Watch thousands of birds of prey migrate over the Straits of Gibraltar from Tarifa or Gibraltar
· Climb El Torreón (1,654 m), the highest peak in Cádiz province, in the Sierra de Grazalema and, on a clear day, see the whole province and the African coastline.
· Have a pint and a pub lunch in Gibraltar

exporting minerals from the interior. Its strategic position also attracted the Romans, who called it Gades (the inhabitants of Cádiz are still known as *Gaditanos*) and Julius Caesar was given his first public office here. The Moors, whilst occupying the area, were not great seafarers, and there followed a period of decline until the 16th century when Spain became an important maritime power. With the colonization of the Americas Cádiz was ideally placed to benefit and when the river to Sevilla began to silt up, it became a great sea port once again. This strategic importance inevitably attracted the attentions of rival seafaring nations such as England, France and Holland, who regularly came to sack, pillage and "singe the King of Spain's beard", as Sir Francis Drake supposedly did. Much of the wealth from the Americas ended up in Cádiz and a large area of the older part of the city, including the cathedral, dates from the 18th century. In the early part of the 19th century, during the Peninsular War, some of the radical citizens of Cádiz set up the first Spanish Parliament or Cortés. It was shortlived, but was the blueprint for the Spanish democracy of today, which ironically took more than 150 years to evolve.

Sights

The entrance to the old part of the city is marked by the city walls, dating back to 1757. Traffic swirls round the **Plaza de la Constitución**, before passing through the **Puerta de Tierra**, the old land gate to the city. Further west and opposite the container dock is the **Plaza de España**. Here, in the middle of the square, stands the **Monumento a las Cortes Liberales**, built for the centenary of the short-lived Liberal constitution of 1812. It is an impressive white stone monument, crowded with dignitaries and inscriptions and topped with a book representing the constitution – this itself is now capped with a large untidy storks' nest. Close by is the elegant and busy hub of **Plaza de la Mina**, where you will find the excellent **Museo de Cádiz** (see below) and several good tapas bars nearby. One of the busiest squares in Cádiz is **Plaza Topete** (also known as **Plaza de las Flores**), the site of a Phoenician temple where first-born babies were said to be sacrificed. The square is now almost completely occupied by the covered **Mercado Central**, with its appetizing displays of fruit, vegetables, *jamón* and fish. There is also an outdoor flower market and many ad hoc stalls selling secondhand tat. The swish, newly restored post office is also here and there are a number of cheap bars in and around the plaza offering no-nonsense *jamón y queso bocadillos* and lunchtime tapas – a good bet especially during the week. Equally bustling is the somewhat asymmetrical **Plaza de San Juan de Dios,** dominated by the

Plazas & parks

Cádiz Province

Manuel de Falla

Down in the crypt of Cádiz Cathedral is the tomb of one of the city's best-known sons, Manuel de Falla, the most important Spanish composer of the 20th century. Born in Cádiz in 1870, Falla initially studied music with his mother and local teachers before coming under the influence of Felipe Pedrell. He eventually moved to Madrid, where he taught the piano, before moving on to Paris. Here he knew and was influenced by Ravel and Debussy.

De Falla returned to Spain in 1914, where he lived mainly in Granada until 1939, when, disenchanted with the Franco regime, he left for Argentina, where he died in 1946.

De Falla developed a nationalistic style

of music, based on the traditional Spanish folk song, while he always fought against the use of Italian and German in operas. His best-known works were Nights in the Gardens of Spain, *the opera* La Vida Breve *(1913); and the ballets* El Favor Brujo *and* El Sombrero de Tres Picos *(1919). He also wrote music for puppets and concertos for harpsichord and guitar.*

On his death, de Falla's body was brought back to Cádiz (despite the claims of Granada, where he wrote most of his better works) and placed in the cathedral crypt along with that of the poet José María Pemán. The theatre in Cádiz is named after de Falla.

Ayuntamiento, the impressive neoclassical town hall, and numerous bars and restaurants. Immediately to the west are the main pedestrianized shopping streets. At the other end of the city, looking out over the Atlantic, is the rather mysterious **Parque Genovés**, with its dark green palms and extraordinary spiral-sculpted cypresses contrasting vividly with the creamy buildings and brilliant blue sea and sky, a spectacular and venerable Dragon Tree and an outdoor theatre where performances are held on summer evenings. Nearby to the east is the extensive university quarter.

Catedral

Undoubtedly the city's most prominent landmark, the cathedral is best viewed from the shore to the south, where the gold dome contrasts with a row of colourwashed houses

Known officially as the Catedral Nueva because it replaced the earlier Cathedral of Santa Cruz, which was largely destroyed by fire in 1596, it was begun in Gothic style in 1722. It was not until 1853, however, that it was finally completed, with the construction of the two towers at the western end. The older, lower parts of the cathedral are built of the local coarse brown *ostionera* sandstone, which is suitable for fine masonry work, but the later, upper construction was of a light grey limestone, giving the building a curiously patchwork appearance. Windows are almost non-existent, while the 'gold' dome is in fact composed of yellow glazed tiles. The main west front has an interesting combination of concave and convex lines, while its impressive steps leading to an attractive café-lined square give the building a much less cramped environment that other Andalucían cathedrals. Don't bother to climb the steps, because the main doors are usually locked unless a service is taking place. To gain entry, go to the side of the cathedral to a door marked 'museum'.

The numbers in brackets refer to the map on page 160

The interior is plain and rather severe but well lit and lacking in the ornate gilding of many Andalucían cathedrals. The **choir** stalls (**1**) are the highlight. They are carved in cedar wood and date from 1702, being brought here in 1858 from the Carthusian Church of Las Cuevas at Sevilla. Above are the busts of over 40 saints and musicians. At the other end of the nave is the circular **Presbytery** (**3**) with the **high altar** (**2**) in the form of a temple supported by Corinthian columns in grey marble and red jasper. There are some 14 side chapels, of which five are worth a closer look. The **Capilla de la Asunción** (**4**) has an interesting *retablo* supported by barley sugar columns, plus two statues attributed to Ignacio Vergara. Next to it is the **Capilla de San Sebastián** (**5**) with an *Ecce-Homo* by Luisa Roldán (daughter of the better known Pedro Roldán) dating from 1684 and more Vergara images. There are three chapels of note in the ambulatory. On either side of the entrance to the Museo are the **capillas de San Servando y San Germán** (**6** and **7**) with more work by Luisa Roldán. Further around the ambulatory is the **Capilla del Sagrario** (**8**) with an *Immaculate Conception* by Vergara.

A glance towards the roof will show areas of wire netting – the limestone has been affected by the salt air and pieces of the rock have been known to fall on worshippers. A restoration programme is now underway, with the stonework being sealed in a protective film to prevent further decay. Having paid to see the Museo as well as the Catedral, it is worth having a quick look. The room is dominated by a 3 m high silver monstrance, said to contain a million jewels, plus a collection of uninspiring artwork, silver and vestments. Steps from the Presbytery lead down to the circular crypt with its flat vault. The altar here is made of Genoa marble with an impressive image of the Virgin of the Rosary, but the main reason for coming here is to see the tomb of Manuel de Falla, the composer, born in Cádiz in 1870 (see box, page opposite). Also here is tomb of the local writer and poet José María Pemán. ■ *Tue to Fri, 1000-1300 and 1600-1900, Sat-Sun 1000-1300. €3, children €1.30. T956259812.*

Museo de Cádiz Housed in a restored mansion in the Plaza de Mina, this fine arts and archaeological museum has excellent lighting and information. Its ground floor has a magnificent collection of archaeological remains from the Cádiz region. There are some significant Phoenician artefacts from the necropolis at Gadir, but it is the Roman rooms which are absolutely outstanding. There is a comprehensive collection of sarcophagi from the Roman necropolis at Gades showing the gradual evolution of shapes, while in Room 5 there is a wide range of amphorae, some shown in the reconstructed wreck of a Roman boat. Household and domestic items are well represented, including some fine mosaics and coins. There are busts, sculptures and a model of the Roman theatre in Cádiz and the Roman city of Baelo Claudia. The fine arts collection is on the first floor, where the most important paintings are the 18 by Zurbarán, including a series of panels from the Carthusian monastery at Cartuja, near Jerez. The faces of the saints were painted from monks which Zurbarán had met. Also here is Murillo's *Los Desposorios de Santa Catalina*, his last work; he fell to his death from

Museums
One of the best museums in Andalucía

Cádiz Province

Catedral at Cadiz

scaffolding and the painting was completed by a pupil. Most of the modern pictures are by local artists and of mixed quality, although those by Godoy and Prieto are notable. The second floor contains an unusual ethnographic section, including the Tia Norica marionettes, from Cádiz's long established and popular satirical marionette theatre. Note that this floor is often closed. ■ *Wed-Sat 0900-2000, Tue 1430-2000, Sun 0930-1430. Free wih EU passport, otherwise €1.50. Detailed guides available in languages other than Spanish. T956212281.*

Cádiz

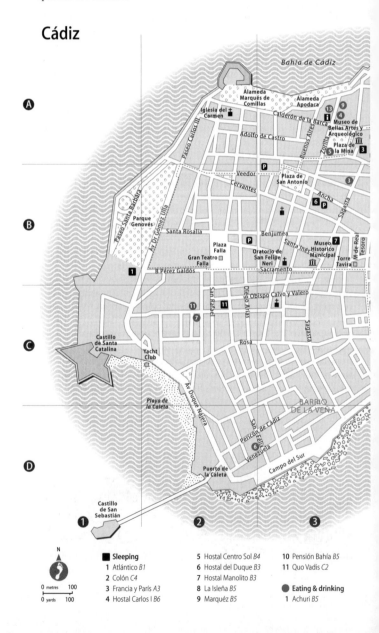

■ Sleeping

1 Atlántico *B1*
2 Colón *C4*
3 Francia y París *A3*
4 Hostal Carlos I *B6*
5 Hostal Centro Sol *B4*
6 Hostal del Duque *B3*
7 Hostal Manolito *B3*
8 La Isleña *B5*
9 Marquéz *B5*
10 Pensión Bahía *B5*
11 Quo Vadis *C2*

● Eating & drinking

1 Achuri *B5*

Torre Tavira This tower, the tallest of over 60 watchtowers in Cádiz, is built in Baroque style and was part of the Palace of the Maquis of Recano, whose first watchman, Antonio Tavira, gave it its name. In 1778, this tower was appointed the official watchtower for the town. Today, above the reception area, there are two exhibition halls. Well worth a visit is the **camera obscura** room, where a moving image of the spectacular rooftop view of the city is projected. ■ *Jun-Sep, 1000-2000, Sep-Jun 1000-1800. €3. C Marqués del Real Tesoro 10, T956212910.*

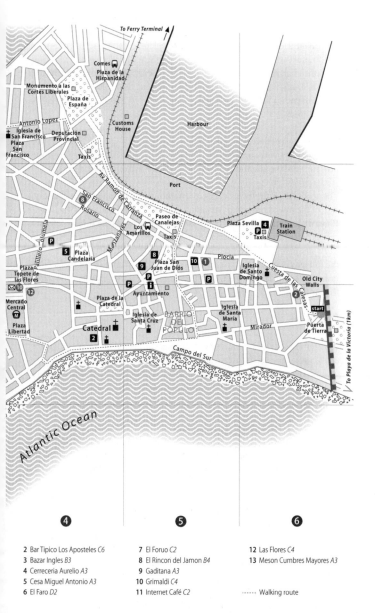

Cádiz Province

Other sights

Gran Teatro Falla The modern brick-built Falla Theatre is designed in Mudéjar style. Located in the northwest of the old city in a square of the same name, it is named after Manuel de Falla, the musician, who was born in the city. See also under Entertainment, page 165.

Oratorio San Felipe Neri This building is located at the junction of Calle Sacramento and Calle San José, where the 1812 Declaration of Independence was made by a group of refugees from Napoleon's occupation of the rest of Spain. The Baroque, oval-shaped building has a fascinating façade covered with plaques sent from other countries. There is a double row of balconies, above which a series of windows allow light to flood into the blue dome. A Murillo *Inmaculada* dominates the High Altar's *retablo*, while a series of seven chapels surround the oval nave. ■ *Daily, at service times only 0830-1000 and 1930-2200. It may be possible, however, to latch on to a group visit, between 1000 and 1330. €0.90.* T956211612.

Barrio del Pópulo Just to the east of the cathedral is the so-called Peoples' Quarter, a labyrinth of narrow streets, with some houses dating from the 13th century, having somehow survived the attention of Sir Francis Drake and other plunderers.

Beaches The north side of the town borders the harbour, but the full length of the south side of the town consists of Atlantic beaches. The original town beach is the **Playa de la Caleta**, which is tightly sandwiched between the ruined defensive castles of Santa Catalina and San Sebastián, but this is not particularly clean. Most *gaditanos* prefer to use the longer **Playa de la Victoria**, which extends the full length of the newer part of the city. It has plenty of sports facilities, beach bars, hotels, apartments and restaurants and can get very crowded in the summer.

Essentials

Sleeping
■ *on map, page 160*

You need to book well in advance for accommodation during Carnaval in Feb. At other times of year, however, there is no problem finding accommodation, budget or otherwise. However, the quality of the accommodation often leaves a lot to be desired – in all price brackets. Most of the more expensive hotels are modern and severely lacking in any discernible charm. You are probably better off saving your centímos and staying in one of the more atmospheric *pensiones* in the old town. Some are admittedly very scruffy, but you can find some good, cheap and clean places as well, particularly in the alleyways leading off Plaza San Juan de Dios. Make sure you see the room first. For the cheapest accommodation, look for the *camas* (rooms) signs in windows. There are plenty of these around and it might be possible to haggle over a price.

AL *Atlántico*, Av Duque de Nájera 9, T956223908, F956214582, cadiz@parador.es. Cádiz's most upmarket hotel located at the point of the isthmus. This modern, rather squat concrete block has great views over the Atlantic and the Bahía de Cádiz, but its 153 a/c rooms are pretty soulless. Has all the usual luxury hotel facilities including pool, garage, wheelchair access. Its restaurant does some pretty decent seafood, at not overly extortionate prices. **AL** *Husa Puertatierra*, Av Andalucía 34, T956272111, www.hotelesmonte.com 98 rooms. Garage, a/c, wheelchair access, modern chain hotel in new part of city. **AL** *La Caleta*, Av Amilcar Barca s/n, T956279411, F956259322, www.melialacaleta@solmelia.com 143 rooms. Garage, a/c, restaurant, wheelchair access, in the newer part of the city. **A** *Playa Victoria*, Plaza Glorieta Ingeniero La Cierva 4, T956205100, F956263300, hpv@teleline.es www.palafoxhoteles.comLarge modern hotel close to the main beach. Rooms with sea views, TV, a/c, safe, minibar. Garage, pool, restaurant, wheelchair access. **A-B** *Francia y Paris*, Plaza San Francisco 2, T9562223498, F956222431. Smallish hotel (55 rooms) in charming square in a quiet, old part of city. A more stylish option than the more expensive 'luxury' places. **B** *Regio I*, Av Ana de Viya 11, T956279331 and *Regio II*, Av Andalucía 79, T956253008. Both with 40 rooms in newer part of town. Regio II is the newer of the two and slightly more expensive.

C-D *Pensión Bahía*, C Plocia 5, T956259061. Just off the main plaza, this is a good, if slightly more expensive option. Its 21 good value rooms, some with a/c and TV, are welcoming and the service is friendly. **C-D** *Hostal Carlos I*, Plaza de Sevilla s/n, T956286600. 30 rooms. A hostal that thinks its a hotel, this is another good place to stay and good value for money. A/c, good facilities, very near the train station.

D *Hostal Centro Sol*, C Padre Elejal de Manzanares 7,T956283103. Spic and span place with 19 light rooms all with bath, TV, and facing onto a central patio. Breakfast and bar available. **E** *Hostal Colón*, C Marqués de Cádiz, 6, T956285351. On a street with several *hostal* options (all in the same price bracket), this is a good deal. Clean rooms, some with balconies overlooking the street. Some rooms have bath. **D** *Inmares*, C San Francisco 9, F956212257. 37 rooms. Centrally placed in one of the main shopping streets. **E** *Hostal del Duque*, C Ancha, 13, T956222777. A more interesting location to stay in away from the other main *hostal* area, just off Plaza San Antonio, this place has big, light rooms with balconies overlooking the street, but is pretty basic. Rooms with shower but no toilet and no towels. **E** *La Isleña*, Plaza Juan de Dios 12, T956287064. Definitely a no-frills establishment with 10 simple rooms (some overloooking the square), very cheap given its central location, but not especially friendly. **E** *Manolita*, C Benjumea 2, T956211577. Small, family run hostal. **E** *Hostal Marqués*, C Marqués de Cádiz, 1, T956285854. Some rooms with bath in this clean but slightly crumbly place. Friendly owner who speaks English.

Youth hostels *Quo Qádis*, C Diego Arias 1, T/F956221939. An innovative and excellent hostel with courses (from language to flamenco) and excursions available. Breakfast included in price. Double rooms or dorm options from €10. **Camping** There are no campsites around Cádiz itself, but plenty near Puerto de Santa María, Puerto Real and Rota. *El Pinar*, Ctra NIV, Km 666, Puerto Real, T956830897. Second category, open Apr-Oct only. *Punta Candor*, Ctra Rota-Chipiona, Km 13, T95681330. First category, good facilities.

Expensive Cádiz boasts 2 of the most outstanding (and pricey) fish restaurants in Andalucía. *Achuri*, C Plocia 15, T956253613. An established favourite and it's worth shelling out for some of the freshest and best prepared seafood you'll eat in the city. A popular lunchtime restaurant. Book ahead. *El Faro*, C San Felix 15, T956211008, has some excellent house specialities including a delicious and locally renowned paella, but also a moderately priced *menú del día*. A warm taberna-style restaurant and also a separate classy tapas bar with excellent and affordable wines and sherries. Phone to book a table and check opening times.

Eating

Not surprisingly, fish comes top of the menu in Cádiz

Mid-range *Grimaldi*, C Libertad, 9, on the Plaza de Topete (de las Flores) by the Mercado Central, T956228316. The rather bizarre faux bodega interior, decorated with old photographs of Cádiz shouldn't put you off this reasonably priced predominantly seafood restaurant. Specialities include *pimientos rellenos con gambas* (prawn stuffed

Cádiz Province

peppers) and other seafood, as well as *pulpo a la Gallega* (Galician-style octopus). *El Rincón del Jamon*, Plaza San Augustín, 5, T956250183. A busy, down-to-earth tapas bar and restaurant, again better on the seafood than meat, although it does a decent seared pork fillet. Delicious *gambas* and a good grilled *dorado* are particularly recommended. The house wines (both white and red) are also very good. Delicious ingredients, cooked simply.

Cheap For inexpensive seafood, try the *freidurías*, of which *Las Flores*, Plaza las Flores, is one of the best. *Chino Marco Polo*, Paseo Marítimo, near the main beach in the new part of town. Chinese restaurant with a *menú del día*, €5.45. This area is also excellent in summer for *heladerías*.

Tapas bars Unsurprisingly for a port, fish and shellfish are the dominant ingredients in tapas in Cádiz and if you are after a tasty meat nibble, you may be disappointed – that said, the *jamón serrano* here is invariably delicious. For a tapas crawl head for **C Zorilla**, which runs from Plaza de la Mina to the northern shore and is made up almost entirely of small tapas bars. This really is the best place to come for tapas in Cádiz. On this street is *Mesón Cumbres Mayores*, where you can eat great non-seafood tapas surrounded by a forest of *jamones* hanging from the ceiling. It is a friendly and relaxed place despite the frantic pace of the waiters serving demanding *Gaditanos*. Great *albondigas* (meatballs) in *salsa*, *jamón* and *chorizo*. *Cervecería Aurelio* is *the* place to come in Cádiz for seafood tapas. You can smell the freshness of the *gambas* halfway down the street – you can't miss it – and there's a stall outside selling shellfish to those who don't have time to stop in for a *copa* and a bite to eat. *Gaditana*, also on C Zorilla, is worth a look, and on nearby Plaza Mina, you should try *Casa Miguel Antonio*, a calm and friendly environment in which to eat some decent *jamón* or delicious paella. There are plenty of other tapas bars in the Plaza de San Juan de Dios and the surrounding alleyways. Also try *El Faro* (see Expensive eating above) and the cheap and friendly *El Forno* bar, C Doctor Marañón, south of the Gran Teatro Falla. *Bar Tipíco Los Apostoles*, on Cuesta de las Calesas, is a large, busy and bright tapas bar with a good selection of wines and sherries. *La Manzanilla*, C Feduchy 9, is a serious sherry bar offering over 100 types of manzanilla.

Nightlife Outside of *Carnaval*, the Cádiz club scene can appear rather staid, but things liven up in the summer along the **Playa Victoria**, where there are a plethora of rather tacky bars, *cervecerías* and clubs heaving with locals and visitors alike all doing their thing to the latest Eurodisco. And the beach is only a stone's throw away if you need some fresh air and space. Try the following: *Las Pergolas*, Paseo Marítimo 11, T956280949 or *Holiday*, Nereidas, Paseo Marítimo, T956273775. In the **old town**, the bars and clubs are more small scale, but this does not stop things from going on well into the early morning hours, in summer and winter. *Bazar Inglés*, C San Pedro, is about as English as you are likely to get in Cádiz (ie not very). It's a late-night hang out with a young *Gaditano* crowd and some decent music (with a little Eurotrash thrown in for good measure) and a long wooden bar to hold on to. **Plaza España** and around is a good bet for live music bars and late night drinking, including *Club Ajo*, Plaza España, and *Poniente*, C Beato Diego de Cádiz, a fun and lively gay club with drag shows most nights. *La Cava*, T956211866, is a popular flamenco *taberna* on C Antonio López, where you can munch on decent simple tapas, washed down with a good Rioja and watch a spectacular show at very close quarters. Phone to check which nights have live shows. Nearby, the area around Plaza Mina also stays lively until late. One of the best music bars in town, *Persígueme*, is on the corner of C Tinte and Sagasta, playing jazz and blues live later on in the week and at weekends, it's a firm local favourite. For more hectic (and tacky) club action within the old city walls, head up to **Punta San Felipe**, north of Plaza España, where you'll find a strip of clubs and bars, all with hit and miss nights, and where you might not be admitted if you're wearing trainers – you have been warned. Start at *Bar Comanche*, C Paseo Pascual Pery, a friendly place, and ask there for local tips on what's going on that night.

See local press, **www.infocadiz.com** or contact *Turismo* for details of what's on where. **Entertainment**
Cinema There are no fewer than 7 cinemas in Cádiz, 2 of which are multiscreen. **Theatre** Cádiz has 3 excellent theatres. Teatro Andalucía, C Londres 2, T956223029, **Teatro José Pemán** (open-air theatre in Parque Genovés, summer only), T956223534; and **Gran Teatro Falla**, Plaza de Falla s/n, T956220828.

Feb *Carnaval* Cádiz is famous for its 10-day carnival. Dating from the 19th century, **Fiestas &** even Franco was unable to suppress it. The Carnaval is a riot of eating, drinking, danc- **festivals** ing, singing and masquerades with a certain South American flavour. A distinctive fea- ture are the bands – groups of people who parade around the city in fancy dress making music with any instruments they can lay their hands on, singing satirical songs, particularly about politicians. The large gay element in the city plays an important part and prizes are awarded for the most original and outrageous presentations. **Mar/Apr** *Semana Santa* The week leading up to Easter is a much more devout affair but nevertheless a busy time in the city. **Early Aug** *La Velada de los Angeles* A popular fair which has been revived in recent years. **7 Oct** *La Virgen del Rosario* Celebrations for the city's patron saint. **1 Nov** *Todos Los Santos* On the eve of All Saint's Day the Mercado Central receives some elaborate decoration.

The chief shopping streets are San Francisco, Nueva, Columela and San José. The more **Shopping** gaudy tourist items seen in other Andalucían cities are happily rarely in sight. There are a number of shops selling local handicrafts including: *Cerámica Popular La Cartuja*, C Nicaragua 2; *Cerámica Compañia*, C Compañia s/n; and *Esterería Acuaviva*, C Rosario 21. This is also a good place to look for leather shoes. For food, head for the central mar- ket on Plaza Topete (de las Flores).

Tennis *Real Tenis Club*, Av Doctor Gómez Ulla, T956221945. **Watersports** Not sur- **Sport** prisingly, watersports figure prominently in Cádiz: *Club Nautico Deportivo Alcázar*, Plaza de San Lorenzo 2, T956260914. *Club Marítimo Gaditano La Caleta*, C Duque de Nájera, s/n, T956213680. *Club Nautico Deportivo*, Bda Puntales s/n, T956260914. *Real Club Nautico de Cádiz*, Plaza de San Felipe s/n, T956212991.

Long distance Air: The nearest **airport** is 30 km north, just outside Jerez (see page **Transport** 179). **Bus**: The main company is *Comes*, Plaza de Hispanidad, near Plaza de España and the port, T956807059. *Comes* has frequent buses to **Algeciras** (12 daily, 2¾ hrs, €7.90), **Jerez** (at least every hour, 45 mins, €2.30), **Sevilla** (11 daily, 1½ hrs, €8.85) and **Tarifa** (8 daily, 2 hr, €6.45). There are also services to **Almería** (2 daily), **Córdoba** (1 daily, 4½ hr, €15), **Granada** (2 daily, 8 hr), **Huelva** (1 daily), **Málaga** (6 daily, 5 hr, €14.50) and **Ronda** (3 daily). *Los Amarillos* terminal is on Paseo de Canalejas, T956285852. It runs frequent buses to **Sanlúcar** (1¼ hrs, €2.45) and **El Puerto de Santa María** (40 mins), as well as buses at 1230, 1700 and 1915 to **Arcos** (1 hr, €3.65) and **Ubrique** (2¼ hrs, €6.65). Time- tables are available at the tourist office. **Taxi**: T956212121/22/23. **Boat**: The port is next to Plaza de España. There are ferries to **Almería**, **Genoa** and the **Canary Islands**. A boat to the Canary Islands leaves Cádiz weekly on Tue at 1800, arriving Las Palmas, Gran Canaria, on Thu at 0845; Tenerife Thu 1500; and Santa Cruz de la Palma, La Palma, on Fri at 0800. Tickets cost €220 and are available from travel agents or *Transmediterránea*, Av Ramón de Carranza, T902454645. There is a local ferry service to and from Puerto de Santa María; a leisurely *vapor* that takes 45 mins or a faster catamaran (see page 168). **Train**: There are 20 trains a day to Jerez (including El Puerto de Santa María), 12 to Sevilla and 3 to Granada. For information, T902240202.

Cádiz Province

Directory **Banks** The main banks have branches close to the Plaza de San Juan de Dios and C Nueva area. Some savings banks may be reluctant to cash TCs or Euro cheques. **Communications** Post office: the main Correos is in Plaza Topete, T956211878. **Internet**: *El Navigante*, C Doctor Marañón, south of Gran Teatro. €2 per hr. **Embassies and consulates** *Denmark*, Alameda Apodaca 21, T956221364. *France*, Ctra Madrid-Cádiz, Km 634, T956302354. *Holland*, Plaza Tres Carabelas 5, T956224500. *Italy,* C Ancha 8, T956211715. *Norway*, Alameda Apodaca 21, T956221364. **Medical services** *Residencia Sanitaria* (for urgent cases), Av Ana de Viya 21, T956279011; *Cruz Roja*, C Santa María de la Solidad 10, T956222222; *Hospital de Traumaticos/Clínica de San Rafael*, C Diego Arias 2, T956226408. **Useful addresses** Garages/repairs: all firms listed below are clustered together in the Zona Franca industrial area on the southeast edge of the city. *Citröen*, C Algeciras s/n, T956281438. *Fiat*, C Cdad de San Roque s/n, T956251309. *Ford*, C Algeciras s/n, T956271054. *GM*, Tainy SA, Ronda de Puente s/n, T956276298. *Renault*, Ronda del Puente s/n, T956280300. *Rover*, C Gibraltar s/n, T956264308. *Seat/VAG*, Automóviles Bahía, C Algeciras s/n, T956250207.

North from Cádiz

The area north of Cádiz as far as the estuary of the Río Guadalquivir consists of rolling farmland given over largely to the production of grapes. Along the attractive coastline are a series of fishing ports and holiday resorts, the latter being very popular with Sevillanos, many of whom own villas along the shore.

El Puerto de Santa María

Colour map 4, grid B1
Population: 73,728

Immediately across the Bahía de Cádiz is El Puerto de Santa María. Known locally as El Puerto, this was the port from which Columbus's flagship the *Santa María* came from. One of the three towns making up the so-called sherry triangle, it is also a fishing and commercial port as well as being a minor resort. The tourist office is at Calle Luna 22, T956542413, open daily 1000-1400 and 1800-2000 (summer); 1730-1930 (winter). The *turismo* runs free guided tours of the town at 1100 on Tuesday and Saturday in summer and on Saturday only in winter.

Worth noting by the *muelle* is the ornate 18th-century stone fountain, El Fuente de las Galeras, with its four spouts, built to provide water for the sailing ships leaving for the New

El Puerto de Santa María

To Railway Station

C Caldevilla
C Virgen de los Milagros
C Chanca
C tuja
C Javier de Burgos
Plaza de Isaac Peral
C Ribera del Río
C Ribera del Marisco
Río Guadalete
Parque Calderón
Muelle de Vapor
Fish Docks
Plaza de las Galeras Reales
C Luna
C Jesús de los Milagros
Bar del Puerto
C Palacio
C Misericordia
C Santo Domingo
Castillo de San Marcos
C Federico Rubio
C Palma
C Aurora
Av de la Bajamar
To Cádiz
Ayuntamiento
To Plaza de Toros
BODEGA AREA
To Camping Las Dunas
To beaches
Catamaran to Cádiz
To Camping Guadalete & Cádiz

N

0 metres 100
0 yards 100

■ Sleeping
1 Pensión Manola
2 Santa Maria

● Eating
1 Romerijo

The Virgen del Carmen festivals

For more than 100 years the Virgen del Carmen has been revered by fishermen and sailors as their patron saint. The Virgen del Carmen festival takes place on 16 July each year and is one of the highlights of the calendar in all the fishing ports around the coast of Andalucía.

After early morning mass the Virgen is taken from her hermitage or church bedecked with flowers on a procession through the streets. The float is carried by local fishermen and the procession may last for most of the day. It eventually arrives at the beach or harbour and the Virgen is either carried into the sea on the shoulders of fishermen or taken out in a boat. Most of the population assemble on the beach where there is a party atmosphere and giant paellas and grilled

sardines are cooked. The fiesta continues with dancing, singing, fireworks and often the election of the festival queen.

The festival is believed to have originated in the ports along the Costa de la Luz and it is here that the most impressive fiestas take place. At El Puerto de Santa María, the Virgen is loaded onto a boat called the Bonanza and taken across the bay to Cádiz and back accompanied by a flotilla of small boats with their horns blaring. Wreaths are thrown into the water in memory of local fishermen who have lost their lives at sea. The whole idea of the festival is to gives thanks to the Virgen for protecting those who follow what is still a very hazardous profession. But, typical of Andalucíans, the event is turned into a riotous and bucolic celebration.

World. Nearby in Calle Federico Rubio is the 13th-century **Castillo San Marcos**, containing a Mudéjar church with the Moorish *mihrab* still intact. ■ *Today, the building is a conference centre, but there are guided tours Mon-Fri at 1000, 1130 and 1300; Sat 1100 and 1330. €1.80.* The tours end at the castle's bodega, where sherry can be sampled and bought. Other buildings of note include the Baroque **Iglesia de San Francisco**, with a fine south door in Plateresque style and some sculptures by Pedro Roldán and the monastery of Nuestra Señora de la Victoria built in the 12th century. There are also a number of impressive *palacios* dispersed around the town, built largely with the profits of the trade with the Americas. The Plaza de Toros, built in 1880, is one of the most important in Andalucía and can hold 15,000 people. The *corrida* is celebrated in great style during the May *feria*, when some of the best-known *matadores* perform. Note the mosaic in the entrance area which has a quote from the famous bullfighter Joselito 'He who has not seen the bulls in El Puerto does not know what bullfighting is'. ■ *Tue-Sun 1100-1330 and 1800-1930. Free.*

A familiar sight in El Puerto are the huge sherry warehouses lining the river front. It is possible to visit some of the bodegas by reserving first. **Terry**, Calle Toneleros sin número, T95685700. Open for visits between 0900-1300 Monday to Friday, €3. **Osborne**, Calle Fernán Caballero 3, T956855211. Visits at 1030 in English, 1100 and 1200 in Spanish, €3. The Osborne family also breed many of the fearsome fighting bulls that can be seen in the fields in the area, as well as providing the large metal black bulls which are the advertising hoardings for Osborne *coñac* – a common feature of the Andalucían countryside.

AL *Puerto Sherry Yacht Club*, Av de la Libertad s/n, T956812000, F956853300. Top of the range in every respect is this exclusive hotel with 58 rooms and every possible facility (and prices to match). **AL** *Meliá Caballo Blanco*, Av de Madrid 1, T956562541, F956562712. 94 rooms. With all the usual features one associates with the Meliá chain.

Sleeping

Cádiz Province

E *Manolo*, C Jesús de los Milagros 18, T956857525. Simple rooms over a delightful patio. **E** *Tiburón*, C Sudamérica s/n, T956875334. Basic rooms. **Camping** *Las Dunas*, Playa Puntillo, T956872210. First category site on the beach with excellent facilities (including pool, restaurant, bar, tennis, fishing and launderette) and within walking distance of the Cádiz ferry, but can get very crowded in the high season.

Eating El Puerto de Santa María is famous for its *marisquerías* which line the river front in C Ribero del Marisco. Select your seafood, which is then weighed and given to you in a paper bag. The largest of the *marisquerías* is *Romerijo*, but another place worth trying is *Bar del Puerto*, opposite the Muelle del Vapor.

Transport **Boat** A pleasant way to arrive at the town is to take the *vapor* from Cádiz. *Adriano 111* is an elderly wooden tub with an equally ancient crew and pitches and rolls alarmingly if there is an Atlantic swell in the bay. It leaves Cádiz at 1000, 1200, 1400 and 1830 daily; departs from El Puerto at 0900, 1100, 1300 and 1530. On Sun and holidays there are supplementary services leaving Cádiz at 1630 and El Puerto at 1730. No sailings Mon, except holidays. The 10 km trip takes 40 mins and costs €1.35. The *vapor* docks at the Muelle de Vapor in El Puerto, where there is parking. The speedier catamaran *Rápido del Puerto* has 8 sailings daily each way; single €2.25, return €4.25. T956255728. In El Puerto, the catamaran is berthed opposite *Hotel Santa María*; parking €1.20 per day.

Puerto Sherry Just outside El Puerto is this new British-built luxury development. There are the usual apartments, chandlers and restaurants around the harbour, plus an enormous 'multi storey car park' for small boats and dinghies, which is a landmark for miles around. Nearby is the **Aquasherry Parque Acuatico** with a range of slides, shoots and other water attractions plus dolphins and free flying birds of prey. ■ *May to Sep, 1100-1800. T956870511. Getting there: On the NIV at 647 km, it can be reached by bus from El Puerto.*

Just south of El Puerto is the Cádiz commuter suburb of **San Fernando**. The main reason to stop here, especially if you have children, is to visit the **Expo Marine Aquarium,** located on the Paseo Marítimo La Magdelena. There are nearly 30 tanks with the marine flora and fauna of the Bahía de Cádiz. ■ *Daily 1000-1400 and 1800-2200. Reduced hours in winter. €3.65, children €2.45, family ticket €7.25.*

Rota & The A491 leads along the coast, looping inland to avoid the US naval base at
Chipiona **Rota**, one of three in Spain. If the graffiti in the area is to be believed, relations between the Americans and the locals is not always smooth, but at least the base provides employment and sustains local businesses. The town of Rota itself is a small, pleasant holiday resort with a good sandy beach, an elegant *paseo marítimo* and a small marina. The Castillo de Luna dates from the 13th century, but has been much restored. The Torre de la Merced is all that remains of the convent of the same name that was built in 1600 and largely destroyed by a hurricane in 1722. The only other historical feature is the 16th-century parish church of Nuestra Señora de la O, displaying a mixture of Gothic, Plateresque and Baroque styles.

The coast road runs north to Punta del Perro and the town of **Chipiona**. A quiet family resort with some Roman remains and pretensions to be a spa, Chipiona is popular with Spanish holidaymakers and during the height of the season its many *pensiones* are usually fully booked.

Sanlúcar de Barrameda

The road, with its accompanying railway line, now runs along the estuary of the Río Guadalquivir to the town of Sanlúcar de Barrameda, the third point of the so-called sherry triangle, specializing in *manzanilla*. Sanlúcar has Roman origins and the Moors built a defensive fort here, while later under the Christians it became an important port. Columbus left here on his second Atlantic crossing and it was Magellan's last port of call before his attempt to circumnavigate the world.

Colour map 4, grid B1
Population: 61,382

The town is divided into the older **Barrio Alto**, occupying the higher ground and containing most of the monuments, and the newer **Barrio Bajo** towards the river, the two being linked by a treelined avenue, the Calzada de Ejército. The **tourist office** is located here, T956366110, F956366132, www.aytosanlucar.org It's open daily 1000-1400 and 1800-2000 (summer), 1600-1830 (winter). *Eurotur* run guided tours of the town, €3 including visits to sights and a bodega; contact the tourist office for more information.

The centre of the old town is the charming **Plaza del Cabildo** and just to the north of here are the main monuments. There are numerous churches worth a visit, particularly the **Iglesia de Nuestra Señora de la O** in the small Plaza de la Paz, with a 16th-century Mudéjar doorway. It also has a curious tower, with a three-tier belfry, which if you can gain admittance gives marvellous views over the town. Another church of interest is the **Iglesia San Francisco** in Calle Ancha. It was built by Henry VIII of England while he was married to Catherine of Aragon and it was meant to be a refuge for British sailors. Today it is usually firmly locked. Adjacent is the *palacio* of the dukes de Medina Sidonia. The present incumbent is the Duchess of Medina Sidonia, a larger-than-life character known as the 'Red Duchess' for her political views. A direct descendant of Guzman 'El Bueno' of Tarifa, she has made herself a thorn in the side of authority in her defence of the less fortunate of the area. Today, the *palacio* functions as a

Cádiz Province

Sleeping
1 Doñana
2 Los Helechos
3 Pensión Blanca Paloma
4 Tartaneros

0 metres 100
0 yards 100

small, exclusive guest house. Just to the west is the Moorish Castillo de Santiago. At the time of writing, the castle was closed for renovation to convert it into a wine museum.

Sanlúcar is famous for its very dry *manzanilla* sherry, its flavour caused by the salt laden winds blowing off the ocean, giving a *flor* (the yeasty skin within the barrels) throughout the year. The largest of the sherry producers is the Barbadillo family, who make four varieties – a Fina, an Olorosa, a Pasada and Solear Muy Vieja, plus an excellent table wine from Palomino grapes. The bodega is located at Calle Sevilla, in the old town. ■ *Mon-Sat 1200, 1300. Tours available in Spanish or English. €3 including tasting. T956385521 in advance for a tour.*

Sanlúcar is also noted for its horse racing, Carreras de Caballos de Sanlúcar, which has taken place for over 150 years during August. The thoroughbred horses race along a 1,800 m stretch of sand at the mouth of the Río Guadalquivir.

Bonanza   Up river from Sanlúcar is the small fishing village of Bonanza, which is the actual spot where both Magellan and Columbus left on their voyages. Today, a busy auction takes place each afternoon when the fishing fleet returns. North of Bonanza is an area of commercial salt production, the Salinas de Bonanza, which is an excellent area for birdwatching, particularly for migrant and wintering wildfowl and waders. The salinas are private, but the owners are sympathetic to responsible birdwatchers. A day permit is essential, however, and should be obtained at the company's office at the entrance.

Coto Doñana   Across the river from Sanlúcar is the nature reserve of Coto Doñana (see page 128). Foot passengers can cross the river by motor boat from the fishing quarter of Bajo de Guía, but to get there by car, however, requires a 150 km, three-hour round trip via Sevilla, which is the lowest bridging point of the river.

It is now possible to visit the Coto Doñana from Sanlúcar on the river boat *Real Fernando* (named after Spain's first steamship). Real Fernando is a substantial boat, with a snack bar and other facilities. The excellent guides are multilingual and there is a video on the Coto Doñana shown on board. The price includes two guided tours around the park; of one hour and 30 minutes, respectively. The first stop is at La Plancha, a restored settlement of thatched huts originally occupied by charcoal burners. The second stop is at the *marismas* where salt was once produced. The heat can be searing here in the summer as there is a total lack of shade. Wild boar and deer are more or less guaranteed, plus a wide range of birds including terns, little owls, egrets, black kites and a variety of waders along the river's edge. Binoculars are useful and can be hired on board. ■ *Departures are at 1000 and 1600 Mar-May, 1000 and 1700 in September, 1000 and 1600 in October and at 1000 only in November and February. Check with the Centro de Interpretación located opposite the departure jetty, T956363813, for any changes and to reserve tickets. Cost €13.25, children €6.25. No sailings on Monday.*

The return journey to Cádiz can be made inland following the A440 to Jerez and then using the NIV.

Sleeping
See inside front cover for price codes

There is a good choice of accommodation in Sanlúcar, apart from budget places. Everything is likely to be taken in Jul and Aug. **A** *Doñana*, Av Cabo Noval s/n (at Bajo de Guía), T956365000, F956367141. 100 light and reasonably large but soulless rooms in a modern resort-style hotel popular with tour groups. Its brochure advertises 'background music' as one of the hotel's advantages! Has a swimming pool, garage, a/c,

Sherry – amber nectar Spanish style

Sherry is produced largely within a triangle formed by the towns of Jerez de la Frontera, El Puerto de Santa María and Sanlúcar de Barrameda, covering some 20,000 ha of agricultural land. Any fortified wine grown outside this area cannot officially be termed sherry. The best growing areas have a white chalky soil called albariza. Its porosity soaks up the winter rains and gradually releases the moisture to the vine roots during the long, hot summer. Two-thirds of the grapes are of the palomino variety, while the remaining one third are of the Pedro Ximénez variety which are used to give sweetness, particularly in cream sherries.

The grapes are harvested in early September and taken to special houses for pressing. The resulting pulp goes into vats, where the juice is separated by gravity. It is only now that the amber liquid arrives at the bodegas where it spends several weeks in fermentation. By January it is clear and a thin crust of flor begins to grow on its surface. The flor del vino or flower of the wine is a type of yeast which is unique to the area. It grows most strongly in spring forming a crinkly white skin on the surface of the wine. Flor is only allowed to continue to grow on the fino, a light dry sherry. In the case of the heavier, darker olorosos the flor is killed by increasing the volume of alcohol in the wine to 18%. The design of the bodegas helps to develop the cool humid environment needed to encourage the flor. They have thick walls and high roofs, while windows are shaded with esparto grass. The floors are made of hard packed soil, which is sprayed with water during the heat of the summer.

Sherry does not have a vintage. The essence of its production is the blending using the solera system. This consists of hundreds of barrels (or butts) made of American oak and arranged in rows called scales. Three times a year 10% of each barrel in the bottom row is drawn off. This is replenished by 10% of the row above, known as the criadera or nursery casks; this is topped up by 10% from the row above and so on. The top row is then filled up from the current vintage. The solera system

ensures that the wine keeps the characteristics of the older stock and maintains its quality and taste. The success of the solera system relies on the skills of the bodega manager and the foreman, the capataz. Samples of wine are taken from the butts by means of a venencia, a small silver cup attached to a flexible stick. The amber liquid cascades down into tall glasses called cavatinos and by taste, sight and smell the capataz decides on the future of the wine and its route through the barrels. The main sherry types are:

Fino *- a very dry, delicate sherry, drunk cold and very popular in Andalucía as an accompaniment to seafood and tapas. It has a light straw-like colour.*

Oloroso *- darker, sweeter, with a higher alcohol content and matures without flor.*

Amontillado *- inbetween a fino and an oloroso, it carries flor throughout its maturing, but is darker and sweeter with a rather nutty aroma.*

Manzanilla *- comes from the coastal bodegas of Sanlúcar where the higher humidity, lower temperatures and salt-laden air produce flor throughout the year, giving a very distinctive flavour. Usually drunk with seafood.*

Cream sherries *- smooth and sweetened by the addition of muscatel or Pedro Ximénez grapes. Very popular in northern European countries such as UK and Holland.*

Certain well known sherries are a blend of different sherry types. Williams and Humberts Dry Sack, for example, is a blend of oloroso, amontillado and Pedro Ximénez. Surprisingly, apart from in Andalucía, sherry is not a popular drink in Spain, but this has not affected production as most of the sherry is exported. Some 70% goes to Britain, continuing the connection that has lasted since the 14th century. The members of the sherry dynasties often appear more English than the English, with their polo horses, tweeds and British public school education, leading to the derisive description of them as señoritos or little gentlemen - the nearest you will get to snobbery in this land of the amber nectar.

Cádiz Province

restaurant, wheelchair access. **B** *Tartaneros*, C Tartaneros 8, T956385378, F956385394. A smaller and considerably more pleasant option than the Doñana, this place has 22 simply decorated rooms in a 19th-century building in the town centre and an outside central patio in which to eat lunch. Garage, wheelchair access, a/c. **B** *Guadalquivir*, C Calzada de Ejército 10, T956360742, F956360745. 80 rooms. Disco. **B** *Posada de Palacio*, C Caballeros 11, T956364840, F956365060, www.sleepinspain.com 11 rooms. Restaurant. **C** *Los Helechos*, Madre de Dios 9, T956361349, F956369650. 56 rooms. Garage, a/c, restaurant. **D** *Las Marismas*, Plaza La Salle 2, T956366008. A small *pensión* close to the bus station, this is probably the best place to stay in town with a very pretty courtyard with rooms looking onto it and a roof terrace. Very good value (in the lower end of C category. **E** *Blanca Paloma*, Plaza San Roque 9, T956363644. Small, economical *pensión* in the older part of town.

Eating **Expensive** *Casa Bigote*, Bajo de Guía s/n, T956362696. One of several excellent fish restaurants along the same road, one back from the river. Others include *Casa Juan*, *Marisquería*, *Poma* and *Arante Claro*.

Jerez de la Frontera

Colour map 4, grid B2
Population: 181,602

The name Jerez is synonymous with sherry and the town is famed for its numerous **bodegas***, which are all close to the town centre. These have mostly been taken over by multinational companies, but the sherry dynasties remain and continue to ape the British upper classes, with their tweeds, polo horses and public school education. But Jerez has much more to offer than the 'amber nectar'. There are a number of historical monuments and museums, all within easy reach from the town centre, while in the suburbs there is southern Spain's best* **zoo** *and the world famous* **Equestrian School***. It also has a sizeable gypsy population mainly living in the Barrio de Santiago and providing some of the most authentic* **flamenco** *in Andalucía.*

Ins and outs

Getting there
See page 179
Conveniently the **train** and **bus stations** are close to each other a few blocks to the east of the city centre. Bus No 10 runs to the town centre. The **airport** is 7 km out of Jerez near the NIV and surprisingly there is no bus service to the city, so a taxi is needed and this will cost around €9.65. **Parking** is difficult to say the least and it is advisable to use the central pay parks.

Getting around
You can hardly miss the lilac coloured local buses, but most sights are in easy walking distance of the town centre.

Tourist offices
The municipal *turismo* is at Plaza del Arenal s/n, T956355654. Another office is in the main street, C Larga 39, T956331150, F956331150. Open Mon-Fri 0800-1400 and 1700-2000, Sat 1000-1400. It has a good range of brochures and maps. See also www.webjerez.com, www.diariodejerez.com and www.jerez.org

The area

Jerez de la Frontera lies 83 km south of Sevilla and 30 km northeast of Cádiz, in the agricultural plains south of the Río Guadalquivir. The city was known as Ceret in Roman times, but renamed Scherish by the Moors. This later changed to Xeres and finally Jerez. The 'de la Frontera' element of the city's name, as with many other towns in the area, dates from around 1380 when it marked a Moorish frontier and also reflects the fact that Jerez changed hands numerous times during the course of the Reconquest. Despite being outnumbered by almost 10 to one, the Moors under Tarik first captured Jerez in 711 following a battle against its Visigoth residents on the plains to the east of the town. Jerez was reconquered in 1251 by Fernando III, but subsequently lost in 1264 by his son Alfonso X. The commander of the Christian forces, García Gómez Carillo, so impressed the Moorish victors that they spared his life. This was clearly a mistake, because after a major siege lasting five months, Alfonso and Carillo were able to recapture the town permanently.

The white, chalky soil in the area, known as *albariza*, has proved ideal for cultivating the Palomino grapes which produce the sherry for which Jerez has been famed for centuries, although, curiously, its vineyards are found many kilometres out of town. Many of the powerful sherry families were originally English, some having been involved in sherry production since the time of England's Henry VII. Today the town presents deep contrasts, with sterile high-rise suburbs and a fascinating ancient centre, with a close knit gypsy barrio and the upper-class villas of the sherry barons.

Sights

Cádiz Province

Fortunately all the places of interest and most of the sherry bodegas are within easy walking distance of the *main square*, the Plaza del Arenal. It is said that this name originated when two knights accused each other of treason and fought for two days and nights in the sandy arena, before King Alfonso stopped the fight personally and pardoned both knights.

Just to the south of the Plaza del Arenal is the Alcázar, which dates back to **Alcázar** the 11th century when it was built by the Almohads. It was once the residence of the Caliphs of Sevilla. It has been heavily restored and consists mainly of walls and the 12th-century octagonal tower. The interior contains a mosque that was transformed into the **Iglesia de Santa María la Real** by Alfonso X when he recaptured the town. Within the grounds is the 18th-century Palacio de Villavicensio, which has a camera obscura show. Also worth seeing at the Alcázar are a Moorish bath house (see below) and some attractive gardens. ■ *May-Sep 1000-2000, Oct-Apr 1000-1800, €1.50 (extra for the camera obscura show).*

Located on the Plaza de la Encarnación, the cathedral, although sited on a **Catedral de** mosque, dates only from the 18th century and is Baroque in style. Amongst its **San Salvador** treasures are a 14th-century figure of Christ, *Cristo de la Viga* and Zurbarán's painting *La Virgen Niña* (Our Lady as a Child). ■ *Daily 1730-1800 during Mass.* In the same area a further reminder of Jerez's past role as a defensive outpost can be seen in the fragments of the original city walls from the Almohad-Almoravid period which still remain, including the **Puerta del Arroyo** at the junction of Calle Calzada del Arroyo and Puerta del Rota.

On the same hill as the Alcázar, these *hammam* date back to the period when **Baños Arabes** Jerez was part of the Caliphate of Córdoba. ■ *Mon-Sat 1100-1330 and 1700-2000, Sun 1100-1330. Free.*

Iglesia-Convento de Santo Domingo Originating from the time of the Reconquest, the convent is an odd mixture of architectural styles. It was badly damaged by fire during the Civil War, but has been carefully restored. Note the 17th-century *retablo*, which has the town's patron, the *Virgen de la Consolación,* as its centrepiece. ■ *0730-1000 and 1730-2130.*

Museums **Centro Andaluz de Flamenco** Located in an 18th-century building, the Palacio de Penmartín, at Plaza San Juan 1, this museum has a collection of musical instruments and the history of the art of flamenco, which *Jerezanos* claim began in their town. Video presentations every hour on the hour; you can also watch videos from their archive of famous flamenco performers. ■ *Mon-Fri 0900-1400. Free.*

Museo de Relojes This museum in La Atalaya Palace, Calle Lealas has a fascinating collection (once owned by disgraced tycoon Ruiz-Mateos) of more than 300 clocks from the 16th to the 19th centuries. Be prepared for the

Cádiz Province

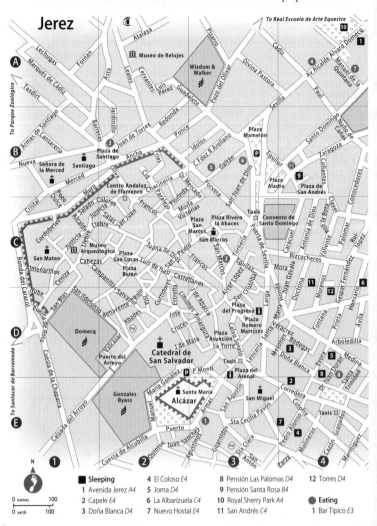

Jerez

■ Sleeping	4 El Coloso *E4*	8 Pensión Las Palomas *D4*	12 Torres *D4*
1 Avenida Jerez *A4*	5 Joma *D4*	9 Pensión Santa Rosa *B4*	
2 Capele *E4*	6 La Albarizuela *C4*	10 Royal Sherry Park *A4*	● Eating
3 Doña Blanca *D4*	7 Nuevo Hostal *E4*	11 San Andrés *C4*	1 Bar Tipico *E3*

0 metres 100
0 yards 100

noise when they are all striking on the hour! ■ *Mon-Sat 1000-1400. €2.40.*

Museo del Vino Located in the Casa del Vino, Avenida Domecq, this museum traces the history of sherry making. ■ *Sun-Fri 1000-1300.*

Museo Arqueológico Based in an 18th-century mansion in the Plaza del Mercado, the displays are in rooms around an attractive plant-filled patio. There are exhibits from the Chalcolithic, Iberian, Roman, Visigothic and Moorish periods. Among the numerous highlights, don't miss the collection of Roman amphorae, the Moorish ceramics and the chronological collection of old coins. ■ *Jun-Aug daily except Mon 1000-1430; Sep-May Tue-Fri 1000-1400 and 1600-1900, Sat and Sun 1000-1430. €1.50.*

Parque Zoológico, on Calle Taxdirt on the northwest suburbs of Jerez, has botanical gardens and a park in addition to the zoo. One of the few decent zoos in Andalucía, making a big effort to preserve and breed endangered species. ■ *Tue-Sun all year, summer 1000-2000, winter 1000-1800. €2.55.*

Other sights

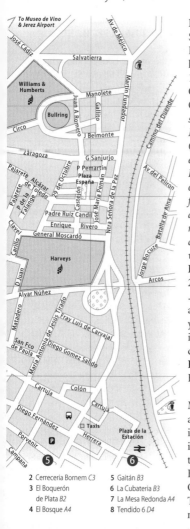

2 Cerrecería Bornem *C3*
3 El Boquerón
  de Plata *B2*
4 El Bosque *A4*
5 Gaitán *B3*
6 La Cubatería *B3*
7 La Mesa Redonda *A4*
8 Tendido 6 *D4*

The **Real Escuela de Arte Equestre,** or Royal Andalucían School of Equestrian Art, on Avenida Duque de Abrantes sin número is located in the Palace of the Cadenas, a 19th-century mansion built by Garnier, the architect of the Paris Opera. ■ *You can see Training sessions and have a tour of the stables, on Mon, Wed and Fri 1000-1300. €6, OAPs, students and children €3. An equestrian ballet is performed by the Dancing Horses of Andalucía at 1200 on Thu and 1200 on Tue Mar-Oct, from €12, students and OAPs 40% discount. T956319635, www. realescuela.org Many tour companies combine the horse show with a bodega visit.* Jerez is hosting the **World Equestrian Games** in September 2002. See www.jerez2002weg .com and make sure you book your accommodation well in advance if you are planning to be in the city during this period. Jerez's equestrian tradition is further demonstrated at the **Feria del Caballo** (Horse Fair), see Fiestas and festivals below.

Bodegas

Most sherry cellars offer guided tours and free tastings. The bodega buildings themselves are of considerable interest as each has a unique character. The domed structure at González Byass, for example, was designed by Gustav Eiffel, architect of the Eiffel Tower, while the Domecq bodega is a mass of rounded arches based on the

Cádiz Province

Mezquita at Córdoba. Note that the bodegas may be closed in late August and early September when the grape harvest or *vendimia* takes place, which in itself is a marvellous festival.

There is usually a demonstration by a vintner who dips a*venencia*, a silver cup on the end of a long pole, into a barrel and pours the sherry into the four glasses in his or her left hand without, of course, spilling a drop. It is best to phone beforehand as the largest bodegas may be fully booked with organized tours. Most bodegas have their own websites.

González Byass, Calle Manuel María González, conveniently located next to the Alcázar, is one of the largest bodegas. The tour used to feature a drunken mouse until he was devoured by a snake. There are now two equally inebriated replacement rodents. ■ *Daily 1½ hr visits, at 1100, 1200, 1300, 1630 and 1730 in Spanish and 1130, 1230, 1630 and 1730 in English. €6. Book in advance, T956357016, or see www.gonzalezbyass.es*

Harveys, Calle Arcos 57. ■ *Mon-Fri 0900-1300. €3. T956346004, jerez@domecq.es*

Pedro Domecq, Calle San Ildefonso 3, is near González Byass bodega. ■ *Visits from 1000 to 13300 by prior reservation, T956151500. €2.50. See also www.domecq.es*

Sandeman, Calle Pizzaro 10, is one of the smaller bodegas and is highly recommended. ■ *Visits Mon-Fri between 1030 and 1330; also Sat Mar-Oct. Book in advance, T956151700. See also www.sandeman.com*

Williams and Humbert, Ctra NIV, Km 641.75. Visits include a tour of the their gardens and stables. ■ *Visits between 1000-1400 Mon-Fri, T956353406. €2.40. See also www.williams-humbert.com*

Wisdom and Walker, Calle Pizarro 7. ■ *Visits at 1315 and 1400, except Thu, and 1400, T956184306. €2.40.*

Essentials

Sleeping
■ *on map, page 174*

There are a number of luxury hotels in Jerez, all of which are recommended, and plenty of cheap *pensiones* near to the town centre, conveniently close to both the bus and train stations. There is little choice, however, in the intermediate range. High season rates in Jerez tend to be charged during the *feria* rather than in high summer.

AL *Guadalete*, C Duque de Abrantes 50, T956182288, F956182293. 137 rooms. Garage, pool, a/c. **AL** *Jerez*, Av Alcade Alvaro Domecq 35, T956300600, F956305001. 120 rooms. Quiet location on north side of town, pool, sports facilities. **AL** *Montecastillo*, Ctra Jerez-Arcos, Km 9.6, T956151200, F956151209. 120 rooms. Pool, a/c, wheelchair access, quiet location. **AL** *Royal Sherry Park*, T956303011, F956311300. 173 rooms. Modern, pool, gardens, a/c, wheelchair access, quiet but central location. **A** *La Albarizuela*, C Honsario, 6, T956346862, F956346686. A brand spankingly new hotel, all white minimalism (a nod of respect for the white chalky soil known as *albariza,* the natural Palomino grape habitat) with spic and span bathrooms. Friendly management and interestingly shaped, light and airy rooms.

B *Capele*, C Corredera 58, T956346400, F956346242, 30 rooms. Garage, a/c, central position. **B** *Doña Blanca*, C Bodegas 11, T956348761, F956348586. There's a modern, but faintly gone-to-seed feel about this hotel, with its canned musak in the lobby and sometimes stuffy rooms. But some have balconies and pleasant views over the city and it's central, so not too bad a choice in this price range. Garage, a/c. **B** *Joma*, C Higueras 22, T956349689. Close to the town centre, this hotel is again modern and rather characterless but has some light rooms with decent views. 29 rooms. **B** *Trujillo*, C Medina,

36, T956342438. A more unusual hotel in a late 18th-century building with Moorish-style staircase and carved wooden ceilings. Last refurbished in the 1960s so a bit crumbly, but with considerably more character than most of the hotels in Jerez – especially in this price range – and has all the same facilities of a/c, garage and TV etc. A very good deal in low season – €35 for a double.

C *Aloha*, Ctra Jerez-Madrid, Km 637, T956302500. A/c, pool, quiet out of town location. **C** *Avila*, C Avila 3, T956334808, F956336807. 32 rooms. A/c. **C** *El Ancla*, Plaza Mamelón, T956321297, F956325005, www.helancla.com Basic, modern rooms with bath or shower and a/c. Pleasant service and a convenient, central location. **C** *El Coloso*, C Pedro Alonso, 13, T/F956349008. Simple rooms in modern hotel that could perhaps do with some redecoration, but also has self-catering apartments to let, leading off a pleasant white courtyard; a good deal if you're planning to stay for a week or more. Relaxed and friendly management.

D *Nuevo Hostal*, Caballeros 23, T956331600. 27 rooms. In an elderly building of some charm, in the shadow of the Iglesia de San Miguel. **D-E** *San Andrés*, C Morenos 12 y 14, T956340983. Undoubtedly the best option in this price range, this is a delightful place to stay, with a beautiful tiled tropical coutryard and garden that is the owner's pride and joy and rooms with balconies looking both on to it and out over the town. 26 rooms. Often used by students of flamenco staying in Jerez, ask around if you want to have some lessons. **D** *Torres*, C Arcos 29, T/F956323400. A/c, wheelchair access. **E** *Las Palomas*, C Higueras 17, 956343773. 41 rooms. Quiet location, cheap, but not especially friendly. **E** *Santa Rosa*, C Gaspar Fernández 8, T956347082, F956323400. 42 rooms. Garage, central position. **Youth hostels** *Albergue Juvenil*, Av Carrero Blanco 30, T956342890. South edge of town (take the No 9 bus). 128 beds, shared rooms, meals available, suitable for wheelchair users, sports facilities. IYHF card required.

As in nearby El Puerto, it is the local habit to buy fresh fish and shellfish from *freidurías* and *marisquerías* and take them to a bar to eat with a drink. One of the most popular *freidurías* is **El Boquerón de Plata**, Plaza de Santiago. **Expensive** The best restaurants are undoubtedly in the *comedores* of the luxury hotels, such as: *El Cartujano*, Hotel Jerez, Av Alvaro Domecq, T956300600; *El Abaco*, Hotel Sherry Park, Av Alvaro Domecq, T956303011; *El Lagar*, Hotel Montecastillo, Ctra Arcos, Km 8, T956189210. **Mid-range** For a more local flavour at reasonable prices try these below. *El Bosque*, Av Alvaro Domecq, T956303333. Traditional Andalucían specialities served in this popular Jerez restaurant. *Gaitán*, C Gaitán 3, T956345859. Modern and traditional cuisine, with especially good seafood, this is another classic place, popular with locals; closed Sun. *La Mesa Redonda*, C Manuel de la Quintana 3, T956340069. More local cuisine in an established and traditional Jerez restaurant which has gained a well-deserved reputation for itself. Well worth the few extra euros you will have to shell out for it. *Tendido 6*, C Circo 10, T956344835. Located near the bullring serving fish specialities. A recommended Chinese restaurant is *Hong Kong*, Plaza San Andrés 5, T956343851.

Eating
● *on map, page 174*

Tapas bars There is a multitude of tapas bars to choose from, with the local *fino* the usual accompaniment. Try *Bar Juanito*, C Pescadería Vieja 4 (just off the Plaza del Arenal), a great introduction to Jerez. If you arrive at lunchtime head straight for this bar and your first impressions of Jerez will never leave you. Delicious *carne* and *jamón* dishes as well as *gambas*. *Bar La Valencia*, C Larga 3, right in the main commercial area, is a decent place to recharge your batteries after shopping. *La Abacería*, Plaza Rafael Rivero s/n, is another gem, where you can sit outside at lunchtime in a pretty square and eat *boquerones con pimiento* (anchovies with pepper), delicious patés and *tostados* and sip a decent *fino* or beer. In the evening it is a lively meeting place for young locals. Nearby is another decent place, *Bar El Barril Plaza*, C Rafael Rivero. If you are wandering around the Alcázar at night, stop in for some excellent fino at the small *Bar Tipíco de Jerez* on Puerto Armas, when all the tourists have gone home. Surrounded by sherry barrels and some tourist kitsch, this place is actually an old timers' joint where the regulars are happy to ignore you or talk to you as you please. Also serves excellent *jamón y queso*. If you find that *fino* is getting too much for you, *Cervecería Bornem*, C Horno 1, is a specialist beer bar in a sherry town. Serves beers from all over the world in a bizarre central European/Spanish bodega/beer cellar. Also has an extensive Spanish wine list. *Café Teatro*, Plaza Romero Martínez, next to the Teatro Villa Marta, is a good stop-off for a coffee during the day. Strangely decorated with photos of Hollywood film stars of yesteryear rather than today's Spanish stars of the stage next door, this place is nevertheless a bar without any pretentions to grandeur.

Bars & clubs Much of the club nightlife of Jerez goes on in the area around and to the north of the bullring, especially C Nuño de Cañas. Other more relaxed, but late night, bars worth checking out include the low key *La Cubatería*, Plaza Mamelón 9. A small, slick looking bar with a down-to-earth owner who enjoys a chat (so long as you speak Spanish) well into the early morning and has a huge and varied record collection of music from the last 3 decades. A great place to try the wonderfully smooth and plum-like Jerez Cardinal Mendoza brandy. See also *La Abaceria* above.

For **flamenco**, go to the Barrio Santiago and *La Taberna Flamenca*, C Angostillo de Santiago 3, which is a reasonable place to start. Performances here are highly regarded, but it is a considerably less spontaenous affair than you may find elsewhere in this district. For the real thing, try the *peñas* (flamenco clubs) of *Peña la Buena Gente*, C Lucas 9; *Peña Antonio Chacon*, C Salas 2; or *El Laga de Tío Parilla*, Plaza del Mercado. There's no point in arriving before 2230 at any of these venues and expect to pay around €12 for your first drink. Flamenco festivals are often held in the town during the summer. Ask the tourist office or Centro Andaluz de Flamenco (see page 174) for details.

Entertainment **Cinemas** There are 3 cinemas in Jerez: *Delicias*, Paseo de la Delicias s/n, T956349642; *Jerezano*, Plaza de San Andrés s/n, T956341845; *Luz Lealas*, C Lealas s/n, T956183347. **Theatre** Jerez's only theatre is the *Teatro Villamarta*, C Romero Martínez s/n. The tourist office will have details of performances.

Fiestas & **May** *Feria del Caballo* This impressive Horse Fair has races, shows and competitions **festivals** featuring the locally bred Cartuja horses and 17th-century traditions. **The week before 24 Aug** *Fiesta de la Vendimia* This is the celebratation and blessing of the grape harvest. **Sep** *Circuito de Jerez* The city's race track hosts the Spanish Grand Prix. During the first fortnight is the *Fiesta de la Bulería*, a festival of song and dance. The month ends with the feast day of the patron saint of Jerez, *La Virgen de la Merced*.

Shopping The main shopping streets are between Plaza del Arenal and Plaza Romero Martínez, particularly C Larga and C Veracruz. Shops selling local craftwork including *La Espartería*, C Ramón de Cala 17, for wickerwork; *Cerámica Amaya*, Av Carrero Blanco 16, for pottery; and *Ferros*, C La Torre 4, for lanterns. There is a street market in the Plaza de la Asunción on Sun. **Sherry** The fino and brandy for which the town is renowned can be bought direct from the bodegas (see above) or from supermarkets, alternatively go the specialist sherry shop, *La Casa Del Jerez*, C Divina Pastora, 1, opposite the Escuela de Arte Equestre, T956335184, where you can sample before you buy.

Sport There is an olympic standard all-purpose stadium, *Complejo Deportivo Chapin*, located on the east outskirts of the town, T956342131. **Swimming** There are 2 pools – *Piscinas Jerez*, Ctra Arcos, T956340207; and *Piscina Cubierta*, C Poseidón s/n, T956312245.

Ecuador, C Consistorio 8, T956331150; Marsans, C Larga 53, T956341010; *Sherrytours*, **Tour operators**
Plaza de la Yerba 4, T956343912.

Air The airport, T956150083, is 7 km east of Jerez near the NIV. Iberia, T956150009, flies **Transport**
to Madrid and Barcelona and Buzz, T917496633, flies to Stansted, UK. **Bus** The bus sta-
tion is on C Cartuja, 1 km from the centre, T956345207. *Comes* buses, T956342174, go to
Cádiz hourly between 0700-2200 Mon-Fri, with 9 buses a day on Sat and Sun (50 mins,
€2.30); El Puerto de Santa María (12 daily, 30 mins, €0.95); Ronda (4 daily, 2½ hr, €8.25);
Málaga (1530, 5 hr, €15.95); Córdoba (1800, 3½ hr, €20). *Linesur-Valenciana*,
T956347844, go to Sanlúcar de Barrameda (30 mins) and Sevilla (1½ hr). *Los Amarillos*,
T956347844, go to Arcos de la Frontera and Ubrique. **Car hire** At the airport are *Atesa*,
T956150014; *Avis* T956150005; *Europcar* T956150060; *Hertz* T56150038. **Train** The sta-
tion is southeast of the bus station, at Plaza de la Estación, C Cartuja, T956342319. There
are frequent trains to Cádiz (45 mins, €2.35) and Sevilla (1 hr, €5.60). A RENFE office is at
C Larga 34, T956334813; open Mon-Sat 0900-1400, 1700-2030.

Banks These are found around the Plaza Romero Martínez and in C Larga and **Directory**
Porvera. There are numerous ATMs. **Communications** Post Office: Correos, C
Veracruz, off C Santa María. Open Mon-Fri 0800-2100, Sat 0900-1400, T956349295.
Internet: *Kerenet*, C Zaragoza, T956348598. Cheap internet access in this newly
opened space that isn't really a bar – more of a youth club. **Embassies and consul-
ates** *Denmark*, C Manuel González 12, T956340000; *France*, Ctra Madrid-Jerez, Km
634.6, T956302354; *Germany*, C Pizarro Bodegas Sandeman, T956301100; *Italy*, C
Manuel González 12, T956340000; *Portugal*, C Manuel González 12, T956340000.
There are no British or American consulates in the area. The nearest are in Sevilla. **Medical services** First Aid from *Casa de Socorro*, C Diego Fernández Herrera 5,
T956341349; **Cruz Roja**, C Alcubillas s/n, T956341549. For urgent treatment: *Sanitorio
de Santa Rosalia*, C Cañada de Miraflores, T956181650; also *Hospital de Santa Cruz*, Av
de la Cruz Roja s/n, T956307454. **Useful addresses** Garages/car repairs: most of the
large car firms cluster along the Ctra Madrid-Cádiz on the northern outskirts of the
town. *Citroën*, J Paez SA, Ctra Madrid-Cádiz s/n, T956344401; *Ford*, Ctra Madrid-Cádiz,
Km 634, T956305200; *GM*, Ctra NIV, Km 635, T956304766; *Peugeot*, Autosherry, Ronda
Muleres 12, T956344663; *Renault*, Ctra Madrid-Cádiz, Km 634, T956306900; *Seat/VAG*,
Ctra Madrid-Cádiz, Km 635, T956306300.

Around Jerez

This small fresh water lake, popular with birdwatchers, is located by the C440 **Laguna de**
Jerez-Medina Sidonia road, about 11 km from Jerez. Look for the large **Medina**
cement works opposite the lake. It is well signposted and there is a small car
park. In the generally monotonous rolling landscape around Jerez the path
along the south side of the reserve provides a pleasant walk, even for
non-ornithologists. In winter, there can be large concentrations of wildfowl
including rarities such as marbled ducks and crested coots. Breeding birds
include black-necked grebes and purple gallinules, while raptors such as
marsh harriers, red kites and Montagus harriers are often around. The margins of the lake are particularly attractive to waders in periods of migration.
This is also an excellent spot for dragonflies, butterflies and wildflowers.
Visitors are requested to keep to the path and avoid the north shore, which is
privately owned.

Lying 4 km along the C440 to Medina Sidonia is the Carthusian monastery of **La Cartuja**
La Cartuja. It has a long history, being founded in 1477. During the

Peninsular War it was used as a barracks by French soldiers, who caused considerable destruction to the building and in 1835 it was closed down. It was given back to the Carthusians in 1949 and now supports a small closed order that continues its archaic traditions by refusing to allow women to participate in its late afternoon visits. The grounds are entered through an impressive gateway that leads to the church, which has a marvellous Baroque façade dating from the 1660s and is rich in carved stonework in a golden sandstone with a colony of Lesser Kestrels breeding among the niches and gargoyles. ■ *Guided tours of the interior on Tue, Thu and Sat, 1700-1830.*

The White Towns and the Parque Natural Sierra de Grazalema

'Oh, white walls of Spain!' wrote Federico García Lorca in one of his deeply felt poems, presenting this colour as one of the most personal characteristics of the popular architecture of Spain. Andalucía typifies this architecture and the classic pueblo blanco - more like a village than a town - is best seen in the triangle of land between Málaga, Sevilla and Algeciras, including Ronda (see page 273). One White Town route described below starts in Medina Sidonia near Jerez and follows the A393 to Arcos and then the A372, through colourful rolling hills of intense greens, soft greys, reds, browns and blues where olives and holm oaks grow, to the bustling and ancient white-walled town of Ubrique and Ronda.

It is also possible to head north of this road at El Bosque into the Parque Natural Sierra de Grazalema through an area that is both rocky and mountainous, green and forested and remote in parts. Until recently it was bandit territory – read Washinton Irving's account in Tales from the Alhambra *of his trip from Sevilla to Granada – today, however, you are more likely to be taken for a ride by the prices in some of the more tacky restaurants of the various villages on the route. But despite the tourists, the pueblos blancos have managed to retain their Moorish character and the Grazalema park can provide a refuge if village life gets too much, as well as some wonderful walks, as well as some excellent walking.*

Ins and outs

Getting there & around All the villages below are serviced by *Los Amarillos* **buses**. There are services from Jerez (T956329347), Cádiz (T956285852), Sevilla (T954989184), Ronda (T952187061), Málaga (T952363024) and between each village, including Ubrique (T956468011). Telephone their offices in the above places (numbers in brackets) for up-to-date timetable information. More frequent services are from Jerez and Cádiz; between villages, buses are sometimes only once daily and not on Sun.

It is also possible to **walk** from El Bosque to Benahoma and from there through the Parque Natural Sierra de Grazalema to Grazalema via the Sendero del Pinsapar. You need a permit for this, obtainable from the park office in El Bosque (see below), or from the smaller offices in Grazalema or Zahara de la Sierra. See the individual towns below for more information. Other walks in the area include the Sendero de la Garganta Verde (see Zahara de la Sierra below).

Medina Sidonia
Colour map 4, grid B2
Population: 10,985

About 35 km southeast of Jerez along the C440 is the ancient hill town of Medina Sidonia. Here a dukedom was created in the 15th century to the family of Guzmán el Bueno of Tarifa fame, who led the capture of Medina Sidonia from the Moors. It was one of the early dukes who led the Spanish

Armada in its ill-fated attack on England. The town is dominated by the 15th-century Iglesia de Santa María, built on the site of an old castle, parts of which still survive. The interior is dominated by the massive Plateresque *retablo*. Look for the painted wood carving *Cristo del Perdón,* which was carved either by Pedro Roldán or his daughter Luisa. The church tower can be climbed and it's worth the exertion for the impressive views north over the cliff edge and across the plains towards Arcos. Other places of interest include the three surviving Moorish gates, the churches of San Agustín and Santiago, the 18th-century Ayuntamiento and the ducal palace. There is little in the way of accommodation – Medina Sidonia is not really used to tourists – but if you reach the top of the hill you'll find that the small square outside the church has a good restaurant, *Mesón Bar Machín,* T956410850, with a dining room full of farming antiques, a terrace providing a wonderful view over the rooftops of the town and an economical *menú del día*.

Arcos de la Frontera

Arcos, the most westerly of the *pueblos blancos,* has an unrivalled position sitting on a long ridge above a steep limestone cliff dropping down to the Río Guadalete. There is a sprawl of white houses, comparing dramatically with the brown sandstone of the castle and the churches. Remote from the Mediterranean coast, Arcos doesn't have as many visitors as, say, Ronda, but is all the more pleasant as a result. The town goes back to Roman times, when it was known as Arco Briga, but it was during the Moorish occupation that it began to assume importance. It was once part of the Córdoba Caliphate and then later an indepedent *taifa* until in 1103 it came under the influence of Sevilla. It held out against the Christian forces until 1264 – an indication of its wonderful strategic location.

Colour map 4, grid B3
Population: 27,897

Cádiz Province

The **Barrio Antiguo** or old part of the town is a maze of narrow streets that retain their Moorish pattern and is more suitable for donkeys than cars. The centre of the old quarter is the Plaza del Cabildo, with a mirador looking out over the cliff to the rolling countryside to the south. On the west side of the square is the 11th-century **Castillo** established by the Ben Jazrum dynasty and now privately owned and closed to the public. The **tourist office** is also here (see below). Also in the square is the **Iglesia de Santa María de la Asunción**. It was built on the site of a mosque in Gothic-Mudéjar style. The original bell tower fell during the 1755 Lisbon earthquake and the replacement was never completed, giving a certain asymmetry to the overall effect. The Plateresque south side is impressive. The interior is rather dismal, although the magnificent choir stalls carved in a variety of woods by Roldán should not be missed. ■ *1000-1300 and 1600-1900,* €*0.90.*

Sights

Moving east is the **Convento de la Encarnación** with just the church surviving, and on the right the Convent of the Mercedarías Nuns (*dulces* available). Ahead is the **Church of San Pedro,** built in the 15th century over a Moorish fort in Gothic style with pointed arches. It is worth looking around inside where the *retablo* is believed to have been designed by Luisa Roldana, the daughter of Pedro Roldano. It's worth climbing the tower for the spectacular view over the town and away to the Bornos reservoir to the northeast. A further walk to the east end of the old town brings you to the Church of San Agustín, a former convent dating from 1539, and the Puertas Matrera, with an 11th-century wall and tower.

The helpful **tourist office** is on the Plaza del Cabildo sin número, T956702264. In summer it's open Monday to Saturday 1000-1500 and 1600-2030 (in winter 1000-1900); on Sunday 1030-1500 (same hours all year). They can give you a map of the old town and useful information on tours of the town or the surrounding area. There is also a tourist information kiosk in the Paseo Andalucía, open daily 1000-1400 and 1800-1930 (summer), 1630-1800 (winter). Guided tours of Arcos, costing €3, are held Monday to Friday at 1030, 1200, 1700 and 1830 and Saturday at 1030 and 1200.

The Holy Week processions are impressive and the floats have to be specially customized to negotiate the narrow streets. On 29 September is the **Feria de San Miguel**, when fighting bulls rampage through the streets. The local teenagers run before them, dodging into doorways and jumping up on street signs and balconies to evade the horns.

Cádiz Province

Sleeping
See inside front cover for hotel price codes

Most of the accommodation in the old part of the town is at the upper end of the range. Budget options are in the newer area to the west. **AL** *Parador Casa de Corregidor*, Plaza del Cabildo s/n, T956700500, F956701116. The usual comfort you'd expect from a parador: 24 attractive, light and airy rooms with terrace-balconies with spectacular views over the cultivated, fertile plain below. A good but expensive restaurant. **A** *Cortijo Faín*, Ctra de Algar, Km 3, T/F956701167. A small luxury alternative on the southeast outskirts of the town, in a converted 17th-century *cortijo*. **B** *Los Olivos*, C San Miguel 2, T956700811, F956702018. A/c, small hotel at quiet end of the town with good views over the cliff. Easily accessible by car. **C** *El Convento*, C Maldonado 2, T956702333. 8 rooms. Atmospheric accommodation in the old 17th-century convent at the back of the parador. Good restaurant (see below). **D** *Andalucía*, Polígno Industrial El Retiro, T956700714. 5 rooms, restaurant, on the edge of an industrial estate on the Jerez road. **D** *Málaga*, C Luis Cernuda 1, T956702010. 14 a/c, traditional rooms with TV. **D** *Callejón de las Monjas*, C Deán Espinosa 4, T956702302. A simple and cosy *pensión* with 8 rooms in the centre of the old town. **D** *San Marcos*, C Marqués de Torresoto, 6, T956700721. A tiny *hostal* with just 4 rooms, all with bath; this is your best bet in this category. Also has a bar.

Outside Arcos C *Mesón de la Molinera*, Ctra Arcos-El Bosque (A382), Km 6, T956700511, F956702967. Located at a development on the banks of the Bornos reservoir, with watersports, fishing and a replica Mississippi paddle steamer, is this chalet accommodation with 20 rooms and a pool. **Camping** *Lago de Arcos*, Santiscal s/n, just off the A382 to Ubrique, T956708333. Camping or basic *hostal* accommodation with a pool.

Eating
See inside front cover for restaurant price classifications

Expensive *El Convento*, C Marqués de Torresoto 7. The classy but low key restaurant of the hotel of the same name, local game dishes a speciality. **Cheap** *Mesón Las Callejas*, C Callejas 19. Hostal restaurant with an economical *menú*. *Los Faraones*, C Debajo del Corral, T956700612. Genuine Turkish restaurant with regular belly dancers to aid the digestion; *menú del día* €7.85. *La Gran Muralla*, C Josefa Moreno Segura 2, T956704120. Chinese restaurant offering a *menú* €4.85.

Transport

Bus *Comes* buses run regularly to Cádiz, Jerez and Ronda. The bus station is in the newer part of the town, in C Corregidores. Contact the tourist office (see above) for timetable information. **Car** If arriving by car, follow the advice on the signs and leave your car in the parking spaces in the square on the western edge of the town and walk from here.

El Bosque

Shrouded in the dark green pine woodland of the Sierra de El Albarracín and at an elevation of nearly 385 m, the white walls of El Bosque are perhaps not as dramatic as some of the other *pueblos* in the park, such as Grazalema and Zahara further north (despite the fact that the latter has recently won a national award for visual improvement). It is, however, a bustling village and the administrative centre (and gateway) of the **Parque Natural de Sierra de Grazalema**. The El Bosque river flows through the town and fresh trout is on the menu everywhere (although you can fish in the river, the fish are also farmed here). There is also a popular hang-gliding take-off point above the town in the Sierra de El Albarracín and as a result there are plenty of accommodation options including a youth hostel and a campsite.

For details of **walking** in the park, visit the **park office**, in the Centro de Visitantes de El Bosque on Avenida de la Diputación sin número, T956727029, pn.sgrazalema@cma.junta-andalucia.es They will give you a map of the park (although not a decent topographical one, for this you will need to go to Ubrique – see below) and you can find out if you need a permit. Certain areas to the north of Benahoma (see below) have restricted access and although you do not need to pay, you will not be allowed in if there are 30 people already there. In the height of summer there are also sometimes restrictions to prevent forest fires. You can apply for a permit to enter the park from the visitor centres in Grazalema and Zahara de la Sierra too, where they will contact this main office for you and fax the permit back. ■ *Daily 1000-1400 and Fri-Sat 1600-1800.*

Sleeping **B-C** *Las Truchas*, Av de la Diputación s/n, T956716061, F956716086, www.tugasa.com The only posh option in town, this, a largish, modern riverside hotel with 24 spacious rooms. It's very comfortable, but a little institutional and impersonal. Part of the *Tugasa* chain. A short drive from the beginning of the Benamhoma - El Bosque walk described on page 189. **D** *El Tabanco*, C La Fuente, T956716081. Rather small and sometimes dark rooms, but all have TV and bath, so this is not a bad deal. Restaurant attached serving fresh trout and basic fried meat dishes with chips. **E** *Casa Gil*, Av de la Diputación, T956716008. Apartments and rooms to rent in this large and friendly family home. An apartment sleeping 6 costs €90 per night. **Youth hostel**: *Albergue Molino de En Medio*, Av de la Diputación, in the park behind *Las Truchas* hotel, T956716212. 37 beds in double and triple rooms and you can **camp** as well. Undergoing extensive renovation at time of writing. **Camping**: *La Torrecilla*, 1km out of town on the road to Ubrique, T956716095.

Eating The 2 hotels above have reasonable restaurants serving basic meat (mainly pork) dishes and fresh trout (both **mid-range**). *Juan Calvillo*, Plaza del Andén s/n, T956716010, is a large and friendly place with a basic menu.

Benahoma From El Bosque you can either travel south to Ubrique or east on the A372 to the small and tranquil village of Benahoma. From El Bosque it's also a pleasant 4 km walk along the Sendero del Río Majaceite through the park. Surrounded by a cloak of pinsapo Spanish firs, this isolated settlement has a very watery feel to it with streams tumbling down the peaks that protect it. There's a trout farm (open the the public) fed by the source of the Majaceite river and next door is the Museo de Agua, a small but interesting homage to how humans have used water over the last three millennia. A small but intriguingly diverse market is held on Wednesdays, where you can buy anything from Bob Marley CDs to locally produced furniture.

Sleeping *Camping Los Linares*, Camino del Nacimiento s/n, T956716275. An extensive campsite (€3.50 a night) and wooden cabins sleeping 4 (€63 total per night) with a large pool and restaurant.

Ubrique

Twelve kilometres south of the A372 on the A374 this white town spreads along the valley of the Río Ubrique. Ubrique is a friendly, urban base for exploring the Sierra de Grazalema, as well as the more peaceful rolling cork and holm oak countryside of the Parque Natural de los Alcornocales further south, which extends into Málaga province. Noted for producing guerrilla fighters, Ubrique was one of the last Republican strongholds in the Civil War. Today, with its thriving traditional leather industry, the town has a busy working community and, some say, an almost industrial feel to it; something lacking from the more tourism driven economies of smaller villages in the Sierra de Grazalema. Its setting, protected by the sheer limestone rock faces of the sierra to the north and east, which helped the Republican cause, also make this one of the area's most underrated destinations.

Castillo de Fátima Ubrique's only remnant of its Moorish past. The Casco Antiguo, or old town, is mainly 18th century, but there are some interesting examples of 16th- and 17th-century Christian architecture in the churches of **Jesús** and **San Juan de Letrán**. In the 19th century the town, prospering as a result of its newfound wealth from the fledgling leather industry, expanded down towards the river, where you will find most of the shops and **leather factories**. To visit one, organize a tour through the tourist office; see below. On the El Bosque Road just to the left before you come into town lie the second century AD Roman ruins of the town of **Ocurris.** Come here at sunset for great views over the plain to the south of the town.

The helpful and informative **tourist office** is at Avenida Dr Solís Pascual 19, T956464900, F956463941, www.ayuntamientoubrique.es You can arrange guided visits to Occuris or the leather factories here for €4.25. They can also provide town plans and are happy to answer questions about Ubrique's history. For large-scale maps of the area, go to *Editorial Tréveris*, a multimedia, book and map shop, Calle San Sebastián, T956463370, www.treveris.es which is a mine of information about the area. It also has **internet access** (€0.5 for 15 minutes).

Sleeping Ubrique is not overburdened with accommodation options; there's only 1 hotel and a handful of small *pensiones* within the town itself. **C** *Ocurris*, Av Dr Solís Pascual 51, T956463939, F956463925. A modern hotel just at the edge of the lower part of the town on the main high street, this place is convenient and comfortable, and has a friendly bar and a large restaurant. **C-D** *Posada El Molino* and *Casa del Panadero*, Camino del Castillo de Fátima s/n, M667942894, T956463953, elmolino @sierradecadiz.com Rural self-catering accommodation is available at 2 adjoining, sensitively restored and simple, but very comfortable, old whitewashed houses, surrounded by wild olive trees, 1 km outside Ubrique on the road to Benaocaz. *El Molino* has 4 doubles and *Casa del Panadero* 2. Rates depend on length of stay. **D-E** *Pensión El Cepo*, Av Dr Solís Pascual 16, T956462549. In the new part of town opposite the tourist office is this basic place, with bath. **D-E** *Pensión Rosario*, C José Antonio Primo de Rivera 3, T956461046. Small *hostal* with basic double rooms in the old town up the hill near the main plaza – definitely the best option in terms of location.

Casa Juan, Av de España 28B, in the new town, T956464077. Old fashioned and estab- **Eating**
lished unpretentious restaurant serving good grilled meat and *revueltos* (**mid-range**).
For a cheap tapas snacks during the day, try *Terraza El Jardín*, Plaza del Jesús s/n,
which also serves vegeburgers! Way up in the old town, a locally recommended tapas
bar worth tracking down is the simple *Bar Nuevo*, C Toledo 41. Another no-frills place
worth checking out in the same area is *Bar Torremolinos*, C Sanjuijo, next to the
16th-century Iglesia de San Antonio.

Grazalema

The gem of all the *pueblos blancos*, Grazalema is notorious as the wettest loca- *Colour map 4, grid B4*
tion in Spain. The rain ensures lush vegetation throughout the year. It is the *Population: 2,256*
main centre for the Parque Natural Sierra de Grazalema, a UNESCO biosphere *Altitude: 823 m*
reserve of 51,695 ha, which supports a wide range of birds (including a growing
population of Egyptian vultures), flowers and mammals. The Park is an ornithological wonderland. Most notable are the raptors: eagles (booted,
short-toed and golden) are easily spotted and it is not unusual to see 100 or
more griffon vultures on the wing: the largest colony in Europe inhabits the
rocky ledges of the 'Garganta Verde' close to Zahara de la Sierra (there are
exceptional views of the gorge on the Benamahoma-Zahara walk described
here). Numbers are being maintained thanks to various feeding sites in the high
Sierra. And one of the major migratory roots between Europe and Africa runs
along the western fringe of the park. Within the park in the Sierra del Pinar, near
Zahara de la Sierra (see below), is Spain's largest expanse of pinsapo, the rare
Spanish Fir. The traditional industry in Grazalema is the making of blankets
and ponchos (they are even exported to Argentina) and woodwork. The British
sociologist Pitt-Rivers wrote a classic study of the town called *People of the
Sierra*. The village has become an important tourist centre over the last decade
and many come to walk in the park and explore the varied flora and fauna, especially during summer. But with its two beautiful 17th-century churches, cottage
industry and sensitive development, the town still has a strong community feel
about it and makes an excellent base for visiting the park.

The park representative, or *Oficina de Información*, is at Calle Piedras 11, **Park**
T956132225, open Tuesday-Sunday 1000-1400 and 1600-1900 (winter), **information**
1800-2000 (summer). You can obtain permits for the restricted areas of the
park here (which entails a phone call to the main office in El Bosque (see
above) and then receive a permit by fax) and a map of the park explaining the
various walking routes from the town and which areas are restricted. For a
decent topographical map of the park, you will need to go to *Editorial Treveris*
in Ubrique (see above), but all the paths within the park are well signposted.

AL *Puerta de la Villa*, Plaza Pequeña 8, T956132376, F956132087. A large, swish, mod- **Sleeping**
ern hotel that has recently appeared and seems out of place with its surroundings,
although it's very comfortable and luxurious. An expensive restaurant serves hearty
mountain fare and the bizarre sounding 'frugal octopus salad'. **C** *Peñon Grande*, Plaza
Pequeña 7, T956132434, F956132435. A modern hotel built in keeping with the village
architecture. Rooms, although not huge, have pretty views of main square and church
or the sierra. A good mid-range option with restaurant. **D** *Casa de las Piedras*, C Las
Piedras 32, T956132014. Pleasant family run hotel with a relaxed atmosphere, restaurant and a pretty courtyard at the heart of Grazalema. Good value: a no-frills place,
rooms have tiny shower rooms but are comfortable. **Camping** at *Tajo Rodillo*, Ctra
C344 Km 49 (follow C Las Piedras to the end), T956132063. €5.75 for 2 adults and car.

Cádiz Province

Eating **Mid-range** *El Pinsapar*, C Doctor Mateos Gago. A decent wine list to go with a simple menu on which grilled trout is a good option. There are several *bares de copas* on
and near the main square serving basic tapas (try the goat's cheese in the spring and
early summer) and there's also a more modern saloon-type bar (with wide screen
TV), *Circulo de la Unión*, which gets lively with hikers needing a beer after a hard
day's walking.

Walks in the Sierra de Grazalema

The area around Grazalema and Ronda offers some of the most beautiful and
varied walking in Spain; it is for good reason that nearly every English walking
company offers tours based in the area. In spite of this - with the exception of
bank and school holidays - you'll meet with few walkers and it's not unusual to
spend a whole day in the hills without meeting another soul. The region's
popularity means that more documentation is available than is the case in
other areas - although most of this is in Spanish. The tourist offices of both
towns are good starting points and stock the excellent 1:50000 map of the area
(see below).

The Sierra de Grazalema park straddles the provinces of Cádiz and Málaga
and encompasses the most southwesterly mountain range in Europe, the very
tail-end of the Cordillera Bética. This rugged massif, predominantly composed of limestone and dolomite, rises dramatically up from the rolling farm-
lands around Jérez to a height of nearly 2,000 m. Although the park is
comparatively small compared to others in Andalucía– it covers an area of
just 500 sq km – its terrain is extraordinarily varied. Jagged formations of karst
give way to poplar-lined valleys, thick stands of cork and evergreen oaks alternate with old groves of olives and almonds and with fields of wheat and barley.

Continental, Mediterranean and Atlantic influences are all present and
Grazalema, plum in the centre of the park, receives more rainfall per square
inch than anywhere else in Spain. It is a remarkable micro-climate: villages
just 8 km from Grazalema receive a quarter of the rainfall. Don't let this put
you off coming to walk. The rainfall is markedly seasonal – November, April
and May tend to be the wettest months – and at other times of the year the
chances are that of the weather will be good. And the high level of precipitation means that the area is remarkably green by Andalucían standards.

What makes the park a double treat are not only the walks but also the *pueblos blancos*: narrow streets of whitewashed houses drop steeply down the hillsides and often just walking from the bottom to the top of a village is a hike in
itself. Grazalema, at the centre of the park and one of the very prettiest villages
in the area, has long been a popular destination for walking groups from the
UK for many years and also with the Spanish from Sevilla and Cádiz who flock
in at the weekends. So book ahead unless you are staying out of season, on a
weekday. Or you could stay in one of the quieter villages at the edge of the park
like Zahara, Montecorto, Benaocáz or Montejaque. And Ronda, of course,
offers a wonderful base, too.

The best **map** of the area is the 1:50000 *mapa/guía* of the Junta de
Andalucía/Instituto Geográfico Nacional which you can normally find at the
Grazalema newsagents and the two park offices in El Bosque and Grazalema.
The map covers all the itineraries listed here. The next best alternative are the
standard I.G.N.1:50000 maps. Sheets (*hojas*): Ubrique 1050, Olvera 1036,
Cortes de la Frontera 1064.

As well as places to stay in Grazalema itself and Zahara, there is **A** *Hotel
Molino del Santo* in Benaoján Estación, T952167151, F952167327, which is a

pleasant riverside hotel popular with Brits. You can get plenty of local knowledge and help with route-planning from the owner, who is a keen ornithologist. Vegetarian food available. The best base from which to explore the park, however, is C *El Tejar* in Montecorto, T/F952184053. Picnics can be prepared and the owners have unparalleled knowledge of local walks and are well used to walkers. They also have four horses.

This is one of the Sierra's most beautiful walks. There are constant changes of terrain, great views to the west across the rolling countryside that leads down towards Jerez and on clear days, to the Atlantic. You'll have a steep climb first thing if you leave from Grazalema (longer route) but you can avoid this by taking a taxi up to the Puerto del Boyar (call Rafael at the *Casa de las Piedras*, T956132014). Due to its popularity this walk is best undertaken on a weekday. Get going by 0930 to allow plenty of time for stops and a picnic along the way and to make the 1540 bus from Benaocáz back to Grazalema (Monday-Saturday). You could have a late lunch in Benaocáz. Beautiful stands of ancient oaks, interesting karst formations, exceptional flora and good raptor-spotting possibilities make this an exceptionally varied excursion. Map 1:50000 Parque Natural Sierra de Grazalema or 1:50000 Series L 1050 Ubrique.

Grazalema to Benaocáz via El Salto del Cabrero

Distance: 11-14½ km
Time: 4-4½-
5½-6 hours
Difficulty: medium (short route) – medium/difficult (long route)

Itinerary Longer route: leave Grazalema's square by passing between the Unicaja bank and the Ayuntamiento along Calle José María Jiménez. Bear left at the end past *Bar La Cabaña*, climb to the top of Calle Real then turn into Calle Portal. Take the next right and continue climbing to the top of the village where you should bear left past the Fromental cheese factory and then turn right onto the Grazalema-El Bosque/Zahara road. Just before reaching a bridge turn left off the road then follow a new path up through the pine trees all the way to the top of El Puerto del Boyar (50 minutes). Here pick up the itinerary below.

Shorter route: take a taxi to the parking area at the top of the pass between Grazalema and El Bosque, El Puerto del Boyar. Just behind a sign for 'Peligro de Incendio' go through the wire-and-post gate to the left of a second, larger gate then follow a track gently downwards. Just before reaching a farm (20 minutes) bear left, away from the track, towards two old oaks where dogs may be tethered. Go through a wire-and-post gate and head across a large, flat area past some magnificent old oaks. At the far end the path crosses a tumbledown wall then winds through thicker undergrowth, at times dividing. Keep left at any fork, sticking close to the cliff. The path soon swings sharply right, drops down by a wall, passes through a graffiti-covered gate, then descends. Be careful not to drop too far to your right; if in doubt, keep left at any fork, staying fairly close to the base of the cliff. The path eventually leads through another gate (50 minutes) where a walker symbol marks your way. After the gate bear right and climb to a flatter area; a lovely spot for a first break. The path now passes to the left of a fallen oak then climbs up through the brambles before reaching a large field. Head for the water trough at the bottom of the field then bear left and climb, following the same line as that of the trough. An indistinct path loops to the top of this open area then arcs right past a fallen oak (ignore a path which bears left and crosses a tumbledown wall). The path bears left to a wall and reaches a gate. Go through and continue, roughly parallel to the wall before angling right across open, rocky land towards the back of El Salto del Cabrero, or the Goatherd's Leap, whose grey massif is now directly ahead. Look for clumps of peonies between the rocks. Near the bottom of this rocky descent you climb over a wall then break out onto a vast, flat area (one hour 40 minutes) at the eastern base of the Salto. You emerge by a clump of oaks where there is welcome shade: a great spot for a picnic. It's possible to scramble up to the top of the Salto from here. A lot of the climb is hands-on, there's no clear path and you should allow an hour to get up and down. Otherwise you should bear left, away from the Salto across this vast open area.

At its far side you pick up a path which crosses a wall before climbing gently across another open tract of land. The path soon levels and Benaocáz comes into view. You'll shortly see a farm ahead of you which you should leave well to your left. The path soon descends, passes to the right of an old lime kiln then zigzags down through the rocks to a gate (two hours 15 minutes). You may spot griffon vultures perching on the cliff face to your right: look for their tell-tale guano. After the gate the path (loose underfoot) loops down to a flatter area then runs along beside a hawthorn-topped wall, passes through a green gate then follows the old drover's path whose ancient cobbling is still visible in parts. After crossing a stream by way of a pretty bridge it swings right, climbs, then widens to become a track which soon passes by some ugly, modern housing then the *Hostal San Antón*. At a garish villa bear left to the centre of Benaocáz (three hours) where *Bar La Palmera* is the best place to slake your thirst. Later head down Calle San Blas (by the Caja de San Fernando) and take the first left to reach the bus stop. The bus passes by at 1540, arriving at Grazalema 20 minutes later.

Benaoján Estación to Jimera de Líbar Estación
Distance: 9 km
Time: 2½-3 hours
Difficulty: easy

This short, easy walk follows a pretty riverside path linking the sleepy villages of Benaoján Estación and Jimera de Líbar Estación. It begins at the Molino del Santo, a hotel and restaurant just up from railway line, one of the very nicest places to stay in the Ronda mountains. You could set off after a late breakfast, dawdle along the way, have a lazy lunch in the excellent *Quercus* restaurant in Jimera de Líbar Estación then return by train later in the afternoon to the Molino or to your car. Departure from Jimera is at 17.33, arriving Benaoján Estación 17.39: times are liable to change so be sure to check. You could turn this into a longer walk by retracing your footsteps back along the Guadalete valley from Jimera or by continuing further south to Estación de Cortes: the train back to Benaoján leaves there at 17.24. Map 1:50000 Parque Natural Sierra de Grazalema or 1:50000 1050 Ubrique and 1064 Cortés de la Frontera.

Getting there If driving from Ronda take the A376 towards Sevilla then turn left on the MA555 towards Benaoján. After 12 km cross the railway and river bridges then turn left for Estación de Benaoján and follow signs to Hotel Molino del Santo. There is a train from Ronda to Estación de Benaoján at 0938. You'd have time enough to make the 1241 train back from Jimera to Ronda.

Itinerary The walk begins at the Molino del Santo in Benaoján Estación. Turn left out of the Molino's main entrance and walk down the hill to a stop sign at a level crossing. Turn left along the railway line, cross over a fast-flowing river and at a second level crossing turn right and cross the railway track. The road drops down, crosses the river Guadiaro and leads up to a sign marking the beginning of the walk, which recommends allowing a generous four hours. Turn right, away from the road at this sign, then follow a dirt track which runs along the left bank of the river. Soon you pass by an abandoned farm with three magnificent old palm trees. The railway to your right was the creation of a British engineer, Mr Henderson, who as well as constructing the Ronda-Algeciras line was also responsible for the one linking Lake Titicaca and Cuzco in Peru. The train that plied this route was known as the Smugglers' Express; it went so slowly that contraband butter, cocoa and rolling tobacco from Gibraltar would be sold from the train windows.

The track narrows to become a path which shortly crosses a small wooden bridge and then bears round to the right and passes a ruined farm. Shortly after the farm the path divides; take the left fork which leads slightly away from the river. The path leads through a gate and shortly afterwards you'll see that the railway is now on your side of the river. Don't deviate from this path. You eventually drop down, cross a (dry) stream (one hour 15 minutes) and after a short distance a concrete water channel runs to the left of the path. Soon you'll see a sign for 'Vía Pecuaria'; you are on the old drovers' path that lead from Cortés to Ronda. You reach a small olive grove: keep to its left hand edge and pass behind a pig-shed. Just past this shed your path comes in to meet with a driveable track. Continue on along this track then cross over a bridge where old bedsteads have been used as railings. You come to a fork by a telegraph pole. Here go right, ignoring the sign 'Camino de Huertas Nuevas'. The track descends, passes a modern house to the right then swings left to the station of Jimera de Libar (two hours). If planning to lunch at the Quercus restaurant you need to cross the tracks and turn right. After lunch either return by this same route or take the train; it's just a 10-minute ride back to Benaoján Estación along Mr Henderson's railway line.

If you don't mind walking along tracks rather than paths this makes for a truly great full day's excursion. The hardest part comes first thing, a long pull up from 500 m to 925 m via a well-surfaced track which hugs the course of the Breña del Agua stream. There are great views of the Sierra del Pinar and the Sierra del Labradillo. The second half of the walk is nearly all downhill with views eastwards into the gorges of Garganta Seca and Garganta Verde, home to one of Europe's largest colonies of griffon vultures. You'll almost certainly see several dozen of these enormous raptors during the walk. Steel yourself for a steep final haul up to Zahara. This route links two of the Sierra's prettier villages; if staying overnight, Zahara is recommended. The predominance of track rather than path means that you can forget where your feet are going and concentrate on the amazing views. Map 1:50000 Parque Natural Sierra de Grazalema or 1:50000 1050 Ubrique and 1036 Olvera. Take plenty of water. You'll need to take a taxi to the beginning or end of the walk. This is easily arranged in Zahara (Diego T956123109) or Benamahoma (Oracio T956 716199).

Itinerary The walk begins at the bottom of Benamahoma at the bus stop, next to Venta El Bujío. From here walk away from the village and take the first right turn at a sign for 'Molino de Benamahoma'. Cross the river and after some 40 m, where the road swings right, turn left. Follow a fence along for 50 m then swing right and climb straight up between two fences on a rough track to a white sign. Here turn right and go through a large, rusting gate. Ignore a left fork just after the gate and stick to the main track: prepare yourself for nearly 1½ hours of climbing. The track goes through a metal gate (45 minutes) and ten minutes later swings right past a ruined farmstead then arcs to the left. Shortly you reach a goat pen and drinking troughs to the left of the track. Careful! At the first large oak to the left of the track after the troughs look for a small cairn. Here bear left away from the track (one hour 15 minutes) following a path which climbs, indistinctly at first, to the top of a small pass (one hour 30 minutes) where it divides. Take the left fork and drop down between

Cádiz Province

Benamahoma to Zahara de la Sierra
Distance: 14 km
Time: 6 6½ hours
Difficulty: medium/difficult

the oaks. As you descend, looking ahead, you'll see a gently convex hillside. Head for its left side and soon you'll spot the track that you will later follow, cutting down across it. Sticking to this same course a building with a white-posted gate comes into view. Head for it keeping the Sierra Margarita to your left. You reach a gate which may be locked but you can go through a second smaller gate to its left. Soon to your right you'll see the Laguna del Perezoso, a shallow watering hole which is often dry. The track reaches a farm where it arcs right and a well-surfaced forestry track leads you down through lovely stands of ilex oaks overgrown with hawthorn, wild olive, ivy and gorse. You go through a wire-and-post gate (two hours five minutes) and continue your descent. Eventually the track bears sharply right then zig-zags down to the valley floor where it swings left and crosses a (dry) stream. Shortly you go through another wire-and-post gate then climb through old groves of olives to the pass of El Puerto de la Breña (two hours 55 minutes) where you break out into the next valley.

Ahead of you now are the rocky crags of Garganta Seca and Garganta Verde. Once over the pass the track bears left and descends, passing through another wire-and-post gate. Follow the main track down, ignoring tracks branching right or left. Eventually you go through a green gate (three hours 25 minutes) and continue your descent. The track crosses the Bocaleones stream, bears left and climbs through the olive groves. Prepare yourself for today's second steep haul! You reach a pretty farm to the left of the track with a palm tree. Here, just before reaching a green gate, turn right away from the track and follow a path steeply up through the olives. You cross a (dry) stream. The path improves and continues to climb then meets with a steep concrete track that leads up towards a pylon. You pass behind a row of modern houses then turn left and almost immediately sharp right and head up a street with a no-entry sign. The road bears left and you reach a wider street which swings right then left. Follow this street and you will reach the main square of Zahara (four hours 15 minutes).

Other walks **El Pinsapar** The classic Grazalema itinerary takes you through the heart of the Pinsapo forest. This full day excursion begins on the road leading from Grazalema to Zahara. After a stiff climb of nearly 1,000 feet a broad path leads through a large stand of pinsapos. You need a permit to do the walk which you can get from the park offices in Grazalema or El Bosque. Get going early to avoid school parties and other groups.

Other routes around Grazalema There are two recently waymarked routes – both half days - which begin near to the campsite on the road above the village. A good and easy-to-follow day's walk is to follow the river Campobuche (sometimes called the Gaduares) to Montejaque and then return by taxi. It is also easy to follow the route from Grazalema to Zahara which drops down the Gaidovar valley, skirts round Monte Prieto to Arroyomolinos where a track begins which leads you nearly all the way to Zahara. And *Walking in Andalucía* by Guy Hunter-Watts (Santana Books) lists further walks in the area

Benaoján to Ronda Details of this half-day walk can be obtained from the *Molino del Santo* in Benaoján Estación (see Walking in the Sierra de Grazalema above). It follows the old drovers' path and the final approach to Ronda, via a narrow gorge, is magnificent.

Zahara de la Sierra

An alternative route to Ronda is via the *pueblos blancos* of Zahara, Olvera and   *Population: 1,552*
Setenil, among others, by taking the road north to Zahara just before Grazalema.   *Altitude: 511 m*
Reached by the stark and silent Puerto de las Palomas, or the Pass of the Doves,
which is the highest pass in Andalucía, Zahara is a fortified Moorish hill village
overlooking a reservoir and dam which has flooded the valley below. The
Moorish castle (taken by the Catholic Monarchs in 1483) has been subject to
some rather severe and insensitive reconstruction and more is in progress. Below
this is an unexpected 18th-century Baroque church at one end of the main street,
with an impressive *retablo*. Just outside the village is the largest surviving stand of
pinsapo fir trees. Like Grazalema, the town is becoming increasingly popular with
tourists and has been declared a national monument, but there are pleasant bars
to relax in and the town is ideally placed for walking in the park.

   The Centro de Visitantes de Zahara de la Sierra is on Plaza del Rey,
T956123004, open daily 1000-1400 and 1600-1800. You can obtain a permit to
enter the restricted areas of the park from here (via a fax from the El Bosque
office) and there is a useful information point where you can find out all sorts of
interesting facts about the area's flora and fauna and what's on in town.

The most interesting walk from the town is the restricted **Sendero de la**   **Walking**
Garganta Verde, starting 3 km from Zahara up the road to Grazalema. Within
minutes of leaving the car park you enter a pristine, almost prehistoric, valley
with no sign of human interference except the odd sign requesting silence in a
breeding area for griffon vultures or giving information about nearby rock formations. After about 30 minutes of gentle walking the path descends rapidly,
passing a cliff where you can see vultures nesting (during the summer, access to
this area may be prohibited by the park authorities), into a canyon with sheer
rock faces rising above, up to 400 m in some areas. The air becomes cooler as
you follow the old river bed filled with huge boulders and unusual rock formations and descend deeper into the canyon. The route becomes slightly more
hazardous at this point as you are required to clamber over rocks to a large cave
called the Cueva de la Pileta. It is well worth the effort; the cave is made of an
unusual pink rock with stalagmites and stalactites and is some 30 m high and
approximately 75 km wide. Rock climbing equipment and a special permit are
required to continue beyond this point as the route along the canyon becomes
increasingly steep. The return journey is almost entirely uphill. Allow approximately four to five hours from the road for a round trip; only 30 people are
allowed access at any one time.

C *Arco de la Villa*, Camino Nazarí on the road just in front of the castle, T956123230. A   **Sleeping**
modern, intriguingly designed hotel with troglodyte pretensions, the building built into   **& eating**
the mountainside. Rooms are rather cell-like although the views of the reservoir and valley below make up for it. Despite a slightly institutional air, this is a good deal for the services on offer. Restaurant mid-range. **D** *Marqués de la Sierra*, C San Juan, 3, T/F956123061.
An old, refurbished, family run inn with 11 simple rooms some with views overlooking the
main street (can be noisy). Internet access and TV in each room. Small cave-like mid-range
restaurant attached for guests' use only. Horse treks available (€10.80 per hr), as well as
other tours. **E** *Los Tadeos*, Paseo la Fuente, T956123086. Basic rooms in a small *hostal* with
bar and restaurant. *Bar Nuevo* on C San Juan has some good *serrano* ham.

Cádiz Province

Olvera
Colour map 4, grid B4
Population: 8,884
Altitude: 643 m

North of Zahara on the A382 is Olvera, which is located, as its name suggests, in an olive growing area. The church, despite being built over a mosque, is 19th century. The Moorish castle, dating from the 12th century, is of more interest and the keep and defensive walls are in good condition.

Setenil de las Bodegas
Population: 3,310
Altitude: 640 m

This is a curious village with cave-like streets with houses built into the overhanging rock, which was once carved out by the river Guadalporcun. Setenil was formerly the centre of a wine producing area (the caves were used as wine cellars), but the industry was decimated by the phylloxera disease. The Moorish castle, which was conquered by the armies of Ferdinand and Isabel in 1485, is largely in ruins. The Iglesia de la Encarnación is 15th-century Gothic.

South from Cádiz

*This part of Cádiz province along the Atlantic coast is known as the **Costa de la Luz** and remains mercifully underdeveloped, containing fine beaches, flower strewn meadows, salt flats, rolling farmland, mountains and a number of small, but fascinating villages.*

Bahía de Cádiz

The shore of the Bahía de Cádiz is an officially designated natural park, covering some 10,000 ha. The bay itself is outstanding for its wintering wildfowl and seabirds. The shoreline has patches of dunes merging into salt marsh, much of which is used for the production of salt, so that entry is often forbidden. Although the NIV and the N340 cross the salt pans and birdwatching is possible from a car on the hard shoulder, this is not encouraged and those who stop will often be subjected to a barrage of horns from passing motorists. The banks between the *salinas* are also of interest for botanists with a wide range of halophytic plants.

Chiclana de la Frontera
Colour map 4, grid B2
Population: 55,494

Leaving behind the salt marshes, this is the first town of note, which is increasingly becoming a dormitory of Cádiz. Once known for its manufacture of traditional dolls, it now has a broader manufacturing base, with a ring of industrial estates to the south and east. The main development is to the southwest of the town, where a road cuts through the pine woods to the Barrosa beach area. Offshore stands the island of Sancti-Petri, with the remains of a Temple of Hercules, a 13th-century castle and a more modern lighthouse. Novo Sancti-Petri is a new tourist complex, with a 27-hole Ballesteros designed golf course (a contender for the 1997 Ryder Cup venue), apartments and luxury hotels. There are two campsites here including the first category site of *La Rana Verde*, Pago de la Rana sin número, in Chiclana, T956494348.

Conil de la Frontera
Colour map 4, grid B1
Population: 17,089

Back on the coast road, the N340, known here as the *Ruta de los dos Mares*, runs south past the luxury development of **Roche**, where a road runs through pine woods and villas to the beach which is backed by low cliffs. The next settlement is Conil de la Frontera, surrounded by a prosperous market gardening area. It was once a minor fishing village but is now developing as a holiday resort, although is as yet still unspoiled. It has two things in its favour – the old part of the town, which has plenty of character, and the broad sandy beach stretching for miles in each direction. The mouth of the small river Salado has been cleaned up from its formerly disgusting state with the construction of a new sewage works a km or so upstream. To the northwest of Conil are low cliffs and a scattering of small hotels, while to the south the dunes extend all the way through the hamlet of El Palmar to Cape Trafalgar.

Sleeping and eating The following are recommended: **A** *Flamenco*, C Fuente de Gallo s/n, T956440711, F956440542. 120 rooms. A/c, pool, wheelchair access, clifftop location, closed Jan-Feb. **C** *Garum*, Ctra N340, Km 24, T956443131. 19 rooms. Recently opened on the main coast road. **C** *Tres Jotas*, C San Sebastián 27, T/F956440450. Small, comfortable hotel with 39 rooms, located on the road into town. Garage. **Camping**: there are 6 campsites here, including *Camping Pinar Tula*, T956445500, with a good range of facilities, including pool, on N340 near Conil.

Further along the coast road is the hill village of Vejer de la Frontera, located on a cliff above a gorge eroded by the Río Barbate. Occupied by the Phoenicians and the Carthaginians, it was later the Roman Besipo. It then became the Moorish settlement of Bekkeh and it certainly retains its Moorish character, with its labyrinth of narrow streets, whitewashed patios and a ruined Alcázar.

Vejer de la Frontera
Colour map 4, grid C2
Population: 12,731

Worth visiting is the 13th-century Church of El Salvador. Built on the site of a mosque, it has a strange mixture of architectural styles, with gothic dominating. Look out for the reredos, containing statues and tilework. ■ *Daily 1100-1300 and 1900-2100.* Also of interest is the Castillo, originally Moorish, but extensively rebuilt in the 15th century. There is some recently uncovered Moorish plasterwork, a horseshoe arch and a small archaeological museum. ■ *Daily 1100-1400 and 1700-2200. Free, but donation appreciated.* The joy of Vejer is to wander around the maze of alleyways and narrow streets and if you've got a car, it's best to leave it in the newer part of the town. If you arrive by bus you'll probably be dropped on the main road in the gorge. To get to the old part of Vejer on the clifftop will involve either a taxi, a long walk up the winding road or tackling a rough track. Each Easter Sunday, Vejer holds its annual *encierro* or running of the bulls. There are runs at midday and 1600. The good news is that this is a *toro embalao*, where the points of the bulls horns are wrapped in a protective sheath.

Sleeping A *Convento de San Francisco*, Plazuela s/n, T956451001, F956451004. Unique accommodation at a restored 17th-century monastery with 25 atmospheric rooms. The hotel was previously occupied by Franciscan monks. Good restaurant in the former refectory. **E** *La Posada*, C Los Remedios 21, T956450258. 6 rooms above a restaurant. Garage. **Camping**: there are 3 campsites, including *Camping Vejer*, Ctra N340, Km 39, T956450098. Good range of facilities including pool.

A minor road leads south from Vejer to the Cabo de Trafalgar, where the Battle of Trafalgar took place in 1805. It was probably the most decisive sea battle of the Napoleonic war as nine French and nine Spanish ships were either captured or sunk without the loss of a single British ship. The British commander, Admiral Nelson, was unfortunately killed, his body being pickled in rum and taken to Gibraltar before being returned to London and the pomp of a burial in St Paul's Cathedral. Cape Trafalgar today displays no such drama. The actual cape is a small island marked by a lighthouse and linked to the mainland by a road along a sandy spit. Immediately to the east is the rather scruffy village of **Los Caños de Meca**, with windblown sand often covering the streets. Its beach is magnificent but the overall effect is spoilt by unattractive apartment blocks. There are a couple of good campsites and three *pensiones*, while some of the bars can get lively during the height of summer. The *Caños de Meca* campsite is close to the beach and Cabo de Trafalgar on the Vejer-Caños road, at Km 10, T956437120.

Cabo de Trafalgar & Los Caños de Meca

Cádiz Province

Cádiz Province

☞ Migrating tuna

It is not just birds that migrate, fish also undertake long marine journeys. In particular the bluefin tuna or tunny, which spends most of the year in the high seas, moves in shoals to warmer, shallower waters to breed. This involves swimming from the Atlantic through the Straits of Gibraltar between mid-April to early June and making a return trip from the end of June to mid-August. For the small fishing communities in the southwest of Andalucía, these are the times to catch the tuna by methods that have changed little since Roman times. Indeed it is believed that tuna was the main ingredient of the garum *fish sauce factory, the ruins of which can be seen at Bolonia.*

The method of catching the tuna is known as an almadraba, *its name suggesting that it was also used by the Moors. Today, the main villages using the* method are Zahara de los Atunes and Barbate on the Costa de la Luz. The migrating tuna are encircled in huge nets, and are then hauled in by teams of fishermen in boats. The fish are then gaffed and pulled up into the boats – a bloody and messy business. The almadraba *is not without its dangers. Tuna are often more than 3 m long and can weigh as much as 400 kg. With several of these creatures being hauled aboard or thrashing around in the bottom of a boat, accidents are not uncommon. With a good* almadraba, *however, there are fine profits to be had for the fishermen, because almost all of the tuna can be used, whether it is eaten fresh or canned or frozen. Much of the tuna goes to Japanese and Korean factory ships waiting offshore, but the catch has dwindled in recent years, probably due to overfishing.*

Barbate de Franco
Colour map 4, grid C2
Population: 21,916

From here a road winds up into the pine woods and heads east to Barbate. Beneath the woods are some precipitous sandstone cliffs, the site of a large colony of over 2,500 pairs of nesting cattle egrets, along with smaller numbers of little egrets, peregrines and ravens. The road eventually drops down into Barbate de Franco, which must be one of the least attractive towns in Andalucía. Situated to the west of the estuary of the none-too-clean Río Barbate, Barbate is a fishing port with an important canning industry. The fish dock spreads for 2 km between the town and the cliffs, while the town itself has few attractions. The fishing and canning industries provide jobs for many inhabitants of Conil, Zahara and Barbate, with tuna the most important catch (see box, page 194). Southeast of Barbate is an area of rubbish dumps and salt pans, before an extensive area is reached which is occupied by the military. The magnificent beach is unfortunately out of bounds and you should not stop on the road.

Zahara de los Atunes

After 5 km is Zahara de los Atunes. The place name literally means 'Flower of the Tuna Fish' and the village has, along with Barbate and Tarifa, an important tuna fishing industry. Its chief attraction is its broad sandy beach, which for much of the year is totally deserted. Hotels include **B** *Gran Sol*, Calle Sánchez Rodriguez sin número, T956439301, F956439197, with 22 spotless a/c rooms in a beachside location; excellent restaurant. Garage. **C** *Doña Lola*, Calle Thompson 1, T956439009, by the bridge over the tidal estuary, has 11 a/c rooms and a garage. The major monument in Zahara is the Almadabra, a huge walled fish market. East of Zahara is a small upland area known as the Sierra de la Plata, whose main claim to fame is that it was the first European breeding site of white-rumped swifts, which use the old nests of red rumped swallows. The sierra also has breeding colonies of griffon and Egyptian vultures.

Bolonia and Baelo Claudia

Further military land means returning to the N340 before coming back to the coast at Bolonia, the road leading through the famous 'painted fields', noted for their wild flowers attracting botanists from throughout Europe. In January the paper white narcissus are in full display and the colours and varieties increase during the spring. By late April the verges and fields, which have never experienced weedkiller or plough, are a riot of colour, with squills, clovers, lupins, irises, vetch and many more.

Reaching Bolonia itself, the major attraction (apart from the magnificent beach) is the remains of the old Roman town of **Baelo Claudia**. Thought to have been founded in 171 BC, the town was at the height of its importance during the first century AD. Under Emperor Claudius it was given the rank of 'municipum' thriving on the salting of fish and production of fish sauces, as well as being an administrative centre for the surrounding area. Its decline came with the fall of the Roman Empire, hastened in all probability by earthquakes. The excavations began in 1917 and have continued intermittently since then. The remains have been partially excavated from the sand, revealing a main street; temples to Jupiter, Juno and Minerva; and a rectangular forum, on one side of which is a basilica and lines of shops or *tabernae*. The town extends further up the hill, where a theatre has been discovered, and this is now included in the official tour. The baths are in the east of the city and were probably private. Three aqueducts brought water to the city, where it was stored in tanks. The necropolis was situated, as was the custom, outside the city walls. One of the most interesting features is the fish factory, which is located right on the beach. Large stone vats have been discovered, which apparently contained *garum*, a type of soupy fish paste composed of the otherwise unwanted bones, heads and entrails, which were stored in the vats with salt until mature. *Garum* was highly regarded and exported in amphorae throughout the Roman Empire. ■ *Tue-Sat 1000-1330 and 1630-2000 Jul and Aug; 1000-1430 and 1600-1730 during the rest of the year. Free with EU passport, otherwise €1.50.*

The village of Bolonia itself is rather a scruffy sprawl, redeemed only by some good fish restaurants. The 4 km long beach is superb, although wind can be a problem. There is a naturist area to the south and, apart from during July and August, your only companions are likely to be the local cattle, who seem to be allowed to wander around at will. For simple solitude in Bolonia, try **D** *Ríos*, T956684320, a small *pensión* on a remote part of the beach with some modern rooms overlooking the sea and a good fish restaurant.

Playa de los Lances

Approaching Tarifa, the coastal road nears the beach. This is the Playa de los Lances, the best of the many fine sandy beaches along the Costa de la Luz. Behind the dunes, several small rivers form a shallow lagoon, backed by rough pasture with a wide variety of spring flowers. This is now a nature reserve and, as it is on a main migration route, it is usually productive, while the rivers here are said to contain otters. The beach is highly popular with windsurfers, but the same wind which makes this sport so thrilling here also means that anyone just wanting to loaf around on the beach will have to put up with an element of sand blasting.

An alternative inland route to the coast road runs through **Facinas**, where on 24 June the Fiesta of San Juan is celebrated with bonfires, past the Almódovar reservoir and over the Puerto de Ojén pass and down to **Los Barrios**, an attractive dormitory town for Algeciras. A good base for walking and

Cádiz Province

birdwatching in Los Barrios is the English owned **AL** *Monte de la Torre*, Apto 66, T956660000, with four rooms plus two apartments. This English-style estate is located in one of Europe's largest cork oak forests. Breakfast only is available. Delightful as this inland route is, it is currently in a very bad state, with some of the best potholes in Andalucía. The laying of pipes has also damaged the surface and a four-wheel drive vehicle is recommended for this route at present.

Parque Natural Los Alcornocales The road passes through the southwest part of this park. *Alcornocales* are cork oaks and these trees clothe the lower slopes, along with white poplars, myrtles, ash and alder along with a variety of ferns, contrasting with the bare rock of the upper slopes. A wide variety of mammals inhabit the park, including mongooses, otters, polecats and wildcats. Among the birds, there is a good selection of birds of prey, such as griffon vultures, short toed eagles, booted eagles and goshawks. There are also great walks in the park; for details, contact the park's information centre, the Centro de Visitantes de Huerta Grande, T956679161. This is situated about 3 km from Algeciras and 10 km from Tarifa beside the N340 at Pelayo, Km 96. It's open Thursday, Friday and holidays 1000-1400 and 1800-2000 1 April to 30 September; Thursday 1000-1400 and Friday 1600-1800 in winter. The centre also has details of accommodation in the area and there is a cafeteria.

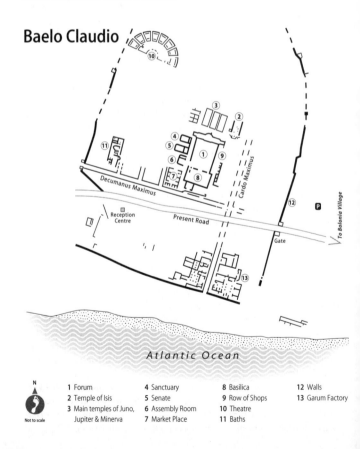

1 Forum	**4** Sanctuary	**8** Basilica	**12** Walls
2 Temple of Isis	**5** Senate	**9** Row of Shops	**13** Garum Factory
3 Main temples of Juno, Jupiter & Minerva	**6** Assembly Room	**10** Theatre	
	7 Market Place	**11** Baths	

Cork in the bottle

The native evergreen cork oak or alcornoque, which flourishes in the humid and gentle hill slopes of southwest Iberia is highly prized for its commercial value. It has a distinctive orange brown smooth trunk if the bark has been recently stripped of its cork bark from the ground up to the main branches. Growing to a height of 10-15m, the cork oak can live for up to 800 years, although harvesting its bark can reduce its life span by up to 200 years. It takes 20 years for the first bark to be ready to cut and thereafter it takes another seven years for the bark to regenerate, although it will not be until the third harvest, when the tree is approaching 50-years-old, that the top quality cork is produced.

Peladores, working in pairs, can cut around 600 kg of bark a day. The cylinders of bark are cut off with axes and the tree immediately starts to bleed resin. This protects the tree until the new bark begins to grow the following spring. The flattened slabs of bark called planchas are taken away by lorry to processing plants, such as those in the Jimena valley and near San Roque, where they are left in the sun to season before being boiled to reduce the tannin content and soften the material. The sheets are then taken away to factories for the final processing.

Cork is, of course, best known as a stopper in wine bottles, a practice widely introduced in the 17th century, thereby revolutionizing the storage of wines. Previously the wine had been stored in barrels and was only poured into bottles for consumption, where it could not be kept long before deteriorating. The advent of corks meant that the wine could now mature in the bottle. It is essential that the stopper is kept in contact with the wine, which is the reason why the bottles are usually stored on their sides. The corks are often printed with the bodegas name or crest, usually branded under heat. Despite much research, no synthetic substitute has yet been produced which is better than natural corks.

Campaigners in northern European countries are trying to persuade wine drinkers to only buy wine that has a cork stopper rather than a plastic one. The idea is to preserve the cork forests rather have them felled and replaced by the less environmentally friendly wheat or sunflowers.

The acorn or bellota of the cork oak is the main food of the black Iberian pig, which gives the gourmet ham known as Jamón ibérico. The bark, of course, has many other uses as well as a bottle stopper. Its lightness, buoyancy and resistance to burning means that it makes an excellent material for insulation, while it is also been used for floor tiles, wall covering, gasket seals and formerly for cricket balls. Furthermore, there is evidence that the ancient Egyptians, seeking comfort to the end, used this most versatile of materials for lining coffins.

Tarifa

Outpost town Tarifa occupies the most southerly tip of the Iberian peninsula. Only 14 km from Morocco, there is a distinct North African flavour about the place, with its narrow Moorish alleyways leading into mysterious cave-like houses, bars and shops. As with many towns on the extremity of continents it experiences unrelentingly strong winds, which until recently kept Tarifa as an windswept backwater. (But now the town is one of the world's major windsurfing sites and the influx of north Europeans and Americans has given the town a cosmopolitan air enhanced by it's main function as a ferry port linking Spain with Tangiers. Despite a rather shockingly rapid and haphazard development over the last decade, the old town of Tarifa is an intriguing place to explore and there is a

Colour map 4, grid C3
Population: 15,118
www.tarifa.net

relaxed and friendly atmosphere in the town's many bars, although you may be overwhelmed by windsurfers and tourists in the summer.

History

Tarifa has both Carthaginian and Roman origins (when it was known as Julia Traducta). Although its name is said to mean wind in Arabic, it is generally accepted that Tarifa was named after Tarif Ibn Malik who in 710 led the first Moorish exploratory raid across the straits with 500 Berbers, returning the next year with a force of 12,000 men. The town was recaptured from the Moors in 1292 by Sancho IV, but their attempt to regain it two years later is more memorable. During the siege, the Moors threatened to murder the young son of the Christian commander, Alonso de Guzmán, unless Tarifa surrendered. Guzmán's response was to throw down his own dagger preferring 'honour without a son to a son without honour'. Nobody apparently asked the opinion of the son who was duly murdered, while Guzmán acquired the title of *El Bueno* (the Good) and the lands that later formed the dukedom of Medina Sidonia under his descendants. Guzmán did not live much longer, however, for he was killed in the Battle of Sierra Gaucín in 1309. 50 years later Tarifa was again threatened by the Moors, led by Yusuf I of Granada. This time King Alfonso XI defeated them in the decisive Batalla del Salado in 1340.

The fact that much of the land around Tarifa has historically been in the hands of the military and the fact that the exfoliating *levante* wind is blowing for much of the time explains why the magnificent beaches to the north of the town have remained undeveloped. On the hills to the northeast of Tarifa, wind farms take advantage of the conditions to generate enough electricity for Tarifa and a surplus to export to Morocco. From two or three experimental windmills in 1981, there are now thousands covering the hillsides as far as the eye can see. Environmentalists are divided – they are certainly a clean and renewable form of energy – but it can be argued that they are a form of visual pollution, which certainly provide a hazard for the migrating storks, vultures and eagles. No research on the effect on the birds was carried out before the expansion.

Sights

The Castillo de Guzmán el Bueno was built between 950 and 960 when the Caliph of Córdoba, Abd Al-Rahman III, decided that the area needed defending against any invasion from North Africa. A small town grew up around the castle, in the quarter now called the Barrio de Jesús. The tower known as the **Torre de Guzmán** is more modern. There are superb views from the tower and battlements. ■ *Tue-Sun 1000-1400 and 1800-2000.* €1.20. The **Iglesia de Santa María** stands in a delightful square of the same name adjacent to the castle. Also in the square is the Ayuntamiento and a small museum. ■ Free. East of the square is a charming promenade with a mirador looking out towards North Africa. Close to the town walls is the **Church of San Mateo,** a 15th-century Gothic church built on the site of a mosque. Unusual for a church in this position, it has some interesting stained glass windows, while the rib vaulting in the nave is also of importance. ■ *Daily 0900-1300 and 1800-2030.*

Following the success of Gibraltar's dolphin and whale watching trips, Tarifa can now offer two of its own – *Whale Watch*, T956684776, and *FIRMM*, T956627008. Both claim to be non-profit making organizations. Early booking is essential.

The **tourist office** is at the northern end of the Paseo de la Alameda, T956627027. Also see the town's excellent website, www.tarifaweb.com The office is open Monday to Friday 1000-1400, 1700-1900 and 1000-1400 Saturday all year round, as well as Saturday afternoons and Sunday during summer. There are two good websites with up–to-date listings of events, bars and clubs, wind and kitesurfing information and accommodation: www.tarifa.net and www.tarifainfo.com

Essentials

It is very difficult to find cheap accommodation in Tarifa; even the most basic *pensiones* have inflated prices due to the massive influx of tourists during the summer season. Beach hotels are often closed in the winter, but those that remain open have much reduced rates, although, depending on how much winsurfing you are planning on doing, it is more fun to stay in the old town if you can find a good deal.

Sleeping
See inside front cover for hotel price categories

Beach hotels west of Tarifa A *Balcón de España*, Ctra N340, Km 77, T956684326, F956680472. 40 rooms. Garden, pool, beach, riding, tennis, parking. Resort-style hotel outside Tarifa on the road to Cádiz. A *Dos Mares*, Ctra N340 Km 79, T956684035, F956681078, dosmares@cherrytel.com 17 rooms. Pool, tennis, bike hire, restaurant, windsurfing school, parking. A *Hurricane*, Ctra N340, Km 77, T956684919, F956680329, www.hotelhurricane.com 28 rooms. Garden, pool, squash, horse riding,

Cádiz Province

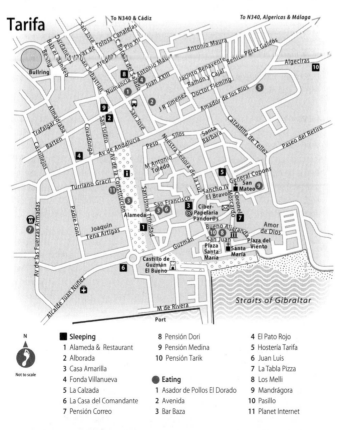

Tarifa

N — Not to scale

Sleeping		
1 Alameda & Restaurant	8 Pensión Dori	4 El Pato Rojo
2 Alborada	9 Pensión Medina	5 Hostería Tarifa
3 Casa Amarilla	10 Pensión Tarik	6 Juan Luis
4 Fonda Villanueva		7 La Tabla Pizza
5 La Calzada	**Eating**	8 Los Melli
6 La Casa del Comandante	1 Asador de Pollos El Dorado	9 Mandrágora
7 Pensión Correo	2 Avenida	10 Pasillo
	3 Bar Baza	11 Planet Internet

windsurfing, health club, beach, parking. **C** *La Cordoniz*, Ctra N340, Km 79, T956684744, F956684101, www.lacodorniz.com 35 rooms. Wheelchair access, parking. **C** *La Ensenada*, Ctra N340, Km 76, T956680637, F956650649. 22 rooms. Garage, pool. **C** *Mesón de Sancho*, Ctra N340, Km 94, T956684900, F956648721. 17 rooms. Garage, pool, tennis.

In town C *La Casa Amarilla*, C Sancho IV El Bravo, 9, T956681993, F956684029, lacasaamarilla@lite.eunet.es If you can afford it, and they have rooms available, this is by far the best and most interesting option in town, with refreshing Art Nouveau and modern North African interiors in a brilliantly yellow-tiled 19th-century town house. More an aparthotel, all 11 units (8 apartments sleep 4 and 3 sleep 2) have kitchen and bath and it's cheaper if you stay a week or more; at €39 for a double in high season, this is a very good deal. **C** *Casa del Comandante*, C Alcalde Juan Núñez 8, T956681925. Attractive and colourful rooms in this modern *hostal* near the port. **C** *Tarik*, C San Sebastián 36, T956685240. Pleasant owners at this *hostal*, which is in the rather dreary main drag north of the old town and neither on the beach nor in the interesting part of town. **D** *Alameda*, Santísima Trinidad 7, T956681181. 11 rooms. Popular choice in central position; a pretty good deal. **D** *Hostal Alborada*, C San José, 52, T956681140, www.hotelalborada.com A light and popular *hostal* outside the centre of town. All double rooms with bath or shower set around an attractive courtyard. Although not in the more picturesque town centre, this is still an option worth considering. **D** *La Calzada*, C Justino Pertiñez 7, T956680366. In the old town. **D** *Correo*, C Coronel Moscardó 9, T956680206. Located opposite the post office, the best room in this popular *pensión* is at the top with great views (and costs slightly more). **D** *Dori*, C Batalla Salado 55, T956685317. 8 rooms in a depressing concrete block off the main street north. Closed for what looks like much needed renovation at time of writing. Can be noisy, but close to the beach and a short walk from the centre of town. **D-E** *Fonda Villanueva*, Av Andalucía 11, T956684149. Some rooms with bath; basic, secure and modern.

Camping There is plenty of choice of campsites on or near the beach to the north of Tarifa. One of the best is *Paloma*, Ctra N340, Km 70, T956684203. www.tarifa.net/paloma Pool, windsurfing, horse riding, mountain biking, rock climbing and hang gliding available. Bunglow-cabins **D-E**, tent with 2 people and car €15. All the others mentioned below are located on the beach and have their own bar, restaurant and pool and all charge roughly the same as Paloma. *Río Jara*, Ctra N340, Km 80, T956680570. Horse riding. *Tarifa*, Ctra N340, Km 79, T956684778. Launderette. *Torre de la Peña I*, Ctra N340, Km 78, T956684903. Launderette. *Torre de la Peña II*, Ctra N340, Km 75, T956684174.

Eating
● *on map,*
page 199

Expensive *Alameda*, Paseo de la Alameda. Good position, great seafood and *platos combinados*. *Méson de Sancho*, Ctra N340, Km 94. For those with transport it's worth the drive a few kilometres east to this excellent roadside restaurant. *El Rincón de Manolo*, Ctra N340, Km 76, T956643410. Probably the most expensive restaurant in Tarifa, with outstanding fish and shellfish.

Mid-range *Avenida*, C Batalla del Salado. Reasonable *platos combinados*. *Hostería Tarifa*, C Amador de los Rios, T956684076. Steakhouse. *Mandrágora*, C Independencia 3, T956681291, is a chilled, low-lit Moroccan restaurant, serving delicious dishes such as kid with quince and cous cous for around €12, accompanied by an excellent CD collection of jazz and north African music. *Mesón Juan Luis*, C San Francisco 15, T956681265, makes a refreshing change from seafood. You can eat well here as long as you like pork. Also owned by Juan Luis is the excellent

The windsurfers' mecca

Windsurfing, sail boarding or fun boarding – whatever you like to call it – is probably the world's fastest growing sport. Surfing, as such, probab ly goes back two centuries or more to the Polynesian Islands, and by the 1960s it had become part of the hippie way of life in California. It was not until the early 1970s that the idea of fitting a sail to the board was put into motion with the first windsurfing board being constructed in Holland. In the early days sailboarding could only take place on calm waters and changing direction was a fraught manoeuvre, but gradually there have been considerable technological advances to cope with rough water and strong winds.

Windsurfers have increasingly searched for areas with strong and reliable winds, and eventually they discovered Tarifa, transforming it from a sleepy frontier town to the mecca of European windsurfers within a matter of 15 years. Today it ranks alongside Fuerteventura in the Canary Islands and Hookipa in Hawaii as one of the top three locations in the world. The winds, the eastern Levante and the western Poniente, can be so persistent as to drive local people to suicide, but these same conditions make windsurfing an all-year round sport at Tarifa.

With the growth of the sport have come the trappings, such as shops selling windsurfing equipment and clothes, as well as campsites, hotels and other accommodation, and a string of windsurf schools. All this has worked wonders for the economy of Tarifa and the surrounding area. The Playa de los Lances, immediately north of Tarifa, s the main location for the windsurfing, but there are also good spots further north at Bolonia, Zahara, Barbate, Caños de Meca, Conil, Chiclana and even off the Playa de Victoria at Cádiz, although the wind strength tends to lessen the further north you go.

It's worth heeding the advice of local windsurfing schools, who always stress these 10 commandments:

- *Familiarize yourself with local conditions before taking to the water.*
- *Check your equipment thoroughly before going out.*
- *Never go sailboarding alone.*
- *Be very careful of offshore winds.*
- *Never sail too far from the coast.*
- *Always tie the board to the sail.*
- *Never let go of the board.*
- *Always wear a wetsuit.*
- *Never go out late in the afternoon - latest is two hours before sunset.*
- *Do not put others at risk, such as swimmers and other surfers.*

Cádiz Province

---

hole-in-the-wall tapas bar opposite at 16a serving mainly *jamón*. A treat for bullfighting enthusiasts, the walls are covered in photographs of the unfortunate bulls at *corridas* over the last few decades.

Cheap The most economical food is found along and around the C Batalla del Salado, the old main road west out of Tarifa. *Asador de Pollos El Dorado*, C Batalla del Salado 37. Chicken and chips to take away. *Bar Freiduría Parame*, C Huerta del Rey. Fresh fish. *El Pato Rojo*, C Batalla del Salado 47. Cheap *menú del día*. *Freiduría Sevilla*, C Sancho IV El Bravo. Fried fish specialities. The *Al-Medina Bar* in C Almedina off Plaza Santa María is also worth a visit for a quick drink since it has an entrance arch which was originally a point of access to the castle.

Tapas bars *Los Melli*, C Guzmán el Bueno 16, just south of Plaza Capitán Menéndez Arango, is a local favourite for decent meat as well as seafood tapas, all washed down with good house *tinto* and flamenco canned music in a lively stand-up bar. Next door is *Pasillo*, another worthwhile stop, also specializing in seafood. See also Juan Luis above. Nearby on C San Francisco is *Bar Baza*, a dark, cave-like hangout specializing in mean *mojitos* and *caipirinhas*.

Clubs The club scene in Tarifa has a very seasonal feel to it (there's little going on in the winter) and places come and go every year. Check tarifainfo.com for the latest. *Far out*, a 10 min walk on the main road heading towards Cádiz, this is the latest and biggest club to hit town, and it's open all year round (although only on Fri and Sat during the winter). International DJs play house, techno, trance and funk. *La Jaima* and *Jungle Playa* are open-air clubs on the beach, open only in high season, and playing a mix of mainly commercial house, trance and jungle.

Entertainment **Bullfights** The Plaza de Toros is in C Bering, check locally for the next bullfight. It is also the venue for live music in the summer. Mad Professor played here in 2001. Check tarifainfo.com for up-to-date listings.

Fiestas & festivals Feb *Carnaval* This is marked by dancing, costumes, masquerades, etc. **15 May** *Romería del Conejo* Pilgrimage in honour of San Isidro. **First fortnight of Jul** *Feria de Tahivilla*. **16 Jul** *Fiesta del Carmen* The statue of the Virgen del Carmen is taken out to sea in a fishing boat to bless the waters (see box, page 167). **First fortnight in Aug** *National Folk Music Festival*. **Early Sep** *Fiesta de Nuestra Señora de la Luz* Fair and pilgrimage in honour of Tarifa's patron saint.

Shopping **Handicrafts** The *Bazar Hispano Arabe* in Av de Andalucía sells leather goods, mainly imported from Morocco and other North African countries.

Sport **Horse riding** *Hotel Dos Mares*, T956684035, or *Hotel Balcón de España*, T956684326. **Windsurfing** There are 21 recognized spots locally requiring varying degrees of expertise. There are numerous windsurfing schools and many shops in the town devoted to windsurfing gear. *Spin Out Surf Base*, Casa de Porro, Ctra N340, Km 75, T/F956680844/Beach T956236352, M639139060, info@tarifaspinout.com Lessons from €48 for 2 hrs tuition. Board rental €28 for 2 hrs. Also arranges surf safaris to Essaouira in Morocco.

Tour operators *Norafrica Tours*, Estación Marítima, T956681830, www.tarifa-tanger.com Excursions to Tangiers, for 1-2 days (1 night in Morocco) from €48 per person.

Transport **Local Bike hire**: available at the *Hotel Dos Mares*, T956684035. **Taxi**: there is a taxi rank in Av de Andalucía, T956684241. **Long distance Air**: the nearest airport is at Gibraltar for flights from London Heathrow with *British Airways*. Jerez Airport, with flights to London Stansted with *Buzz*, is 120 km away and can be reached by the daily *Comes* bus. The journey takes 2 hr by car. Málaga airport is 164 km east along the coast road. **Bus**: the station is in C Batalla del Salado. There are frequent *Comes* buses, T956684038, to Algeciras (30 mins, €1.45) and Cádiz (2 hrs, €6.45), as well as 2 to Málaga (0830 and 1730, 3½ hrs, €9.95) and 4 to Sevilla (1½ hrs, €6.25) and 1 to Almería (0830, 9 hrs, €22.25). **Boat**: ferry tickets for Tangier are available from *Marruecotur*, C Batalla del Salado 57, T956684751. Catamarans leave daily at 0930, 1130, 1300, 1600 and 1830 in summer and at 1130 and 1800 in winter. The journey takes 35 mins and costs about €21 single.

Directory **Banks** There are 2 banks on C Sancho IV el Bravo, 2 on C Nuestra Señora de la Luz, one on Av de Andalucía and one on C Batalla del Salado. **Communications** Internet: *Ciber-Papelería Pandor@'s*, C Sancho IV el Bravo 5, T956681645. Expensive at €6/hr, but central. *Planet Internet*, Av de la Constitución, near the tourist office, is marginally cheaper. **Post office**: Correos, C Colonel Moscardó 9. Mon-Fri 0900-1400, Sat 0900-1200. **Telephones**: there are numerous private *locutorios*, including *Estudio 21*, C Batalla del Salado 35; *Baelo International*, C Sancho IV El Bravo 19. **Medical services** Cruz Roja, C Juan Nuñez 5, T956684896; **Servicio de Urgencia** (emergencies),

C Calzadilla Téllez s/n, T956680779. **Useful addresses** Garages/repair workshops:
Ford, Frandomar Auto, C Braille 5, T956681443; *Renault*, Auto-Silva, Ctra N340, Km 84.

East from Tarifa

*The N340 rises quickly out of Tarifa eastwards, reaching 340 m at the Puerto de
Cabrito, surrounded by the ubiquitous wind farms. Just past this point is a mirador,
with a small kiosk, giving fine views of North Africa. On clear days, individual
buildings and minarets can easily be picked out on the Moroccan side of the straits.*

Algeciras

The road continues eastwards dropping quickly down to the city of Algeciras. A
busy container port with an important petro-chemical industry, Algeciras can
hardly be called an attractive place and few would think of lingering, unless they
were waiting for a ferry (see Transport below). Pollution frequently hangs over
the town and its high-rise suburbs are dreary in the extreme. Algeciras is notable
chiefly for its position at the end of the train line from Madrid and its proximity
to Morocco. It has views across Algeciras Bay towards Gibraltar and the
equally depressing town of La Linea. The recent opening of the
long-awaited Algeciras bypass has helped to relieve the town's traditional
traffic congestion. As a major embarkation point for Tangier and Ceuta
with frequent daily ferries to both, Algeciras becomes congested during the
summer months as migrant Algerians and Moroccans return home from
France, Belgium, Germany and the Netherlands.

> *Colour map 4, grid C3*
> *Population: 101,972*

Today, you can find a few attractive corners of the town, mostly in the area
around Plaza Alta, with two interesting churches, Nuestra Señora de la Palma,
dating from the 18th century, and Nuestra Señora de Europa with a neat
Baroque façade.

Algeciras gained its name from the Moorish el Gezira el-Khadra (Green
Island). The Moors landed here when they first invaded Iberian soil in 711
under their commanders Musa and Tarik. The 'Pillars of Hercules' at either
side of the Straits of Gibraltar are named after the Moorish leaders – Jebel
Tarik (Gibraltar) on the European coast after the general who led the invasion
and Jubel Musa on the African coast after Musa Ibn Nusayr, his lieutenant.

> **History**

A major Christian victory was achieved by Alfonso XI in 1344. Participa-
tion in this assault was referred to by a character in Chaucer's *Canterbury Tales*
as an indication of knightly valour. A few decades later, in 1379, Algeciras was
destroyed during a Moorish raid and had to be reconstructed by Carlos III.
Consequently, the Moorish place names are the only remaining traces of the
centuries they spent in the town.

There is plenty of cheap accommodation to choose from, with over 30 *pensiones*. Many
of these are pretty tatty – check the room first. **AL** *Reina Cristina*, Paseo de la
Conferencia, T956602622, F956603323. 162 rooms. A/c, pool, faded Victorian elegance. **A** *Alborán*, C Alamo, Colonia San Miguel, T956632870, F956632320. 79 rooms.
A/c, wheelchair access. **A** *Al-Mar*, Av de la Marina 2, T956654661, F956654501. 192
rooms. Garage, a/c, wheelchair access. **E** *González*, C José Santacana, T956652843. 19
rooms, modern. **Youth hostels** *Albergue Juvenil Algeciras*, Barriada El Pelayo s/n,
T956679060, F956679017. Located 8 km west of Algeciras on the Tarifa road, with 100
beds, meals, parking, sailing.

> **Sleeping
> & Eating**
> *See inside front cover
> for hotel price codes*

Cádiz Province

☞ Watching the migration

Many birds migrate according to the season in order to take advantage of the optimum conditions for breeding. Whereas small songbirds migrate on a broad front, soaring birds tend to concentrate their routes. This is because their method of travelling is to soar and glide, rather than to fly strongly in a direct line. Soaring birds must therefore constantly seek thermals in order to gain height. This gives them problems when it comes to crossing large stretches of water, so they must seek routes where the water is at its narrowest point. Soaring birds in Europe (including here storks, eagles, vultures and other birds of prey) will either use the Bosphorus in the east or the Straits of Gibraltar in the west. This means that the majority of the soaring, migratory birds of the western side of Europe will pass over the Tarifa/Gibraltar area twice a year, travelling northwards in the spring and southwards in the autumn.

When to watch the migration

Migration across the Straits of Gibraltar takes place, in fact, almost the whole year round, but the most significant northward movements are between mid-March and the end of May, while the most important southbound movements are between late August to mid-October. Some species have concentrated periods of travel - the honey buzzard, for example, will be seen coming north during the first three weeks of May. Other species have a less exact timetable, with the white stork moving north as early as November and as late as May. There are more birds involved in the autumn, southbound migration which follows breeding, but on the other hand during the spring, northbound migration the birds will be seen at lower levels having just drifted across the Straits. Generally speaking, the most rewarding months will be April and September.

Where to watch the migration

The most popular place is the Mirador del Estrecho on the N340 5 km east of Tarifa, a public viewpoint with a small, overpriced kiosk. If this becomes too crowded there are a number of lay-bys nearby. An alternative, especially for the northward spring migration is Punta Secreta, a low headland due south of Algeciras, reached via the coast road from Algeciras to Getares Bay and moving on round the lighthouse. When westerly winds are blowing, Gibraltar can be rewarding. The Upper Rock Nature Reserve is an excellent spot for observing the migration (see page 215). There is, however, an observatory at Jews Gate, just past the entrance to the Reserve, manned by the Gibraltar Ornithological and Natural History Society who welcome visitors and can give information on the latest sightings. In selecting a viewpoint, remember that the wind direction is crucial as soaring birds will drift laterally with the wind. With westerly winds then, Gibraltar is likely to be the best bet, while with winds from the east the area around Tarifa is likely to be more profitable.

Other points to remember

● Binoculars are essential, and likely to be less cumbersome than a telescope.

● Birds of prey are most easily identified by their underwing pattern. A good field guide is therefore desirable. Any of the popular ones will do, but enthusiasts might want to obtain Flight Identification of European Raptors, RF Porter, et al, 1981, Poyser, London.

● Storks and larger raptors will not be active until around 1000 when thermals are starting to form.

● Strong winds and persistent rain will stop movement.

● In very hot weather, the thermals will ensure that raptors will soar to high levels.

What species to expect

The following are the most common and regular migrants: black storks, white storks, honey buzzards, black kites, red kites, Egyptian vultures, griffon vultures, short-toed eagles, marsh harriers, hen harriers, Montagu's harriers, sparrowhawks, buzzards, booted eagles, ospreys, lesser kestrels, merlins, hobbies. Rarer migrants include: black vultures, goshawks, Spanish imperial eagles, golden eagles and Bonelli's eagles.

Algeciras is an important communication centre. **Bus** The main bus station is on C San **Transport**
Bernardo. *Comes*, T956653456, runs frequent buses from here to Cádiz (2 hrs, €7.95),
Sevilla (3½ hrs, €13.25) and Tarifa (30 mins, €1.45), as well as 4 daily to Madrid (8 hrs,
€21.25). For Gibraltar, take a *Comes* bus to La Linea (45 mins, €1.50). *Portillo*, Av
Virgen del Carmen 15, T956651055, runs 7 buses daily to Málaga (2 hrs, €8.45); and 6
to Granada (3¾ hrs, €16.30) and Jaén (5 hrs, €21.75). **Boat** There are frequent daily
ferries to Tangier (2¼ hrs, €45 return)and Ceuta (45 mins, €36.90 return) from 0700,
with seasonal hydrofoils to both of these ports. Note that the hydrofoils may not run in
rough weather, which is a not infrequent occurrence. Tickets can be purchased from
kiosks all round the Campo de Gibraltar and travel agents in Algeciras. For more details,
contact *Transmediterránea*, T902454645. **Train** The station is on C San Bernardo.
There are 2 trains to Madrid at 1500 (6 hrs, €57.25) and 2130 (11 hrs, from 31.95); 3 to
Granada (4½ hrs, €16.35); 6 to Ronda (1 hr 50 mins, €6.15); 3 to Sevilla (5½ hrs,
€19.65). For Córdoba, take the Madrid train and change at Bobadilla junction. Contact
RENFE for more information, T902240202.

San Roque to Jimena de la Frontera

Continuing round the Bay of Algeciras, the hill village of **San Roque** (population 22,322) appears to the left. It was founded in 1704 by people fleeing from
Gibraltar, which had just been taken over by the British. They assumed that
they would one day return to the Rock, but this, of course, was not the case.
There is a pleasant main square, an 18th-century church, an antiquated bullring and very little else. Even the view from the mirador is marred by the hideous petrochemical works.

From San Roque a road leads to **La Linea** (population 59,629), the main
gateway to Gibraltar. If San Roque is dreary, La Linea is even worse. Its prosperity during this century has depended on the state of the border with
Gibraltar. La Linea traditionally provided most of the workers in the naval
dockyard and when Franco closed the border, many of the inhabitants were
deprived of a livelihood. Today there is a poverty-stricken look about the
place, particularly in the litter-strewn fishing suburb to the east. There is,
however, an attractive main square, the Plaza de la Constitución, with some
good tapas bars in the side streets. The bus station is just off the main square
and there is a regular bus service along the Costa del Sol to Málaga.

East from San Roque over hills is **Sotogrande**, a development like a piece of
Surrey stockbroker belt dropped down in southern Spain, with its manicured
lawns, cricket pitches, polo fields and golf courses. On the coast is Puerto
Sotogrande, probably the most upmarket of all the marinas along the *costa*.
The Valderama golf course at Sotogrande hosted the Ryder Cup competition
between Europe and the US in 1997 and this prompted road improvements
along the Cádiz part of the coast.

The A369 runs inland from San Roque following a parallel route to the railway line to Ronda. This is one of the best places in Andalucía for watching
storks, which nest enthusiastically on the railway pylons. After 10 km, a road
branches off northwest to **Castellar de la Frontera** (population 8,948),
perched on a hilltop overlooking the Guadarranque reservoir. The original
inhabitants were moved out in 1971 to Nuevo Castellar in the valley, their
place taken by German and Dutch hippies looking for an alternative lifestyle.
Old Castellar has a 13th-century Moorish castle and considerable architectural interest, but the place has a rather sinister atmosphere and few visitors
stay long. Plans to turn Castellar into a tourist complex with a parador (it has
the potential) seem to have foundered.

A further 25 km away is **Jimena de la Frontera**, another hill town with a Moorish castle. This is in a good condition and has an impressive triple-arched entrance gateway. Jimena is notable for its surprisingly large colony of expat Brits, many of whom have their own businesses. In Jimena is C *Hostal El Anon*, Calle Consuelo 34-40, T956640113, F956641110. Converted from four village houses, it is full of charming nooks and crannies; price includes breakfast. It also has a restaurant and pool. From Jimena, the C341 climbs up through Gaucín, Algatocín and Benadalid to Ronda – one of the great scenic routes in Andalucía.

Gibraltar

Colour map 4, grid C4
Population: 30,000

Gibraltar, the British enclave, has been strategically important for centuries, but in these days of modern warfare, that location is no longer so vital. The atmosphere in Gibraltar was once like that of a British naval town set in the Mediterranean, but since British forces left Gibraltar in 1991, leaving the Rock in the hands of the locally recruited Gibraltar Regiment, the ambience has changed somewhat. Cruise line passengers and tourists from the Costa del Sol have now replaced the British matelot in the pubs and shops of Main Street and Gibraltar is struggling to develop its own identity through financial services and tourism.

*There is plenty to see, including a **Moorish Castle** and the best preserved **Arab Baths** in the southern Iberia. There are many **fortifications** and gateways, a legacy of the sieges that have taken place over the centuries. The Upper Rock area has the impressive **St Michael's Caves**, with its nearby troops of **Barbary Apes**. The Upper Rock is also a good place to spot migrating **birds** of prey in spring and autumn. At a lower level, there are some fine **botanic gardens**.*

Ins and outs

Getting there
See page 217 for further details
No **bus** services cross the border from Spain, but *Portillo* buses run from towns and cities in Andalucía to La Linea on the Spanish side of the border. If arriving at Gibraltar by **car** for a short stay, it might be advisable to leave the car on the Spanish side of the border and walk through. This avoids the customs delays and the problem of finding a parking space on the Rock. Ignore rough looking characters on the La Linea side of the border who wish to park and guard your car, as they have no authority whatsoever. In Gibraltar itself, a pay and display car park on the west side of the entry gates opposite the air terminal costs €0.60 per hr. A **passport** is required for entry into Gibraltar.

Getting around
It now possible again to drive right round the Rock. Turn left at the first roundabout past the airstrip and this road will take you along the east side of the Rock, past the *Caleta Palace Hotel*, Catalan Bay, Sandy Bay, through a long tunnel and eventually to the southern tip of Gibraltar at Europa point. Return along the west side of the rock to the cable car park from where it is an easy walk into the town. **Car hire** is scarcely necessary in Gibraltar – there are a number of bus routes operated by *Calypso Travel* (who have 'midi' buses and even some former London Transport double deckers), 3 minibus firms and over 150 taxis. Remember that parking is difficult and that illegally parked vehicles are enthusiastically wheel clamped. Driving is on the right, the same as in Andalucía.

Tourist offices
The main tourist office, and also the home of the Gibraltar Tourist Board, is at Duke of Kent House in Cathedral Sq, next to the Anglian Cathedral, T74950 F74943. (The Duke of Kent, fourth son of George III and father of Queen Victoria, stayed in the

Dire Straits

Illegal immigrants from Morocco and other North African countries are known as espaldas mojadas or wetbacks because of their journey in often precarious boats across the Straits of Gibraltar between Spain and North Africa. The Straits, whilst only some 20 km wide, are dangerous waters, with swirling currents and strong winds. When the levante wind is blowing at full strength even 5,000 tonne ferry boats may be confined to harbour.

The trade began in the late 1980s. The wetbacks pay anything up to US$1,000 to risk their lives in small open boats known as pateras, powered only by a 50-horsepower outboard motors. Designed for no more than six people and normally used for inshore fishing, some have been intercepted with as many as 40 passengers on board, earning their owners up to US$35,000 a trip. Inevitably, many pateras sink. Sometimes the wetbacks are put over

the side well off the beach and non-swimmers may not make it to the shore. As the pateras have no radios or life saving equipment, they can sink without trace. The Spanish authorities believe that over 1,000 illegal immigrants may have perished in this way over the last 10 years. Immigrants come to Spain in the hope of securing employment and a brighter future, but are ruthlessly exploited by the boat mafia.

But for every wetback drowned, thousands of Moroccans do make it to Spain and quickly disappear into the interior. Many are picked up by the police and held in special camps where they are looked after by the Red Cross. As they have no papers and refuse to say where they have come from, it is difficult for the authorities to expel them. Those who do evade the police face an uncertain future, lacking documents and being confined to low paid work.

building during his time as governor in 1802.) There are also sub-offices at the airport, in the market place and in John Mackintosh Hall. The Tourist Board have produced some excellent free fact sheets on natural history, geology, history and visitor information. The offices are open Mon-Fri 1000-1800, Sat 1000-1400 and their staff are very helpful.

The Gibraltar Tourist Board has sanctioned an 'Official Rock Tour', by taxi or minibus, **Official tours** with drivers as official guides. The tour starts at a number of points in the town and the route initially goes down the east side of the Rock (when this road is open) stopping at Catalan Bay to view the water catchments, before proceeding to the lighthouse at Europa Point at the southern tip of the peninsula. The route then climbs up to the Jews Gate viewpoint. There is a 30-min stop at St Michael's Cave and a further 10 mins at the **Apes' Den**. There is an optional stop at the **Upper Galleries**, but many drivers miss this out, returning to the place of departure. The tour, which takes between 1½-3 hrs and costs £10, is an excellent introduction to Gibraltar for those on a day trip. If you have your own transport you may wish to take longer, but you'd have to cope with the stressful driving conditions on the Upper Rock. A number of firms operate minibuses on this tour, including *Bland Travel* T77012, *Calypso Tours* T76226, *Exchange Travel* T76151 and *Parodytour* T76070. For taxi trips contact the *Gibraltar Taxi Association*, T70027. Taxi prices vary according to the number of occupants, but are usually around £16-£20 per person. At slack periods it is worth trying a little bargaining with the drivers. Some taxi tours do not include the entrance fee to the Upper Rock. **NB** Much of the Upper Rock area is unsuitable for wheelchair users, despite the fact that such people are given free entrance to all the places on the Official Tour.

The area

Gibraltar is at one of the most southerly points of Iberia. It is a peninsula some 6½ km in length and 2 km wide at its broadest point. It is joined to Spain by a low isthmus and is separated from North Africa by the Straits of Gibraltar, some 13 km across at their narrowest point. The town clusters around the lower slopes on the west side, spreading further west in recent years on reclaimed land. Of its 30,000 inhabitants, 20,000 are native Gibraltarians, 6,000 are expatriate Britons and the remainder guestworkers from Morocco or EU countries. However, since the border was reopened in 1985 many Gibraltarians now live in Spain and commute back over the border daily to work. The Moroccans, who were brought over to work in the dockyards when the border with Spain was closed, now find that they have little work or employment protection. They have mounted intermittent demonstrations outside Government House in recent years. The Gibraltarians themselves come from a variety of backgrounds – Spanish, British, Maltese, Jewish, Moroccan and Genoese – and while English is the official language, they will often mix English and Spanish (even within the same sentence) in a curious dialect known as *llanito*. In fact, the mainland Spanish often refer to Gibraltarians as *llanitos*.

The **climate** of Gibraltar is milder and windier than the Costa del Sol. Mid-day temperatures average 14°C in January and 22°C in July. The *levante*, an east wind, forces cloud onto the summit of the Rock, increasing humidity and ensuring higher rainfall figures than in neighbouring Spain. There are no rivers or streams in Gibraltar and as the rock is entirely a grey, permeable, Jurassic limestone, it was necessary to collect water via enormous concrete catchments on the east side of the peninsula. Today, most of the water supply comes from a desalinization plant.

History

Discoveries during the last century of prehistoric remains in a cave on the North Face of the Rock have now been shown to be of Neanderthal Age. More recently, another cave has been excavated on the south of the Rock, near Europa Point. Known as Gorham's Cave, it has provided archaeologists with remains dating from up to 100,000 years ago, including bones of hyena, deer, tortoises and tuna. In later times the Phoenicians knew Gibraltar as Calpe (note the similarity with the Penon at Calpe on the Costa Blanca) and in Greek mythology it formed, along with Mount Ablya on the other side of the Straits, the twin pillars of Hercules.

Moorish influence in the area began in 711 AD, when Tarik Ibn Zeyed invaded the mainland to start his campaign against the Visigoths. He named the Rock Gibel Tarik (or Tarik's Mountain), which has corrupted over time into Gibraltar. Later, under the Almohads, around 1160, Caliph Abdul Mamen constructed some defensive works, reservoirs and a mosque. Gibraltar stayed in Moorish hands until a surprise attack by the Spanish, led by Guzmán El Bueno in 1309, but within 25 years it was regained by the Moors led by the Sultan of Fez after a siege of 4½ months.

The Moors were finally evicted from the Rock in 1462 by the Spanish, led by the Duke of Medina Sedonia. They were to stay for a further 240 years until the War of the Spanish Succession. Although Britain supported the Spanish against the French, Gibraltar was taken by a combined Anglo-Dutch fleet in 1704 led by Admiral Rooke. The inhabitants were told that they had to

Gibraltar

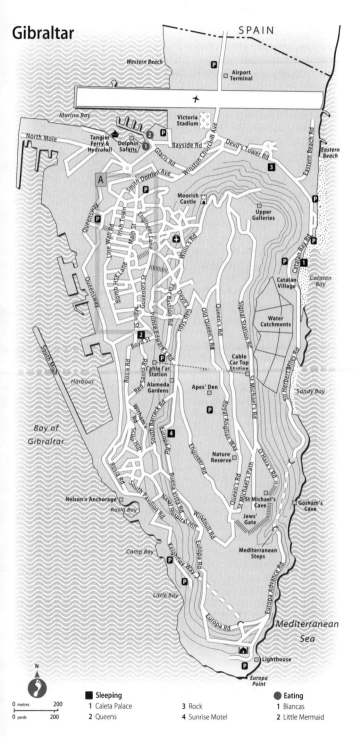

Cádiz Province

SPAIN

Western Beach

Airport Terminal

Marina Bay

Victoria Stadium

North Mole

Tangier Ferry & Hydrofoil

Dolphin Safaris

Bayside Rd

Glacis Rd

Winston Churchill Ave

Devil's Tower Rd

Eastern Beach Rd

Eastern Beach

Smith Dorrien Ave

Moorish Castle

Upper Galleries

Queensway

Irish Town

Main St

Line Wall Rd

Engineer Lane

Willis's Rd

Catalan Bay Rd

Catalan Village

Catalan Bay

Queensway

Bomb House Lane

Governor's St

Prince Edward's Rd

Devil's Gap Stps

Flat Bastion Rd

Old Queen's Rd

Queen's Rd

Signal Station Rd

Water Catchments

Boyd St

Prince Edward's Rd

Cable Car Top Station

St Herbert Miles Rd

South Mole

Harbour

Rosia Rd

Red Sands Rd

Witham's Rd

Scud Hill

South Barrack Rd

Cable Car Station

Alameda Gardens

Apes' Den

St Michael's Rd

Sandy Bay

Bay of Gibraltar

Europa Rd

Royal Anglian Way

Engineer Rd

Nature Reserve

Queen's Rd

O'Hara's Rd

St Michael's Path

St Michael's Cave

Gorham's Cave

Nelson's Anchorage

Rosia Bay

Rosia Rd

South Pavilion Rd

Buena Vista Rd

Naval Hospital Hill

Wildmill Rd

Jews' Gate

Mediterranean Steps

Camp Bay

Keightley Way

Europa Rd

Little Bay

Europa Rd

Europa Advance Rd

Mediterranean Sea

Lighthouse

Europa Point

N

0 metres 200
0 yards 200

■ Sleeping
1 Caleta Palace
2 Queens
3 Rock
4 Sunrise Motel

● Eating
1 Biancas
2 Little Mermaid

☛ **Smugglers' paradise**

Stop at traffic lights in any Andalucían city and the chances are that you will be approached by young men selling cartons of cigarettes. Vendors, known as Winstonistas, will almost certainly be selling contraband cigarettes which have entered Spain through Gibraltar. The Spanish tobacco industry is state controlled and the government claims that it is losing vast sums of money annually to the illegal trade from Gibraltar.

The method is no secret. Gibraltar imports vast quantities of cigarettes from USA, 90% of which are exported illegally to Spain, where a packet of Winstons costs around £1.40 as compared with 54p in Gibraltar. The smuggling is carried out by young men known as the 'Winston Boys' using fast speed boats, painted matt black so that they are almost invisible at night. They land the goods on the beach at La Atunara, a seedy fishing village on the far side of La Linea, where they are speedily secreted away. A cargo of 1,000 cartons can earn a profit of £5,000 - not bad for a night's work. The reason for the growth of smuggling is clearly linked with the closure of Gibraltar's Naval dockyard, which once employed 70% of the colony's 13,000 workforce. Now there is an unemployment rate of 11% and a recent estimate claimed that with 250 speedboats operating, over 1,000 Gibraltarians would be involved directly or indirectly in smuggling. Spain's Guardia Civil try to stop the smuggling, but have achieved only limited success. In a recent attempt to stop a cargo at La Atunara they were pelted with stones and iron bars and had to make an ignominious retreat. The Guardia Civil's helicopters have frequent running battles with the speedboats and there have been fatalities on both sides.

Even more serious has been the move towards the smuggling of drugs from Morocco. The drug runners favourite vessel for this work is the RIB - the inflatables of the type used by the SAS which are capable of speeds up to 120 kph and which can out-run any of the boats used by the Gibraltar or Spanish authorities. Little wonder that articles have appeared in the British press suggesting that Gibraltar is a 'smugglers paradise'.

In addition to the smuggling problem there are also accusations of money laundering. Gibraltar has still to comply with over 50 EU directives on a variety of matters. This has created a situation whereby Gibraltar earns little sympathy from either Britain or Spain. Meanwhile Spain continues its tactic of trying to smother Gibraltar into submission, complaining loudly about the smuggling (though far more drugs and tobacco enter Spain via other routes) and using this to justify its long border delays - an action which simply makes Gibraltarians dig in their heels even more.

The election of a new Chief Minister, Peter Caruana, in 1996 and again in February 2000 with an increased majority, has helped matters to a certain extent. Although committed to maintaining ties with Britain, he wishes to improve relations with Spain and clamp down on the activities of the smugglers. After six years in power, however, his political views now seem to be as entrenched as his predecessors and relations with both UK and Spain seem as abrasive as ever.

support the claimant to the Spanish throne, Archduke Charles of Austria, or leave the Rock. Many did leave and founded a settlement at nearby San Roque, fully expecting to return shortly. Britain, however, gained formal sovereignty over the Rock in the Treaty of Utrecht in 1713 and has remained there ever since, despite Spain's diplomatic and military attempts to regain it. At the start of the next century, Gibraltar's strategic position was fully utilized during the Napoleonic Wars.

Gibraltar played an important strategic role in both world wars, but particularly the second, when the Rock became honeycombed with passages and caverns (augmenting the existing caves) for the storage of ammunition and other arms, making a formidable fortress guarding the western entrance to the Mediterranean. It is an often forgotten fact that most of the inhabitants of Gibraltar were evacuated during the Second World War, ending up in places such as Britain, Madeira and Jamaica. The majority returned when hostilities ceased.

In the post-war period, Franco continued to try to persuade the British to give up the Rock, but in a number of referendums the Gibraltarians have always staunchly wished to remain British. Franco eventually closed the border in 1965; however, this only served to make the *llanitos* even more anti-Spanish. After the death of Franco and the entry of Spain into the Common Market, the borders were re-opened in 1985.

In 1988, the SAS killed three suspected IRA terrorists at the Shell petrol station a stone's throw from the border, and although there had been some collaboration with the Spanish police, the incident did little to enhance cooperation between the two countries. In recent years, since the departure of the British forces, Gibraltar has made attempts to create some economic independence by forming a sort of financial Isle of Man in the Mediterranean, with mixed results. Over 75,000 financial institutions now have a base in Gibraltar and the EU has accused many of drugs money laundering and harbouring Russian mafia money. In the early 1990s, relations with Spain took another turn for the worse with the activities of the young Gibraltarian cigarette and drug smugglers (see box above).

Gibraltar finds itself in a curious political situation. As a British Crown Colony, it is regarded as part of Europe, but with responsibility without representation. Owing to a British Government oversight, Gibraltar is not able to vote for an MEP.

Sights

The most obvious Moorish monument, but not the best location, is the castle. It was built in 1333, probably on the site of an earlier fortress that may have dated from soon after Tarik's initial occupation of the area in 711 AD. Originally, the castle's defences stretched down the edge of the town where Casemates Gate now stands, but they were destroyed in the various sieges. The main part of the castle remaining is the **Tower of Homage**, the walls of which are pitted with some of the scars inflicted during the various local conflicts. The castle can be viewed from the road above it, while below it is hemmed in by recently built blocks of flats. Entry, however, is not permitted as the castle functions today as Gibraltar's prison and the roof overlooks the exercise yard. At the lower end of the old walls is an ancient gatehouse and nearby is **Stanley's Tower**, originally built in 1160 AD, but renovated several times since. Its clock dates from 1845.

In the **museum** are some superbly preserved Moorish baths. They are approached from Room 1 of the museum (containing archaeological remains), which leads into the Main Hall of the baths. It is best to start a tour from the Entrance Hall, thought to have originally been twice its present size, the southern half having been destroyed during the Great Siege of 1779. Part of the main flue or hypocaust has been uncovered, which links with the furnace at the east end of the baths. Note, too, the star-shaped apertures in the

The castle

The oldest buildings and monuments in Gibraltar are Moorish

Moorish baths

Cádiz Province

roof and a vent in the wall that would have let out the steam. Here bathers were given buckets of water to throw over themselves before proceeding into the Main Hall. Here there is a central dome over a series of horseshoe arches, the columns of which are of particular interest, four being Moorish, one Roman and the other three Visigothic. This mixed bag was probably brought here from other sites in the vicinity. The Main Hall originally contained private cubicles for changing and relaxing. Next is a Cold Room, with higher ceilings to retain the cooler temperatures, and containing shallow cold and tepid baths. The next room to the east is the Hot Room, which is entered through a large round arch. It is believed that the steam bath was located at the north end and the hot plunge bath on the southern side. Some of the original lead piping may still be seen and the whole area is in a good state of preservation. ■ *Opening times are the same as for the museum; tour included in entrance fee.*

Shrine of Our Lady of Europa The only other Moorish remnant is the **Nuns Well**, opposite the entrance to Keighley's Tunnel, near Europa Point. The Well is, in fact, an underground Moorish cistern, but acquired its name from the nuns who tended the nearby **Shrine of Our Lady of Europa**. This shrine is built on the site of a mosque and was made into a Catholic chapel in the mid-15th century. The Image of Our Lady was guarded by a permanent light. Despite being desecrated by both the Turks and the British, the shrine remains and there is a pilgrimage to the spot on 5 May (Europe Day). ■ *Mon-Fri 1000-1900, Sat, Sun and holidays 1100-1900; closed for lunch 1300-1400. Free.*

Close to the shrine is a small patch of Moorish pavement. The nearby **Europa Point** has a lighthouse and an observation platform that makes an excellent place for viewing dolphins and migrating seabirds – all with a backdrop of the North African coast when the visibility is clear. The lighthouse, which is 150 years old and rises to a height of 50 m, is the only lighthouse outside of Britain which is regulated by Trinity House. A recent addition to the landscape around Europa Point is the newly-built **Mosque**, built with the help of the Saudi royal family. Its lofty minaret makes an excellent counterpoint to the lighthouse.

Upper rock To view the features of the Upper Rock, it is best to take the **Cable Car**. When the conditions are right, the view from the top of the rock can be superb with vistas of the Costa del Sol, Algeciras Bay and the mountains of Morocco. The lower station is located in Rosia Road close to the Alameda Botanical Gardens and the *Bristol Hotel*. Choose a day when there is no cloud cover on the top of the Rock. ■ *0930-1715, last trip down 1745, weather conditions permitting, closed Sun. £5.00/€8.40 return, with a stop at the Apes Den; £7.00/€12 includes all the sites including St Michaels Caves. £11.70 includes lunch at the upper terminal restaurant.* Probably the best bet is to walk down from the upper station to the caves, a pleasant downhill walk of 1 km, and then rejoin the cable car at the **Apes Den**, a stroll of less than a km.

The so-called Barbary Apes (*Macaca sylvanus*) are in fact a species of tailless monkey, the only ones on the mainland of Europe. Legend has it that they arrived in Gibraltar via an underground tunnel from Morocco, but the truth is that they were imported for pets by British soldiers and some inevitably escaped. They used to live in two packs, one at the Apes Den and the other living on the steep slopes of Middle Hill. During the Second World War, Sir Winston Churchill had a special effort made to maintain the apes' numbers, as the legend said that the British Empire would fall if the apes ever left the Rock. Now they are breeding so enthusiastically that they number around 260 and live in seven packs of around 40-50 in each. As they are causing damage to the natural vegetation and increasingly coming down into the inhabited areas to scavenge for food, it has been decided that their numbers are to be culled. Visitors are warned not to feed the apes or make sudden movements, as they are not as loveable as they look. Take care also of valuables such as cameras, which the apes take great delight in stealing.

A short walk from either the upper station or the Apes Den leads to **St Michael's Cave**, a huge cavern containing stalagmites, stalactites, pillars and flow structures. This cave is just one of a whole maze of natural and manmade caves which honeycomb the Rock. Today, the main cavern is frequently used as an auditorium for concerts. There are also small dioramas with full sized models of both Neanderthal and Neolithic Man.

On the north face of the Rock, overlooking Spain, are some manmade passages, known as the **Upper Galleries**. They were constructed during the time of the Great Siege (1779-1783) by British engineers as gun emplacements, ensuring the rock's impregnability. ■ *1000-1900 in summer and 1000-1730 in winter.*

Botanical Gardens

These gardens, formerly known as the Alameda Gardens, are nearly 180 years old. They were laid out in 1815 and were the brainchild of the governor at that time, Lieutenant General Sir George Don (whose tomb is at the Cathedral of the Holy Trinity). To pay for the gardens, Don had the bright idea of legalizing lotteries in the colony. Some eight lotteries were held, which soon raised the required money, whereupon Don promptly made lotteries illegal again.

The garden's historical features include a small stone ventilation tower in the lower part, which was part of an old Moorish aqueduct. Elsewhere are two Victorian 18-tonne guns. In the upper area there is a memorial to the Duke of Wellington, erected in 1819 and paid for by deducting one day's pay from every soldier currently serving on the Rock - another of Don's money raising ploys. It was little wonder that soldiers often mutinied in those days and ironically the gardens were laid out on the spot where mutineers were often hung. Other features include a 150-year-old fountain and a whalebone arch no doubt originating from the whaling station which used to operate in nearby Algeciras.

As well as native Gibraltar plant specimens, there are flowers, shrubs and trees from other parts of the world which have a similar Mediterranean climate, such as the Cape region of South Africa, Perth in Australia, Madeira and the Canary Islands. Particularly impressive when in flower are the numerous Dragon Trees from Tenerife. ■ *Free. The gardens are situated on the west side of Europa Rd, next to the Cable Car Station.*

More sights in Gibraltar Town

Close to the lower cable car station in Rosia Road is **Nelson's Anchorage,** the spot where Nelson's body was brought ashore from HMS Victory preserved in a rum barrel after the Battle of Trafalgar in 1805. Dominating the site today is a 100-tonne Victorian 'super gun' – one of just four that were cast in 1870. ■ *Mon-Sat 0930-1700. Free with a ticket to the Upper Rock Nature Reserve.*

Gibraltar has many defensive **walls**, **gates** and **fortifications**. Running along the west side of the rock, following the old Moorish sea wall, is **Line Wall**. It stretches from Casemates to Rosia Bay and has been refaced in Portland Limestone, the local limestone being too brittle for this use. All the land between the wall and the sea is reclaimed land. The other important wall is **Charles V Wall**, stretching from the south end of Line Wall up to the old Moorish wall. There are two gates in Charles V's Wall, both overlooking the

Trafalgar Cemetery. The **Southport Gate** was originally built in 1552, probably on the site of Tarik's original fortifications. It is now a series of gates, one for pedestrians bearing the Spanish royal arms and the other, used by traffic, has arms of Britain, Gibraltar and the then Governor. The most recent series of gates commemorates the referendum of 1967, when the Gibraltarians opted to retain their links with Britain. Higher up, **Prince Edward's Gate**, dating from 1790, is named after Queen Victoria's father. The **Ragged Staff Gates**, near the main entrance to the dockyard, are thought to have gained their name from the crest of Charles V. Finally, at the north end of main street, are the **Casemates**, which have always been the main land defence for over six centuries. They were rebuilt extensively after the Great Siege.

The **Governor's Residence** was once a Franciscan monastery. It is an imposing brick and stone Gothic style building with two Dutch Ends and a square Portland stone doorway with roof. It became the official residence of the chief British officer in 1704, before the friars were evicted eight years later. The 16th-century cloisters remain intact, but unfortunately the building is not open to visitors. A colourful Changing of the Guard ceremony takes place monthly outside the residence. (Another tradition, the Ceremony of the Keys, takes place three times a year in Casemates Square.) The convent's Chapel of St Francis was renamed **Kings Chapel** and became the garrison's main Church of England place of worship. Worth visiting, the chapel has the colours of various British regiments plus the tombs of a number of Governors, both Spanish and English.

The Gibraltar Parliament now sits in the **House of Assembly**, which was the old Exchange and Commercial Library. Unfortunately its dignity is somewhat lowered by the plethora of tatty cafes surrounding the building.

Places of worship

The numerous places of worship reflect the varied background of the Gibraltarians

The oldest building is the Catholic **Cathedral of St Mary the Crowned**. Built on the site of a mosque, some of the early Moorish structures can still be seen, particulary on the south side of the building. It was badly damaged during the Great Siege and has been extensively rebuilt, with an imposing yellow and white classical façade and sturdy bell tower. The Anglican **Cathedral of the Holy Trinity** was not built until 1825 and was consecrated as a cathedral in 1838. Located in Cathedral Square, it has an extraordinary design, dominated strangely by Moorish style horseshoe arches. The **Great Synagogue**, Shahar Hashhamayim in Engineer Lane, was founded in 1724, but was destroyed by floods in 1744 and then later during the Great Siege. The present building, for the 750 Jews in Gibraltar today, dates from 1768 and has a Flemish style bell gable.

Gibraltar Museum

This museum is located in Bomb House Lane, off Cathedral Square, in a reconstructed 14th-century building which was formerly officers' quarters. It was chosen as the place for a museum because it was known that Moorish baths lay underneath the site. Rooms 1 and 2 consist of archaeological material covering the Paleolithic to the Moorish periods. The museum's most important archaeological exhibit is now in London's Natural History Museum. This is a female skull discovered in Forbes Quarry on the North Front of the Rock in 1848. Its significance was not realized at the time, but modern dating techniques have revealed that it is of Neanderthal age. As the tour guides like to point out, Neanderthal Man should really have been Gibraltar Woman. In Room 7 is one of the Museum's proudest possessions – an enormous model of Gibraltar as it was in 1850 at a scale of 1:600. It is particularly interesting to see the old Moorish walls before they were swallowed up by the high rise flats. Note, too, how the sea came right up to the town wall before the harbour was constructed in 1894.

The Museum is also the main tourist information office. ■ *Mon-Fri 1000-1800, Sat 1000-1400. £2, children £1. Also at the Museum is a small restaurant.*

Wildlife

One of the best ways of seeing some of the wildlife of the Upper Rock is to take the cable car to the top and then walk down via some of the quieter lanes and steps. On the main route up, high stone walls and speeding taxis and mini-buses shut out any wildlife. But the top of the Rock is an excellent place for observing the migration of eagles, vultures and storks during spring and autumn, particularly when the wind is from the west. There is also an **Information Centre** at Jews Gate. Birdwatchers are usually welcome here, as news of sightings can be passed on. There is a limited amount of walking that can be done from the top of the cable car due to precipitous slopes and old gun emplacements.

Upper Rock Nature Reserve

Much of the upper Rock is composed of either bare rock or scrub consisting of dwarf olives, fan palms and broom, with Aleppo Pines at lower levels. Breeding **birds** include peregrines (which nest on the north face), blue rock thrushes, scops owls and alpine swifts. Gibraltar is the only place in mainland Europe where the barbary partridge is found. Head for the Mediterranean Steps, a precipitous circular walk from Jews Gate. Migration time can be very exciting, contributing to the 270-odd species of birds recorded at Gibraltar. There is a good range of wild **flowers** from Christmas onwards, including paper white narcissus, giant squill and wild gladioli and wild iris. Amongst the more exotic butterflies are the painted lady, Spanish festoon, Cleopatra, swallowtail and the enormous two-tailed pasha. There are plenty of lizards and geckoes, but **mammals**, apart from rabbits and the two groups of Barbary apes, are elusive.

The Gibraltar Ornithological and Natural History Society (GONHS) are pleased to help visiting wildlife enthusiasts. On Saturday at 1400 one of their members is at the Europa Point Observation Platform to the right of the Trinity Lighthouse to help in the identification of sea birds and migrants. On Sunday morning between 0900 and 1000 the Society runs birdwatching walks from Jews Gate up the Mediterranean Steps. ■ *Contact Bob on T78322 (evenings only).*

This has become increasingly popular in recent years. The Straits are rich in sea mammals; in addition to common dolphins, the striped and bottlenosed varieties can be seen, along with occasional whales, such as the fin, sperm, pilot and orca. (In the early 20th century there was a thriving whaling station in Algeciras Bay). *Fortuna* runs dolphin tours on an 80-year-old sailing boat, operating from Queensway Quay Marina, T74598. The *MV Lochlan* has an underwater camera and video monitor and provides excellent food. It operates from Marina Bay, T47333. Most sailings last 2-2½ hours. There is also an evening cruise during the summer when much of the Rock is floodlit. Booking is essential. A branch of the same company, *Ocean Air*, operates a seaplane that runs trips around the rock, the timing linked up with the whale watching boat. *Dolphin Safari*, T71914, established over 30 years ago, runs a small catamaran with the emphasis on touchy-feely encounters with the dolphins. Other firms include *Jolly Joevan*, T74430, and *Nimo*, T73719. *Nautilus VI*, T73400, is a luxury semi-submersible offering underwater views of dolphins.

Dolphin watching

Cádiz Province

Essentials

Sleeping
Price codes in Gibraltar

AL over £100
A £90-100
B £70-90
C £50-70
D £40-50
E under £30

Hotels in Gibraltar are generally more expensive than comparable hotels in Spain. A number of hotels claim to be in the luxury grade, but travellers used to this category may be disappointed. There is little available at the cheaper end of the range and those looking for budget accommodation should consider the *pensiones* in La Linea on the Spanish side of the border. Sleeping rough on the beaches is frowned upon by the local police, who carry out regular checks in the summer.

AL *Whites* (formerly the *Holiday Inn*), Governors Pde, T70700, F70243. 123 rooms. Roof top leisure area with pool, sauna, mini gym. Good restaurant and fine views. **A** *Rock*, Europa Rd, T73000, F73513. 146 rooms. Located on the edge of the Upper Rock overlooking the Botanic Gardens. Good views, pool, restaurant and garage. **B** *Caleta Palace*, Catalan Bay, T76501, F42143, 200 rooms. Beachside location beneath the water catchments on the east side of the Rock. Sandy beach, pool, restaurant and garage. Some package tour use. **B** *Eliot*, Governors Pde, T350 70500, F350 70243, www.gibraltar.gi/ eliothotel Rooftop pool and restaurant with stunning views. **C** *Bristol*, 10 Cathedral Sq, T76800, F77613. 60 recently refurbished rooms. Central location near the cathedral and museum, with garden and pool. **C** *Continental*, Engineer Lane, T76900, F41702. 17 rooms. Modern hotel with central location. No restaurant. **D** *Queens*, 1 Boyd St, PO Box 99, T74000, F40030. 62 rooms. Conveniently placed for the cable car, Botanic Gardens and shopping. Restaurant. **D** *Sunrise Motel*, 60 Devil's Tower Rd, PO Box 377, T41265, F41245. 36 rooms. A/c. Located under the north cliff of the Rock and convenient for the airport. **E** *Cannon*, 9 Cannon Lane, T51711, F51789, cannon@gibnet.gi 18 rooms. Recently opened Swedish owned small hotel in the town centre. Restaurant. **Youth hostels** *Emile Youth Hostel*, Montagu

Gibraltar centre

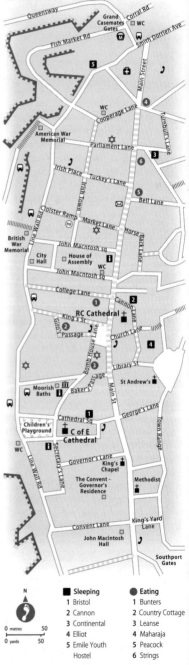

Sleeping	Eating
1 Bristol	1 Bunters
2 Cannon	2 Country Cottage
3 Continental	3 Leanse
4 Eliot	4 Maharaja
5 Emile Youth Hostel	5 Peacock
	6 Strings

0 metres 50
0 yards 50

Bastion, Line Wall Rd, T51106. Communal TV lounge and rooms. Continental breakfast included in the price of £10 a night. **Camping** There is literally no room for a campsite in Gibraltar. The nearest sites in Spain are at Algeciras to the west and Manilva to the east.

Expensive *Bunters*, 1 College Lane, T70482. Sophisticated international fare plus traditional English desserts, evenings only. *Strings*, 44 Cornwalls Lane, T78800. International food, including Moroccan, closed Mon, booking advisable. *The Peacock*, Bell Lane, T40064. Aimed at the lunchtime business community, good fresh fish and Gibraltarian dishes. **Mid-range** *Biancas*, Marina Bay, T73379. Specializes in pizzas, appeals to a youthful clientele, excellent harbour views. *Country Cottage*, 13-15 Giros Passage, T70084. English cuisine including roast lamb and Angus steak. *Little Mermaid*, Marina Bay. Recently opened Danish restaurant with typical Scandinavian specialities. *Maharaja*, 21 Turnbulls Lane, T75233. The best Indian food on the Rock. **Cheap** Pubs are excellent value (see below). For cheap fish and chips try *Casements Fishery* on the second floor of the International Commercial Centre, takeaway or eat in. *Macs Kitchen*, 245 Main St, T71155. Acceptable fast food. *The Leanse*, 7 Bomb House Lane. A kosher restaurant conveniently near to the synagogue, serving international and oriental food (expensive), closed Sat.

Eating

Pubs There are numerous pubs, most of which serve some sort of food, usually with an English flavour. The pubs in Main St, such as *The Angry Friar*, *The Royal Calpe* and *The Gibraltar Arms* are inevitably a magnet for both shoppers and tourists, but *The Clipper* in Irishtown and *Sir Winston's Tavern* in Cornwalls Pde are equally good. **Nightclubs** Try *Sax*, first floor of the ICC, open until 0200. *Penelope*, 3 West Pl of Arms, T70462. Set in one of the old town walls.

Bars & nightclubs

Casinos *International Casino Club*, 7 Europa Rd, T76666. Apart from the gaming tables, there is a restaurant and fine views. Open 2000-0400, entry free. **Cinemas** *Queens*, next to the hotel of the same name in Boyd St. Recently refurbished. Open daily, except Wed; admission £3-4.

Entertainment

Gibraltar is sales-tax free and therefore has considerable attractions, not only to expatriates on the Costa del Sol, but also to Spaniards living over the border who flock in for their petrol and cigarettes. Be warned that there are limits on the goods you are permitted to import back into Spain and there are often long customs delays. For those who can brave the narrow crowded pavements and busy traffic of the main street, there are branches of well-known UK firms such as *Safeway* (3 branches), *Marks and Spencer* and *Mothercare*. In the smaller shops in the town centre, the best bargains are in electrical goods, jewellery, watches and perfume, but don't assume you are getting a bargain just because you are buying in Gibraltar. Shopping hours tend to resemble those of the UK rather than Spain. A popular shopping venue is *Gibraltar Crystal*, located at Grand Casemates, at the north end of Main St, where you can see glass blowers at work and buy their products.

Shopping

Sport fishing trips *Jolly Joevan*, T74430. *Jalex*, T70393. **Scuba diving** *Dive Charters PADI*, T45649. *Dive Hire NUAI*, T73616. *Rock Marine BSAC*, T73147.

Sport

Alpha Travel, 123 Main St, T79281; *Bland Ltd*, Cloister Building, T77012; *Calypso Tours*, 21 Horse Barrack Lane, T76520; *Exchange Travel*, 241 Main St, T76151; *Herald Travel*, Montagu Pavilion, Queensway, T71171.

Tour operators

Local Bike, scooter and motorcycle hire: *Rent a bike*, T70420. **Car**: the best **car parks** are at the cable car centre and a small multi-storey car park near the sports ground on the west side of the town. Approach both of these car parks via

Transport

Queensway, NOT through Main St, which is largely pedestrianized. **Car hire**: most of the international car hire firms are based at the airport, including *Avis*, T75552, *Budget*, T79666, *Hertz*, T42737 and *Europcar*, T77171 (highly recommended). There are a number of local firms who might be cheaper, but will not have the full back-up services in Spain. Car hire is generally slightly cheaper in Spain. If customs delays are bad, drivers may have to pick up their cars on the Spanish side of the border. When returning a car and catching a plane, remember to leave plenty of time for customs delays. Don't worry about leaving the car on the Spanish side of the border – this is normal procedure and the hire firm will collect it if you give precise instructions on its whereabouts. If you choose to drive in Gibraltar, be warned that the locals have, for obvious reasons, taken enthusiastically to scooter ownership. A vast number of these machines buzz around like mosquitoes and make driving a nightmare.

Long distance Air: the underused Gibraltar Airport was built in the Second World War on reclaimed land and a feature of the road into town is that it passes over the runway, which is shared with the RAF, and traffic is stopped as each plane lands and takes off. It is only served by 2 airlines – *GB Airways*, (a subsidiary of *BA*) and *Monarch*. No Spanish companies use the airport, although this could change in the future. *GB Airways* run 14 flights a week from London Gatwick. *Monarch* flies 4 times a week from London Luton. Both companies run a reduced service in the winter. *GB Airways*, T75984, *Monarch*, T47477. There is a £7 passenger tax when leaving Gibraltar. There is a car park opposite the airport, which charges from 30p for 30 mins to £1.50 for 6 hrs. It is worth considering routes via Málaga, which give greater choice and cheaper fares and less expensive car hire. **Boat**: Gibraltar has become an important ferry port with links to Morocco. The *MS Estrella* runs to and from Tangier on 3 days a week. Foot passengers pay £18 single and £30 return, vehicles £40 and £80. The crossing takes approximately 2 hrs. T77666. There is now a daily catamaran service to and from Tangier. Tickets cost £30 for a period return and £25 for a day trip. The crossing takes 1 hr 15 mins. T79200. A hydrofoil service, the *Hanse Jet,* operated by *FRS Maroc* runs 2 return trips to Tangier daily and takes 1½ hrs. A quicker way to travel to Morocco is by *GB Air*, who fly daily to Casablanca and Marrakesh. **Car** Spanish customs are usually awkward in view of the widespread smuggling of cigarettes and drugs, so delays for re-entering Spain are common and can last from 15 mins to 5 hrs, depending on the political situation at the time.

Directory Banks Branches of all the main British and Spanish banks, plus some from other European countries, are mainly based around the Main St/Line/Wall Rd area. There are also a number of bureaus de change, including one at the airport and three in Main St. **Currency**: the official currency is the Gibraltar pound and the colony issues its own notes and coins, but euros and US dollars are widely accepted in all commercial establishments. Gibraltar notes are not exchangeable outside the Rock. **Communications** Post office: the main branch is located at 104 Main St, open 0900-1300 and 1400-1700, Sat 1000-1300. Gibraltar issues its own postage stamps. **Telephones**: when telephoning out of Gibraltar, the international prefix is 00 (except for Spain). To call Gibraltar from Spain dial first 9567 (except in Cádiz province where the code is 7). Faxes can be sent from the offices of *Cable and Wireless*, 25 South Barracks Rd. Telephone cabins in Gibraltar are the traditional British red version. Gibraltar mobile phones cannot be used in Spain, although, ironically, they function perfectly well anywhere else in Europe. **Embassies and consulates** *Belgium*, 47 Irishtown, T78553; *Denmark*, Cloister Building, Market Lane, T72735; *Israel*, 3 City Mill Lane, T75955; *Italy*, 12 College Lane, T78123; *Netherlands*, 2/6 Main St, T79220; *Norway*, 315 Main St, T78305; *Sweden*, Cloister Building, Market Lane, T78456. **Medical services** UK residents are entitled to free medical treatment provided that they have a temporary address in Gibraltar. Day visitors from UK and other EU nationals must provide Form E111. **St Bernards Hospital**, T73941. There is also a **Health Centre** in Casemates Sq, T78337.

Málaga Province

6

Málaga Province

Málaga suffers from an image problem. To many it is no more than the name of the airport closest to the Costa del Sol sunbed and sea resorts. In fact, Málaga is the second most mountainous province in Andalucía – the first being Granada – with a breathtaking variety of scenery. Heading inland from the conspicuous tourist resorts on the coast, you come to such historically heady towns as **Ronda** perched precariously atop a 120 m deep gorge. Further east is the lake district of **El Chorro** with its sparkling blue lakes, surrounded by pine-covered mountains. This is the province where some of the prettiest **pueblos blancos** (white villages) can be found, along with forested valleys, prehistoric caves, salt water lagoons and acres of olive and citrus tree groves. The landscape includes several natural parks, including the **Parque Natural del Torcal** with its lunar landscape of extraordinary limestone formations, which formed a seabed 150 million years ago.

More recent history lives on in the towns and cities. In **Málaga** cupolas jostle for space with spires, minarets and lofty apartment buildings, while, like a grand old dame, the 11th-century Gibralfaro castle sits grandly aloft with the best view of all. The Malagueños are typically Andaluz and the locals have that enviable capacity to live life for the present, and live life to the full. "Every day seems to be a holiday," commented the 19th-century writer Richard Ford on his first visit to this part of Spain. This vibrancy of spirit is contagious throughout the province especially during traditional holidays like Easter Week or **Semana Santa** and the annual **ferias** with their flamenco and fino.

Málaga

Colour map 5, grid B1
Population: 528,079

Málaga has a touch of both the Moorish grandeur of Granada and the casta-net-clicking spirit of Seville. Yet although some 3 million visitors land at the airport each year, most people automatically turn right to the Costa del Sol, rather than left into the city. Admittedly, initial impressions can be discouraging as, like most Spanish cities, the shell is drab and industrial. But the kernel, the historic city centre, is fascinating, with its majestic, if peculiar, unfinished Gothic Cathedral, surrounded by sun-baked ochre buildings, narrow pedestrianized streets and more bars per sq m than anywhere else in Europe.

Málaga flourished in the Muslim era and in the 19th century had a dynamic middle class. Decades later the Costa capital was a favourite winter resort for wealthy Madrileños. Aside from the cultural and historic sights, there are some intriguing old-fashioned shops here, their dusty, dark interiors revealing such treasures as handmade fans, intricately embroidered shawls or counters piled high with local hams and great wheels of local Manchego cheese. When the shops shut, the streets shift into night-time mode with a big-city choice of restaurants, bars and clubs, while the August feria is one of the most vibrant in Spain and a time when the Andaluz spirit of alegria can be appreciated to the full.

Ins and outs

Getting there Málaga's busy **airport**, which handles 7 million passengers a year, is located about 7
See page 236 for km west of the city centre and 4 km east of Torremolinos. There is a bus which runs
further details between the aiport and Málaga every 30 mins which leaves from the 'City Bus' stop outside the arrivals hall. If you're heading for Málaga or the nearer coastal resorts, the best option is the Fuengirola-Málaga train which runs every 30 mins from 0711 to 2345 with stops in Torremolinos and Benalmádena. If you are going to Málaga, stay on until the final Centro-Alameda stop. To reach the centre from here, cross the Puente Tetuán over the Río Guadalmedina and follow the Alameda Principal. To reach the train station from the airport, turn right outside the airport building upper-level exit and follow signs over the footbridge. Tickets are obtained from a machine on the platform or on the train. Leaving the airport by car, follow the exit road. Approaching the N340, the left-hand lane will take you across a flyover and on to Málaga and the right-hand lane will take you on to the N340 heading west for the Costa del Sol resorts and onwards to Cádiz. Málaga's main **bus** station is conveniently close to the RENFE **train** station (5 mins north on Paseo de los Tilos). There are bus connections to all the major Andalucían cities and towns. It is a 20-min walk to the centre from here, but local buses cover the route. A taxi to Málaga costs about €7, and to Marbella €34.

Getting around Most of the monuments and museums of Málaga are located within a compact area and can be conveniently visited on foot. Taxis, however, are cheap and there are ranks at the bus and train stations and in the Alameda Principal. If you fancy a clip clop around the city on a horse-drawn carriage, head for the Paseo de España and expect to pay around €18 for a 45-min trip. There is an open top sightseeing bus tour around the city which takes in the main historic sights and can be picked up at several stops, including outside the bus station and the cathedral.

Tourist offices The main regional tourist office is at Pasaje Chinitas 4, T952213445. Open Mon-Fri 0900-1400, Sat 0900-1300. The municipal tourist office is housed in a wonderful old

Things to do ★

- Have a mint tea in one of Málaga's many *teterías*, or Moroccan tea shops
- Join in with the riotous Verdiales fiesta in late December north of Málaga
- Go for a complete spa treatment at the sulphur baths of Carratraca
- Walk in the Parque Natural El Torcal on a clear day and see the limestone landscape of the entire park and North African coastline from a viewpoint at 1,339 m
- Relax in Ronda in the room located in an 13th-century tower at the *En Frente Arte* hotel

building at Av de Cervantes 1, just off the Paseo del Parque, T952604410. Open Mon-Fri 0800-1500, 1630-1930 (closing 30 mins earlier in winter), Sat 0930-1330. There are smaller tourist offices at the airport and bus station, plus several information kiosks in the centre (Plaza de la Constitución and next to the Correos, near Puente Tetuán). See also the city's website, www.malaga.com

Málaga airport is perfectly safe if you arrive in the early hours, but you will not find any public transport to and from the city. There will be plenty of taxis parked outside the arrivals hall; however, do check the official rate, which is clearly posted, to avoid being overcharged. If you booked a package holiday or are staying at a reputable hotel, there should be a representative to meet you. **Arriving at night**

The area

Málaga is located at the mouth of the Guadalmedina River, which is usually dry, at the head of a broad bay, with its suburbs stretching away to the foot of the surrounding mountains. Climatically, it has one of the most favourable climates in Spain, with the mountains to the north cutting out cold winter winds, so that average January temperatures are around 15°C, while in the summer sea breezes usually make the heat bearable. Rainfall figures for Málaga itself are low, but plentiful rain in the sierras inland, along with a plethora of reservoirs, ensure that water supply is not usually a problem.

Málaga has a long history dating back to the Phoenicians who are credited with planting the area's first vineyards and who founded a settlement called Malaka, a word derived from *malac*, meaning to salt fish. The city became a busy trading port during Roman times, exporting minerals and agricultural produce from the interior. From the eighth century Málaga was occupied by the Moors, when it was the main port for the province of Granada. This was the so-called Golden Age when al-Andalus, and its rulers, or caliphs, rivalled those of Baghdad and Damascus for their wealth and accomplishments. In the 14th century, Málaga's magnificent Gibralfaro fortress was built. The city fell to the Catholics in 1487 after a long and violent siege. The Moorish population was subject to considerable persecution, which led to a revolt in 1568. This was brutally put down and the remaining Moors expelled. **History**

Deprived of its most able citizens, the fortunes of Málaga declined. It was not, in fact, until the 19th century, when an agricultural based revival began, that things began to look up. During the Civil War, Málaga supported the Republicans and saw a considerable amount of vicious fighting. Italian planes bombed the city, destroying part of its ancient centre although fortunately not all.

Málaga Province

Modern Málaga Since the 1960s mass tourism has transformed the area to the west, the Costa del Sol, but has thankfully had little effect on the city itself which remains intrinsically Spanish. Today Málaga is a thriving regional centre with good shops, a healthy nightlife, interesting architecture and historical and cultural appeal. Although most tourists still head straight for the bucket and spade Costa, the city is slowly waking up to its tourism potential and, for example, has recently introduced its first open top city tour bus (see Getting around above). Málaga's old town has also had a good scrub and brush up over the last few years and, thankfully, the crumbling historic buildings that provide much of its character are being restored, rather than pulled down. The new Picasso Museum is similarly likely to boost the city's appeal, while the port is becoming increasingly popular with cruise liners.

Málaga Province

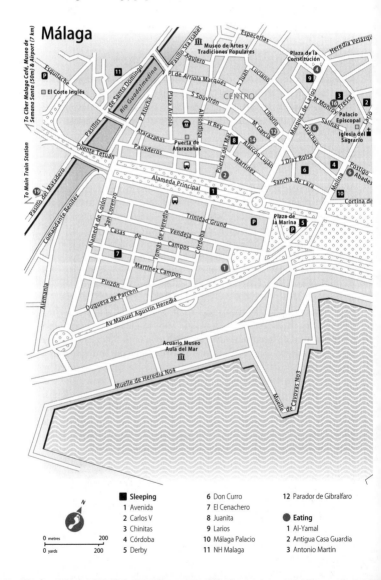

Málaga

Sleeping	6 Don Curro	12 Parador de Gibralfaro
1 Avenida	7 El Cenachero	
2 Carlos V	8 Juanita	**Eating**
3 Chinitas	9 Larios	1 Al-Yamal
4 Córdoba	10 Málaga Palacio	2 Antigua Casa Guardia
5 Derby	11 NH Malaga	3 Antonio Martín

Sights

Most of the sights in Málaga are contained within an atmospheric area of 19th-century streets and squares north of the main east-west thoroughfare. This starts in the east at the Plaza de Toros and passes first through the Paseo del Parque, an attractive tree-lined promenade, past the Plaza de la Marina, along the Alameda Principal. This 19th-century boulevard with its colourful daily flower market leads to the recently landscaped bed of the Río Guadalmedina, ending in the area around *El Corte Inglés* department store, the post office and the Centro Alameda station of the electric railway.

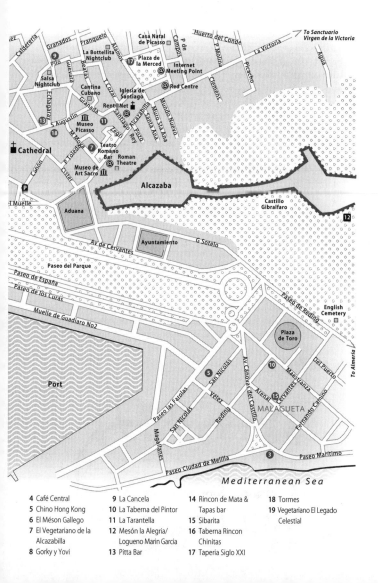

Málaga Province

The Alcazaba This former fortress and palace was started by the Moors in the 700s, but most of the structure dates from the mid-11th century. The site was originally occupied by both the Phoenicians and the Romans, and in fact there is a considerable amount of Roman masonry in the walls. The Alcazaba suffered badly during the Catholic Reconquista, but was carefully restored in the 1930s. Today, it rises impressively above the cramped streets below with a series of terraced, fortified walls and fine gateways, laid out with gardens and running water in typical Moorish style.

The main palace building now houses the Archaeological Museum. Exhibits cover the prehistoric, Phoenician, Roman and Moorish periods, consisting of pottery, statues, coins and mosaics, presented in a rather haphazard fashion. From the terraces of the museum there are fine views over the port and the city. ■ *Tue-Sun 0900-1900. Free. T952216005.*

Classical & Moorish sights
The views from the top of the castle are arguably the best in the city

The **Castillo Gibralfaro** (Lighthouse Hill) is a ruined Moorish castle built by Yusef I of Granada in the early 14th century. It is linked to the Alcazaba below by parallel walls. A path leads up to it from the side of the Alcazaba, but this is a stiff walk and in the summer heat it's better to approach it by the road which leads from the city up towards the Parador via Calle Mundo Nuevo (the fifth road past the Roman Theatre) and Calle Victoria. Alternatively, take the No 35 bus from the Paseo del Parque. ■ *0900-1900. Free.*

There are two other Moorish curiosities in Málaga. In the underground car park at the west end of the Paseo del Parque are the remains of the **Moorish city walls** (plus part of the 18th-century harbour wall). Formerly protected by a brick wall, they have been restored and are displayed behind glass. The Moorish walls are believed to date from the 14th-century Nasrid period. Further west at the entrance to the city market is the Puerta de Atarazanas. This was originally the gateway into the Moorish dockyard and it displays the crest of the Nasrid dynasty.

The **Teatro Romano**, located close to the entrance of the Alcazaba, was unearthed in the 1950s during building work to extend the 19th-century Casa de Cultura (which has now been demolished). It is currently under excavation but the banks of seating are clearly visible from the street.

The Cathedral Málaga's cathedral, as with many others in Andalucía, was built on the site of a mosque and dates from the 16th century, with numerous modifications at later dates. One of its two towers was never completed, giving it a lopsided

Catedral

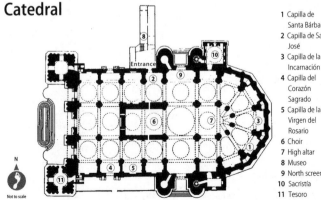

1 Capilla de Santa Bárbara
2 Capilla de San José
3 Capilla de la Incarnación
4 Capilla del Corazón Sagrado
5 Capilla de la Virgen del Rosario
6 Choir
7 High altar
8 Museo
9 North screen
10 Sacristía
11 Tesoro

N

Not to scale

appearance, leading to the nickname of la Manquita, variously translated as 'the cripple' or 'the one-armed lady'. The story goes that funds needed for its completion were diverted to the American War of Independence. The interior is both Gothic and Renaissance, while the exterior is typical 18th-century Baroque, aside from a particularly fine Gothic doorway in Plateresque style dating from the early 16th century. The cathedral has recently undergone considerable restoration after a massive fundraising effort. A large, somewhat gloomy building, its interior has also benefited recently from more imaginative lighting.

The highlight of the cathedral is, without doubt, the Choir. Behind the stalls are some superb carvings of saints, 42 of which are attributed to Pedro de Mena around 1662 (de Mena's house, incidentally, is located in a back street about 500 m from the cathedral). Rearing above the choir stalls are two 18th-century organs. Also worth inspection is the relatively modern, tabernacle-like High Altar, which unusually for Andalucía, does not have a backing *retablo*.

There are 16 side chapels, of which only five have some distinction (see plan). The Capilla de San José has a stone altarpiece with a superb triptych of the Annunciation by the Italian painter Cesere Arbassia. At the east end behind the High Altar is the Capilla de la Encarnación. Probably the most delightful chapel of all is that of Santa Bárbara, which is dominated by a superb retablo, festooned with saints and dating from the mid-16th century. The main feature of the Capilla de la Virgen del Rosario, is the painting of the Virgin attributed to Alonso Cano and dated around 1666. The painting is flanked by statues of San Lorenzo and San Blas. Finally, the Capilla del Corazón Sagrado, closed by a 19th-century bronze grill, contains a Baroque-style *retablo containing 11 panels of 16th-century paintings brought here from* Castille and attributed to Becerril. The altar table also contains some fine silver and gilt work. The admission fee to the cathedral also includes entrance to the **museo**, a rundown affair near the entrance door containing the usual vestments, copes and silver. ■ *1000-1845 Closed Sun. €1.80. C Molina Larios, T952215917.*

There are a number of interesting churches in the central area of Málaga, the best of which are the **Iglesia del Sagrario**, adjacent to the cathedral with a splendid Gothic portal and a beautiful altarpiece (open daily 0930-1230 and 1800-1930), and **Sanctuario Virgen de la Victoría**, in Calle La Victoría, which has further work by de Mana. Also worth a visit is the **Iglesia de Santiago** in Calle Granada, with its 15th-century Mudéjar tower. ■ *Daily 0930-1300, 1800-2000.* Adjacent to the cathedral on Plaza del Obispo is the 18th-century **Palacio del Obispo**, or Bishop's Palace, which has one of the most beautiful façades in the city.

This curiosity is located east of the Paseo del Parque and just past the bullring. It dates from the days when 'infidels' (ie non-Catholics) were buried on the beach, where after storms their remains were often washed up. In the mid-18th century a British consul persuaded the authorities to allow him to start an English cemetery. Look for the small Church of St George. From here a path leads into the leafy walled cemetery, a haven of peace in the noisy city. Hans Christian Andersen once visited the cemetery and observed 'I can well understand how a splenetic Englishman might take his own life in order to be buried in this place'. The inscriptions on the gravestones make absorbing reading. Look for the tombstone of Gamel Woolsey near the eastern wall, an American poet and wife of the British writer and Hispanist Gerald Brenan. He was due to join her here when he died, but his body was pickled in

English Cemetery

Málaga Province

formaldehyde in the anatomy department of Málaga University for some 14 years, before in January 2000 he was eventually laid to rest next to his wife. ■ *Mon-Fri 1000-1400, Sat-Sun 1000-1200. Free.*

Paseo del Parque Between the Alcazaba and the port is a delightful tree-lined avenue, giving welcome shade during the heat of summer days. Built on land reclaimed from the sea, the park itself has a fine collection of rare, well-labelled plants, along with sculptures and fountains (look for the Genoa Fountain, now on a traffic island). There are some distinguished buildings on the north side of the park, including the flamboyant art deco Banco de España, the baroque Ayuntamiento, La Aduana or old customs house, and El Correo, the former post office.

Casa Natal de Picasso Often erroneously described as a museum, Picasso's birthplace is now the recently renovated headquarters of the Picasso Foundation. It is located in the Plaza de la Merced, a once impressive square which is being restored to its former glory. There are several of the artist's earlier paintings and sketches on exhibit; however, the foundations is primarily a research facility for academics. ■ *Mon-Sat 1100-1400 and 1700-2000. Sun 1100-1400. Free. T952060215.*

Museums **Museo de Bellas Artes** This museum, set in the restored 16th-century Palacio de Buenavista, has now closed. It will re-open in late 2002 as the Picasso Museum.(Check with the tourist office for up-to-date information) The Picasso family have 'donated' 182 pictures to the city authorities at what they describe as a 'bargain price' of €7.83 million. Also in late 2002 , the Bellas Artes collection is due to move from its temporary home in the Aduana building to its new quarters in Calle Calzada de Trinidad on the northwest side of the Río Guadalmedina. (Again, check with *turismo* for up-to-date information).

Museo de Artes y Tradiciones Populares Anyone interested in social history should make a particular effort to see this museum which is located at Calle Pasillo Santa Isabel 10 by the recently landscaped bed of the river Guadalmedina, a two-minute walk from the Alameda. Look for the inn sign labelled Mesón de Victoria, as this museum is housed in an old 17th-century hostelry. The museum consists of a somewhat haphazard collection of items of everyday life going back several centuries, including fishing boats, an olive press, guns, farming implements and a whole range of household relics. ■ *Mon-Fri 1000-1330 and 1600-1900. Sat 1000-1330. €12.*

Museo de Semana Santa In the Plaza de San Pedro opposite *El Corte Inglés* department store is this Holy Week museum with exhibits of processional regalia. ■ *Mon-Fri 1030-1230 and 1900-2100.*

Museo de Arte Sacro This museum of religious art dating from the 15th to 18th centuries, including work by Pedro de Mena, is located in the recently restored Palacio del Obispo, near the cathedral. ■ *Only open when an exhibition is being held.*

Acuario Museo Aula del Mar Otherwise known as the Museo Marítimo, on Avenida Manuel Augustín de la Heredia (near the port), this marine museum has aquaria and underwater caves containing turtles, octopuses and coral. It also runs marine ecology courses and boat excursions in Málaga Bay. ■ *Daily 1000 -1430 €3, children €2.40. T952229287.*

Excursions **Jardín Botánico La Concepción** These botanical gardens, 3 km north of Málaga, have an interesting history, being created over 150 years ago by Amalia Heredia and her husband, the American mining tycoon George Loring, who later became the Marquis of Casa-Loring. They collected plants from many parts of the world and also accumulated an important archaeological collection. The estate, covering some 120 acres, eventually passed into the hands of the Echevarrieta family who sold it to the Málaga city hall in 1990. The local authorities then spent four years classifying the plants, restoring the fountains and clearing paths. The gardens were finally open to the public in June 1994. Visits take the form of guided tours, with multi-lingual guides, lasting around 1½ hours. The tone is set at the entrance, which is through a 3-m thick bougainvillea hedge and then follows what resembles a tamed jungle with some 30 species of palms, dragon trees, a huge pergola of wisteria, whole banks of Swiss cheese plants, some in flower, camellia, jacarandas, a Norfolk Island pine claimed to be the largest in Andalucía, a vast variety of rhododendrons and much more. Curiously, this part of the gardens is known as the English garden; nearby is a typical Spanish *paseo* known equally curiously as the French garden. The latter leads to a mirador giving stunning views over Málaga (the cathedral and castle can be clearly seen) and the enormous stone dam of La Concepción reservoir.

The tour returns via a small archaeological museum in the style of a reproduction of a Greek temple, containing artefacts filched from a variety of sites, as was the custom of the time. Particularly impressive are the articles from the first-century Roman site at nearby Cártema, including statuary, mosaics, milestones and a sarcophagus with interior pillow. The museum itself may not always be open, but there are sufficient artefacts lying around outside to provide interest. There is a somewhat sleepy venta 200 m to the north. ■ *Tue-Sun 1000-1630.* €*2.80; children under 14,* €*1.40. T952252148. Access to La Concepción is easy as it lies alongside the Málaga-Antequera N331 autovía, just off the Málaga bypass, and is well signposted. Local buses stop nearby.*

Essentials

Despite its size and importance, Málaga has a surprisingly poor choice of accommodation, although as tourism here increases, this is bound to improve. If you are visiting in the summer, it is essential to book in advance, especially during the August *feria*. There are over 60 *pensiones* to choose from in Málaga, but as is often the case in a sea port, they need to be chosen with care, as some can be rather squalid, particularly in the central area. Insist on seeing the room first.

Sleeping
■ *on map, page 227*

AL Guadalmar, Ctra de Cádiz, km 238, T952231703, F952240385, guadalmar@ trypnet.com This 9-storey modern hotel sits across from a private beach 3 km west of the city centre; all the rooms have a sea-view balcony. This is a hotel geared for families with excellent sports facilities, including indoor and outdoor pools, gym, pool, sauna and tennis. Babysitting service, a/c, garage, TV, restaurant. **AL** *Málaga Palacio,* C Cortina del Muelle 1, T/F952215185. An imposing hotel of 225 rooms opening onto a tree-lined esplanade. Conveniently close to the cathedral, city centre and nightlife. Rooftop pool, a/c, TV. **A** *Don Curro,* C Sancha de Lara 7, T952227200, F952215946, doncurro@ infonegocio.com This 112-room classic hotel has an old-fashioned feel with wood-panelling and fireplaces. Centrally located close to cathedral, the usual city noises are accentuated by the hotel's bingo hall. Parking, TV, a/c, restaurant. **A** *Larios,* C Larios 2, T952222200 F952222407, www.hotel-larios.com Cool, modern hotel with 34 rooms on exclusive shopping street in the heart of the city. Rooms have a hint of art deco. Parking, TV, a/c, restaurant. **A** *Los Naranjos,* C Paseo Sancha 35, T952224317, F952225975. A reasonably priced hotel located near the best beach east of the city. Décor is typically Andaluz with colourful *azuelejos* and ornate wood carving. Parking, 41 rooms, TV, a/c,

☞ Chiringuitos

One of the joys of a beach holiday in Andalucía is to have a lunch al fresco in a beach bar or chiringuito. In the early years of tourism, the chiringuitos were often owned by people who had their main restaurant in the town and just opened up their beach bar for the summer. They were just wooden shacks that blew down in the winter or were destroyed by storm waves and had to be rebuilt again for the following season. Nowadays they are much more permanent structures with impeccable hygiene, but many still have a traditional atmosphere with straw roofs and the statuary fishing boat in which to roast sardines on a spit. Invariably fresh fish figures prominently on the menus with paella and shellfish always popular.

Some chiringuitos have become extremely well-known, such as **El Tintero** on the El Palo beach in Málaga, where the food is taken directly from the trays of waiters who circulate among the tables shouting out the names of the dishes. There are some fine sea food chiringuitos near to the fishing ports of La Carihuela in Torremolinos and at Fuengirola. Those in Marbella tend to be rather more substantial and upmarket, with customers often rubbing shoulders with a Spanish cabinet minister or a celebrity. On the Atlantic coast of the Costa de la Luz, the chiringuitos are usually more rustic and temporary, often being taken down in the winter months.

Everyone has their favourite chiringuito. Try the unique **Sinbad's** on Urbanización Marbesa, near Puerto Cabopino. The whole place is draped with fishing nets, sea shells and nautical artefacts you can even see the owner braving the waves in his flimsy boat. You can't get fresher seafood than that!

---

restaurant. **A** *NH Málaga*, Río Guadalmedina, T952071323, F952393862. The city's newest hotel geared for business travellers with a sleek, modern interior, 129 a/c rooms, TV and all mod cons. Parking, restaurant. **A** *Parador de Gibralfaro*, Paseo García del Olmo, T952221902, F952221902, Gibralfaro@parador.es A superb traditional parador near the castle. The rooms have private entrances and sun terraces with panoramic views of the city and sea. There are just 12 rooms, so advance reservations are essential. A/c, TV, meeting rooms, restaurant, bar, pool.

B *Las Vegas*, Paseo de Sancha 22, T952217712, F952224889. 107 rooms. Large traditional establishment with pleasant leafy garden, located near bullring. Tropical gardens, pool, restaurant, bar, a/c. **C** *Carlos V*, C Cister 10, T952215120. Located in the shadow of the cathedral with an interesting façade decorated with wrought-iron balconies. 51 rooms with TV and a/c. Parking. **D** *Hostal Avenida*, Alameda Principal 5, T952217728. Simple *hostal* with 25 rooms in very central location near the shops and port. **D** *Chinitas*, Pasaje Chinitas 2, T952214683, F952286642. There are just 5 rooms in this small *hostal* located on one of the city's most historic pedestrianized streets. Recommended. **D** *Derby*, C San Juan de Dios 1 No 4, T952221301. 16 rooms. This 4th floor *hostal* is excellent value, located in the heart of town overlooking the port. Recommended. **D** *El Cenachero*, C Barroso 5, T952224088. This clean, no-frills *hostal* has 14 rooms, some with bath. Recommended. st. **E** *Córdoba*, C Bolsa 9-11, T952214469. Small family-run hostal with shared bath. Recommended.

Outside Málaga   AL *Parador del Golf*, Apto 324, T952381255, F952382141. A hacienda-style resort hotel with 60 rooms and golf course, located 10 km west of the city near the beach. Parking, a/c, TV, pool, restaurant. **B** *Humaina*, Ctra del Colmenar, Las Montes de Málaga, T952641025, F9552640115. Away from the city and the coast, surrounded by a natural park, this hotel is ideal for walkers, or those seeking tranquil surroundings. Ochre walls, terracotta tiles and balconies in most rooms add to the appeal. A/c, TV, restaurant.

Youth hostels *Albergue Juvenil Málaga*, Plaza de Pio XII 6, T952308500. 110 beds. Suitable for wheelchair access, meals provided, reservations recommended, near Carranque multisports facilities. The hostel can be difficult to find. Take the No 18 bus from the Alameda Principal to the last stop and ask from there. **Camping** The nearest is *Balneario del Carmen,* Av Pintor Sorolla on the coast road west of Málaga, T952290021. Bar, restaurant, beach, tennis. There are other sites at Torre del Mar and Torremolinos.

There are some superb restaurants and tapas bars in Málaga where you can enjoy traditional local specialities, such as *fritura malagueño* (fried fish) and *sopa de ajo* (garlic soup). Thankfully, few restaurants cater to tourists here, so there is a welcome lack of so-called international dishes advertised by faded photos with a depressing reliance on chips. Menus tend to be only in Spanish; another good sign. The Pedregalejo seafront has some of the best seafood restaurants and *chiringuitos* (see box above) in the province.

Eating
● *on map,*
page 227

Fish restaurants Expensive: head east of the city to the old fishing villages of Pedregalejo and El Palo, now part of the Málaga suburbs. The best known are: *El Cabra*, C Copo 21, and *Casa Pedro*, C Quitapeñas 4, an enormous no-frills fish restaurant which is full of Spanish families on Sun. Back in Málaga, the most celebrated fish restaurant is *Antonio Martín*, Paseo Marítimo. Popular and pricey with a sea view terrace, this traditional restaurant is frequented by matadors from the nearby bullring. **Mid-range**: another favourite in Málaga is *Marisquería Las Dos RR*, C Carpio 4, in the Huelin district which specializes in *pescado frito*, mixed seafood fried in batter. **Cheap**: *La Cancela*, Denís Belgrano 5, is a cosy bistro-style restaurant serving typical local fare with tables outside in the summer. *Café Central*, Plaza de la Constitución. Inexpensive traditional cuisine served in this busy restaurant popular with the locals. Near *El Cabra* and *Casa Pedro* in El Palo on the Playa del Dedo is the remarkable *Tintero*, where the dishes are auctioned as they leave the kitchen. The bill is totted up according to the number of plates left on your table The disadvantage is that the food is not always quite hot enough when it finally reaches you. However, for sheer entertainment value, this restaurant is hard to beat.

Other restaurants Expensive: *La Taberna del Pintor*, C Maestranza 6. Arguably the best meat restaurant in Málaga, but pricey. **Mid-range**: *La Cónsula*, Churriana, T952622562. Restaurant of a well-known cookery school, specializing in Andalucían dishes. Located in an impressive 19th-century mansion where the writer Ernest Hemingway used to stay. *El Corte Inglés*, the department store's top floor *buffet libre* and grill is a popular stop for shoppers. *El Mesón Gallego*, C Casas de Campos 23. Galician specialities. *Rincón de Mata*, Esparteros 8. An atmospheric small restaurant with interesting house specialities. **Cheap**: *Arcos*, Alameda 31. a Good variety of *platos combinados*. Tormes, C San Agustin 13. Located on an attractive pedestrianized street, this old fashioned restaurant has a very reasonable *menú del día*. A number of good value Chinese restaurants and pizzerías have recently begun to appear in Málaga. For Chinese food, try *Chino Hong Kong*, Paseo las Farolas 25, and *La Tarantella*, C Granada 61. There are several vegetarian restaurants in Málaga, including the excellent *El Vegetariano de la Alcazabilla*, C Pozo del Rey 5 near the Roman Theatre, and the Chinese *El Legado Celestial*, C Medelín 3, which has an inexpensive daily buffet.

Málaga Province

Andalucía has more tapas bars than anywhere else in Spain and some of the best can be found in Málaga

Tapas bars Often, the tastiest, most typical tapas are found in unassuming back-street bars. Look for a bar frequented by locals with a crew of friendly fast-moving staff and stay away from English menus! A good place to start is the *Antigua Casa Guardia* on the corner of C Pastora and the Alameda and reputedly the oldest bar in the city. Try the prawns with Málaga wine. Close by is one of the best areas, along the pedestrianized C Marín García. Look for *Mesón La Alegria*, No 15, noted for its *jamón serrano*, and the atmospheric *La Manchega* at No 4. The most famous bar here is *Bar Logueno*; there's no number, but you can find it by the people milling outside sipping their glasses of *fino* or sherry. There is a tantalising choice of 75-plus tapas here, includ-ing many *Logueno* originals, like *setas* (sautéed wild mushrooms) with garlic, parsley and goat's cheese. Round the corner at Esparteros 8 is *Rincón de Mata* where tapas cost just €1 with specialities including *habas con jamón* (broad beans with ham), *gambas al pil-pil* (spicy fresh prawns) and *caracoles* (snails). Near the Picasso Museum at No 8 C Echegaray, the *Pitta Bar* has great Lebanese and Arab tapas, including houmous and falafel. Also recommended is *Gorky & Yovi*, C Stachan 6, which serves quality wines in huge, bulbous, long-stemmed glasses and a range of tempting, if expensive, cheeses and patés. *Tapería Siglo XXI*, Plaza de la Merced 12, is a wonderful old-fashioned bar in the square where Picasso was born, specializing in local cheeses and *jamón serrano*. For the best *berenjenas con miel* (deep-fried aubergines with honey), head to *Taberna Rincón Chinitas*, Pasaje Chinitas 9. Near the Plaza de Toros, *Sibarita*, C Cervantes 12, is a hole-in-the-wall traditional tapas bar with the day's spe-cials chalked up on a board. The adjacent *El Cantillo* is also worth checking out.

Teterias Increasingly popular, particular among students, are Moroccan-style tea-shops, or *teterias*. They are usually cosily cushioned with low tables and oriental rugs and serve dozens of different teas. Two of the most popular are situated on C San Agustin near the cathedral, while the largest is *Teteria Baraka*, housed in a former Arab bakery on the tiny C Horno, near the Plaza de la Constitucíon.

Bars & nightclubs
Nightlife in summer spills out towards El Palo and its beachside discos

Malagueñas love the *juerga* (a good night out), so nightlife is not hard to find, particularly in the summer. Student life centres around C Granada, Plaza de la Merced and Plaza de Uncibay. **Bars** *ZZ Pub*, C Tejón y Rodríguez, has live music on Mon and Thu. Close by the *Warner Bar* on Plaza de los Martínez has a good atmosphere, as does *La Botellita*, C Alamos 38, *El Cantor de Jazz*, C Lascano, and, surprisingly enough, a relatively new Eng-lish pub called *Wish You Were Here*, C Comedias 7, which is popular with Spanish stu-dents and occasionally has live Celtic music. For a Latino sound *Salsa*, C Méndez Nuñez, has live salsa on Wed and *Cantina Cubano*, C Granada, has good taped music and piña coladas. **Nightclubs** There is a host of disco bars in the Malagueta area, south of the bullring, where *Ragtime*, Paseo de Reding 12, is a favourite venue with blues, jazz or fla-menco, depending on the night. *H20*, C Fernando Camino, is another throbbing club in this area. The bohemian crowd focus on *Café Teatro*, C Afligidos 8, while *La Casa del Conde*, C Santa Lucía 9, is the haunt of Málaga's yuppies.

Entertainment **Art galleries** There are surprisingly few galleries, given the size of the city and the soon to open *Museo Picasso* will provide Málaga with a welcome cultural boost. Aside from this, there is the *Colegio de Arquitectos*, Av de las Palmeras – the building itself is worth the visit, but it also stages exhibitions. Open Mon-Fri 1200-1400, 1900-2100. There are also regular exhibitions by artists, photographers and archi-tects at the *Sala de Exposiciones del Museo*, Paseo de Reding 1. The *Sala Miramar* in the old *Hotel Miramar* on the Paseo Marítimo has occasional exhibitions, while the *Fundación Picasso*, Plaza de la Merced 15, often has temporary exhibits. There are regular exhibitions at the *Palacio Episcopal*, on the north side of the Plaza del Obispo, and also at the *Sala Alameda* at Alameda Principal 19. A few doors down,

Any excuse for a party

One of the most bizarre of all the extraordinary fiestas in Andalucía takes place in the hills north of Málaga during the last week in December. Known as the Fiesta de Verdiales, *it is one of the noisiest and most drunken dates in the* Malagueñas *calendar. Groups of folk singers and dancers from the surrounding villages home in on* La Venta del Tunel, *just off the Málaga-Antequera autovía, joined by thousands of merrymakers. The groups are called* pandas *and must have at least eight members, including musicians, dancers and flag wavers. They are led by an* alcalde *(mayor) and wear white shirts, black leggings with a red sash and extraordinary headgear decorated with flowers, beads, mirrors and bells. From these hats fall lengths of multi-coloured ribbons. Their instruments include guitars, fiddles, tambourines and anything else which will make a loud noise – for that is the object of the exercise. The songs are made up by the* pandas *and certainly wouldn't make the Top 10, generally extolling the virtues of their particular* pueblo. *The greatest cacophony occurs when two groups of* pandas *encounter each other (known as a* choque) *when a frenzy of noise and energy erupts in an effort to drown the rivals.*

Although each panda *performs on a stage, they rarely stop playing throughout the festival, lubricated by vast quantities of the sweet Málaga wine. The followers of the Verdiales join in the fun, consuming litres of wine and kilos of sausages.*

The history of the Verdiales is long and complex. Experts believe that they are older than flamenco itself, possibly originating during the time of the Moors, with the songs of the olive pickers. The fiesta was held until 1931 at the shrine of the Virgen de los Dolores, when a mass was celebrated and alms collected. When the shrine was demolished, the groups kept up the tradition by playing at rural inns or ventas. *The permanent site of the* Fiesta de Verdiales *at Venta del Tunel was fixed in 1961 and since then the event has gone from strength to strength. The Málaga city authorities now support the jamboree to the tune of over €6,000 in prize money, but one suspects that who wins is less important than having a good party!*

the Archivo Municipal at No 23 has exhibitions which are usually of an historical and/or religious nature. **Cinemas** There are numerous cinemas in the city, which show the latest films invariably dubbed in Spanish. Films are shown in original version at *Albéniz Multicines*, C Alcazabilla, T952128860. **Football** Games are held at the *Estadio de Futbol La Roselada*, P Martirincos, T952614374. **Theatres** *Teatro Cervantes*, C Ramos Martín 2, T952224100, was restored in 1987 and stages opera, theatre and dance. Check the programme as international performers frequently appear. It is also the home of the *Málaga Symphony Orchestra* and the *Málaga Danza Teatro*. More modest is the *Teatro Estable de Málaga*, whose productions feature at the Casa de Cultura in C Alcazabilla.

Málaga is noted for its fiestas. **Late Feb** *Carnaval*. **Easter** *Semana Santa* Local brotherhoods mount processions each day and a prisoner is released from Málaga jail. The ceremonies rival those of Sevilla and are arguably the best in Spain. See www.semanasanta.tv **23 Jun** *San Juan* Huge bonfires are built on which satirical images are burnt. **16 Jul** *Virgen del Carmen* The Virgin is taken in procession to the sea by local fishermen. **Aug** *Feria* An annual fair which commemorates the incorporation of Málaga into the kingdom of Castille by the Catholic Monarchs who entered the city in Aug 1487. More than an estimated million people come to the city to enjoy the bullfights, flamenco, processions, children's theatre and fireworks. **Dec** *Verdiales* Folk song competitions take place in the mountains north of Málaga.

Fiestas & festivals

Shopping The main shopping area is west of the cathedral and north of the Alameda Principal and in the streets around the Plaza de la Constitución. Further west in the Av de Andalucía is *El Corte Inglés*, the comprehensive department store. It has a popular restaurant, convenient parking and is opposite the Centro-Alameda station for the electric railway. In the central area of the city is the rather more downmarket department store of *Félix Sáenz* in a magnificent building that dates back to 1886. The most expensive shops and boutiques are centred around C Larios, where you will also find most of the well known international franchises. For jewellery try *Tierra*, C Especerías 10, and for perfume visit the tiny *Perfumería y Mercería Lagarterana* in C Careterí 93. There is an interesting group of street stalls between *El Corte Inglés* and the river, with bargain jewellery and souvenirs offering good value. A street market is held every Sun in the Paseo de los Martiricos, 1000-1500. The *Larios Centro* is located between *El Corte Inglés* and the new bus station, with over 100 shops, a hypermarket and a multi-screen cinema.

Sport **Golf** There are a vast number of golf courses to choose from along the Costa del Sol to the west of the city. Nearest is *Club de Golf El Cabdado*, T952299340. **Horse riding** Equestrian centre: Apartado 94, Alhaurín de la Torre, T952412818. **Tennis** *Club de Tenis*, C Pinares de San Antón, T952291092.

Tour operators There are over 30 travel agents' offices in Málaga, so the following are a small selection: *Central de Viajes*, T952218167. *Halcon Viajes*, T952203335. *Melia*, Alameda Principal 1, T952211071. *Viajes Florin*, T952328908.

Transport **Local** **Car hire**: This is most conveniently arranged at the airport, where all the main international firms have their offices (see page 35). The following firms have offices in the city: *Avis*, C Cortina del Muelle, T952216627; *Hertz*, Alameda de Colón 17, T952225597; *Málaga*, Paseo Marítimo, T952210010; *Miramar*, Av Pries, T952226933. **Scooter and motorcycle hire**: *Victoria Racing*, C Victoria 6, T952220483. **Taxi**: there are taxi ranks at the bus and train stations and in the Alameda Principal; *Radio Taxi*, Plaza de Toros Vieja, T952320000.

Long distance **Air**: For airport information, see page 35. **Bus**: the main bus station is on Paseo de los Tilos, T952350061. A number of bus companies use the station, with *Portillo*, T952360191, covering the area to the west of Málaga and *Alsina Graells*, T952310400, running services to the east. Local connections are generally at 30-min intervals and links with other cities every 2 hrs. Printed timetables are, as usual, difficult to obtain and you may have to rely on the information on the wall. **Ferries**: there are regular daily sailings (except Sun) to Melilla, the Spanish enclave in North Africa. The crossing takes around 10 hrs. For information, contact *Transmediterránea*, C Juan Díaz 4, T902454645 Tickets from the Estación Marítima. **Train**: the RENFE station is on C Cuarteles, T952360202, but tickets can be obtained from many travel agencies. Look for the RENFE sign in the window. There is a twice daily Talgo 200 to **Madrid** which now takes only 4 hrs as it joins the high speed AVE track at Córdoba. They leave Málaga at 0635 and 1605. The 4 other daily trains to Madrid might take 2-4 hrs longer. The same trains stop at **Córdoba**, while there is also a direct link with **Sevilla**. Other Andalucían destinations involve a change at Bobadilla junction. The Fuengirola-Málaga stops at the main train station (RENFE) before the final stop, almost opposite *El Corte Inglés* department store, while another branch runs north to **Alora**. Tickets may be purchased on the train. For information on trains to the airport, see page 35.

Directory **Banks** All the main banks have branches in Málaga, mainly concentrated at the west end of the Alameda Principal. ATMs are found at most banks. There are a few change shops in the central area, but the commission can be high. **Communications** Internet: *Ciber Málaga Café*, Av de Andalucía 11. Open 1000-late. €2.5 per hr. *Internet Meeting Point*, Plaza de la Merced 20. Open 1000-2400. €2 per hr. *Red Center*, Plaza de la Merced 5. Open 1000-2000. € 2 per hr. *Rent@Net*, C Santiago 8. Open 1000-2400. €1.30 per hr. *Teatro Romano Bar*, C Alcazabilla. Open 1000-2400. €2 per hr. **Post office**: the main Correos can be found in the Av de Andalucía, almost opposite *El Corte Inglés*, T952359008. **Telephones**: numerous *locutorios* throughout the central area of the city. Open Mon-Sat 0900-2100, Sun 1000-1300. Credit cards accepted. **Embassies and consulates** *Canada*, Plaza de Malagueta 3 – 1°, T952223346; *France*, Duquesa de Parcent 8, T952226590; *Germany*, Paseo de Limonar 28, T952227866; *Italy*, C Palestina 3, T952306150; *Netherlands,* Alameda de Colon, Pasaje Linaje 3P, 2 – 4°D; T952600260; *UK*, Mauricio Moro Pareto 2 T952352300. NB The nearest US consulate is in Fuengirola. Useful addresses **Car repairs**: *Citroën*, Ctra Cádiz 239, T952315400; *Renault*, Ctra Cádiz 178, T952315000; *Volkswagon*, Ctra Cádiz, T952313630; *Ford*, Av Velázquez T952239900; *Volvo*, Av Juan XXIII, T952316108; *Peugeot*, C Bodegueros 19, T952346862; *Seat*, Polígono Santa Bárbara, T952241880.

East of Málaga

The coastline east of Málaga (strictly speaking the eastern Costa del Sol) is in the main an uninspiring stretch of ribbon development with small, unattractive resorts largely free of international tourists, but crowded with malagueñas *at weekends. In the Málaga suburbs there is a* paseo marítimo *(named after Pablo Picasso) fronted by imported sand. There is little to stop for in the old fishing villages of Pedregalejo and El Palo except their fish restaurants.*

Málaga Province

The first resort of any size is **Rincón de la Victoría**, with its newly built *paseo marítimo*. 2 km before Rincón, however, is a road leading inland to the Cueva del Tesoro or Treasure Cave – a name allegedly derived from some Moorish kings' gold which was secreted here. There are stalactites, stalagmites, columns and tufa screens, but the main interest is in the Palaeolithic wall paintings and other remains. Unfortunately, the wall paintings are not always on view, but these caves are refreshingly uncommercialized, compared with those at Nerja further east. ■ *Daily 1000-1400 and 1600-2000.* €3.

Cueva del Tesoro

There are also some ruins of **Roman baths** at nearby Benagalbón. After a halfhearted attempt at some restoration by the regional government, the site has been totally abandoned.

Many of the place names in this area have the prefix *torre*, referring to the *atalayas* (watchtowers) that are found at intervals along the shore. The square towers are probably Moorish in origin, while the round towers were more likely to be built by the Christians. Torre del Mar, the next coastal resort, has made recent efforts to improve its image, but it is a soulless spot with a pebbly beach, backed by a huge promenade and high rise apartment blocks. It has some good seafood restaurants, however, as well as as two small hotels, four reasonable *pensiones* and a rather basic campsite. The tourist office is at Avenida de Andalucía 169, T952541104, and opens daily in the summer 0800-1500 and 1600-2100; Monday to Friday in winter 0800-1500.

Torre del Mar

La Axarquía

La Axarquía (also spelt Ajarquía) is located inland from the coast east of Málaga city. Parts of the region are remote and settlement, by and large, consists of small villages. It was once notorious bandit country and a hotbed of guerrilla activity during the Civil War (and after). Government propaganda after the real threat of guerrillas had passed ensured that La Axarquía continued to be seen as an unsafe place to travel.

Vélez Málaga
Colour map 5, grid B2
Population: 53,816

Four kilometres inland from Torre del Mar is Vélez Málaga, the regional capital of La Axarquía. It gets its name from Ballix-Malace, meaning rock fortress of Málaga, and today there are remains of the Moorish castillo on a steep crag above the town. Fernando's army eventually ejected the Moors in 1487, leaving the way open for the assault on Málaga which then led to siege and capitulation of Granada four years later. Today it functions as the main market town for the fertile Vélez valley. Take a look at the church of Santa María la Mayor, dating from the 16th century and the first building to be erected by the victorious Christian forces. It was built on the site of the mosque and the minaret can still be distinguished. Inside, the triple nave, typical of the period, and the Mudéjar ceiling, are noteworthy. There are several other interesting churches along with the Palacio del Marqués de Beniel, a 16th-century mansion which was once the town hall. For tourist information, contact the *turismo* in Torre del Mar (see above).

Cómpeta
Colour map 5, grid B2
Population: 2,681

Around this village the hill slopes are clothed with vineyards and drying racks for the Moscatel grapes making the strong, sweet wines for which the area is well known. A riotous wine festival, the *Noche del Vino*, is held in the main square in mid-August. Cómpeta has attracted large numbers of northern European ex-pats in recent years, particularly from UK and Denmark, and many have set up craft industries. There is a pleasant main square, dominated by the bell tower of the Iglesia de la Asunción, with several bars serving economical meals. There is a small tourist office on Calle Rampa close to the main square, which is open Monday to Saturday 1000-1400, T952553301. You can obtain local walking maps at the office and also at the *Marco Polo* English bookshop near the main square, just off Plaza de Almijara, T952516423.

Sleeping and eating **A** *Los Caracoles*, T952030680. An unusual hotel built on top of a high ridge just to the side of the road leading to Frigiliana with some extraordinary organic architecture. **D** *Alberdini*, T952516241. On top of a high ridge just outside of the village with exceptional views and some interesting architecture. Best in warmer months since heating is a bit hit-and-miss. **D** *Casa La Piedra*, T952516329. Two bedrooms in an old house in a pretty square with terraces looking down to the sea. Sandra, the British owner, knows a lot about the walking in the area.

Alfarnate
Colour map 5, grid B1
Population: 1,451

In the north of La Axarquía is Alfarnate. The *Antigua Venta de Alfarnate* is claimed to be the oldest inn in Andalucía. Once the haunt of assorted highwaymen and robbers, including the notorious El Tempranillo, it now houses a small outlaws' museum including a prison cell. The *venta* serves excellent country food, although avoid the weekends when it is crowded with the inhabitants of Málaga and Granada.

Walking in La Axarquía

What makes walking in La Axarquía such a treat is the very marked difference in climate, vegetation and terrain between the higher passes and the coastal fringe. The Mediterranean is often visible, sparkling in the distance, and on most of the walks the Sierra de Tejeda provides a spectacular backdrop, especially during the winter months when there is often snow on its higher reaches. Many of the region's walks follow dirt tracks which have been created both by the Forestry Commission and, more recently, the by property developers. Although these don't have quite the same appeal as a narrow footpath does, it means that routes are generally easy to follow. Many walks in the area have recently been waymarked.

The most attractive part of La Axarquía is its eastern end and the three walks described below are in the mountains and lush river valleys close to Cómpeta - perhaps the place to base yourself. The contrast between the land north and south of the village couldn't be greater. Just beyond the steep ridge which dominates the town is a vast arena of limestone peaks where there is virtually no sign of human habitation. This is in marked contrast to the land between the village and the sea which is extensively cultivated, sprinkled with numerous small farmsteads and cut through by lush, subtropical river valleys. Everything, it would seem, will grow here: there are groves of citrus, avocado, mangos, pomegranate – and even custard apples, lychees and sugar cane. These fertile valleys provide welcome respite if you are walking during the hotter months. The section of river valley north of Canillas is particularly attractive. The region's benign climate means that this is an area well suited to winter sorties. Málaga can be reached in little more than an hour and you will meet with few other walkers on your rambles.

The best **maps** of the area are the standard 1:50000 map of the Servicio Geográfico del Ejército, Series L. The walks described below are covered by Sheet (*hoja*): Zafarraya 18-43 and Sheet (*hoja*) Vélez-Málaga 18-44. The *Marco Polo* bookstore in Cómpeta, see above, generally has both maps in stock.

For **accommodation**, see Cómpeta above. Also, the tourist office in Sayalonga has details of a number of village houses for rent, either for just one night or for a longer stay, T952535206. Prices vary according to size of house. In Árchez, try **D** *El Mesón Mudéjar*, T952553106, which has five simple rooms above a popular restaurant in the centre of the village by the church.

Sayalonga Circuit

Distance: 10 km
Time: 3½-4 hours
Difficulty: easy

This half-day excursion links two attractive villages, Sayalonga and sleepy Corombela. The walk takes you through the subtropical orchards of Sayalonga's terraced river valley where there is an astonishing variety of fruit trees. Then comes a steep climb up to Corombela passing by several small farmsteads and on the return leg there are excellent views of the Sierra de Tejeda and the Mediterranean. Nearly all of the walk is along tracks and this is an easy circuit to follow. There is a short section of tarmac road when you leave Corombela but there is very little traffic; don't let this put you off this excellent walk. Map: 1:50000 Vélez-Málaga (1054).

Itinerary This walk begins in Sayalonga's Plaza Rafael Alcoba. Go past the Ayuntamiento into Calle Cristo following signs for 'Cementerio Redondo'. Branch right along Calle Rodríguez de la Fuente then at the end turn left (unless you wish to visit the only round cemetery in Spain in which case go right then later retrace your footsteps). Pass a church to your left then bear right downhill to a sign marking the beginning of the walk to Corombela. A dirt track leads downhill, passing beneath the cemetery, through fertile groves of fruit trees. The route is waymarked with white and yellow stripes. The track meets the river (15 minutes), runs beside it, then crosses it via a narrow bridge. With the river to your right you soon pass the lovely Casa El Molino then begin climbing through lush, well-irrigated terraces. Soon the track changes course, heading away from the river up a side valley past stands of bamboo and a cluster of farm buildings. Look for the *secaderos* or drying platforms used to dry the moscatel grapes. Continue climbing and you pass another group of buildings to your left. You reach a fork (45 minutes). Ignore the track that branches right down towards an ugly goat shed but rather go left and continue climbing. Cómpeta is now visible and Corombela comes into view.

The track runs past several small farms before descending slightly (one hour), crossing a gulley then passing Las Tres Fuentes, or the Three Springs, on your left. After passing a football pitch the track meets a tarmac road. Go straight across into Corombela (one hour 20 minutes). Bear left just past the bakery to *Bar Cantero*, a good place for a drink after your long climb from Sayalonga. Here swing left past a supermarket into Calle Las Pitas. Continue past a garishly painted building along a track that runs just above the Corombela/Daimalos road. The track climbs, passes Villa Alminara, then drops down to the tarmac road which you should follow to the top of the pass. After ten minutes of asphalt-bashing, where the road swings sharply right, turn left on a track (one hour 45 minutes) which leads past a farm where wine is for sale with more *secaderos*. At the next fork go right and soon you pass above four small farms. Follow the ridge along – on a clear there are great views of the Sierra de Tejeda and La Maroma (2,069 m) – past an ugly breeze block building and just before a modern house with arches turn left following a track steeply downhill. Sayalonga is visible across the valley. You pass two pretty farms then a ruin on the right. Continue to descend, swinging sharply left and then right. Just before a ruined farm branch right off the track, pass a

La Axarquía

few yards to the right of the ruin then bear sharp right and drop down to a rough track which zigzags down towards a house with two palm trees, soon merging with a better track which arcs right towards the farm. Here go left and continue down and cross the river (two hours 15 minutes). You may need to remove boots in the wetter months. On the other side bear right and after 100 m, just past a lemon and an orange tree to the left of the track, branch left on a path which winds steeply up through the terraces. It is quite overgrown in parts. Where it becomes less distinct swing left along the top of a vineyard then drop down to a dirt track then bear right and follow a rather messy track up to a breeze-block building. Passing to its left then climbing you return to the sign marking the beginning of the walk. From here retrace your footsteps back to Plaza Rafael Alcoba (two hours 40 minutes).

This enchanting walk takes you out from Canillas de Albaida via a beautiful riverside path which meanders through thick stands of oleander, crossing back and forth across the Cájula river – easily passable unless there has been heavy rainfall. After a steep climb the middle section of the walk takes you along dirt tracks and is quite different in feel. But it is easy to follow and there are fine views of the Sierra de Tejeda. The final section of the walk - there is a steep climb last thing - is along an ancient cobbled path with gorgeous views of Canillas and the Chapel of Santa Ana. Try to do this walk when the oleander are in flower for a real spectacle. There are some prickly plants on the middle section before you reach the forestry track so you could wear trousers. Map 1:50000 Zafarraya (1040).

Canillas de Albaida Circuit

Distance: 11 km
Time: 4½-5 hours
Difficulty: medium

Itinerary The walk begins from the car park at the entrance of Canillas as you come from Competa. Go down the hill from the roundabout past the chemist and supermarket. At the bottom bear left at a sign for 'Finca El Cerrillo'. Head down past the chapel of San Antón then bear right and drop down, cross the river then immediately bear right following a concrete road towards an old mill. The road narrows to a path which runs beside the Cájula river, crossing back and forth several times. Pass a breeze-block building (20 minutes) on your left and continue along the river's right bank. You'll see red waymarking. Cross the river again and climb; there is beautiful old cobbling in places. After passing beneath an overhanging rock face you descend back down to the river, cross it a couple more times then the path climbs up the river's left bank between two fences and becomes a track. Ahead you'll see a white farmhouse.

Careful! Before you reach it branch right (by a small orange tree to the left of the track) at a sign 'Camino del Río' along a narrow path which passes by a grove of young avocados. It winds, passes the stumps of a line of poplars then continues on its rather serpentine course, occasionally marked by cairns. Shortly your path is crossed by another which has black water pipes following its course. Turn right here and then almost immediately left then wind down to the river which you cross via stepping stones. The path climbs up the other bank and soon becomes better defined (occasional red dots mark the way). Where the path divides go left. A ruined house comes into sight on the other side of the river. Cross the river again and climb the path towards the house. You should pass just to the right of the house then climb steeply up the side of the valley. As you climb you'll see a solitary building on the crown of a hill. Remember this landmark – you'll pass by it later in the walk. The path swings right, descends, crosses a (dry) stream then bears right again and winds uphill. You come to an area of terracing where you continue to climb. Above you to your right you'll see a small farmhouse. Head up to the farm which you should pass just to its right. You reach a dirt track. Turn right here (one hour 15 minutes) and head for the solitary building which you saw earlier in the walk. Just past the house the track arcs left towards the head of the Cájula gorge and a small cluster of houses. The track winds, descends, crosses el Arroyo de Luchina via a concrete bridge with rusting railings then climbs again past olive and citrus groves. After passing a house to your right where a row of pines has been planted you cross the river (one hour 45 minutes). Continue past a row of poplars on the main track: don't turn sharp right on a track leading down towards the river. Follow this track, climbing at first, roughly parallel to the Cájula river, heading back towards Canillas. Eventually you pass a water tank then a house to the right of the track with a solar panel (two hours). Just past this house the track swings to the left and another track branches right (it has a chain across it). Ignore this turning, continue for 30 m and then - careful! - turn right away from the track on to a beautiful path which zigzags all the way down to the river Llanada de Turvilla. Somewhere to one side of the path would make a memorable picnic spot. Cross the bridge over the river then bear right and wind up towards the Santa Ana chapel. Pass beneath the chapel - the gorge is now down to your right - and after a steep climb the path becomes a track which leads you just beneath the cemetery where a green mesh fence runs to your right. Bear sharp left past house number 35, go to the end of the street then head up the hill past the supermarket and bank to arrive back at your point of departure (two hours 45 minutes).

Cómpeta Circuit (via the Casa de la Mina)

Distance: 12 km
Time: 5-5½ hours
Difficulty: medium

Although this itinerary follows dirt tracks rather than mountain paths it makes for a memorable excursion. Once you are up and over the pass of Puerto del Collado a stunning panorama opens out before you, a vast tract of virtually uninhabited sierra that stretches for miles to the north and east. It's amazing to consider that the crowded beaches of Nerja are little more than 15 km away. After your steep climb up from Cómpeta you're rewarded with some shade and the chance of a refreshing dip when you pass by the Fábrica de la Luz. You may need to take boots and socks off to cross the river during the wetter months. You have about 1 km of asphalt road at the very end of the walk when you head back to Venta La Palma. Map 1:50000 Vélez-Málaga (1054) and Zafarraya (1040)

Itinerary The walk begins by the Venta de Palma, just 1 km from Cómpeta on the road leading to Torrox; starting here avoids a steep haul up from the village centre. Cross the road and head up the dirt track following signs for 'Casa de la Mina' and 'Finca Monte Pino'. You climb steeply up past a number of villas with satellite-dishes. Eventually you leave the buildings behind and reach a pine forest. Where the track arcs right look for a red mark on a rock just to the left of the track. Here cut left, away from the track, and climb up beside a (dry) stream. Soon you pass an old lime kiln on your right. Follow the stream bed up until you meet with a scree slope which you follow along to the left as far as a water tank. Here the path swings sharp right and climbs, following the course marked by an arrow painted on the tank. You pass a quarry then emerge on the track at the top of El Puerto del Collado. Turn left here (not hard left which leads up a very steep track) following signs for 'Casa de la Mina'. You are now rewarded with wonderful views of the Almijara Sierra. La Casa de la Mina, a white building, is clearly visible up ahead of you. Just past La Casa de la Mina (one hour 15 minutes) branch sharply right on another well-surfaced track which descends towards La Fábrica de la Luz. It loops down and down (tempting short cuts are best avoided because some of them lead to a dead end) passing a large house with arched windows and a cypress and eucalyptus grove just beneath it. Just past this house the track climbs slightly then again descends, passing a second farm with buildings to both sides of the track. The track leads down through olive groves and past a sign 'zona de escalada' which marks an area where rock-climbing takes place.

This is an enchanting part of the walk: the Mediterranean is visible and you pass a number of wonderful old carob trees amongst the olives. You pass a house with an ugly, breeze-block wall then drop down into the shade of the river bed before reaching the Fábrica de la Luz (two hours 15 minutes), the old electricity generating station. This is a good spot for a picnic; there are palm and eucalyptus trees, running water and a steep cliff face. Crossing the (dry) river you come to a fork. Don't take fork left towards El Acebuchal and Frigiliana but rather go right, cross the river once again, then follow the track gently upwards towards the Torrox/Cómpeta road. Eventually, after passing an electricity pylon and then Villa Carlota and Casa Cabra, you reach the main road where you should swing hard right away from the road and head up a track which leads you past Villa Damien. At the first fork in the road, by a palm tree, keep right, go past Casa Pastor then at the second electricity pylon (it has a white base) turn left and climb a footpath which runs just to the left of three olive trees. You again meet with the track which you cross once again, thus cutting out another large loop in the track. The dirt track winds on around the hillside between a number of villas. When you come to a fork go right and head uphill towards a white water tank. Your track merges with a better-surfaced track which runs more or less parallel with the road to Cómpeta, which is down to your left. Eventually it drops down and meets with the road. Bear right here and climb for about ten minutes along the tarmac back to Venta La Palma (three hours 45 minutes).

In an effort to sponsor rural tourism, five routes have been devised by the regional government for visiting La Axarquía by car, each colour coded and waymarked. The **Ruta del Sol y del Aguacate** (the Sun and Avocado Route) starts at Rincón de la Victoria and visits the agricultural villages of the Vélez valley, including Macharaviaya, Benamocarra and Iznate. The **Ruta del Sol y del Vino** (the Sun and Wine Route) starts in Nerja and includes the main wine-producing villages such as Cómpeta and Frigiliana. The **Ruta Mudéjar** concentrates on architecture, looking at villages such as Archez, Salares and Sedilla. The **Ruta de la Pasa** (the Route of the Raisin) looks at the more mountainous villages in the northwest of the area. Finally, the **Ruta del Aceite y los Montes** (the Route of the Oil and the Mountains) examines the olive growing villages such as Periana and Alaucín in the north of the area. Owing to the terrain, most of the routes are not circular and involve retracing your steps in places, but they are, nevertheless, highly recommended. A detailed brochure describing the routes can be obtained from the tourist office in Nerja; see below.

Driving through La Axarquía

Back on the coast the ribbon development continues towards **Torrox Costa**, a featureless resort favoured by Germans and Scandinavians. There are the remains of a roman villa near to the lighthouse. The village of Torrox itself is some 4 km inland and has some Roman remains, while recent archaeological evidence suggests that the area immediately to the west was an important Phoenician stronghold and several graveyards have been found dating from the fourth and fifth centuries. Approaching Nerja, the coastal plain begins to widen out and there are some of the first signs of the *plasticultura* which disfigures the coast further east in Almería.

Torrox
Colour map 5, grid B2
Population: 11,691

Málaga Province

Nerja

Colour map 5, grid B2
Population: 15,326

Some 50 km from Málaga, Nerja is situated on a low cliff littered with sandy coves. Sheltered by the mountains, Nerja has a mild winter climate. Despite tourist development, Nerja has been spared the excesses of the western Costa del Sol, most of the buildings being low rise and the *urbanizaciones* tastefully designed. The **tourist office** is located at the landward end of the Balcón de Europa, T952521531, with very helpful staff who will provide a useful town plan. Check their noticeboard for vacancies and events. ■ *Mon to Fri 1000-1400, Sat 1000-1300. Also see the town's website, www.nerja.net*

Nerja started life as the Moorish settlement of Narixa, suggesting reliable spring waters. Unfortunately, an earthquake in 1884 destroyed much of the town and no Moorish constructions survived. For centuries the inhabitants made a profitable living by making silk, growing sugar cane and fishing. None of these activities thrive today and the sugar refining buildings are part of the industrial archaeology.

Sights The main attraction within the town is the **Balcón de Europa**, a tree-lined promenade jutting out into the sea with fine views along the coast and to the mountains inland. On the east side of the Balcón is the small, former fishermen's beach of Calahonda. There are a few token fishing boats left, but it has

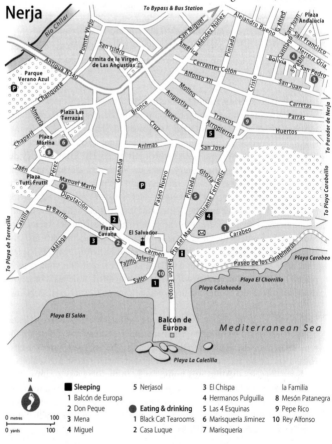

Nerja

N	■ Sleeping	5 Nerjasol	3 El Chispa	la Familia
	1 Balcón de Europa		4 Hermanos Pulguilla	8 Mesón Patanegra
	2 Don Peque	● Eating & drinking	5 Las 4 Esquinas	9 Pepe Rico
0 metres 100	3 Mena	1 Black Cat Tearooms	6 Marisquería Jiminez	10 Rey Alfonso
0 yards 100	4 Miguel	2 Casa Luque	7 Marisquería	

now been largely taken over by tourists. Further east, and out of sight behind a headland, is the popular beach of Burriana. Other beaches near the main tourist hotels stretch away to the west of the town. To the west of the Balcón is a small square at the end of which is the whitewashed **Church of El Salvador**, dwarfed by its Norfolk Island Pine. It has elements of Mudéjar and Baroque work plus an interesting mural representing the Annunciation on a Nerja beach. On the main N340, in the north of the town, is the **Ermita del Virgen of las Angustias**, a 17th-century chapel with Granada style paintings on the cupola. Inland from the Balcón is a maze of small streets, with some quality shops.

Cuevas de Nerja These caves were discovered in 1959 by a group of local schoolboys on a bat hunting expedition and are now a national monument. In addition to the usual features of limestone caves, such as stalactites and stalagmites, there is evidence that the caves were occupied by Cro-Magnon man as indicated by pottery, ornaments, implements of stone bone and flint, and tools of copper and bronze. The boys found a group of skeletons and it is believed that small communities were in occupation from 2000 BC until a major earth tremor blocked the cave entrance and sealed in the occupants and their artefacts. The most important finds were the wall paintings, probably Upper Palaeolithic in age and largely of animals – believed to be part of a magical rite to ensure success in hunting and guarantee the fertility of domestic animals. Regrettably, the paintings are not on public view, but there are a few token photographs and artefacts in a show case just after entering the caves.

The lighting of the caves and the piped music may appear to be somewhat overdone, but the limestone features are genuinely awe-inspiring. In the summer season, the main chamber of the caves is used as an auditorium for a festival of music, often with internationally known performers. Contact the tourist office in Nerja for the programme. There is a restaurant with a terrace giving superb views along the coast, but it can get crowded, particularly in the summer, and a suitable alternative is the delightful *Hotel al Andalus*, just 200 m away and with more excellent views from its terrace restaurant (it may be closed, however, during the winter months). ■ *Open all year daily 1000-1400 and 1600-1830. €4.80, children over 6 €2.40. T952529520. There are regular buses from Nerja.*

Maro This small village is located on the clifftop 4 km east of Nerja, close to the caves. The whitewashed houses stand above an attractive cove. Originally the Roman settlement of Detunda, Maro has three items of particular interest, all dating from the 18th century: the small, but charming village church of *Nuestra Señora de la Maravillas de Maro*; the ruined sugar factory; and best of all, the magnificent four-tiered aqueduct which carried water across a valley to the factory. It looks Moorish, but is in fact 19th century. Regular buses run from Nerja. For accommodation, there is **C** *Playa de Maro*, Apartado Correos 7, T952529598, F952529622; a small, quiet hotel close to the beach with 22 rooms and a pool. **C** *Al-Andaluz*, Carretera de la Cueva sin número, T952529648, F952529557, is another small and peaceful hotel, located near the caves and Maro village, with a good restaurant.

La Axarquía Some of the more southern villages in this area are within easy reach of Nerja; see page 238.

Frigiliana A mere 6 km north, Frigiliana is steeped in Muslim atmosphere and was the site of the last stand of the *morisco* converts who rebelled against Spanish

Excursions

Málaga Province

repression in 1569-70, nearly 80 years after the fall of the last Moorish kingdom in 1492. Ceramic plaques record the events on the walls of the houses in the older part of the town. Frigiliana is a pretty village, with narrow streets and whitewashed houses festooned with hanging plants and geraniums. Accommodation in the village is limited, but there is **B** *Hotel Rural La Posada Morisca*, T952534151, with 12 beautifully furnished rooms, superb views and friendly staff. Price includes breakfast. Recommended. There is also **D** *Las Chinas*, Plaza Capitán Conés, T952533073, with nine rooms and a good restaurant.

Sleeping There is a good choice of accommodation to suit all pockets. It is best to book in advance during the height of the summer and during Semana Santa. **AL** *Parador de Nerja*, C Almuñécar 8, T952520050, F952521997. 73 rooms. Relatively modern parador set on cliff top with attractive gardens, lift to the beach, pool, tennis, a/c, TV and all that one would expect from a parador. **A** *Balcón de Europa*, Paseo Balcón de Europa 1, T952520800, F952524490. 102 rooms. TV, sauna, garage, private beach, convenient for shops but can be noisy from merrymakers and breaking waves. **C** *Portofino*, Puerta del Mar 2, T952520150. 12 rooms. Central location, closed Oct-Mar. If you're looking for an out-of-town location you could try Maro, see Excursions above. **D** *Don Peque*, C Diputación 13, T952521318. Small comfortable, central position. **D** *Nerjasol*, C Arropieros 4, T952522121. Popular *hostal* with en suite rooms and a pleasant roof patio. **E** *Mena*, C El Barrio 15, T952520541. 10 rooms. Good sea views and an attractive garden. **E** *Miguel*, C Almirante Ferrándiz 31, T952521523. 8 rooms. Good ambience in the older part of town, close to the Balcón. **Camping** *Nerja Camping*, On N340 4 km east of Nerja, T952529696. Located near Maro (see Excursions above) and the beach, this campsite has a pool and bar.

Eating There is a wide selection of restaurants to suit all pockets and tastes in Nerja, although those around the Balcón tend to have inflated prices and be directed at tourists. **Expensive** *Casa Luque*, Plaza Cavana 2, T952521004. Spanish and international cuisine, pricey but good value for money. **Mid-range** Seafood restaurants are moderately priced here; try *Hermanos Pulguilla*, C San Pablo 6, T952521892. *Marisquería la Familia*, C Diputación 17, T952520046. *Marisquería Jiménez*, Plaza Marina. *La Noria*, Ctra de Frigiliana, km 1.5. Spanish style *mesón* in an old farm building, good fish and game dishes. *Mesón Patanegra*, Plaza la Marina, T952520222. Good Spanish cooking. *Pepe Rico*, C Cristo 26, T952520247. Good international cuisine. **Cheap** Those on a tight budget could try the lunchtime offerings of fish and shellfish in the *chiringuitos* on Burriana beach, particularly *Ayos*, or *Pizzería Jiménez*, Av de Pescia 17, T952521998. **Tapas bars** Try *El Chispa*, C San Pedro 12 and *Las 4 Esquinas*, C Pintada. *Arte de Azúcar/Black Cat Tearooms*, C Carabeo 13. An English tearoom with a Spanish twist. Homemade cakes and tea served in an airy room or roof terrace.

Bars & nightclubs Disco and karaoke bars are clustered around Plaza Tutti Frutti. For flamenco shows, try *Bar El Colono*, C Granada 6, or *Peña de Flamenco Solea*, C Antonio Millón.

Fiestas & festivals **16-17 Jan** *San Antón* Procession and fireworks in Maro. **Feb** *Carnival* For 3 days with parades and singing of *chirigotas* (popular songs). **3 May** *Cruces de Mayo* Flower crosses made locally with singing and dancing. **14-15 May** *San Isidro Romería*. **23-24 Jun** *San Juan* Beach barbecues, with a local cake speciality 'tortas de San Juan'. **Jul** *Festival de la Cueva* Flamenco, classical music and ballet in the Nerja caves. **16 Jul** *Fiesta de la Virgen del Carmen* The fishermen's fiesta, where the statue of the Virgin is carried down to the sea at Calahonda beach. **7-9 Sep** *Feria Maravillas de Maro* Local saint's day festival with fair in Maro. **9-13 Oct** *Feria de Nerja* Local saint's day week-long festival.

A street market is held every Tuesday. | **Shopping**

Benamar, C G Franco 35, T952521745; *Jaime Tours*, C Pintada 79, T952522790; *Latitud* **Tour**
7, Plaza Cantarero s/n, T952522512; *Verano Azul*, C Castilla Pérez 60, T952523700. **operators**

Local Car hire: *Autos Andalucía*, C Pintada 51, T952521534; *Autos Costasol*, C Jaen, **Transport**
Edificio La Marina, T952522796; *Autos Nerja*, C Cruz 22, T952520694; *Autos*
Unidos-Hertz, C Diputación 7, T952524250; *Lual*, C Castilla Pérez s/n, T952523066.
Taxis: taxi rank at Plaza Ermita on the old N340. **Long distance Buses**: services from
Málaga and Almería stop on the main road in the north of the town or at the bus sta-
tion on C Miguel. There are 12 buses a day to Málaga and the coastal towns to the west;
8 eastward to Motril and Almuñécar; 2 connect directly to Granada, which can also be
reached by changing at Motril. There are daily long distance coaches from Córdoba,
Cádiz and Sevilla, plus local buses to and from the inland villages of the Axarquía, such
as Frigiliana, Torrox and the hospital at Vélez.

Communications Post office: Correos is located near the junction of Puerta del Mar **Directory**
and C Carabeo. **Medical services First aid**: T952520935. **Hospitals**: Cliníca, C Bronce
8, T952520358, open 24 hrs.

North of Málaga

A more interesting route than the N331 *autovía* that heads north to Antequera **Cártama &**
is the A357 west of Málaga. The first town on the route is Cártama, where there **Crocodiles**
is the immensely popular Crocodiles Park. Apart from watching the grue- **Park**
some reptiles, there is a shop, video display and small museum. ■ *Daily*
1000-1800. €4, children under 12 and senior citizens €3.45. Further north is
Alora, a white hill village capped with a ruined Moorish alcazaba (now the
cemetery). It is well worth taking a stroll through the narrow streets – aim for
the main square, where you will find the impressive church of La
Encarnación, dating from the early 18th century and claimed to be the largest
in Málaga province after Málaga's cathedral.

Just north of Alora fork right and after 12 km you arrive at El Chorro Gorge, a **Garganta**
deep ravine cut into the limestone by the river Guadalhorce, a route used by **del Chorro**
the railway which cuts in and out of tunnels along the side of the gorge. Also
following the side of the gorge is a narrow path, El Camino del Rey, which was
built in the early 1920s and used by King Alfonso XIII when he opened the
nearby hydro electric works. The path today is extremely dangerous and is
marked with a 'No Entry' sign. This does not, however, seem to stop people
making the attempt. There is a project to restore the Camino del Rey, but
work has been held up because of a lack of agreement about exactly who owns
the path. The cliffs of El Chorro are popular with rock climbers; see page 55.
There is a small, basic and unofficial campsite at El Chorro.

The road continues north from El Chorro into the Bobastro valley. Look for **Bobastro**
the sign *Iglesia Mozárabe* which leads up the mountain side to the hilltop site
where there are the remains of a Mozarab hill fort, once the home of over
3,000 people. It was the headquarters of Omar Ibn Hafsun, the son of
muwallad (mixed Arab-Christian parentage) nobles who at one time controlled much of Andalucía. In 899 he converted to Christianity and constructed the church where he was interred on his death in 917. The church is

Málaga Province

the only recognizable structure left and the nave, aisles, a transept and some side chapels can be clearly identified. Back in the valley, the rocky walls contain a number of formerly inhabited caves.

Guadalhorce Reservoirs Further north are the Guadalhorce reservoirs, three manmade lakes which supply the drinking water for Málaga and have earned the title Andalucía's lake district. In much of the early 1990s when the winter rains failed, the reservoirs have been well under capacity (as low as 8% in 1995, when 30% is needed to supply Málaga for the summer). When they are full they make a valuable leisure resource. With their blue water, pine-clad shores and perfect swimming they are an obvious tourist attraction. Camping sites, picnic areas and restaurants are gradually appearing, but the area sees few visitors, except on summer weekends, when the reservoirs are best avoided. On the shores of the Embalse de Guadalhorce is the *Parque Ardales* campsite, T952112401, which is 6 km from the village of Ardales. Although the reservoirs themselves are rather sterile from a wildlife point of view, the pinewoods have crested tits and crossbills, while the surrounding hills have a good range of raptors, including golden and Bonelli's eagles, griffon vultures and the occasional migrating osprey. Flowers and butterflies are also outstanding, particularly in the early summer.

Ardales
Colour map 4, grid B5
Population: 2,977

For a different return route, take the MA 444 to the southwest end of the reservoirs at Ardales, a village which clothes the side of a rocky hill capped by the remains of a Roman fort and a Moorish Alcázar. The central square has a number of tapas bars. For accommodation, try **E** *El Cruce*, Carretera Alora-Campanillos, T952459012, which has seven rooms.

Carratraca
Colour map 4, grid B5
Population: 852

Five kilometres southeast of Ardales Carratraca, well known for its sulphur spa, which has attracted bathers since Roman times. The baths were at their most famous during the 19th century, when they attracted nobility and famous figures from all over Europe. When not frolicking in the sulphurous water, the socialites could visit one of three casinos. The elegant *Hostal El Principe* is also a throwback from these times. After being closed for many years, the baths have recently reopened for the summer months between 15 June and 15 October and the water that issues forth at a constant 16°C is claimed to work wonders for skin and respiratory complaints. A complete

Málaga Province

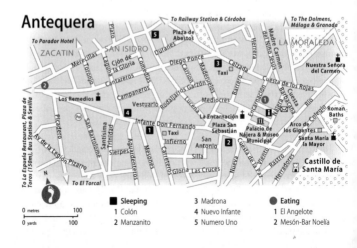

Antequera

■ Sleeping	3 Madrona	● Eating
1 Colón	4 Nuevo Infante	1 El Angelote
2 Manzanito	5 Numero Uno	2 Mesón-Bar Noelía

treatment costs €126.50. In recent years, Carratraca has revived the performance of its ancient passion play, which takes place on Good Friday and Easter Monday in the bullring, with a cast of over 100 villagers. The Passion Play has its own website – www.arrakis.es

Antequera

Located some 45 km north of Málaga, the ancient town of Antequera lies at the junction of the Sierra de Torcal and the highly productive agricultural land to the north. It has always been a religious centre and has numerous convents and churches, plus prehistoric dolmens and a Moorish castle. It is a good base for exploring El Torcal, the fascinating limestone plateau to the south.

Colour map 4, grid A6
Population: 40,239

Getting there The **bus** station is on Paseo García del Olmo, nearer the town centre. The **train** station is 3 km from the town centre in Av de la Estación, T952843226. You can take a taxi to the centre (€3) or it's a 10-min walk. Few trains, however, visit Antequera, the main station being at Bobadilla, several kilometres away. **Getting around** Most of the monuments can be reached without transport, but for the footsore there are taxi ranks in C Infante Don Fernando and C Calzada. **Tourist offices** The municipal tourist office is at Plaza San Sebastián 7, T952702505. Open in summer Mon-Sat 1000-1400, 1700-2000; Sun 1000-1400. In winter, it's open Mon- Sat 1000-1330, 1600-1900; 1000-1330 Sun.

Ins & outs
See page 252 for further details

The area

Antequera today is a modest sized market town serving the fertile plain (*vega*) to the north which grows cereals, vegetables and sunflowers. To the south is the Sierra de Chimenea, rising to over 1,300 m. Antequera's strategic position as a focus of routes has resulted in a long and important history. The clutch of dolmens to the east of the town show that the area was occupied in prehistoric times, while recent excavations to the west demonstrate that Antikaria, or the Ancient City, was an important Roman settlement. The Moorish past is evident in the hilltop Alcazaba, which dominates the town. In 1410, Antequera was the first major stronghold of the kingdom of Granada to be captured and held by the Christian armies and was later an important base for the attacks on other Moorish strongholds. During the next two centuries Antequera built up its wealth and many of its churches and other monuments date from this time.

Sights

The castle hill, close to the centre of the town, makes an excellent starting point as the view over Antequera is outstanding and all the main features can be identified. The area can be reached on foot or by car (there is a small parking place beneath the walls). The Castillo de Santa María is a Moorish Alcazaba built in the 14th century over the remains of a Roman fort. The most impressive features are the two towers, the 13th-century Torre de Homenaje, or keep, and the earlier Torre Blanco, or White Tower. Both are undergoing restoration and should not be entered without the guide (if you can find him). The castle was captured from the Moors by a royal prince, the future King Fernando I of Aragón, in a Christian victory of such significance that he was henceforth known as *El de Antequera*. The courtyard of the Alcazaba now consists of well-kept gardens with welcome shade, while the walls provide

Castillo de Santa María

Málaga Province

panoramic views over the surrounding countryside. Look east towards the oddly shaped hill known as the **Peña de los Enamorados** (Lovers' Rock). Legend has it that two lovers from rival Moorish factions threw themselves off the top when their liaison was forbidden. Next to the Castillo is the **Arco de los Gigantes**, a type of triumphal arch built in 1585 for Felipe II, but believed to incorporate stone from older monuments, possibly Roman. Behind the arch is the church of **Santa María la Mayor**, with an ornate Plateresque façade and recently restored Mudéjar ceilings. Today it functions as an art restoration centre, where students can learn stone masonry and the treatment of iron and woodwork. It is also the site for occasional concerts. A display in the nave shows the development plans for Antequera and future restoration details for the town's monuments. Stripped of all its religious paraphernalia, the church has a wonderful simplicity that gives the visitor a chance to appreciate its basic architecture. ■ *Mon-Fri 1030-1400, 1630-1830; Sat 1030-1400.*

Behind the church are the remains of some **Roman baths** that are currently being excavated. The area involved is quite extensive, with just one small section being dealt with at present. The results are already quite spectacular. It is possible to walk down to the excavations from the front of the church.

The Dólmenes   Antequera was originally a prehistoric site prior to successive occupation by the Romans, Moors and Christians and its Megalithic dolmens, a national monument on the northeast outskirts of the town off the road to Granada, are some of the best preserved burial chambers in Europe. The **Cueva de Menga**, the oldest, dates back to 2500 BC with huge, roughly cut stone slabs, believed to weigh 180 tonnes and originating from a location 8 km away, which form the roof. The gallery leads to an oval burial chamber. Much is made of the fact that Menga's gallery lines up with the Lovers' Rock, behind which the sun rises at the summer solstice. The nearby **Cueva de Viera** is smaller and slightly less ancient, but has better cut stones, while the domed ceiling of **Cueva de Romeral**, circa 1800 BC, 3 km north, is regarded as one of the earliest examples of Spanish architecture. ■ *Tue 1500-1730, Wed-Sat 1000-1400 and 1500-1730, Sun 1000-1400. Free. If the caves are closed you may be approached by some local pensionistas who will show you around for a small tip. Getting there: Menga and Viera can be reached on foot from the town by following the signs for Granada and looking out for the petrol station on the left. The local bus also runs this way. Romeral is a few kilometres further along the main road along a rough track off left in the grounds of a sugar refinery (look for the chimney). The cave itself is on the far side of the railway line (leave your car before crossing the line).*

Singlia Barba   The recently excavated Roman ruins of Singlia Barba are at *Finca Castillón*, 6 km west of Antequera on the old road to Sevilla. A team of archaeologists from Málaga university have excavated a cemetery, theatre, houses and many Roman artefacts. The land is privately owned, but the Ayuntamiento in Antequera may be able to arrange a visit.

Churches &   Just below the Castillo to the east is the **Iglesia de Nuestra Señora del**
convents   **Carmen**, built in the 17th century. It is now being restored – look for the
Antequera has 26   Mudéjar woodwork ceiling, chiaroscuro panel and the main altar's *retablo*,
churches and   over 10 m in height. ■ *Mon-Sat 1000-1400, 1700-2000; Sun 1000-1400.* The
convents and many   16th-century **Iglesia de la Encarnación** also has a Mudéjar ceiling, while the
are well worth a visit   **Iglesia de los Remedios**, a national monument, is dedicated to Antequera's patron saint. Many of the convents sell *dulces*.

Ancient mansions are much in evidence in Antequera, including the Renaissance-style **Palacio de Nájera** on Plaza Coso Viejo, which now houses the **Museo Municipal**. Although many of the displays are uninspiring, the museum is worth visiting for two remarkable exhibits. A bronze Roman statue – a life-size figure of a boy, *El Efebo* – was ploughed up in a field in the 1950s and is believed to date from the first century. An American museum is said to have offered a million dollars for it, but the offer was turned down! The other exhibit is a wood carving of St Francis of Assisi, variously attributed to either Alonso Cano or Pedro de Mena. ■ *Tue-Fri 1000-1330, Sat 1000-1330, Sun 1100-1330. €1.20. Hourly guided visits.* The **Plaza de Toros** also has a small museum. ■ *Sat 1800-2100, Sun 1000-1300 and 1800-2100. Free.*

Museums

Essentials

A *Parador de Antequera*, C García del Olmo s/n, T952840901, F952841312. 55 a/c rooms with TV. Pool, parking, restaurant, garden; avoid during spring and summer fairs if you want any sleep. **C** *Nuevo Infante*, C Infante Don Fernando 5, 2°, T952700293. 12 rooms. Excellent new apartment-style accommodation, garage, quiet, central, bar. **D** *Colón*, C Infante Don Fernando 29, T952844516, F952841164. 35 rooms. Renovated, central. **E** *Manzanito*, Plaza de San Sebastián 5, T952841023. Sizeable *hostal* with 33 rooms with showers, in main square. **D** *Madrona*, C Calzada 31, T952840014. 10 rooms with bath, central, good restaurant with local specialities. **E** *Numero Uno*, C Trinidad de Rojas 40, T952843334. New building with 9 en suite rooms and a roof terrace. **E** *Reyes*, C Tercia 4, T952841028. 14 rooms. Central.

Sleeping
See inside front cover for hotel price codes

There is a wide range of eating places, although nothing particularly inspiring. Some of the best places, including tapas bars, are around Plaza Abastos, where the weekly market is held. **Expensive** *Parador de Antequera*, Paseo García de Olmo, T952840901. Good, but pricey, regional food. **Mid-range** *La Espuela*, Ctra de Córdoba s/n, T952702633. Newish restaurant inside the bullring, atmospheric, local dishes with a good *menú del día*. **Cheap** *El Angelote, Plaza Coso Viejo, T952703456. Local cuisine in an old mansion facing an attractive small square. Madrona*, C Calzada 31, T952840014. Good *pensión* restaurant serving local dishes and tapas. *Mesón-Bar Noelía*, Alameda de Andalucía 12, T952845407. Functional surroundings but good simple food. *Manzanito*, Plaza San Sebastián 5, T952841023. Another good, inexpensive *pensión* restaurant. For **tapas bars** try those around Plaza Abastos. There are also a number of cafeterías and heladerías in the commercial centre serving pastries, ice cream, etc, including *Manolo*, C Calzada 24; *Berrocal*, C Tercia 8; and *Lozano Chico*, C Diego Ponce 29.

Eating

The pick of the rather uninspiring discotheques are *Rockefella*, C La Silla 25; *Top Kapi*, C San Pedro 24 and *Triangulo*, Camino de Santa Catalina s/n.

Bars & nightclubs

Not much goes on in Antequera, except at *feria* times. The 19th-century bullring is used mainly during the *Feria de Primavera* and *Feria Real* (see Fiestas and festivals below). A flamenco contest also takes place during the former, while more of the art can be seen during the *Noche Flamenco de Santa María* in Aug. **Cinemas and theatre** There are 3 cinemas, one at Teatro Torcal plus *Ideal Cinema*, Infante Don Fernando 73, T952842130 and *Delicias*, C San Pedro. There is a small **theatre**, *Teatro Torcal*, C Cantareros 8, T952841196.

Entertainment

Feb *Carnaval* Celebrations include satirical songs and fancy dress parades through the streets. The *Feria de Primavera* (Spring Fair), which includes a flamenco contest, is seen as a practice for the *Real Feria de Agosto* (Royal August Fair)

Fiestas & festivals

Málaga Province

during the **third week of Aug** and marked by bullfights and flamenco. **8 Sep** *Fiesta de Nuestra Señora de los Remedios* Antequera's patron saint is paraded through the streets on her silver platform.

Shopping The main shopping area is along C Infante Don Fernando, the Alameda de Andalucía and C Canteros. A **flea market** is held in Av de la Estación on Sun.

Sport **Gliding** Contact the Ayuntamiento, T952844211. **Football** Estadio de Futbol, close to the bullring. **Swimming** There are 2 pools – *Piscinas Albarizas*, Ctra de Sevilla s/n, and *Piscina Municipal*, C Antonio Mohedano, s/n, T952844153.

Tour operators *Viajes Ibermar*, C Infante Don Fernando 49; *Viajes Toral*, Plaza Pintor Cristobel Toral 2, T952840112.

Transport **Bus** *Alsina Graells*, T952841365, is the main bus company, with services to Málaga (2 daily, 45 mins, €6.35), Sevilla (4 daily, 2¼ hrs, €9.25), Córdoba (2 daily, 2¼ hrs, €7) and Granada (3 daily, 1¼ hr, €5.85). *Casal*, T952841957, also runs buses to Málaga (12 daily). Local buses run to and from Teba, Archidona and Bobodilla Junction. **Taxi** For taxis, T952841008, or visit the taxi ranks in C Infante Don Fernando and C Calzada.

Directory **Banks** The main banks are located in C Infante Don Fernando, though many do not open on Sat in the summer. A few have ATMs. **Communications** Post office: Correos, C Nájera s/n, near Museo Municipal, T952822083, Mon-Fri 0800-1500, Sat 0900-1300. **Telephones**: there are no *locutorios*, but there are plenty of public telephones on C Infante Don Fernando and Alameda de Andalucía. **Medical services** *Casa de Socorro*, C Picadero, T952844411; *Centro de Salud*, Parque María Cristina s/n, T952842929; *Cruz Roja*, Paseo Cristina s/n, T952842283; *Hospital General Básico*, C Infante Don Fernando 135, T952844411. **Useful addresses** Car repairs: these cluster in an out-of-town situation, along the Ctra de Córdoba. *Seat/Audi/Volkswagen*, Ctra de Córdoba s/n, T952843661; *Opel/GM*, Ctra de Córdoba s/n, T952842940; *Renault*, Polígono Industrial, T952841559; *Austin/Rover*, Taller Soto, C Porterías 48, T952841567; *Citroën*, Automobiles Martos, C Camino Villaba s/n, T952843463; *Ford*, Ctra Sevilla-Granada, km 159, T952844051; *Peugeot*, Ctra de Córdoba 7, T952841685.

Around Antequera

Teba
Colour map 4, grid A5
Population: 4,371

This town on a hilltop above the Río Almargen is accessible by bus from Antequera. Lord James of Douglas died here in 1330 in a battle when the Christians defeated the Moors. He may have been encumbered by a casket hanging around his neck that contained the heart of Robert the Bruce. He was taking the heart to the Holy Land, so what he was doing in Teba is anyone's guess. The heart was recovered and returned to Melrose Abbey where it was buried, but in 1989 a monument in Scottish granite was erected in the centre of Teba to mark the connection. The Moorish castle, built on Roman foundations, is largely in ruins, but worth a visit if only for the view. The parish church of Santa Cruz Real is also worth a look, with an imposing interior supported by soaring red marble columns. Search out the gold cross near the altar, said to have been donated to the church by Ferdinand and Isabella.

Three kilometres west of the town is **Garganta de Teba** cut by the Río la Venta. This gorge is a splendid area for wildlife enthusiasts. Bonelli's eagles, Egyptian vultures and eagle owls have traditionally bred in the gorge, but they may have been deterred by rock climbers in recent years. Other birds around in summer include choughs, black wheatears, blue rock thrushes and crag

The Carretera Nacional N340

In the 1980s the N340, which runs along the full length of Andalucía's Mediterranean coastline, was dubbed the most dangerous road in Europe, a reputation which was fully justified. Literally hundreds of lives were lost each year in accidents, particularly in the stretch between Fuengirola and San Pedro.

The reasons for this situation were obvious, except apparently to the Spanish authorities. The N340 was not only a four-lane highway without a central reservation, but it also acted as a local road linking urbanizaciones *with each other. It also cut off* urbanizaciones *from the beach. This led to horrific situations such as cars stationary in the fast lane waiting to turn left and, because of the lack of footbridges, pedestrians running across four lanes of traffic.*

Fortunately, in the early 1990s there was a massive injection of funds to improve Andalucía's infrastructure, spurred on by Expo 92 in Sevilla and the availability of EU money. The N340 is now a two- or three-lane autovía *from Málaga to Estepona, with a central reservation, flyovers, tunnels and pedestrian footbridges. In 2000 a parallel toll road was built between Fuengirola and Estepona. This is underused, especially by Spanish drivers who dislike paying for motoring,*

but it certainly speeds up the journey along the coast.

But the original N340 between Fuengirola and Marbella is still a very dangerous road, for the following reasons:

● *There is no hard shoulder, so there is nowhere to go to avoid an accident or sudden hold-up.*

● *There are few slip roads, so cars cannot join the* autovía *at speed. Cars join the road from STOP signs into traffic travelling at up to 120 kph. Similarly, vehicles must slow down considerably before leaving the* autovía*.*

● *The sheer volume of traffic, especially during the height of the season.*

● *Many tourists collect hire cars from the airport at Málaga and drive straight on to the* autovía *in a strange car (also faced with an unfamiliar left-hand drive if they are British) heading for unknown destinations.*

● *After the summer drought, the heavy autumn rains fall on an oily surface which soon resembles a skating rink.*

● *Moroccan guestworkers returning from France and Germany to the ferries at Algeciras drive often overloaded cars and the drivers have rarely stopped for sleep.*

Drivers are strongly advised to take the utmost care at all times and certainly not drink and drive.

Málaga Province

---

martins. It is also an excellent spot for butterflies. Access into the gorge depends very much on the amount of water running – it can be quite a scramble in winter.

This upland limestone block is 16 km south of Antequera and covers 1,171 ha. The grey limestone has been weathered into fantastic shapes giving an eerie atmosphere. The thin alkaline soil supports stunted trees and bushes such as elder, maple and hawthorn. There is a huge variety of wild flowers, including over 30 species of orchids, dwarf irises, peonies, rock roses and many more. Spring and early summer are the best times to visit, but there are flowers to see at all times of the year. Birdwatchers might see booted and short toed eagles, blue rock thrushes and black wheatears, while there is an abundance of reptiles, including the rare green-eyed lizard. To appreciate the abundant wildlife, it's best to avoid crowded times at weekends and in early summer when school parties visit. **Parque Natural El Torcal**

The **Centro de Visitantes** has excellent displays and audiovisual presentations. It's open daily 1000-1700. Near the centre is a terrace with exceptional views down towards Málaga and the coast.

From the visitors' centre there are three circular **walks** marked with arrows. The green route is only 1½ km and takes 30 minutes. The yellow circuit of 2½ km can be walked in under one hour and includes a panoramic view at 1,200 m. The red path can take up to five hours, with a viewpoint at 1,339 m where you can see the entire park and the coastline of Africa on a clear day. The paths are generally well marked with arrows painted on the rocks, but in thick mist keeping to the trail can be tricky. Consult the weather forecast, as El Torcal can not only be covered in thick cloud, but frost and snow are not uncommon in winter. It's also advisable to wear substantial footwear and if it's hot, take a bottle of water.

Sleeping *La Posada de Torcal*, in Villanueva de la Concepción, T952031006, laposada@mercuryin.es A small but luxurious and beautifully furnished place with a pool, facing the limestone mass of El Torcal. *Camping Torcal*, T952703582, at Río de la Villa on the slopes of El Torcal, which has good facilities, including a pool.

Transport To reach El Torcal by **car**, take the C3310 from Antequera towards Villanueva de la Concepción, turning off after about 12 km towards the visitors' centre at the foot of the mountain, which reaches 1,369 m at its highest point. **Buses** towards Villanueva de la Concepción are infrequent and drop you at the turn off with several kilometres still to walk. The best options are hitchhiking or a taxi.

Archidona
Colour map 5, grid A1
Population: 8,168

Fifteen kilometres east of Antequera lies the once strategic town of Archidona. Occupied by the Iberians, the Romans and the Moors and defended by a hilltop Castillo, it was captured by Christian forces in 1462. Later it was the chief town of the Counts of Ureña and the dukes of Osuna. Today it is a backwater, bypassed by both the main road and the *autovía* to Granada. Its pride and joy, however, is the Plaza Ochavada, a late 18th-century octagonal square, surrounded by buildings using ornamental brickwork and stone. One of the main aims in building the plaza was to provide work for the many unemployed at that time. Surprisingly, apart from the Convent of las Minimas, which is not open to the public, there are few monuments of interest in the town. A good place to eat is *Mesón El Bobión de Oro*, Calle Grande 6, T952748063.

The surrounding hills contain a significant reminder of the area's Moorish past in the shape of a church high in the Sierra de Archidona. The **Santuario de la Virgen de Gracia** is signposted up a steep, narrow tarmac road from the town. It was originally a ninth-century mosque, Moorish settlements having been established in the area under Emir Abd Al-Rahman in 756 AD. Following the reconquest of Archidona in 1462 the mosque was converted into a Christian church, although there may have been a church on the site prior to the arrival of the Moors, since the three arches inside the door are Visigothic. The mosque's *mihrab* was converted by the Christians into an altar to the Virgen de Gracia, the local patron saint whose fiesta is celebrated on 14 August. Restoration work began in 1988 and still continues. ■ *Nov-Jan 0900-1400 and 1500-1900, Feb-Apr 0800-1400 and 1600-2000, May-Oct 0700-1400 and 1700-2200. Free. There is very limited parking at the summit.*

Nearby are the scant remains of an Arab fortress, the scene of much fighting amongst various factions of the occupying Moors and later between the Moors and the Christians during the Reconquest.

Málaga Province

Laguna de la Fuente de Piedra, located close to the town of the same name, lies just off the A92 to the west of Antequera. The lagoon is eliptical in shape and covers around 1,300 ha. In winter, this saline lagoon extends up to 14,000 ha. In summer, however, the heat and the wind induce high levels of evaporation. Until the 1950s it was used as a *salinera* producing salt commercially and in 1963 the first recorded breeding took place. By 1982, the importance of the lagoon was officially recognized and it was listed under the Ramsar convention as a wetland of international significance. By 1984 it was a fully protected reserve and controlled by the environmental agency of the Andalucían government. The lagoon now has an information and display centre with information panels, audio visual and computer displays regarding the way of life of the flamingoes and the other wildlife of the reserve. ■ *Daily 1000-1500 and 1600-1900.* Next to the centre is a mirador located under a shady tree giving perfect viewing.

Laguna de la Fuente de Piedra
One of only two regular breeding sites for greater flamingoes in southwest Europe

The breeding success of the flamingoes depends entirely on the amount of winter rainfall. In spring 2001, the reception centre claimed that there were 80,000 flamingoes present, although many would dispute this claim. The demands by local farmers for irrigation water has not helped the overall situation. The chicks are counted by photographs taken from the air and then about 10% are rounded up before they can fly and are ringed. This process has shown that the flamingoes are amazing wanderers and birds ringed at Fuente de Piedra have been recorded on the Camargue, in Tunisia and even in Senegal.

The lagoon also has 200 breeding pairs of gull billed terns, plus black winged stilts, avocets, kentish plovers and the rare white headed duck. The small lake next to the reception centre has a colony of black headed gulls, while another ornithological delight close to the viewing platform is a chalk cliff face with breeding beeeaters. During the winter months there are a host of waders, wildfowl and even cranes. Within the lake's zone of influence are haplophytic plant communities which can cope with the saline conditions. On the sandier stretches, tamarisk is abundant. ■ *The best time to visit Fuente de Piedra is between Jan and Jun. Try to arrive before 1100 as the heat haze and sun shining from the south make watching difficult later in the day.*

Sleeping Fuente de Piedra: D *La Laguna*, Autovía Sevilla-Málaga, km 135, T952735292. Restaurant, a/c. There is a **campsite** in the village close to the reserve – *La Laguna de Fuentepiedra*, Camino de la Rábita s/n, T952735294. Open throughout the year, with pool, bar and restaurant.

The Costa del Sol

The stretch of coast west from Málaga to Gibraltar is a narrow coastal strip of ribbon development that since the late 1960s has grown into a collection of resorts, urbanizaciones and leisure complexes which on first sight can be quite a shock to the uninitiated. It is difficult to explain the success of the costa. It is certainly not the quality of the beaches, which are generally gritty or rocky; nor is it the access provided by the coast road, which is one of the most dangerous in Europe; it cannot be the cultural background, which, with a few notable exceptions, is sparse. The climate, however, particularly in winter, is the best on mainland Europe, attracting thousands of northern Europeans in the colder months. Inland, the scenery can be spectacular. Drive for two or three hours and you can be in Sevilla, Granada or Córdoba.

Many of the worst architectural features in the form of tower blocks were put up in the 1960s and 1970s; since then the main trend has been to build low rise

Málaga Province

urbanizaciones, which in the 1980s and 1990s have been dominated by the time share business. Many of these developments have been stylish and well designed, but often the original landscape of dunes, heath and pine woods has been destroyed. Nevertheless, it is estimated that around 350,000 foreigners live on the Costa del Sol, either legally or illegally, with vast numbers owning their own property. Tourist numbers have fluctuated and the early 1990s were lean years with European recession, high Spanish inflation and the attraction of other package venues such as Florida and the Caribbean. By the late 1990s, however, the building cranes were back and the recovery was well under way, with over three million visitors passing through Málaga airport annually and high hotel and apartment occupancy rates.

Torremolinos

Colour map 4, grid B6
Population: 37,235

The first of the resorts west from Málaga, Torremolinos was also the earlier to be developed, with a thriving hippie scene in the 1970s. Known as 'Torrie' to the first English package tourists, it is loud, brash and dedicated to hedonistic culture. Many might be appalled by its vulgarity, but out of season it is far less offensive, appealing to North European winter retirees. The local authorities are working hard to raise the image of Torremolinos and dispel its largely undeserved 'lager lout' reputation.

The main **tourist office** is in the Ayuntamiento on Plaza Blas Infante 1,

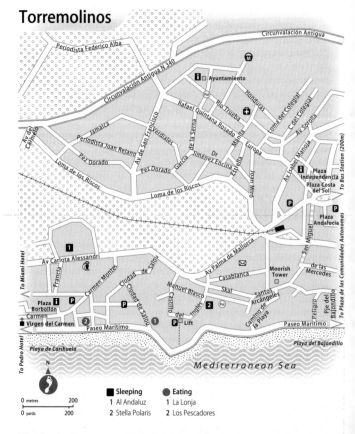

Torremolinos

Sleeping	Eating
1 Al Andaluz	1 La Lonja
2 Stella Polaris	2 Los Pescadores

0 metres 200
0 yards 200

TRAVELBAG

Adventures

Off the beaten track...

T952379512. It's open Monday to Friday 0930-1330 in winter and daily 0900-1400, 1700-2000 in summer. There are smaller offices in Plaza Independencia, T952374231, open Monday to Friday 0930-1400; Plaza Borbollón in La Carihuela district, T952372956, open Monday to Friday 0930-1430; and Plaza de las Comunidades Autonomas near the Playa del Bajondillo, T952371909, open daily in summer 1000-1400, 1700-2000 and Monday to Friday 0930-1430 in winter.

It is difficult to appreciate that 40 years ago there were hardly any buildings here apart from the water mills which gave Torremolinos its name (and which only stopped working in 1924) and a few fishermen's cottages behind La Carihuela beach. The centre of what old town existed is Calle San Miguel, now a busy pedestrianized alley full of boutiques, and restaurants, varying from the grotty to the chic, and even a Moorish tower. Torremolinos has four beaches, separated by rock headlands. To the east are the Playa del Bajondillo and the Playa de Playamar, while to the west are Playa de Carihuela and Playa de Montemar. All four are identically heaving with browning bodies during the height of the season. A surprisingly pleasant promenade links up all the beaches.

The most interesting area in Torremolinos is undoubtedly La Carihuela, the old fishermen's quarter. There are a few token fishing boats still hauled up on the beach, but the majority now operate out of Benalmádena marina to the west. While in La Carihuela, look in at the simple little fishermen's church of the Virgen del Carmen, in Calle Carmen, one block back from the Paseo Marítimo.

There are plenty of rooms except at the height of the season. Most of the large package tour hotels are located behind the eastern beaches. A further clutch of hotels are found behind the Montemar beach including: **A** *Al-Andaluz*, Av de Montemar s/n, T2381200, F2381906. 164 rooms. Pool, a/c, tennis. **B** *La Barracuda*, Av España 1, 3 and 5, T952385400, F952389121. 234 rooms. A/c, pool, restaurant, tennis. **B** *Finca La Mota*, Ctra de Míjas, Alhaurín El Grande, T952490901. 12 rooms in a 300-year-old converted farmhouse. **D** *Miami*, C Aladino 14, T952385255. 26 rooms. Quiet, small hotel in suburban road, nice gardens, pool. **D** *Pedro*, C Bulto 1, T2380536. 12 rooms. Simple but clean, right on the Paseo Marítimo in La Carihuela. Recommended. **D** *Stella Polaris*, Urbanización La Roca, T952382911. 117 rooms. A/c, wheelchair access, cliff top location. **Camping** The town's campsite is 3 km west of Torremolinos on the N340, T952382602. It has limited facilities, including a bar.

Sleeping
See inside front cover for hotel price codes

There are some excellent fish restaurants in La Carihuela, including *La Lonja* and *Los Pescadores*, both right on the beach. Try also *La Langusta* and *La Cantana* on the Paseo Marítimo.

Eating

If you are looking for a lively night out, then Torremolinos is the place to be. Gay bars, discos, sports bars and nightclubs abound and music throbs until daybreak. Most venues centre around Plaza Costa del Sol and Av Palma de Mallorca.

Bars & nightlife

Bus Regular Portillo buses run along the coast road between Málaga and Fuengirola every 15 mins. There are also buses to Ronda, Granada, Córdoba, Tarifa, Cádiz and other destinations; T952382419 for more information. **Taxi** There is a taxi rank in Plaza Costa del Sol. **Train** Torremolinos is on the Fuengirola-Málaga electric railway, with trains every 30 mins in each direction. The train station is on C La Nogalera (C La Nogalera, a pedestrianized offshoot of C San Miguel).

Transport

Málaga Province

Hedonistic harbours

Andalucía has a long seafaring tradition. Some of the world's oldest civilisations came across the seas to its shores, while it was largely Andalucían sailors who crewed the ships of Columbus and others who discovered and mapped the New World. Of the eight provinces of Andalucía, six have a coastline, either on the Atlantic or the Mediterranean. There are major sea ports such as Cádiz or Málaga, which have had to adapt and convert to the container trade or cater for cruise liners. There are also countless smaller fishing ports, such as Barbate or Fuengirola, which are suffering from the problem of over fishing and the consequent depletion of stocks.

In more recent history a major change has been the adaptation to the demands of the thriving tourist industry and this has led to the growth of puertos deportivos or marinas. There are now over 30 of these, with more under construction. They range from small harbours, such as that at Garrucha in Almería province, which caters for little more than a tiny fishing fleet, to the large, glitzy and rather vulgar Puerto

Banús, which can cope with nearly a thousand boats, many of them floating gin palaces with their own on-board helicopters. Some harbours have become tourist attractions in their own right - coachloads of pensioners flock to Benalmádena port during the winter months.

Successful marinas generate their own spin-offs. Apart from chandler's shops and the provision of fuel and repairs, many have popular restaurants, bars, boutiques and discos, while the attraction of water has led to the development of upmarket apartment blocks. Benalmádena has a thriving sea water aquarium. Many have regular flea markets and other popular attractions, while in many cases, as at Estepona, the local fishing fleets have moved into the marinas and no longer have to haul up on the beach. Along with the tourists come others who feed off them, such as the jugglers, street musicians and pickpockets. But the emphasis is on pleasure and they have rapidly become an integral part of the Andalucían tourist scene.

Río Guadalhorce Just to the east of Torremolinos and quite close to Málaga airport is a quite unexpected nature reserve at the mouth of the Río Guadalhorce. This area consists of the narrow estuary and a series of ponds and scrub. Although protected by the region's environment agency, the site suffers from industrial pollution, sewerage and human disturbance. Despite these problems this minute wetland site has a remarkable number of birds, particularly during migration periods. There is a wide range of winter wildfowl, waders, heron and egrets. No fewer than seven varieties of terns have been recorded. Access is via the old N340 just east of the river at Finca La Isla.

Benalmádena
Colour map 4, grid B6
Population: 28,479

Torremolinos merges imperceptibly into Benalmádena, its less frenetic neighbour to the west. There are some well-kept beaches which are less gritty than those at Torremolinos while most of the developments are low rise with tasteful villas straggling up the hillside. Benalmádena's most noticeable feature is its marina, see box. Try to find *Restaurante La Resaca*, a bodega serving excellent fish dishes and tapas. Within the marina is *Sea Life*, a submarine park with plastic tunnels taking you into the aquariums for eyeball-to-eyeball contact with sharks and other sea creatures. ■ *Daily 1000-1800 daily, €5.75, children €4.* There are two regular pleasure boats operating out of the port. The *Super Goleta* heads to Málaga (1¼ hours), while the *Joven María II* goes to Fuengirola. Both boats charge €9 return. Some 3 km inland is Benalmádena village with a small archaeological museum and a folly type castle, the Castillo de Aguilas, where birds of prey are flown daily at 1300, 1900 and 2000. There are some 150 raptors on display, including eagles, owls, falcons and vultures. ■ *1100-1900. €5.15, children €3.35.*

Travelling along the N340 you can't miss the Costa's latest attraction, the **Benalmádena cable cars**. The *telecabinas* run from Tivoli World to the top of the Calamorro mountain, 769 m above sea level. The journey takes 15 minutes and gives fantastic views along the coast from Gibraltar to the Sierra Nevada, while in clear weather you can glimpse the North African coast. There is a restaurant at the top and 3 km of paths amongst some interesting *maquis* vegetation, with a good variety of butterflies. ■ *Return trips cost €5.45 and €4 for children. T952575038.*

Fuengirola

The thriving resort of Fuengirola is quieter than Torremolinos to the east and has fewer 'beautiful people' than Marbella to the west. It is basically a family resort, which appeals to Northern European retirees in the winter and attracts large numbers of Spanish visitors, particularly from Córdoba in the summer. Dominated by Sohail Castle, it is very much a working town, with a thriving fish dock and light industry in the suburbs to the north.

Colour map 4, grid B6
Population: 44,924

Fuengirola is located at the mouth of the Fuengirola River, which forms a broad valley extending inland. It has a climate similar to that of Málaga, but being further west, it is more open to Atlantic influences and has slightly cooler summers. The municipal tourist office occupies the old railway station in Avenida Santos Rein, T952467457, and has helpful multi-lingual staff. It's open Monday to Friday 0930-1400 and 1600-1900, Saturday 1000-1300.

Fuengirola is linked by a 7 km promenade with Los Boliches and Carvajal to the east. The name Los Boliches was derived from the Bolicheros, who were sailors and traders from Genoa and who are believed to have settled here in the early 14th century. It is from Los Boliches that the Virgen del Carmen fishermen's fiesta takes place every July.

Unlike Torremolinos, Fuengirola has a long history. Roman remains are currently being excavated at Torreblanca, while at Los Boliches on the Paseo Marítimo a Roman arch has been erected from remains recovered from the sea bed by divers. It was the Romans, too, who probably built the first structure at the **Castillo de Sohail** on a hill by the river at the west end of the town. In the eighth century it was extensively rebuilt by Caliph Abd Al-Rahman III. The castle was destroyed in 1485 in the Christian Reconquest of the area, the Moors surrendering on the day of San Cayetano, the patron saint of Fuengirola today. In 1730 the castle was rebuilt to defend the coast against the British who had taken Gibraltar in 1704. During the Peninsular War in 1810, a British expedition of 800 men under General Blayney landed at the Castle and advanced on Mijas, but later they retreated to the Castle, where, humiliatingly they were obliged to surrender to 150 Polish mercenaries. It is interesting to note that at this time the population of Fuengirola was a mere 60 people. The town became independent of Mijas in 1841; the big expansion did not happen until the tourist boom of the 1960s and 1970s.

Sights

The Castillo de Sohail has recently been renovated and turned into a cultural centre. The interior is now an outdoor auditorium where concerts take place and there is also a small exhibition centre and museum. You can get to the castle, which is floodlit at night, via the path from the river mouth.

Zoológico de Fuengirola is in Calle Camilo José Cela, next to the bull-ring. This small zoo was closed down by the local authority in 1999 after

Málaga Province

concern over the way the animals were being kept. The American company *Rainforest* reopened the zoo in 2001. It has four different habitats and opens at night so that the public can see nocturnal animals. ■ *Daily 1000-1800. €8.43, children under 12 €5.40.*

Aquaparks can be found on Torremolinos and Fuengirola bypasses with similar opening hours, attractions and entrance fees. **Parque Aquático Mijas** at Fuengirola, for example, has a variety of pools, watershoots including a 'kamikaze', slides and rapids, restaurant, free parking. ■ *Daily at 1000, closure according to season, full day tickets €10.85, children 4-12 €6.95 (no charge for second child). Connections from Fuengirola bus station, T952460404.* The larger **Aquapark Torremolinos** has a wave pool, twisters,, kamikaze, an impressive Black Hole and body ski slopes. ■ *Daily May-Sep 1000-1800 (Jul-Aug open until 1900). €14, children €10.25. T952388888.*

Tivoli World is a large amusement park at Arroyo de la Miel, near Benalmádena with gardens, computerized fountains, rides, restaurants, flamenco shows and a large outdoor theatre featuring internationally known stars. ■ *Daily 1800-0200. €3.65, including all entertainment plus the cost of rides. Alternatively, a SuperTivolino ticket for €13.85 allows entrance and up to 30 rides. T952441896. The nearest railway station is at Arroyo de la Miel. Substantial reductions can be made on entrance fees to places such as Tivoli World and the Aquaparks by booking through travel agents such as* Maxy's *on Paseo Marítimo.*

A popular **boat trip** runs from Fuengirola harbour to the marina at Benalmádena. The *Joven María II* runs approximately hourly in each direction. ■ *€4.80 (return €9), children under 10 €2.40 (return €3.65).*

Fuengirola

A *Las Pirámides*, C Miguel Márquez 43, T952470600, F952583297. 320 rooms. At the quieter end of the Paseo, restaurant, parking, pool, tennis, convenient for the beach, often live entertainment in the evening. **C** *Más Playa*, Urbanización Torreblanca del Sol, T9524753. Pool, restaurant, tennis, wheelchair access. **C** *Stella Maris*, P Principe de España s/n, T952475450. 196 rooms. A/c, restaurant, pool, wheelchair access. **C** *Villa de Laredo*, Paseo Marítimo 42, T952477689 F952477950. Spanking new Art Deco style hotel opposite the port. Restaurant has its own shellfish pond. All the above hotels have much reduced winter rates. **D** *Agur*, C Tostón 4, T952476662, F952488708. 33 rooms. Parking, conveniently situated for town and beach. **D** *El Amigo*, Av los Boliches 71, T952470333. 20 rooms. On the main street. **D** *El Cid*, Av Conde San Isidro s/n, 100 m west of the bus station. 46 rooms. Breakfast available. **E** *Cuevas*, C Capitán 7, T952460606. 13 rooms. Small, well kept and handily placed. **Camping** There are numerous sites close to the sea to the west of Fuengirola. *La Roselada*, Ctra N340, Km 211, Camino la Salina, Loma Baja, T952460191. Bar, pool, tennis, beach. *Fuengirola*, Ctra N340, Km 207, T952474108. Bar, restaurant, games area, beach. *Calazul*, Ctra N340, Km 200, Míjas Costa, T952493219. Bar, restaurant, beach, watersports. All three sites can get extremely busy and noisy during the summer months.

Sleeping
See inside front cover for hotel price codes

There is a vast and cosmopolitan range of choice in Fuengirola, varying from simple Spanish seafood through to Indian, Chinese and exotic Indonesian. **Expensive** *La Langosta*, C Lopa de Vega, T952475049. Shellfish specialities. *Portofino*, Paseo Marítimo, T952470643. Italian and international menu, booking recommended. *Valparaíso*, Ctra Fuengirola-Míjas, Km 4, T952485996. International menu, dancing, terrace, closed Sun.

Eating
See inside front cover for price codes

Mid-range *Bélgica Antiqua*, Av Condes San Isidro 67, T952471596. Danish and Belgian cuisine and fish dishes. *City Grill*, C Juan Sebastian Elcano, T952474369. Steak specialities.

4 Ku Damm
5 La Gondola
6 Portofino
7 Rajdoot
8 Romy

Finca la Fuente – to find it is an initiative test in itself. Take the Míjas-Coín road. 3-4 km after the Alhaurín crossroads, turn left at the small sign. Follow a rough track for around 2 km (you will be grateful for a 4WD). This English-owned converted *finca* is located by a bubbling stream with rock pools for swimming; a perfect place to laze away a summer afternoon. The food is good too! *Ku Damm*, Fuengirola Porb, T952472864. Popular German restaurant overlooking the harbour. *Menú del día* €5.85. *El Potro*, Urbanización Sierrazuela, Av de Míjas, T952470284. Steaks cooked at tables. Flamenco on Sat. *Rajdoot*, C Lamo de Espinosa, T952462910. Tandoori specialities. *El Sultan*, Parque Doña Sofia, C Heroes de Balar. Well-established Moroccan restaurant, house specialities including lamb and couscous.

Cheap For those who enjoy simple Spanish food, especially fish, the pedestrianized C Moncayo and the alleyways leading off it can be recommended. There are numerous restaurants here, such as *La Gondola*, *Sal y Pimiento*, *Europa* and *Romy*, with an

Málaga Province

excellent *menú del día* with wine for under €6. There are also small fish bars for *raciones* around the marina. Cheaper still are the *buffet libre* restaurants, where for a set price of around €6 you can eat as much as you like. The following are located along the Paseo Marítimo: *Buffet Saturno*, *Top 20* and *Buffet Versalles*. In the summer, locals and foreign residents head for the *ventas* on the Míjas Golf Rd, including *Venta Perea* and *Venta La Marena*, which has a good grill. At the Míjas-Alhaurín crossroads, the *Venta Los Morenos* is as good. All offer good basic Spanish country cooking at reasonable prices, but they can be crowded at weekends and at the height of the golfing season.

Tapas bars are mainly located in the area to the west of the train station and in C San Rafael, which leads off the main square. Try *La Campana El Parillo*, *Casa Flores* and *Sol y Sombra*.

Bars & nightclubs **Nightclubs** Discotheques are mainly found either along the Paseo Marítimo, try *Disco/Night Club Maxy*. Nearby is the lively *Mai Tai* in the basement of *Hotel Puerto Sol*. At the west end of town close to *Hotel PiráMles* is a cluster of discos including *La Marcha* and *Jaguar*.

Entertainment **Casino** *Casino Torrequebradna*, Ctra de Cádiz, Km 226, Benalmádena-Costa, T952442545. Games room, Fortuna nightclub with cabaret, piano bar and restaurant, open Fri and Sat from 2230. **Theatre** *Salon Varietes*, C Varietes. A small but highly popular theatre with entertainment in English. Performances from mid-Sep to mid-Jun.

Fiestas & festivals 16 Jul *Fiesta de la Virgen del Carmen* One of the best of its type along the coast. The statue of the virgin is carried from the church in Los Boliches in a 2-hr procession to the beach and into the sea. An amazing spectacle, with half the inhabitants on the beach and the other half in the sea, either swimming or in boats. **Late Sep** Romería This is a small affair with decorated carts and horseriders heading for the hills. **First 2 weeks of Oct** *Feria del Rosario* Celebrated on the permanent showground site between Los Boliches and Fuengirola, where there are *casetas* for the various societies and brother-hoods. All this is accompanied by fireworks, bullfights and flamenco.

Shopping There is a daily indoor market located in a modern building at the junction of Av Suel and Av Santos Rein. The huge outdoor weekly market is held on Tue at the permanent feria site on Av Santos Rein. There is also a large flea market held on Saturday and a smaller but popular Sunday market held by the port, which has handy nearby cafés and tapas bars. The large *hipermercado* **Euromarket** is situated on the Fuengirola bypass and also has a regular Sunday car boot sale. The main fashion shops are located around the Plaza de la Constitución. The leather market, close to *Hotel Palmeras Sol*, sells a variety of goods in addition to leatherwork and you can bargain.

Tour operators *Centro*, Las Rampas, T952470208. *Benamar*, Paseo Marítimo, Edificio El Yate, T952473762. *Maxy*, Paseo Marítimo, T952470610. *Perla Travel*, Paseo Marítimo, T952463076. *Rusadir*, C Marbella 37, T952474885.

Transport **Local Car hire**: *Helle Hollis*, T952479800, and *Marinsa*, T952382180. **Taxi**: there are taxi ranks opposite the bus station and near the port. **Coches de Caballo** (horse drawn carriages) can be picked up outside the port. **Long distance Bus**: the station is on the corner of Av Ramón y Cajal and C Alfonso XIII, T9522475066. Take care here as it is a favourite bag-snatching spot. *Portillo* buses run every 30 mins along the coast road and also to Míjas. There are 4 daily buses to Granada, Ronda and La Linea; 11 daily to Algeciras, with 3 continuing to Cádiz; 1 daily to Jerez and Almería and 5 daily to Madrid.

Train: the station of the electric railway to Málaga is in Av Santos Rein, opposite the indoor market. Trains for Málaga leave at 15 and 45 mins past the hour (€2 to Málaga, €1.50 to airport).

Directory

Banks All the main Spanish banks, many with ATMs, have branches here, mainly close to the Plaza de la Constitución. **Communications** Internet: *Internet Café Daytona*, Edificio Solplaya 6 , C Martínez Catena. *Hello*, conveniently placed at the rear of the bus station. There is also the friendly *Café Olé*, C Maestra Angeles Aspiazu. **Post Office**: new building on the site of the old indoor market in C España, T952474384. **Telephones**: *locutorios* containing several booths and accepting credit cards are located on the Paseo Marítimo and next to the tourist office in Av Santos Rein. **Embassies and consulates** Most of the nearest consulates are located in Málaga, except *USA*, Centro Comercial Las Rampas, T952474891 and *Ireland*, Av los Boliches, T952475108. **Medical services** Ambulance: T952472929. **First aid clinic**: T952472929. **Hospital**: T952307700. **Cruz Roja**: T952250450.

Around Fuengirola

This village is geared to catering for the tourist, with donkey rides, garish souvenirs and English-run restaurants. Despite all this, Mijas has a certain charm and is well worth a visit. It has a long history, certainly going back to Roman times, while the Moors built the defensive walls which partially remain today. The village is located 425 m above sea level at the foot of pine-covered mountains, superb views along the coast from the well-kept gardens above the cliffs. You can't miss the imposing new Ayuntamiento, largely built with taxes from foreign residents, who, in the Mijas administrative district which stretches to the sea at Mijas-Costa, outnumber the Spanish by two to one.

Mijas
Colour map 4, grid B6
Population: 37,490

Above the car park on top of the nearby cliff is the **Ermita de la Virgen de la Peña** (Shrine of the Virgin of the Rock), where there is a tiny image of the patron saint of Mijas. The image may date back to 850, but was hidden when the Moors approached the village. It was discovered in an old wall in 1586 and returned to the Ermita. Inside the grotto today are numerous *ex votos* – small models of arms and legs, many made of silver, left by people who claim to have been cured following prayer to the Virgin. Head for the Plaza de la Constitución, which leads to the cliffs and old walls. The **Iglesia de la Concepción Immaculada** was built in the 17th century on the site of a Moorish mosque (the town fell to the Christian armies in 1487 and most of the Moorish population were expelled). Most of the church was built in Mozarabe style. While it was being renovated in 1992, some ancient wall paintings were discovered on the main pillars. Inscriptions in Old Spanish date them as early 17th century.

To the north of the church is the tiny **bullring**. Built in 1900, it is one of the very few square bullrings in Spain. Because it is so small, traditional bullfights with mounted picadors cannot take place here, so it is restricted to the fighting of novice bulls on foot. Don't miss the **Casa Museo,** the village museum located in an old town house near to the Plaza de la Libertad. Village traditions are shown, with rooms devoted to a bakery, wine bodega, a typical bedroom and kitchen. ■ *Daily 1000-1400 and 1700-2000*. High above Mijas in the wooded hillside is the **Shrine of the Calvario.** It was built in 1710 and used by the barefooted Carmelitas brothers for spiritual retirement. The shrine is only open on Good Friday, but it's well worth the steep walk (follow the small iron crosses) for the superb view over Mijas to the coast beyond.

Málaga Province

Sleeping AL *Byblos Andaluz*, Mijas Golf, T952473050, F952476783. 144 rooms. One of the top hotels in Spain, with outstanding sports and leisure facilities. **A** *Club Puerta del Sol*, Ctra de Fuengirola, Km 4, T952486400, F952486441. 330 rooms. Large new hotel in Andalucían style, fitness centre. **A** *Mijas*, Urbanización Tamisa, T952485800, F952485825. 101 rooms. A well appointed establishment in a quieter part of the village. **D** *El Mirío Blanco*, Plaza de la Constitución 13. Small, cosy, on the main square. **E** *Romana*, C Coín 47, T952485310. Good value *pensión*.

Eating Mijas village has some excellent restaurants in amongst the 'chips with everything'places. **Mid-range** The new development above the Plaza de la Constitución has a series of restaurants with fine views down to the coast. Overlooking the Plaza Virgen de la Peña is *The Snug*, T952485732, with a good atmosphere and friendly service. Try also *El Padastro*, Paseo de Compas, T952485000. International food in a picturesque tower. **Cheap** For a meal under €6, go to *La Malagueña*, Plaza de la Paz, T952485128 or *Restaurante Mirlo Blanca*, which also offers rooms.

Marbella

Colour map 4, grid B5
Population: 98,377

The attractive resort of Marbella is a social step above its neighbours to the east and west. Backed by a distinctive limestone mountain, it has a superb beach, historic old town, swish shops and fine restaurants, as well as the chance of spotting a famous face.

Ins and outs

Getting there
See page 268 for further details
The nearest **airports** are at Málaga and Gibraltar, which can be reached by road in less than 1 hr. The nearest **train** stations are RENFE in Málaga and the electric railway in Fuengirola. A new bus station has opened in C Trapiche, T952764400, next to the bypass, but most local buses still pass through the town centre en route.

Getting around There are **taxi** ranks in the main street, Av Ricardo Soriano, and in C Arias Maldonado, next to the Parque de la Constitución.

Tourist offices The main tourist office is located in the Ayuntamiento in the Plaza de los Naranjos, T952823550, open Mon-Fri 0900-2100, Sat 1000-1400. It can provide town plans. Another *turismo* is on Glorieta de la Fontanilla s/n, T952771442, and is open Mon-Fri 0930-2100, Sat 1000-1400. An additional office is under the 'triumphal arch' at the eastern entrance to Marbella, T952822818, and is open daily 1000-2400. Another summer-only office is in Av Principal, Puerto Banús, T952817474.

The area

Marbella has a long history, having been populated at various times by Phoenicians, Visigoths and Romans, as well as being the most important Moorish town between Málaga and Gibraltar. Historians suggest that Moorish Marbella was a fortified town, with an oval-shaped, 2 m thick encircling wall containing 16 towers and three gates – to Ronda, Málaga and the sea. The town was taken by the Christians in 1485 and they set about remodelling the layout of the fortress, but much of the Moorish street plan remains today. In the early 20th century Marbella was little more than a large village struggling to earn a living from agriculture and iron mining.

The iron industry is believed to have employed over 1,000 men in the mid-19th century, with main centre of operations along the banks of the Río

Verde. An iron pier was built near the present docks to export the finished product and a few stanchions remain today. The industry finally closed in 1931, not through shortage of iron ore, but because of the depletion of local trees which provided the charcoal for the smelting process.

The changes began in the mid-1950s when a Spanish nobleman named Ricardo Soriano introduced his friends to the area. His nephew, Prince Alfonso von Hohenlohe, built the Marbella Club, attracting a wealthy international set to the area.

Marbella's inhabitants include Arab kings, arms dealers, media stars, famous sportsmen and notorious criminals. Marbella was in danger of becoming rather seedy in the late 1980s, particularly when the property market collapsed, but the new, larger-than-life mayor, Jesus Gil, has given the town a facelift and it continues to thrive. Amongst his many grandiose schemes is a plan to build a millionaires' island off the shore at Puerto Banús.

Sights

Marbella's old town is a compact area located to the north of Avenida Ramon y Cajal. In its centre is the **Plaza de los Naranjos** (Orange Square), opened up in the 16th century by the Christian town planners by demolishing the maze of alleyways which constituted the Moorish *medina* (and incidentally finding Roman remains on the site). On the north side of the square is the 16th-century **Ayuntamiento**, or town hall. In the southwest corner of the square is a delightful stone fountain, the **Fuente de la Plaza**, which dates from 1604. Nearby is the **Ermita de Nuestro Señor Santiago**, Marbella's first Christian church, a small and simple building thought to date from the late 15th century. Look also for the **Casa Consistorial**, built in 1572. It has a fine wrought iron balcony and Mudéjar entrance, while on its exterior stonework is a coat of arms and inscriptions commemorating the bringing of water to the town. Finally in the square is the **Casa del Corregidor**, with a 16th-century stone façade, now a café.

Head for the northeast corner, particularly around Calle Trinidad, where there are good stretches of the old Moorish walls and at the western end of this street stands one of the towers of the original **castillo**, built by the Moors in the ninth century. The old walls continue into Calle Carmen and Calle Salinas. Also at the east end of the old town are two hospitals. **Hospital Real de San Juan de Dios**, in Calle Misericordia, was founded by the Catholic Monarchs at the time of the Reconquest to minister to foreign patients. It has a chapel with a panelled Mudéjar ceiling and a tiny cloister. The **Hospital Bazán**, with its attractive exterior of pink stone and brickwork, dates from Renaissance times. Inside, there is a chapel, large rooms with intricate ceilings and a gallery. Originally a palace, the building was bequeathed by its owner Don Alonso de Bazán to be a local hospital; today, it is an art gallery. Don't miss the fine **Church of Santa María de la Encarnación**. Started in 1618, it has an impressive stone Baroque doorway, three sizeable naves and an interesting upper choir loft. Try to ignore the ghastly modern organ and concentrate on the high altar, where you will find the image of San Bernabé, the patron saint of Marbella.

Museo del Grabado Español Contemperáneo Exhibition of contemporary Spanish prints in the sympathetically restored Palácio de Bazán with strong Mudéjar influence. ■ *Mon 0930-1400, Tue-Fri 0930-1400 and 1730-2030, Sat 1000-1400. Winter and summer opening times may vary. €2, children under 14 €0.60. T952825035.*

Casco Antiguo
The main enjoyment of the old town is its maze of narrow alleyways, small squares and whitewashed houses festooned with flowers

Museums

Málaga Province

Museo de Bonsai This museum is an absolute gem and has become very popular. Housed in a modern building surrounded by landscaped gardens and lakes, the miniature trees are imaginatively displayed on a wooden raft-like structure over water containing turtles and fish. Parking is easy; indeed this is a good place to leave a car when visiting Marbella's old town. ■ *Daily 1000-1330 and 1600-1930. €3, children €1.50. Parque Arroyo de la Represa, T952862926.*

Parks

Marbella prides itself on the number of parks & open spaces around the town

La Alameda, close to the main street, has now been extended into the **Avenida del Mar**, linking the town centre with the Paseo Marítimo. Further west is the **Parque de la Constitución**, with attractive gardens and a large outdoor auditorium. **Parque Arroyo de la Represa** occupies a dry valley in the east of the town and has a series of terraced gardens and lakes with a modern suspension bridge.

Marbella

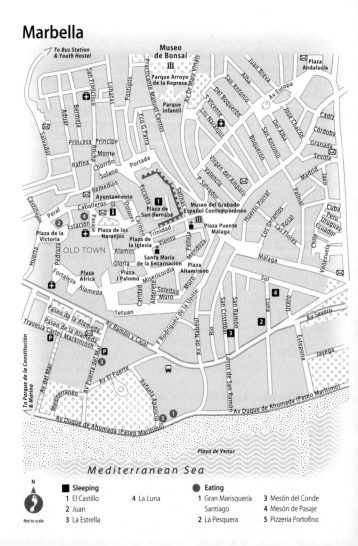

Sleeping
1 El Castillo
2 Juan
3 La Estrella
4 La Luna

Eating
1 Gran Marisquería Santiago
2 La Pesquera
3 Mesón del Conde
4 Mesón de Pasaje
5 Pizzeria Portofino

N

Not to scale

Essentials

Most of Marbella's hotels are in the outskirts. Cheaper accommodation is mainly located around the fringes of the old town, particularly in C Luna. If you want to be near Marbella without paying inflated prices, there is San Pedro de Alcántara just 10 km west (see page 270). **AL** *Meliá Don Pepe*, Finca las Marinas, T952770300, F952770300. 202 rooms. Faces the sea with a sports and leisure complex which include 18-hole golf course, indoor and outdoor pools, TV, parking, garage, restaurant, squash and tennis courts. **D** *La Estrella*, C San Cristóbal 36, T952779472. Some with bath and balcony. **E** *El Castillo*, Plaza de San Bernabé 2, T952771739. 26 rooms. Simple and clean, marvellous location in small square in old town. **E** *Juan*, C Luna 18, T952779475. Good value; some rooms with bath. **E** *La Luna*, C Luna 7, T952825778. 10 rooms, all well-equipped with balconies.

Sleeping
■ on map, below
Price codes:
see inside front cover

Outside Marbella **A** *El Castillo de Monda*, 29110 Monda, 15 mins by car from Marbella, T952457142, F952457336. 23 rooms in sympathetically converted ruins of a Moorish castle, pool, restaurant. **A** *Club Pinomar*, Ctra de Cádiz, Km 189, T952831345, F952833948. 46 rooms. Located 5 km east of Marbella, small beach hotel with watersports facilities. **B** *Artola*, Ctra de Cádiz, Km 194, T952831390, F952830450. 31 rooms. Small traditional Andalucían hotel 12 km east of Marbella with modern extension and 9-hole golf course, pool, restaurant, parking. **B** *Refugio de Juanar*, Sierra Blanca, Ojén, T952881000, F952881001. 20 rooms. Formerly a hunting lodge and parador, now a cooperative, in a peaceful mountain location with ibex and eagles and good walking possibilities, functional but comfortable, cosy fires in winter, tennis, pool, no dogs allowed. **B** *Santa Fé*, Ctra de Monda, Km 3, Coín, T952452916, F952595524. 5 rooms in a converted olive mill, gourmet restaurant.

Youth hostels Albergue Juvenil, C Trapiche 2, T952771491. 113 beds, suitable for wheelchair users, meals provided, kitchen, pool, central location. **Camping** There are 3 excellent campsites near Marbella, all on the main coast road but close to the beach. All are open all year round and winter use by recreational vehicles is high. Booking is advisable in Jul and Aug and on fiestas. *La Bouganvilla*, Ctra N340, Km 188, T952831973. Top category, bar, restaurant, laundry, beach, pool, watersports, golf, riding tennis. *Marbella 191*, Ctra N340, Km 184. Bar, laundry, beach, watersports; *Marbella Playa*, Ctra N340, Km 190, located 12 km east of town despite its name, close to one of the best beaches in the area. Bar, restaurant, pool, and supermarket.

It is no surprise to find that there is a huge variety of eating places in Marbella and the surrounding area. Despite the affluent reputation of the town it is possible to find reasonably priced food.

Eating
● on map,
opposite
Price codes:
see inside front cover

Expensive *Gran Marisquería Santiago*, Paseo Marítimo, T952770078. At the top of the range with good seafood and other dishes, favoured by locals. *La Hacienda*, Urbanización Las Chapas, T952821267. Inaugurated by the late Paul Schiff, the famous Swiss chef, unique menu, very pricey. *La Meridiana*, Camino de la Cruz, Las Lomas, T952776190. Modern restaurant with inventive international cooking, one of Marbella's top eating spots, very expensive. *Mesón del Conde*, Av del Mar 18, T952771057. Swiss restaurant specializing in meat and cheese fondues. *El Castillo*, Urbanización Pinomar, Ctra de Cádiz, Km 189, T952832746. Castilian style restaurant with 8 types of paella, suckling pig and much more. **Mid-range** Albahaca, C Lobotas 31, T952863520. A rare Andalucían vegetarian restaurant in a 400-year-old town house, lunchtime *menú* €585. *El Mesón del Pasaje*, C Pasaje, T952771261.

Málaga Province

Traditional restaurant in the old town. *El Palenque*, Ctra de Cádiz, Km 176, T952823112. Argentinian style steaks. *La Pesquera*, Plaza de la Victoría, T952778054. Reasonably priced fish dishes served under a thatched roof in a quiet square in the west part of the old town. *Pizzería Portofino*, Paseo Marítimo, T952775043. Pizzas, couscous and great sea views. **Cheap** Locals looking for cheap food served outdoors head for the three *ventas* on the mountain road 3 km south of Ojén on the C337, which specialize in game dishes, especially rabbit and partridge.

The following **tapas bars** are recommended: *Bar Figuerado*, C Haza del Méson (opposite municipal market); *El Mediterranito*, C Tetuán; *Los Tres Pepes*, C Peral, good ambience; *Trebol*, C Ancha, always busy; *Bodegón El Chorrón*, C Chorrón, good seafood.

Entertainment **Football** Marbella's team is in one of the lower divisions of the Spanish league. Stadium located in the northeast of the town 1 km from the *autovía*.

Fiestas & festivals **Jun** *Feria y Fiesta de San Bernabé* Celebrations for Marbella's patron saint, with concerts and firework displays.

Shopping Good quality shops abound in Marbella, particularly along Av Ricardo Soriano and in the alleyways of the old town. Many of these specialize in expensive, good quality jewellery and fashion goods. There are also numerous art galleries and craft shops. There is an indoor fruit and vegetable market in C Benevente, open daily. There is also a large outdoor market held on Mon near the football stadium, which is well worth a visit - but beware of pickpockets

Sport **Golf** Marbella is surrounded by golf courses, including *La Dama de la Noche*, T952812352, the first floodlit course in Europe. Others include *Río Real*, T952779509; *Aloha*, T952812388; and *Los Naranjos*, T952815206. **Horse riding** *Club Hípico Elvira*, T952835272. *Club Hípico Los Monteros*, T952770675. *Centro de Equitación*, Lakeview, T952786934. **Tennis** *Manola Santana*, Hotel Puente Romano, T952770100. *Club Deportivo Sierra Blanca*, T952863829. *Los Granados*, Puerto Banús, T952818832. In addition, the majority of upmarket hotels in the Marbella area have tennis courts with equipment to hire.

Tour operators *Marbesol*, Av Ricardo Sorriano 10, T952773139; *Tourafrica*, Av Ricardo Sorriano, Edif Molino, T952771596; *Viajes Meliá*, Av Ricardo Sorriano, T952773548.

Transport **Bus** Local buses run every 30 mins along the coast in each direction, while 5 buses a day go inland to Ojén, Coín and Monda. There are 8 coaches daily to Algeciras, 4 to Ronda and La Linea. Cádiz, Sevilla and Jerez are also served and there are 5 coaches daily to Madrid.

Directory **Banks** These are mainly along Av Ricardo Sorriano. Cash dispensers abound. **Communications** Post office: Correos is located in C Alvaro de Bázan, T952772898. **Telephones**: *locutorios* are placed at intervals along the seafront, Av de Duque de Ahumada. Payment can be made by credit card. **Medical services** Chemists: open on Mon-Fri 0900-1400 and 1700-2030, Sat 0900-1400. The name of the duty night chemist is shown on the window of each shop. **Hospitals**: *Marbella Clinic*, T952774282, is located on the Av de Severo. A new hospital, *Hospital Comarcal*, has recently opened 5 km east of Marbella on the N340, opposite *Los Monteros Hotel*. *Marbella Medical Services*, T952823135, have British trained doctors and do not charge travel insurance holders. **Useful addresses** Garages/workshops: showrooms and workshops of all the major European car firms are clustered along the

Ventas

The inland areas of Andalucía are full of small country restaurants known as ventas. They are nearly always family owned and operated and are simply furnished. Although often serving a limited choice of dishes, the emphasis is on freshly cooked local produce, including country meat dishes, such as rabbit, partridge and kid, using recipes that have been handed down through the family.

Ventas can become crowded at weekends with Spanish families. Don't let this put you off – the whole atmosphere will be vastly entertaining. Some ventas *become so well-known that they rise to the status of successful restaurants. For details of some of the better* ventas *near the Costa del Sol, see* Ventas, *by Bob Carrick, published by Santana Books.*

N340 on the east fringe of the town. *Ford*, T952776450; *Renault*, T952771616; *Seat*, T952778800; *VAG*, T952828409. Should your car be parked illegally and towed away, contact **Municipal Car Tow**, T952773692.

Around Marbella

The village of Benhavís is in an attractive setting just north of a picturesque gorge. It is the home of a number of artists and sculptors and has a number of excellent restaurants, of which the following can be particularly recommended: **Mid-range** *La Sarten*, T952855577, with good Spanish cooking accompanied by twice monthly jazz and flamenco. *Las Griegas*, T952855465, with authentic Greek cooking. *Cuarto Hondo*, T952855136, international cuisine, includes suckling pig. **Cheap** *Venta Román*, T952886421, typical country style, popular on Sunday lunchtimes.

Benhavís
Colour map 4, grid B5
Population: 1,710

Málaga Province

Just 8 km north of Marbella is the expanding village of Ojén, which has a history going back to Roman times. A number of springs rise in the village and this attracted the Moors who were in power here until 1570 and Ojén still retains much of the flavour of that time. It was once famous for the production of *aguardiente*, a powerful anis, but its main claim to fame today is that the singer Julio Inglesias lives here. Don't bother looking for his house, however - it's way out in the wilds. There is a highly regarded annual *Fiesta de Flamenco* held during the first week in August. Ojén also has an interesting parish church that was built on the site of a mosque. The spire was once the minaret. The local tourist office is in the Plaza de Andalucía. Here you can book four-wheel-drive tours in the Sierra de las Nieves with *Monte Aventura,* an organization committed to conserving the environment, T952881519.

Ojén
Colour map 4, grid B5
Population: 1,961

Continue through Ojén and over the pass and after 4 km turn left through the pine forest. From here a narrow, scenic road leads to the **Refugio de Juanar** (see page 267) and a walking track leads through woodlands of sweet chestnut and almond trees and on past olive groves to a mirador at 1,000 m, from where there are stupendous views over Marbella, the coast and, on clear days, Morocco. Allow 1½ hours for this walk. Just before the mirador another track leads up to the top of the limestone peak at 1,215 m that overlooks Marbella. There are many other walking trails, mostly leading from the Refugio. You could even walk back down through the woods to Ojén. The wildlife is incredible, with a wide range of flowers, including orchids, butterflies and birds. Small family groups of ibex are not uncommon; if these are elusive there is a compensatory bronze statue of one set on a rock above the mirador. During the spring

Baring all on the Costa

Even during the Franco dictatorship, topless sunbathing was beginning to appear on the Costa del Sol, despite warnings by the patrolling Guardia Civil to cover up. Today, the practice is commonplace and full nudism is permissible in certain areas.

Nudism (or naturism) probably began in Scandinavia in the early years of the 20th century, but the first purpose-built nudist resort did not appear on the Costa del Sol until 1979 at Costa Natura, just to the west of Estepona. Here, there are apartments, a supermarket, watersports and many other facilities. Local authorities have recently begun to realize that nudist beaches can be part of the wide range of facilities a resort might offer and they have officially designated certain sites for naturism. Indeed some sites may have signs banning the wearing of costumes (a good ploy to deter the peeping Tom). Other

beaches, whilst not official sites, are widely accepted as locations for nudism.

Such locations often attract the poseur and voyeur, but the atmosphere is generally healthy, particularly at weekends, when Spanish families appear in droves. If you want to sample the delights of nudism (and don't forget to apply high factor cream to the parts which the sun does not normally reach!), you could try the following sites in Málaga province: Benalnatura, beneath the cliffs to the west of Benalmádena; the dunes to the west of Puerto Cabopino; Almarat beach, Vélez Málaga district. In Cádiz province there is the southern part of the beach at Bolonia and Caños de Meca near Cape Trafalgar. There are also a number of sites in Almería province, where the Andalucían Nudist Association has its headquarters; for further information, contact the association at Calle Principe Felipe 11, Apartado de Correos 301, Almería.

and autumn migrations birds of prey can be seen en route to and from the Straits of Gibraltar, while booted and Bonelli's eagles breed in the vicinity. Other breeding birds include crossbills, Dartford warblers, blue rock thrushes, firecrests and crested tits. The area can be crowded with picnickers on Sunday.

Puerto Banús

Floating gin palaces alongside gold Rolls Royces and tourists hoping to glimpse the famous are just some of the sights here

The area between Marbella and Puerto Banús is known as the golden mile and is lined with expensive properties including that of King Faud of Saudi Arabia with an adjacent mosque – a return of the Arabs to the area bringing the history full circle. Puerto Banús itself is a marina development some 6 km west of Marbella and the haunt of the famous and the notorious. The harbour is backed by expensive apartments, boutiques, restaurants and nightclubs.

Casino Nueva Andalucía at *Hotel Andalucía Plaza*, Nueva Andalucía, T952810919, has got a games room with American and French Roulette, Black Jack, Punto y Banca, fruit machines and a restaurant.

The chief aim of the **Centro de Observación Marina** is to study marine species, but the centre is open to the public. There are 22 tanks holding 50 different species, including sharks, conger eels and sun fish. ■ *1000-2400. €4.25. T952818767.*

A flea and antique market is held next to the bullring on Saturday mornings.

San Pedro de Alcántara

About 10 km west of Marbella is San Pedro de Alcántara. San Pedro is largely undeveloped, being a kilometre or so back from the beach. This area of wasteland, however, is rapidly becoming urbanized, with a planned marina and a promenade running all the way to Marbella. Market day is Thursday. For accommodation, try **A** *El Cortijo Blanco*, Carretera de Cádiz, Km 172, T952780900, F952780916; an Andalucían style hotel with 311 rooms, pleasant gardens, pool and wheelchair access. There is also

D *El Cid*, Calle Extremadura 11, T952780639, which has 28 simple but good value rooms.

There are three important archaeological sites in the area west of Marbella dating from Roman times. All are easily accessible.

The centre of the **Basílica de Vega del Mar** site consists of a seventh-century Roman basilica. The plan is still clear to see, with three naves which would have separated major clergy, men and women, and the bases of some substantial pillars. The basilica is aligned east/west and at each end are semi-circular apses, showing the link with the North African churches of the time. At the north end of the westerly apse is a remarkable baptismal font, some 2 m deep and often filled with rain water to give a realistic idea of the total immersion practised at that time. Surrounding the basilica is a necropolis where 187 tombs have been unearthed, which are aligned east-west. The earliest tombs were triangular in cross section and probably made of wood. They were later square-shaped and lined with round stones. Later still there were family tombs of brick. The more affluent had their tombs lined with marble. There are some small tombs, apparently of children who died in infancy. ■ *Getting there: leave the N340 at the roundabout at San Pedro Alcántara and take the beach road. Turn along the last road on the right before the beach. After 500 m look for a grove of mature eucalyptus trees on the left. Alternatively go to the end of the beach promenade and walk along the beach for 150 m before turning inland to the eucalyptus trees.*

The second site is 400 m along the beach to the west of the basilica next to the *urbanización* of Guadalmedina. Look for the round watch tower, which is adjacent. These are third-century Roman baths, the **Termas de las Bovedas** (or vaults), which were possibly part of the town of Silniana, destroyed by an earthquake in 365 AD. It is a building of two octagonal floors, using a durable mortar of limestone and beach sand. The building was constructed around an octagonal patio nearly 10 m in diameter. Parallel to the walls are the remains of a 1½-m deep octagonal pool. The upper floor consists of a circular gallery with access to several small rooms. Discovered in the subsoil are the remains of a hypocaust and a praeforium (where the water was heated). Assuming that they are in fact baths, then they are clearly some of the most important discoveries of early Roman times, but archaeologists are divided and some experts consider them to be storage tanks for water carried in nearby aqueducts (these were noted in a manuscript by a historian in 1663 who described them as 'over a league in length', but which have now been lost). Having survived since the third century, Las Bovedas are now, ironically, in danger of falling down and a planned €24,000 has been allocated to secure the structure.

The third site is the large Roman villa at **Río Verde**, located to the south of the coast road between Marbella and Puerto Banús. It dates from the late first century or early second century. The remains show the *peristilo* (round patio with columns) surrounded by three corridors and five rooms. The main interest is in the mosaics, which are mainly in black and white. The room which faces north (and can easily be seen from the road) contains a splendid mosaic of Medusa's head, with four snakes among the strands of her hair and two more coiled around her neck. She is surrounded by geometrical patterns enclosing ducks and herons. The other rooms have mosaics showing culinary items and nautical themes. The mosaics suggest that the owner of the villa was of the dominant social class at the time and probably involved in commerce and trade. ■ *Getting there: owing to the problems of turning left from the* autovía, *approach from the* west. If arriving from Marbella, go to the Puerto Banús underpass and return. After crossing the Río Verde bridge, take the first road to the right and follow the signs. The remains are tucked in amongst modern-day villas.

All three sites are enclosed by railings, but you can still get a good view. For a closer look it's worth getting keys from the tourist office in Marbella or San Pedro. The Marbella office organizes occasional guided tours of all three sites.

Estepona
Colour map 4, grid C4
Population: 39,178

The most Spanish of the Costa resorts, Estepona has an attractive seafront with a promenade backing a shingle beach, with a few low-rise apartment blocks. The town itself has some interesting corners, including two attractive squares, the Plaza Arce and the Plaza Las Flores. The **tourist office** is at Avenida San Lorenzo 1, T952802002, and is open Monday-Friday 0930-2100, Saturday and Sunday 0930-1330. The main restaurants and tapas bars are along Calle Terraza.

Sleeping Book ahead for accommodation in Jul and Aug. Both luxury hotels are on the main road but close to the beach: **AL** *Atalaya Park*, Ctra de Cádiz, 168.5 km, T952884801, F952885735. 246 rooms. Pool, golf, tennis, a/c. **AL** *El Paraíso*, Ctra de Cádiz, Km 167, T952883000, F952882019. 195 rooms. A/c, pools, tennis, golf. **C** *Diana Park*, N340 Km 168, T952887659. The first ecological hotel on the Costa del Sol, which boasts anti-allergy paint, use of natural fibres in furnishings, no fitted carpets, environmentally friendly soap and detergents and the treatment of its swimming pool water with ozone instead of chlorine. **C** *Santa Marta*, Ctra de Cádiz, 167 km, T952888177, F952888180. 37 rooms. Pool, restaurant. There are 10 *pensiones* of which the following near Plaza las Flores can be recommended: **E** *La Malagueña*, C Castillo s/n, T952800011. 14 rooms. **E** *San Miguel*, C Terraza 16, T952802616.

Costa Natura

Three kilometres west of Estepona is Costa Natura, a long established naturist complex. Casual visitors are discouraged and membership cards from naturist clubs in your own country must be produced. For information, T952801500.

Casares
Colour map 4, grid C4
Population: 3,144

Three kilometres west of Estepona a winding road leads inland for 18 km to Casares, claimed to be the most photographed village in Spain. Its whitewashed houses clothe the side of a hill which is capped by the ruins of a 13th-century Moorish fortress on Roman foundations built in the time of Ibn al Jatib. The fort was a centre of resistance against the French during the Peninsular War. Next to the fort is the Iglesia de la Encarnación. It was built in 1505 and has a brick Mudéjar tower (the remainder of the church is constructed of brick and stone, partly covered in plaster). The interior has three naves and a small chapel, but as it was partially destroyed during the Civil War, it is nowadays boarded up. The castle and church share their hilltop position with the local cemetery, which is meticulously kept (the view from the hill top shows a new one being built on the outskirts). On the cliff below is a breeding colony of lesser kestrels, while there are spectacular views down to the coast towards Gibraltar and North Africa.

Casares is said to have derived its name from Julius Caesar, who may have been cured of his liver complaints by the sulphur springs at nearby Manilva. The 17th-century Church of San Sebastián, which can be visited on the way to the fortress, is a simple whitewashed containing the image of the Virgen del Rosario del Campo. In the adjacent square is a statue of Blas Infante who was a native of Casares and leader of Andalucía's nationalist

Sweet chestnuts

Sweet chestnut trees (Castenea sativa), or castaños, can be found in many mountainous parts of Spain, but nowhere are they more important than in the Serrania de Ronda, where they cover an area of over 4,000 ha. Their autumn colours also add to the attraction of the sierra landscape. The trees can grow to over 30 m in height and have dark glossy narrow leaves with toothed edges. The twigs bear long yellow catkins in the spring and their fruit are flattened triangular nuts borne in threes within a prickly case. There are actually several varieties of sweet chestnut, including tempranas, which ripen early and pilongas, which produce a drier fruit. Sweet chestnuts get their distinctive shape (a short trunk with branches sprouting directly above) from the somewhat aggressive pruning process that happens every three years, aimed at optimizing the crop.

In the Serranía de Ronda, the chestnut woods are family-owned and the crop forms a major source of income for many people. In a good year, when rain falls at the right time, the annual harvest can weigh as much as 5,000,000 kg. All the family members, augmented by casual workers, help with the picking and packaging using traditional methods, including donkeys for transport.

The chestnuts are said to have important nutritional and medicinal qualities and they are usually eaten raw or roasted. There are, however, a number of local recipes, some of which may go back to Moorish times. These include chestnuts in brandy, chestnuts in syrup and chestnut cream.

Much of the crop is exported, mainly to the UK, France and the US. The wood is also highly prized for its resistance to disease and changes in the weather, but it is used increasingly less due to its high price relative to other wood. It is still used, however, to make furniture in some parts of Andalucia, like the Sierra de Aracena in Huelva province.

movement. He was executed by Franco's supporters. In the square *Bar-Restaurant Claveles*, with farming implements festooning its walls, is a good place to eat, specializing in game dishes such as rabbit, partridge and quail. Across the road is *Bar Los Amigos*, popular with locals and providing a good range of tapas.

The alternative route back to the coast at Manilva passes through attractive vineyards and limestone scenery, although the road surface is poor. There are two buses a day from Estepona to Casares, but should you decide to stay overnight, the only viable possibility is the **E** *Pensión Plaza*, in the main square, T952894088, with nine rooms. From Casares, it is an exciting 20-minute drive to Gaucín (see page 282), the road initially dipping down into the valley of the Río Genal before climbing up a series of hairpin bends to the village.

Ronda

This charming, historic town is located on a limestone plateau in the Serranía de Ronda mountains, astride a spectacular gorge – El Tajo – some 120 m deep. Ronda is divided into two contrasting districts on each side of the gorge. To the south is **La Ciudad,** the old town containing many Moorish remains including its haphazard street plan. To the north of El Tajo is **El Mercadillo**, a largely modern district graced by what is claimed to be the oldest **bullring** in Spain. Ronda has a more extreme climate that the coast, with colder winters (snow is not uncommon on the surrounding mountains) and very hot summers when mid-afternoon temperatures average 33°C.

Colour map 4, grid B4
Population: 33,806

Málaga Province

Ins and outs

Getting there
See also page 281
Portillo **buses** arrive at Plaza Concepción García Redondo, T952872262. The **train** station is on Av Andalucía. Both are near the Mercadillo area of Ronda. **Parking** is always a problem in Ronda. The best choice is the underground car park in the Plaza del Socorro, but you will need a street plan well in advance. The most suitable alternative is to head for the centre of town, cross the gorge and use the car park to the left of the bullring. You will need a parking ticket, but the helpful attendants will help you with the machines.

Getting around
Ronda is easily explored on foot, but there is a **taxi** rank in Plaza Carmen Abela. Bicycles can be hired from *Biciserranía*, opposite the bus station.

Tourist offices
The tourist office in Plaza de España, T952871272, and the staff are usually very helpful, unless harassed by hordes of tourists. It's open Mon-Fri 0900-1900, Sat-Sun and holidays 1000-1400. It has town plans plus details of firms offering walking and horseriding tours in the nearby sierras. There is also a small tourist office in the Casa de Mondragón, see page 278. For more information on Ronda, see www.andalucia.org

History
Ronda has a long and fascinating history. The Iberians named it Arunda; the Romans' name for Ronda was probably Arundo. It enjoyed its most prosperous times, particularly under Abu Nur, during the Moorish occupation, which lasted nearly eight centuries. The Moors' fortification of Ronda, their regional capital, was legendary but, due to internal divisions, it took a Christian army of 13,000 cavalry and 25,000 infantrymen only seven days to capture it in 1485. What remained of the Moorish Alcazaba was almost totally destroyed by the French during the Peninsular War in 1809. Ronda also saw plenty of action in the Civil War, when representatives of both sides were thrown into the Tajo. In the early years of the 19th century Ronda was a popular retreat for British officers based in Gibraltar. Now the British come in coachloads from the Costa, but this does not seem to spoil the essential charm of the town.

Sights

The Tajo, formed by the river Guadalévin, splits Ronda into two unequal sections. To the south is the small old town, known as La Ciudad, and its suburb of San Francisco, which lies outside the old walls. To the north is the much more recent El Mercadillo.

Around El Tajo
The Tajo is spanned by three bridges. The lowest and oldest is the **Puente Arabe**, a Moorish structure which has been much restored. Next is the **Puente Viejo**, dating from the 17th century and still taking vehicles. Thirdly, there is the so-called **Puente Nuevo** or new bridge. Beneath the Puente Nuevo was the former prison and then a tapas bar. Despite its foul smelling raw sewerage, the photogenic Tajo makes for excellent birdwatching, with rock doves, choughs and crag martins whirling through the gorge. To view the Tajo from El Mercadillo side of town, leave Plaza España along Calle Villanueva. At the end turn right along Calle Los Remedios and proceed downhill. After 150 m, any small alleyway to the right will lead to a series of beautifully terraced gardens known as **La Mina,** giving stupendous views of the gorge.

Ronda

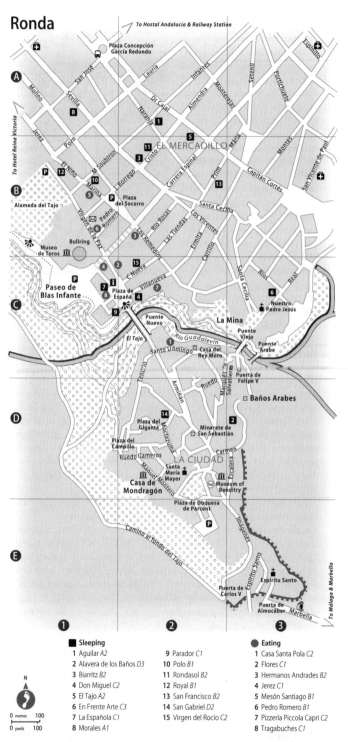

To Hostal Andalucia & Railway Station

Plaza Concepción García Redondo

A

To Hotel Reina Victoria

EL MERCADILLO

B

Alameda del Tajo

Plaza del Socorro

Bullring

Museo de Toros

Paseo de Blas Infante

C

Plaza de España

Puente Nuevo

El Tajo

Río Guadalevín

Casa del Rey Moro

La Mina

Nuestro Padre Jesús

Puente Viejo

Puente Árabe

Puerta de Felipe V

Baños Árabes

D

Plaza del Gigante

Minarete de San Sebastián

Plaza del Campillo

LA CIUDAD

Santa María Mayor

Museum of Banditry

Casa de Mondragón

Plaza de Duquesa de Parcent

E

Camino al fondo del Tajo

Espíritu Santo

Puerta de Carlos V

Puerta de Almocábar

Marbella

To Málaga & Marbella

Málaga Province

1　　**2**　　**3**

N

0 metres 100
0 yards 100

■ **Sleeping**
1 Aguilar *A2*
2 Alavera de los Baños *D3*
3 Biarritz *B2*
4 Don Miguel *C2*
5 El Tajo *A2*
6 En Frente Arte *C3*
7 La Española *C1*
8 Morales *A1*
9 Parador *C1*
10 Polo *B1*
11 Rondasol *B2*
12 Royal *B1*
13 San Francisco *B2*
14 San Gabriel *D2*
15 Virgen del Rocío *C2*

● **Eating**
1 Casa Santa Pola *C2*
2 Flores *C1*
3 Hermanos Andrades *B2*
4 Jerez *C1*
5 Mesón Santiago *B1*
6 Pedro Romero *B1*
7 Pizzería Piccola Capri *C2*
8 Tragabuches *C1*

La Ciudad You can cross the gorge by the **Puente Viejo,** originally a Roman bridge, but rebuilt in 1616. Note to the left the Iglesia de Nuestro Padre Jesús, outside of which is the water trough known as El Fuente de los Ocho Caños – the fountain of the Eight Springs. Cross the bridge and pass under the arch of the **Puerta de Felipe V.** From here the distinctive roof of the **Baños Arabes** can be seen with its cupolas and star-shaped roof windows. The building is made of brick and inside are octagonal columns supporting typical Moorish arches. The usual hot and cold rooms were fed from a nearby stream.

After years of neglect and erratic opening, the baths have had a major renovation and are now open on a permanent basis. Information boards have recently been installed and guides can occasionally be seen, so that you can tag onto a group that is being shown around. ■ *Tue 0900-1330 and 1600-1800, Wed-Sat 0930-1530. Free. T952873889.*

Return to the arch and climb up the steep hill of Calle Santo Domingo. Further up the hill to the right is the **Casa del Rey Moro**, the House of the Moorish King, an 18th-century mansion built on Moorish foundations. At the rear of the house is a stairway cut into the rocky side of the gorge, said to have been used by Christian slaves to bring water to their Moorish masters. Hopefully the water was less polluted in those days than it is today. The Casa del Rey Moro has recently been opened to the public, who can view the 'water mine' from the hanging gardens, which were constructed by a French landscape gardener in 1912. Take care with the 365 steps, which are steep and often slippery. The stench of the river at the bottom, and the thought of climbing back, may make you conclude that the entrance fee is as steep as the steps. ■ *Daily 1000-2000. €3.60. T952187200.*

Calle Santo Domingo now reaches the top of the hill at the Puente Nuevo, where there are some antique shops that are well worth a browse.

Calle Armiñán leads through La Ciudad from Puente Nuevo to the edge of town. Worth seeking out on the right is the tiny Plaza del Gigante, with the **Casa del Gigante** (the Giant's House), a 14th-century Moorish palace. Sadly, the house is not at present open to the public. Further along Calle Armiñán on the right is another Moorish feature, the **Minarete de San Sebastián,** a 14th-century Nazrid style tower that has survived from a mosque. At the end of the same road are two gates in the town walls. The oldest is the **Puerta del Almocáber** with a horseshoe arch and two matching towers. The name is believed to have derived from the Arabic word for cemetery, and presumably the arch led to burial grounds, which would have been outside the walls. Alongside is the **Puerta de Carlos V**, dating from the 16th century and named after Ferdinand's successor. Close to the two arches is the **Iglesia del Espíritu Santo** (Church of the Holy Spirit), a sturdy edifice dating from 1505. ■ *1000-1830. €0.60.*

The focal point of the Ciudad is the leafy square of the **Plaza de Duquesa de Parcent,** which is dominated by the **Iglesia de Santa María Mayor**.

All Andalucía loves a bandit

Banditry or bandolerismo *has always, until quite recently, been an acceptable occupation in Andalucía. With its rugged countryside, dense forest, caves and mountains, Andalucía has been profitable territory for the brigand and smuggler. Many of the* bandoleros *were Robin Hood-like characters, who stole from the rich but made sure that the less fortunate in society were well looked after. Many were forced into banditry because of the appalling social conditions in the rural areas. As such, their activities functioned as a safety valve against social dissent, a point noted by the English writer Gerald Brenan, 'In the eyes of the country people he was a hero, the friend of the poor and a champion against their oppressors'. The more privileged in society were not, however, so appreciative and their protests led in 1844 to the formation of the Guardia Civil, whose main role was to protect the affluent against the brigands.*

Undoubtedly the most notorious bandit was José María Hinojosa Cobacho – known as El Tempranillo – who was born near Lucena in Córdoba province in 1800. At the age of 22 he claimed that 'the king may reign in Spain, but in the sierra I do'. He was referring to the Sierra Morena, which runs along the entire length of northern Andalucía and through which all transport to Madrid had to pass as it delivered the riches from the New World. Profitable territory for a bandit, especially as El Tempranillo demanded an ounce of gold for each wagon or carriage which crossed his land. Said to be blond (he may have been a descendant of one of the German

settlers who came to the area in the mid-18th century), El Tempranillo was noted for his gallantry towards women (kissing their hands as he removed the rings) and for his sense of humour. It is said that on one occasion he arrived at a venta *and asked to share some soup. He was told by the diners that there were no spoons left, so he fashioned a spoon from a piece of bread and consumed the soup and his bread. He then produced a gun and revealed his identity, requesting that the terrified diners eat their spoons, as he had done, until their teeth cracked. El Tempranillo was eventually treacherously murdered by a former comrade.*

The last of the notorious bandoleros *was José Mingolla Gallardi, known as Pasos Largos. This nickname means, literally, 'Big Feet', but translates more aptly as 'Strider' or 'Loper' after José's father. Both had a characteristic loping gait that enabled them to cover huge distances on their hunting trips in the Serranía de Ronda. Hailing from the village of El Burgo, Pasos Largos took to the hills after committing several murders. He quickly became a legendary figure and although once captured and imprisoned, he soon returned to his bandit's way of life. He was eventually killed in 1934, after a shoot out with the Guardia Civil.*

This long history of banditry does much to explain the Andalucían's tolerant attitude towards law breaking. A person who can get away with a swindle or a scam is often respected, while someone who can put one over on bureaucracy or authority is something of a hero.

Málaga Province

Originally a 13th-century mosque, it was rebuilt by the Christians but retains much of the Moorish architecture. It has a late Gothic nave and heavily carved wooden Baroque choir stalls and an impressive *retablo*. There is also a *tesoro* – a museum of church treasures, including a large amount of silverware and ancient bibles. In the entrance porch are some Moorish arches covered with Arab calligraphy and nearby part of a *mihrab* has been exposed. On the frontal exterior of the church is a balcony facing the square, which provided a position for dignitaries to watch bullfights before the main ring in the Mercadillo was built. ■ *1000-1800. €1.50.*

At the far end of the plaza is the site of the **Alcázar**, destroyed by the French in 1809. Completing the square are the Ayuntamiento (in a building which was formerly the 18th-century barracks), the police station, law courts and two small convents.

Leave the Plaza Duquesa de Parcent via the narrow Calle Manuel Montero and head for the **Casa de Mondragón**, undoubtedly the most important civil monument in Ronda. It was believed to be the residence of Abomelic, son of the Sultan of Morocco in the early 14th century. From the mid-13th century Ronda was mostly part of the kingdom of Granada and the last Moorish governor of Granada also resided in the palace. When Ronda fell to the Christians, Fernando and Isabel adapted the palace for their use. The outer façade of the building dates from the 18th century, but much of the interior is Moorish or Mudéjar, with filligree work and horseshoe arches and mosaics. There are a number of delightful patios with fountains and stunning views over the Tajo.

Much of the Casa de Mondragón is taken up with the **Museo Arqueológico**. The history section looks at the world of caves, Roman and Moslem funeral remains, and the historical evolution of Ronda. The ethnography section has displays on the production of cork oak, cheese and pig products. The third section deals with the environment and in particular the local Parque Natural de Grazalema. The audio visual displays are well presented and include a walk-in cave and a metallurgy room. ■ *Mon-Fri 1000-1800, Sat, Sun and holidays 1000-1500. €1.80, children under 14 free.* A return to the Puente Nuevo could be made via the Plaza del Campillo, from where there is a path down into the Tajo through fields that are full of wildflowers in the spring.

Museums Back in Calle Armiñán at Number 29 is the newly opened **Museo de Bandolero**. Ronda is an apt place for such a museum to be located as the mountains around the town abounded with Robin Hood characters in the 18th, 19th and even the early 20th centuries (see box). There are five rooms in the museum displaying documents, weapons, maps and a mock tavern of the times. Some of the great figures of banditry are illustrated, including José María Hinojosa Cobacho, alias 'El Tempranillo', José Mingolla Gallardi, alias 'Pasos Largos' and 'Shotgun Getares'. The forces of law and order are also not forgotten. ■ *Daily 1030-1800. €2.40.*

Nearby, are two other small museums. In Callejón del Arto is the gruesome **Museo de Instrumentos Europeos de Tortura**, which exhibits instruments of torture from the Middle Ages to the 17th century. ■ *Daily 1000-2100. €3.* At Number 65 Calle Armiñán is the **Museo Histórico Popular de la Serranía**, displaying folk artefacts of the region. ■ *Daily 1000-1830. €1.20.*

El Mercadillo This part of the town has less in the way of monuments, but is not without interest. It is dominated by the **Plaza de Toros**, or bullring, built in 1785 and claimed to be the oldest in Spain. It holds 5,000 people and was used as the setting for the film *Carmen*. Outside are the statues of the *toreros* Antonio and Cayetano Ordóñez. Under the bullring is a small **Museo de Toros** and whatever your feelings are about bullfighting, this is a fascinating place, full of torobilia such as photographs, posters, toreadors' clothing and bulls' heads, all with suitable background music. ■ *Daily 1000-1800. €3.60. Tickets can be obtained from the souvenir shop to the right of the bullring entrance.*

Between the bullring and the Puente Nuevo is the **Plaza de España,** which has undergone something of a facelift in recent years. On the east side of the Plaza de España is Ronda's **Parador,** sympathetically converted from the shell

The modern bullfight

The original bullfights were fought from a horse using a long spear. The modern form of bullfighting on foot began in Ronda, when Francisco Romero jumped into the ring to save a dismounted rider who was being gored by distracting the bull with his hat. But it was his grandson, Pedro Romero (1754-1839), who laid down the ritual of modern bullfighting using a sword and red cape. With his formal style, Romero killed nearly 6,000 bulls without once being gored. Today there is a monument to Romero in the Alameda. The nearby bullring was opened in 1785 and it is

unusual in that the seating is fully covered. There has been a long string of famous toreros from Ronda, the latest being Antonio Ordóñez, who owns a nearby estate.

The artist Goya painted a number of pictures at the Ronda bullring. Every September there is a Pedro Romero festival, when corridas goyescas *take place with the bullfighters wearing the costumes of Goya's time. The Ronda style of bullfighting is regarded by aficionados as rather severe and ascetic, compared with the more exhibitionist approach of, say, Sevilla.*

---

of the old town hall. At the rear of the parador is a landscaped pathway with viewing terraces known as the **Paseo de Blas Infante.** This forms a sort of linear mirador running almost to *Hotel Reina Victoria*, with superb vertiginous views over the cliff edge, down to the river Guadalévin and away to the distant sierras. Apart from the view, this is a marvellous birdwatching spot as peregrine falcons breed on the cliffs and during the summer alpine swifts and crag martins zoom along the rock face. Further along the *paseo* is a new concert hall and next to it a shady park, the **Alameda del Tajo,** with fountains and a small aviary. At *Corpus Christi* the central pathway of the Alameda is covered with flower carpets laid out in patterns.

The commercial centre of Ronda is to be found in the streets opposite the bullring. The main shopping street is the pedestrianized Calle Carrera Espinal, which leads to the pleasant Plaza del Socorro, lined with restaurants and tapas bars. Several blocks away to the east, but worth the walk is an old 16th-century inn, the **Posada de las Animas** (the Inn of souls). It is claimed that Cervantes once slept here. Nowadays the only sleepers are the *pensionistas* of the town, as this is now an old peoples' home.

Essentials

AL *Parador de Ronda*, Plaza de España, T955590069, F952878080, 71 rooms. Built within the original façade of the old town hall with spectacular views over the gorge; restaurant. **A** *Alavera de los Baños*, C San Miguel s/n, T952879143, www.andalucia.com /alavera Delightful small hotel with a restaurant, located between the town walls and the Baños Arabes. Tasteful rooms and good food. **A** *En Frente Arte*, C Real 40, T952879088, www.enfrentearte.com A combined hotel, art school and gallery. Converted house with 11 rooms, one in a 13th-century tower, in the old part of town. Price includes breakfast (served until 1500), lunch, internet use and free 24-hr bar. Rooms with bath, TV, minibar; some with own terrace. Great views, beautiful patios, pool, sauna, games and music rooms, restaurant. **A** *Reina Victoria*, C Jerez 25, T952871240, F952871075, www.ronda .net/usuar/reinavictoria 90 rooms with bath, TV, a/c and heating. Beautifully located Edwardian hotel built by the English, one room is a small museum dedicated to the poet Rainer María Rilke, good views, particularly from the terrace, pool, garage. **A** *San Gabriel*, C José Holgado 19, T952190392, F952190117,

Sleeping

See inside front cover for hotel price codes

Most of the cheaper places are located in the heart of the Mercadillo area

Málaga Province

www.hotelsangabriel.com One of only 2 hotels in La Ciudad, this is a superb restoration of an 18th-century town house.

B *La Española*, C José Aparicio 3, T952871051, F952878001. Renovated *fonda*, now a modern hotel. Good views over the Tajo from some rooms. **B** *Don Miguel*, C Villanueva 8, T952877722, F952878377. 19 rooms. Small hotel adjacent to the gorge, comfortable, clean, excellent restaurant, garage. **B** *Polo*, C Mariano Soubirón 8, T952872447, F952872449, hpolo@ronda.net. 33 rooms. Traditional town-centre hotel, restaurant, a/c. **C** *El Tajo*, C Dr Cajal 7, T952876236, F952875099. 67 rooms. Garage, in the centre of the Mercadillo. **D** *Royal*, C Virgen de la Paz 42, T952871141, F952878132, www.ronda.net /usuar/hotelroyal 29 rooms with a/c, heating and bath. On main road opposite Alameda, can be noisy, restaurant. **D** *Morales*, C Sevilla 51, T952871538. 13 rooms. Clean and reliable. **D** *San Francisco*, C Prim 8, T952873299. Good value, all 16 rooms with bath. **D** *Virgen del Rocío*, C Nueva 18, T952877425. Close to the Plaza de España and recently refurbished. **E** *Aguilar*, C Naranja 28, T952871994. 17 rooms. **E** *Andalucía*, Av Martínez 19, T952875450. 11 rooms. Opposite railway station, clean, with bath. Highly recommended. **E** *Biarritz*, C Cristo 7, T952872910. 21 rooms. Pets accepted. **E** *Rondasol*, C Cristo 11, T952874497. 15 rooms, some with bath.

Camping A number of campsites have sprung up in the Ronda area in recent years. The best is the highly recommended *Camping El Sur*, just out of town on the Algeciras road, T952875939. Open throughout the year. Pool, bar, restaurant and bungalows.

Eating
The better restaurants in Ronda serve the traditional food of the area, including cocidos and game dishes

Expensive *Don Miguel*, Plaza de España, T952871090. Probably the best food in Ronda, certainly the best view, with its terraces overlooking the bridge and gorge. *Tragabuches*, C José Aparicio 1, T952190291. Often claimed to be one of the best restaurants in Andalucía. Sophisticated ambience and complex cuisine. *Pedro Romero*, C Virgen de la Paz, opposite bullring. Regional décor and food. **Mid-range** *Jerez*, Paseo de Blas Infante 2, T952872098. By the bullring, happily caters for both tourists and locals alike. *Hermanos Andrades*, C Los Remedios 1. Good value. *Mesón Santiago*, C Marina 3, T952871367. Traditional Ronda restaurant with local dishes. *Pizzería Piccola Capri*, C Villanueva 18, T952873943. One of the few restaurants in Ronda serving international food, good atmosphere and views over the Tajo. *Tenorio*, C Tenorio 1, T952874936. Local dishes. **Cheap** *Casa Santa Pola*, C Santo Domingo 3, T952879208. Diners greeted with free sherry, view over gorge, *menú del día* €7.25. *Cervecería El Patio*, C Carrera Espinel 100, T952871015. Patio dining area. *Flores*, C Virgen de la Paz 9. Popular with tourists, cheap *menú del día*; *La Ibense*, C Espinel 42. Good for ice creams and snacks. The restaurant at the railway station is good. Try also the café at the bus station for a small snack and a large slice of Spanish life. For the best **tapas bars** try the Plaza del Socorro, particularly *Marisquería Paco*. Elsewhere, the following are recommended: *Bodega La Esquina*, C Remedios 24 and *Bodega La Giralda*, C Nueva 19.

Fiestas & festivals
24 Jan *Fiesta de la Virgen de la Paz* Patron saint of Ronda. **May** *Feria de Mayo*, or May Fair, celebrates the Reconquest. **Early Sep** *Pedro Romero Festival* with *corridas goyescas* (bullfights in Goyaesque attire). There is also an *International Folk Festival* in **Sep** and a *flamenco* festival on the last Sat in **Aug** as part of the *Feria de Ronda*.

Shopping
The main pedestrianized shopping street is the C de la Bola (confusingly shown on some maps as C Carrera Espinel) which runs east from the bullring for approximately 1 km. Regional specialities including saddlery, wrought iron work and antiques. There is a street market held on Sun at the Barrio de San Francisco near the south walls of the old town. Shops on the C Nueva sell equipment for camping. Local craft shops include *Artesanía Arte Ronda*, Plaza del Teniente Arce s/n, and *Cerámica Rondeña Ramón*, Plaza de España s/n.

The municipal sports stadium is on the industrial estate to the north of the town, **Sport**
T952870506. **Hot air balloon flights** Contact Aviación del Sol, T952877249. **Tennis** T952871438.

Bus The *Portillo* **bus** company runs frequent services to Marbella, 4 coaches a day to **Transport**
Málaga, 1 to La Linea and 3 to Cádiz (one of which proceeds to Jerez). The *Comes* and
Lara bus companies serve the *pueblos blancos* to the north and west of Ronda.
Train The town is on the Algeciras to Bobodilla **railway** line and 5 trains a day run in
each direction. The train journey from Algeciras runs through a number of picturesque
towns and villages including Gaucín, Castellar de la Frontera and San Roque and is a
highly recommended way of reaching Ronda.

Banks The main bank in the town is the *Caja de Ahorros de Ronda* in C Virgen de la **Directory**
Paz opposite the bullring. Other banks have appeared in recent years, but they are still
rather thin on the ground, while the commission they charge on TCs varies enormously. There are also a few establishments offering change facilities in the bullring
area. **Medical services Emergencies**: Clínica Espinillo, T952875882; *Cruz Roja*, C Jerez
56, T952871464. **Hospitals**: *Hospital General Básico de la Serranía*, Ctra del Burgo 1,
T952871540. **Communications Post office**: Correos, Virgen de la Paz 20,
T952872557. Open Mon-Fri 0800-1500, Sat 0900-1300. **Telephones**: *locotorios* on C de
la Bola and C El Niño. **Useful addresses Garages/repairs**: filling stations are scarce.
One is located on the south edge of the town, another on the north bypass. There are
no petrol stations between Ronda and the coast. There are several garages and repair
workshops on the El Fuerte industrial estate.

Around Ronda

The so-called *pueblos blancos*, or white towns, including Grazalema, the gateway to the Sierra de Grazalema with some excellent walks, are easily reached
from Ronda; see page 185.

These are the ruins of the first-century Roman town of Acinipo, once a Neo- **Ronda La Vieja**
lithic and later a Phoenician settlement. Its peak period as a Roman town was
in the first century AD, when it was a prosperous agricultural centre. Much of
the site is rubble-strewn and only the Roman theatre survives in any recognizable form. There are superb views of the surrounding countryside, particularly
towards Olvera. ■ *Tue-Fri 1000-1800, Sat, Sun and festivals 1200-1830. Free.
Getting there: take the A473 Arcos road out of Ronda towards Algodonales. Turn
right after 9 km along a minor road signposted to Ronda la Vieja. 6 km later you
will arrive at a farmhouse, where the farmer will give you a plan of the site.*

This prehistoric cave is located some 20 km southwest of Ronda and was dis- **Cueva de la**
covered in 1905 by José Boullón, while searching for guano to use as a fertil- **Pileta**
izer. Later exploration found skeletons of Paleolithic Man plus shards of
pottery and other artefacts dating from 25,000 BC, but the most significant
finds were the wall paintings of fish, a goat, a deer and a pregnant mare,
which had been executed in charcoal and red and yellow ochres. There are
also some abstract signs and symbols, which it is suggested might be connected with magic ritual, but most visitors will come to the conclusion that
they are some form of tallying system. There are also some fine limestone
formations, such as stalactites and stalagmites, but as these are not lit they
are difficult to appreciate. There are also thousands of bats hanging from the
roof of the cave.

Your guide will be one of the Boullón family, who live in the farmhouse in the valley. If there is nobody around when you arrive, don't worry, you will be seen from the farmhouse and a guide will eventually appear. If a party is inside the cave there will be a notice on the grill at the entrance. One in every two or three visitors will be given an oil lamp to carry. Extra torches are useful. The lack of commercialization of the cave adds to its charm. For accommodation there is **B** *Molino del Santo*, Barriada del Estación, 29370, in Benaoján, T952167151, F952167327, which has 12 rooms in a renovated water mill close to the cave. It is a good base for walking. ■ *Daily 1000-1300 and 1600-1800 in theory, but be prepared to wait for enough people to arrive to form a group. Visits last approximately 1 hr. Take warm clothing. €4.85-5.45, depending on the size of the group. The caves can get extremely busy during the summer, so arrive early to ensure gaining entry. Getting there: either take the A473 and turn left after 6 km south through Montajaque and Benaoján, or by taking the A369 towards Gaucín and Algeciras and turning right just after passing through Atajate. (If you take the Montajaque route, look out for the huge dam built in the 1920s, which lacks a reservoir because the water insists on seeping underground.) The nearest train and bus stops are in Benaoján.*

Benalauría
& Gaucín

The A369 from Ronda passes through Atajate, Benadalid, Algatocin and Gaucín. Just south of Benadalid a side road leads to the delightful hamlet of Benalauría, where the villagers have made their contribution to rural tourism by reviving local crafts and traditions. They have converted an old olive mill into a museum and put on the best Moors versus Christians battle in the region. For eating, try *Mesón La Molienda*, Calle Moralera 59, located in a rustic village house and offering mouthwatering local specialities.

Gaucín, which is set on a ridge, is worth a stop, although it looks considerably better from a distance than by closer inspection. Its Moorish castle, the Castillo de Aguila, so-called for its eagle's views to Gibraltar and North Africa, has been partially restored, and it was here that Guzmán el Bueno of Tarifa fame died in 1309 while attempting to capture the fortress. If you're driving, the one-way system around the narrow streets can be a considerable challenge. There are few accommodation possibilities in Gaucín, including **D** *Pensión Moncada*, Calle Luis Armillán sin número, T952151324, or you could try one of two English-owned farmhouses offering bed and breakfast in peaceful surroundings: **C** *Cortijo El Puerto del Negro*, Apartado 25, 29480 Gaucín, T/F952151239, four rooms plus two cottages in wilderness surroundings; and **C** *Finca la Almuña*, Apartado 20, 29480 Gaucín, T/F952151200, with six rooms, good home cooking and local riding and walking possibilities. A *turismo rural* office in Gaucín, T952151600, has details of houses to rent around Gaucín and sells maps of the area.

Córdoba Province

7

Córdoba Province

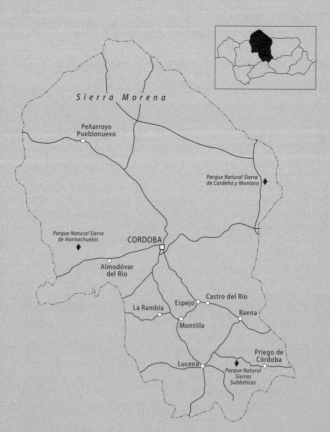

Sierra Morena

Peñarroyo
Pueblonuevo

Parque Natural Sierra
de Cardeña y Montora

Parque Natural Sierra
de Hornachuelos

CORDOBA

Almodóvar
del Río

Castro del Río

La Rambla   Espejo

Baena

Montilla

Priego de
Córdoba

Lucena

Parque Natural
Sierras
Subbéticas

The province of Córdoba is the most northerly of Andalucía's provinces and has a relaxed, unhurried appeal, particularly after the clamour of the Costa resorts. Even its main city, Córdoba, evokes a sense of calm. The province is completely landlocked; a patchwork of pine-clad hills, open plains and prosperous agricultural land with its broad valley neatly dissected by the Río Guadalquivir. At a lazy bend on the northern banks lies Córdoba with its magnificent Mezquita, the winding alleyways of the Judería and the ancient Arab quarter. More Moorish grandeur can be found a few miles away with the ruins of **Medina Azahara**, once the finest palace of the Caliphs.

In the north of the province is the **Sierra Morena**, which forms the border with Extremadura and Castilla provinces, rising in places to over 900 m. In the extreme northwest of the Sierra is the region known as **Los Pedroches**, famous for its ruined castles, Renaissance churches and unexpected storks' nests. The Sierra Morena has two **natural parks**: in the northeast is the Parque Natural de Sierra Cardeña Montoro, while in the west is the Parque Natural de la Sierra de Hornachuelos. Despite its raw and rugged beauty, the Sierra Morena attracts few tourists, as good a reason as any for a visit.

In the south of the province is the **Sistema Subbético**, consisting of limestone ranges and narrow valleys carpeted with cork oaks. There are four ranges within the Subbético rising to over 1,000 m, the whole forming a parque natural. In the west of this region is an unexpected group of wetland sites or zonas húmedas, covering some 10 sq km.

Córdoba

*The zenith of Córdoba's influence came in the 10th and 11th centuries when it was the western capital of the Islamic empire rivalling Baghdad in culture, sophistication and power. Although it is little more than a minor provincial capital today, the **Moorish** legacy lives on in the winding alleys of the old quarter. This area encompasses the equally fascinating **Judería** (Jewish quarter), and flows seamlessly into the new part of town. Here, plazas such as the grandiose Plaza Tendillas are lined with pavement cafés and sophisticated shops equalling the vibrant flip-side of this city's appeal. Dominating the lot is the **Mezquita**, probably the most stunning mosque ever built by the Moors and one of the world's great buildings, despite the fact that a Christian **cathedral** has been built slap in the middle of it. The Guadalquivir, now silted up and no longer navigable, retains one of the many Moorish waterwheels that kept Queen Isabella awake at night. The riverside is also is home to a large flock of egrets, which swirl around the **Roman bridge**, adding to the magic of Córdoba's historic core.*

Ins and outs

Getting there
See page 298 for further details
The main **bus** companies are *Alsina Graells*, Av de Medina Azahara, and *Ureña*, Av de Cervantes (both near the train station). Buses run to the centre every 15 mins and a taxi costs approximately €5. Visitors arriving by **car** will find that parking is a nightmare. Check in early to a hotel with a garage or, if just making a day trip, park to the south of the river to the west of the Roman bridge. If you park illegally, you car will certainly be towed away. The **train** station is on Av de América, on the north edge of the town, a 30-min walk from the old town via the commercial centre. There is an information point in the concourse, where you can book accommodation. Taxis and local buses connect the station with the old town.

Getting around
Fortunately, most of the monuments are located in a compact area on the north bank of the river and can easily be reached on foot. The nearest **taxi** rank to the old quarter is located at the Paseo de la Victoría, opposite the *Meliá hotel*. Another rank can be found near to the main shopping area in the Plaza de Colón. **Coches de Caballo** (horse drawn carriages) can be hired right outside the Mezquita and cost approximately €4 for a 30-min trip around the historic quarter of the city.

Tourist offices
The main tourist office is in the Palacio de Congresos, C Torrijos, alongside the Mezquita, T957471235, F957471778; open summer Mon-Sat 0930-2000, winter 0930-1800, Sun 1000-1400. There is also a small municipal tourist office, a block west of the Mezquita in Plaza Judá Levi, T957200522; open Mon-Fri 0900-1400 and 1630-1830. Both offices have opening times and fees for the main monuments, and as these change frequently, it's worth visiting one of the tourist offices first. The tourist offices provide free maps and a comprehensive guide which lists useful information, such as hotel, restaurant and bar listings. Also ask for a free copy of the monthly what's on guide, *Welcome Olé*.

History

The history of Córdoba is thought to date back to Neolithic times. The city's verifiable history begins with a Bronze Age settlement, as evidenced by the minerals of the Sierra Morena, but it was during Roman times that it sprang to prominence. Founded in 152 BC, it was known as Corduba and soon became

Things to do in Córdoba

★

- After exploring the delights of Córdoba's Mezquita, continue the Moorish theme with lunch at *Los Califas* restaurant, with its great views over the mosque
- Go bodega-hopping in Montilla to sample some of the town's eponymous wines
- Hear the competing rolling drums of the Black and White Tailed Jews during Baena's Semana Santa processions
- Become a Baroque church buff in Priego de Córdoba by visiting its many fine religious buildings

a regional capital. Later it was the administrative centre for the wealthy province of Baetica. The city was then overrun by both the Vandals and the Visigoths and had to wait for the Moors to take over for its golden age to come. In late 711, Córdoba was captured by Moorish troops led by Mugueiz El Rumí. By 756 Córdoba had become the capital of Moorish Spain and for several centuries it was the main centre of Muslim culture and learning, producing poets and philosophers such as Averoëss and Miamonides. In 758, Abd Al-Rahman I of the Ommayyad Dynasty arrived from Damascus and established an independent Emirate.

Much of the Iberian peninsula was ruled from the city which was the capital of the western Caliphate from 929 to 1031 following independence from Baghdad. By now the city was the largest in western Europe with as many as 500,000 inhabitants and an estimated 3,000 mosques. Córdoba grew in importance and influence under Abd Al-Rahman's successors, especially Abd Al-Rahman III and Hakkam II, until internal disputes and a revolt by the Berbers began to weaken the Ommayyads, leading to the abdication of Hisham II in 1031. The Caliphate of Córdoba then split up into a number of minor *taifas* (kingdoms), while the city itself came into the hands of first the Almoravides in 1094 and subsequently the Almohades in 1149. Córdoba was captured by the Christians led by Fernando III in 1236 and with the Reconquest the decline soon set in. Little of the wealth from the New World found its way to Córdoba, and by the time the French occupied the city during the Peninsular War, the population had dropped dramatically.

During the Civil War, Córdoba was captured by the Nationalists, who perpetrated some appalling atrocities. The Córdobeses proved, however, to have long memories and in the first post-Franco elections voted for a communist local authority; the only major city in Spain to do so. Today the city reflects a progressive prosperity and is, once again, a centre of learning with a large university and the more recent establishment of a centre devoted to the study of Muslim history and culture.

Sights

The mosque is Córdoba's most famous example of Arab architecture. **The Mezquita** Although not quite as remarkable as Granada's Alhambra, it is in its own way an equally significant remnant of Spain's Moorish heritage and is a must for any visitor to Andalucía.

There are in fact four distinct stages in the construction of The Mezquita, representing distinct styles and periods corresponding to the Moorish rulers of the time. The building began in 785 in the time of Abd Al-Rahman I on the site of a Visigoth church and a Roman temple, with the intention of building Islam's most grandiose mosque. The architect, whilst demolishing the

Córdoba Province

original church, had a ready source of building materials. To save time the west-facing wall was retained, but this meant that the *mihrab* does not exactly face Mecca. (An alternative explanation is that the *mihrab* was designed to face Damascus, from where many of the inhabitants had fled.) There were a vast number of pillars available for use, both from the Visigoth church and also the earlier Roman temple, plus many more brought to the site from other places. They were of a variety of types (marble, jasper and porphyry), colours and lengths. The longer pillars were buried in the floor to match the height of the shorter ones, while a second row of pillars and arches were constructed to support the roof, a design that resembles a Roman aqueduct. A distinctive

Mezquita

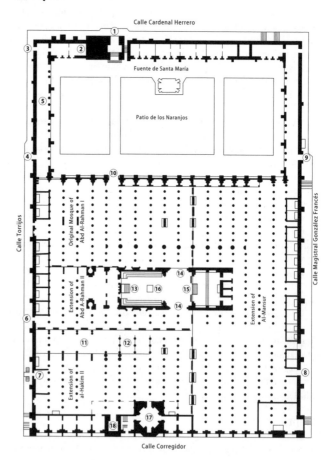

1 Puerta del Perdón	10 Puerta de la Palmas
2 Bell Tower	11 Site of Visigoth Cathedral
3 Puerta de la Leche	12 Capilla Real
4 Puerta de los Deanes	13 Choir
5 Cloisters	14 Transepts
6 Puerta de San Miguel	15 High Altar
7 Puerta del Palacio	16 Capilla Mayor
8 Puerta del Sagrario	17 Mihrab
9 Puerta de Santa Catalina	18 Tesoro

Córdoba Province

Understanding the mosque

On account of the Moors, there are many mosques in Andalucía. Large cities such as Córdoba would have had scores of mosques. The Grand Mosque or alijama was always built in the centre of the urban area, surrounded by its commercial area known as the medina. Nearby would be the madraza or college, while a maze of surrounding alleyways would contain numerous small shops.

The mosque itself would consist of three distinct elements – the minaret, the courtyard and the prayer hall. The minaret, from where the muezzin calls the faithful to prayer, is a square, narrow tower decreasing in size as it rises. Usually made of brick or stone, it is decorated with small arches, tiles and brickwork. It is capped with three golden spheres or yamur. The courtyard or shan, which was often shaded with trees and had fountains playing, was the place for the ritual

washing or ablutions. There was frequently a covered gallery running around the outside. The prayer hall or liwan is little more than an empty space held up by arches and pillars forming parallel naves, with prayer mats on the floor. The mihrab is in the centre of the wall that faces Mecca. In small mosques, the mihrab, which amplifies the voice of the prayer leader, might be a simple hollow niche, but in the Grand Mosque the area might be ornately decorated. The exterior of the Mosque (and Córdoba is an excellent example) usually has high stone walls with minimal decoration and no windows, as the mosque might need to be defended. There would be a small number of doors, invariably with horseshoe arches.

The mosque also acted as a central point for many of the activities of the city such as teaching, law enforcement and community administration.

feature of the arches is the striped red and white pattern produced by using red brick and white stone.

Abd Al-Rahman II extended the mosque during the period 833 to 848 with nine more arches added to the south. The third enlargement came in the time of Al Hakkim II, who demolished the south wall to add another 14 rows of columns, transforming the building into a huge rectangle. He also used Byzantine craftsmen to construct a new *mihrab*. The prayer niche, whilst indicating the direction of Mecca, also has the function of amplifying the voice of the prayer leader. Today, the *mihrab* is railed off, but try to see the ceiling, which is carved into a shell from a single piece of marble, and also the *maksura* or anti-chamber, where the Caliph and his party would pray. This is distinguished by some richly coloured mosaics.

The fourth and final expansion of the Mezquita was during the time of Al-Mansur, the minister of the child-ruler Hisham II. This final enlargement added seven rows to the east side, which it can be claimed destroys the symmetry of the mosque, since the *mihrab* no longer occupies a central position. The building today comprises a huge rectangle measuring 129 m by 179 m.

To the north of the mosque is the **Patio de los Naranjos**, a courtyard of orange trees and fountains where the ritual ablutions took place before prayer. None of the original fountains remain today but their more modern successors give the flavour of Moorish times. Set into the north wall of the patio is the **bell tower**, built at the same time as the cathedral. The climb to the top is rewarded with fine views over the city.

After Córdoba was captured by Fernando III in the Christian Reconquest, the mosque was gradually converted into a church, initially by adding a **Capilla de Villaviciosa** built by Mudéjar craftsmen in 1371. The most drastic

Conversion of the mosque

alterations took place in 1523 under Charles V (also renowned for his inter-ference with the Alhambra in Granada) who sanctioned the building, despite local objections, of a **Capilla Real** (Royal Chapel) and the **Cathedral Coro** in Renaissance style. On inspecting the finished work he did have the decency to comment: "You have built what you or others might have built anywhere, but you have destroyed something that was unique in the world". The cathedral is not without its worth, however, and of particular interest are the choir stalls, ornately carved in mahogany by Pedro Duque Cornejo in the 18th century. There are also some items of interest in the Christian side chapels. In the Capilla de la Concepción are some fine carvings by Pedro de la Mena, while in the Capilla de Cardinal Salazar is an impressive statue of Santa Teresa, sculpted by José de Mora. In the *Tesoro* (treasury) is a monstrance by Enrique de Arfe, which was first seen in the Corpus Cristi procession of 1518. It is more than 2½ m high, weighs 200 kg and is a mass of jewels, crosses and relics. Nev-ertheless, having viewed the cathedral sitting awkwardly within the Moorish mosque, one is reminded of a famous Royal observation in a similar context that it is 'like a carbuncle on the face of a well-loved friend'.

The Mezquita can be crowded with visitors, but this need not be a disad-vantage. Some of the tour guides are a fund of knowledge and it is quite easy to tag on to a group and get the benefit of an expert commentary. Go in the late afternoon for a more peaceful tour. ■ *Mon-Sat 1000-1930, Sun and festivals 1400-1900. Winter opening times may vary. Entrance, via the Puerta del Perdón.* €6.50.

Palacio Episcopal The Palacio Episcopal, on the west side of the Mezquita, was originally con-structed by the Visigoths, then became an Alcázar which the resident Caliphs had linked to the mosque by means of a bridge. The Omayyad court aban-doned this alcázar when they moved to Medina Azahara. However, the oldest surviving part of the building today is 15th-century in age, but it is due to the existence of the early Moorish fortress that the nearby Christian building is known as the 'Alcázar Nuevo'. The Palacio is today partly used as a museum (mainly religious art, sculptures and tapestries) and partly as a venue for exhibi-tions and congresses. ■ *Mon-Fri 0930-1330 and 1530-2000, Sat 0930-1330, winter Mon-Fri 0930-1730. Free with a Mezquita ticket, otherwise* €1.20.

Alcázar de los Reyes Cristianos Also known as Nuevo Alcázar, work was started here in the 13th century for Alfonso X and was later enlarged and used as a palace by the Catholic Mon-archs. Ferdinand and Isabel received Columbus in this building, before he departed on his first voyage to the New World, while it was also the prison of Boabdil El Chico, the last of the kings of Moorish Granada. Along the river-side, opposite the palace, were a series of water wheels and flour mills. The wheels also brought water to the alcázars, but they are said to have infuriated Isobel as they prevented her from sleeping. One reconstructed wheel remains today. The Alcázar became a centre for the Inquisition from 1490 until 1821. Even as late as the mid-20th century, the building was functioning as a prison, so it is perhaps not surprising that there is little to see from its Golden Age. There is now a small municipal museum here, in which the locally-discovered Roman mosaics are the most important exhibit. The most enjoyable pastime here is wandering around the gardens to the south of the building, with its pools, fountains and rose beds, which are illuminated during the summer evenings. ■ *Tue-Sat 1000-1400 and, 1630-1830, Sun 0930-1430. Gardens only Tue-Sun 0800-2400.* €2.55, *Fri free.*

Between the Mezquita and the city walls to the west lies the Judería, Córdoba's old Jewish quarter is a warren of narrow lanes and alleyways, sadly overdosed with souvenir shops. However you can still find some delightful corners, such as the flower-filled Callejón de las Flores. The best approach is via the 14th-century Puerta de Almodóvar. From here turn right into Calle Judías, which leads to the **Synagogue**, one of only three in Spain and the only one in Andalucía. Built in 1315, this tiny building has some fine Mudéjar plasterwork of Hebrew texts and retains its women's gallery. The fact that

Judería

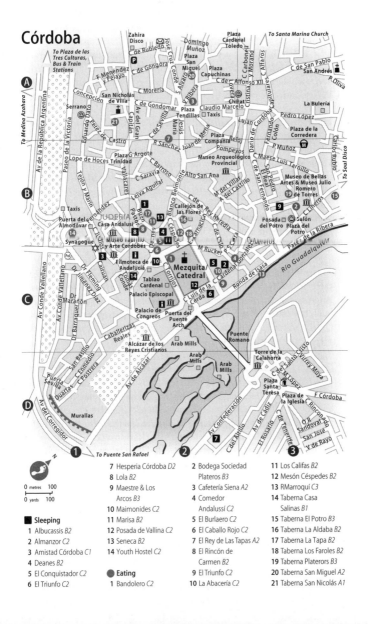

Córdoba

Córdoba Province

7 Hesperia Córdoba *D2*
8 Lola *B2*
9 Maestre & Los Arcos *B3*
10 Maimonides *C2*
11 Marisa *B2*
12 Posada de Vallina *C2*
13 Seneca *B2*
14 Youth Hostel *C2*

Eating
1 Bandolero *C2*

2 Bodega Sociedad Plateros *B3*
3 Cafetería Siena *A2*
4 Comedor Andalussí *C2*
5 El Burlaero *C2*
6 El Caballo Rojo *C2*
7 El Rey de Las Tapas *A2*
8 El Rincón de Carmen *B2*
9 El Triunfo *C2*
10 La Abacería *C2*

11 Los Califas *B2*
12 Mesón Céspedes *B2*
13 RMarroquí *C3*
14 Taberna Casa Salinas *B1*
15 Taberna El Potro *B3*
16 Taberna La Aldaba *B2*
17 Taberna La Tapa *B2*
18 Taberna Los Faroles *B2*
19 Taberna Platerors *B3*
20 Taberna San Miguel *A2*
21 Taberna San Nicolás *A1*

Sleeping
1 Albucassis *B2*
2 Almanzor *C2*
3 Amistad Córdoba *C1*
4 Deanes *B2*
5 El Conquistador *C2*
6 El Triunfo *C2*

both the Judería and the Synagogue survived after the expulsion of the Jewish community by Ferdinand and Isabel in 1492, says much for the traditional religious and cultural tolerance of the Córdobeses. ■ *Tue-Sat 1000-1330 and 1530-1730, Sun 1030-1330. Free to EU citizens otherwise €0.30.*

South of the Synagogue, in a small *plazuela*, is a statue of Maimónides, the Jewish philosopher, who was born in Córdoba in 1135.

Also in the Judería is the **Museo Taurino y Arte Cordobés** in the Plaza de Maimónides, devoted largely to *tauromaquía* (the art of bullfighting), with special attention given to Manolete, the famous local matador killed by the bull Islero in 1947. (There is a statue to Manolete in Plaza Lagunilla.) ■ *Tue-Sat 1000-1400, 1630-1830. Sun 0930-1430. €2.95, free Tue. EU students free.*

Puente Romano
This Roman Bridge crosses the Río Guadalquivir from the Triumphal arch and Bridge Gate to the Torre de Calahorra on the other side. It has 16 arches and was built after Caesar's victory over Pompey. First restored by the Moors in the eighth century, it has been renovated many times since.

Torre de Calahorra
Located on the south side of the Roman Bridge, this defensive tower is now an Interpretation Centre, giving an audiovisual history of Córdoba in addition to displaying some armour which once belonged to El Gran Capitán – Gonzalo Fernández de Córdoba, and items connected with the local 16th-century poet Luis de Góngora. The audiovisual show uses some 18 projectors and other electronic wizardry, showing amongst other things 'The song of the waters of the land of Andalucía', and a 'Magic model of the Alhambra of Granada'. Don't let this put you off – it gives a good introduction to the Mezquita. ■ *Daily 1000-1800. €3.65; €4.80 with full audiovisual programme.*

Baños Arabes
In a private house at the rear of a shop in Calle Velázquez Bosco in the Judería, there is a 10th-century *hamman* or sauna, claimed to be the oldest baths in Andalucía. Adjacent to a small open patio surrounded by arches, they certainly have plenty of atmosphere. There was once a passage between the baths and the nearby Mezquita. ■ *Opening hours are dependent on the presence of the friendly and informative owner, who will deliver a 2-min lecture in rapid fire Spanish and leave you to it. €0.60.*

Callejón de las Flores
This small narrow street, just a stone's throw from the northeast of the Mezquita, is worth seeking out. Its whitewashed walls are festooned with pots and flowers. At the small plaza at the end of the alley, look back to see the belfry of the Mezquita perfectly framed. This street sets the scene for the rest of Córdoba, which maintains the patios from the Romans and the Moors – from the humblest cottage to the grand *palacios*. Often framed by wrought iron doorways and complimented by decorative tiles and gentle fountains, the patio is an essential feature of the city, culminating in the annual Festival of the Patios during the first fortnight in May.

Museo Arqueológico Provincial
The archaeological museum is undoubtedly the best of its kind in southern Spain
Located in the Plaza de Jerónimo Páez in a Renaissance mansion with an Italian-style porch, the museum is entered via a delightful patio with a fountain and surrounding arches containing Roman capitals and assorted mosaics. There is much to appreciate in the Neolithic, Roman and Moorish periods, but certain items stand out, such as the Christian sarcophagus, its side beautifully carved in marble, and the bronze stag from the Moorish ruins of nearby Medina Azahara. The mosaics throughout are excellent and

some were, in fact, discovered on the site, the mansion having been built over a Roman villa. The museum is off the tourist track, which of course means you can enjoy it in peace. On the downside the Plaza Páez, outside the museum, is the meeting place of some of the more dubious youths of Córdoba – this is probably the only place in the city that you're likely to feel even remotely threatened. ■ *Tue 1500-2000, Wed-Sat 0900-2000, Sun 0900-1500. €1.50, free with EU passport.*

Plaza del Potro & environs

This is a delightful square about a kilometre east of the Mezquita, and well worth the walk. The square is named after the fountain, dating from 1577, which is decorated with a *potro* (or colt). At the south end of the plaza is a monument to San Rafael, behind which is the Guadalquivir and the country-side stretching away in the distance. The square was once a livestock market and in the 16th and 17th centuries it was a popular meeting place for the wheeler-dealers of the city. The square was certainly known to Cervantes, who mentioned it in *Don Quixote*. An interesting and balanced set of buildings, mostly in honey-coloured sandstone, surround the square. To the west is the **Posada del Potro**, a carefully restored inn where Cervantes probably stayed, with a courtyard surrounded by former stables and a wooden balcony containing the inn's rooms. The building is now the Casa de la Cultura and you're welcome to wander around.

Opposite, on the east side of the square, is the **Museo de Bellas Artes** in a building which was once the Hospital de la Caridad. Entry is through an attractive sculpture-filled garden. The galleries contain works by all the usual names such as Valdés Leal, Zurburán, Alonso Cano and Murillo, although not their better works. There are also refreshingly, some works by modern painters, such as Benedito, Chicharro and Solana. ■ *Tue afternoon 1500-2000, Wed-Sat 0900-2000, Sun 0900-1500. Free to EU citizens, otherwise €1.50. T957473345.*

On the other side of the same building's courtyard, as you enter on the right, is the **Museo Julio Romero de Torres**. This museum is devoted to the work of the local Córdoban artist Julio Romero de Torres. Largely unheard of outside the city, this exponent of modernism and symbolism claims to provide 'a personal glowing serenade to the women of Córdoba'. Most of his work consists of semi-erotic nudes and smouldering gypsy women. He does, however, have a big following in the city, although probably mainly the male section of the population. Local feminists possibly think otherwise. ■ *Tue-Sat 1000-1400 and 1630-1830, Sun 0930-1430. €2.95, Fri free.*

Plaza de la Corredera

Just east of the Museo Arqueológico and north of the Plaza del Potro is the remarkable Plaza de la Corredera, which is an extraordinary colonnaded square. It was enclosed in the 17th century and formed a multi-purpose arena, which has been used for bullfights and even burnings during the Inquisition. Today, it has a rather faded air about it and is the location for an open and a covered market.

Palacio de Viana

Located in Plaza Don Gome, this is an opulent mansion dating originally from the 14th century, which until quite recently was the home of the Marquess of Viana. The guided tour takes in the various rooms of the house, including art galleries, bedrooms, and a particularly fascinating kitchen, as well as 14 flower-filled patios. ■ *Mon-Fri 1000-1300 and 1600-1800, Sat 1000-1300. €3.*

Córdoba Province

Casa Andalusí   Although this place at Calle Judios 12, near to the Synagogue, is not widely known, many who visit here describe Casa Andalusí as the highlight of their visit to Córdoba. It consists of an old house with a range of patios and a number of rooms or suites with an historic theme and an exhibition including a collection of Arabic coins going back over 10 centuries. Although the Casa has become rather more commercialized recently, it should not be missed. ■ *Mon-Sat 1030-2000. €1.80.*

Churches   After the Reconquest, Fernando III built 14 parish churches in Córdoba, mainly between the late 13th century and the early 14th century and incorporating a mixture of architectural styles including Gothic and Mudéjar. They were usually built with three naves, often with many-sided apses and built in the local cream-coloured sandstone. Several had additions in the Baroque style in the 17th and 18th centuries. The following are the most rewarding: **Iglesia de San Nicholás de Villa**, in Plaza San Nicholás on the edge of the main shopping area, has an octagonal tower and battlements and, unusually, four square apses. **Iglesia Santa Marina**, in the plaza of the same name in the north part of the city, is a stout building with three porches with pointed arches, above which is a delicate rose window. Outside the church is a monument to Manolete, the bullfighter who was born in the Santa Marina barrio. **Iglesia San Lorenzo**, located again in a square of the same name, has a distinctive tiled porch with three pointed arches. Above this is an ornate rose window surrounded by six rows of mouldings. The bell tower has a curious belfry set at an angle to the main structure. Finally, there is the **Iglesia de San Andrés** located in the old silk-making district. Built mainly in the 18th century, it retains only its vaults from the times of the Reconquest.

Essentials

Sleeping   Places, as you would expect, are generally cheaper away from the historic quarter.
■ *on map, page 291*   **AL** *Amistad Córdoba*, Plaza Miamonides 3, T957420335, F957420365, nh-cordoba@nh-hoteles.es Centrally located, stylish hotel built around 2 former 18th-century mansions with Mudéjar courtyard, carved-wood ceilings and 84 large, comfortable rooms with a/c. Restaurant, bar, garage. **AL** *El Conquistador*, Magistral González Francés, T957481102, F957474677, conquist@teleline.es Tastefully decorated former private villa with marble and granite lobby overlooking a colonnaded courtyard with fountain and flowers. Try for a room overlooking the mosque which is floodlit at night. 99 rooms, a/c, garage, café, bar, babysitting, garage, sauna, solarium. **AL** *Hesperia Córdoba*, Av Confederación, T957421042, F957299997, hotel@hesperia cordoba.com A relatively new luxury hotel south of the river near Puente Romano. The 108 rooms are spacious and modern with good night time views of the floodlit city. Garage, a/c, pool, restaurant. **AL** *Maimonides*, C Torrijos 4, T957471500, F957483803, maimonides@arrakis.es Recently renovated and comfortably luxurious with a definite Andalucían style. The cafetería has a typical patio and the granite and marble lobby is superb. 82 rooms, garage, internet access in all rooms, wheelchair access, a/c, right next to the west side of the Mezquita. **AL** *Posada de Vallina*, Corregidor Luis de la Cerda 83, T957498750, F957498751, hotel@hotelvallina.com Recently opened as a small hotel-cum-restaurant across from the Mezquita, the building is magnificent with Roman columns and an ancient well. The 15 rooms are decorated in contemporary Andalucían style with small balconies. A/c, restaurant, laundry service, welcome drink.

A *Tryp Los Gallos*, Av de Medina Azahara 7, T957235500, F957231636, sol.inngallos@solmedia.com Modern hotel crowned by a roof garden originally

See inside front cover for hotel price categories

If you arrive by car look for a hotel with a garage - street parking is very difficult

constructed by the bullfighter El Cordobés. Located on shady street just west of the centre. A/c, garage, 115 rooms, pool. **A** *Lola*, C Romero 3 T957200305, F957422063, hotel@hotelconencantolola.com A charming, cosy new hotel with 8 individually decorated rooms and a home-from-home salon with plants, pictures and sink-into sofas. A/c, garage. **B** *Albucassis*, C Buen Pastor 11, T957478625. Tucked away in the Jewish quarter, close to the synagogue, this 3-storey hotel is hundreds of years old but has been tastefully restored. Rooms open onto a pretty interior patio and have marble floors and attractive tiled bathrooms. 15 rooms, garage, a/c, bar, wheelchair access. **B** *Marisa*, C Cardinal Herrero 6, T957473142, F957474144. Fabulous neo-Moorish lobby with traditional arches sets the tone for the décor throughout this 36-room hotel in the heart of the Jewish quarter. A/c, garage, wheelchair access. **C** *Maestre*, C Romero Barros 4/6, T957472410, F957475395. Rooms are positioned around an attractive inner patio and the furnishings and décor are traditional with Castilian-style furniture and quality oil paintings. The position is perfect, tucked down a quiet cul-de-sac close to the Plaza del Potro. The management also run a cheaper hostel next door, which is similarly good value. A/c, garage, 26 rooms.

D *Almanzor*, C Cardenal González 19, T957485400. In the centre of the historic quarter, this simple hostel is a real find. Comfortable and well-furnished rooms; several with balconies. A/c, TV, garage. **D** *Deanes*, C Deanes 6, T957293744. Good-value choice in typical Córdoban house with plenty of old-fashioned charm. A large central patio has comfortable appeal and the tapas bar is popular with locals and serves some highly original specialities, like thistles in almond sauce! **D** *Séneca*, C Conde y Luque 7, T957473234. Excellent value at lower end of this price category with stunning patio, complete with original Moorish pavement. Breakfast available as optional extra. Book ahead as it fills up fast, even out of season. **D** *El Triunfo*, C Luis de la Cerda 79, T957475500. Priced at the top end of this price range, but still a good deal and close to the mosque. 50 recently-renovated and sturdily-furnished rooms with brightly tiled bathrooms, a/c, garage, TV. **D-E** *Los Arcos*, C Romero Barros 14, T957485643. 16 simply furnished rooms in a central location close to the Plaza del Potro with attractive patio. Cheaper with shared bath. **E** *Fonda Agustina*, C Zapatería Vieja 5, T957470872. Cheapest accommodation in town and spotlessly clean with basic rooms in a quiet location; definitely a bargain. **Youth hostel** *Plaza Judás Leví*, T957290166, F957290500. Impressive new building, 163 beds (2-5 beds to a room), meals, no maximum stay. **Camping** *Campamento Municipal*, Av del Brillante 50, T957278481. First category site, pool, 1½ km north of town; take bus No 11 or 12 from centre.

Córdoba lies in the centre of a rich agricultural region and the local cuisine uses a wonderful range of raw ingredients. Vegetables and fruit are eaten when in season and, as is the case throughout Spain, the Cordobéses are inordinately fond of garlic. They also love green and red peppers, sweet as well as hot, fresh as well as dried, and their beloved *jamón serrano* which is not only eaten as a tapa, but is incorporated into a wide variety of local dishes. Meat and fish are frequently found in combination while ground almonds in soups and sauces lend a subtle savour to the local cuisine. Typical dishes to try are *salmorejo*, a much thicker version of *gazpacho* made with more garlic and bread; *rabo de toro* (oxtail stew), *churrasco* (grilled pork dish served with pepper sauce) and *cordero a la miel* (lamb in honey).

Eating
● *on map, page 291*
See inside front cover for hotel price categories

Expensive *El Blasón*, C José Zorilla 11, T957480625. Set in charming old house with less expensive ground-floor bar and café and more formal dining room upstairs. Menu features classic Cordoban recipes made with innovative flair. *El Caballo Rojo*, C Cardenal Herrero 28, T957475375. The oldest restaurant in Córdoba, just behind the Mezquita tucked down a cul-de-sac flanked by potted geraniums. It prides itself on a

Moorish inspired menu. Try the lamb with honey, fish with raisins and pine nuts and their particularly tasty dessert, *canutillo de almendra* (almond pastry). *La Almudaina*, Campo Santo de los Mártines 1, T957474342. A former 15th-century palace in an unbeatable location, facing the river in the old Jewish quarter. Formal dining in lace-curtained rooms or al fresco in a glass-roofed central patio. Specialities include hake with shrimp sauce and pork loin in wine sauce. Booking is essential.

Mid-range *Cafetería Siena*, Plaza de las Tendillas s/n, T957473005. Great location on bustling main square in the centre of the shopping district, serving good value light meals, *platos combinados*, as well as breakfast and tapas. *El Burlaero*, Calleja de la Hoguera 5, T957472719. Famous throughout Spain for its game dishes, this restaurant is spread over several rooms with low, beamed ceilings and typical Córdoban patio. Traditional dishes based on the freshest of ingredients. *El Rincón de Carmen*, C Romero 4, T957291055. A romantic restaurant in early 18th-century building in the Jewish quarter. There are several interesting rice dishes, including black rice (coloured by squid ink) and various paellas. *Los Califas*, C Deanes 3, T957471320. Great atmosphere and popular with locals. Warm limestone décor with brilliant blue tiles and old brick, plus outside terrace with stunning Mezquita views. Traditional Córdoban cuisine, as well as several Moroccan-inspired dishes. *RMarroquí*, C Ronda de Isasa 6, T957492871. New Moroccan restaurant with colourful ethnic décor, outside tables and popular dishes including couscous, kebabs, chicken and almonds, lamb *tadjin* (stew), followed by Moroccan sweets and mint tea.

Cheap *Bandolero*, Torrijos 6. Right next to the tourist office offering basic international and Spanish dishes, with a menu del día for €7. *Comedor Andalussí*, C Alfayatas 6, T957327667. A hole-in-the-wall Moroccan restaurant with falafel, couscous, homous and pitta bread sandwiches, eat in or takeaway. *Mesón Céspedes*, C Céspedes 12, T957483229. Bright, cheery restaurant with a choice of 4 daily *menú del días*, priced €7-12, plus a daily special for just €5. *Taberna Platerors*, San Francisco 6 T957470042. Opposite *Hotel Maestre*, this 17th-century bar and restaurant has a large patio decorated with colourful tiles and several small rooms, including one dedicated to the late, local bullfighter Manolete. The food is solid homestyle cooking with the starters a meal in themselves. *El Triunfo*, Corregidor Luis de la Cerda 79, T957498484. Next to the hostal of the same name, this restaurant has *platos combinados* for €5, a choice of 3 daily menus and pizza.

Tapas bars There are many excellent tapas bars in the old part of Córdoba. The local tipple is Montilla, an unfortified mellow, dry sherry which according to the locals, is less likely to lead to a hangover - or so they say.

Judería: Close to the synagogue is the cavernous *Bodega Guzmán* frequented by crusty old men in flat caps and bullfight aficionados, hence the small *taurino* museum in the back. Great authentic atmosphere. Nearby, the *Taberna Casa Salinas*, Puerta de Almodóvar, has a central patio and is known for its *pescaito frito* (fried fish). If you're lucky you may experience an impromptu flamenco session.

Around the Mezquita: *Taberna La Tapa*, C Deanes 1, short on elbow room with a long list of tapas, is a local hang out. *Taberna Los Faroles*, C Velázquez Bosco, has a vast central patio, is popular with tourists of every nationality and is a great place to just hang out and people-watch, while enjoying excellent tapas and raciones, including *boquerones en vinagre* (anchovies in vinegar) and wedges of *tortilla* (potato omelette). Still in the same area, the lively *Taberna La Aldaba*, C Velázquez Bosco, offers a slice of *tortilla* and a *cerveza* for €3 and a choice of 4 tapas and a *cerveza* for €6. *La Abacería*, C

Corregidor Luis de la Cerda 73, may be a little too tourist orientated for some, but does have a good selection of tapas, including *patatas a la brava* (fried potatoes with spicy tomato sauce), *berenjenas a la miel* (aubergine slices with honey), *salmorejo* (gazpacho with guts), tortillas with various fillings, and fried *boquerones* (anchovies).

Around Plaza del Potro: *Taberna El Potro*, C Lineros 2, is a little heavy on the super-kitsch art reproductions of Julio Romero de Torre but serves wonderful tapas. *Bodega Sociedad Plateros*, C San Francisco 6, is the headquarters of the Sociedad Plateros, a silversmiths' benefit society which has branched out into the running of bodegas. This bar is in a century-old former convent with a delightful *azuelejo* clad patio, serving up a good tapas selection and well-kept montilla range.

Around Plaza Tendillas: *El Rey de Las Tapas*, C Rodríguez Sánchez 5, is a friendly bar built around an airy patio with a good tapas selection. *Taberna San Miguel*, Plaza San Miguel 1, is legendary and not to be missed. Tapas here include *callos en salsa picante* (tripe in a spicy sauce) and *patatas a lo pobre* (fried potatoes with onion and garlic). Next to the Plaza de San Nicolás, the *Taberna San Nicolás* is a fine old bar serving up a superb range of tapas and raciones, including all kinds of fried fish.

Discos and the main nightlife in Córdoba, particularly during the summer, is centred in the El Brillante area, northwest of the Plaza de Colón. *Pub DSO*, Llanos del Pretorio 1, has a large outside terrace and live music most weekends, while *El Burlaero* a few doors down is popular for early-evening cocktails. Round the corner on C Molinos Alta 7, the *Gallery* bar is hopping from dawn to dusk on Sat. Av Gran Capitán is also throbbing with late-night action. *O'Donoghue's* at No 36 is an Irish bar, while a few doors down *Riff* is a lively foot-tapping music bar, popular with students. Closer to the centre, *Soul* on Alfonso XII (next to the Ayuntamiento) was described by the *Daily Telegraph* as being 'the coolest bar in town' and attracts a vibrant, arty crowd. Also in the centre of town is *Zahira* disco on C Conde de Robledo 3, which has Thu party nights and plays mainly latin and rock.

Bars & nightclubs

Bullfights Take place throughout the season at the Plaza de Toros de los Califas, which is in the modern part of the city to the northwest of the historic quarter. **Cinema** *Filmoteca de Andalucía*, C Medina y Corella 5, T957472018. Regular screenings of subtitled foreign films. **Concerts** These take place on Sun in the Alcázar and there are open-air shows in the *Teatro Municipal* (see below), including the International Guitar Festival. Check with the tourist office for details. **Flamenco** Córdoba is famed for its flamenco. A national flamenco competition takes place every 3 years and there are numerous festivals during the summer months. One of the best venues with an authentic ambience and delightful patio is *Tablao Cardenal*, C Torrijos 10, T957483112. Flamenco starts 2230, closed Sun. Another good flamenco venue is *La Buleriá*, C Pedro López 3, T957483839, near Plaza de la Corredera. Starts 2230. Summer only. **Theatre** *Gran Teatro*, Av de Gran Capitán s/n, T957480237, www.teatrocordoba .com Stages excellent music, drama and dance productions. Pick up the monthly programme from the tourist office. *Teatro Góngora*, C Jesús y María 12, T957472165. The tourist office will have details of performances.

Entertainment

Feb *Carnaval*. **Easter** *Semana Santa* There are some 28 traditional Easter processions. **5-12 May** *Fiesta de la Patios* This is marked by concerts and flamenco, as well as a competition for the best decorated patio. The tourist office will have a map of the patios open to the public, alternatively, you'll notice 'patio' signs in the streets and alleyways, which means you are invited to enter. The patios are a stunning example of a beautiful Cordoban tradition. **25-28 May** *Feria de Nuestra Señora de la Salud* The city's women

Festivals

Córdoba Province

dress in traditional costume. **Sep** *Fiesta de Nuestra Señora de la Fuensanta* Celebrations for Córdoba's patron saint. **24 Oct** *Fiesta de San Rafael Arcangel.*

Shopping The main shopping streets are to the north of the historic quarter, concentrating along Av Ronda de las Tejares, Plaza Tendillas and C Cruz Conde. There are numerous shops around the Mezquita aimed at the tourist trade, but selling some of the traditional craftwork of the Córdoba area such as silverwork, jewellery, leather (known simply as 'cordobanes'), pottery and guitars. There is a flea market every morning in the Plaza de la Corredera, with a larger affair on Sat.

Sport **Golf** *Club de Golf los Villares*, Ronda Tejares 1, T957350209. **Horse riding** *Club Hípico*, Ctra Trassierra, Km 3, T957271628. *Cortijo la Ventilla*, Hacienda El Cordobés, Gran Cápitan 14001, Córdoba, T957474794. **Squash** *Squash Córdoba*, C Alonso el Sabio 22, T957480981. **Swimming** *Piscina Municipal*, Av del Brillante.

Tour operators *Viajes El Corte Inglés*, Av Ronda de los Tejares 39, T957200182. *Viajes Vincit*, Av Burgos 1, T957472316.

Transport **Air** Córdoba has a small airport for internal flights, but the nearest international airports are at Málaga or Sevilla. The *Iberia* office is in Ronda de los Tejeres 3, T957490968. **Bus** The main bus station is at Plaza de las Tres Culturas, T957404040. There is a daily bus to **Cádiz** at 1900 (4½ hrs, €14) and several daily buses to **Madrid** (4½ hrs, €10.), Málaga (3 hrs, €9.80), **Jaén** (1½ hrs, €6) and **Sevilla** (0700 and 0900, 1hr 40 mins, €7.95). **Train** The RENFE office is on the same square as the main bus station, Plaza de las Tres Culturas, T957400202. There are frequent connections from many destinations, with 12 trains daily to **Sevilla**, 3 to **Algeciras**, 2 to **Jaén** and 3 to **Ronda**.

Directory **Banks** Banks are in the Av del Gran Capitán and the Ronda de los Tejeres area. **Communications** Internet: *Ch@t*, C Claudio Marcelo 17. Open 1000-2200, Sun 1600-2200, €1.80 per hr. *Ciberplanet*, Centro Comercial, El Arcangel. Open 1000-2200, €1.50 per hr. *Salón Internet*, Hostal El Pilar del Potro, C Lucano 12. Open 1000-2400. €2.40 per hr. *Serrano*, C Eduardo Dato 9. Open 1000-2200. €2.10 per hr. **Post office**: Correos, C Cruz Conde 15, open Mon-Fri 0800-2100, Sat 0900-1400. **Telephones**: *locutorio* at Plaza Tendillas 7. Open Mon-Fri 0930-1400 and 1700-2300, Sat 0930-1400. **Embassies and consulates** *France*, C Manuel de Sandóval 4, T957472314. **Medical services**

MEDINA AZAHARA - CORDOBA PROVINCE

Ambulance: T957295570. Emergencies: T957217903 Hospitals: *Hospital Reina Sofia*, Avda Menéndez Pidal s/n, T957217000. *Cruz Roja*, Paseo de la Victoria, T957222222. *Hospital General*, T957297122. **Useful addresses** Garages/car workshops: *Citroën*, Ctra Madrid, T957260216. *Ford*, Polígono las Quemadas, T957255800. *Peugeot*, Av de Cádiz. T957292122; *Seat/VAG*, Polígono la Torrecilla, T957295111.

Medina Azahara

Also known as Madinat al-Zahra, these Moorish ruins are about 7 km northwest of Córdoba. The complex was begun in 936 by the Caliph Abd Al-Rahman III in honour of his favourite wife, Azahara. No expense was spared in its construction and historians have provided some amazing statistics: 10,000 men and 1,500 camels and mules were used to construct the palace and the associated buildings, which included houses, barracks, baths, markets, mosques, ponds and even an aviary and a zoo. The affluence of the place amazed visitors, some rooms having visual effects (extraordinary for the time) involving crystals providing rainbows and moving bowls of mercury sending sunbeams around the walls. The building materials were varied in origin, with tiles and bricks taken from Roman sites in Andalucía and marble brought in from North Africa and other places. When complete, Medina Azahara measured 2,000 m long by 900 m wide, spreading over three terraces leading down to the Guadalquivir valley, while it is estimated that 20,000 people lived within its double walls.

After the death of Abd Al-Rahman III, his successors Al-Hakim II and Al Mansur continued to live at Medina Azahara, but when the latter died, decline set in. There was a popular revolt in 1010 and the Medina was looted and then finally destroyed by retreating Berber mercenaries; it had lasted a mere 75 years. Over the succeeding centuries the site was frequently ransacked for its building materials, which have turned up in, among other places, Sevilla's Alcázar.

Today, most of the site consists of ruins and foundations, but excavations continue and there has been some controversial reconstruction, mainly to the

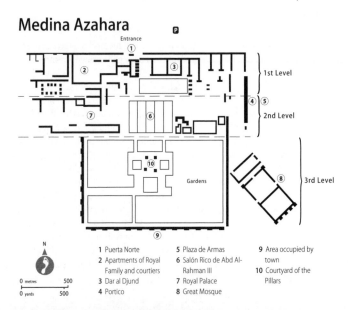

Medina Azahara

1 Puerta Norte
2 Apartments of Royal Family and courtiers
3 Dar al Djund
4 Portico
5 Plaza de Armas
6 Salón Rico de Abd Al-Rahman III
7 Royal Palace
8 Great Mosque
9 Area occupied by town
10 Courtyard of the Pillars

Córdoba Province

palace. This does, however, give some scale and atmosphere to the place. Entry through the Puerta Norte gives a view down over the location. The first level consists of the royal apartments with the rooms built around patios; there were believed to be some 400 houses for courtiers here. To the east is the main military area, the *Dar al-Djund*, including the barracks. This leads to the portico, which was obviously the grand entrance to the Medina, while beyond this was the Plaza de Armas, probably a military parade ground.

Dominating the second level is the Royal Palace, with its restored audience chamber where guests were received. Painstakingly pieced together, the chamber shows some delightful plaster carving, which unusually for Islamic art work, shows figures of men and animals. Finally, on the lower level, are the foundations of the Great Mosque, revealing five naves. The paths in the gardens act as a 'store room' for thousands of pieces of carved plasterwork, some of which are used in the reconstruction. There is a small exhibition area showing archaeological items. ■ *May-Sep Tue-Sat 1000-1400 and 1800-2030, Oct-Apr Tue-Sat 1000-1400 and 1600-1880, Sun 1000-1400. Free to EU citizens otherwise €1.50. To reach Medina Azahara, take the Av de Medina Azahara out of Córdoba. After leaving the industrial suburbs behind, turn right after 4 km. It is another 3 km to the site. Bus No 01 will drop you at the main road intersection. There are also all-inclusive tours organized by Cordoba Vision, T957760241 for current schedule and prices. Don't confuse Medina Azahara with the privately-owned 15th-century Monastery of San Jerónimo, which is clearly seen in the woods on the hillside above the Medina.*

Almodóvar del Río
Population: 7,155

On a day's excursion it is possible to drive on from Medina Azahara a further 15 km along the C431 to Almodóvar del Río, following the Guadalquivir with the Sierra Morena to the right. Dominating the town is the eighth-century Moorish castle fortified by Abd Al-Rahman III, but heavily restored by the Christians in the 14th century. Today it is privately owned, but visits are possible if you can find the guardian. The sleepy town below livens up only during the second Sunday in May when the Romería de la Virgen de Fátima takes place.

North from Córdoba

Leaving behind the fertile *vega* of the Guadalquivir, the land rises gradually into the Sierra Morena, a landscape similar to that in neighbouring Jaén and Huelva provinces. Initially rolling farmland with cereals, the succeeding higher land is well wooded with four species of oak, two of pine, plus areas of garrigue scrub, with deep ravines in places. Although this is popular hunting country (particularly for wild boar and deer), it has a good range of wildlife and has the advantage of rarely being visited by tourists. Amongst the mammals are small numbers of mongoose, lynx and wolves, while there are otters in the rivers and reservoirs. Birds of prey are outstanding, with all three varieties of vultures and five species of eagles. Black storks also breed. Spring flowers and butterflies are prolific.

There are two natural parks in this section of the Sierra Morena, the **Parque Natural de la Sierra Cardeña y Montoro** in the northeast and the **Parque Natural de la Sierra de Hornachuelos** in the northwest. Hornchuelos has the additional scenic attraction of some large reservoirs. There are no towns of any size in the area and the villages tend to be uninspiring. Accommodation, too, can be a problem, the only hotels being in the villages of Peñarroya-Pueblonuevo and Villanueva, while *pensiones* are sparse on the ground and there are no official campsites.

Not just a sherry lookalike

The wines of the Montilla region in Córdoba province have suffered for years by being considered a cheap version of sherry. Indeed, until 1944 the Montilla region sent much of its production to Jerez (the description amontillado *is derived from Montilla), but after that date 'sherry' had to be produced within a certain area of Cádiz province. Montilla now has its own denominación, and certainly within Córdoba province it is the norm to drink Montilla rather than sherry. Although it does not have the worldwide distribution of sherry, Montilla has become popular in the UK, which imports around 100,000 cases a year, and to a lesser extent in the Netherlands.*

Aficionados of Montilla are quick to point out the differences with sherry. Firstly, there is the grape. Whereas sherry is made largely with the Palomino grape, Montilla uses the Pedro Ximénez grape, which is thought to have been brought to the area by a soldier serving in Flanders in the 16th century. Secondly, the climate around Montilla is hotter than in the Jerez area which receives

more sea breezes. Consequently, the Montilla develops more sugar and therefore more alcohol content, removing the necessity to fortify the wine with more spirits. Thirdly, the wine is fermented in a slightly different way. There are three pressings, after which the juice is clarified and pumped into tinajas - huge pottery Ali Baba type jars, where it remains for nine months.

After this, the differences in production cease. The wine may develop a flor (a yeast cap several inches thick), in which case the wine becomes a fino. If not, it becomes the darker oloroso and is sweetened. Like sherry, Montilla is blended using the solera system, mixing wines of different ages to produce uniform quality and is then aged in oak barrels. The end product is claimed to be a more natural drink than sherry and what is more it is retailed at a cheaper price.

Like the bodegas in Jerez, the equivalents in Montilla offer tours and tastings. Try the following: Bodegas Cruz Conde, *Calle Márquez 3;* Bodegas García Hermanos, *Av Marqués de la Vega de Armijo 4;* Bodegas Tomás García, *Llano de Palacio 7; and* Bodegas Pérez Barquero, *Av Andalucía 31.*

South from Córdoba

Known as the **Campiña Cordobesa**, this is a landscape of rolling olive groves and vineyards. On the N342 road to Granada, the first settlement of importance is Espejo, a small town which has been inhabited since Iberian times. Both the Romans and Moors had important sites here and after the Reconquest it had an important role in defending the frontier against the Kingdom of Granada. It was Ferdinand IV who gave the town its name from the word *specula*, meaning watchtower. There is the inevitable hilltop castle, in this case a 15th-century Gothic-Mudéjar building, with an impressive keep. If spending some time in the town, try to visit the Gothic parish Church of San Bartolomé and the Palacio of the Dukes of Osuna.

Espejo
Population: 4,023
Altitude: 418 m

From Espejo, the route follows the valley of the Guadajoz River to Castro del Río, another town with Roman origins. Its castle, of which a fair amount still remains, would have seen much fighting between the Christians and the Moors, the latter having laid siege to it unsuccessfully for several months in 1331. Today there are a number of interesting churches and the town's main industry is the making of olive wood furniture.

Castro del Río
Population: 8,015

Córdoba Province

☞ Best of the bunch

In Córdoba province rolling olive groves stretch for endless hectares. Olive trees were first introduced to Andalucía by the Romans, worshipped the product back to Rome. (The best Spanish oil is still exported to Italy and often re-exported as an Italian product.) The Moors extended the cultivation and called the oil az-zait, meaning 'juice of the olive'. Today, Spain is the world's largest producer of olive oil and Andalucía accounts for 20% of this amount, producing some 550,000 tonnes of oil annually.

Andalucíans are proud of their 1,000-year-old trees, which are very fire- and drought-resistant. Methods of harvesting and processing have barely changed since Roman times. The tree blossoms in spring and the green, unripe olives are harvested around September. Ripe olives turn black and are harvested later. Some 10% of the harvest is picked for consumption as a fruit and widely used, often stuffed with pimiento or almonds, as a tapa or in salads. The remaining 90% is used for the production of oil. These olives will be taken to local factories where they are washed and then ground under cone-shaped stones. The resulting pulp is spread on esparto mats and pressed, so that the oil flows out and the 'cheese', which is the residue of the pips and pulp, is left behind. The oil is then filtered through a series of settling tanks, giving pure virgin olive oil.

Selecting a bottle of olive oil from the supermercado shelf, however, is not so simple. It's important to check the percentage of acidity. The best oil, virgen extra, comes from olives which are picked ripe and milled immediately and which can contain a maximum 1% acidity. Fino is

allowed 1.5% and corriente 3.3%. The higher the acidity, the stronger will be the flavour and therefore the lower the price. Aceite de Orujo is made by repressing the cheese left over from the first pressing. This is mainly used for industrial purposes, for instance in the production of Castille soap and in carding wool. Some aceite de orujo is also refined for cooking oil. To encourage production of high quality oil, a control board, as with wine, issues some denominación de origen labels. Of the four already issued, two are in Andalucía, at Sierra de Segura (Jaén) and Baena (Córdoba). In some parts of the south of Spain, oil-tasting takes place in the same way that wine is sampled.

It's a sad fact, however, that olive oil consumption in Spain has dropped considerably in recent years. Producing olive oil is expensive as it is a labour-intensive industry, whereas alternatives such as corn and sunflower oil lend themselves to the use of machinery in the farming methods and are therefore much cheaper on the supermarket shelf.

Olive oil does, however, have one saving grace – it is healthy. Folklore has always claimed that olive oil contributed to good complexions, efficient digestion and strong hearts. The people of Spain, Italy and Greece have a markedly lower incidence of coronary disease. Modern nutrition, with its emphasis on the Mediterranean diet seems to be confirming this belief. Olive oil contains no cholesterol.

The Essential Olive Oil Companion, by Anne Dolamore, published by Grub Street, includes information on varieties, history, cultivation and recipes.

Montilla
Population: 22,792
Altitude: 379 m

Eighteen kilometres south of Castro del Río, just off the N331, is Montilla, which is famed for its wine, giving its name to the drink, and bodegas (see box, above). Otherwise, there is little else of interest. A little to the west is **La Rambla**, a pottery centre specializing in the spouted drinking vessels known as **botijos**.

Laguna de Zonar & other lakes

Just southwest of the town of **Aguilar**, 8 km south of Montilla on the C329, is the largest lake in the Campiña Cordobesa, the Laguna de Zonar. Covering some 66 ha, this protected area comes complete with a hide and an information centre (which regrettably is often closed) and is outstanding for its winter wildfowl. It used to be one of the best spots in Andalucía for seeing the rare white-headed duck, until the recent introduction of carp which have decimated the subaquatic vegetation. Just off the Moriles-Jauja road is the **Laguna Amarga**, comprising some 16 ha of permanent water surrounded by abundant vegetation, including tamarisk and reeds. Wildfowl are again the main attraction, while purple gallinules occasionally breed in the reeds. Both marsh and Montagu's harriers hunt over the lake. Just off the Aguilar-Moriles road is the small, but permanent **Laguna del Rincón**. Fringed by often dense vegetation, this lake is reliable for white-headed ducks, plus a whole range of other winter wildfowl, while water rails and purple gallinules breed in the reeds. There is an information centre and public hide, but both may be closed during the week. The remaining lakes (the **Laguna de Tíscar** near Puerto Alegre, and **Laguna Salobral** close to Baena) are semi-permanent and can be dry by May, but often attract flamingoes and passage waders. Because of the salinity of the water, the surrounding vegetation is of the halophytic type. The permanent lagoons have an interesting range of amphibians, including striped-necked terrapins and painted frogs, while viperine water snakes are common.

East of Montilla is the town of Baena, a centre for the production of olive oil and having its own *denominación de origen* (see box, above). The huge oil storage tanks can be clearly seen as you approach Baena. The name of the town comes from a Roman called Baius who had a villa in the vicinity. Baena has Moorish origins and there are a number of interesting buildings, including the Church of Santa María, which has a Moorish tower, believed to be the minaret of a former mosque, while there are three Plateresque doors. Unfortunately the building was partially destroyed during the Civil War, when many of its treasures were lost. The castle was built in the ninth century and had many later extensions. There are still some stretches of its walls which form the boundaries of the old quarter and which feature two Almohad horseshoe gates. The centre of the old part of the town is the Plaza de la Constitución, around which are a number of buildings of historical importance, including an 18th-century colonnaded warehouse, which now operates as the Casa de cultura. Holy Week is spectacular in Baena, with two notable fraternities, the 'White Tailed Jews' and the 'Black Tailed Jews', who parade, rolling their drums, on alternate days. Should they meet (and this is usually arranged) they try to 'out-drum' each other. The din is predictable.

Baena
Population: 20,057
Altitude: 407 m

Córdoba Province

Sistema Subbético region

The south of the province becomes hillier as you get closer to the Sistema Subbético. The largest town of this region is **Lucena**, a centre of light-industry specializing in furniture, with some 40 retail outlets. The only reason for stopping here would be to look at the church of San Mateo, which is one of the finest Baroque churches in the province.

East of Lucena, on the N331, is the remarkable, but little visited town of Priego de Córdoba. An early Moorish settlement, Priego had its heyday in the 18th century, when it produced great quantities of silk and other textiles, creating a wealth that led to the construction of superb Baroque churches.

Before touring the churches, obtain a town plan from the tourist office just off the **Plaza de la Constitución**. The building in which the tourist office is located was the birthplace of Niceto Alcalá Zamora, who was the first

Priego de Córdoba
Population: 22,196
Altitude: 649 m

president of the Spanish republic between 1931 and 1936. In the square is the 16th-century fountain with its 180 jets. For sheer atmosphere, head next for the **Barrio Villa**, which is the oldest part of Priego and retains much of its original Moorish street plan. There are a number of delightful *plazuelas* linked by winding alleyways festooned with hanging pots of flowers and a promenade, the **Paseo de Adarve**, which gives wonderful views over the surrounding countryside. The Moorish castillo, with its dominating keep, has been heavily altered and is now privately owned.

Priego has a whole host of Baroque churches and in a short visit it will be impossible to cover all of them. The following are recommended: the **Iglesia de San Francisco**, in Calle Buen Suceso, with many examples of the work of Juan de Dios Santaella, born in Priego in the early 18th century; the **Iglesia de la Asunción**, in the Plaza de Abad Palomino, with its amazing *retablo* and *sagrario* (now national monuments); and **Iglesia la Aurora** in Calle Argentina, with a pillared façade and more gems from Santaella inside. This only scratches the surface – there are another half a dozen churches to satisfy Baroque buffs. There are four *pensiones* (one extremely cheap), but no hotels. There is a municipal campsite near the bullring.

Parque Natural Sierra Subbéticas In the extreme southeast of Córdoba province, to the east of Lucena and Cabra and to the west of Priego, is this protected area. It consists of limestone sierras, four of which are over 1,000 m in height, reaching a maximum of 1,570 m in the Sierra Tiñoso, and separated by narrow valleys. The area is lightly wooded, mainly by cork oaks, with poplars along the rivers. At the higher levels, raptors are the main attraction with perhaps some 20 pairs of griffon vultures. Short-toed eagles are common in summer, while with luck Bonellis and golden eagles may also be seen. The lower levels have a range of typical Mediterranean birds, such as hoopoes, the magnificently-coloured bee eater, red-rumped swallows, black wheatears and blue-rock thrushes. Pot holing and paragliding are available; check with the Reception and Nature Interpretation centre at km 23 on the road between Cabra and Carcabuey. There is also an information centre on the road to Zuheros.

One of the main gateways to the park is the small town of **Luque** to the north, which was at the centre of Moorish and Christian skirmishes in the 12th and 13th centuries. Its castle dates from the ninth century and a good section of the town walls are still standing. Worth looking at is the parish church of La Asunción in Gothic and Renaissance styles.

Granada Province

8

Granada is Andalucía's most mountainous province, with around half the area over 1,000 m in height and boasting Iberia's highest peak, of 3,481 m. With a snow cover for much of the year, the Sierra Nevada is Spain's premier skiing location and in 1996 it hosted the World Championships. The **Sierra Nevada** mountains, snow capped in winter, form a perfect backdrop to the city of Granada itself. It's worth stopping here for the magnificent Moorish **Alhambra** alone, but the rest of the city offers much more besides.

The beautiful mountainous region of the Alpujarras south of the Sierra Nevada has some of Andalucía's best walking country, as well as some of its most characterful villages.

The province's short stretch of Mediterranean coastline, known as the **Costa Tropical**, is the best bit of coastline in Andalucía, with tall cliffs, coves and attractive resorts such as **Salobreña** and **Almuñécar**.

Granada

Colour map 3, grid C1
Population: 241,471
Altitude: 685 m

There is a Spanish saying 'Quien no ha vistado Granada, no ha vistado nada' *(The person who has not seen Granada has seen nothing) Few who visit the city would disagree. Easily reached from the Costa by motorway, Granada should not be missed. Undoubtedly the jewel in the crown is the Moorish **Alhambra Palace**, regarded by many as the most dramatic and evocative monument in Europe. It was the palace-fortress of the last Muslim kingdom in Spain and reveals Moorish building and art at its sublime peak. The setting is magnificent. Built on a low hill between the rivers Genil and Darro, the Alhambra has as its backdrop the **Sierra Nevada**. But there is much more to see in Granada. On the far side of the Darro valley is the **Albaicín**, an old Moorish ghetto of atmospheric alleyways and squares, which straggles up the hill to the gypsy caves of **Sacromonte**. Down in the city, the Renaissance **Cathedral** has a Royal Chapel containing the tombs of* Los Reyes Católicos, *Ferdnando and Isabel. There are also many links with the Granadino writer and poet **Federico García Lorca** throughout the city, ranging from historic bodegas where he used to drink with his literary chums, to his summerhouse, now a Lorca museum.*

Ins and outs

Getting there
See page 330 for further details
The national **airport** is 17 km to the west of the city, T958245200. The *José Gonzalez* company runs 5 buses daily connecting the airport to the centre of Granada, stopping at the Palacio de Congresos and the Gran Vía (30 mins, €2.50). Taxis cost €15. The nearest international airport is at Málaga. The main **bus** station is on Ctra de Jaén, 3 km north-west of the town centre. A No 3 bus will bring you into the city. The **train** station is on Av de Andaluces, T958271272, reached by the No 11 bus, which follows a circular route.

Getting around
Once in Granada, it is easiest to travel on foot around the lower part of the city, since most main sights are close together and parking can be a problem.

Tourist offices
The main tourist office is a tiny office in the atmospheric Corral de Carbón, C Libreras 2. It opens Mon-Sat 0900-1900, Sun 1000-1400, T958221022, F958223927. The municipal tourist office, which is larger and more people friendly, is at Plaza de Mariana Pineda 10, T958247128, open Mon-Fri 0930-1900, Sat 1000-1400. Both can provide city maps, accommodation lists and a free *¿Qué Hacer? What's On?* booklet. There are additional tourism kiosks located in Plaza Nueva and Plaza Bib-Rambla, open from Mar-Oct. Useful websites: www.moeibus.es/ii/granada/; www.lingolex.com/granada.htm

History

Historical records go back to the **Iberian** tribe known as the Turdulos, who made coins on which Granada is named Iliverir. Then came successively the **Phoenicians**, the **Greeks** and the **Carthaginians**. The famous sculpture, the Dama de Baza, dates from the latter period. The **Romans** established a town, known as Illiberis, roughly in the location of the Alhambra. The settlement grew in importance under the **Visigoths**, at which time a **Jewish** suburb, named Garnatha Alyehud, became established on the southern slopes of the Alhambra. This was significant, because it is believed that the Jewish population assisted the **Moors** in their invasion of the city.

★

Things to do in Granada

- Avoid the crowds at the Alhambra – visit outside summer months a few hours before closing
- Ramble through the streets of the Albaicín and have a cuppa in a *tetería*, or Moroccan teashop
- Stay in a cave in Guadix
- Relax in the hot springs of Santa Fé
- Snowboard in the Sierra Nevada
- Go on the *romería* to Mulhacén Mountain from Trevélez in the Alpujarras in August

The Moors gave Granada the name Karnattah (both names mean pomegranate, the fruit which has now been adopted as the city's symbol). For three centuries it was under the control of the Caliphate of Córdoba, but when this declined the capital was moved in 1013 to Granada where it was to remain for fourth and a half centuries until it was ended by the Catholic Monarchs in 1492. Granada thrived under both the Almoravids and the Almohads, so that by the late 13th century its territory stretched from the coast at Tarifa in the west to Almería in the east. It could survive, however, by paying allegiance to the various Christian kings established to the north and occasionally using Arab power from North Africa. Its most affluent period came during the reigns of **Yusef I** (1334-54) and **Muhmmed V** (1354-91), the rulers who were largely responsible for the construction of the Alhambra.

Towards the end of the 15th century, however, things were to change for the worse. Firstly, in 1479, the Christian forces became united with the marriage of Ferdinand and Isabel and their combined armies had, within 10 years, taken Almería, Ronda and Málaga. At the same time the Moors were weakened by internal strife which led to civil war between rival supporters of the Sultan Muley Hassan's two most influential wives, Ayesha and Zoraya. The feud caused Ayesha to flee to Guadix with the heir Abu Abdullah (better known as Boabdil). He was proclaimed king there in 1482. Known as *El Rey Chico*, Boabdil eventually overthrew both his father and his uncle to become the last king of Granada. The Catholic Monarchs began to make impossible demands on **Boabdil**, who tried in vain to rustle up support from the Islamic world. War was declared in 1490 and Granada quickly laid to siege. After seven months Boabdil gave in and formally ceded the city to the Catholic Monarchs, thus completing the Christian Reconquest.

Harsh times followed for the city, with the Jewish and Moorish inhabitants eventually being expelled. Deprived of many of its craftsmen, traders and merchants, decline set in. There was a brief revival during the Baroque period, when several important monuments were built, such as the monastery of La Cartuja. As with many parts of Andalucía, the Peninsular War was a disaster for the city, with Napoleon's barbaric troops actually using the Alhambra as a barracks, causing untold damage to this monument and many others. Granadinos have always had a reputation for being staid, middle class and right wing (a distinct contrast with neighbouring Córdoba) and during the Civil War the local fascists slaughtered literally thousands of left wingers and liberals, including the writer Federico García Lorca – a blemish which the city still struggles to live down.

Granada Province

Alhambra

The Alhambra comprises four separate groups of buildings. The **Alcazaba** is a ruined 11th-century fortress, which was the only building on the hill when the Nazrids made Granada their capital. They extended the walls and towers, which are largely intact today. The **Casa Real** or Royal Palace was built much later during the 14th century, mainly during the reign of Muhammad V. The **Generalife** on the northeast side of the hill was the extravagant pleasure palace of the Nasrid rulers, recreated today as a series of beautiful flower-filled terraces, cool fountains and pools. Finally, there is the **Palace of Carlos V**, a Renaissance building that would stand as an impressive structure on its own, but is a grandiose intrusion amongst the Moorish surroundings. The name

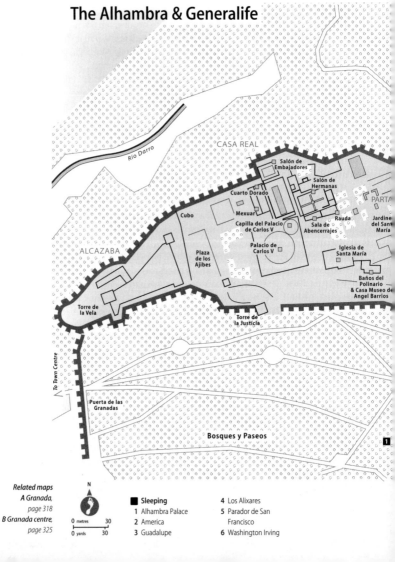

The Alhambra & Generalife

Rio Darro

CASA REAL

Salón de Embajadores

Salón de Hermanas

Cuarto Dorado

PARTA

Cubo

Mexuar

Capilla del Palacio de Carlos V

Rauda

Jardine del Sant María

Sala de Abencerrajes

ALCAZABA

Palacio de Carlos V

Iglesia de Santa María

Plaza de los Ajibes

Baños del Polinario & Casa Museo de Angel Barrios

Torre de la Vela

Torre de la Justicia

To Town Centre

Puerta de las Granadas

Bosques y Paseos

1

Related maps
A Granada,
page 318
B Granada centre,
page 325

N

0 metres 30
0 yards 30

■ Sleeping
1 Alhambra Palace
2 America
3 Guadalupe

4 Los Alixares
5 Parador de San Francisco
6 Washington Irving

Alhambra comes from the Moorish *Qalat Alhamra*, meaning the red palace or fort, which could refer to the red building stone or soil, although some Arab chroniclers claim that it derives from the fact that it was rebuilt at night by the reddish light of flaming torches.

Only 8,800 visitors a day are allowed into the Alhambra so it's advisable to book in advance, particularly during the high season. A small number of tickets may be on sale at the entrance early in the morning, but the vast majority of tickets are sold up to a year in advance through the Banco Bilbao Viscaya (BBV), at any of their branches, or by ringing T902224460 from within Spain, and T00341374 5420 from abroad. Alternatively, see http://decompras. bbv.es choosing the day and time you wish to visit. At the peak season you may be allocated a time. Tickets

Admission

The Alhambra is best avoided during the heat of summer when it is most crowded, although it's better to see it in the summer than not at all

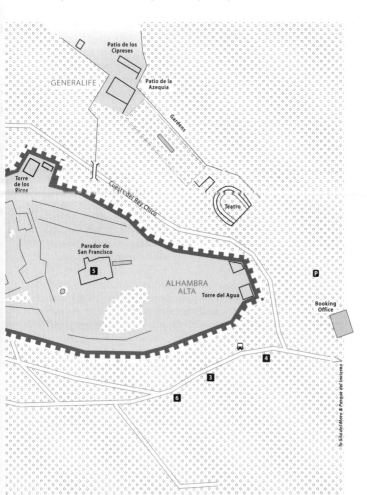

Granada Province

are payable by credit card (Visa and Mastercard only); collect them from any branch of BBV or from the Alhambra office well before you allocated slot. In an effort at crowd control, the tickets to the Alhambra will have a 30-minute time slot for entry to the Casa Real (once in you can stay as long as you like) and as this is likely to be some time after your initial entry to the Alhambra, there will be time to see first the Generalife and the Alcazaba. ■ *The Alhambra area is open Mar-Oct 0830-2000 (floodlit visits Tue-Sat 2200-2330); Nov-Feb 0830-1800 (floodlit visits Fri-Sat 2000-2130). €7, EU senior citizens €5, under 8s and disabled free.* The ticket office opens at 0800.

Getting there To reach the Alhambra on foot from the city, leave Plaza Nueva by the steep Calle Cuesta de Gomérez, reaching after about 200 m the **Puerta de las Granadas**, a stone gateway capped with three large pomegranates, the symbol of the city. Take the left-hand fork and you'll eventually reach a modern block which is the main entrance to the complex. If arriving by car you can no longer use the Calle Cuesta de Gomérez route. Instead follow the brown signs marked ALHAMBRA, which takes you round the ring road, towards the Sierra Nevada, before turning back up the hill to approach the Alhambra from the east. Take a ticket from the car park machine on entry and pay at the kiosk or automated machine before leaving.

Alcazaba The **Plaza del Aljibes** was once a gully separating the palace from the fortress, but was filled in after the Reconquest to contain *aljibes* or large water cisterns. Later the whole area was flattened out to form a parade ground. You can inspect the cisterns on Monday, Wednesday and Friday mornings. The Alcazaba is the oldest part of the whole complex, but most of it was destroyed by Napoleon's departing troops. Much of the central area is taken up with the **Jardín de los Ardaves**, a garden dating from the 17th century. Cross this to reach the **Torre de la Vela**, the top of which gives magnificent views over the city, the Río Darro and over to the Albaicín and the caves of Sacromonte, with the snow capped hills of the Sierra Nevada in the opposite direction.

Casa Real Recross the Plaza de los Aljibes to reach the **Casa Real**, the Royal Palace, dating largely from the 14th century, particularly during the rule of Muhammad V. It can be divided into three distinct sections. The Mexuar was a series of chambers used for business; the Serallo was where important guests were received; and the Harem consisted of the private living quarters. Having fallen into decline over the centuries, serious restoration work began in 1860 and is still underway, so that some areas may be closed to the public. Although its exterior is simple, the interior is highly intricate with a variety of ornamented ceilings and walls made of tiles, carved plaster work and Arabic inscriptions. There is clever use of light and space, with courtyards and delicate archways set off with fountains and water channels drawn off the nearby Genil and Darro rivers. Water is skilfully used as the central theme throughout the palace, with many pools mirroring the surrounding carvings.

The entrance to the Casa Real leads into the **Mexuar** (1), the place where the Moorish kings held court with their subjects and dispensed justice. It had a similar function immediately after the Reconquest. At the far end is a small **Oratorio** (2), set at an angle to Mecca. This leads to the **Cuarto Dorado** (3) or Golden Room, which was re-vamped by Carlos V, although originally Mudéjar. The **Patio de Cuarto Dorado** (4), a simple courtyard with an ornate façade, leads into the Serallo section of the Casa, which was built in the time of Yusef I – and mainly to his design.

The first section of the Serallo is the **Patio de los Arrayanes** (5), named after the neat myrtle hedges alongside the sizeable pool with its simple fountain. Notice here the beautifully carved filigree plaster work. The route now moves into the **Sala de la Barca** (6), which has an exceptional, restored *artesonado* wooden ceiling, thought by some to be in the form of a boat, although the name probably derives from a corruption of the Arabic word *baraka* (blessing or luck). Just beyond here is the **Torre de Comares** (7), the most impressive of the Alhambra's towers, 45 m high with walls 2½ m thick. Inside is the **Salón de Embajadores** (8), by far the largest room in the palace with a ceiling soaring to a height of 20 m. The carved walls here are quite stunning, set off by a large number of windows, doorways and arches, complementing the cedarwood ceiling. The original floor was probably marble, but this has been replaced at some time with earthenware tiles around a centre of glazed tiles with a coat of arms. The room has a strong sense of history, for it was here that Boabdil signed the document handing the city over to the Christians. It is also probable that this was the place where Columbus was received by Ferdinand to discuss his proposed travels to the New World.

The Harem section of the Casa Real is the **Patio de los Leones** (9), or the Court of the Lions, which is undoubtedly the most photographed part of the palace – although you would need to be there out of season to obtain a photograph which excludes the crowds. This beautiful courtyard represents a symbolic Islamic paradise with a central fountain supported by 12 small grey lions from which four rivers of paradise flow into four restful pavilions. The fountain is a recent addition and it has been argued that the triangles on the heads of two of the lions would make the Star of David, suggesting Jewish origin. The same theory claims that it could not have been Moorish because they represent living animals, although as the nearby ceiling has both men and animals represented, perhaps this argument should not be taken too seriously. The patio is surrounded by arches resting on a marble forest of 124 pillars, each with a different capital.

Casa Real

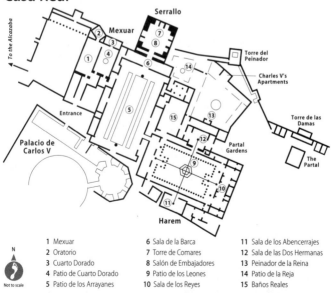

Granada Province

N

Not to scale

1 Mexuar	6 Sala de la Barca	11 Sala de los Abencerrajes
2 Oratorio	7 Torre de Comares	12 Sala de las Dos Hermanas
3 Cuarto Dorado	8 Salón de Embajadores	13 Peinador de la Reina
4 Patio de Cuarto Dorado	9 Patio de los Leones	14 Patio de la Reja
5 Patio de los Arrayanes	10 Sala de los Reyes	15 Baños Reales

There are a number of rooms leading off the Patio de los Leones. At the far eastern end is the **Sala de los Reyes** (10), the Hall of the Kings, entered by three porches with triple arches. Of particular interest here are the drawings in leather of men and lions, the 10 Moors possibly representing kings, hence the name. These drawings, which have been attached to the beams, are in direct contradiction to Islamic law and it is believed that they may have been the work of a Christian during the latter years of the Moorish rule. To the south is the **Sala de los Abencerrajes** (11). In the fountain at its centre it is said that Abu al-Hassan, the father of Boabdil, beheaded some 16 members of the Abencerraj family whose leader had fallen in love with his favourite wife Zoraya. Although there may be no more to this story than the red streak in the marble of the fountain, that are probably due to rust, this room certainly saw some acts of considerable cruelty. Don't miss the ceiling in this room; with 16 sides, each lit by a window and sta-lactite vaulting to the sides. On the north side is the **Sala de las dos Hermanas** (12), the Room of the Two Sisters, named after two slabs of white marble in the floor, but possibly the room of the sultan's favourite wife. The honeycomb of stucco work on the dome is dazzling. This room opens out onto a mirador, known as the 'eyes of the sultana', with a tranquil garden patio below.

Continuing along a rather tortuous route you eventually arrive at the **Peinador de la Reina** (13), the Queen's Pavilion, which was originally an ora-tory for the sultanas, but later the dressing room for Carlos V's wife. Moving through the **Patio de la Reja** (14), a 17th-century addition, the route moves to the **Baños Reales** (15), the Royal Baths, which are in the Roman style rather than Arabic. The entry room contains four arches forming a square area in the centre surrounded by galleries, the walls of which are richly decorated in mosaic tiles. The baths themselves have white marble walls and floor, with an upper gallery, possibly for musicians who were reputedly blind. The baths are only open to visitors on specific days which change throughout the year. An up-to-date timetable can be obtained from the tourist office or by calling the Alhambra information office, T902224460.

The exit from the Casa Real takes you into the **Partal Gardens** (named after a pavilion or portico) with its central pool guarded by two large stone lions. Rising over the gardens is the **Torre de las Damas**, via which Boabdil is said to have escaped from his father Muley Abul Hassan. The gallery of the tower has an ornamental wood ceiling with a cupola decorated with stars, domes and shells. The highest part of the tower forms a belvedere giving fine views over the Darro valley below.

Palacio de Carlos V This building was begun in 1526 after Carlos V had pulled down a significant part of the Casa Real to make way for it. The palace was designed by Pedro Manchuca, who was once a pupil of Michelangelo, and is in strong Renais-sance style. The work was stopped in 1568 due to a Moorish rebellion and did not resume until 1579, but has never been completely finished. Although claimed to be the best Renaissance palace outside Italy, it sits uncomfortably amongst the delicate Moorish buildings around it (in much the same way the Christian cathedral seems out of place in the Moorish Mosque at Córdoba, which was also the work of Carlos V). The interior is dominated by the central courtyard in the form of a circle surrounded by a portico of 32 Doric columns, with a similar number of Ionic columns in the upper gallery, which is a pattern repeated on the exterior of the building. The courtyard was often used as an arena and even staged bullfights. The ground floor of the palace now houses the Museo Hispano-Musulmán, while the upper floor is the site of the Granada's Museo de Bellas Artes.

Washington Irving

As hordes of visitors wander around the carefully restored Alhambra, few realize how much they owe to the 19th-century American humourist and writer Washington Irving, who created the character Rip van Winkle.

Irving was born in New York in 1783 and after rejecting his early legal career, turned to writing, providing literary pieces for New York newspapers. In 1809 he wrote The History of New York, supposedly the diary of an early Dutch immigrant. It was claimed to be the first American contribution to comic literature and earned instant fame and fortune. In 1815, he came to England and was part of a literary circle that included Sir Walter Scott. During this period, he wrote a book of short stories called Sketch Book, which included Rip van Winkle and The Legend of Sleepy Hollow, made into a successful Hollywood film starring Johnny Depp in 2000, and was widely acclaimed for its whimsicality and humour.

Between 1826 and 1829, Irving was a member of the staff of the US Legation in Madrid. During this time, he hired some rooms in the Royal Palace of the Alhambra and wrote the romantic Tales of the Alhambra. Published in 1832, it is still on sale in many of the shops in Granada. The Alhambra had been used as a prison in the 18th century and had been badly damaged by Napoleon's troops during their occupation in 1812. In fact, they tried to blow up the whole complex during their retreat and were only foiled by a soldier who returned to remove the fuses. Washington Irving's Tales of the Alhambra brought the Spaniards' attention the treasure on their doorstep and it was quickly proclaimed a National Monument and has been cosseted ever since. Meanwhile, Irving's only memorial in Granada is the rather uninspiring hotel named after him just beneath the Alhambra's walls.

Granada Province

The **Museo Hispano Musulmán** contains many items from the Alhambra, most notably a spectacular 15th-century vase, the Jarrón de la Alhambra, 1½ m in height, together with Moorish ceramics, stucco, carvings, jewellery, etc. There is also an 11th-century stone trough with strong relief work on its sides showing antelopes and lions fighting at the foot of a tree. The **Museo de Bellas Artes** has sculptures that are generally better than the paintings, with works by Diego de Siloé, Alonso Cano, Pedro de Mena and the de Mora brothers. One of the most important items is a triptych of El Gran Capitán, a 15th-century raised enamel from Limoges attributed to Nardon Penicaud. After the beauty of the Alhambra, this museum does not get the attention it deserves. ■ *Both museums are open Tue 1430-1800, Wed-Sat 0900-1800, Sun 0900-1430. The Alhambra entrance fee does not cover these museums and tickets must be bought at the door. Each museum is free with EU passport, otherwise €1.50.*

Generalife

Above the Alhambra on the slopes of the Cerro del Sol is the Generalife, the summer palace of the monarchs of Granada. The name is derived from the Arabic *Gennat-al-Arif* (Garden of the Architect). It was probably built in the 13th century, although it has since been altered several times, particularly after the fall of Granada, although this work was almost certainly carried out by Arab workers. It can be reached from the upper car park entrance and also from the Alhambra via a bridge which crosses the Cuesta del Rey Chico.

The grounds of the Generalife consist of a soothing interplay of pathways, gardens and fountains, with clever use of shade and running water – ideal for a relaxing hour or two in the heat of summer. The best known area is the **Patio**

de la Acequia (Court of the Long Pond), with its arched walkway and stretch of gently playing fountains, framed by flowerbeds. At its end is the delightful little palace full of latticed plasterwork and an upper galleried belvedere. The other main courtyard is the **Patio de los Cipreses**, where the ancient trees are said to have been the setting for romantic intrigues over the centuries, most notably the affair between Boabdil's favourite wife Zoraya and the head of the Abencerrajes clan which led to the supposed bloody execution in the Sala de los Abencerrajes.

It should be remembered that a sizeable city was contained within the walls of the Alhambra and whilst most of this has since been reduced to ruins, there are a few other buildings remaining. Of these, by far the most interesting is the **Convento de San Francisco**. Built by Fernando and Isabel in the late 15th century on the site of a Moorish palace, it is now a parador. The chances of getting a room here are slight unless you book several weeks ahead, but it is worth strolling around and having a drink on the delightful patio. Nearby are the remains of a chapel where Fernando and Isabel were originally buried, before being removed (against their instructions) to the cathedral in the city.

Sights

Albaicín Clinging to the hillside across from the Alhambra on the far side of the Río Darro is the evocative Moorish ghetto of Albaicín, its name meaning 'district on the slope of a hill'. It is believed to have been originally occupied in 1227 by Moors driven out of Baza by Ferdnando III and became one of the busiest areas of Moorish Andalucía, shown by the remains of 30 or more mosques and numerous water tanks and fountains. Flanking the winding, narrow streets are villas with Moorish decoration and beautiful gardens tantalisingly concealed by their high walls. The air is scented with jasmine, orange blossom and, at night, the distinctive musky perfume of *dama de noche*. The best approach is by taking the Carrera del Darro from the Plaza Nueva, alongside the river which leads past fine facades and crumbling bridges. There are stunning views of the Alhambra to the right (particularly when it's floodlit at night). Then strike off left up the Cuesta del Chapiz or the Calle de Zafra to ramble along the narrow cobbled streets and alleys, through tiny plazas buzzing with life, past Moorish ramparts and cisterns and the traditional *cármenes* (a combination of houses and gardens). If you keep climbing you will eventually arrive at the Mirador de San Nicolás, from where you can experience a glorious view of the Alhambra, particularly at dusk.

There are also however a number of interesting sights in the valley, including the **Church of Santa Ana**, a brick church in Mudéjar style, which seems to rise out of the side of the Río Darro. Dating from the 16th century and located just above the point where the Río Darro disappears under the city, it was built in 1537 by Diego de Siloé and has a strong Mudéjar influence. Look, in particular, for the dazzling ceiling in the main chapel. Nearby, on the left at No 31, are the **Baños Arabes**, 11th-century public baths entered via a tiny patio garden. Some of the columns in the brick built rooms are Roman and there are typical starred and octagonal skylights. ■ *Tue-Sat 1000-1400. Free.*

Also on the Carrera del Darro at No 41 is the **Casa de Castril**, a 16th-century mansion with a splendidly ornate Plateresque façade and now housing the city's **Museo Arqueológico**. There are some important and well-displayed Neolithic remains from the caves at Los Murceliegos and an excellent Roman section, which includes some fourth-century Christian lamps. Make sure you see the Moorish room featuring a fourth-century bronze astrolabe,

Federico García Lorca

Lorca, undoubtedly the most popular poet of the Spanish speaking world, was born in 1898 in the village of Fuente Vaqueros, a village on the vega to the west of Granada. His childhood was spent in Granada and on the family farm, Huerta de San Vincente, where he absorbed the flavour of the Andalucían countryside and the way of life of its people, especially the gypsies. He attended the university in Granada, where he published his first book of poems, and later went on to Madrid University where he studied philosophy. When he was 30, he achieved national fame for the first time with his book of gypsy ballads, El Romancero Gitano. On the strength of this success, he went to New York for a year learning English, intermittently attending Columbia University and working on a book of poems, Poeta en Nueva York, which was published after his death.

Lorca returned to Spain in 1931 and ran a popular travelling theatre for the Spanish government. During the next five years he produced his best known stage works, including Bodas de Sangre (Blood Wedding, 1933), Yerma (1935) and La Casa de Bernarda Alba (1936), which dealt with the passions and emotions of country people. His most famous set of poems was Lament for the Death of a Bullfighter and other poems (1935), stressing throughout the nobility of the gypsies.

Lorca was proud of his Moorish ancestry and despised the post-Reconquest activities of the Christians, suggesting that Los Reyes Católicos had destroyed a culture superior to their own. He was also strongly critical of Granada's middle class, believing them to be northerners rather than true Andalucíans. Lorca was an accomplished musician and recognized the historical importance of

flamenco to the Andalucían culture, organizing Granada's first festival of cante jondo, the deep gypsy song.

Lorca was an open homosexual, with Republican sympathies. Neither trait appealed to the middle classes of Granada, where Lorca had expected to be safe during the Civil War. He was mistaken. In August 1936 he was assassinated by a group of Franco's followers in a gully in the village of Viznar, some 10 km northeast of Granada. His body was never found.

The Granada authorities have been slow to appreciate the worth of their most famous son, but if you're after a Lorca pilgrimage there are three places which you can visit. The house where Lorca was born in Fuente Vaqueros is now a museum to his memory (see Museums below). Secondly, the Huerta de San Vicente in Calle Arabial, a former orchard where the Lorca family spent the summer, is now transformed into a beautiful rose garden. "From the Huerta de San Vicente, where I live among magnificent fig trees and sturdy walnut trees, I have the best mountain view in Europe," Lorca wrote to a friend. In front of the house, beside the lane, you can still see the two cypresses planted by Federico and his brother Francisco. The house on the plot is a small museum containing Lorca's original furniture, paintings and other objects; among the most interesting is his piano, a drawing by Salvador Dali and Lorca's desk, where he wrote some of his most accomplished works, such as Diwan of the Tamarit and Blood Wedding, amongst others. ■ Tue-Sat 1000-1230, 1600-1830. €1.30, Wed free. Finally, at the village of Viznar, where Lorca was shot, there is a monumental garden with a small granite memorial.

which was used to position stars in order to orientate mihrabs towards Mecca, as well as converting Muslim dates into Christian ones. ■ *Tue 1500-2000, Wed-Sat 0900-2000, Sun 0900-1430. Free to EU citizens, otherwise €1.50. T958225640.*

Behind this building is the **Convento de Santa Catalina**, housed in an old Moorish palace – the nuns' *dulces* have a mean reputation. The main mosque

Granada

To Casa Aljarife,
Hostal Veronica & Cool

Hospital
Real

Ancha de Capuchinos

Aceta de San Ildefonso

Av Cap Morena

Avenida de Pastor

Av Hospicio

14

Fuente
del Triunfo

9

Cuesta de San Antonio

Walls of the
Albacín

Carretera de Murcia

Pagés

6

Pardo Horno

Las Minas

Panadéros

ALBAICIN

Larga San Cristóbal

Veredilla de San Cristóbal

Ceniceros

Alhacaba

Aljibe de la Gitana

7

Callejón Campañas

2

San Nicolás

12

Nuevo San Nicolás

Monjas

Pilar Seco

Natalio Rivas

Nueva Santísimo

Mendoza

10

Lavadero la Cruz

San Juan de Dios Gran

Mano de Hierro

Iglésia de San
Juan de Dios
& Hospital

6

Arriola

Rector López Argueta

San
Jeronimo

Cuesta Colegios

Plaza
del Triunfo

Carrera de Toma

Calle

Almona del Boqueron

Los Santos

Gran Via de Colon

Calle de Elvira

Carrera de San Juan

Calle de la Duquesa

9

Eshavira tapas

Zenete

Santa Isabel
la Real

10

8 **5**

San José

San José

3

Carro Chavel

Rosar

Guimiel San Jose

San Gregorio
Betico

Santa Ana

7

Tendillas Santa Paula Marqués

B

San Jerónimo

Calle Augustin

Calderería Nueva

Calderería Vieja

Cetti Meriem

Almireceros

Plaza
Nueva

Plaza
Santa Ana

Cuesta de
Gomerez

Paredón
Jesús Peñas

@
Freenem

12

Conde de Tendillas

Horno de Haza

Montalbán

Horno de Abar

Plaza
Lobos

Carril del Picon

Cuenca Colegios

Triana

Tablas

Santa Teresa

13

Calle del Buensuceso

13

La Paz

Plaza
Trinidad

Colegio Catalino

Pescadería Salamanca

Los Meisones

Alhóndiga

Iglésia de la
Magdalena

Cathedral

Capilla
Real

Palacio
de

Plaza Isabela
Católica

Plaza
Descalzas

Estribo

Alcaicería
area

Alcaiceria

Calle Reyes Católicos

M Pineda

Corral del
Carbón

1

Campo
Verde

Plaza
Bib-
Rambla

Pavaneras

Escudo del Carmen

Laurel

Jardín

Tomita

San Rafael

Piedra Santa

11

Las Navas Rosario

C Sarabla

Plaza
Mariana
Pineda

Cta del
Progreso

Obispo

Veronica de la Magdalena

Gracia

Puentezuelas

Párraga

Angel Gavinet

Cervantes @

San Miguel Alta

Casillas del Prats

Música Vieja
Zarzo

Moral de la Magdalena

Solarillo de Gracia

La Cruz

Agulla

Angel

7

Calle de Recogidas

Los Frailes

Plaza de
Campillo

3

5

Pino

Pte
Castañeda

2

Acera de Darro

4

San Jacinto

San Pedro Mártir

Martinez

Pasaje
Recogidas

Luis Braille

Graf Navíraez

Afán de Ribera

San José

Nueva San Antón
Baja

Horno Esperado

Padre
Alcover

Calle de San Antón

Duende

San Isidro

Nuestra Señora de
las Angustias

To Restaurant Raíces

To Mezquita

To Mezquita

Calle de Sócrates

Granada Province

Detail maps

*A The Alhambra &
Generalife,* page 310

B Granada centre,
page 325

N

0 metres   100
0 yards   100

■ **Sleeping**	6 Hostal San Joaquin	12 Pension Los Iznajenos
1 Alhambra Palace	7 Hostal Veronica	13 Reina Cristina
2 Carmen	8 Lola del Castillo	
3 Carmen de Santa Inés	9 Luz Granada	● **Eating**
4 Casa Marisca	10 Pensión Las Cumbres	1 Bar Chirimeras
5 Dauro	11 Pensión Lisboa	2 Bar La Mancha Chica

of the Albaicín now has the **Iglesia de San Salvador** built on its site, but the original *Patio Arabe* was fortunately preserved. The best views of the Alhambra and the distant Sierra Nevada are obtained from the mirador at the top of the hill beside the **Iglesia de San Nicolás**, which can be reached on bus no 12. The church has little of interest, but note the Moorish fountain outside.

Other fine, historic churches in the Albaicín include the **Iglesia de San Juan de los Reyes** with a bell tower that was the original minaret of the mosque over which the church was built. Close to the Casa Castril is the **Iglesia de San Pedro**. It dates from 1570 and has an open cloister overlooking the Río Darro. In the northwest of the Albaicín is the **Iglesia de Santa Isabel la Real**, founded by the Queen in 1505 and built on land belonging to the Nazarí kings. Also in the west of the Albaicín is the **Iglesia de San José,** dating from 1525 and housing some valuable art and sculpture, and the **Iglesia de San Gregorio Bético**, built by the Catholic Monarchs on the site of a Christian cemetery during the time of the Nazarí kings.

■ *University students lead tours of the Albaicín on Fri, Sat and Sun leaving at 1200, 1600, 1800 and 2000. Tours depart from the Real Cancille ría close to Plaza Nueva, T670634837.*

North Granada

Once up here the **Puerta Nueva** gateway is nearby to the north. From here west, parallel with the Cuesta de la Alhacaba, are some 13th-century Moorish walls, marking the oldest area of Moorish Granada. Near the west end is the **Convento of Santa Isabel** on Calle San Juan de los Reyes, named after the Queen who received the city at Boabdil's capitulation in 1492. Partially built within an old Nasrid palace of which some arches still remain, the convent's church has a Mudéjar ceiling and a fine Plateresque doorway. Beyond it on

Granada Province

3 Café Suizo
4 Chikito
5 El Alcebreche
6 El Ladrillo
7 El Mirador

9 Mare Nostrúm
10 Mesón Blas Cas
11 Mirador de Moraya
12 San Nicolas
13 Taqueria Mexico

Callejón de las Monjas, formerly part of the convent, are the remains of the 15th-century Moorish palace of Dar al-Horra built for Boabdil's mother Ayesha la Horra, whose feud with her husband was largely responsible for the Moors loss of Granada. The style of the surviving tower and patio overlooking the Albaicín is reminiscent of the Alhambra itself. ■ *This convent is temporarily closed for restoration, but the convent church is open daily 1000-1800.*

Two churches worth a visit are the **Iglesia de San Miguel** on the east side of the attractive Plaza de San Miguel Bajo, built over a mosque and preserving the original ablutions fountain, and the **Iglesia de San José**, in Calle Cauchiles, also built over a mosque and maintaining the minaret as a belfry. If you can't manage the walk, take the Alhambra bus, which runs every 15 minutes linking Plaza Nueva with the Albaicín, dropping you off at the central Plaza San Miguel El Bajo.

Sacromonte This area of gypsy caves has been inhabited for hundreds of years. Although some still do live here the majority of the *gitanos* have been rehoused in the city after the floods in 1962. The gypsies return in the evening to perform contrived flamenco shows to coachloads of tourists, who are outrageously fleeced with over-the-top prices for drinks and tatty souvenirs, often with a spot of professional pick-pocketing and amateurish fortune telling. Nevertheless, Sacromonte has plenty of atmosphere and you can have a good, if pricey, evening out.

Catedral Claimed to be one of the finest Renaissance churches in Spain, most might find this description extravagant, but there is much of interest, particularly in the interior. The Cathedral is located in the centre of the old Moorish city or medina. When the Catholic Monarchs conquered the city the cathedral was accommodated in the main mosque, but this was demolished in 1508 and work began on a new cathedral in 1518. The construction was directed by a number of people, the most notable of whom was Diego de Siloé, between

Catedral

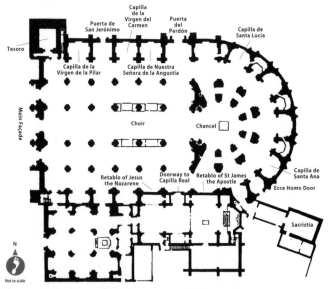

Granada Province

1528 and 1563. Squat, towerless and hemmed in by other buildings, the exterior, which is made of brown sandstone, is dull, with only the main façade by Alonso Cano of some merit. The two doors to the north, the Ecce Homo and San Jerónimo are worth seeing. The interior, however, has some redeeming features, being light, airy and, unusually for Andalucía, possessing some fine stained glass windows at higher levels by Theodore of Holland. The interior stonework of the cathedral is painted white and this makes a sharp contrast with the gold of the Capilla Mayor, where on the columns of the main arch are statues of the Catholic Monarchs at prayer, carved by Pedro de Mena. There is a triple nave, with two side aisles, supported by sturdy pillars. In the south aisle, the Doorway to the Capilla Real, or Royal Chapel, is flanked by *retablos* to St James the Apostle and Jesus the Nazerene, both dripping with gold leaf. Equally noteworthy is the High Altar, in cupola style, and the choir stalls carved by an anonymous 16th-century craftsman. There are 20 side chapels, with art works by Bocanegra, Cano and Ribera. The Capilla de Nuestra Señora de las Angustias has a magnificent Baroque *retablo* and a 15th-century carving of the Virgin brought by the conquering Christian army. Also worth looking at are the chapels of the Virgen del Pilar, the Virgen del Carmen, Santa Lucía and Santa Ana. There is also a small museum, with the usual vestments silverware and tapestries.

Part of the Cathedral-Capilla Real complex is the **Church of El Sagrario**, which is a 1704 reconstruction. There are some 15th and 16th century paintings and a delightful Renaissance baptismal font carved in white marble. Entry to the Cathedral is along an alleyway from Calle Gran Vía de Colón. ■ *Mon-Sat 1000-1330 and Mon-Sun 1600-1900.* €*2.10.*

The **Capilla Real**, begun in 1506 and completed in 1521, was designed as a sepulchre for the Catholic Monarchs. Isabel died in 1505 and Fernando 11 years later, both being buried at the Alhambra, but in 1521 their remains were taken to the Capilla Real. The Gothic style building actually has only one façade (it adjoins three other buildings), which has a Plateresque portico embellished with shield and emblems of Los Reyes Católicos. Inside, the tombs are found in the transept enclosed by a fine Plateresque *reja* by Maestro Bartolemé of Jaén. The tombs are carved from Carrera marble and the Catholic Monarchs are flanked by their daughter Joana la Loca (the Mad) and her unfortunate husband Felipe el Hermoso (the Fair). The actual coffins are in the crypt underneath, but whether they still contain the monarchs' bodies is debatable as they were desecrated by Napoleon's troops during the Peninsular War. Other features of note are the *retablo* by Felipe de Vigarny containing a

Capilla Real

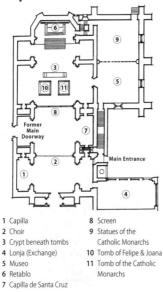

1 Capilla	8 Screen
2 Choir	9 Statues of the
3 Crypt beneath tombs	Catholic Monarchs
4 Lonja (Exchange)	10 Tomb of Felipe & Joana
5 Museo	11 Tomb of the Catholic
6 Retablo	Monarchs
7 Capilla de Santa Cruz	

Granada Province

wealth of gilded figures and scenes including the handing over of the keys of the city by Boabdil, and the Sacristy which contains Fernando's sword, Isabel's crown and her personal art collection including several Medieval Flemish paintings and her impressive royal jewels. All in all the Capilla Real is of more interest than the cathedral itself. Enter from Calle Oficios. ■ *Mar-Sep Mon-Sat 1030-1330 and Sun 1100-1300, Mon-Sun 1600-1900; Oct-Feb daily 1030-1300 and 1530-1830. €2.10*

Alcaicería This is an arcade of souvenir shops, formerly the Moorish silk market, located around Calle Zacatín which was next to the mosque (now under the cathedral). Unfortunately, little of the original market remains following a fire in 1843. Restoration work has been carried out reviving some of the atmosphere, but substituting expensive gift shops for the Moorish bazaars. South of the Alcaicería is the charming **Plaza Bib-Rambla**, with its central area lined with flower stalls plus an impressive fountain. The buildings around the square include part of the old university dating back to the 16th century. There are a number of cafés and restaurants to provide a peaceful break from sightseeing.

Palacio de Madraza Also in Calle Zacatín at the north end is this rarely visited palace which was built in the early 1300s for Yusef I and was the prayer college attached to the mosque. Although much restored, it is still possible to see the old prayer hall with its elaborately decorated *mihrab*. Gaining further entry, however, may be a problem.

Corral de Carbón This is the oldest surviving Moorish building in Granada. It was originally a 14th–century inn, before being successively adapted as a granary, a theatre, a centre for charcoal sellers (hence its present name) and now a craft centre with artisan workshops. Entry is through a magnificent Moorish horseshoe arch backed by a double gallery arch into a courtyard with a marble horse trough, surrounded by two upper galleries made of brick. The municipal tourist office is now located here in the office to the left of the entrance.

Hospital de San Juan de Dios Situated in the west of the central area of Granada and about 10 minutes' walk from the cathedral is this building. It was founded by the Catholic Monarchs in 1492 and has been on its present site since 1504. Entry is through a fine portico with Doric columns, but the most impressive features are the two patios. The outer, larger one has a lower arched gallery decorated with coloured tiles and a typical Andalucían pebble patterned floor with central fountain. The smaller inner patio is full of orange trees and crumbling frescoes. The building is still a working hospital and entry should be discreet. Next door is the **Church of San Juan de Dios**. Begun in 1737, it has an imposing façade capped with two spires. The entrance door has two sets of Corinthian

columns, the upper set framing a statue of San Juan by Ponce de León. The interior is dominated by the high chapel with frescoes and a spectacular *retablo* by JF Guerrero dripping with gold, marble and glass.

Monasterio de San Jerónimo One block away from San Juan de Dios in Calle Gran Capitán is this monastery. It was founded by the Catholic Monarchs in 1492 and the building was completed in 1547, much of the work directed by Siloé. Of exceptional importance are the cloisters, with a double layer of 36 arches, and the church, which has some 18th-century frescoes and a magnificent gold *retablo*. On either side of the *retablo* are statues of the so-called El Gran Capitán, Gonzalo de Córdoba, and his wife María Manrique at prayer. ■ *1000-1330 and 1500-1830. €2.10.*

Monasterio de la Cartuja Not far from the university on the northwest side of the city on Calle Real de Cartuja is this impressive Carthusian monastery. It is located in the Ainada Mar (Fountain of Tears) area of Granada where the Arabs once built their summer residences on land given by El Gran Capitán, Gonzalo de Córdoba. It took over 300 years to complete and is a mixture of the styles spanning this period resulting in an overall impression of jumbled opulence, with Baroque dominant. Entry is through a Plateresque porch, with an arch bearing the coat of arms of Spain, over which is a vaulted niche with a 16th-century wooden statue of the Virgin. Within, there is a large courtyard full of orange trees and box hedges, with the monastery on one side and the Church on the other. The church's wealth almost overwhelming, but note in particular the 18th-century sacristy in brown and white marble and rich decorations. The Sagrario is almost as impressive, while next to the choir stalls are a pair of paintings by Cotán surrounded by gilded carving. ■ *Daily 1000-1300 and 1600-2000 Mar-Sep; 1030-1300 and 1530-1800 Oct-Feb. €1.80, free Sun mornings. The monastery is a good 30 mins' walk from the centre, but bus no 8 bus passes nearby.*

Museums
Many museums are now free for EU citizens, but you'll need your passport as proof

Casa Museo Federico García Lorca, located 17 km west of the city in the village of Fuente Vaqueros, is the birthplace and former home of the dramatist and poet Federico García Lorca, who was shot by right-wing Nationalists in 1936. He was born in June 1898 in the house of the village schoolmistress, his mother. The house is now a museum and the neighbouring granary turned into an exhibition and cultural centre. The building is located in Calle Poeta García Lorca, just off the main square, and is full of Lorca memorabilia. See box, page . ■ *Tue-Sun 1000-1300 and 1800-2000 in summer and 1000-1230 and 1600-1830 in winter. €1. T958258466. Ureña buses go here approximately hourly from Av Andaluces by the train station.*

Casa Museo Manuel de Falla was Gaditano composer's home for a number of years at Calle Antequeruela Alta 11. ■ *Tue-Sun 1000-1500. €1.50.*

Museo Angel Barrios was the home of this 20th-century guitarist. It is inside the Alhambra grounds and contains information about his life. ■ *Sat only, 1000-1400. Free.*

Casa de los Tiros, located in the Plaza del Padre Suarez, was formerly the Palace of the Princes of Granada and now houses the Museo de Historia y Artesanía de Granada. A fortress-like building, it gets its name from the *tiros* or muskets projecting from the upper windows. Also adorning the exterior are a number of statues of Greek deities such as Hercules, Theseus, Jason, Hector and Mercury. Inside, the Golden Hall has a beautifully painted coffered ceiling. Alongside the small courtyard with its Moorish columns and

Granada Province

capitals there is an Alpujarras-style kitchen of the type typical of inns in this region. There are other rooms devoted to the gypsy culture, local bullfighting memorabilia and Washington Irving. Local ceramics and wrought iron are well represented, but the painting is generally disappointing. ■ *Mon-Fri 1430-2000. Free. T958221072.*

Parque de las Ciencias Located on the Avenida del Mediterráneo, Granada's Science Park, is well worth a visit. This interactive, hands-on museum has themes such as the Biosphere, Perception, the Earth's Movement and Physical Tests. There is an Astronomical Observatory and a Planetarium. There are some wonderful exhibits for children, such as seeing inside a beehive, experiencing a tornado or a volcano and following a piranha fish around with a camera. ■ *Tue-Sat 1000-1900, Sun 1000-1500. €3, with an extra €1.50 for the Planetarium. T958131900, cpciencias@parqueciencias.com*

Churches Granada's numerous fine churches mostly date from the period immediately after the Reconquest and they were usually built on the site of a mosque. In the city centre and just a stones's throw from the cathedral, is the **Iglesia de los Santos Justo y Pastor**. It was built by the Jesuits as a collegiate church in 1575. The elegant dome contrasts dramatically with the Baroque bell tower. South of the cathedral, in Calle Acera del Darro, is the **Iglesia de Nuestra Señora de las Angustias**, the patron saint of Granada. Built in the 17th century, it has an ornate façade flanked by grandiose towers. The interior is distinguished by some priceless sculptures, including some by José de Mora and Pablo de Rojas. Don't miss the sumptuous Baroque *retablo*. Finally, in the east of the city, is the impressive Gothic hulk of the **Iglesia de Santo Domingo**, which was built in the early 16th century along with the adjacent convent.

Essentials

Sleeping
■ *on maps,*
pages 310 and 325
See inside front cover
for hotel price codes

Accommodation is more expensive around the Alhambra area; cheaper, and probably noisier options are in the city. If arriving by car look for somewhere with a garage or parking space. With over 50 hotels (including 12 in the luxury **AL** range) and around 100 *pensiones*, there is certainly loads of choice. There are, surprisingly, no *pensiones* in the Albaicín area. Most are located in the district to the southeast of the cathedral. Strange as it may sound, especially to sun-starved northern Europeans, Granada's high season is spring and autumn, whereas during Jul and Aug most hotels drop their prices considerably.

Within the Alhambra AL *Parador San Francisco*, T958221440, F958222264, info@parador.es Magnificent and luxurious accommodation inside the Alhambra complex, within a former convent, although there is more modern annex. Try and get a room in the older section but book well in advance, especially in summer, as this is the most famous parador in Spain. 38 rooms, garage, TV, gardens, restaurant, bar, a/c. **B** *América*, Real de la Alhambra 53, T958227471, F958227470. 13 rooms. Delightful small hotel, formerly a hostel, close to the parador, with a shady patio where home-cooked meals are served during the summer. Booking essential, expensive for the facilities but well worth it. Closed Jan-Mar. 13 rooms, parking nearby, a/c.

Near the Alhambra Other hotels in a quiet location close to the Alhambra include: **AL** *Alhambra Palace*, C Peña Partida 2, T958221468, F958226404, alhambrapalace.es Luxury in pseudo-Moorish style complete with crowning dome and Arabian Nights décor. Try for a room with a balcony overlooking the city; particularly stunning at sunset. 144 rooms, a/c, wheelchair access, restaurant, bar, parking, garden. **A** *Los Alixares*, Av Alixares del Generalife s/n, T958225506, F958224102, alixares@hoteles porcel.com This is a modern hotel with all creature comforts, cool beige and cream décor and good views, particularly from the 4th and 5th floors. 162 rooms, a/c, pool, parking, restaurant. **A** *Guadalupe*, Av de los Alijares s/n, T958223423, F958223798, guadalupeh@infonegocio.com A comfortable old-fashioned hotel close to the Generalife car park with good views from some rooms, so check in advance. 58 rooms, a/c, parking, restaurant, cafetería. Several good-value *hostales* nearby, including: **D** *Suecia*, **C** *Moninos 2*, Huerta Los Angeles, T958225044, F958225044. Tucked away in quiet cul-de-sac, a 15-min walk from the Alhambra, seductive small hotel, very homey with pretty rooms in varying sizes and décor. Priced at top end of category.

Within the city AL *Carmen de Santa Inés*, Placeta Porras 7, T958226380, F958224404, sinascar@teleline.es A delightful intimate hotel with small walled garden complete with bubbling fountain, lemon tree, vines, roses and goldfish. Rooms are individually furnished with lovely tiles, modern art and fine fabrics. A/c, 5 rooms. **AL** *Luz Granada*, Av de la Constitución 18, T958204061, F958293150. 174 rooms. Wheelchair access, a/c, garage, disco. **AL** *Princesa Ana*, Av de la Constitución 37, T958287447, F958273954, reservas@hoteles-ma.es. Balconied 5-storey hotel in the centre with plush interior of marble and soft pink and white. Dark wood furnishings and American-style dual sink bathrooms, at the lower end of this price range. 61 rooms. Garage, a/c, restaurant, bar, cafetería. **A** *Casa Morisca*, Cuesta de la Victoria 9, T958221100, F958215796, casamorisca@terra.es On a steep hill in the Albaicín with Alhambra views, this 15th-century converted house has Moorish-inspired décor with a

Granada centre

Granada Province

■ **Sleeping**	● **Eating**	10 Hamman Baños
1 Hostal Landázuri	1 Alcaicería	11 La Gran Taberna
2 Los Tilos	2 Al-Andalus	12 La Riviera
3 Maciá	3 Boabdil	13 Marisquería Cunini
4 Pension Britz	4 Bodega Casteñeda	14 Mesón Andaluz
5 Pensión Romero	5 Bodega La Mancha	15 Samarcanda
6 Plaza Nueva	6 Casa Cepilla	16 Seis Peniques
7 Viena	7 Casa Julio	17 Sevilla
8 Zacatin	8 Corral de Carbon	18 Taberna Salinas
	9 El Retable	

Related maps
A Alhambra and Generalife,
page 310
B Granada,
page 318

N

0 metres 50
0 yards 50

pretty central patio, stucco work arches, multicoloured tiles and wooden ceilings embellished with arabic calligraphy. A/c, 14 rooms. **A** *Cóndor*, Av de la Constitución 6, T958283711, F958283850, condor@maciahoteles.com Pleasant hotel near the cathedral with pale wood furnishings and balconies in most rooms. You may need earplugs on a Sat night. 104 rooms. A/c, garage, restaurant, cafetería. **A** *Reina Cristina*, Tablas 4, T958253211, F958255728, clientes@hotelreinacristina.com Grand 19th-century townhouse close to the lively Bib-Rambla square. Elegant lobby with neo-mudéjar ceiling, a fountain and marble columns. Famous local restaurant and excellent tapas in the café. 43 rooms, a/c. **B** *Macía*, Plaza Nueva 4, T958227536, F958285591, maciaplaza@maciahoteles.com Simple hotel in bustling plaza which can be noisy. Small functional rooms. Breakfast included. 40 rooms, a/c. **B** *Plaza Nueva*, Plaza Nueva s/n, T958501897, F958501813, hotelplazanueva@wanadoo.com Open in spring 2002, this smart new hotel promises to be a winner, with slick upbeat decór and balconies overlooking the square.

C *Casa del Aljarife*, Placeta de la Cruz, Verde 2, Albaicín, T/F958222425, most@wanadoo.es. Idyllic location in tiny square in the heart of the Albaicín with views of the Alhambra from the rooftop terrace. The 4 small rooms in this 17th-century house are individually furnished with lots of charm. A/c, TV, use of fax and email. **C** *Los Tilos*, Plaza de Bib-Rambla 4, T958266712, F958266801, www.hotellostilos.com Excellent value, no-frills hotel with comfortable, modern interior overlooking pleasant square where there is a daily flower market. Good views from small 4th-floor terrace. 30 rooms, a/c. **D** *Residencia Britz*, Cuesta de Gomérez 1, T958223652. Basic comfortable rooms, some with terraces, with brightly tiled en-suite bathrooms. Choice of pavement cafés a short stroll away. 22 rooms **D** *Landázuri*, C Cuesta de Gomérez 24, T958221406. 15 rooms. On the hill leading up to the Alhambra, restaurant and roof terrace with views of the Alhambra. English speaking owner. **D** *Lisboa*, Plaza del Carmen 27, T958221413 F958221487. 28 rooms. Clean and modern, on busy square near to the cathedral. **D** *Hostal San Joaquín*, C Mano de Hierro 14, T958282879. A cosy rambling *hostal* with 2 shady patios and spacious rooms. **D** *Verónica*, C Angel 17, T958258145. 14 rooms. Small friendly *hostal* south of the cathedral. **E** *Pensión Castril*, Darrillo de la Magdalena 1, on corner of Alhóndiga, T 958259507. Central, clean, friendly, shared bath. Recommended. **E** *Pensión Los Iznajeños*, C Lucena 1, T958278255. No-frills *hostal* in tiny cul-de-sac near Plaza de la Trinidad with friendly owner and spotless rooms. **E** *Zacatín*, C Ermita 11, T958221155. Right in the centre of the Alcaicería market in centre. Basic but large rooms, some with bath. **E** *Viena*, C Hospital de Santa Ana 2, T958221859. 3 rooms. Small Austrian owned hostel off the Cuesta de Gomérez.

Self-catering D *Lola del Castillo*, Plaza de San Miguel Bajo 14, T958282904, corralon@mixmail.com One apartment (2 double rooms) with well-equipped kitchen and pretty courtyard garden with palms and orange trees. Buzzy location in the centre of the Albaicín. **Outside Granada: D** *Cortijo La Solana*, La Solana Alta, 18650 Dúrcal, T/F958780575. 4 rooms with balconies and great views in this comfortable country guest house overlooking the Lecrín valley, south of Granada close to the Puerta del Suspiro del Moro, price includes breakfast, American run.

Youth hostels *Camino de Fuente*, 18779 Viznar, T958543307, F958543448, 108 beds, 12 km from Granada in peaceful woodland setting, pool, facilities for the disabled. *Camino de Ronda 171*, F958272638. 78 beds. Meals provided, pool, in a sports complex on the edge of town, suitable for wheelchair users, bus No 11 300m, reservations essential. **Camping** All sites are on bus routes. *Los Alamos*, Ctra A92,, Km 290, 5 km from city, T958275743. Pool, open Apr-Oct. *Cubillas*, Ctra Bailén-Motril, Km 115, 10 km from city, T958453328. *Granada*, Peligros, 3 km from city, T958340548. *María*

Eugenia, Ctra N342, Km 286, 3 km from city, T958200606. Pool, 4 km further out, open all year. *Suspiro del Moro*, Ctra Bailén Motril, 12 km from city, T958555411.

Eating out is no problem in Granada, where there are restaurants and bars to suit all tastes and pockets. Hotel restaurants tend to be pricey, while the Alhambra and Plaza Nueva areas have the inevitable tourist rip-off establishments. There are a number of regional specialities – try Trevélez ham, cured in the mountain air of the highest village in Spain; omelette *al Sacromonte* and almond soup. Regional desserts contain more than a hint of the Moorish past, with *huesos de santo* ('saints bones') and *barettas*.

Eating
● *on maps,*
pages 310 and 325
See inside front cover
for restaurant price
codes

Expensive *La Colina de Almanzora*,C Santa Ana 16, T958229516. Next to the new Baños Arabes with sensational views of the Alhambra and Albaicín. Dishes include eggplant with honey and stewed partridges with chestnuts. *Corral de Carbón*, Mariana Pineda 8, T958223810. Fabulous 14th-century *mesón* with brick and beam interior specialising in game dishes. *Cunini*, C Pescadería 14, T958250777. Pricey seafood restaurant with tables outside. *Mirador de Morayma*, C Pianista García Carrillo 2, T958228290. Marvellous location overlooking the Albaicín and the Alhambra – a must for all romantics, specialities include *tortilla de Sacromonte*. The nearby restaurant *Tomasas* has similarly stunning views and menu. Try the *ajo blanco* (chilled almond soup). *San Nicolás*, C San Nicolás 3, T958804262. Sumptuous décor and scrumptious nouvelle-Andaluz dishes like leg of pork filled with lavender and honey. Pricey, but more good views justify the expense.

Mid-range *Alcaicería*, C Oficios 8, T958224341. Atmospheric location in the old Arab market close to the cathedral, good regional specialities. *El Alcebreche*, Plaza San Miguel El Bajo 6, T958273101. Pretty square in the Albaicín where Moroccan owner dishes up healthy, tasty dishes with no preservatives and plenty of veggie choice. Closed Jan. *Mesón Andaluz*, Cetti Meriem 10, T958227357. Smart popular restaurant serving a good value *menú del día* at €10 with a couple of splash-out specialities on the menu and a better than average wine list. *Mesón Blas Casa*, Plaza San Miguel Bajo 15, T958273111. In the heart of the Albaicín, one of the few restaurants open year round serving up tasty dishes, with an emphasis on grilled meats. *Chikito*, Plaza Campillo 9, T958223364. Attractive historical restaurant in a central location east of the cathedral with a medium priced *menú del día*. *Las Perdices*, Av Andalucía 24, game specialities. *Raices*, Pablo Picasso 30, T958120103. The longest established vegetarian restaurant in Granada (quite possibly in Spain!), with a daily changing menu, and imaginative desserts. *Samarcanda*, Calderería Vieja 3, T958210014. Excellent Lebanese restaurant with all the predictable favourites, as well as a few international dishes. *Seis Peniques*, Plaza de los Tiros, T958226256. Regional and international food. *Sevilla*, C Oficios 12, T958221223. Open since the 1930s with 4 picturesque dining rooms and an outdoor patio overlooking the Capilla Real. As you'd expect, dishes are traditional Granadino with a *menú del día* of around €16. *Taquería México*, Buensuceso 49, T958520097. A fairly authentic Mexican *cantina*, popular with locals with a busy bar out front. *Velázquez*, Emilio Orozco 1, T958289109. Near the Plaza del Triunfo and popular with locals, intimate dining room with brick-wall bar serving sturdy local cuisine, like lamb with honey and braised monkfish.

Cheap *Al-Andalus*, C Elvira, T958226730. Mainly for eating on the go, although there a couple of bar stools and a table, but the Arabic food selection is good with falafel, houmous, kebabs, and pitta bread sandwiches followed by diet-busting Arabic cakes and sweets. *Boabdil*, Hospital de Peregrines 2, T958228136. A family style friendly restaurant with several *menú del días* from just €5. Small outside terrace and tapas at the bar. *El Ladrillo*, Placeta Fátima. Lively restaurant with outside terrace specialising in seafood. If you don't care if you're unable to identify all the tentacles on your plate,

Granada Province

order the vast seafood platter *barcos* for €8, which is easily enough for 2. *Bar La Mancha Chica*, Camino Nueva de San Nicolás, T958202623. Hole-in-the-wall, family run bar and restaurant serving excellent and cheap Arabic food, like couscous and tabbouleh. *Mare Nostrum*, Gran Vía 45, T958279890. Cut-price Chinese and Japanese cuisine with plenty of vegetarian choice. *Menú del día* from just €4.5. *Pizzería Burger Goffi*, C Pedro Antonio de Alarcón. Fast food and takeaways. *Reyes Católicos*, Placeta Sillería 3, T958223928. Friendly service and a range of fixed price *menús*. *Café Suizo*, Acera del Darro 26. Particularly good for breakfast, with all the normal choice, plus a vast selection of coffees and teas.

Tapas bars   Granada has some great atmospheric tapas bars particularly around Plaza Nueva and along C Acera del Darro. Typical tapas including *tortilla al Sacromonte* (omelette with potatoes, peas and peppers), brains in batter and testicles (all finely chopped!), *habas con jamón* (beans with ham) and fried fish and other seafood. *Bodegas Castañeda*, C Almireceros 1 y 3, T958223222. This long established and classy Granadinos joint serves classic tapas dishes simply, as well as baked potatoes with a tasty choice of fillings. Also a popular restaurant (mid-range) later on. Book in advance or you'll wait a long time for a table. The bar opposite is lively late into the night. In the same area, *La Riviera*, C Cetti Meriem 7, is a new bar with good tapas and a popular early evening haunt; round the corner at C Elvira 13, *Taberna Salinas* has an old-fashioned bodega atmosphere with hams hanging over the bar (gently curing in cigarette smoke) and is dimly lit and cosy, with a choice of traditional tapas. Serious *jamón* aficionados should check out *Bodegas La Mancha*, C Joaquín Costa 10, or *El Retablo*, C Elvira, which also has a good range of sandwiches. For seafood tapas, the old-fashioned *Casa Julio*, Hermosa 5, is excellent while *La Gran Taberna*, Plaza Nueva 12, specialises in a more upmarket choice. Choose from a vast selection, including trout with cottage cheese, Roquefort with beets and goat's cheese canapés, as well as the more standard selection. **Albaicín**: On Carrera del Darro, *Bar Chirimias* and *Rabo de Nube* both have a good range of tapas with the added plus of a drop-dead view of the Alhambra from the outside tables. For the best view, head for *El Mirador*, Placeta San Nicolás, where you can reward yourself with an ice-cold *cerveza* and a tapa (or 2) while enjoying arguably the best view of the Alhambra painted against a Sierra Nevada backdrop.

Cafés   There are some wonderful cafés and cake shops in Granada. One of the best is *Pastelería Lopez-Mezuíta*, Reyes Católicos 39. The home-made meringues are to die for. **Teterias**: these Moroccan-style teashops first emerged in Granada and are now equally popular in Sevilla and Málaga, particularly among students. The only catch is that they can be expensive, so do check the price of your cuppa before you order. The highest concentration is, fairly obviously, in the old Moorish quarter. Several of the most atmospheric are on C Calderería Nueva where, within a few doors from each other, you can find *Teteria Oriental*, *Teteria Alfaguara* and *Le Renez Vous* which also sells delicious crêpes. For a truly 5-star teteria check out the top floor of the newly opened *Hammam Baños Arabes*, C Santa Ana 16, T958229978, not to be confused with the ancient Moorish baths nearby, which are now a historical sight. The Hammam teteria has dreamy views and you can truly pamper yourself and have a bath, aromatherapy session or massage in the adjoining baths afterwards. **Heladerías**: for a good ice-cream parlour, try *La Perla* in Plaza Nueva.

Bars **Centre**: if you are suffering from draught Guinness deprivation, kick off the evening at *Hannigan* & Sons Irish pub on Cetti Meriem 1, near Plaza Nueva. For live music, head towards the Gran Vía where jazz fans will enjoy *Eshavira*, Postigo de la Cuna 2, where there is also the occasional impromptu flamenco evening. Not to be confused, the similar sounding *Entresuelo* on nearby C Azacayas 16 is a lively disco-bar, particularly popular with resident *extranjeros*. Still in the centre, *Mystic*, C Pedro Antonio, has weekly party nights on Thu while *Mezquita* V, C Pinto López Mezquita 5, is a laid-back bar with music at weekends. **Albaicín**: here, nightlife centres around Carrera del Darro. The following bars and clubs are within a few doors of each other and worth checking out if you are looking for places where the locals hang out: *Rincón de San Pedro*, No 12; *Fodo Reservado*, Santa Inés 4 (just off Carrera del Darro) and *Huerto del Loro*, across from the first bridge. **Nightclubs** Try *New York*, C Portón de Tejiero, or *El Cid*, C Luis Braille 3. Discos mainly flourish in university term time, when some of the lower Sacromonte caves are turned into lively discos. In town there are a couple of large discos: *Granada 10*, C Cárcel, opposite the cathedral, and *Cool* (formerly *Oh Granada*), on C Dr Guirao, which is the city's largest with 3 dance floors.

Bars & nightclubs

Like all Andalucían cities, Granada has a lively nightlife, although don't even think of going club cruising until close to midnight

Bullfights The bullfighting season is Mar-Oct. For more information, contact the tourist office or the Plaza de Toros ticket office, Av Dr Oloriz 25, T958272451. **Cinemas** There are also 6 cinemas. The *Cine Club Universitario* at the university occasionally screens original soundtrack films, T958243000. **Flamenco** Popular and reliable flamenco theatre run by noted dancer at *Jardines Neptuno* on C Arabia from 2200 daily, book in advance, entrance includes drink, €21, T95851112. The shows in the caves of Sacromonte are heavily tourist orientated; however, the Fri and Sat show at *Los Tarantos*, Sacromonte 9, is more authentic than most, €21. T958224525. Far more rewarding is the impromptu flamenco that takes place at the annual fiestas and *feria*. Alternatively, check the programme of the annual International Music and Dance Theatre where some of the top professionals often appear, under the stars in the Alhambra. **Theatres** Concerts, dance and theatre productions take place in a number of venues in Granada, including historic buildings; pick up a *Guía de Granada* at the tourist office to check what's on where. There are also 3 theatres which have a year-round programme. *Teatro Isabel la Católica*, C Acera del Casino 2, T957274000. *Teatro Estable de Granada (Universitario)*, C Gran Capitán 16, T958202725. *Teatro Alhambra*, C de Molinos 56, T958220447. The *Auditorio Manuel de Falla*, Paseo de los Mártires, T958220022, also has orchestral concerts most weeks.

Entertainment

Jan A fiesta on the first 2 days of Jan celebrates the end of the Reconquista and the arrival of the victorious Fernando and Isabel in Granada. **Early Feb** *Romería Popular de San Cecilio* A celebration of the city's patron saint, with a pilgrimage to Sacromonte Abbey in his honour. **Easter** *Semana Santa* Traditional processions take place and special viewing stands are erected in Plaza del Carmen. **May** *Las Cruces de Mayo* Squares and patios are decorated with floral crosses. **Jun** *Corpus Cristi* A major festival with bullfights and other celebrations. **Late Jun or early Jul** *International Music and Dance Festival* This highly recommended festival takes place in the Palacio de Carlos V; information from the tourist office. **29 Sep** *Romería a la Ermita de San Miguel Alto*. **Last Sun in Sep** *Fiesta de Nuestra Señora de las Angustias*. **Nov** *International Jazz Festival*.

Fiestas & festivals

The main shopping streets are to the east of the cathedral, particularly along C Reyes Católicos and around the square of Puerta Real. The main department store is *El Cortes Inglés* on Acera del Darro, the broad continuation of C Reyes Católicos. There are a variety of craft items that are typical of the area, including carpets, marquetry work, brass lanterns and *jarapas*, the traditional rugs from the Alpujarras. There are artisan workshops in the Corral de Carbón adjacent to the tourist office. For Arabic spices,

Shopping

Granada Province

perfumes, bakery goods and souvenirs, head for *Calderería Vieja* and *Calderería Nueva* in the heart of the Albaicín.

Sport **Climbing and hiking** *Ocio Aventura Granada*, Colonia San Sebastián 2, T958816185. Provides information on trails. **Horse riding** *Real Sociedad Hípica*, Ctra de la Zubia, T958811006. **Mountain biking** *Escuela Montalbán*, C Conde Cifuentes 11, T958256875. **Squash** *Abarles Club*, Santo Tomás Villanueva 5, T958227910. **Swimming** There are no fewer than 8 pools in the city. *Parque Acuático Aquola*, Ctra de la Sierra, Km 4, T958486186. **Tennis** *Real Sociedad de Tenis*, Cno Conejeras, El Serrallo, T958125302.

Tour operators *Bonanza*, C Reyes Católicos 30, T958229777. *Ecuador*, C Angel Ganivet 8, T958223566. *Marsans*, Gran Vía de Colón 20, T958222088. *Sacromonte*, C Angel Ganivet 6, T958225598. *USIT Unlimited*, Navas 29, T902252575, www.usitunlimited.es Specialists in student travel.

Transport **Local Bus**: the local intercity bus company is *Alsina Graells*, at Camino de Ronda 97, T958251358. Free bus maps and timetables are available from the tourist office and *bonobus* tickets for 10 journeys can be bought from tobacconists and kiosks for €3.01. No 2 bus runs to the Alhambra and can be picked up from beside *El Cortes Inglés* or in Plaza Bibataubín. **Car hire**: *Atesa*, Plaza Cuchilleros 1, T958224004. *Autos Fortuna*, Infanta Beatríz 2, T958260254. *Autos Gudelva*, Pedro Antonío de Alarcón 18, T958251435. *Ital*, Plaza Cuchilleros 12, T958223524. **Parking**: It is best to use one of the underground car parks; cars parked illegally will be towed speedily away. The Alhambra car park next to the main entrance is convenient, because after seeing the Alhambra it is possible to take the regular shuttle bus to and from the city centre. **Taxi**: there are taxi ranks in Plaza Nueva, Puerta Real and outside the Alhambra. **Coche de Caballo**: Horse drawn carriages are available near the Correos on C de los Mesones.

Long distance Bus: *Bacoma*, Av de Andaluces 10, T958284251, runs long distance coaches. There are daily buses to Almería (10), Almuñecar (9), Baza (8), Córdoba (8), Guadix (11), Jaén (8), Madrid (1), Málaga (15), Motril (7), Nerja (2), Salobreña (7), Sevilla (9) and Ubeda/Baeza (7). Buses marked *directo* are slower and cost slightly less. There are also daily buses to the Sierra Nevada, €4.22 return. A full set of timetables can be obtained from the tourist office. **Train**: there is a RENFE office at C Reyes Católicos 63, T958223119. Daily trains run to Algeciras (4), Almería (3), Antequera (4), Cádiz (4), Córdoba (3), Guadix (3), Madrid (2), Málaga (1), Ronda (4), and Sevilla (6).

Directory **Banks** All banks are closed on Sat from 15 Jun-15 Sep. Numerous banks and ATMs in Plaza Isabel la Católica, along Gran Vía de Colón and C Reyes Católicos. **Communications** Internet: *Cervantes*, Plaza del Campillo 5, T958228583. Open Mon-Sun 1000-2300. €1.5 per hr. *Freemem*, C San Jerónimo 14, T958806080. Open Mon-Fri 1030-2300, Sat-Sun 1700-2200. €1.5 per hr. *Madar*, C Calderería Nueva 12, T958229429. Open Sun-Fri 1000-2400, Sat 1200-2400. €1 per hr. *Navegaweb*, C Reyes Católicos 55, T958210528. Open daily 1000-2300. €1.8 per hr. **Post office**: Correos in Puerta Real. Open Mon-Fri 0800-2100, Sat 0800-1400. **Telephones**: there is a public call centre at C Reyes Católicos 55. Open Mon-Sat 0900-1400 and 1700-2200. **Embassies and consulates** *Belgium*, C Recogidas 66, 1°A, T958251631; *France*, C Carlos Pareja 5, T958261447; *Italy*, C Dr Martín Lagos 3, 1°, T958261361. The nearest *British* Consulate is in Málaga. **Medical services** Hospitals: *Cruz Roja* (emergencies), C Escoriaza 8, T958222222/958222024; *Hospital General*, Av Coronel Muñez, T958292856; *Hospital Clínico San Cecilio*, Av Dr Olóriz 16, T958275900; *Hospital San Juan de Dios*, C San Juan de Dios 15, T958241724.

East of Granada

East of Granada the N342 towards the border with Murcia province, initially through outstanding scenery with superb views of the Sierra Nevada to the south. There are two natural parks, the ***Parque Natural de la Sierra de Baza*** *in the south and the* ***Parque Natural de la Sierra de Castril*** *in the more remote north, forming part of the Sistema Subbético. There are two major towns in this eastern part of the province,* ***Guadix*** *and* ***Baza****.*

Guadix

Colour map 3, grid C2
Population: 20,322
Altitude: 949 m

Located some 58 km east of Granada on the Río Guadix in a fertile farming region is the town of Guadix. Some 10,000 people in Guadix still live in well furnished caves dug out of the soft tufa rock of the hillside. It is thought that this troglodyte community, in the Barrio Santiago, was established following the Christian Reconquest of Spain, when fear of Felipe II caused local Moors to seek safety underground. There is a **Cave Museum** in the barrio showing traditional implements and furniture. ■ *Mon-Fri 1000-1400 and 1600-1800; Sat 1000-1400.*

Julius Caesar is said to have founded the town in 45 BC, setting up silver, iron and copper mines. Later, the Moors, who called it Wadi-Ash (the river of life), established a silk industry here and remained until 1489. Guadix achieved notoriety during the Civil War, when some horrendous atrocities were committed. Today, it is an agricultural centre, with industries based on esparto grass and the production of cutlery.

The town's old quarter is almost entirely walled, with an impressive Moorish gateway, the Puerta San Turcuato. The ruined Moorish **Alcazaba** dates from the 10th and 11th centuries. Its red sandstone walls are capped with battlements and a central tower, the *torre gorda*, gives magnificent views towards the Sierra Nevada. ■ *Daily 0900-1300 and 1600-1800. €0.60.*

Also built of red sandstone is the **cathedral**, which although started in 1492 on the site of a mosque, was not completed until the 18th century. Not surprisingly, it shows a variety of styles, with Baroque dominant. The main façade is dominated by Corinthian columns and designed by Vicente Acero. The late-Gothic interior, which is largely the work of Diego de Siloé, is somewhat gloomy, the best features being the Churrigueresque choir stalls. ■ *Mon-Sat 1030-1300 and 1630-1800, Sun 1030-1400.*

Outside is the **Plaza Mayor**, arcaded in Renaissance style and much restored after damage during the Civil War. There are a number of interesting churches in the town, including El Sagrario, with a Plateresque façade, and Santiago, which has Mudéjar ceilings. The bus station is only five minutes from the main sights (*Autodía* buses in Calle Rector Marín Ocete 10), but the train station is 20 minutes from the town centre.

Sleeping

There are 3 small hotels and a *pensión*. The best of these is **D** ***Mulhacén***, Av Buenos Aires 41, T958660750, F660661. The best *pensión* in town with 39 rooms and a garage. Recommended. **E** ***Carmen***, Ctra Granada, 226 km, T958661500, F958661401. Garage, a/c. Recommended.

Around Guadix

There are some interesting villages worth visiting around Guadix, including **Graena**, where there are thermal baths that have been used since Roman times, **La Pexa**, with ruins of a ninth-century Moorish castle, and the pottery village of

☞ Troglodyte tendencies

There are still some 35,000 cave dwellers in Andalucía, the largest proportion of them in the Guadix area of Granada province. In most cases, however, these are not natural caves, but dwellings which have been excavated by humans in the hard, brown Pliocene clay of the area. The custom is believed to date originally from the 16th century, when the Moriscos were fleeing from the persecution of Felipe II. Today, the Andalucían government has embarked on a cave improvement programme.

There is a long history, however, of cave dwelling in Andalucía. Caves at Boquete de Zafarraya, Málaga province, Pinar in Granada and Vera in Almería show evidence of Neanderthal man, possibly dating back 85,000 years. Relics include bones, tools, ceramics and cooking implements. The cave wall paintings at Pileta near Ronda showing fish, goats and horses are dated as Bronze Age, while the caves at Nerja in Málaga show that after the Ice Age, Cro-Magnon man inhabited the caves of Andalucía.

Many of the better caves in the Guadix area have seven or eight rooms, electricity, sewage disposal, television and even a cave garage. Many of these troglodytes have resisted the pressure to be rehoused in high rise flats. After all, caves do not leak or collapse, they are quieter than apartment living, the temperature is a constant 17°C throughout the year and extra room is easily available. The caves have title deeds like more conventional property and are bought and sold in the same way. Community life is often good, with caves converted into discos, bars and churches.

It is often thought most cave dwellers are gypsies, but this is not the case. The most famous gypsy troglodytes are those of Granada's Sacromonte district, but, in fact, most of these have been rehoused in apartments in town and only return to their caves at night to fleece the flamenco-seeking tourists.

The caves have become tourist attractions in recent years and it is not unusual to find a tour bus including a visit to a cave on its itinerary. You can even rent-a-cave. Promociones Turísticas de Galera have 14 caves available for daily or weekly rent (€25 a night or €130 a week). The caves take up to seven people in two double or three single rooms. Contact Turismo Rural Casas Cuevas, Promociones Turísticas de Galera, Avenida Nicasio Tomás 12, 18840 Galera, Granada, T958739068.

For cave luxury try the Cuevas Pedro Antonio de Alarcón, a newly built cave hotel in a complex of 19 caves. The hotel has richly furnished rooms and all mod cons, as well as an excellent restaurant. The price of a two-room cave sleeping four is €50. Contact Cuevas Pedro Antonio de Alarcón, Barriada San Torcuato, 18500 Guadix, Granada, T958664986, F958661721.

Cave lodgings are now available in Granada's Sacromonte district, with prices per week at €40 to €90. Contact Cuevas El Abanico, Verea de Enmedio 89, Sacromonte, Granada, 18010, T958226199. Another alternative is the UK-based Mundi Color, T020-78286021, who offer some 50 cave rooms and apartments in cave country around Guadix.

Purullena. Southwest of Guadix is a large flat semi-arid depression known as the **Hoya de Guadix**. This steppe area has chalky ground, dissected with gullies and ravines, with esparto grass and a little cereal farming. Although the site has no special protection or status, this is one of the better areas of Andalucía for steppe birds including little bustards (probably 100 pairs), stone curlews, black bellied sand grouses, tawny pipits and Dupont's larks.

Baza

Fifty kilometres northeast of Guadix is the town of Baza, which has a long history. Iberian tribes occupied the area and their most important relic is the *Dama de Baza*, a sculpture which is now in Madrid, although a copy is in the local archaeological museum. The Romans named the town Basti, while during Moorish times Baza was a silk producing centre and from 1234 onwards it was part of the Nasrid Kingdom of Granada. It was taken by the Christians in 1489 after a long siege. Today it is mainly an agricultural centre, but has a number of interesting remains. Baza also has its **cave dwelling area**, located to the east of the town and easily spotted from the main road. The **tourist office** is at Plaza Mayor 2, T958861325. It's open daily 1000-1400, 1600-1830.

Colour map 3, grid C3
Population: 20,113
Altitude: 848 m

The 10th-century Moorish **Alcazaba** is well and truly ruined, but the **Baños Arabes** are better preserved. Dating from the 10th century, these Moorish baths are among the oldest in Spain, but they are now privately owned. They are closed until 2003 for restoration. Elsewhere, the **Iglesia de Santa María de la Encarnación**, with its façade attributed to Diego de Siloé, is worth a visit, while the **Palacio de los Enríquez**, a privately owned 16th-century Mudéjar mansion, still retains some ceilings in the Moorish style. ■ *For admission ask at the tourist office. Groups of 10-15 only. €1.80. Getting there: the bus station is on Av de los Reyes Católicos, T958185010, 8 buses a day to Guadix and Granada.*

The best hotel in town is **D** *Robemar*, on the Carretera de Murcia, Km 175, T958860704, F058700798, with 46 rooms, wheelchair access and a pool.

Sleeping

South of Baza is the **Parque Natural de la Sierra de Baza**, some 52,000 ha of woodland full of oaks, pines, rowans, maples and ilex. There is a good variety of Mediterranean birds, with important colonies of Egyptian vultures and golden eagles. Mammals include genets, beech martens and badgers. North of Baza is the large semi-arid depression of the **Hoya de Baza**, covering some 80,000 ha. Much of the area is covered with tamarisk and scrub, with poplars along the watercourses. The area has no special protected status and contains similar species to the Hoya de Guadix, which is better for birdwatching.

Around Baza

Twenty kilometres northeast of Baza the A330 leads to the remote town of **Huéscar**, a town of some 10,000 people in a mainly agricultural area. It was an important Roman and Carthaginian settlement. The Moors also occupied it until it fell to the Christians in 1488. There are the remains of a Moorish castle and some watchtowers, while there are a number of 16th and 17th century fine mansions. The collegiate church of Santa María de la Encarnación, with its impressive façade, dominates the town. Huéscar makes a good base to explore the sierras to the north, including the **Parque Natural de la Sierra de Castril**, a deeply incised limestone block with a number of peaks over 2,000 m, with griffon vultures and golden eagles as well as other birds of prey.

Granada Province

West of Granada

Fifteen kilometres from Granada and close to the airport, a minor road leads north to the village of Fuente Vaqueros, the **birthplace of Federico García Lorca**. The house where he was born is now a museum, see page 323.

Fuente Vaqueros

Santa Fé Nearby, and close to the airport, is the small town of Santa Fé. There is little worth stopping for here, but about 15 minutes' drive south of the main square are some **hot springs**, tucked in amongst the olive groves. These consist of a series of clear pools connected by waterfalls, with a water temperature of around 38-39°C. The springs are very relaxing in winter, with superb views of the Sierra Nevada. The springs are not commercially exploited or advertised, but local people use them and can give directions.

Loja

Population: 20,143
Altitude: 482 m

Some 30 km further west is the small town of Loja. A flourishing trading centre in Phoenician times, Loja was a strategic military base under the Moors, guarding the western end of the *vega* or plain. It was eventually captured by Ferdinand in 1486 following a long siege after which it is said that over 5,000 Muslims left the town for Granada. The Moorish Alcazaba has been in ruins since the time of Felipe II, but still retains the walls, the Ochavada tower and a finely preserved well. There are a number of churches of interest in Loja, all built in local brown sandstone. The Iglesia de Santa María de la Encarnación was built over a mosque to the design of Ventura Rodríguez and has an imposing tower, but it is the Church of San Gabriel that is most impressive. The work of Diego de Siloé, it is one of the best examples of Renaissance in Granada province. Other buildings worth a look include the 'New' Granary dating from the 16th century and the Palacio de Narváez, a 19th-century building in French style with superb gardens.

Los Infiernos de Loja Just outside Loja, off the minor road to Ventorros, are Los Infiernos de Loja, a series of waterfalls and rapids flowing through a ravine cut by the Río Genil in the last part of the Subbético range before going on the Iznájar reservoir. They are particularly impressive in the spring, when the water levels are high.

Río Frio A few kilometres west of Loja is the small hamlet of Río Frio, where the river of the same name flows north to join the Genil. A number of *piscifactorías*, or trout hatcheries, have sprung up here and they in turn have spawned several *ventas* and restaurants, featuring trout as their speciality dishes. This is a favourite stop for Granada bound coaches, while on Sunday Río Frio is a popular lunchtime venue for Granadinos and Malaguenos. There is a shady walk along the riverside.

Alhama de Granada

Colour map 5, grid B2
Population: 5,894
Altitude: 883 m

Perched on a cliff top overlooking a deep gorge created by the Río Alhama, the town gets its name from the Moorish *Al Hamman* meaning thermal waters or baths. In fact, its history goes much further back than the Moors as it was occupied in turn by the Iberians, Phoenicians, Carthaginians and Romans (who called it Artigi). Both the Romans and the Moors valued Alhama highly as a spa and the baths are still in operation today. To find them take the C340 north out of town (noting the old Roman bridge) and fork right to find a complex of gardens, fountains, a hotel and the baths themselves. Some of the old Moorish 11th-century constructions remain, but the present day buildings date from the Middle Ages. The staff at *Hotel Balnaerio* can show you some of the original Moorish sections of the baths.

The town itself is a delight and one can appreciate Muley Hacen's cry of sorrow '*Ay di me Alhama*', when he lost the battle here against Christian forces in 1482. Most of the places to see are near to the Plaza de la Constitución, close to which is the **Barrio Arabe**, with a maze of alleyways following the original street plan. The Moorish **castle** is largely ruined and privately owned. Close by is the 16th-century **Iglesia del Carmen**, which looks out over the gorge. The church which dominates the town, however, is the **Iglesia de la Encarnación**, a 15th-century Gothic building with a Mudéjar pulpit and an *artesonado* ceiling, which the ubiquitous Siloé had a hand in designing. Other buildings worth seeing include the **Pósito**, or granary, in the Plaza de los Presos, which was built in the 13th century and used for a time as a synagogue, and the **Casa de la Inquisición**, a delightful stone building with a Plateresque façade.

There are a limited number of accommodation possibilities. Both hotels listed here close in the winter. **B** *Balneario Alhama de Granada*, Balnearios s/n, T958350011, F958350297. A spa hotel at the baths with pool and tennis. The best, but still reasonably priced, in town, with 116 rooms. **D** *Baño Nuevo*, Balnearios s/n, T958350011. Another hotel on the same site as the main hotel, with 66 rooms. **E** *Hostal San José*, Plaza de la Constitución 17, T958350156. 14 rooms.

Sleeping

South of Alhama the road runs through the Zafarraya Pass at the summit of which there is a clutch of *ventas*. Nearby is an enormous Karstic depression, which is excellent for wild flowers, particularly orchids, in the spring. Also nearby is the Boquete de Zafarraya cave, where a Neanderthal skull was discovered in 1883. The route continues south into the Axarquía region of Málaga province, reaching the coast just south of Velez-Málaga.

Zafarraya Pass

South of Granada

The Sierra Nevada

The Sierra Nevada has several unique features. It is the most southerly ski centre in mainland Europe, but also one of the highest. This means that it has a long season, often lasting until late May, but also long hours of sunshine. It is exposed to high winds, but it also has excellent views, even to Africa on clear days. Access is easy. Infrastructure improvements for the world championship mean that the 35 km road from Granada has been much improved and the journey takes only 45 minutes. Its accessibility from Granada and the Costa del Sol, however, also means it can get very crowded, particularly at weekends and holidays. The purpose-built resort, formerly known as Pradollano but now expanded and renamed Solynieve (sun and snow), is not an attractive place by alpine standards – the treeless slopes around give it little ambience – but this is more than made up for by the excellent skiing facilities. A trip to the Sierra Nevada in summer makes a pleasant change from the oppressive heat in Granada. The Sierra Nevada is a national park and the park information centre is located on the Carretera de Sierra Nevada, Km 23, T958340625. It's open daily 1000-1400 and 1600-1800. It sells maps and guidebooks of the area and has a bookshop and cafeteria. See also www.nevadensis.com for more park information, or contact the *Nevadensis* office, T958763127.

Colour map 5, grid B4

The mountains are snow capped for most of the year and sufficient snow for skiing from December to April, but surprisingly there are no glacial features such as pyramidal peaks or even glaciers. Three peaks rise above the general level, **Alcazaba** (3,366 m), **Veleta** (3,470 m) and **Mulhacén** (3,481 m). The latter is the highest mountain on the Iberian peninsula, but most of the

Granada Province

skiing takes place on the slopes of Veleta, above Solynieve. Summer activities include mountain walking, hang gliding and horse riding. The whole area is a national park, covering nearly 170,000 ha. The lower slopes were once covered in oak and pine woodland, but some deforestation has taken place. There is some agriculture in the valleys. The higher areas are rather barren with alpine moorland, scree and bare rock. Despite having national park status and being declared a Biosphere Reserve by UNESCO in 1983, these titles have failed to prevent the degradation of much of the alpine terrain as developers in the ski industry have run roughshod over the conservation interests.

Prior to the second half of the 20th century, few Granadinos would have had any reason to go to the Sierra Nevada, particularly in winter. An exception were the 'icemen' who would toil up to the snowline and bring down blocks of ice on mules to sell in the streets of Granada. A few local enthusiasts, however, started to ski on the mountains in the early part of the 20th century, again accessing the Sierra Nevada by mule. They eventually formed the Sierra Nevada Society in 1912 (Spain's third oldest skiing club), but it was not until the 1960s that any serious development started. A 10-year plan began in 1985 and further expanded facilities to a standard which enabled Sierra Nevada to successfully apply to host the 1995 World Skiing Championships. Unfortunately fate intervened in the form of the climate - untypically mild weather not only led to a lack of snow, but temperatures were not cold enough to operate the hydrants for 'artificial snow'. This led to the cancellation of the championships, but they were held successfully the following year. It is now bidding for the 2010 world championships.

Wildlife There are some 2,000 species of plants, of which around 70 are unique to the area; the 200 species of the alpine zone include 40 endemics, such as the white flowered buttercup, Nevada daffodil, glacier toadflax and the Nevada violet. There is also a fine range of **butterflies**, including the Nevada blue, which is only seen above 2,000 m, and there are three or four other blues which are only found in this area. Amongst the 35 species of **mammals** in the park, the Spanish ibex, once almost extinct in the area, has now recovered to number over 3,000. In the woodlands of the lower slopes are wildcats, beech martens and badgers. With regard to **birds**, the high peaks and cliffs contain several hundred pairs of alpine choughs and other mountain species such as rock bunting, alpine accentors, ravens and black wheatears. The elusive wallcreeper is also occasionally reported. The lower slopes have a good range of Mediterranean woodland birds, including nightingales, subalpine warblers, roller and golden orioles. Birds of prey are not particularly common and are confined to golden eagles, peregrines and Bonelli's eagles, with goshawks in the more wooded areas.

Skiing &
snowboarding
Try to avoid weekends
and fiestas, when
the resort can be
intolerably crowded

There are some 2,500 ha of skiable area with 19 lifts (cabins, chairlifts and t-bars) capable of carrying 30,000 people an hour reaching 54 km of marked slopes. There are additionally six off-piste itineraries and a skiable vertical drop of 1,300 m. A total 3½ km are floodlit for night time skiing at weekends. Snow boarding (practised on a broad single ski, a direct descendant of the skate board) is the latest craze and has its own circuit. Cross country skiing is also catered for, but is less popular than in other areas. Equipment hire is no problem and costs around €13.86 a day, €45.18 for six days. A lift ticket costs between €13.86 and €18.98 per day according to the season and up to €80.72 a week. Lifts operate 0900 to 1615-1700, according to conditions. Most lifts run up to the Borreguiles area where there are plenty of bunny slopes. Further lifts then run up to more challenging pistes. Lift tickets can be obtained from kiosks in the Plaza de Pradollano and in the lower Al-Andaluz gondola terminal. Ticket windows are open from 0900 to 1720 on Monday to Saturday and Sunday until 2000. There are around 20 ski schools, including one for infants. The best times for skiing are between 0900 and 1100 and 1300 to 1500, when the slopes are almost deserted. Associated facilities include ski schools, banks, supermarkets, boutiques, ski rental and taxis. Après ski is typically Spanish, with heavy emphasis on fiestas. For a recorded daily update in both Spanish and English of ski conditions T958249119. A useful website is www.sierranevadaski.com

Walking & climbing

The upper reaches of the Sierra Nevada give some scope for mountain walking and scrambling during July and August, when most of the snow has gone. A dirt road runs from near the parador down to Capileira in the Alpujarras, but it is best to have a four-wheel drive vehicle for this journey. The ascent of Veleta begins from this road and should take about three hours to the summit. The ascent of Mulhacén normally starts from Trevélez in the Alpujarras and you should allow six hours for this climb. The *Ruta Integral de los Tres Mil* is an attempt on all the peaks over 3,000 m and starts at Jeres del Marquesado to the north of the Sierra Nevada and finishes three or four days later in Lanjarón in the southwest. Although expert rock climbing skills are not required for these routes, walkers should obviously be well kitted out; get an up to date weather forecast (T958249119) and have a detailed map – there is a 1:50,000 map produced by the *Federación Española de Montañismo* which can be bought in bookshops in Granada and in Solynieve.

Sleeping
See inside front cover for price codes

Hotels are generally modern and many have jacuzzis, squash courts, fitness centres, saunas and indoor pools. There are some 15 hotels and just one *pensión* in Solynieve. Almost all open only 1 Dec-30 Apr. Those that remain open in the summer may reduce their prices from 25-60% of the winter price. For the central reservation agency T958249111. Self catering apartments are also available.

Solynieve is not a pretty place even with a covering of snow, so it's worth staying below, particularly in summer. During the skiing season accommodation is quite expensive, whilst many of the hotels close from Jun to Nov. The few which stay open all the year may halve their prices during the summer and include: **A** *Parador Sierra Nevada*, Ctra de Sierra Nevada, Km 34, T958480400, F958480458. Small and modern. **AL** *Kenia Nevada*, Pradollano s/n, T958480911, F958480807. 67 rooms. Garage, pool, sports. **B** in summer. **AL** *Nevasur*, Pradollano s/n, T958480350, F958480365. 62 rooms. Few facilities. **C** in summer. Cheaper accommodation is provided by the **D** *Albergue Universitario*, Carretera de Veleta Km 36, T/F958480122, with 83 beds. It is open all year round.

Around Km 22-25 on the road from Granada in an area known as Guejar Sierra, are a cluster of hotels and *pensiones*, of which the best are: **A** *Don José*, Ctra Sierra Nevada, Km 22, T958340400, F958159458. 26 rooms. Good restaurant. **C** in summer. **A** *Santa Cruz*, Ctra Sierra Nevada, Km 23, T958470800. 66 rooms. Pool, sports. **B** in summer. **A** *El Nogal*, Ctra Sierra Nevada, Km 21, T958484836, F958470836. 37 rooms. Restaurant, pool. **C** in summer. **C** *Puentes de Sierra Nevada*, Ctra Sierra Nevada, Km 17, T958753219. The best of the 3 *pensiones* with a pool and restaurant. **E** in summer.

Youth hostels *Estación de Pradollano*, near the top of Solynieve, T958480305. Situated 35 km from Granada, with 104 beds, cafeteria and sauna.

Granada Province

Transport **Road** The Sierra Nevada is 161 km from Málaga. Wheel chains can be rented at garages on the Granada-Sierra Nevada road. There is a petrol station 8 km from the ski station, at Km 22 on the Granada-Sierra Nevada road. There are several viewpoints en route, including one giving views over the Genil reservoir. **Bus**: *Autobús Viajes Bonal*, T958273100, runs a daily bus service to the Sierra Nevada, leaving at 0900 from the Palacio de Congresos, on Paseo del Violón on the east bank of the Río Genil, and returning at 1700, with tickets available at the *Bar El Ventorillo* beside the Palacio. The departure point changes periodically, so check with the bus company or tourist office. *Alsina Graells* run an hourly bus service between Málaga and Granada. For details of direct buses to Madrid from the Sierra Nevada, T958249111 and T915484400. **Taxi**: T958151461 or 958280654. A taxi from Granada to the Sierra Nevada costs around €40.

The Alpujarras

Colour map 5, grid B4 *This area stretches across the southern slopes of the Sierra Nevada. It is a region of superb natural beauty, with deeply eroded valleys, lush meadows, terraced slopes and villages of great character. The air is clear and the backdrop of the Sierra Nevada is snow capped for much of the year. The Alpujarras undoubtedly provide the best walking and hiking opportunities in Andalucía (see page 344). Said to have an Iberian origin, the name Alpujarras comes from alp meaning high place, and Ujar, the goddess of clear light. This may be fanciful, but it summarizes the beauty of the area, which Richard Ford described as the 'Switzerland of Spain'.*

The Alpujarras

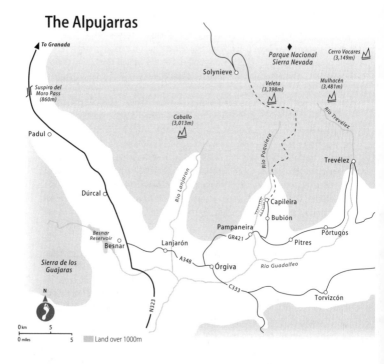

Ins and outs

The road south from Granada towards Motril, the N323, leaves the *vega* and climbs steadily to a height of 860 m at the **Puerto del Suspiro del Moro** – the Pass of the Moor's Sigh, named after Boabdil the last Moorish King of Granada, who paused here for a last look at the city before his exile. The road continues south for another 20 km before the A348 leads east to Lanjarón, the gateway to the Alpujarras. From Granada, there are three daily buses to Pitres that stop in Lanjarón, Órgiva, Pampaneira, Bubión and Capileira. Two of these go beyond to Pórtugos, Trevélez and Bérchules. Buses also run to Motril.

The scenery and clear air of the Alpujarras means that the region receives a steady stream of visitors throughout the year. Spring and early summer are undoubtedly the best times, with flowers at their best, birds in full song and plenty of snow on the peaks. Even in spring, however, the area can be crowded at weekends. There are fewer visitors in autumn, but there is little in the way of bird life and flowers, although the colours of the trees in the valleys can be attractive. The weather in the winter is unreliable and snowfall can be heavy in the higher areas with poor visibility.

The area and history

This remote area is bordered to the north by the Sierra Nevada and to the south by a series of lower ranges, including the Sierras de Lújar, Contraviesa and Gádor. A broad valley runs east-west drained by the rivers Guadalfeo and Andarex. A series of smaller rivers run north-south fed by melting snow from the Sierra Nevada, creating deep valleys and gorges and ensuring that the area stays green for most of the year. The silt laden valleys are extremely fertile, so that agriculture thrives, helped by an equable climate due to the mountains keeping out extreme cold from the north and extreme heat from the south. The original forest of the Alpujarras, consisting of ilex and pyrenean aak, is less common now owing to clearance for agriculture, but there is a wealth of introduced species such as poplar, chestnut, cork oak and olive. The white and black mulberry trees, introduced by the Moors for feeding the silk worms, are still found extensively.

When Granada fell to the Christians, many of the Moors fled to the Alpujarras, which under the Nasrids had been divided into administrative areas known as *taas*. Boabdil lived in the *taa* of Laujar. The Moors terraced the valley sides and built irrigation channels and generally left their stamp on the landscape, with street patterns in the villages unchanged

Válor
Bérchules GR421 Yegen
Cádiar Ugíjar
Juviles

Sierra de Contraviesa

over the centuries. The domestic architecture, too, is distinctive. The roofs are invariably flat and constructed of large blocks of the local schist laid horizontally. This is covered with a depth of several inches of slate shards. The flat roofs or *terraos* are often used for terraces and cross alleyways making small tunnels. Chimneys are circular in shape with a small mushroom-like capping. The walls are made of *launa*, a paste of magnesium and clay, covered with whitewash. Another feature is the exterior gallery or *tinao,* which is usually festooned with flowers. Their craftwork, such as ceramics, esparto work and textiles, still survive, as does their food, particularly delicious sweetmeats known as *pestiños* and *roscos.*

The Christians continued to make demands to force the Moors to adopt Christianity, which eventually resulted in the abortive revolt in 1570 and this eventually led to the final banishment of all Spanish Moors in 1610. The Alpujarras were repopulated with Christians from north Spain, but a certain number of Moors were obliged to remain to instruct them in the intricacies of the irrigation systems. The area gradually fell into rural poverty, which centuries later the Civil War did little to change.

It was not until the second half of the 20th century that the fortunes of the Alpujarras began to revive. This recovery is based largely on tourism and on the influx of new Northern European residents. The popularity of Chris Stewart's best selling book *Driving Over Lemons,* which tells of an expat's life in the Alpujarras, is also bound to attract even more visitors to the area.

Many environmentalists, however, consider that the Alpujarras are under threat, with quarries scarring the hillsides and inappropriate urbanizations springing up, reflecting the lack of planning restrictions. The biggest threat of all is the proposal to dam the headwaters of the Río Trevélez and pipe the water to the south of the region, but as the capacity of the pipe is seven times the needs required, the suspicion is that the water will be used for the *plasticultura* industry on the coast, which will leave the aquifers in the Alpujarras permanently low.

Sleeping Whilst most of the villages will boast a *pensión* or two, decent hotel accommodation is hard to find and it's worth booking in advance during the summer and fiesta weekends. The best bets are in Lanjarón and Órgiva, but don't expect anything in the luxury range. There are three official **campsites** in the Alpujarras, all second category: *Camping Órgiva*, Valle de Guadalfeo, Órgiva, T958784307; *Camping Trevélez*, Haza de la Cuna, 1 km from the village, T958858735; and the highly recommended *Balcón de Pitres*, Carretera Órgiva-Ugijár Km 51, T958766111.

Lanjarón
Population: 3,877
Altitude: 659 m

This has been a spa town since Roman times. There are eight springs in all, each containing a different chemical make-up which can help a variety of ailments. The bottled water from these springs is marketed all over Spain, while there is a plethora of shops selling herbal remedies to the elderly, who throng the streets in summer. The main street, the Avenida de Andalucía, is elegant and shady, while close by is the Moorish castle on top of a rocky hill flanked by a long rugged escarpment. Largely ruined today, it was the scene of a major battle in the Moorish uprising of the late 16th century. The hermitage of Tajo de la Cruz is worth a look, as is the 16th-century Church of La Encarnación. There is a tourist office at the west end of the village, with helpful multilingual staff. It also acts as a travel agency and will book accommodation. Places to stay include **C** *Andalucía*, Avenida Andalucía 15-17, T958770136, with 58 rooms, pool, restaurant and gardens; and **C** *Miramar*, Avenida Andalucía 10, T958770161, with 59 air-conditioned rooms, garage, pool and gardens.

Ten kilometres east of Lanjarón is Órgiva, the administrative centre of the region, which was made capital of the Alpujarra by Isabel II in 1839. It is also an important market town. It was frequently mentioned by the Arab chroniclers and although the sons of Muley Hassan and Zoraya lived here, there are few remains of its Moorish heritage around today. The town is dominated by the twin towers Iglesia de Nuestra Expectación, which dates from the 16th-century, while the somewhat dilapidated Palacio de los Condes de Sástago looks Moorish, but is in fact 17th century. On Thursday is the lively weekly outdoor market, which attracts people from throughout the area, both locals and many of the numerous New Age travellers who now live in the region. For accommodation there is C *Alpujarras Grill*, C Empalme sin número, T958785549, with 22 air-conditioned rooms and a garage.

Órgiva
Population: 5,039
Altitude: 450 m

North from Órgiva, are three villages of the High Alpujarras, Pampaneira, Bubión and Capileira, which cling to terraces on the side of the Poqueira valley.

Pampaneira is approached through the **Poqueira Gorge**, cut by the river of the same name which rises on the slopes of Mulhacén. Pampaneira is an attractive little village and it is no surprise to learn that it has won the Best Kept Spanish Village Award on a number of occasions. There is a pleasant square next to the 16th-century, largely brick built, Baroque church. Look for the *retablo* and the Mudéjar coffered ceiling. The Plaza de Libertad has bars, craft shops and the Sierra Nevada Natural Park Visitors' Centre. Here there is a small display showing the natural history, geology and wildlife of the Alpujarras, while there is also a comprehensive collection of books and pamphlets. Particularly recommended for serious trekkers are the handbooks *Andar por Sierra Nevada* and *Andar por La Alpujarra*. Also available are 1:25,000 maps covering Pico de Veleta, Trevélez and Bérchules. The multilingual staff also have details of accommodation to rent and arrange treks in the Sierra Nevada on foot or by four-wheel drive vehicle. A recommended place to stay is the **D** *Hostal Ruta del Mulhacén,* Avenida de la Alpujarra 6, T958763010, which has attractive rooms with bath and balcony. Opposite, and near where the bus stops, is the **D** *Hostal Pampaneira,* Calle José Antonio 1, T958763107, with a friendly owner and clean spacious rooms. It also has a good value *menú del día*.

Pampaneira
Population: 337
Altitude: 1,058 m

Just outside the village, perched on the side of the gorge, is the incongruous **Tibetan Buddhist Monastery of Clear Light**, also known as O Sel Ling, the birthplace of the young Osel, who is supposed to be the successor to the Dalai Lama. It can be visited from 1500 to 1800 daily, T958343134.

In a stunning position backed by the snows of the Sierra Nevada, this is the next village along the valley. It is rapidly acquiring the trappings of tourism, but it has a long way to go to catch up with Capileira. For accommodation, there is **A-B** *Villa Turística de Bubión*, Barrio Alta sin número, T958763111, F958763136, with self-catering apartments (no kitchen) for two to four people, as well as hotel facilities including a restaurant and pool. A cheaper option is **D** *Las Terrazas*, Plaza del Sol, T958763034, F958763252. Simple accommodation and friendly owners. Good value. Mountain bikes available. Also contact Concha, Calle Buenavista 2, T958763220, for short or long stays in roomsor apartments with great views (**E**). Highly recommended. An attractive and friendly Moroccan style internet café, *CiberMonfi*, is at Calle Alcalde Pérez Ramón 2, with a pleasant garden and belly dancing on some Saturday nights.

Bubión
Population: 376
Altitude: 1,300 m

Granada Province

☞ Sorting out your hams

The English words 'ham' and 'gammon' both originate from the Spanish word **jamón**. The thin slices of ham available in Britain and North America are known as jamón york in Spain, where they are thought of as only being fit for a toasted sandwich or a roll. In Andalucía jamón serrano is the real thing and it has attracted around it a certain mystique and tradition. It is also extremely popular. Spain consumes 27 m joints of ham annually and no bar or bodega worth its salt would be seen without festoons of jamónes hanging from the ceiling. The production of jamón serrano, cured mountain ham, has traditionally been a cottage industry, with small farmers keeping a number of free range pigs under oak trees where they eat the fallen acorns. The slaughtered pigs would then be taken to the local curing factory, a small scale affair where the joints would be kept for two or three months for the curing process. This involves covering the meat with sea salt to sweat, in a carefully controlled micro climate.

Some areas of Andalucía, such as Trevélez in the Alpujarras, are noted for the excellence of their hams. The ham, par excellence, however, is the pata negra from the Sierra Morena of Huelva province, which is produced from Iberian pigs with characteristic black patas, or feet. They give a fatty meat, but this helps to tenderise during the curing stage, which may last for as long as 18 months. As a result pata negra can be extremely expensive.

There is a complicated etiquette to produce the wafer thin slices of jamón. Ingenious wooden racks with screws and clamps hold the ham steady while it is carved with long, thin, razor sharp knives. Accompanying the jamón will be bread or a type of bland biscuit which will not detract from the taste of the ham. Add a glass of cold fino and you have a meal fit for a king.

However, you should enjoy the traditional jamón serrano while you can, because the old time cottage industry may not last much longer. The lines of jamones in bars and bodegas may soon be a thing of the past, owing to EU hygiene laws. Some 60% of ham is now sold boned in vacuum sealed bags, produced by huge marketing consortiums in the cities of the north. Connoisseurs may sniff, but at least jamón serrano will be cheaper.

Capileira
Population: 560
Altitude: 1,436 m

This village at the head of the valley marks the start of the summer dirt road that climbs up to the upper slopes of Mulhacén and Veleta and down to Solynieve. It is also an excellent centre for walking and horse trekking holidays. In Moorish times it had a mosque and two baths and was well known for its silk production. The Church of Nuestra Señora de la Cabeza was in Mudéjar style but was rebuilt in the 17th century. It has a carving of the Virgin, which was a gift from Ferdinand and Isabel. There is also a museum devoted to the writer Pedro Antonio de Alarcón, who travelled widely in the 19th century and wrote a book about the Alpujarras. For accommodation, there is **C** *Finca Los Llanos*, T958763071, an attractive place at the top of the village off to side of road to Sierra Nevada with pool. Three other options in the **D** range are *Hostal Ruta de las Nieves*, Carretera Sierra Nevada sin número, T958763106, with great views from its terrace, *Hostal Atalaya*, Calle Perchel 3, T958763025, rooms with bath on the edge of town and *Hostal Paco López*, Carretera de la Sierra, T958763011, which has newish rooms with bath and balcony. There are plenty of restaurants in town. *Restaurante La Pizzería*, Plaza de la Constitución, has an interesting selection of pizzas.

In the tiny, unspoiled village of **Ferreirola**, close to Bubión and Capileira, is **D** *Sierra y Mar*, T958766171, F958857367. A delightful guesthouse but often fully booked. Owners José and Inge have exceptional knowledge of walks and the area. If *Sierra y Mar* is full there are rooms and apartments to rent in the village from Fernando of *Nevadense*, based at the Centro de Visitantes in Pampaneira, T958766253.

Returning south to the main east/west high road, there is a cluster of villages, including Pitres, Pórtugos, Mecina Fondales, Ferreirola and Busquistar, which collectively make up what in Moorish times was known as the *Taa* or *taha* group (a word derived from the Arabic word for obedience). All five villages show the typical domestic architecture of the area, with the gallery-like *tinaos* and walls and roof made of *launa*. **Pitres** is the largest of the group and although less attractive than the villages in the Poqueira valley, it's worth stopping here. Its name is thought to come from the Latin *petra*, meaning stone, so it was probably occupied by the Romans before the Moors, but remains of the latter can be seen around the village, with the ruins of an old hilltop mosque, a derelict mill and a well.

Just to the east of Pitres is the well-kept village of **Pórtugos**, which itself is unremarkable, but 400 m to the east is a hermitage containing the image of *Nuestra Señora de las Angustias*. A steady stream of villagers walk down the hill to look through the grill and pray. A plaque on the wall has a verse attributed to the local writer Pedro Antonio de Alarcón (1872-1972). Alongside the hermitage is a wooded valley where a spring emerges, the Fuente Agria, which is rich in iron minerals giving the stream bed a reddish brown tinge.50 m away, next to a picnic site, the stream drops over a cliff known as El Chorreón and through a remarkable vegetated gorge like something out of a rain forest. There are two good accommodation possibilities in Pórtugos, which makes a convenient centre for exploring the area: **B** *Nuevo Malagueno*, Carretera Órgiva-Trevélez sin número, T958766098, F958857337, with stunning views from rooms, a garage, bar and restaurant. A *pensión* sited on a terrace at the entrance to the Trevélez valley, with, as its name suggests, some marvellous views is **C** *Mirador de Pórtugos*, Plaza Nueva 5, T958766014, with a good restaurant.

The next valley has been cut by the Río Trevélez and with terraces lining the valley sides, this is not so dramatic as the Poqueira. A road leads up one side of the valley to the village of Trevélez, returning down the other side. The name Trevélez means 'three districts' and the village is divided into the *alto, medio* and *bajo barrios.* While it has little of real interest, its main claim to fame is that it is the highest village in Spain (and indeed the whole of the Iberian peninsula). Trevélez is also the main starting point for treks to the top of Mulhacén and the other peaks of the Sierra Nevada. Next to the bridge over the river Trevélez is a rather charmless square, surrounded by bars, tacky craft shops and *jamonerías.*

The mountain ham of Trevélez is famous throughout Spain and is produced from white pigs rather than the usual Iberian black strain (see box). The climate is said to be ideal for the microbial flora required for the curing. Legend has it that Rossini was once prepared to swap his Stradivarius for a Trevélez ham! Certainly the small square reeks with the aroma of hams and sausages that hang in profusion from the ceilings of every house and shop. A Fiesta de los Jamones is held every year in August. The other big event is the *romería* to Mulhacén which is held on 5 August, in honour of the Virgin of the Snow. Good budget accommodation in Trevélez is provided by **D** *Hostal Fernando,* Trevélez Alto, T958858565; a small establishment with friendly staff. Recommended. Alternatively try **D** *Hotel La Fragua*, T958858626, which is a fairly basic, small hotel at the top of the village with an excellent restaurant just a few yards away. Popular with walking groups from the UK.

Pitres & Pórtugos

Trevélez
Population: 793
Altitude: 1,476 m

Granada Province

East of Trevélez The high road continues through the unremarkable, but pleasantly attractive villages of **Juviles**, a silk producing centre in Moorish times, **Bérchules**, overlooking a gorge, and, just off the main route, **Cádiar** with an attractive central square. In Bérchules is **D** *Hotel Los Bérchules*, T958852530, a very comfortable small hotel on the village outskirts and a perfect base for walking the Bérchules circuit (see Walking in the Alpujarras below). The English owner Wendy is exceptionally kind and helpful. Good views out across the valley. Cádiar marks the end of the Western Alpujarras and heralds a change in the scenery to a more arid, undulating landscape, particularly as you get closer to the border with Almería.

In the north, the town of **Válor** is worth a visit. Surrounded by well-wooded farmland, the village is characterized by its steep winding streets with the houses covered by the dark grey *launa*. The village is well known for the exploits of one of its 16th-century residents, Fernando de Córdoba y Válor who led the Moorish revolt against the Christians in the Alpujarras in 1569. The family's house still stands in the village, which is the venue for the best Moors and Christians festival in the region. The nearby village of **Yegen** was the home for many years of the British writer Gerald Brenan, who wrote the observational study *South of Granada* (see box). His house, El Casa del Inglés, can be found in the upper part of the village.

Southern Alpujarras The lower sierras in the south of the Alpujarras are less visited. With a drier climate, agriculture is more difficult and there are consequently fewer villages. Villages like **Haza del Lino**, **Albuñol** and **Albondón** (all of which have great views of the Mediterranean) tend to concentrate on wine growing, producing a deceptively strong *rosé*, which is usually available from barrels on the counters of most bars in the Alpujarras.

Walking in the Alpujarras

The Alpujarras are attracting an increasing number of walkers. The recent waymarking of the GR-7 route (see under Other walks below) which loops all the way across the region and of a number of PR (*pequeño recorrido* or short distance) footpaths has made the area more accessible to less experienced walkers. Several companies based in Britain and Germany are organising walking holidays in the area. And people are coming to climb the higher peaks and to undertake higher traverses of the Sierra; there is a good sytsem of mountain refuges with more on the way.

Thanks to the isolation of the Alpujarras and the comparatively recent arrival of paved roads, the footpaths linking the villages are mostly intact and make for some wonderful walking. Routes described here all have some steep climbing involved - there is no such thing as a gentle *barranco* or ravine - but the walking is varied and often spectacular. Two of the routes stick to the lower network of footpaths whilst the walk up to Siete Lagunas gives you a taste of the wonderful scenery of the high Alpujarras.

Because of the altitude of the villages – they are amongst the highest in Europe – you can walk comfortably in the Alpujarras in June and September although you should get going early. During the winter snow rarely settles for long below 1,200 m and this can be an excellent time to visit, especially when the almond trees are in blossom. Spring is a double treat: the flowers are at their best and temperatures mild enough for lazy picnics along the way.

The most detailed **maps** available of the area are the 1:25000 series of the Instituto Geográfico Nacional but you will need several of them to cover the

Gerald Brenan

On the wall of a house, just off a small square in the Alpujarran village of Yegen, is a tiny plaque which proclaims in blue letters that the English writer Gerald Brenan lived here in the 1920s and 1930s. This is a modest tribute to someone whom many consider to be the greatest English Hispanist.

Brenan was born in 1894 and after a public school education (where according to his biographer he developed most of his hang-ups), he fought in the First World War, gaining a Military Medal and the French Croix de Guerre. After the war he settled in Spain, mainly it seems because of the cheap wine and cigarettes, which were lifelong addictions. He ended up in the then remote village of Yegen, with his collection of over 2,000 books, having married the American poetess Gamel Woolsey. It was here that he had a steamy relationship with a 15-year-old peasant girl, resulting in his only daughter Miranda – who the long-suffering Gamel agreed to bring up. Don Gerardo, as he was known to the locals, was quite wealthy owing to a number of legacies which came his way, so he did not need to publish work to survive. Study and scholarship were more important and it was not until he was 40 that his first book was published. This was South From Granada, a perceptive insight into everyday life in an Andalucían pueblo (village) and since regarded as a sociological masterpiece. Then followed the scholarly The Spanish Labyrinth and the Literature of the Spanish People. Meanwhile, Brenan had developed a strong Andalucían dialect and a love for the Spanish, admiring their dignity in poverty and their emotions which they carried on their sleeves. It was a two way rapport and his passionate writing found an appreciative readership in Spain. Brenan was also an assiduous correspondent and wrote at length to contemporaries in Britain, especially the Bloomsbury circle. Indeed, his recent biographer, Jonathon Gathorne-Hardy, believes that his brilliant letters will

'eventually prove Gerald's most lasting memorial'.

Gerald Brenan moved to England at the outbreak of the Civil War, and he did not return to Spain until 1949, settling in Churriana near Málaga. He continued his writing, preferring this to the academic world and turning down offers of chairs in Spanish Studies at both Oxford and Boston. In his later years Brenan's behaviour became increasingly bizarre. Gathering material for his novel The Lighthouse Always Says Yes, he enthusiastically embraced the hippie culture of Torremolinos, despite being in his late 60s. After the death of his wife, he moved in with an Englishwoman 49 years his junior in the village of Alhaurín el Grande. Finally at the age of 90 he returned to England, staying in an old people's home in Pinner.

Brenan was always more highly regarded in Spain than in England and the Spanish press spread the idea that he had returned to England against his will. Eventually a delegation from Alhaurín came to Pinner and virtually kidnapped Brenan and returned him to Andalucía. He was installed in a home in Alhaurín and the Regional Government provided a nurse and covered his living expenses. There he lingered on like an ailing Russian president, kept alive as a literary trophy. Brenan eventually died in Alhaurín in January 1987.

Today, there is little for aficionados of Don Gerardo to see. The home in Yegen has a small plaque. The houses in Churriana and Alhaurín el Grande have both changed hands several times. His manuscripts and books are kept in a locked room in Alhaurín's public library, the key controlled by the moribund Brenan Foundation. There is not even a grave or monument at which to pay homage. Brenan had paid for a plot next to his wife in Málaga's English Cemetery, but awkward to the end, he made a late change in his will and donated his body to medical science. His corpse remains pickled in formaldehyde in the Anatomy department at Málaga University.

Granada Province

walks listed here. It is probably best to stick with the Instituto Geográfico Nacional's 1:50000 map (*mapa/guía*) - Sierra Nevada. If you choose to go for the individual 1:50000 series you'll need numbers 1027, 1042 and 1043. Trevélez falls right on the border of two maps, 1027 and 1042 but 95% of the route which leave from the village is covered by the 1027 map (Güéjar-Sierra). Alpina's 1:40000 map Sierra Nevada/La Alpujarra isn't bad although some tracks are missing from the map. The best place to pick up maps and guide books is in the Centro de Visitantes in Pampaneira where the excellent Nevadense guides are based (see page 341). The amount of assembled litertaure and maps is really impressive (some of it is in English, too). Try to drop in at beginning of your visit: Pampaneira is one of the first villages you pass through as you arrive from the west.

Trevélez Circuit
Distance: 14½ km
Time: 7½/8 hours
Difficulty:
medium/difficult

This long all-day walk takes you up to the beautiful high cirque (2,900m), which lies just beneath mainland Spain's highest peak, the Mulhacén (3,479 m). From Trevélez you have a climb of nearly 1,500 m so to enjoy this walk you should be reasonably fit and get going at a reasonable hour. You can shorten the walk by almost three hours or 6 km by ending the climb at the ruins of Cortijo La Campiñuela. In the colder months there is often snow on the higher sections of the walk so check before leaving Trevélez. The path followed on the circular option from La Campiñuela is steep and loose at times; if in doubt you can simply make this an up-and-down walk for as far as the mood takes you. Map 1:50000 Sierra Nevada General Map or 1:50000 Lanjarón (1042) and 1:50000 Güéjar-Sierra (1027).

Itinerary The walk begins in the square at the bottom of Trevélez in front of Bar Rosales. Go up the hill to Mesón La Fragua. Here bear left, pass *Hotel La Fragua*, turn right beneath an archway then turn right into Calle Horno. After 40 m, at a yellow arrow on a telegraph pole, go left. A narrow path leads up through the terraces then merges with a second path before crossing a stone bridge. You cross a (dry) stream, continue up past a small white building then cross a second bridge. When the path divides (20 minutes) go straight on following red and white marker posts. You pass a farm with solar panels then cross another (dry) stream. About 200 m after passing a threshing circle the path divides. Bear left and climb: a rock with a white arrow points the way. Careful! At a small cairn (45 minutes) bear left following red dots. This narrower path bears left then meets with a fence then passes through a gate. You now follow cairns up across looser terrain. Soon a fence runs to your left and Trevélez is visible way down below. After a longish climb the path swings right and runs beneath a water channel, Acequia Gorda, and a fence. You reach a second fence, go through a gate then cross the water channel and continue along its left bank. After 200 m bear left, go through a gap in a fence and climb steeply through an area of young pines. The trees thin out and the path zigzags up to another fence. Here go through another gate (sometimes open) and follow the fence along. Where it ends climb towards a low wall which lies between you and the rocky massif of Mulhacén. The path swings right, crosses a water channel (Acequia del Mundo) and red dots lead you to a flat area and a ruined farm: Cortijo La Campiñuela (two hours 15 minutes). The path bears right between the farm and a threshing circle then climbs past a tumbledown corral. Where it divides go left, continuing up over looser shale. Cairns and red dots mark the path. The path eventually descends and crosses the Río Culo de Perro at a point where its banks have been shored up with concrete. On the other side bear left: the path is indistinct at first but soon cairns lead you slightly to the right, away from the stream. After climbing for about 15 minutes the path divides. Bear left and climb the Culo de Perro's steep, rocky right bank, marked on some maps as 'Chorreras Negras' – literally, the small, dark waterfalls. You cross the rocky river bed just before the top of the ridge and reach the beautiful glacial cirque of Siete Lagunas (three hours 45 minutes) which lies between Alcazaba (3,360 m) and Mulhacén (3,479 m) both of which can be climbed from here. This walk finishes here, at 2,900 m, on the flat, grassy area between the Siete Lagunas, or Seven Tarns, which is a perfect picnic spot.

You now have a choice. The easiest option is to retrace your footsteps back to Trevélez (six hours 15 minutes). A slightly more difficult option is to return to the ruins of Cortijo La Campiñuela (four hours 45 minutes) where you bear right on a good path which descends through terracing then crosses the Acequia del Mundo. Follow it along then cross once again to its upper bank. Trevélez comes into view. Soon a fence runs to your left and your path drops into the Barranco Madrid, which you cross just up from the fence. The path narrows then divides. Go left, following cairns down a looser-surfaced path. Go through a fence, descend to a flatter area and when you reach another fence, go right; don't go through the gap. The path runs indistinctly just to the right of the fence, descends to another flat area then passes beneath a small dry-stone hut and then a second tumbledown building. Cairns help to guide you down. At a grassy area bear left, drop down just to the left of a barbed-wire fence then go through a wire-and-post gate. The path narrows before contouring right, slightly away from Trevélez, towards an isolated farm. Just before reaching it (five hours 45 minutes) swing hard left and drop down through the terraces east of the farm. Soon you'll be heading towards a stone platform at the end of the ridge. You reach a slope where the path bears right, drops down its right bank, then goes through a gate. A clearer path now leads down beneath a stone wall then crosses the slope. Continuing your descent you cross a water channel then bear right. The path passes a threshing circle, drops down a (dry) gulley, passes beneath another threshing circle then reaches another water channel, Acequia Nueva. Here swing left and follow the narrow bank of the channel until you reach an ugly breeze-block building. Here turn right, descend, and you'll meet with the path that you followed earlier in the day which leads you back to Mesón La Fragua (six hours 15 minutes).

This longish walk follows a loop of the GR7, the long-distance path which crosses the southern flank of the Sierra Nevada. It is an astonishingly varied walk and you visit no fewer than five villages along the way. Although there is one slightly dull stretch as you pass Cádiar, some sections are as pretty as any in the Alpujarras. Remember that between the Río Guadalfeo and Juviles you'll have to negotiate a climb of nearly 450 m. If you are reasonably fit and get going early from Bérchules you'll have ample time to picnic along the way and still be in Juviles to make the late afternoon bus back to your point of departure. Much of the walk is along muleteers' tracks which cut up and down the sides of steep-sided barrancos. There are a few short sections of tarmac as you pass through the villages. Map 1:50000 Sierra Nevada General Map or 1:50000 Lanjarón (1042) and 1:50000 Berja (1043).

Bérchules to Juviles
Distance: 12 km
Time: 6½-7 hours
Difficulty: medium/difficult

Itinerary The walk begins at *Hotel Bérchules* at the bottom of the village. Turn left out of the hotel then right and walk down to the adjacent village of Alcútar. Here branch right at a sign 'Centro Población', pass a fountain then a

Granada Province

church, then fork left into Calle Cantera. Take the next left into Calle Real and continue to number 30. Here bear right then left along Calle Churre. Follow the road round the bottom of Alcútar to a fountain. Here turn right on to a beautiful path (the camino del río) which drops down through fig, almond and olive groves to the river which you cross via a pretty stone bridge. The path bears right then reaches the outskirts of Narila (35 minutes) where it is concreted. You pass a fountain, cross a bridge then come to a square by a church. Cross the square to a phone box then drop down a narrow alley to a pylon then turn sharply right. The path zigzags back down towards the river. At the end of a breeze-block wall turn left and continue along parallel to the river. At a point where its banks are shored up (55 minutes) you pick up a track which leads to a fenced-off irrigation tank. Turning left you come to the outskirts of Cádiar. Here bear right, skirting round the bottom of the village. After passing a fountain a wooden sign points your way to Lobras. At the next fork swing left along a track which hugs the river's left bank. You pass several irrigated allotments. Continue past the football pitch, cross an ugly concrete bridge over the Guadalfeo, then continue along its right bank. You'll see red and white GR waymarking. After passing a ruined farm to the right of the track you climb steeply on a narrower path. It crosses a water channel, descends, then arcs round to the right and climbs steeply up the Loma de San Agustín. You reach another barranco where the path bears right; you are now rewarded with great views of the Contraviesa Sierra. At the top of the ridge (two hours) Lobras comes into view. The path now drops down to the (dry) river of the Barranco de Albayar. Here bear left along the river bed for 100 m to a marker post then swing right on a steep path that climbs towards Lobras. The path eventually levels then meets with a tarmac road. Here turn right.

As you enter Lobras the road divides. Branch left into the village and at the church bear left again, descend, then turn right past the Consultorio to meet once again with the tarmac road. Pass the ugly Villa Rodríguez Martín and opposite a water tank (two hours 35 minutes) bear left at a sign for Timar. Careful! Just past the village rubbish tip fork right on a path which at first follows a water channel. It crosses a (dry) stream and climbs. At the next fork go left and zigzag steeply upwards. The path merges with a track which leads to the top of the pass and a GR marker post. After this narrow pass bear sharp right on to a track. At the very next fork turn right again on a path which descends for a short distance then climbs up through the terraces beneath Timar. Heading towards a water tank, the path crosses an irrigation channel then an old threshing circle. After passing a ruin to your left you reach a track which bears right, passes a cemetery and reaches Timar (three hours). Keep to this track which runs just below a concrete road, passes a tiny chapel and skirts round the bottom of the village. Just past the church branch left and just past a lone cypress tree bear left again to reach a marker post where you branch right at a sign for Juviles. As you climb, a wall and a fence run to your left. Where they end bear sharp left. The path climbs steeply to the top of the narrow pass then on its far side bears left and climbs again over rather looser terrain. After crossing an irrigation channel the path levels before descending and crossing the stream beneath Juviles. A final steep haul leads up to the village along a cobbled path then a track. When you reach a Chacinería bear right up the hill to reach the road to Bérchules. Turn left to reach the bus stop and Bar Alonso where you could treat yourself to a beer and a tapas (four hours). It makes a good rendezvous point if you are returning by taxi.

This loop walk begins and ends in the pretty village of Capileira and takes you up to the generating station of La Cebadilla. Although your destination is at a height of over 1,600 m the walk begins in one of the highest villages of the Alpujarras (1,432 m) so there is not too much climbing. The views down the Poqueira river valley are exceptional and there is the possibility of extending this walk (see below) from a point above La Cebadilla. Most of the walk follows old footpaths which cut across the old terraces of the valley. There is also a 30-minute stretch of track on the return leg before you pick up the loveliest of paths which drops steeply down to Capileira. Map 1:50000 Sierra Nevada General Map or 1:50000 Lanjarón (1042).

Capileira Circuit

Distance: 9 km
Time: 4-4½ hours
Difficulty: medium

Itinerary The walk begins outside the village's Ayuntamiento, to the right of the road as you arrive from Bubión. Cross the road and take the street leading into the village by a phone box. Turn left at *Restaurante El Tilo* then take the next right and pass *Bar El Tilo*. At the end of a small square head along Calle del Cubo then bear right past *Apartamentos Vista Veleta* until you reach a viewing point to the left of the road. Here keep right and pick up a path which descends towards the river. You pass a swimming pool to the left of the path then reach a fork (15 minutes) where you bear left and continue down to the valley floor. Here you cross a bridge over the river Poqueira by a sign 'Aguas de Alta Montaña'. The path swings right, climbs and after 50 yards a wooden-posted barrier runs to your right. Follow the course of the barrier ignoring a path which leads up to a threshing circle. You climb gradually up through the terracing, roughly parallel to the river. At times you'll see marker posts but they are sometimes absent when you might most expect to see them. The path leads past a ruined farmstead with a threshing circle and continues running more or less parallel to the river, every so often looping up to a higher level. The path swings left (40 minutes) in front of the wall of a terrace then right again and continues climbing. You pass a row of poplars then a renovated farm building to your left. The path now loops more sharply upwards and you should spot a transmitter mast up ahead which you will later pass by. When the path reaches a small barranco it bears left then crosses it a little higher up. Soon a ramshackle fence runs to the right of the path and leads up to a farm with solar panels and barking dogs (one hour). Passing to the left of the farm the path drops down, crosses a small bridge and after 100 m reaches a fork. Here branch left and climb. After crossing a terrace you pass another tumbledown farm before reaching a line of poplars where you swing left, following the line of trees upwards. You pass a threshing circle, climb more steeply, pass one more stone building to your left before reaching the transmitter mast (one hour 15 minutes). Just to its right is an ugly modern building with a bridge leading to its front door. A few yards past the house turn right and pick up a wide track that leads down to the river and the HEP buildings. You come to the bridge crossing the Río Poqueira. Carry on up the track by the river to the power station (one hour 45 minutes), the furthest north that this walk takes you.

You could continue further up the track, cross a second higher bridge to a sign that marks various higher circuits up the Poqueira river valley. Otherwise, retrace your footsteps to the bridge (two hours) below the generating station, cross it then swing right past the houses, school and church that were built for the workers from the generating station. The track climbs gradually, heading south towards Capileira. Ignore a track branching right to Cortijo Roble but be ready to branch right off the track approximately 100 m after passing beneath the electricity lines (two hours 20 minutes). You drop down,

Granada Province

pass a house and head towards a second, slate-built house. Soon a water channel runs to the left of your path. You pass a threshing circle and the path follows the fence of the house along before climbing and running along just beneath a pine plantation. Continue past a large water tank towards Capileira; don't swing downhill to the right at a marker post! You soon reach a second fork in the path. Turn right and go down past two small huts. At the outskirts of the village bear right at the first house, drop down Calle Castillo, head straight over at the next crossroads and you arrive at the telephone box next to *Restaurant El Tilo*. Here turn left and retrace your footsteps back to the town hall (three hours).

Other walks **The GR-7** This long distance route, running all the way from Andorra to Algeciras, cuts across the middle of the Alpujarras (the walk described from Berchules to Júviles follows a part of this route). You could easily follow the GR-7 from village to village for five or six days but you should make sure to have a good map and compass since the waymarking is sometimes confusing.

Eastern Alpujarras There are some wonderful walks at the eastern end of the Alpujarra. A good base in this area is *Casa de Las Chimeneas*, T958760352, in Mairena, owned by a young British couple, David and Emma Illsley.

Southern Alpujarras There are a number of lower walks out from the **C** *Alquería de Morayma*, T958343221, a beautiful small inn close to Cádiar. The owner, Mariano, has a number of route descriptions.

Shorter Routes Elma Thompson's leaflets *'Exploring the Alpujarras'* describe a series of more gentle walks, most of them radiating out from Bubión and Poqueira.

The Costa Tropical

The 60 km coastal stretch of Granada province is known as the Costa Tropical, consisting of the most attractive coastal scenery within Andalucía. Apart from the area around Motril, where the Río Guadalfeo has built up a flat plain, the shoreline consists largely of tall cliffs with the occasional small cove or fishing village. Motril, set slightly inland, is the main town of the area, while the only sizeable resorts are Almuñecar and Salobreña. Because of the physical nature of the coast line and the distance from major airports, the Costa Tropical has resisted the developments which have afflicted the areas to the west, but it is extremely popular with weekenders from Granada.

Motril
Colour map 5, grid B3
Population: 50,025

Motril is the main town of the Costa Tropical and is the second largest town in Granada province. It has always been an important route centre, lying at the intersection of the east-west coast road and the north-south Granada road. Motril is actually some 3 km inland, separated from its port by the sugar cane fields. The Carthaginians brought sugar cane to the area in the third century, but it was not until the 10th century that the Moors developed the refining process. More recent development has been due to the Larios gin family and because of the dominance of the sugar cane crop around Motril, the area has often been dubbed 'Little Cuba'.

Motril is generally an uninspiring town, but you can't miss the **Iglesia Mayor de la Encarnación**, which is located in the tree-lined avenue at the entrance to the town. Construction began in 1510 and shows a variety of architectural styles including Mudéjar, Baroque and Gothic. The church also doubled as a fortress against Berber pirates, so the overall effect is rather windowless and austere. In the Plaza de España, next to the church, is the dominating statue of Cardinal Belluga, a native of Motril. The imposing Ayuntamiento was built in Baroque style by Isidro de la Chica in 1631. A fascinating example of the 'sugar culture' is the **Casa de la Palma**, a colonial style house, which includes one of the few remaining pre-industrial sugar mills in Spain. The **Calderón de la Barca Theatre** dates from the late 19th century and is in Neoclassic style.

The main bus company serving the area is *Alsina Graells*, with the following daily services: 10 buses to Granada; three long distance coaches to Sevilla via Córdoba; one to Jaén and Cádiz; and two to Madrid. The bus station is a 10-minute walk up the hill out of town. There are **taxi** ranks in Avenida de Andalucía and in Plaza Aurora.

Salobreña

Some 4 km west of Motril is the small resort of Salobreña. It is in two parts, an old hill village and a modern beach development, both surrounded by sugar cane fields. The older part has the most spectacular location on the Granada coast. The **tourist office** is in Plaza de Goya, T958610314. It is open Monday to Friday 0930-1330 and 1630-1900; Saturday 0930-1330. On Thursday and Friday there are guided tours of the town, costing €5.10 including entry to the castle and museum; contact the tourist office for reservations.

Colour map 5, grid B3
Population: 10,053

Salobreña has a long and interesting history. Founded by the Phoenicians in the eighth century as a trading post, it was known as Salambina. It was later occupied in turn by the Carthaginians and the Romans, when it was integrated into the province of Bética. In 713 the Moors arrived and were to stay for seven centuries, calling it Salubania. It was one of Granada's 30 districts and an area of some agricultural and industrial importance. During the Nasrid period (1166-1247), Salobreña was used by Granada's royal families for summer holidays. In 1489 it was conquered by Francisco Ramírez of Madrid, who was made governor by the Catholic Monarchs when he later successfully defended the town against the siege of Boabdil.

After languishing for years in poverty, Salobreña has gained a modicum of prosperity through tourism. The newer coastal area of Salobreña is a purpose-built tourist development, but is inoffensive, well planned and consists mainly of low rise apartment blocks and villas. The sandy beach is divided into two by a large rock – Peñon Beach and Guardia Beach.

The **Castillo** was built by the Moors and later remodelled by the Christians. Despite some damage by earthquakes, it was the most important fortress in the coastal part of the province. With steep cliffs on three sides, the only approach was through the houses, making it resistant to siege, especially as a fountain within the castle gave a reliable water supply. It is kidney shaped and consists of two enclosures, one of which contained the prison, which at one time or another held a number of disgraced Moorish kings such as Muley Hacen and Yusef III. A large flattened tower contained the armoury, while another tower protected the entrance. Moorish ceramics and glass have been found on the site. ■ *Tue-Sun 1030-1350 and 1600-1900. €2.41, including entry to the museum. Follow the signs marked 'Castillo' through the narrow roads and alleyways.*

Sights

The **Iglesia de Nuestra Señora del Rosario** is also worth a visit. It is located on the east side of the Castillo at a lower level. It was constructed in the first half of the 16th century in Mudéjar style on the site of a former mosque and was

Granada Province

extensively restored in the 17th and 18th centuries. As with many churches in this area, it has three naves separated by square pillars. The sculptures inside date from the 17th century.

Sleeping The main hotel accommodation is found close to the main coast road. There are a number of cheaper *pensiones*, both on the seafront and in the old town. **C** *Salobreña*, Ctra N340, Km 326, T958610261, F958610101. 151 rooms, marvellous position on a spur overlooking old Salobreña, pool, tennis, parking, garden. **C** *Salimbina*, Ctra N340, Km 328, T958610037. 13 rooms, restaurant, hill top location looking over town and sea. **D** *Mari Tere*, Ctra de la Playa 7, T958610126. 20 rooms, restaurant, handy for the beach. **D** *Palomares*, C Fábrica Nueva 44, T958610181. 12 rooms, friendly. **E** *Pérez*, C del Cristo 28, T958610127. The cheapest in town. **Camping** *El Peñon*, Paseo Marítimo. 2nd category beach side site.

Eating **Expensive** *Mesón Duran*, Ctra Málaga, Km 341. International cuisine, sea views. **Cheap** *Mesón la Bodega*, Plaza de Goya, has ambience along with sherry from the barrel and a reasonable *menú del día*. *Chiringuitos* on the beach, such as *Flores* and *Tres Hermanos*, provide good, inexpensive fish dishes.

Fiestas & **Easter** week is marked by traditional *Semana Santa* processions through the old part of **festivals** town. **End Jul** *Fiesta de San Juan y San Pedro*. **Aug** *Cultural Week* Exhibitions and talks. **First week in Oct** *Fiesta de Nuestra Señora del Rosario*.

Transport Buses stop at the town entrance, just off the coast road. There are eight local buses in each direction, hourly to Motril, seven buses a day from Almería, Málaga and Granada, with less frequent connections with Sevilla.

Almuñécar

Colour map 5, Thirteen kilometres west of Salobreña lies Almuñécar, the largest resort on
grid B3 the Costa Tropical. It was founded by the Phoenicians some 3,000 years ago
Population: 21,500 and later occupied by the Romans, who left behind an aqueduct and the rather improbable name of Sexi Firmun Julium. The Moors wisely dropped that name and called it Al-Munnakkah. It was the Moors who built the Castillo de San Miguel on the foundations of a Roman ruin, although it was extensively reconstructed during the time of Carlos V and until quite recently served as the local cemetery. In 755, Almuñécar was the spot where Abderramán I landed after he fled from Damascus. Heir to the Omeya Dynasty, he soon became Emir of Córdoba and reigned for over 30 years. Recently, a huge bronze statue in his memory has been erected beneath the castle.

Laurie Lee in *As I Walked Out One Midsummer Morning* described Almuñécar in withering terms at the start of the Civil War, when he was rescued from its rather stony beach by a British destroyer. Today, he would be surprised at Almuñécar's development as a holiday resort, although its future expansion will probably be limited by its distance from Málaga Airport, some 75 km to the west. A headland, the **Peñon del Santo**, divides the coastline into two, with the Playa de San Cristóbal to the west and the Playa de Puerta del Mar to the east. Both beaches are of stone or shingle, but backed by attractive *paseos* with a number of *tapas* bars. The inevitable apartment blocks and hotels do not seem to have drastically ruined Almuñécar, which still retains a Moorish atmosphere in the old town behind the castle.

The Municipal **tourist office** is at Palacete de la Navarra, an interesting **Sights**
Neo-Moorish building at the coastal end of Avenida Europa, near Playa
Cristóbal, T958631125. ■ *1000-1400, 1600-1900, www.almunecar-ctropical.org*

It is well worth visiting the small **Museo Arqueológico**, in the Plaza de la
Constitución. Known as the *Cuevas de las Siete Palacios* (Cave of the Seven
Palaces), the place is thought to have been a cellar of Roman construction,
probably used for water storage. Local artefacts are displayed from Phoenician, Roman and Moorish periods, but the star exhibit is an inscribed Egyptian vase dating from the reign of the Pharoah Apophis I. ■ *Tue-Sat
1030-1330 and 1600-1800, Sun 1030-1330. €2, including entry to castle.*

The **Castillo San Miguel** is perched on the headland that separates
Almuñécar's two main beaches. The Castillo was built in the reign of Carlos V
on the site of a Roman fort and a later Moorish Alcazaba. Dominating the site
is the tower which acted as a prison for many years. It suffered under the
French during the War of Independence and was then battered into ruins by
the British navy in 1808. For years it was the town's cemetery, until quite
recently when its inhabitants were dug up and relocated elsewhere. The site
was then renovated and is now the home of the town **museum**. ■ *Opening
times and entry fee same as Museo Arqueológico above.* Beneath the walls of the
Castillo is the site of a newly excavated Roman fish factory making *garum*, a
kind of fish sauce, in similar style to that at Baelo Claudia in Cádiz province.

The excavations form part of the **Botanical Gardens**, which display more
than 400 varieties of subtropical plants, mainly from Latin America. The Parque
Ornithológico is Almuñécar's most popular attraction. It is widely advertised as
the 'Loro Sexi' (the Sexy Parrot). ■ *1100-1400 and 1600-1800. €2.*

Almuñécar also has a **Parque Acuatico** with all the usual water features
located on Paseo de Reina Sofia, which is very popular with children.
■ *Jul-Sep. €9, children €4.50. T958634016.*

There are some good walks in the hills behind Almuñécar. Take the road **Walking**
towards Torrecuevas, then turn left for a private nature reserve called Peña
Escrita, which is a good place to start a walk. There is a small café here and
wooden cabins for rent.

There are plenty of rented apartments are available. **A** *Helios*, Plaza de San Cristóbal **Sleeping**
s/n, T958634459, F958634469. The largest hotel with 232 rooms, pool, garage, a/c, **& eating**
wheelchair access. **B-C** *La Najarra*, C Guadix 12, T958630873, F958630391,
hotel_lanajarra@jet.es 30 rooms. Pool, tennis. **D** *Carmen*, Av Europa 19, T958631413,
h_carmen@teleline.es Central. **D** *Tropical*, Av Europa s/n, T958633458. 11 rooms.
Small, comfortable and central. Recommended. **D** *Victoría II*, Plaza Damasco 2,
T/F958631734, hotelvictoria@teleline.es 40 rooms with bath and TV in central location. Recommended.

Just to the west of Almuñécar is **La Herradura**, set on a beach between the **Around**
headlands of Cerro Gordo and La Mona. Once a fishing village, it is now **Almuñécar**
becoming a distinctly upmarket residential area. The beach at La Herradura is
rather stony, but the water is clear, which has led to a lively diving trade, with
four diving equipment stores on the front and a number of boats available. Sea
canoes, sail boards and jet skis can also be hired and there is paragliding from
the cliffs above the town. Nearby is the recently built marina development of
Marina del Este. The Marina has a number of dive shops. Dives cost €30 with
full gear.

Granada Province

Otívar and **Lenteji** are a couple of attractive villages about 30 minutes' drive on the old Granada road which winds through the Sierra Nevada from Almuñécar.

Jaén Province

9

Jaén Province

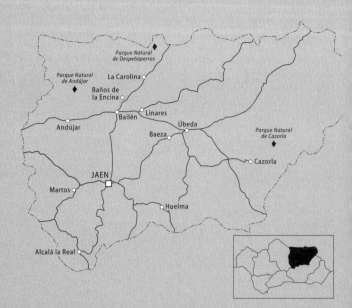

The landlocked province of Jaén in northeastern Andalucía is one of the region's least visited areas, yet it has some interesting cities and protected areas. In its city architecture, it is more like central Spain, with which it is linked to by the Despeñaperros Pass. Like **Baeza** and **Úbeda**, the capital city, **Jaén**, has some fine Renaissance buildings, including the cathedral. These monuments, funded by textile production, were largely designed by the famed Andrés de Vandelvira.

The history of the province, however, goes back way beyond Renaissance times. Moorish castles abound in Andalucía, but two of the best examples are found in Jaén province – at **Baños de la Encina** in the north, guarding the Despeñaperros Pass, and at **Alcala la Real** in the south.

The mountainous east of the province is dominated by the **Parque Natural de Cazorla**, a series of limestone ridges running northeast-southwest, forming the largest protected area in Andalucía. Other natural parks include the **Sierra Mágina**, immediately southeast of Jaén and part of the Subbética mountain range, while in the north of the province is the **Parque Natural Despeñaperros**, part of the Sierra Morena.

Jaén Province

Jaén

Colour map 3, grid B1
Population: 107,184
Altitude: 574 m

*Situated in hills beset by more olive trees than you can shake a stick at, Jaén offers a refreshing glimpse of an Andalucían city free from the usual trappings of tourism. The impressive Renaissance **cathedral** on Plaza Santa María, the well-preserved **Baños Arabes** and a handful of other monuments and museums can easily be seen in a day. The 13th-century **Castillo de Santa Catalina** looms above the city, presenting a spectacular view of Jaén and its surroundings.*

Ins and outs

Getting there
See page 364 for further details

The nearest national **airport** is at Granada and the nearest international airport is at Málaga. The city's **bus** station is at the Plaza de Coca de la Piñera in the centre, T953255014. The road system around Jaén has improved with the completion of the N323 *autovía* which runs from Granada, linking up with the Despeñaperros Pass and central Spain. The huge RENFE **train** station is in Plaza de la Estación, T902240202, which is 20 mins walk from the centre.

Getting around

You can visit most of the worthwhile monuments on foot as they are clustered to the northwest of the cathedral, but the footsore will find **taxi** ranks in Plaza de las Batallas and at the rear of the cathedral. The *Castillo* bus company runs regular services around the town from the bus station in Plaza de Coca de la Piñera, stopping in the Plaza de la Constitución. **Parking** in the city is horrendous and it is best to use the well-signposted pay car parks. The underground car park at Parque Victoría is convenient for all the main sights.

Tourist offices

The **municipal tourist office** is at C Maestra 13, near the cathedral, T953242624/T953190455. It's open Mon-Fri 1000-1900, Sat-Sun 1000-1300.

Background

Jaén was probably an Iberian town, but the first major settlement was built by the Romans who were attracted by local deposits of silver. They named it Aurigi, and it was here, legend has it, that Euphrasius introduced Christianity. The Moors took the city in 712 and called it Yayyan, turning it into a strategic centre along local caravan routes. The Moorish armies under Muhammad II al-Nasir stopped in Jaén *en route* to the disastrous **Battle of Las Navas de Tolosa**, in which they lost much of their territory to Alonso VIII (see box, page 367). Jaén itself, which had become part of the Nasrid Kingdom of Granada, was ceded to Fernando III by Muhammad Ibn Nasr in 1246, after which time it played a key role as a Christian frontier town during the final stages of the Reconquest. Jaén was, in fact, used by the Catholic Monarchs as a meeting point by their army prior to the thrust to expel the Moors from Granada. As in many parts of Andalucía, decline then set in, a situation which was not helped by the steady emigration of its citizens to the colonies of the New World.

Today, Jaén is the poorest of the provincial capitals of Andalucía, with chronic unemployment both in the city and the surrounding agricultural area.

★

Things to do

- Check out the view of Jaén and the surrounding area from the city's Castillo de Santa Catalina
- See live flamenco at the *Peña Flamenca de Jaén* in Jaén city
- Join the *romería* in late April to see La Morenita in the shrine of Nuestra Virgen de la Cabeza in Parque Natural Andújar
- Stroll around Baeza's Renaissance palaces
- Explore the Parque Nacional de Cazorla on foot or horseback

Sights

Jaén's outsize cathedral was built on the site of the Great Mosque. It was begun in 1492, largely to the design of Andres de Vandelvira who spent the last 30 years of his life on the building, but was not completed until the early years of the 19th century. The exterior is dominated by the west front in Baroque-style with Corinthian columns and twin-towers capped with small domes. The statues are by Pedro Roldán. The architecture elsewhere is undistinguished. The Renaissance interior is typically gloomy, due to the lack of windows. Worth looking at are the choir stalls, dating from the 16th century and richly carved, and some of the many side chapels, which have the occasional notable work of art. Kept behind the high altar, in a glass case, is a holy relic, a cloth with which St Veronica is reputed to have wiped the face of Christ. Locals are allowed to kiss the glass case on Friday afternoons. ■ *0830-1300 and 1700-2000. There is also a small Sacristy Museum, Sat and Sun 1100-1300, which has a few sculptures and other items of interest.*

Catedral

If you walk 20 minutes northwest from the cathedral along Calles Martínez and Molina (passing to your left the **Arco de San Lorenzo**, all that remains of the church of the same name), you come to the Palacio de Villadompardo in Plaza Santa Luisa Marillac. The Palace was built in the 16th century over the **Baños Arabes**, which have now been re-opened. The building also contains the **Museo de Artes y Costumbres Populares** and the **Museo Internacional de Arte Naif**.

Palacio de Villadompardo

This palace houses Andalucía's largest surviving Moorish baths

The area of the Palacio occupied by the **Museo de Artes y Costumbres Populares** was a bank in the 17th century. It now includes two of the courtyards of the palace and a columned gallery on two levels. The museum gives a fascinating view of everyday life in the province over the last few centuries. The basement concentrates on agriculture, particularly the production of wine, cereals and olives, with a comprehensive collection of carts and farming implements. The first floor deals with ceramics, textiles and traditional house-building techniques. Here you can see the first cast-iron bed, which won first prize at the 1851 Great Exhibition in London. The second floor looks at various aspects of religion, plus a handful of trades.

The **Museo Internacional de Arte Naif** was opened in 1990 to occupy the remainder of the palace and was the first of its kind to be set up in Spain. Naive or primitive art has always been underestimated and this museum makes a refreshing change from the heavy religious-based art found in most of Andalucía's fine art museums. Naive art is characterized by being created by people who paint with no established methods or ideas learnt at art school. Their work is generally flat with bright colours, detailed background, foreground and lack of perspective. The simplicity and fantasy make them easy to

Jaén Province

Jaén

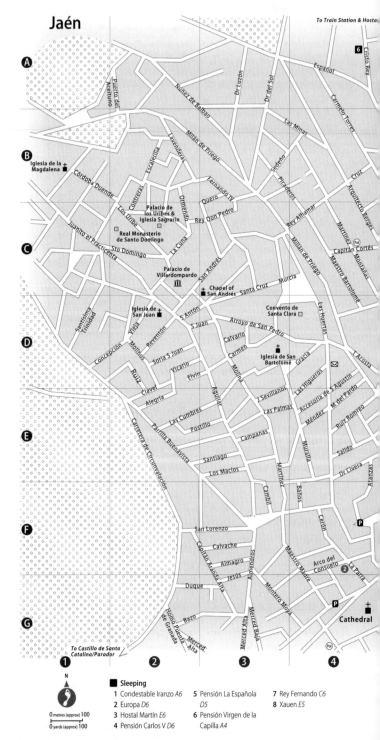

Jaén Province

A

To Train Station & Hosta

6 Cristo Rey

Puerto del Aceituno

Núñez de Balboa

Dr Luzón

Dr del Sol

Español

Carmelo Torres

B

Iglesia de la Magdalena

Córdoba Duende

Escalerilla

Contreras

Los Uribe

Lavanderas

Fernando IV

Millán de Priego

Picaderos

Sedeño

Las Minas

Cruz

Arquitecto Berges

C

Juanito el Practicanta

Sto Domingo

La Cuna

Palacio de los Uribes & Iglesia Sagrario

Real Monasterio de Santo Domingo

Ollmendo

Quero

Rey Don Pedro

San Andrés

Rey Alhamar

Millán de Priego

Martínez Montañés

Capitán Cortés

Maestro Bartolomé

D

Santísima Trinidad

Concepción

Molinos

Vieja

Reventón

Soria S Juan

Vicario

Iglesia de San Juan

S Antón

S Juan

Santa Cruz

Murcia

Convento de Santa Clara

Palacio de Villardompardo

Chapel of San Andrés

Arroyo de San Pedro

Calvario

Carmen

Iglesia de San Bartolomé

Gracia

Las Huertas

T Acosta

Ruiz

Clavel

Alegría

Elvín

Aguila

Molina

J Sevillanos

Las Palmas

Accesoria de S Agustín

Méndez

Mt del Pardo

Ruiz Romreo

Salido

E

Carretera de Circunvalación

Parrilla Buenavista

Las Cumbres

Postillo

Campanas

Santiago

Los Macios

Martínez

Cambil

Baños

Muralla

Dr Civera

Araña

F

San Lorenzo

Calvache

Capitán Maeda Alta

Almagro

Jesús

Almendros

Maestro Madre

Arco del Consuelo

La Parra

P

2

G

To Castillo de Santa Catalina/Parador

Duque

Honda Puente de Granada

Bazo

Merced Alta

Merced Alta

Merced Baja

Montera Moya

Cerón

P

Cathedral

Pol

1   **2**   **3**   **4**

N

0 metres (approx) 100
0 yards (approx) 100

■ **Sleeping**

1 Condestable Iranzo *A6*

2 Europa *D6*

3 Hostal Martín *E6*

4 Pensión Carlos V *D6*

5 Pensión La Española *D5*

6 Pensión Virgen de la Capilla *A4*

7 Rey Fernando *C6*

8 Xauen *E5*

understand. The collection is based on the legacy of Manuel Mozas, who donated his own collection, which included his works and those of other artists. Paintings of numerous Spanish and foreign artists have since been added.

The **Baños Arabes**, or Moorish baths, were built in the 11th century and the Almohad decoration suggests that they were restored a century later. After the Reconquest in 1246, they fell into disuse and later the buildings became a tannery. In the late 16th century, the palace of Don Fernando de Torres y Portugal was built on the site, filling the basement of the ruined baths with soil. A local archaeologist rediscovered the baths in 1913 and until their reopening to the public in 1984 they were diligently restored. The site consists of an entrance hall and rooms for cold, tepid and hot baths. The floors are largely of marble, with brick walls and stone pillars supporting brick horseshoe arches. The ceilings are either cupolas with star-shaped windows or half-barrel vaults. Their lack of decoration suggests that they were for public rather than private use.

■ *The Palacio de Villadompardo is open from Tue-Fri 0900-2000, Sat and Sun 0930-1430. Closed fiestas. Free with EU passport, otherwise €0.60. Visits to the Baños Arabes are by guided tour only, every 30 mins.*

Other sights around the Palace

On the other side of Calle San Andrés is the 16th-century **Chapel of San Andrés**. Its star attraction is the magnificent altar screen by Maestro Bartolomé, the notable local craftsman. On the far side of the small square in front of the Palace is the **Iglesia of San Juan**, notable for its gracious Romanesque tower. Its interior is also worth a glance, with sculpture by Martínez Montañes and Sebastián de Solís. Just north of the palace is the **Monasterio de Santo Domingo**, in Calle Santo Domingo. It was built in the 14th

● **Eating**
1 Batavia *C4*
2 Casa Vicente *E3*
3 La Gamba de Oro *C4*
4 Méson de Río Chico *C5*

Bathing the Moorish way

Andalucía is particularly rich in examples of medicinal baths and spas, which was always a strong Mediterranean tradition, particularly with the Romans. It was the coming of the Moors to Spain, however, which made this a fine art, because in the Islamic world bathing was not just for hygiene or pleasure, but part of the religious practice. Known to the Moors as hamman, *each town would have several public baths, with the main baths close to the central mosque. Wealthy and powerful individuals would have their own private and often luxurious baths. Today, many of these baths have survived, like those at Alhama de Granada, where the spring water used has medicinal qualities. Others, such as those in Jaén, were excavated in the 20th century after being built over. There are further baths at Ronda, Alhama de Almería and Córdoba, with some of the best preserved in Gibraltar.*

The organization of the baths followed a fairly standard pattern. Entry was through an open-air courtyard and then into an entrance hall, where the visitor was welcomed and moved into the separate areas for men and women. There were then three rooms – the cold, warm and hot. The cold room (or al-maslaj) was for undressing. Clothes were taken off and replaced by towels, slippers and bath robes. The warm room (or bait al-wastani) would have had pools, as would the hot room (or bait al-sajuni), where the humidity caused perspiration in order to clean out the pores. At the side of the pools were areas to rest and have a massage or haircut. The water and air were heated by a wood furnace from which a hypocaust system distributed the warmth under the floor.

The architecture of the baths was also standard. The roofs of the baths were simply vaulted, with star-shaped apertures. Other parts of the building would have had traditional tiled roofs. Inside, the floors were of absorbent flagstones, while the walls had decorative glazed tiles. Pillars and rounded arches held up the roof. The pillars were often taken from Roman remains, where these were available.

The baths were usually well staffed with attendants supplying all the bathers' requirements. Others would stoke the furnace or have cleaning duties. Barbers and masseurs would ply their trade. For the bathers, however, the baths were a place for lounging, relaxation, gossip and doing business.

MOORISH BATHS, JAEN

century and was later the city's university. It then carried out the dealings of the Inquisition, before becoming a school. It has an imposing 16th-century façade by Vandevira, but gaining entrance may be frustrating – if you manage to get in you will be impressed by the elegant patio. ■ *Mon-Fri 0900-1530. Free.* Also close to the Baños Arabes is the **Palacio de los Uribes**, a 16th-century mansion. Further north is the **Iglesia de la Magdalena**, the city's oldest church. Full of history and atmosphere, the church was built over a mosque and retains the minaret as its bell tower. Also preserved in the patio at the rear is the pool that was used for ritual ablutions. There are the remains of some cloisters. The church was built in the centre of the old Roman town, and it is claimed that parts of the cloisters are constructed of old Roman tombstones. Also worth a look is the ornate altar screen inside.

This castle stands on the hill overlooking the town. It was once an Arab palace built by Ibn Nasr, but, after its capture from the Moorish King Al-Hammar during the Reconquest, it has been much altered and restored. Some secret passages have been discovered leading down to the *barrio* of La Magdalena in the town below, which still has its winding Moorish street plan. The castle is now a parador and a path from its car park leads along to a mirador, giving magnificent views of the city below. ■ *Jun 15-Sep 15 Mon-Sun 1030-1330, rest of the year 1000-1400 and 1430-1800. Closed Wed.*

Castillo de Santa Catalina

This museum at Paseo de la Estación 27 contains a fine collection of archaeological exhibits, the most important of which are the Iberian fifth-century stone-sculptures which were found in the west of the province. The Moorish room has a good collection of coins and ceramics, the latter in the green style that is still prevalent in the pottery of today. The Fine Arts section of the museum is upstairs, but is hardly worth the walk. ■ *Tue 1500-2000, Wed-Sat 0900-2000, Sun 0900-1500. Free.*

Museo Provincial

To the east of the cathedral is the late 14th-century **Church of San Ildefonso**, within which is the image of the Virgen de la Capilla, Jaén's patron saint. A little to the east of the route from the cathedral to the Baños Arabes is the **Iglesia de San Bartolomé**, which boasts a fine Mudéjar coffered ceiling. Finally, there is the 13th-century **Convento de Santa Clara**, in Calle Las Huertas. Founded by Ferdinand III, it has a figure of Christ with Bamboo, which may be of 16th-century Ecuadorean origin.

Other churches & monasteries

Essentials

Considering Jaén's importance as a regional centre, the amount and variety of accommodation is surprisingly small, with only 7 hotels and 5 *pensiones*, all near the centre and on bus routes. **AL** *Parador Nacional*, Castillo de Santa Catalina, T953230000, F953230930. 45 a/c rooms, restaurant, pool, in heavily restored section of the castillo, quiet with stunning views. **B** *Condestable Iranzo*, Paseo de la Estación 32, T953222800, F953263807. 159 rooms, garage, a/c, disco. **B-C** *Rey Fernando*, Plaza de Coca de la Piñera 7, T953251840, F953265122. Central position near the bus station. Garage, a/c, restaurant. **C** *Europa*, Plaza de Belén 1, T953222700, F953222692. 36 a/c rooms with bath, newly-decorated, garage, restaurant, centrally located off Av de Granada. **C-D** *Xauen*, Plaza de Deán Mazas 3, T953240789, F953190312. 35 rooms, central location, also a university residence, restaurant (closed during holidays). **D** *La Española*, C Bernardo López 9, T953230524. Interesting old house, cheaper without bath, located very near cathedral in quiet pedestrianized area. **D** *Hostal Renfe*, Paseo de la Estación, T953274704, F953274604. Handy for the train station but quite a way from the centre. The most expensive *hostal* in this category. **E** *Carlos V*, Av de Madrid 4, T953222091. No rooms with bath, noisy main road. **E** *Hostal Martín*, C Cuatro Torres 5, T953191431, F953243678. 12 rooms, rough and ready. **E** *Virgen de la Capilla*, C Cristo Rey 2, T953220024. 29 rooms, a/c, cheapest rooms with bath in town, restaurant, near the Museo Provincial.

Sleeping
■ *on map, page 361*
See inside front cover for hotel price codes

Jaén Province

Eating

● on map, page 361
See inside front cover
for restaurant price
classifications

Local dishes include *gazpacho* with, unusually, grapes and apples, and *ensslada de pimientos asados* – roasted pepper salad. **Expensive** *Restaurant Castillo de Santa Catalina*, T953264411. At the summit for altitude, price and ambience with local specialities. *Casa Vicente*, C Arco del Consuelo 1, T953262816. Priciest restaurant in town, in old mansion specializing in game and other local dishes. **Mid-range** *Batavia*, Paseo de la Estación 31, T953266032. Traditional cuisine. For reasonable *platos combinados* and *raciones* there are plenty of places in C Nueva like *La Gamba del Oro*, No 5, T953261613, for seafood and *Mesón del Chico*, No 12, T953228502. Another couple of economical places are *Bar Mesones* and *Taberna La Posada* on pedestrianized C Federico de Mendizabal, 13-14, where you can sit outside. **Tapas bars** The best place in town is the *Peña Flamenca de Jaén*, C Maestra 11, T953231710. Located in the pedestrianized old part of town, this bar has a good atmosphere and serves great tapas; it has occasional lovely flamenco music. Also try *Grana y Oro* and *El Pósito* in Plaza del Pósito, off Joaquin Carniceros.

Entertainment

Nightclubs There is nothing in the way of wild nightlife in Jaén. There are a few lacklustre discos, mainly along the Av de la Estación. **Bullfights** The most important bullfights take place during the festivals of *San Lucas* and *Nuestra Señora de la Capilla*. **Cinemas** There are 3 multi-screen cinemas, the best of which is *Avenida Multicines*, Av Muñoz Grandes 4, T953264706.

Festivals

Night of 16 Jan *Fiesta de las Lumbres (fires) de San Antón*; 1st week in May *International Piano Competition*; 2nd Sun in May *Romería del Cristo del Arroz* is a pilgrimage to the Fuente de la Peña; 11 Jun *Fiesta de Nuestra Señora de la Capilla* is a celebration for Jaén's patron saint, with flowers, processions and dances; 12-20 Oct *Feria de San Lucas* is Jaén's most important fair, with bullfights and sports events. It dates back to the 15th century, having been established by the Constable of Castille, Miguel Lucas de Iranzo; 25 Nov *Pilgrimage to the Castillo de Santa Catalina*.

Shopping

Cottage industries thrive throughout the province, producing ceramics, rugs, wickerwork, ironwork and guitars. There is a flea market on Thu next to the train station. The main shopping streets of the city are those branching off the Plaza de la Constitución, such as the Paseo de la Estación, Vía de la Capilla and C San Clemente.

Tour operators

Ecomar, C Navas de Tolosa 14, T953256650. *Halcon*, Plaza Coca de la Piñera s/n, T953259600. *Sacromonte*, Pasaje Mazas s/n, T953222212. For the hire of tourist guides ring *María de la Cruz Lomez Guidsa*, T953257987, or *Fernando Gallardo Carpio*, T953261468.

Transport

Bus There are at least 12 buses daily to **Baeza/Úbeda** (1 hr), 2 going onto Cazorla (2½ hrs), 4 to **Córdoba** (2 hrs), 14 to **Granada** (1 hr), 4 to **Málaga** (4 hrs) and 3 to **Sevilla** (5 hrs). There are restricted services at weekends. There are also buses to **Madrid**, 2 of which don't stop at every village on the way. **Train** Jaén has rail links with other Andalucían cities. There are trains to **Madrid** (0610, 0920 and 1540; 4 hrs; €19), **Cádiz** (0755, 4 hrs 40 mins, €21), **Córdoba** (0755, 1 hr 35 mins, €7.50) and **Sevilla** (0755, 3 hrs, €14).

Directory

Banks Banks are concentrated around the Plaza de la Constitución. **Communications** Post office: Correos, Plaza de Jardinillos, T953191112. Open Mon-Sat 0900-1400. **Telephones**: no *locutorios*, but cabins in most of the squares, including Plaza de la Constitución and Plaza de San Francisco. **Medical services** Hospitals: *Centro Hospitalario Princesa de España*, Ctra de Madrid, T953280650; *Hospital del SAS Ciudad de Jaén*, Av del Ejército Español, T953222408. **Red Cross**: *Cruz Roja*, C Carmelo

Torres 1, T953251540. **Useful addresses** Garages/car repair workshops: many of the main garages/showrooms are located on the Los Olivares industrial estate. *Citroën*, C Ortega Nieto 9, T953251576. *Ford*, Pol Los Olivares, C Mancha Real 2, T953280554. *Peugeot*, C Ortega Nieto 3, T953280405. *Renault*, Ctra de Granada, Km 336, T953243649. *Seat*, C Ortega Nieto 3, T953281722. *Volvo*, Pol Los Olivares, C Beas de Segura 18, T953281521.

South of Jaén

The main road from Jaén south to Granada, the N323, initially follows the valley of the Río Guadalbullón through the Sierra Mágina. This mountain region rises to 2,167 m at Pico Mágina and forms the Parque Natural Sierra Mágina covering nearly 20,000 ha. There are three distinct vegetation zones in this limestone area. At lower levels is evergreen forest with holm oaks, juniper and holly. The middle zone comprises Mediterranean forest with largely deciduous trees, while above the tree-line is open grassland with brooms. The lower levels support a variety of mammals including wild boars, beech martens, polecats and genets, and the recently introduced red deer. Mammals will be elusive, but the birdlife is abundant, including raptors such as golden eagles, Bonelli's eagles, griffon vultures and eagle owls. Golden orioles are found along the wooded river valleys and there are blue-rock thrushes and ring ouzels in the higher spots.

Parque Natural Sierra Mágina

There are a couple of villages in the area worth a diversion. Some 10 km from Jaén, just off the N323 to the west, is the hilltop village of **La Guardia**, dominated by its eighth-century Moorish castle, which, unusually, is in the shape of an equilateral triangle. Its ruins have much older elements in its walls, possibly going back to Visigoth times. You can get the key from the Ayuntmiento. The other building of note in La Guardia is the ruined church of Santo Domingo, designed by Vandelvira and once part of a Dominican monastery. Further to the southeast is the village of **Huelma**. Located on the south side of the Sierra Mágina in wild scenery, the village has a Moorish castle with several round towers. Below it are narrow whitewashed alleyways with the original Moorish street pattern, leading to the sandstone Renaissance Iglesia de la Immaculada.

Villages between Jaén & Granada

A more leisurely route south from Jaén to Granada goes via Martos, Alcaudate and Alcalá la Real. South of the rolling landscape of olive groves is the village of **Martos**, dominated by its ruined Moorish castle of La Virgen de la Villa, on the crag which overlooks the town. This particular fortress fell to the Christians in 1225 on St Marta's Day – hence the present place name. The keep and Tower of Almedina are still in good condition. While in the village, take a look at the Ayuntamiento which was built in 1577 and the 13th-century Church of Santa María de la Villa (although later additions in Baroque style dominate).

Twenty-five kilometres further south is the small town of **Alcaudate**. Known to the Moors as Al-Qabdaq, it changed hands several times during the Reconquest, before finally falling to Alfonso XI in 1340. The ruined fortress of Albendín, which towers over the town, was built in the 10th century with the stones from a former Roman settlement, but only the massive keep remains in good condition. There are various other defensive walls and towers scattered around Alcaudate, particularly along the road to Granada. Nestling beneath the castle is the Church of Santa María, with a mixture of architectural styles, a staggered tiled roof and strongly built tower.

A further 26 km south is the town of **Alcalá la Real**, which was first set-tled by Yemanis in 713. It was later a Moorish stronghold (known as Al-Kalaat Be Zayde) with its peak of influence coming in the 12th and 13th centuries when it was an independent *taifa*. It changed hands several times during the Reconquest, finally falling to Alfonso X, who added the suffix *Real* to the place name.

The views from the castle over the town and the surrounding olive groves and mountains are stupendous

The hilltop castle, the *Castillo de la Mota* and the adjacent church of Santa María la Mayor, covers some 3 ha, with rocky cliffs forming part of the exter-nal walls. There were seven gates to the fortress, one of which, the Puerta de la Imagen, is now the main entrance. The walls were supported by a series of watchtowers, of which 15 still exist – six Christian and the remainder Arab. The keep now houses a small archaeological museum, with Roman, Moorish and Christian remains. Coins, skeletons, pottery and weapons, mostly obtained on the site, are all carefully displayed. A few metres away is the Church of Santa María de Mayor, which was built during the time of Alfonso XI on the site of a mosque. It has been gutted and is in process of being restored by an enthusiastic group of architectural students. There are guided tours of the whole site (a tip is deserved and appreciated). Access is easy – follow the signs from the town cen-tre to the top of the hill. Overnight accommodation, however, is restricted to the *Pensión Zacatín*, Calle Pradillo 1, T953580568.

North of Jaén

*The area north of Jaén is largely agricultural, with a rolling landscape covered with olive groves. On the north side of the Guadalquivir valley are the three, largely nondescript, industrial towns of Linares, Bailén and Andújar. **Andújar**, the most attractive of the three, has some parts of its walls and towers still stand-ing, plus a few examples of Baroque and Renaissance architecture. Today, Andujar is well-known for its ceramics and sunflower oil bottling industries.*

Parque Natural de Andújar

Immediately north of Andújar is the Parque Natural de Andújar, covering some 60,000 ha. This is one of the most heavily-wooded parts of the Sierra Morena, with cork oaks, encinas and stone pines along with large areas of scrub. Woodland birds include golden orioles, azure-winged magpies, crested tits and woodpeckers. There is a good range of raptors including all three vultures, golden eagles and buzzards, while there is a good chance of see-ing the rare Spanish imperial eagle. This park also includes the location of Andalucía's second most important *romería* (after El Rocío), to the 13th-cen-tury shrine of **Nuestra Virgen de la Cabeza**. The original shrine was destroyed during the Civil War by a combination of Guardia Civil occupation and Republican bombardment. The hermitage which replaced the shrine has little to commend it, but this does not deter the thousands of pilgrims who converge on the spot at the end of April from all over southern Spain to see *La Morenita* (the little dark one).

Baños de la Encina

The small hill village of Baños de la Encina has a wonderfully preserved Moorish castle. Archaeological remains show that Baños was a Prehistoric settlement. Bronze Age paintings and remains have been found in the nearby caves of la Moneda and Peñalosa. It was occupied by the Arabs in the eighth century and in 967 Al-Hakim II had the fortress built, naming it Burch al Hamma, or the tower of the baths. The castle, composed of golden, sandy conglomerate and shaped like a ship, is in an excellent state of

The Battle of Las Navas de Tolosa

It was in the year 711 that the Moors led by Tarik, General of the Caliph's Governor in North Africa, left Tangier with an army of 9,000 men and landed in Gibraltar. Within five years they had occupied almost the whole of the Iberian peninsula. By the year 1065, the taifa kingdoms still occupied two thirds of Iberia. The Almohad empire at the start of the 13th century covered most of the southern half of Spain and Portugal, with what is now Andalucía firmly in Moorish hands. Whenever the Christians in the north threatened, the Moors were always able to call on reinforcements from North Africa to fight for their cause. But by now the Christian armies were beginning to unite and the allied forces of Castille, Aragon and Navarra faced up to the Almohads in 1212.

The battle was fought some 9 km northeast of the village of Las Navas de Tolosa, which guarded the Despeñaperros Pass to the north. The Christians had amongst their forces a contingent of mostly French crusaders, along with the men of Pedro II of Aragon, Alfonso VIII of Castille and the army of Sancho 'the Strong' of Navarre. The Moorish army of Granada was led by the fourth Almohad caliph, Mohammed al-Nasir. The Moors were soundly defeated and now the fragile balance between the Moors and the Christians was broken, with the Christians having the upper hand. In addition, the people of the Maghreb, seeing the first signs of weakness in the Almohads, decided that they were no longer prepared to come on further military journeys into Al-Andalus.

Although the Moors held on in Granada for a further 250 years, largely through the payment of taxes and tributes, the Battle of Las Navas de Tolosa was the beginning of the end – but a battle which continues to be re-enacted today throughout Andalucía in the fiestas of the Moors versus the Christians.

preservation, despite the fact that it was won and lost six times by the Christians. Entry is through a double horseshoe arch. The walls, with their crenellated tops, have restored battlements and no fewer than 14 towers. There is a huge courtyard which was used as a parade ground in more military times and now used for village dancing at fiestas. The impressive keep gives spectacular views over the village and the nearby reservoir, the Embalse del Rumblar. Viewing hours are informal and depend entirely on the ancient guardian and his equally antique key. His surprising agility around the rickety steps usually earns him a tip. If he is not around, enquire at the Ayuntamiento in the main square. The village itself is worth a stroll around. Take a look at the pretty Plaza de la Constitución and the imposing Iglesia Parroquial de San Mateo, with its Gothic 15th-century nave and octagonal Renaissance tower, dated 1596. There are also one or two mansions with coats of arms over their doors.

Parque Natural de Despeñaperros East of the Despeñaperros Pass is this small reserve covering 8,000 ha. The natural vegetation and the animal and birdlife are similar to the nearby Parque Natural de Andújar (see above) and because access is difficult from the *autovía*, if you're pushed for time, you may wish to give this one a miss.

East of Jaén

*About 50 km east of Jaén are the hilltop towns of **Baeza** and **Úbeda**, justifiably described as architectural gems. It has often been claimed that little of architectural significance in Andalucía came after the Moors, but these remarkable*

Jaén Province

towns are surely the exception, and anyone seeking the Renaissance style should head in this direction. Aided by wealth created by the 16th-century wool trade, Úbeda and Baeza were developed by two men – the architect Andrés de Vandelvira and the nobleman Francisco de los Cobos, secretary to Carlos V. Together they provided a number of civic and public buildings, ranging from churches and universities to granaries and abattoirs, which form classic Andalucían Renaissance masterpieces.

Baeza

Colour map 3, grid B2
Population: 15,635
Altitude: 790 m

Baeza was known as Viata to the Romans and was later an important Moorish settlement. Called Bayyasa in Arabic, it was the civilian and religious capital of the upper Guadalquivir region, but, in 1227, it was one of the first Andalucían towns to be captured during the Reconquest. For the next two centuries it became a warring centre between rival Christian families, earning it the title of the 'Royal Nest of Sparrow Hawks', until Isabel became so exasperated that she tore down much of the Alcázar and the defensive walls. Baeza's main development came in the 16th and 17th centuries, with the wealth produced from textiles and agriculture. Today, it gives an overwhelming impression of sleepy Renaissance charm, set off by the honey-coloured sandstone of its buildings.

Sights

Fortunately, most of the worthwhile buildings in Baeza are concentrated within a small area, so that it is possible to see the best features within half a day if necessary, although a longer stay would certainly be more rewarding. The first stop should be at the charmingly old-fashioned **tourist office** located in the 16th-century former law courts, an attractive Plateresque building called the *Casa del Pópulo*, T953740444. It is open Monday to Friday 0900-1430, Saturday 1000-1300. It has maps and brochures, including a detailed description of the many monuments in the town.

The centre of the town is the Plaza de España and this merges southeastwards into the long, tree-lined Plaza de la Constitución. At its southeast corner is the delightful little **Plaza del Pópulo** (also known as the Plaza de los Leones), surrounded by a clutch of interesting buildings. The **Casa del Pópulo** (House of the People) now houses the tourist office (see above). On

the west side of the square is the double-arched **Jaén Gate**, part of the original walls, and built in honour of Carlos V, who passed this way en route to his marriage with Isabel of Portugal. Opposite the arch is the old **Abattoir**, dating back to 1540 and displaying the enormous coat of arms of Carlos. Today the town archives are kept here. In the centre of the square is the **Fuente de los Leones** (fountain of the Lions), which is believed to have been built with stones from the Roman ruins of

BAEZA - Plaza de los Leones.

Castulo. Now badly eroded (the lions look more like coypus). The female statue in the centre of the fountain is thought to be that of Hannibal's Iberian wife, Imilce.

From Plaza del Pópulo take Calle San Gil and then Calle Obispo Mengibar to **Plaza de Santa María**. In the centre of the square is another imposing stone fountain, dated 1569, with a small triumphal arch and the coat of arms of Felipe II. Designed by Ginéz Martínez, who was also responsible for the town's water supply, it is now Baeza's symbol. Dominating the square is the 13th-century **Cathedral**, which was built on the site of a mosque, but comprehensively updated by Andrés de Vandelvira 300 years later. The nave has three

Walking tour

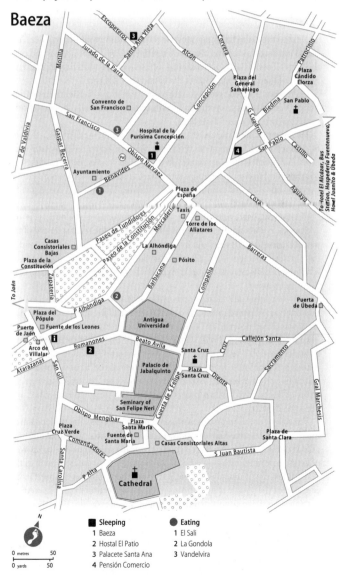

Baeza

Jaén Province

Sleeping	Eating
1 Baeza	1 El Sali
2 Hostal El Patio	2 La Gondola
3 Palacete Santa Ana	3 Vandelvira
4 Pensión Comercio	

0 metres 50
0 yards 50

aisles, the sturdy columns supporting low semicircular vaulting. The oldest part of the cathedral is the *Puerta de la Luna* (Door of the Moon) in 13th-century Gothic-Mudéjar, while the other door, in the south wall, is the 15th century *Puerta del Perdón*, from which an alleyway leads to a mirador giving fine views over the rolling landscape of olive groves to the southeast. The cathedral is lighter and airier than most and shows to good advantage the 14th-century Gothic rose window above the Puerta de la Luna. Don't miss the painted wrought iron grill by Maestro Bartolomé, which encloses the choir. There are also four fine Mudéjar side chapels leading to a small cloister, where part of the old mosque can be seen. If you have €0.60 to spare, you can persuade a picture to move aside to reveal a silver monstrance which then revolves to the accompainment of choral music. ■ *1000-1300 and 1600-1800 in winter and 1600-1900 in summer*.

Next to the cathedral is perhaps the most beautiful building in Baeza, the **Casa Consistoriales Altas**, also known as the *Palacio de los Cabreras* and once the upper Town Hall. Now a national monument, the walls display the coats of arms of Juana the Mad and her husband Felipe the Fair.

On the opposite side of the square to the cathedral is the **Seminary of San Felipe Neri**. Dating from the 16th century, the stone walls show the traditional graffiti of successful students.

Heading northeast the Cuesta de San Felipe leads on the right to the **Iglesia de Santa Cruz**. This small church is the oldest in Baeza, being constructed immediately after the Reconquest in 1227 in Romanesque style, although with later additions. The simple white-walled interior has some 16th-century frescoes, but is free of monuments and ornamentation – and consequently tourists. ■ *1100-1300*.

On the opposite side of the road and joined to the Seminary is the 15th-century **Palacio de Jabalquinto**, undoubtedly the most splendid of the palaces in the town. It was built by Juan Benavides, a relative of Ferdinand; it has a richly ornamental Isabelline Gothic façade topped with an arched gallery, while inside there is an impressive Renaissance courtyard and a majestic Baroque staircase.

Turn left into Calle Beato Avila by the **Antigua Universidad**. This old university was opened in 1542 and classes were held for over three centuries, but it was closed down in 1824. Since then it has been a high school and during July and August it holds classes as part of the Granada International Summer School. The famous Spanish poet Antonio Machado gave French grammar lessons here from 1912 to 1919 and many of his best works come from this period of his life. 'I dream of you when I can no longer see you', he wrote of Baeza. Also worth a look is the Mudéjar ceiling in the main hall and the superb patio.

Turn right at the end of the Antigua Universidad, passing under an arch into Calle Barbacana. Shortly on the right is the **Pósito**, the old communal granary. At the end of the street is the **Torre de los Aliatares**, or clock tower, once incorporated into the old walls of the town. You are now back in the Plaza de la Constitución, where there are two other buildings of note. On the east side of the square is **La Alhóndiga**, the 16th-century Corn Exchange, with an impressive façade including a double arcade. A third flat gallery was added later and all three were glassed in. On the opposite side of the plaza is the **Casas Consistoriales Bajas**, or the Lower Town Hall, built in the 17th century with impressive arched windows fronted by iron work. The tour ends, where it began, in the Plaza del Pópulo.

Just to the southwest of the Plaza España is the **Convento de San Francisco**. Designed by Vandelvira, it is still impressive, despite the ravages of an earthquake and French troops in the 19th century. Along with part of the **Hospital de la Purísima Concepción** next door, it has been converted into the *Hotel Baeza* (see Sleeping below). Also worth looking at is the **Ayuntamiento**, located to the west of the Plaza de la Constitución. Having also acted as the law courts and a prison, it dates from 1559 and has an elaborate Plateresque frontage.

Essentials

A *Confortel Baeza*, C Concepción 3, T953748130, F953742519. Newly-decorated hotel in central location, with wheelchair access, restaurant. Price includes breakfast. **B** *Baeza*, C Concepción 3, T953748130, F953742519. Central position, a/c, restaurant, located in a sympathetically-converted convent. **B** *Hospedería Fuentenueva*, Av Puche Pardo, T953743100, F953743200. Near the bus station is this former prison with 12 rooms (formerly the cells), a good restaurant and pool. Price includes breakfast. **C** *Palacete Santa Ana*, C Santa Ana Vieja 9, T/F953741657. Recently renovated, crammed full of Renaissance-style furniture, a little over the top. There's a huge restaurant with a roof terrace up the road that gives discounts to its guests. **D** *Alcázar*, Av Puche Pardo, T953740028. 34 rooms, located above a restaurant near the *Juanito* and bus station. **D** *Comercio*, C San Pablo 2, T953740100. All rooms with bath, on main pedestrianized street. The only *pensión* in the centre apart from *El Patio*. **D** *Juanito*, Av Puche Pardo s/n, T953740040, F953742324. Modern hotel with 37 a/c rooms, wheelchair access. **D** *La Loma*, Ctra de Úbeda, Km 321, T953743402. 10 rooms, a/c, restaurant; small modern hotel 1 km from centre on the Úbeda road. **E** *Hostal El Patio*, C Conde Romanones 13, T953740200, F953748260. An old Renaissance mansion in the historic quarter of the town. It is built around a covered patio with potted plants and a fountain. Cheapest place in town without bath.

Outside Baeza **B-C** *Rural*, 9 km from Baeza on the Jaén N321 road in the Complejo Hacienda La Laguna, Puente del Obispo, T953127172, F953127174. There is a good, but expensive, restaurant serving international cuisine attached to a catering college; open Mon-Fri term-time only, T953765084. Also here is the Museo del Aceite, T953765100.

Expensive *Juanito*, Av Arca del Agua, T953740040. This hotel restaurant is the most popular place in town and has good local dishes. **Mid-range** *El Arcediano*, C Barbacana, T953748184. Good value *menú del día*. Recommended. *La Gondola*, Portales Carbonería 13 (on main plaza), T953742984. Bargain *menú del día*, which you can have on their pleasant terrace. Recommended. *Sali*, C Cardenal Benavides 9, T953741365. Opposite the Ayuntamiento, this place has a good value *menú del día*. *Vandelvira*, C San Francisco 14, T953748172. The *Hotel Baeza* restaurant in the reconstructed ruins of the Convento San Francisco, serves good food in its terrace and courtyard. **Cheap** *Casa Pedro*, C Cardenal Benavides 3, a former Chinese restaurant, and *La Bodega*, C San Francisco, both have simple but inexpensive menus. Cheaper still are pizza slices at *Pizza Viena*, C San Francisco 49, or a huge *bocadillo* at *El Estudiante*, opposite the Antigua Universidad on C Beato Avila. **Tapas bars** Generally most places serve excellent tapas, like the bars on C San Pablo or on the main plaza. The liveliest *terraza* in Baeza is *Cafetería Mercantil* on Plaza de España. It is somewhat of an institution among the locals; word has it that this is the place for buying or selling a mule or tractor. It serves tasty *raciones* and ice cream.

Sleeping
■ *on map, page 369*
See inside front cover for hotel price codes

Eating
● *on map, page 369*
See inside front cover for restaurant price codes

Jaén Province

Transport **Bus** There are services to **Úbeda** (14 daily, 15 mins), **Jaén** (12 daily, 45 mins), **Córdoba** (1 daily, 2½ hrs), **Sevilla** (1 daily, 4½ hrs) and **Madrid** (2 daily, 4 hrs). The entrance to the bus station is on Av Puche Pardo, also known as Paseo del Arca del Agua (just beyond C Julio Burell), T953740468. There isn't a taxi rank here but you could try T953740006, which puts you in touch with the taxi rank on Plaza de la Constitución. **Train** The nearest railway station, called Linares-Baeza, T953740444, is some 12 km away and bus connections are sparse, particularly at weekends. A taxi to Baeza costs around €15. There are trains to **Córdoba** (1447 and 1708, 1½ hrs, €12), **Granada** (1110, 1145 and 2020; 2½ hrs; €17.50), **Sevilla** (1708, 3 hrs, €17.50) and **Almería** (1137 and 2013, 3 hrs 20 mins, €21).

Úbeda

Colour map 3, grid B2
Population: 32,524
Altitude: 757 m

Despite its large area of modern suburbs, Úbeda's delight is its large and architecturally outstanding old quarter, full of Renaissance richness. It is a mildly prosperous market town, producing agricultural machinery, along with the more traditional olive oil, esparto and ceramics. Cereals, vines and olives are the main crops grown locally, helped by the Jaén Plan, which has developed irrigation schemes in the area. Despite its obvious historical attractions, Úbeda remains something of a tourist backwater, largely due to its geographical remoteness.

Ins & outs
See page 376 for transport details

The **tourist office** can be found in the elegant *Palacio del Marqués del Contadero*, C Baja del Marqués 4, T953750897, F953792670. It is open Mon-Fri 0800-1900, Sat-Sun 1000-1400. For guided tours of the city, contact *Artificis*, T953758150, or the province's

Úbeda

Sleeping
1 Castillo
2 Consuelo
3 La Paz
4 Palacio de la Rambla
5 Parador
6 Sevilla

Jaén Province

tourist guide association, T953792851. Both the Ayuntmiento and the reception of the *Hospital Santiago* can also provide information. The latter can arrange guided tours of the old quarter.

History

It was known to the Romans as Betula because of its location near to the Bethis, the Roman name for the Río Guadalquivir. On its foundations Abd al-Rahman II built the Moorish town of Ub-badat al-Arab. It was walled in 852 and later occupied by both the Almoravids and the Almohads. It was during Moorish times that the craft industries of pottery and esparto work were developed, which still survive today. It was eventually conquered by Ferdinand III in 1234. The situation in Baeza repeated itself in Úbeda – noble families came to the town, built their mansions and then fought each other for power, causing Ferdinand and Isabel in 1503 to demolish the defensive walls and towers of the town. Úbeda's heyday came in the 16th century, during the times of Carlos I and Fellipe II, when the area's textiles were traded throughout Europe, bringing great wealth to the town. The patronage of two noblemen, Francisco de los Cobos (who was Carlos V's secretary) and Juan Vásquez de Molina, plus the genius of the architect Andrés de Vandelvira, led to the construction of the wonderful Renaissance quarter of the town. Decline set in, however, in subsequent centuries.

Sights

Úbeda is neatly divided into old and new quarters, the latter being of little interest. Following the signposts, head straight for the historic section (*Zona Monumental*), but remember that there are 46 classified historical buildings and it's impossible to see them all in a day. If time is limited, concentrate on a few of the suggestions below.

Eating
1 El Gallo Rojo
2 El Olivo

Flanked by a collection of honey-coloured Renaissance buildings, the Plaza Vásquez de Molina must be one of the most attractive squares in Spain. There are two churches. On the southeast side is the **Church of Santa María de los Reales Alcázares**, which was built on the site of a mosque, its cloisters enclosing what was the mosque's patio. The church is, in fact, a hotchpotch of different styles and epochs. The main walls belong to the 17th century, the double belfries to the 19th and the cloisters are Gothic. Inside, there are five naves topped with barrel vaulting, plus a number of interesting chapels. The main chapel stands on the

Plaza Vásquez de Molina

Jaén Province

spot where the first mass following the Reconquest was celebrated. Look also for examples of the wrought-iron grilles of Maestro Bartolomé. At the back of the church is the **Cárcel del Opispo**, the Bishop's Prison, which was founded as a convent and is now the law courts.

The other church is Vandelvira's **Sacra Capilla del Salvador** at the northeast end of the plaza. Ordered by Francisco de la Cobos and originally designed by Diego de Silóe (who was responsible for Granada and Málaga cathedrals), it was built by Vandelvira and the stonemason Alonso Ruíz. The church was originally the chapel of Cobos' mansion, which later burnt down. The main west-facing façade is a mass of ornate Plateresque detail, but it is worth strolling round to the north door to see in the tympanum Vandelvira's trademark, Santiago the Moor slayer. Inside, the single nave has Gothic ribbed vaults and is dominated by the *retablo*, the work of Michelangelo's pupil Alonso de Berruguette. It is capped with a cupola and fronted by yet another grill by Bartolomé. ■ *Entry to the church is via the sacristy on the north side, but you may have to find the caretaker for the key*.

Behind the Capilla is the **Hospital de los Honrados Viejos del Salvador**, designed by Vandelvira and constructed in the 16th century for the honoured elderly of the town. Continue past this building to the end of the street to the **Redonda de Miradores**, where a paseo gives superb views of the rolling olive-treed landscape and the Cazorla mountains beyond. Back in the square on the other side of the Capilla is the **Condestable Dávalos Palace**, a large 16th-century mansion, originally the residence of Fernando de Ortega, Dean of Málaga. It is now a parador and if you cannot afford to stay there, at least look in for a drink and admire the magnificent arcaded patio with a gallery above. At the west end of the Plaza de Vásquez de Molina is the **Palacio de los Cadenas**, named after the chains which were once attached to the columns on the façade. The palace was built for Juan Vásquez de Molina, secretary to Felipe II, and whose family arms are found over the main doorway. Also designed by Vandelvira, the building now houses the Ayuntamiento, entry to which is via the Plaza de Ayuntamiento to the rear, where you will find a **tourist office** (see above). Also here is the **Palacio del Marques de Mancera**, now a convent, and the **Antiguo Pósito** or old granary, which in its time has been a prison and is now the police station.

Plaza del Primero de Mayo & around

The Plaza del Primero de Mayo is easily reached from the Plaza de Vásquez de Molina by heading northwest along either of the streets on each side of the parador. The Plaza del Primero de Mayo (sometimes known as the Plaza del Mercado) has a totally different atmosphere from the previous square. It is tree-lined and has a delightful bandstand in the centre, along with a palm-tree-shaded monument to San Juan de la Cruz. Near the Plaza at the end of Calle San Juan de la Cruz is the **Oratorio de San Juan de la Cruz**. St John of the Cross was a small friar (reputed to be only 1½ m tall) who was a writer, poet and mystic. He came to Úbeda in 1591 from the Convent of La Peñuela for treatment to a cut on his foot, but died a painful death from gangrene. The Oratory has a small museum in which the cell where he died can be visited. Various relics and personal objects are on display. ■ *Tue-Sun 1100-1300 and 1700-1900. €1.20.*

Back in the square, the **Iglesia de San Pablo** comprises a variety of styles. The main façade faces south and on either side of its sturdy portal are balconies dating from the 13th century. The west wall is the oldest part of the church and is in the transitional Romanesque style. The north wall is Gothic and is dated 1485, while the tower is Plateresque and therefore later. The main interest in the interior is in the chapels, one of which, the Chapel of Camarero Vago, was possibly the first work carried out in Úbeda by Vandelvira. The Chapel de las Mercedes is earlier and in Isabelline style. On the southwest side of the square is the 16th-century **Ayuntamiento Viejo**, which dates from the 16th century. Italianate in style, it has a number of arches resting on Corinthian columns and from its balconies the local dignitaries presided over the *autos de fé* on the orders of the Inquisition. Ironically, the site of the fires is now marked by the bandstand.

There are a number of buildings of note in the streets leading off the Plaza del Primero de Mayo. The **Casa de los Salvajes** (House of the Savages) in Calle Horno Contado, was built in the 15th century for the Chamberlain of the Bishop of Jaén, Francisco de Vago. The house has acquired its name from the figures on the coat of arms, which possibly depict natives brought back from the Indies by the successors of Columbus. In the same street is the **Casa de los Manueles**, with an impressive Renaissance façade and Baroque coat of arms. Southwest from the Plaza del Primero de Mayo and close to the Plaza de Ayuntamiento is the **Palacio de Vela de los Cobos**, built in the mid-16th century by Vandelvira for Francisco Vela de los Cobos and with a superb arcaded gallery. North of the Plaza del Primero de Mayo, in Calle Cervantes, is the **Casa Mudéjar**, a 14th-century building with pointed horseshoe arches, which now houses an archaeological museum. ■ *Tue 1500-2000, Wed-Sat 0900-2000, Sun 0900-1500. Free.*

The Hospital de Santiago is located in the west of the town, some 10 minutes' walk from the Plaza de Andalucía along Calles Mesones and Cobos. It is probably Vandelvira's finest work and was commissioned by Diego de los Cobos y Molina, the Bishop of Jaén in the mid-16th century. Described as the 'Andalucían Escorial', it is a disciplined and subdued work for Vandelvira. The entrance steps are flanked by lions and above the arch Santiago again slays some Moors. The interior features a graceful arcaded patio with 20 marble columns brought from Genoa in Italy, a superb vaulted staircase and another Vandelvira chapel. The hospital is now a cultural centre and provides tourist information.

Hospital de Santiago

Other churches and convents in the old quarter include the **Iglesia de San Pedro**, which has a Romanesque apse, the **Convento de Santa Clara**, dating from 1290, and the **Iglesia de la Trinidad**, with an exuberant Baroque frontage. Also of interest are the **Potters' Quarter** in Calle Valencia, and some remnants of the old walls in the south of the town, including the gateway, the **Puerta de Granada**. Finally, on the border of the old and new areas in the Plaza de Andalucía, is a modern statue of a fascist Civil War general, which after the war was riddled with bullet holes that remain today.

Other churches & convents

Jaén Province

Essentials

Old quarter There are now 3 stunning palaces to stay at in this area: **AL** *Álvar Fáñez*, C Juan Pasquau 5, T/F953796043. 12 rooms, restaurant, much cheaper during lower season (**C**). **AL** *María de Molina*, Plaza del Ayuntamiento, T953795356, F953793694. Slightly less tastefully decorated is this hotel overlooking the plaza, very close to the major sights, with 22 rooms and restaurant. **AL** *Palacio de la Rambla*, Plaza del Marqués 1, T953750196, F953750267. The present Marquesa de la Rambla, Elena Meneses de Orozco Gallego de Chave, lets out some of the rooms in her sumptuous mansion in the historic quarter. All 8 rooms have TV, minibar, some with their own

Sleeping
■ *on map, page 372*
See inside front cover for hotel price codes

Most of the pensiones are located on the west side of the town centre

fireplace, family antiques and old-fashioned bath with legs. The most impressive room has its own patio. Situated in an impressive Renaissance square located in the centre of the old quarter is **AL** *Parador Nacional Condestable Dávalos*, Plaza Vásquez de Molina 1, T953750345, F953751259. This luxurious and atmospheric parador is undoubtedly the best place to stay in Úbeda. 31 a/c rooms and restaurant. Also in the old quarter is **A** *Rosaleda de Don Pedro*, C Obispo Toral 2, T953796111. 32 rooms, restaurant, patio and pool.

More modern and cheaper accommodation is in the newer and considerably less picturesque part of the town, mainly on and around Av de Ramón y Cajal

New quarter **AL** *Ciudad de Ubeda*, Ctra de Circunvalación s/n, T953791011. Large, modern hotel, part of the Meliá Confort chain, with all mod cons plus wheelchair access, but located a bit out of the way on the town's bypass. **C** *La Paz*, C Andalucía 1, T953750849, F953750848. Newly decorated but impersonal. **D** *Consuelo*, Av Ramón y Cajal 12, T953750840, F953756834. 39 rooms, a/c, wheelchair access, good restaurant, near bus station. **D** *Dos Hermanas*, C Risquillo Bajo 2, T953752124, F953791315. 30 rooms, garage, a/c, restaurant, upgraded *pensión* on the northern outskirts of the town, a good walk from the centre. **D** *Sevilla*, Av Ramón y Cajal 9, T95750612. 23 rooms, mostly with bath, near the bus station. **D** *Victoría*, C Alaminos 5, T953752952. The best of the *pensiones*, closer to the sights and in a better part of town. Small, a/c, all rooms with bath. **D-E** *Castillo*, Av Ramón y Cajal 20, T953750430. Modern, cheaper rooms without bath, close to the bus station. **E** *Martos*, C Vandelvira 3, T953756178. Close to the bus station. **E** *Miguel*, Av Libertad 69, T953752049. In the north of the town, cheapest rooms in town with bath.

Eating
● on map, page 372
See inside front cover for restaurant codes

Most of the hotels have good restaurants and many serve a *menú del día*. The best value is *Hotel Álvar Fáñez*; *Hotel Consuelo* also has a good *menú*. **Expensive** The best restaurant in Úbeda is undoubtedly at the *Parador*, which serves excellent, but pricey, regional dishes. *El Porche*, C Redonda de Santiago 7, T953757321. Attractive covered patio. **Mid-range** *Gallo Rojo*, C Ramón y Cajal 3, T953752038. Good regional dishes. *El Seco*, C Corazón de Jesús 8, T953791472. Opposite a pleasant plaza. Nearby on the Plaza del Ayuntamiento is the cheaper *Mesón Navarro*, which has a bit of a dingy dining room. **Cheap** There is a distinct lack of good budget options. *El Olivo*, Av Ramón y Cajal 6, T953752092. Reasonably priced *menu del día* and *platos combinados*. *Pizzería Venecia*, C Huelva 2, T953755813. Good value pizzas and *menú del día*, popular with locals. *El Estudiante*, Av Cristo del Rey 8, T953754402. Good value. **Tapas bars** *El Patio*, C San Francisco 9, T953791801. Great views of the valley from the patio. *Puerta Graná*, tucked Hawai next to Puerta de Granada to the south of town. Trendy bar serving good tapas and raciones on a lovely patio. Recommended.

Festivals **1 May** *Romería* A pilgrimage to the Virgen of Guadalupe. On 1 May, the day of the patron saint, San Miguel, is celebrated with a large fair, fireworks and a flamenco festival.

Shopping The main shopping area of the town is in the newer section in the roads leading off the Plaza de Andalucía. There is a street market on Fri. Local craft specialities include ceramics, esparto mats and baskets (established in Moorish times), ironwork, carving and gilding.

Transport **Bus** These run from Jaén via Baeza and from Linares. Also to **Granada**, **Sevilla** (2 daily, 4½ hrs), **Córdoba** (2 daily, 2½ hrs), **Málaga** (1 daily, 2½ hrs) and **Madrid** (2 daily, 4 hrs). The bus station is on C San José, T953752157. **Taxi** There is a taxi rank in the central Plaza de Andalucía. **Train** The nearest station is Linares-Baeza, T953740444, is about 14 km away. There are 7 buses from Úbeda to the station (30 mins) Mon-Fri, 5 on Sat and 2 (0745 and 0830) on Sun. Contact the bus station for more information.

Banks These are located in the newer part of the town, mainly in the roads leading off **Directory**
the Plaza de Andalucía. **Communications** Post office: Correos, C Trinidad 4,
T953750031. **Medical services** Hospitals: *Hospital General*, Ctra de Linares,
T953797100. **Red Cross**: *Cruz Roja*, C Santiago s/n, T953755640. **Useful
addresses** Garages/car repairs: *Citroen*, T953790379, and *Peugeot*, T953751154,
have garages on Ctra de Circunvalación. *Seat*, T953754108, and *Volkswagen-Audi*,
T953751031, are on Ctra Linares.

Parque Natural de Cazorla

The natural park of the Sierras of Cazorla, Segura and Las Villas forms the *Colour map 3, grid A4*
largest of the Spanish natural parks, covering a surface area of 214,336 sq km.
This mountainous area connects the Sierra Morena with the Subbética chain,
closing off the Guadalquivir valley and stretching all the way to the border with
Murcia province. The park consists of a series of parallel limestone ridges run-
ning from northeast to southwest and there are a number of peaks over 2,000 m.
It is one of the wettest areas in Spain with an annual rainfall of over 2,000 mm,
plus regular snowfall which ensures that the headwaters of the Guadalquivir
are well supplied.

Climate For the most abundant flowers and birdlife the best time to visit the park is **Ins & outs**
May and June. Avoid summer weekends and July and August, when the park is satu-
rated with visitors. Autumn can be very pleasant, but lacks flowers and birdsong. Dis-
ruption from snow is not unknown during the winter months. **Park essentials** There
is an Interpretation Centre at Torre del Vinagre, which is in two sections. The first is the
Educational Centre and next door is a hunting museum (including a mounted stags'
heads bagged by General Franco). For details of the tourist office in Cazorla, see page

Parque Natural de Cazorla

Sierra de Cazorla
Sierra de Segura
Sierra del Castril

Tranco Hornos
Villanueva del Arzobispo
Iznatorof
R Guadalimir
Villacarrillo
R Guadalquivir
Park Boundary
Embalse de Tranco de Beas
N 322
1,830m
Torreperogil
Torre del Vinagre
1,577m
Barrossa Valley
To Jaén
Úbeda
Baeza
1,736m
La Iruela
Peal de Becerro
Cazorla
R Guadalquivir
R Quesada
R Guadiana Menor
Quesada
Los Rosales
2,028m
Park Boundary
Collejares
Tiscar
Huesa
Belerda
R Guadalentin
To Baza
To Jaén

N

0 km 5
0 miles 5

■ **Sleeping**
1 Parador El Adelantado

▨ = Land over 1,000m
➤ = Recommended route

383. There is very little public transport in the park, and no petrol stations within the park boundary. Signposting is also poor. Beware of the maps of the park in the official glossy brochures, as they can be inaccurate in places.

Wildlife and vegetation

The park is heavily wooded, with aleppo pines at lower levels and maritime and laricio Pines higher up. Patches of mixed woodland include *encinas* (holm oaks), olives and junipers, with poplars and willows in the wetter valleys. The whole area is a naturalist's delight, with some 1,300 flowering species, including some 30 endemics such as the Cazorla violet and the hoop petticoat daffodil. Wild peonies and gladioli plus a host of orchids are among the outstanding flowers.

There is a lot of game – many were introduced when the park was a shooting reserve. The bellows of the rutting red deer are a typical sound in autumn. Also found are roe and fallow deer, while ibex can be seen, usually above the tree line. Predators include beech martens, polecats and genet and the occasional pardel lynx. Other mammals include foxes, badgers and wild boars, while otters frequent many of the rivers.

Over 100 bird species nest within the park. Raptors are outstanding and include all three vultures, four varieties of eagle, honey buzzards and peregrines. The Cazorla is the only place in Spain outside the Pyrenees where the Lammergeier can still be seen, although there is probably only one breeding pair left. Some attempts at re-introducing immature birds have been made. There is also a wide range of woodland birds, including crossbills and firecrests. Butterflies are outstanding in spring and early summer, including the mother of pearl blue and the Spanish argus. Reptiles and amphibians include three species of snake and several lizards and skinks, of which Valverde's lizard is endemic to the area. The rivers and lakes of the park, on which there are no motorized watersports, are rich in fish such as carp, trout, barbel and black perch. Anglers will need a permit from the tourist office.

Walking

Most people coming to walk in the park base themselves in Cazorla, at the southeastern tip of the park. The area immediately to the east contains some of the park's most dramatic scenery and somewhere in or close to the town would provide the best base for walking here - although you will be a fair drive from the start of the Río Borosa itinerary described below. If you don't have your own transport you'll need to rely on taxis or buses to get you up into the park.

For **maps**, the Pentathlon 1:50000 Plano Topográfico de las Sierras de Cazorla, Segura y Las Villas, based on the IGN series 'L', covers the whole of the area in just one map but it is rather unwieldy. Other good maps easily found in Cazorla are the Alpina 1:40000 series. If planning to do all of the walks detailed here you will need three maps: Sierra de Cazorla, Sierra de Segura I and Sierra de Segura II/Las Villas.

Río Borosa Gorge
Distance: 19 km
Time: 7-7½ hours
Difficulty: medium/difficult

The Sierra's best-known walk takes you along a beautiful section of the impressive gorge of the Río Borosa. You follow a dirt track and then a spectacular wooden walkway eastwards through the gorge which opens out into a huge, natural ampitheatre of soaring limestone crags. From here a steep climb takes you to a high reservoir which you reach by following the course of a mill race, tunnelled out of the mountainside. The walk can be as far up and down

Jaén Province

as you like but remember you'll climb for 600 m should you do the whole lot. It is best done on a weekday out of holiday season. Remember that the upper section of the walk is sometimes impassable in winter; check with the park rangers at Torre de Vinagre centre (see above) or with one of the agencies in Cazorla. Take a torch for negotiating the tunnels and in the warmer months remember your bathing costume – there are lovely river pools for swimming. **Map**: Alpina 1:40000 map: Sierra de Segura I or Penthalon 1:50000 Plano Topográfico de las Sierras de Cazorla, Segura y Las Villas.

The start From Cazorla take the road that leads via La Iruela then Brunchel, up into the park, then turn left for Coto Ríos/Embalse del Tranco on the A319. When you reach the Centro de Interpretación Torre del Vinagre, turn right and follow signs for 'Central Eléctrica', the electricity generating station. Cross the river and leave your car in the park to the left of the road just before the *piscifactoría*, or trout farm.

The walk begins from the car park to the left of the road just before the piscifactoría of the Río Borosa. Walk past the fish farm, cross a bridge, then turn right and follow a track along the left bank of the river. Soon you cross a concrete bridge; swing left along the river's right bank, then cross back again to the left bank via a wooden bridge. Where the track bears left and climbs, you branch right (35 minutes) on a path marked 'Cerrada de Elías'. You twice cross the river via narrow footbridges. The Borosa's gorge narrows and you follow a hanging cake-walk above the river. Eventually the path meets the track again. Continue up the gorge which begins to open out. There are wonderful views of the twisted strata of La Cuerda de Las Banderillas and La Peña Plumera and, when the track bears slightly right, of the towering massif of Castellón del Haza de Arriba (1,504 m). Soon you'll catch sight of the pipeline that funnels the water down the side of the valley to the Central Eléctrica. You cross over a bridge (1¾ hours) then follow a fence that runs just to the right of the station and its outbuildings. You pass a spring, cross a narrow bridge, then pick up a path at a sign for 'Laguna de Valdeazores'. You now climb steeply up the left bank of the river. Steel yourself: you have a climb of about 300 m if you wish to follow the walk all the way. To the left you'll spot the Picón del Haza; for much of the year a waterfall runs off its eastern flank. The path climbs up into the spectacular ampitheatre of the gorge's higher reaches: the mountains rise almost sheer to 1,500 m. Red dots mark your way and soon you'll see a second waterfall to your right: El Salto de los Órganos. The path passes over loose scree, bears right and, where you can see the remains of a dam, swings sharply to the left towards an electricity pylon. Just before the pylon bear right at a sign 'Nacimiento de Aguas Negras' and 'Laguna de Valdeazores'. The path leads through one of the tunnels which were cut to bring water to the mill race: this one is almost 350 m long! After passing through a second, shorter tunnel you come to the reservoir called Embalse del Borosa, La Laguna de Aguas Negras or Embalse de los Órganos – according to which map you are following! (2¾ hours). Where the path divides, bear left and climb away from the water channel and head up the valley of the Arroyo del Infierno to the Nacimiento de Aguas Negras (three hours), where the Rio Borosa rises from beneath the rocks. This is a great spot to picnic. Retrace your footsteps all the way back down the gorge to arrive back at your point of departure (5½ hours).

Vadillo Castril to Cazorla
Distance: 9 km
Time: 4-4½ hours
Difficulty: medium

This walk follows a wonderful mountain trail which cuts up from the Guadalquivir valley through a high pass, before winding its way down and around the Escribano peak, to Cazorla. There are wonderful views up the valley and out across the sea of olive groves which stretches west from Cazorla. Don't give the taxi fare of €18 a second thought: the ride up into the park alone is memorable enough to justify the expense. Be prepared for a long climb of almost 400 m up and past the Fuente del Oso. **Map** Alpina 1:40000 map: Sierra de Segura I or Penthalon 1:50000 Plano Topográfico de las Sierras de Cazorla, Segura y Las Villas.

The start Because this is a linear walk you'll need to take a taxi from Cazorla to El Puente de la Herrerias. The jouney takes about 30 minutes and costs approximately €18 (recommended taxi driver: *Urbano* T608854701). An alternative for early risers would be to catch the bus which takes the Forestry Commission workers from Cazorla to Valdillo Castrillo; from here you could walk along the road to Puente de las Herrerias beside the Guadalquivir river. It takes just 20 minutes. Bus departure times vary according to the season, so check with the tourist office in Cazorla.

The walk begins on the Valdillo Castrillo side of the El Puente de la Herrerias. Cross the Guadalquivir, then turn immediately right down towards a bar. Cross a small bridge and look for a path which heads up the hill from just behind a spring, to the left of the bar. You zigzag up the right side of the stream to a fork where you should bear right. The path widens and soon you reach a marker post where you have three choices. You should take the middle path which swings right and climbs up to the Forestry Comission buildings of La Fuente del Oso. Climb past these buildings to the road (30 minutes) then turn right, cross a bridge and – careful! – swing immediately left across an open space before bearing right on a path which heads up through the pines. At first you follow a line of pylons: to your left is the Cerro de la Torquilla. When you come to the next fork, branch left and climb through the pine forest towards El Collado del Oso. This is a stunning section of path with marvellous views up the Guadalquivir valley over to your right. Eventually you pass through El Puerto de los Arenales at 1,358 m (45 minutes) which would be a great spot to picnic. On the other side of the pass the scenery completely changes: you now look out across the endless olive groves to the east of Cazorla. The path winds steeply down through the pines on the eastern side of the pass. There is waymarking. Soon the forest opens out and the path bears right then passes to the right of a small building. You continue to contour round the Escribano mountain and shortly the Templar's Castle of La Iruela comes into sight. After descending steeply down, the path drops to cross a (dry) streambed and – careful! - on a rock you'll see a red arrow pointing upwards (2¼ hours). Here you should swing right off the main path (a red GR cross suggests that you are going the wrong way but ignore it) and continue your descent. As you approach the castle, keep close to the cliff on your left and follow a narrow path down which meets with the road by a swimming pool. The last 20 yds are steep and loose. Turn left onto the road, pass beneath the castle (it is well worth a visit), then branch left again and then head through the centre of the village. At the far end of the village go straight across the road, which leads from La Iruela to the Ermita de la Virgen de la Cabeza, and drop steeply down to return to the square at the north end of Cazorla (three hours).

This circular walk from Cazorla, mostly along high mountain trails, is one of the Sierra's 'classic' itineraries and is well worth its reputation. A long climb of nearly 900 m up from the village leads you to a high pass from where the peak of El Gilillo (1,848 m) is easily climbed: the views on a clear day of the distant Sierra Nevada alone make this walk worth the effort. From here a beautiful high mountain trail brings you back to Cazorla in a long, lazy loop – a wonderful reward for your efforts earlier in the day. If you find the long climb intimidating, you can avoid the initial 3 km of mountain road above Cazorla by taking a taxi to the barrier by the Hotel Ríogazas. **Map** Alpina 1:40000 map: Sierra de Segura I or Penthalon 1:50000 Plano Topográfico de las Sierras de Cazorla, Segura y Las Villas. You should be prepared for cold conditions on the higher, often windy section of this walk. If climbing Gilillo add an hour to the timings below.

Cazorla circuit

Distance: 16 km
Time: 7-7½ hrs
Difficulty:
medium/difficult

The start The walk begins in the main square of Cazorla, the Plaza de la Corredera. From the square, head up Calle del Carmen, and opposite a church, turn right into Calle Mercedes Gómez. At the end of the street bear left, climb, then bear left again and climb up Calle del Herrón, which narrows to become a path as you pass the last of the village houses. At a water tank go left and follow white and red waymarking up through the pines. You meet with a track by a viewing platform (25 minutes). Turn right here and continue round the bowl of the valley on the track. Eventually you cross the Ríogazas river, then pass a spring to your left before reaching a Stop sign/barrier (one hour 5 minutes). Continue past the barrier for 60 m to a sign on the left of the track. Here turn left off the track and climb. At first the path is indistinct but it soon improves. After winding through the pines you meet the track again which you cross and continue climbing. You meet the track a second time. Cross it once more and zigzag upwards to more open terrain where the path divides by a cairn. Turn left and climb up through the pines. Shortly you reach a cliff face where you cross a rockfall, descend slightly then bear right and again climb upwards. Cairns mark the path. On a clear day you can see the distant Sierra Nevada and– much closer – the plateau of El Chorro. The vegetation becomes sparser and the path looser underfoot. You eventually reach the top of the Gilillo pass, at 1,740 m (2½ hours). From here you could climb Gilillo (1,848 m). The trig point at the top is clearly visible: allow a minimum of 45 minutes. Otherwise, go over the pass, descend for 20 yards, then turn left towards a mountain refuge. Just above it you pick up a narrow footpath which runs to the left, of the Loma de Castellones. Cairns help you to negotiate this rather indistinct path which climbs then crosses the ridge at its far end (three hours). Stick to the most obvious path and soon you'll pass through a stand of pine and juniper. After passing two large cairns to its left, the path descends for a short distance, then once again runs uphill. At the next large cairn it swings right and descends. You reach another stand of pines and, following cairns, come to a more open area of jagged and strangely beautiful outcrops of limestone: a great spot for a picnic. Just beyond this flat area, the path descends, bears left (you should spot the red roof of the *Parador* hotel to your right), then comes to the El Puerto del Tejo pass where it divides. Turn left following the green arrow. The path contours round the mountain, descends, passes beneath some power lines, then reaches the ruined farm of Prado Redondo (four hours 20 minutes). Just before the farm swing left, descend, bear left again along the bottom of a threshing circle, then follow an indistinct path up into the pines. It soon improves; there are cairns and waymarking reappears. The landscape opens out and the path passes a pylon and the castle of La Iruela comes into view. A final steep, stony section brings you to the Ermita de La Virgen de la Cabeza. Head for the metal cross to the left of the chapel and just beyond it pick up a steep path which drops down to the track which you followed at the start of the walk. Cross this track to the mirador, bear sharp right and follow a path back down into the village, then retrace your footsteps back to the main square (5½ hours).

Other walks Don't waste time contacting the park office in Cazorla who have absolutely no written or even verbal advice to offer! The 'tourist offices' in Cazorla are really just private travel agencies which try to sell you one of their own guided walks. The Penthalon guide *Andar por El Parque Natural de las Sierra de Cazorla, Segura y Las Villas* by Gonzalo Crespo lists (in Spanish) routes in the park (nearly all up and down walks) but most require a lengthy drive to get to the start of the walk. At the northern end of the park a number of routes have been waymarked out from the village of Siles. It is an attractive area although rather less dramatic than that around Cazorla. The Alpina 1:40000 series of maps (see above) includes a booklet describing (in Spanish) a number of walking routes. These are highlighted on the individual maps. *Walking in Andalucía* by Guy Hunter-Watts lists other walks in the park two circular walks out from Hornos and Segura, two of the most attractive villages at the northern end of the park.

Circular route by car

If you only have one day in the park and have your own transport, the route below is recommended and is shown on the map, page 377

Leave Úbeda eastwards on the N322, bypassing **Villacarillo** after 32 km. After another 6 km, a side road leads north to the hill village of **Iznatoraf**, which is well worth a diversion. There is a pleasant square, an imposing Renaissance church, a ruined Moorish castle above some narrow alleyways and some spectacular views from a mirador on the north side of the village. Back on the main road turn right just before Villanueva del Arzobispo on a minor road which leads to the park. The scenery improves dramatically and after about 10 km the road enters a spectacular wooded gorge, eventually arriving at the hamlet of **Tranco**, scattered around the dam of the Tranco reservoir. There are a number of bars and restaurants here, many of which have some accommodation, set amongst the trees overlooking the reservoir. To follow the reservoir southeast, you need to cross the dam, but another recommended diversion is to carry straight on northeast to the hill top village of **Hornos**, perched on a crag dominated by a castle, which, though mostly in ruins, makes an excellent viewpoint over the reservoir. The village has a strong Moorish flavour, with narrow streets and a small stretch of the original walls, complete with a horseshoe arch.

To go southeast into the park, don't take the road shown on the tourist office map on the east side of the reservoir – it does not exist! Instead return to Tranco, cross the dam and pass through the park gates (your entry and departure will be noted and you'll be asked if you're going to stay the night, and if so, where). The road now continues along the north side of the Tranco reservoir, giving spectacular views of the island in the centre of the lake, the **Isla Cabeza de la Viña**, which in the early 1990s was no longer an island, owing to the low winter rainfall and subsequent drop in water levels. The road continues past the end of the reservoir, now following the Río Guadalquivir towards its headwaters, passing through the hamlet of **Coto Ríos**, before arriving at the Torre de Vinagre Interpretation Centre (see page 377).

The main route through the park now leaves the Guadalquivir valley and climbs over the **Puerto de las Palomas** (Doves Pass), where a mirador gives superb views back through the valley. The road then drops down past the park boundary and into the villages of, firstly, **La Iruela** and then to **Cazorla**.

Jaén Province

Essentials

Remember to book accommodation well ahead in the park, especially during the summer months. **A** *Parador El Adelantado*, Sierra de Cazorla, T/F953727075, cazorla @parador.es 33 rooms, pool, restaurant, functional building in hunting-lodge style in a superb setting. **B** *Noguera de la Sierpe*, Coto Ríos, T953721601, F953721709. 20 rooms, wheelchair access, pool, restaurant, disco. **C** *Los Enebros*, Ctra El Tranco, Km 7, La Iruela, T953721610. Pool, tennis. **C** *Río*, Paraje de la Teja, La Iruela, T953720211. 21 rooms, most with delightful views. **C-D** *Apartamentos Reiza,* Hornos de Segura, T953495106. Small well-equipped apartments at the edge of the village which sleep from 2-6. **Camping** There are 3 sites in the Sierra de Segura and 6 in the Sierra de la Cazorla. Most are well-equipped and in unspoilt surroundings. The only first category site is *Fuente de la Canalica*, Ctra las Acebeas, Siles, T953491004. There are also a number of *camping libre* sites which are free, but have no facilities. Contact the park information centre in Torre del Vinagre or Cazorla for full details.

Sleeping & eating See inside front cover for hotel price codes

The main tourist centre of the park, Cazorla stands at a height of 900 m beneath a steep limestone cliff, the Peña de los Halcones. The town has a long history, with both Iberians and Romans living here. It was the Moors who recognized its strategic position and originally built the two castles which dominate the village. The municipal tourist office is in Paseo del Santo Cristo 17, north of Plaza de la Constitución, T953710102; open in summer only. *Quercus Turismo*, Calle Juan Domingo 2, T953720115, www.excursionquercus.com, sells maps, guidebooks and tours of the park.

On the Plaza de la Corredera, known locally as the Plaza del Huevo because of its egg shape, is the Ayuntamiento, located in a Moorish-style palace. Plaza Santa María is the most lively square and is named after the ruined church, which was designed by Andrés de Vandelvira, but regrettably destroyed by Napoleon's troops in the Peninsular War. The square is overshadowed by La Yedra, the tower of one of the Moorish castles. Also in this square is the small Museo de Artes y Costumbres, which gives a glimpse of local history crafts and folklore. ■ *Tue-Sat 1000-1400*. These two squares, as well as Plaza de la Constitución, have a wealth of tapas bars.

Cazorla

Sleeping and eating **A** *Villa Turística de Cazorla*, Ladera de San Isicio, T953710100, www.villacazorla.com A pueblo-type development of 32 cottages in traditional style, on the hillside overlooking the village of Cazorla. Pool, gardens, restaurant, all rooms have fireplace, terrace, kitchen and TV. Breakfast included in price. **C** *Molino la Farraga*, T953721249. A beautiful converted mill just outside of the town and by far the nicest place to stay in Cazorla; wonderful food and welcome. **D** *Hostal Guadalquivir*, T953720268. A friendly, family-run hostal close to Cazorla's main square. Popular with walking groups from the UK. Rooms are basic, but clean. **D** *La Finca Mercedes*, just outside of Cazorla on the road to La Iruela, T953721087. Excellent rooms with views, food available. Good value. The owners have another 6 rooms in a farm just 5 minutes away. Pool and garden. **D** *Hotel de Montaña Los Parrales*, between Cazorla and Hornos/Segura, T953126170. A small hotel in a peaceful location looking out across the reservoir of El Tranco. Pleasant rooms, simple home cooking, chaotic service. Price includes breakfast. **E** *Hostal Betis*, Plaza de la Corredera 19, T953720540. Some rooms looking over the square but can be noisy. **Youth hostels** *Albergue Juvenil Cazorla*, C Mauricio Martínez 6, T953720329. 76 beds, pool, meals available. **Camping** *Camping Cortijo*, 1 km from centre, T953721280.

Segura de la Sierra Just outside the park boundaries in the north of the area is Segura de la Sierra, which is easily reached from Hornos and which can be seen from kilometres around, sitting on the top of its conical hill. Its strategic position meant that it was occupied in turn by all the groups who invaded Andalucía, from the Phoenicians through to the Moors. The castle, built by the Almoravids and eventually destroyed by French troops during the Peninsular War, has been heavily restored, consisting of two main precincts, several towers, gates, a keep and a well. To look around, you'll need a key from the tourist office. They will also arrange for entrance to the Moorish Baths in the main square, where you can see cold, tepid and hot rooms, with double horseshoe arches at each end and a barrel vault with star-shaped ventilation holes. C *El Mirador de Messía de Leiva,* T953482101, has beautifully decorated apartments at the heart of this pretty village. Attractive restaurant serves regional specialities. To the south of the park, a road runs from **Peal de Becerro**, through **Quesada**, another old Moorish settlement, and over the **Tíscar Pass** through spectacular scenery, before joining the Granada-Basa A92N some way to the south.

Almería Province

10

Almería Province

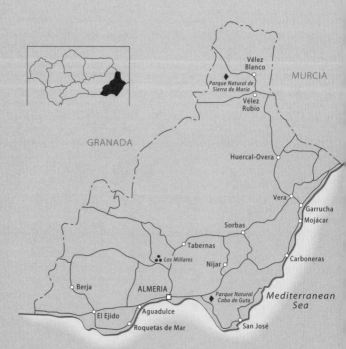

This is the most easterly of the provinces of Andalucía. It is the hottest, sunniest, driest and least populated province, with only 400,000 people living in its 8,000 sq km of arid landscape. Despite the airport at Almería and the low rainfall, tourism has not made much progress here, especially when compared with the Costa del Sol. There are few towns of any size in the interior, which is often mountainous, rising to its highest point at Chullo, 2,609 m. Almería has a **semi-desert** landscape with low rainfall, under 100 mm annually. Today, brief spring showers encourage a plethora of wildflowers to briefly bloom.

The arid landscape, near constant sunshine and the clear light have attracted film producers, with spaghetti westerns made by the score. Some of the sets have been preserved at **Mini Hollywood**, 12 km north of Almería. East of the provincial capital, Almería, there is an ever-changing coastline of towering cliffs, remote coves and occasional dunes. The **Parque Natural Cabo de Gata** is noted for its wetland birds, desert plants and excellent diving conditions. Further east, the ancient hilltop village of **Mojácar** has spilled down to the coast to form the modern resort of Mojácar Playa.

The west of the province is marred by vast areas of plasticultura centred on the town of El Ejido, with market gardening produce supplied both to Spain and much of northern Europe. Tourism here struggles, with the resorts of Roquetas de Mar and Aguadulce hemmed in by the advancing plastic.

Almería

Colour map 5, grid B6
Population: 168,025

It is an interesting fact that the city of Almería is further south than both Algiers and Tunis in North Africa. Crowded in to the north by the semi-desert, this busy sea port has a strong African flavour about it and the well-preserved Moorish **Alcazaba,** *which looms over the city, adds to this feeling. With ships from many nations using the port and busy ferries plying to other Mediterranean cities, Almería feels more like a seaport than any other Andalucían coastal town. As with many ports, Almería has its seedy areas, but these are fairly obvious and the friendly locals will gently guide you away from them. The main shopping and commercial areas are around the attractive tree-lined* **Paseo de Almería,** *with most of the best eating places. Try and visit the solid, almost windowless,* **cathedral***, which had to double as a sanctuary when pirate raids threatened.*

Ins and outs

Getting there
See page 394 for further details
Almería has its own international **airport**, just off the N344, 8 km to the east of the city, T950221954. Bus no 14 runs from the airport to the town every 30 mins Mon-Fri 0700-2130 and every 45 mins Sat and Sun. If returning to the airport, catch the bus outside *Pizza Hut* on Av de Federico García Lorca. The **bus** station is a few minutes' walk away at Plaza de Barcelona. **Trains** arrive at the station on Ctra de Ronda, about 20 mins' walk from the centre, T902240202 for information.

Getting around
The main **taxi** rank is in Parque Nicolás Salmerón, near the port, where **Coches de Caballo** (horse drawn carriages) can also be picked up for sightseeing tours.

Tourist offices
The tourist office is at Parque Nicolás Salmerón, on the corner of C Martínez Campos, opposite the port, T950274355, F950274360. Open Mon-Fri 1000-1300, Sat 1000-1200. The staff are multilingual and extremely helpful. This should be an essential stop for all first time visitors to the city. There is also a municipal tourist office in Av Federico García Lorca s/n, T950280748. Open Mon-Fri 1000-1300 Sat 1000-1200. There is an information point at the airport, T950292918. Also see www.almeria-turismo.org

History

The city was probably founded by the Phoenicians and later occupied by the Romans, who called it Portus Magnus. A major expansion came in 10th-century Moorish times, when the newly built port at the mouth of the river Andarax was known as Al-Mariyat (the mirror of the sea). Under Abd ar-Rahman III the magnificent **Alcazaba** was built. Later, after the collapse of the caliphate at Córdoba, it became capital of a separate *taifa*. By the 14th century it had a population of over 300,000, with prosperity based on ship building and silk weaving. This period of affluence ended with the Christian Reconquest in 1490 and the expulsion of the Moors. Decline set in, not helped by the earthquake of 1522, which destroyed much of the town and the castle. By the 17th century the population had fallen to under 600. Recovery came in the 20th century with the construction of the railway line and a new harbour to export minerals such as iron and lead from the interior. Almería did not escape unscathed during the Civil War. It was staunchly Republican, which led to the bombardment of the harbour by German warships in 1937. It was not until the last two decades of the 20th century that prosperity returned to Almería, spurred on by horticulture and tourism.

Things to do ★

- Enjoy the view from the mountain road over the Puerto de la Virgen pass in the Sierra de los Filabres
- Visit spaghetti western land and see a cowboy shoot-out
- Buy some pottery or *jarapas* in Níjar
- Go scuba diving round the Cabo de Gata headland
- Sleep at El Dorado hotel, Carboneras, in a room decked out as a famous film set
- See a three-day mock battle between the Moors and the Christians in Mojácar

Sights

Although the Alcazaba can be easily seen from most parts of the city, it can be quite complicated to find the entrance. The historic parts of the city are clearly signposted, but the streets in the old part are narrow and confusing, so obtain a town plan from the tourist office first. Approach via the cathedral and Calle Almanzor. If you are lost you will find the local inhabitants very helpful. There is limited parking at the entrance of the Alcazaba and also in the nearby Plaza Vieja.

The Alcazaba has had a chequered history reflecting that of the town itself. Work on the building started in 955 under Abd ar-Rahman 111 of Córdoba, who gave the city the classification of 'medina'. Its most glorious period was during the 11th century during the reigns of Jayran, Zuhayr and Almotocin, but it has also experienced periods of total neglect. Although in the beginning the Alcazaba served as the headquarters of the governors and the Muslim kings and in later times as the residence of the Christian rulers, it was always first and foremost a military base. This use, combined with the effects of the earthquake in 1522, plus subsequent renovations, has substantially altered the original appearance.

It consists of three defensive compounds, all containing construction from different periods of history. The **first compound**, the largest of the three, is approached through an exterior gate, then up a zig-zag ramp (a defensive ploy not uncommon in Moorish fortifications) before arriving at the **Puerta de Justicia** (1), overlooked by the **Torre de Espejos** (2) which was added in the 15th century. The mirrors were apparently used to contact ships approaching the harbour. This compound originally served as a military camp and could also house several thousand people in times of siege. A constant supply of fresh water was pumped up through wells by **windmills** (3). Today the first compound is a garden with attractive areas of flowing water. To the east is the **Saliente Bastión** (4) which was used as a lookout point. The ramparts

The Alcazaba
The largest Moorish castle in Andalucía & its hill site dominates the city of Almería. Numbers in brackets refer to the map, page 390

Almería Province

'The Alcazaba'

eventually arrive at the **Wall of the Watch** (5) which served as a bell tower. From here the massive **Muralla de la Hoya** (6) stretches away to the northeast spanning a deep valley and up to the mirador of San Cristóbal on the hill of the same name, somewhat reminiscent of the Great Wall of China.

The **second compound** served as a residence for the Muslim kings and governors and also housed their guards and servants. You can only wonder at its former magnificence, for there are only scant remains today. You can identify the remnants of **Albijes Califales** (7), a former **mosque** (8) (converted into a Mudéjar style shrine by the Catholic Monarchs), some **Muslim houses** (9) and **military baths** (10) in the Roman style. Archaeological work is continuing in this compound, concentrating on the ruins of the **Palacio de Almotacín** (11) and the **Ventana de la Odalisca** (12) in the north wall. There is a poignant tale concerning the latter. Apparently a prisoner fell in love with a Moorish slave girl who tried to help him escape, but the plot was discovered and he jumped to his death from the window, the girl inevitably dying from a broken heart some days later.

The **third compound** is entirely post-Muslim. After the Reconquest of Almería, the Catholic Monarchs, seeing the earthquake wreckage, ordered the construction of a castle with thicker walls in the westernmost and highest part of the Alcazaba. Entrance was by a bridge over a moat protected by three semi-circular towers. The interior **Patio de las Armas** (13) is dominated by the **Torre del Homenaje** (keep) (14). The two other buildings are the **Windmill Tower** (15) and the **Torre de Pólvora** (16). There are excellent views from these towers over the port and the gypsy area below the castle known as **La Chanca**. ■ *Daily, summer 1000-1400 and 1700-2000; winter 0930-1400 and 1630-1900. Free with EU passport, otherwise €1.50. T950271617.*

Cathedral & The Cathedral is a large uninspiring building begun in 1524 on the site of an
churches old mosque, but most of the work was carried out in the 17th century. Designed by Diego de Siloé, it was built for defence against attacks by Berber pirates as well as for worship. It consequently has massive stone walls and small high windows, while its corner towers had positions for cannons. The only exterior feature of note is the stylish Renaissance doorway, the Puerta Principal. Inside, amongst the severity, look for the altar designed by Ventura Rodríguez and paintings by Alonso Cano. Note, too, the 16th-century choir stalls carved in walnut by Juan de Orea. There is also a small cloister surrounding an attractive garden, but the entry door is often locked.■ *Mon-Fri 1000-1700, Sat 1000-1300. €1.80.*

Alcazaba

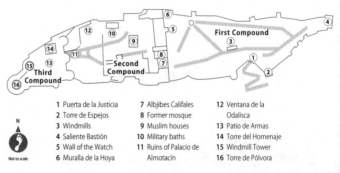

1 Puerta de la Justicia	7 Albjibes Califales	12 Ventana de la
2 Torre de Espejos	8 Former mosque	Odalisca
3 Windmills	9 Muslim houses	13 Patio de Armas
4 Saliente Bastión	10 Military baths	14 Torre del Homenaje
5 Wall of the Watch	11 Ruins of Palacio de	15 Windmill Tower
6 Muralla de la Hoya	Almotacín	16 Torre de Pólvora

N

Not to scale

Of the other churches worth mentioning in Almería, the best is the **Iglesia de San Juan**, just to the west of the cathedral, which was built in the 17th century on the site of a mosque. There is a mihrab on the south wall.■ *Entry only at service times.*

Cerro de San Cristóbal This hill is the best vantage point in town. Next to the mirador is an enormous figure of Christ and an outdoor altar. This area can be reached from the town centre via the Puerta de Purchena and Calle Antonio Vico. Unfortunately there is a lot of vandalism and graffiti at the site.

Other sights

Centro de Rescate de la Fauna Sahariana The Sahara Wildlife Rescue Centre is located in the valley behind the Alcazaba and was established in 1971 with help from the World Wildlife Fund to save Saharan species in danger of extinction. The surrounding scenery ensures that the desert species feel at home and the venture has been extremely successful. The centre is not generally open to the public, but it is possible to obtain a permit from the organization's headquarters close to the tourist office.

Los Alijibes Town plans of Almería show these old Moorish water cisterns at Calle de los Alijibes 20. The location is actually a flamenco bar, which is usually closed until mid-evening. Some performances actually take place partially within the cisterns – certainly a unique venue.

Hospital Real Built in the mid-18th century, this building on Calle Hospital is still a working hospital. If you can get inside, look for the delightful tiled patio.

La Plaza Vieja With only one access road, it is easy to miss this delightful pedestrianized square, also known as the Plaza de la Constitución, with its late 19th-century Ayuntamiento. One block away to the north is the 17th century Church of Las Claras.

Calle de las Tiendas Just south of the Puerta de Purchena, this is the oldest street in Almería and during the 19th century it was full of fashionable shops, but it now looks somewhat run down.

There have been plans for many years to open a new **Archaeological Museum** to display the artefacts from the Chalcolithic site at Los Millares. Indeed many town plans show the museum sited at Carretera de Ronda 13. It is still not open, however, but meanwhile there are artefacts on show in the Prehistory room at the Public Library – Biblioteca Pública Francisco Villaspesa, Calle Hermanos Machado sin número. ■ *Tue-Fri 0900-1400, Sat 0930-1330. T950264492.*

Museums

Essentials

Most *pensiones* are in the central area in streets leading off the Puerta de Purchena. **AL** *Gran Sol Almería*, Av Reina Regente 8, T950238011, F950270691. 117 rooms. Traditional, comfortable, Andalucían city centre hotel, located between the town and the port, a/c, TV, garage, disco, pool. **AL-C** *Torreluz*, Plaza Flores, T/F950234799. This is in fact a series of 4 hotels, offering various prices and facilities. **A** *Sol y Mar*, Ctra Málaga 110, T950234622, F950277010. 15 rooms. Small modern hotel in good location overlooking the port and the Moorish castle; good but expensive restaurant. **B** *Costasol*, Paseo de Almería 58, T/F950234011. 55 rooms. Good value, convenient for bus and train stations. **C** *Indalico*, C Dolores R Sopeña 4, T950231111, F950231028. 52 rooms. Central location, can be noisy, a/c, garage. **C** *La Perla*, Plaza del Carmen 7, T950238877, F950275816. The city's oldest hotel, just off the Puerta de Purchena. Recently redeveloped with attractive 44 a/c rooms.

Sleeping
See inside front cover for price codes

D *Hostal Americano*, Av de la Estación 4, T950258011. Garage, TV lounge, close to train and bus stations. **D** *Hostal Bristol*, Plaza San Sebastián 8, T950231595. 27 en suite rooms. Central, good value. **D** *Embajador*, C Calzada de Castro 4, T950255511, F950259364. On the train station side of the city centre, with 67 a/c rooms. **D** *Estación*, C Calzada de Castro 37, T950267239. Modest *pensión* close to both the bus and train stations. **D** *Nixar*, C Antonio Vico 24, T950237255, F950237255. Probably the best of the *pensiones*, 40 a/c rooms, some with bath. **E** *Andalucía*, C Granada 9, T950237733. 76 rooms. Large and faded but clean and good value. **E** *Maribel*, Av Federico García Lorca 153, T950235173, 16 rooms. Adequate cheap rooms on the Rambla de Belén.

Youth hostels Albergue Juvenil, C Isla Fuerteventura s/n, T950269788, 173 beds. Meals available. New building, suitable for wheelchair users, open all year. Can be reached using the No 1 bus, from Rambla de Obispo Orbrera, at Av Federico García Lorca end. **Camping** *La Garrofa*, Ctra Motril-Almería, Km 8, T950235770. Second category site, open all year round, located 4 km west of the centre on the Aguadulce road. There are other sites nearby at San José and Roquetas de Mar, both second category.

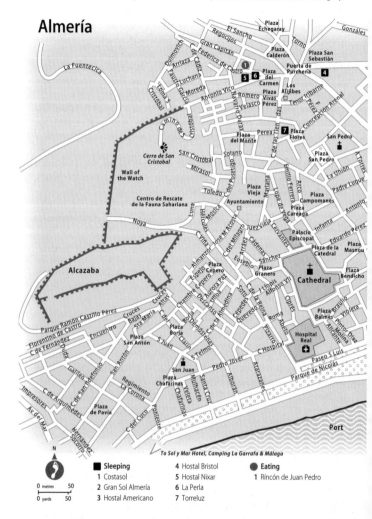

Almería

Sleeping
1 Costasol
2 Gran Sol Almería
3 Hostal Americano
4 Hostal Bristol
5 Hostal Nixar
6 La Perla
7 Torreluz

Eating
1 Rincón de Juan Pedro

To Sol y Mar Hotel, Camping La Garrafa & Málaga

The best restaurants are either on, or just off, the Paseo de Almería. Local specialities to look for including *gachas* (a hot clam stew), *trigo* (a stew with grains of wheat, pork, beans and herbs), *choto al ajo y en ajillo* (kid with garlic or garlic sauce) and spiced sardines. Almería is not noted for classical wines but small cellars can be found in the villages of Alboloduy, Berja, Fondón, Luajar and Ohanes.

Eating

Expensive *Rincón de Juan Pedro*, Plaza del Carmen 5, T950235184. Local specialities. **Mid-range** *Anfora*, C Acosta Lainez 3, T950231374. Specializes in local produce. *Asador Torreluz*, Plaza Flores, C Fructuoso Pérez, T950234799. Outstanding meat restaurant in the *Hotel Torreluz*. *Club de Mar*, C Muelle 1, T950235048. Wharfside setting, semi-international cuisine. *Mesón la Reja*, C Arapiles 7, T950235702. Local dishes. *Los Gauchos*, C Granada 25, T950273594. Specialist steak restaurant. **Cheap** *Buffet Libre Almería*, C Jerez 10, T950260137. Eat as much as you like for a set price. *Hong Kong*, C Hermanos Machado 2, T950264338. The best of the Chinese restaurants in the city. *Meh Hua*, C Altamira. Good value multi choice *menú*. There are also a number of bar-restaurants offering cheap *menús* in the Parque de Nicolás Salmerón opposite the port.

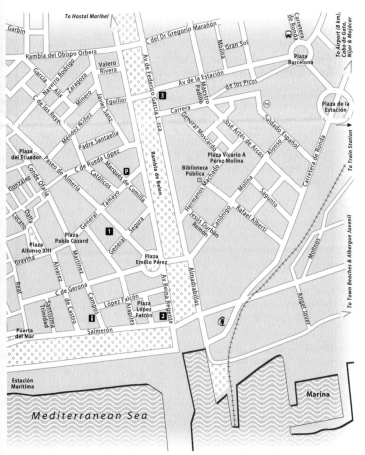

Almería Province

Tapas bars There are good bars for tapas in and around the Puerta de Purchena at the north end of the Paseo de Almería. Try *Bodega las Botas*, C Fructuoso Pérez 3, which has a good atmosphere with sherry barrels and legs of *serrano* ham hanging from the ceiling – you may even get a free tapa. Also *Bar El Alcázar*, Paseo de Almería 4, with good seafood tapas. *Bar-Restaurant Imperial*, Puerta de Purchena, is spoilt only by the traffic noise. In the cathedral area there are numerous bodegas catering mainly for lunchtime trade, of which *Bodegas Montenegro* is highly recommended.

Bars & nightclubs **Discos** *Lord Nelson*, C Canónigo Molina Alonso 1, T950254026; *Grants Club*, C Reina Regente s/n, T950241099. During the height of the season, the local authority erects disco marquees along part of the Paseo Marítimo, which at least keeps the noise in one place.

Entertainment **Cinemas** Almería boasts 4 cinemas, of which the *Imperial*, Av de Pablo Iglesias s/n, is probably the best. **Flamenco** The only spot worth mentioning is *Peña El Taranto*, C Los Aljibes 20. **Theatres** *Cervantes*, C Poeta Vilaespesa s/n, T950237093. *Auditorio Municipal Maestro Padilla*, Av del Mediterráneo s/n, T950276922.

Fiestas & festivals Feb *Festival of Puppet Theatre*. **Last week in Aug** *Feria* This is marked by sports events, bullfights and dancing. in. Also in **Aug** is an *Iberian and Mediterranean Folklore* event. **Nov** *International Jazz Festival* This is held in the Cervantes Theatre. **Late Dec-early Jan** *Winter Festivals* These culminate in the *Romería de la Virgen del Mar* when the virgin of the sea is taken in procession to Torre García beach.

Shopping The commercial centre is in the Paseo de Almería, the Puerta de Purchena, the C de las Tiendas and the surrounding area. Handicraft items typical of the region including ceramics and pottery, *jarapas* (blankets made from rough cloth and rag strips), bedspreads, esparto grass items, basketwork and small carved marble goods. There are street markets on Tue in Av Mediterráneo; on Fri at the Plaza de Toros; and on Sat at the Plaza del Zapillo.

Sport **Golf** The nearest golf courses are at Almerimar, T950480234, Roquetas de Mar, T950333055 and Turre, T950479164. **Scuba diving** The Cabo de Gata area is popular for scuba diving and underwater fishing. **Watersports** Contact the *Centro de Actividades Náuticas*, Av de Cabo de Gata. The Municipal Sports Centre is in the Av de Mediterráneo, T950229820.

Tour operators *Koral*, Paseo Almería 47, T950251133; *Indamar*, Paseo de Almería 73, T950237883; *Paris*, Paseo San Luis 2, T950265022; *Viajes Alysol*, Paseo de Almería 34, T950237622; *Viajes Sur*, Paseo de Almería 4, T950244677.

Transport **Bus** The station is in the Plaza de Barcelona, T950210029, and is a modern building with a cafeteria and a comfortable waiting room. *Alsa* bus company, T950281660, has services to Mojácar (8 daily, 1 hr 15 mins, €5.15), Níjar (1500 and 1800, 1 hr 20 mins, €1.90) and Tabernas (6 daily, 40 mins, €1.75). *Alsina* runs buses to Algeciras (0800, 3½ hrs, € 21.10), Málaga (3 daily, 3½ hrs, €12.40), Granada (6 daily, 2¼, €8.50) and Sevilla (0930, 5½ hrs, €23.50). There are hourly buses to and from the resorts of Roquetas de Mar and Aguadulce the west. **Train** It is difficult to mistake the station on Ctra de Ronda, T950251122, with its neo-Moorish style frontage and ultra modern extension. There are four *talgos* a day from Madrid and other connections from Barcelona, Granada and Valencia. Overnight trains come from Sevilla and Córdoba. **RENFE** have an office in the town centre, C Alcalde Muñoz, T950231207, or

T902240202. **Boat** Ferries to Melilla are run by *Transmediterránea*, Parque Nicolas Salmerón 19, near the port, T902454645. Ferries run daily except Sat, leaving at 2330 and arriving in Melilla at 0800. Tickets cost €25.15 and are available from travel agents.

Banks Banks are mostly at the north end of the Paseo de Almería. **Embassies and** **Directory**
consulates *Finland*, Av Cabo de Gata, T950243238; *France*, Av de Cabo de Gata 81,
T950252284; *Germany*, Centro Comercial Satélites Park, Ctra de Málaga s/n,
Aguadulce, T950340555; *Netherlands*, C Reyes Católicos 26, T950268504; *Sweden*, C
Dr Aráez Pacheco 2, T950250033; *UK*, contact Málaga, T950217571. **Communica-**
tions Post office: Correos, Plaza J Casinello 1, Paseo de Almería, T950237207. **Tele-**
phones: *Locutorio* in C Navarro Rodríguez 9. Open Mon-Sat. **Medical services** Emer-
gencies: T950257198. Hospitals: *Cruz Roja*, T950222222; *Hospital Provincial de*
Almería, Plaza Dr Gómez Campana 1, T950241455. **Useful addresses** Garages/car
repairs: *Ford*: Automecánica Almeriense, Ctra N340, Km 117, T950237033; *Peugeot:*
Talleres Sur, C Padre Santaella 4, T950238101; *Renault*: Ctra N340, Km 446,
T950259312; *Rover:* Codasa, C Doctoral 16, T950224266; *Volvo*: Ctra de Granada,
T950238963.

North of Almería

The Chalcolithic, or Copper Age, archaeological site of Los Millares was dis- **Los Millares**
covered in 1891 when the Almería-Linares railway line was being con-
structed. The early excavations were carried out by two mining engineers,
Louis and Henri Siret, who were employees of the railway company. They
found a Chalcolithic fortified settlement dating from circa 2700 BC. The excavations spread over 5 ha and show a series of defensive walls enclosing circular
huts, a foundry, a simple aqueduct bringing water from Alhama and a silo.
Most remarkable of all, however, is the Necropolis, where over 100 tombs
have been discovered. Artefacts recovered include pottery, jewellery,
basketware and a variety of utensils. The inhabitants, who may have numbered 2,000, were hunters and farmers. The evidence suggests that the climate
and vegetation were much kinder than the barren semi-desert which sur-
rounds the site today. The farm stock included sheep, goats and pigs, while it
is clear that cereals and vegetables were grown. The surrounding forest sheltered wild boar and deer. It also seems that the Río Andarax, the dry bed of
which runs round part of the site, was navigable in those days and was used for
bringing the copper ore from the Sierra de Gador to the southwest.

To get there from Almería, take the A92 north out of Almería and after 12
km fork left along the N324. Just after the village of **Gador**, fork left again
along the A348 towards **Alhama de Almería**. This is a small spa town which
dates back to Moorish times and you can still take the waters here today,
which explains the unexpectedly grand *Hotel San Nicolas*, which is located at
the site of the original baths. Just 4 km away is Los Millares, which is poorly
signposted. Look for a plain building on the right hand side of the road at Km
24. ■ *Wed-Sat 0930-1430 and 1600-1800, Sun 0930-1430.*

Paraje Natural del Desierto de Tabernas

Back on the A92 heading north, the road runs through the Paraje Natural del
Desierto de Tabernas, a fascinating area of semi-desert, the bare treeless
mountain slopes showing the rock structure, dried up river beds and flat

Almería Province

topped plateaux. This is probably the only area of true semi desert on mainland Europe and not surprisingly it has some desert birds more common in North Africa, such as trumpeter finch and Dupont's lark, of which there are believed to be around 150 pairs. The desert area now has no fewer than three spaghetti western theme parks.

Mini Hollywood Twelve kilometres along the A92 and just past a junction with the N340, almost immediately on the right hand side of the road, is Mini Hollywood, the oldest and the best of the three theme parks. This is a relic of the golden age of spaghetti western films, such as *A Fistful of Dollars* and *The Good the Bad and the Ugly* (also *Indiana Jones*) which were made in this area in the 1960s and 1970s. The film makers were attracted by the arid scenery, reminiscent of the American Midwest, plus the clear air and almost unbroken sunshine, all of which were ideal for shooting. The film makers have now moved on but the sets remain, with bars, a bank, stables and Red Indian encampments. At noon and 1700, 'cowboys' enact shoot-outs and stunts. There is also a rather depressing zoo. ■ *1000-2100 in summer, 1000-1700 in winter. €10.25, €13.25 if the zoo is included, children €3.95. The car park is equally expensive at €2.50.* Further along the road to Tabernas is **Texas Hollywood,** which is somewhat less commercialised and includes amongst its features an Indian village complete with wigwams and a US cavalry fort. Shows at 1430 and 1730. ■ *Open same times as Mini Hollywood. €5.75.* A third site has opened up recently known as **Western Leone.** Horses can be hired here. ■ *Daily Jul-Sep, with shows at 1200, 1500, 1730 and 2000. €5.75.*

Gérgal & Sierra de los Filabres At the road junction near Mini Hollywood the A92 leads northwards passing the road to the village of Gérgal after some 12 km, which has a ruined castle and is the main gateway to the Sierra de los Filabres. A winding road from Gérgal leads up to Calar Altar, which at 2,168 m is the highest point in the sierra. Just beneath the summit is the **Observatorio Astronómico**, which clearly benefits from the cloudless skies of the region. From the observatory, a network of tracks, passable with four-wheel drive vehicles, fans out over the Sierra linking with the villages to the north on the Heurcal-Baza road, such as Purchena, Tijola and Olula. The east part of the Sierra de los Filabres can be seen by passing through Tabernas and after 11 km taking the 3325 road north towards Uleila. Then follows a spectacular mountain drive over the Puerto de la Virgen pass (1,070 m) before descending into Albánchez and joining the C323 near Cantoría.

Tabernas
Population: 3,241 Tabernas lies 2 km beyond Mini Hollywood on the N340 and is dominated by a conical hill capped by a small Moorish castle. While the town itself has little of interest, the castle, where Ferdinand and Isabel stayed during the siege of Almería, looks more promising. There is no tourist office and, although the Ayuntamiento is helpful, there is no information about the castle. It is best approached by heading for the municipal sports stadium and taking the wide, but rough, track to the summit. There has been some half-hearted restoration work on the castle, from where there are superb views, but you're left with the feeling that the town could make more of this asset.

There are no hotels in Tabernas, but three *pensiónes* are located on the N340, which bypasses the town. **D** *Hermanos García* is probably the best of the three, but is a bit overpriced for what it is.

Almería Province

Eighteen kilometres east of Tabernas is the small town of Sorbas, located on a deep gorge, over which houses hang alarmingly. Sorbas is a pottery making centre and, at the lower part of the town, there are a number of shops in front of small workshops where the goods are sold at wholesale prices. There is a popular weekly market in the main square on Thursdays. Just south of Sorbas is the **Parque Natural de Karst en Yesos,** a limestone area with a number of caves eroded away during wetter climatic times. The caves, which have the usual stalactites and stalagmites, can only be visited on a guided tour organised by the local tourist office. ■ *2 hr tours with equipment provided take place hourly in summer and cost €6.65.*

Sorbas
Population: 2,748

You could return to Almería by missing out Sorbas and instead encircling the Sierra Alhamilla, turning off the N340 to **Lucainena de la Torres** and following a dramatic scenic road before dropping down into **Níjar**. This is an attractive little town with some scant remains of a Moorish castle, but most come here for its craftwork. It produces some distinctive handmade pottery, a craft carried on from Moorish times. Look for the studio of the English potter Matthew Weir (Calle Lavadero 2) who puts a modern interpretation on the traditional styles. Níjar is also a centre for the production of *jarapas*, the rugs and blankets made from wool and rags. The main street of the newer part of the town is named after the writer Federico García Lorca, who based his work *Blood Wedding* on a local scandal that took place in Níjar in 1928. It involved an heiress named Francisca who was being forced to marry a labourer named Casimiro. On the eve of the wedding she eloped with her cousin, but they were intercepted by Casimiro's brother, who shot the cousin dead and was later convicted of murder. The humiliated Casimiro never married, nor did Francisca, who lived as a recluse in Níjar until her death in 1978. There are a surprising number of accommodation possibilities in the town, with several small hotels and five *pensiones*. Good value is **C** *Venta de Pobre*, T/F950385192, with 21 rooms, air conditioning and wheelchair access. Return to Almería by joining the N340, 6 km to the south.

Níjar
Population: 15,406

East of Almería

Parque Natural Cabo de Gata-Níjar

Shortly after Almería airport, fork right to **El Cabo de Gata**, a small undeveloped resort with a long beach of coarse sand. There is little in the way of accommodation here. The village takes its name from the vast area of succulents growing around it. This is the Parque Natural de Cabo de Gata-Níjar, which covers 29,000 ha. There are two distinct types of landscape: coastal dunes with saline lagoons behind them (the first line of dunes are mobile, but further inland the dunes are fixed by vegetation) and hills of volcanic origin, known as the Sierra de Cabo de Gata and still exhibiting some laval columns. There are some interesting flora within the park, including the thorny jujube tree, the dwarf fan palm or palmetta, which is Europe's only native palm and sand wort which occurs in the dunes. Reptiles found here are the Italian wall lizard (the only place in Spain where this is found), the tawny lizard, viper and grass snake. Hares and foxes are common. The Mediterranean monk seal last bred here in 1974, but has recently been re-introduced. It is the birds, however, which are the main attraction of this reserve.

Almería Province

Las Salinas The most rewarding location is the area known as Las Salinas, a series of salt pans which are still commercially operated just south of Cabo de Gata village. Fortunately Andalucían environment agency has an arrangement with the owners and large parts of the 350 ha of water are undisturbed and they form a wetland of major importance. Greater flamingoes have attempted unsuccessfully to breed here, but there can be as many as 2,000 non-breeders around in the summer. Breeding birds include black winged stilts, avocets and little terns, while passage species include ospreys, storks, purple herons and egrets. There is a good range of wildfowl in the winter, while the rarer gulls include slender-billed and audouins.

For access, look for the lifeguards' tower on the side of the coast road; immediately opposite this is an entrance with a sign saying *Entrada Prohibida* (Entry Forbidden). Ignore this and drive into the car park, which is alongside the hide which overlooks the *salinas*. The park has a visitors' centre located on the Almería road, with displays describing the geology, flora and fauna of the park. ■ *Tue-Sun 0930-1530.* Unfortunately, much of the low lying part of this park is litter strewn – mainly the debris of the *plasticultura* industry and it is sad to see such a starkly beautiful landscape ruined by humans.

South of the hills of salt, the road continues to the headland of Cabo de Gata with its lighthouse. The mirador is a good spot for observing migratory birds, while the clear waters off the point are a favourite spot for scuba divers. The Cape actually protrudes further south than the northern tip of Tunisia. Beneath the headland is a rocky reef, El Arrecife de la Sirenas – the Mermaids' reef – named not after mermaids, but the monk seals which were once found here in large numbers. The road from here on is narrow and tricky with numerous hairpin bends.

San José To reach the small resort of San José it is probably wise to return inland from Cabo de Gata. San José can also be reached by bus from Almería. The resort is fairly unspoilt still, but the newly built marina will probably alter that. There are some accommodation possibilities here, including **C** *San José*, Barriada San José, T950380116, which is curiously decorated but has fine sea views; and **C** *Bahía Vista*, Correo sin número, T950380019, which is an economical alternative. The *Hotel San José* has a good restaurant, while there are two good fish restaurants, *El Ganandero* at nearby Retamar and *Bar Fonda Mediterráneo* on the beach at San Miguel.

Carboneras The coastline now runs to the northeast, with a series of cliffs, inaccessible
Population: 6,312 coves and cliff top tracks which might prove challenging even for four-wheel drive vehicles. It may be better to head back inland and return to the coast at Carboneras, which has an enormously ugly cement works at the south end of the town. The village centre is dominated by the sturdy 17th-century Castillo de San Andrés surrounded by landscaped gardens. There is a broad beach with a large number of fishing boats, backed by a collection of bars and *pensiones*. A new marina is under construction and behind it is a small resort area. Carboneras has a lively Moors versus Christians fiesta in mid-June. Ask at the small tourist office in the Plaza del Castillo. Amongst the *pensiones*, **B** *Felipe*, T950454015, has the best facilities, while **E** *La Marina*, T950454070, is the cheapest. There is one unusual hotel: *El Dorado*, Playa de Carboneras, T950454050, F950130102, info@eldorado-carboneras.com, with 17 rooms. Different parts of the hotel are decorated as film sets, such as *Dr Zhivago* and the *Three Musketeers*; pool, restaurant.

From Carboneras the road towards Mojácar is one of the most spectacular coastal drives in Andalucía, winding along the cliff top with hairpin beds and tantalizing views of isolated coves, some with access along rough tracks.

Mojácar

A settlement at Mojácar goes back to Iberian times and during the Roman occupation it was one of the most important towns of Baetica, when it was believed to be known as Murgis, a name the Moors later changed to Muxacra. The Moors defended Mojácar stoutly against the armies of the Catholic Monarchs, who eventually allowed them to keep their customs provided they swore allegiance to the Christian crown. Mojácar prospered in the early years of the 20th century and in the 1920s it had a population of 9,000, but after the Civil War and the years of emigration, it fell as low as 400. Its recovery began in the 1960s when it was discovered by an intellectual set of artists and writers. In 1969 it was declared Spain's Prettiest Village, which resulted in the intellectuals mostly moving away to fresh untouched paradises. In their place came an English travel company who were largely responsible for developing Mojácar Playa. The travel firm soon went into liquidation, but by then the boom was well underway. Today, half of Mojácar's population are foreign residents, mainly British, with a significant number of artists and potters. A long established English language magazine is produced monthly.

Colour map 6
Population: 4,525

There are two parts to Mojácar – the Old Mojácar Pueblo and the new Mojácar Playa. The old part is the more interesting as it is a hill village with a distinctly Moorish flavour, with its cube like, sugar lump, whitewashed houses, Arab gateways and the original Moorish street pattern. The Moorish atmosphere of the alleyways and squares is attractive and there is a mirador on the north side giving fine views over the countryside inland towards Turre. The Church of Santa María dates from the 15th century, but has been vastly restored. Bars, restaurants and souvenir shops abound. Despite the picture postcard views, Old Mojácar is a little disappointing.

Sights

Until quite recently, the women half-covered their faces with *cobijas* (triangular shawls) and drew *indalos* on their doors to keep away bad luck. *Indalos* are stick-like figures holding an arc above their heads, thought to have originated in Neolithic times in the caves at Vélez Blanco. Although no longer seen over doorways, the *indalo* sign figures on just about every souvenir in the town's shops.

Mojácar Playa spreads for several miles along an excellent sandy beach. The rather ugly *Centro Comercial El Cruce* is located at the intersection of the coast road and the route up to Mojácar Pueblo. To either side of the centre are hotels, pensions, discos and restaurants.

In Plaza Nueva at the entrance to Old Mojácar, is the very helpful **tourist office**, T950475162. Bus timetables are posted on the window when the office is closed on Saturday afternoon and Sunday. Town plans are available.

There are some excellent hotels in Mojácar Playa, but the lower end of the accommodation scale tends to be overpriced. **Mojácar Playa A** *Continental*, Playa de Palmeral, T950478225, F950475136. Only hotel on the beach side of the road, 23 a/c rooms, wheelchair access. **A** *Parador Reyes Católicos*, Playa s/n, T950478250, F950478183. Modern building on seafront in landscaped grounds, with 98 rooms, pool, tennis, garage. **C** *Río Abajo Playa*, Playa de Mojácar, T950478928. 18 rooms. Small beach front hotel with pool. **D** *Flamenco*, Playa Mojácar (Puntal del Cantal), T950478227, F950475195. 25 rooms.

Sleeping
See inside front cover
for hotel price codes

Almería Province

☞ ## Sightings in Las Salinas

At first sight the area west of Roquetas, dominated by market gardening and tourism, would seem unpromising for wildlife, but in fact this is a prime location for birdwatching with some rich wetland sites. There are four salinas or old salt production sites, most of which have nearby dunes, reeds and scrub. The first is Salinas de San Rafael, which is to the east of Roquetas and is partly overgrown and rubbish strewn, but there are a few salt pans left near the sea. West of Roquetas and south of the village of San Agustín is the largest complex of Salinas Viejas and Salinas de Cerillos, divided by a raised bank. The most westerly site is the Salinas de Guardias Viejas, just to the east of

Almerimar. Watching is rewarding throughout the year, but less so between June and August, when the heat can be blistering, especially with the lack of shade. A wide range of gulls and wildfowl visit the salinas during the winter, but it is the passage periods of spring and autumn when the real rarities appear, including six varieties of tern, collared pratincoles and cream-coloured coursers. Breeding water birds include white-headed ducks, marsh harriers, black-winged stilts and avocets, while the surrounding reeds and scrub hold water rails, great reed warblers, lesser short-toed larks and woodchat shrikes. This list is just a fraction of the species which could turn up.

D *Hostal Puntazo*, Paseo Mediterráneo s/n, T950478265. 36 rooms (includes a modern extension). **D** *Provenzal*, Playa de Descargador, T950478308. 26 rooms. A/c. **Mojácar Pueblo D** *Mamabels*, C Embajadores 1, T950475126. Only 4 rooms, but good sea views and a decent restaurant. **E** *La Esquinica*, C Cano s/n, T950475009. **E** *Casa Justa*, C Morote 5, T950478372. **Camping** *El Cantal de Mojácar*, Ctra N340, Desvío Vera-El Cantal, T950478204. Second category, restaurant. On the beach front 1 km from the *Centro Comercial El Cruce* and rather scruffy. Campers looking for a little peace and quiet may prefer *Camping El Quinto*, a second category site on the Ctra Mojácar–Torre and within walking distance of Old Mojácar.

Eating
See inside front cover for price codes

The vast range of eating places reflects Mojácar's international character. **Expensive** *Bistro Breton*, Playa Mojácar, T950478008. French cuisine, closed Thu. *La Lubina*, Pueblo Indalo, T950458376. Terrace, fish dishes. *Palacio*, Plaza del Cano, in old town. Nouvelle cuisine and traditional dishes. *Tito's*, Playa de Ventanicas, T950478711. Beachside fish restaurant. **Mid-range** *El Bigote*, Mojácar Pueblo. International and Spanish food. *Estrella de Mar*, Rambla de Cantal. Excellent seafood restaurant, with tapas. **Cheap** For cheap tapas, try those round the main square in Mojácar Pueblo, such as *Bar Indalo*. There are also a number of ice cream parlours (*heladerias*), such as the Italian *Alberto's*, near the *Hotel Indalo*, where fresh ice cream is made daily along with excellent cappuccino.

Fiestas & festivals

The highlight of the year is the *Fiesta Moros y Cristianos*, on the weekend closest to 10 Jun, a mock battle between the Moors and Christians, lasting 3 days and accompanied by fireworks, music and giant paellas. One of the best on the coast.

Tour operators

Aysol, Urb El Cruce, T950478175; *Indalo*, Ctra Carboneras, T950478700; *Solar*, Urb Gaviota, T950478700.

Transport

Car hire *Autos Mojácar*, C Glorieta 3, T950478125; *Indalo*, Playa de Mojácar, T950478376; *Solvicar*, C Plaza Nueva, T950478246.

Almería Province

North from Mojácar

Five kilometres inland from Mojácar, the agricultural village of Turre is a delightful change after the coast. There is an attractive church with a Mudéjar tower and a Wednesday street market. Nearby is a Bronze Age site, although the archaeologists from Almería seemed to have removed most things of interest. In Turre is **A** *Finca Listonero*, Cortijo Grande, T/F950479094, listonero@wanadoo.es, an away-from-it-all British-run country farmhouse, offering a relaxing holiday with gourmet cooking and an imaginative wine list.

Turre

Back on the coast, Mojácar merges into Garrucha, a small fishing port with pretensions of grandeur. The marina stubbornly refuses to take off, but villas are appearing thick and fast in the hills behind the port. The fair-sized fishing fleet ensures that the fish restaurants around the port at least serve fresh food, but it does not come cheap. There is a beach of coarse sand and more than acceptable litter.

Garrucha

The coast road now swings inland to the agricultural village of Vera, with 5,000 inhabitants and an interesting collection of monuments, including the 16th-century parish church of La Encarnación; the Real Hospital de San Agustín built in 1521 for Carlos V; the early 17th-century convent in Calle Juan Anglada; and the Casa Consistorial which was completed in the early 18th century. The latter also houses a small historical museum. ■ *Tue-Sun 1000-1400 and 1700-2200. Vera also has a stretch of beach east of Garrucha, with a Parque Aquatico (daily 1000-1900), and 3 typical beach hotels, one of which is a naturist complex –* **C** Vera-Hotel, *Carretera Vera-Garrucha, Km 2, T950390382, F950390361, with 20 air-conditioned rooms, restaurant, 2 pools, and sports facilities.*

Vera

East of Vera, close to the estuary of the Río Almanzora, is the village of **Palomares**, which achieved notoriety in 1966, when after a mid-air collision an American B-52 lost its cargo of H-bombs. Three fell in fields outside the village and were quickly recovered. The fourth fell in the sea and it took a sizeable US fleet several weeks to reclaim it. None, fortunately, exploded.

Twenty kilometres north of Vera is the unremarkable agricultural town of **Huercal-Overa**. The N340 leads north and then the A92 west into the northeast corner of Almería province to the area known as Los Vélez, flanked by the Sierra María. On the N342 is the town of **Vélez Rubio**, which is a rather ordinary spot apart from its magnificent Iglesia de la Encarnación, claimed to be the largest parish church in the province. It dates from the mid-18th century and its construction was funded by local noblemen, whose crests appear on the superbly carved façade. Look for the impressive *retablo* inside. **Vélez Blanco** has rather more interest. It is located below a hill capped by a Renaissance castle which envelops the original Moorish structure, mostly dating from the early 16th century. It is, however, a mere shell, the interior having been gutted and transported stone by stone to the USA by an American millionaire. It is now in the New York Metropolitan Museum. Other buildings of note include the 16th-century Convent of San Luís, , the Church of Santiago and some fine mansions in Calle Palacios, while the narrow streets of the old Moorish quarter are worth wandering around. Between Vélez Rubio and Vélez Blanco is the **Cueva de los Letreros**, approached by a rough track and some concrete steps. The cave is

Vélez Rubio & Vélez Blanco

Almería Province

☞ Life and death in the greenhouse – plasticultura

With some 15,000 ha of the Almería coast covered in greenhouses, creating a mirage of an ocean of plastic, it's often difficult to see where the land ends and the sea begins. In Moorish times the coastal area was extremely fertile, but after the Reconquest the agricultural infrastructure began to crumble away, so that by the early years of the 20th century the area was barren and desolate.

Things began to change in the 1950s when the 'sand-plot technique' of cultivation was introduced. This involves firstly levelling the land and then surfacing it with a layer of compacted clay, followed by well-rotted manure and finally a layer of well-washed beach sand. The clay prevents water percolating downwards, while the sand prevents evapotranspiration. The manure is replaced every three or four years. In 1962 the first sand plot was covered with a greenhouse, but the plastic explosion did not occur until the mid-1970s.

The typical greenhouse is 25 m long and 3½ m high in the centre and supported by eucalyptus poles and wire. The crops are watered by drip (or trickle) irrigation, which cuts down on evaporation. The plants are dependent on soluble fertilizers and pesticides are added to the water. Crops are mainly grown between October and June (the summer temperatures being too high). The main crops are peppers, cucumbers, courgettes, tomatoes, water melons and flowers, which are transported to the countries of northern Europe by refrigerated lorry. In recent years lettuces have been flown to

the US and Canada. The produce is marketed by co-operatives known as alhondigas (derived from the Arabic word for corn exchange).

Despite its economic success, plasticultura is not without its problems. The biggest difficulty is with water supply. Most supplies come from wells, but the aquifers are becoming exhausted and the remaining water more saline. There are plans to divert water from the High Alpujarras, and even from Central Spain, but this has led to protests by environmentalists and the farmers in the mountains. Desalinization plants may be a solution, but this is an expensive option. Secondly, pesticide residues have built up and some northern European countries have refused to accept some consignments due to high chemical levels. The third problem concerns transportation. There is no rail link westwards, while the road system in Almería, though improving, is still poor. Finally, the rapid growth of plasticultura has led to serious social problems, particularly in the plasticultura centre of El Ejido, including alcoholism, drug abuse, bankruptcies and particularly suicide. Many of the plasticultura farmers are from the hill villages of the Alpujarras, and they have lost their close knit support systems when moving to the coast and have been unable to cope with the sudden wealth and tensions of a highly competitive industry. Many of the farmers now employ illegal immigrants from Africa in the greenhouses, which has led to racial tension in the area.

in fact a rock overhang, shielded by an iron grille, from where you can just about see some drawings of animals and the famous *indalo* sign.

Parque Natural de la Sierra de María Just west of Vélez Blanco is the Parque Natural de Sierra de María, consisting of some 19,000 ha of dolomitic limestone covered with Mediterranean scrub at lower levels and pines and oaks higher up. Its highest point is María, at 2,045 m. It is excellent for wild flowers, particularly orchids in the spring and early summer, the area has a wide range of butterflies including rarities such as the Spanish argus and the Nevada grayling. Red squirrels are not uncommon in the pines. The sierra is noted for its raptors, such as golden eagles, goshawks, buzzards and peregrines, joined in the summer by short toed and booted eagles. There is also a wide range of other birds, with nightingales in the denser scrub and little bustards and stone curlews in the semi-steppe areas. For the best access, take the local road from Vélez Blanco to María. Just past this village is a small road south to the Ermita de la Virgen de la Cabeza. From here there are tracks leading up into the higher parts of the sierra.

West of Almería

Eight kilometres west of Almería is Aguadulce, a long-established and sedate holiday resort, originally the domain of weekenders from Almería, but with increasingly more international clientele. There is a large marina, a tree-lined promenade backing a beach of rather gritty sand and a range of mainly low rise apartment blocks and hotels.

Aguadulce

From Aguadulce, leave the N340 and follow the coast road to Roquetas de Mar. This was originally a small agricultural and fishing village. The port still operates, but the fishing boats now have to compete with yachts. There are a number of fish restaurants adjacent to the port, but these are surprisingly expensive, considering their location. The main development has been 3 km to the south, where a huge new resort has been built, known as Playa Serena, with a collection of package tour high rise hotels, apart hotels and apartments.

Roquetas de Mar
Colour map 5, grid B6
Population: 40,582

The route continues west running between the *invernaderos*, or plastic greenhouses, of the *plasticultura* industry and the coastal dunes, lagoons and salt marsh, until down to the left is the new, purpose-built resort of **Almerimar**. Started by British developers, it suffered from the economic downturn of the early 1990s, but has had its fortunes revived by the Japanese and by the *plasticultura* millionaires from nearby El Ejido who regard it as their playground. The whole complex seems under siege from the acres of plastic surrounding it.

Almerimar, El Ejido & Adra

The road now swings inland to **El Ejido**, the centre of the *plasticultura* industry (see box). It has grown rapidly to become the second largest town in Almería province. developing into a linear conurbation along the N340 of over 5,000 people. Largely unplanned, El Ejido is an ugly place with its convoys of refrigerated lorries carrying fruit and vegetables.

Eighteen kilometres west of El Ejido is the equally depressing **Adra**, whose main claim to fame is that it was the place where Boabdil, the last Moorish King, stayed before leaving Spain for good. Some 20 km inland along the A337 is the small agricultural town of **Berja**, the slopes around covered with orchards and vineyards. Steeped in history, there is a ruined Moorish Alcazaba and some remnants of Moorish baths, while a little to the north is the hermitage of La Virgen de Gádor. Berja's neighbour to the east, **Dalías**, is sited on the Roman town of Murgis.

Background

11

Background

History

Located at the junction of land and sea routes, Andalucía has always been open to invasion and colonization. The influence of this settlement often spread to the rest of the Iberian peninsula, as in the case of the Moors. In the 15th century the role was reversed as Andalucía sent sailors and explorers on their conquests of the Americas.

Europe's oldest human remains, probably dating from one to two million years ago, were found in 1976 in Orce, Granada province. The caves of Andalucía have revealed further considerable evidence of prehistoric inhabitants. A female skull found in a cave in Gibraltar has been dated as Neanderthal. (Its significance was not realized at the time, otherwise we might have been talking about 'Gibraltar Woman' rather than 'Neanderthal Man'). In Palaeolithic times, homo sapiens reached the area. The caves of Nerja and the cave at Pileta, near Ronda in Málaga province, both have fine cave paintings which give an indication of the way of life of those times. In the Neolithic period, the cave paintings at Vélez Blanco, Almería province, have been dated at around 4000 BC. The remains of the Chalcolithic settlement at Los Millares near Almería show that 1,000 years later metal was being used for weapons and utensils. The dolmens at Antequera in Málaga province also probably date from this period.

The prehistoric scene

The Iberians established their kingdom of Tartessus during the first millennium BC, possibly located around the mouth of the Guadalquivir, although its exact location has so far failed to be unearthed by archaeologists. However, evidence of its excellence in gold, silver and copper production can be seen in Sevilla's Museo Arqueológico. It is known that they were literate and had skills in music and art. The most valuable artefact from this time is the **Dama de Basa**, a statue found at Basa in Granada province and believed to date from the fourth century BC.

The Iberians & Tartessians

The Phoenicians came to Andalucía in a trading capacity, establishing coastal ports at Cádiz, their most significant settlement, which they called Gadir, as well as Málaga (Malaka) and Almúñecar (Sexi). They dealt in metals, fish, salt and dyes. Both the Phoenicians and the Tartessians were superseded by the Carthaginians, who set up their capital at Cartagena, Murcia, but eventually occupied the whole of Andalucía.

Phoenicians & Carthaginians

The second Punic War ended the domination of Carthage and the Romans soon occupied completely the Iberian peninsula. Their most southerly province was called **Hispania Baetica**, which was approximately the area of modern Andalucía, with its capital at Córdoba, and this became one of the wealthiest parts of the Roman empire. The Romans developed the mines at Río Tinto in Huelva province and grew a variety of agricultural produce, particularly along the Guadalquivir valley. Their settlement at Baelo Claudia in Cádiz province exported *garum* – a type of fish sauce – throughout the empire. Baetica provided two Roman emperors during this period, Hadrian and Trajan from Itálica, plus philosophers such as Seneca. Other Roman sites include the Necropolis at Carmona and their first Spanish city, Itálica, near Sevilla. Before the decline set in, the Romans had built temples, amphitheatres, aqueducts, baths and a network of fine roads linking the major cities.

    As the Roman domination weakened from the fifth century AD, there were invasions from the north by firstly the **Vandals** (incorporated in the name Andalucía) and later by the **Visigoths**. Although they first brought Christianity to the area, their hold was never strong and they were weakened by internal divisions. By the eighth century the way was open for the Moorish invasion.

Romans & Visigoths

Background

The Moors The first move in the Moorish Conquest took place in 711 when **Tarik**, the governor of Tangier, crossed the straits from North Africa with a force of 7,000 Berbers and defeated the Visigoth ruler King Roderic by the Río Guadalete near Tarifa. Within the decade the invaders conquered most of the peninsula which became part of a vast Muslim empire known as **al-Andalus**, which they then controlled, to a greater or lesser extent, for nearly eight centuries.

When the Ommayyad Dynasty in North Africa was overthrown by the Abbasids, the sole surviving Ommayyad prince, **Abd Al-Rahman**, escaped to al-Andalus and set up an independent Caliphate with its capital at Córdoba, which became one of the largest, wealthiest and most cultured cities in the western world. A power strug-gle within the régime led to civil war after 1008 and the last of the Ommayyad caliphs was expelled in 1031.

Al-Andalus split up into a number of petty principalities or *taifas*, with several of their rulers patrons of high culture and art and who thereby played a crucial role in the transmission of Greek thought, via Arabic, to Europe at the start of the Renais-sance. Córdoba´s importance then became secondary to that of Sevilla.

The *taifas*, however, were caught between the expanding Christian powers to the north and the Islamic revivalism of the **Almoravid** rulers of Morocco, who particu-larly objected to the *taifa* rulers' payment of tribute to the Christians. In 1086 Almoravid troops crossed the Straits to help the *taifas* defeat Castilla. The newcom-ers then overthrew the taifa rulers and re-established unity in al-Andalus. The defeat of the Almoravids in 1145 by the **Almohads** led to fresh invasions both from the Christian kingdoms and from Africa. The high point of Almohad power in al-Andalus was reached around 1200 with a series of attacks on Castilla and Aragón, but in 1212 the severe defeat by Christian forces at Las Navas de Tolosa was the beginning of the end of Moorish domination in Spain.

How should one evaluate the Moorish period of occupation? The main point to remember is that it was not so much a military conquest as a benevolent occupa-tion, typified by a tolerant attitude towards other religions. Jews and Christians (known as *Mozarabs*) were allowed to retain their faiths, while their places of wor-ship were rarely destroyed. From the social point of view, the Moors – who in fact were not only Arab muslims who occupied Spain but also Berbers, Syrians and Egyptians - made a tremendous impact not only in scholarship, but in trade, cul-ture and urban life. Their agriculture was aided by complex irrigation projects, which were more sophisticated versions of the existing Roman models. It is their architecture, however, which has left the strongest influence, as shown in the impressive monuments – including palaces, mosques and baths - in Córdoba, Granada and Sevilla.

The Christian Reconquest The reconquest of Moorish lands by the Christians was a gradual process and advances intermittent. The frontier between the opposing forces was always chang-ing and this accounts for the place name 'de la frontera' which is common in south-west Andalucía. After the crucial battle of Las Navas de Tolosa in 1212, the Christian forces led by Fernando III (el Santo) quickly captured Córdoba in 1236 and then Sevilla in 1248. Only Granada survived as a Nasrid Kingdom for, remarkably, another 250 years, protected by a chain of castles and paying heavy tribute to Castilla. The decline of **Marinid** power in Morocco after 1415 left Granada without allies. The marriage of Isabel I of Castilla and Fernando V of Aragón - known as Los Reyes Católicos, or the Catholic Monarchs - united the two Christian kingdoms and paved the way for the final assault on Granada, led by Gonzalo Fernández de Córdoba, El Gran Capitán, who had developed the Christian army into a large and effective force. The advance culminated in a nine-month siege in 1491. In January 1492, Boabdil sur-rendered the keys of the city and fled to the Alpujarras.

The Spanish Inquisition

The Spanish Inquisition was established in 1480 by King Fernando V and Queen Isabel I, Los Reyes Católicos, with the authority of the Pope. It was introduced initially to meet the supposed threat posed by the conversos, Jews who through coercion or social pressure had converted to Christianity. Many were suspected of continued secret observance of Judaism. Later attention turned to converted Muslims or Moriscos and in the 1520s to suspected Protestants. Its authority did not extend to non-Christians. Within a few years of the founding of the Inquisition, the Papacy relinquished virtually all supervision to the sovereigns. Thus the Spanish inquisition became more an instrument of the state than of the church, furthering the absolute monarchy and abridging the power of the nobles.

The Spanish Inquisition continued actively in the time of Felipe II, who further oppressed the Protestants, particularly in Holland and the Moriscos. The latter rebelled in 1568 and after suppressing the revolt, Felipe expelled the entire group, to the great detriment of the country.

The inquisition, with powers to investigate and try suspects, worked through tribunals in the principal towns and was controlled by an Inquisitor General appointed by the king. The harshest tribunal was in Sevilla, seen as a hotbed of conversos, where 20,000 cases were tried between 1481 and 1524.

Each region was visited annually by an Inquisitor who published an Edict of Faith, a type of questionnaire for all adult Christians, covering their beliefs and requiring them to report known heretics. Those accused of serious crimes were imprisoned to await investigation and trial, which could take years. The accusers were never named, but the prisoner could produce a list of his or her enemies whose evidence was supposedly ignored. The most notorious inquisitor was Tomás de Torquemada, who was said to have executed thousands of supposed heretics.

Although there were controls on interrogation methods, three forms of torture were allowed - the rack, the hoist and water torture. Those who confessed were given lighter sentences. Various fates awaited those who were found guilty – absolution, flogging, fines, galley service, confiscation of property or being burned at the stake. As a consolation, those who confessed after being sentenced to death were strangled before being burnt.

About 5,000 people were executed up to 1530, thereafter the Inquisition's ferocity declined and between 1560 and 1700 only 500 death sentences were passed from 50,000 cases. The Inquisition was not suppressed in Spain, however, until 1834.

Although Muslims were promised the right to practise their religion the expulsion of the Jews in 1492 indicated religious intolerance in Spain. Forcible mass baptism of Muslims began in 1499, provoking a quickly suppressed rebellion. Muslims in Granada had the choice of conversion or emigration on unfavourable terms (with children and property to be left behind). In 1502 the same policy was extended to Castilla and in 1525 to Aragón. Many converted Muslims, known as Moriscos, practised their faith in secret. In 1609 Felipe III expelled all Moriscos. The 300,000 people who left included many of the country's finest craftsmen and artisans (Moors who had worked on Christian buildings producing an architectural style known as Mudéjar). Thus the 780-year Muslim presence in Iberia came to an end, leaving its firm imprint on the Spanish language, in place names and in the few remaining examples of its architectural greatness.

The fall of Granada in 1492 coincided with the first voyage of Christopher Colum - bus to the New World. Over the next three decades there was a systematic explora - tion and exploitation of the Americas, followed later by colonisation. Power in Andalucía now moved to Sevilla, where the riches of the New World were brought ashore. Little of this wealth, however, found its way to the ordinary people.

Background

Disraeli's Andalucía

It is not widely known that Benjamin Disraeli, the 19th-century British prime minister and favourite of Queen Victoria, visited Andalucía as a young man. His experiences there were vivid, and, he claimed, coloured his future life.

Disraeli's early years were not distinguished. His proposed career in law did not work out and his first political novel, Vivien Grey, was only moderately successful. He was constantly in debt and often on the verge of mental breakdown - which he described as 'the great enemy'. The solution seemed to be a change of scene. Financed by the father of a publishing friend, he decided on a tour of the Middle East.

Aged 26, Disraeli set out from Falmouth on a steam packet, HMS Messenger, in 1830. The first port of call was Gibraltar, which was meant to be a brief stopover, but in the event he stayed several weeks and the Rock was his base for numerous sallies into Andalucía. He made the Griffiths Hotel his base.

Disraeli, at this stage of his life, was at the height of his dandyism and his foppish demeanour was the talk of the officers on the Rock. Disraeli used two canes, one for the day and one for the evening, changing with a flourish at the night gun. The evening paseo was, of course, much to his liking.

Disraeli's first venture into Spain was a journey on horseback to Ronda. It was in the Sierra de Ronda that he had his first encounter with bandits, describing in a letter to his father how they 'commit no personal violence, but lay you out on the ground and clean out your pockets'. Disraeli had a certain sympathy with the brigands, writing to his sister that 'robbery had become more honourable than war, in as much as the robber is paid and the soldier is in arrear'.

Then came a longer excursion, travelling from Gibraltar to Cádiz on horseback in 2 days, via Tarifa and Medina Sidonia. Disraeli was captivated by Cádiz, with its white houses and clear air. He left reluctantly, travelling up the Guadalquivir by steamer to Sevilla. The intense heat was good for his constitution and he loved relaxing in the shady patios. He was introduced to the paintings of Murillo ('the most original of artists') and saw his first bullfight, which he described as 'a magnificent, but barbarous spectacle'.

In Córdoba he was suitably impressed with the Moorish mosque. The next leg of his journey was to Granada, through even more dangerous bandit country. Granada was the climax of his tour and he was surprised to find that the Alhambra was not a ruin, but in remarkably good condition.

Disraeli returned to Gibraltar via Málaga, where he saw his first sugar cane growing. Catching up on his letter writing, he described Andalucían women with great enthusiasm – 'her eyes gleam rather than sparkle, she speaks with a quick vivacity but in sweet tones, and there is in all her carriage, particularly when she walks, a certain dignified grace which never leaves her'. He depicted the fan as the most wonderful part of the whole female scene, calling it a 'magical instrument'. He enthused – 'now she unfurls it with the slow pomp and the conscious elegance of a peacock. Now she flutters it with all the languor of a listless beauty, now with the liveliness of a vivacious one. Now in the midst of a very tornado, she closes it with a whirr which makes you start'.

Disraeli was less enthusiastic about Spanish cuisine, noting that garlic and bad oil preponderated. He liked its freshness and acknowledged that it had been good for his health.

The vitality of Andalucía had left its mark on him and many of his experiences were reproduced in his future novels. In Coningsby, there is a character called Sidonia, while the heroine, Edith Millbank, is of Spanish descent and frequently plays the guitar. Henrietta Temple contains 'a serenade of Seville', while in Contarini Fleming there is a vivid description of a bullfight.

The 16th and 17th centuries found Spain, and Andalucía in particular, in the dol - **16th to 20th**
drums. The Inquisition had led eventually to the expulsion of the Jews and the **centuries**
Moriscos, which created a void in the labour force and in commerce and trade (see
box above). Financially in huge debt, despite the New World riches, Spain lost its
possessions in France and the Netherlands.

When Felipe V, a Bourbon, succeeded to the Spanish throne in 1700, a rival claim -
ant, Archduke Charles of Austria, was supported by British forces, leading to the War
of Spanish Succession. The war ended in 1713 with the Treaty of Utrecht, whereby
Spain lost its territory in Belgium, Luxembourg, Italy and Sardinia. Gibraltar, which
had been taken by the British during the war, was to remain in their hands. The
Bourbon connection meant that Spain was drawn into the Napoleonic Wars and the
Spanish fleet was defeated by Nelson at the battle of Trafalgar, near Cádiz in 1805.
Within three years Napoleon had installed his brother Joseph on the Spanish throne
and the French army set out on a systematic destruction and theft of much of the
country's artistic heritage, which Andalucía was unable to escape. This led to the War
of Independence, when the Spanish initially defeated the French at the Battle of
Bailen in Jaén province. Later, helped by Wellington's army, the French were finally
driven out of Spain. Meanwhile, in 1812, the first democratically elected parliament
was set up in Cádiz and although this was not to last long, the written constitution
was to form the basis of future democracy in Spain.

The remainder of the 19th century saw the political turmoil continue, the further
loss of overseas territories and, in Andalucía, the phylloxera plague which severely hit
the wine and sherry industry.

Protest from the landless peasants in the early years of the century led to calls for **The early 20th**
more regional autonomy and agricultural reform. Spain remained neutral during the **century**
First World War and the post-war recession led to disillusionment with the parlia -
mentary government. General Primo de Rivera sensed the feeling of the time and
organized a successful military coup in 1923. He later organized the Ibero-American
Exhibition of 1929 at Sevilla. This was something of a fiasco as it coincided with the
Wall Street crash and led to the collapse of the peseta and Rivera's departure.

The success of the anti-monarchist parties in the 1931 elections forced Alfonso
XIII off the throne and the Second Republic was born. Republican and moderate
Socialist leaders were released from jail to form a government. Two features of the
new constitution were particularly controversial: home rule for the Basque country
and Catalonia, which was opposed by Spanish nationalists and the army; and separa -
tion of the Church and the State which antagonized many Catholics. A mild land
reform and other social policies stirred up right-wing hostility. Disputes between
Socialists and Republicans led to their defeat in the 1933 election and the coming to
power of the right who reversed earlier reforms. Left-wing groups rose in revolt in
1934 and were brutally put down by Franco's Spanish Foreign Legion. The February
1936 general elections were held in an atmosphere of extreme tension. The narrow
victory of the left-wing coalition, the Popular Front, over the right-wing National
Front was followed by the formation of a minority Republican government and
growing violence as Socialists and Anarchists seized land while right-wing leaders
plotted with army officers to seize power.

The military uprising on 18 July 1936 failed in the main cities but succeeded in the **The Civil War**
Catholic North. In Andalucía and Catalonia workers seized land and factories. General
Franco borrowed planes from Hitler to transport his best Spanish troops, then sta -
tioned in Morocco, into Andalucía to crush the revolt before marching them north
towards Madrid. With the accidental death of General Sanjurjo, Franco became
leader of the rebel Nationalist forces.

Background

The Civil War was prolonged and bloody. The Nationalists enjoyed the assistance and weaponry of Nazi Germany and Fascist Italy. Despite the support of the volun - teer International Brigade, the Republicans could not compete against the profes - sional army, and their resistance collapsed in March 1939. The war had turned factions within villages and towns against each other and reprisals on both sides were violent. It was also the first modern war, when aircraft showed their ability to wipe out whole populations, as the example of Guernica showed. Franco 's revenge was harsh and many were sent to labour camps or executed.

Modern Andalucía

Post war Spain Spain was too weak and exhausted to be anything but neutral during the Second World War and post war recovery was slow. Conditions for workers on the land in Andalucía was appalling and many emigrated to Madrid, northern Spain and to Latin America. US aid in the mid-1950s initiated a recovery, but it came with a price - the establishment of US nuclear bases, such as that at Rota in Cádiz province. The aid did, in fact, kickstart the economy, and with the growth of tourism, such as that along Andalucía's Costa del Sol, prosperity began to increase.

When Franco finally died in November 1975, he had already nominated Juan Carlos, grandson of Alfonso XIII, as his successor. He duly became king and success - fully steered Spain towards parliamentary democracy. The centrist Christian Demo - crat UDC party won the elections in 1977 and drafted a new constitution. In 1978 a former Franco minster, Manuel Fraga, founded the conservative Alianza Popular. The King showed his authority in February 1981 when there was an attempted army coup led by Colonel Tejero, whose men stormed the Cortes. When it was clear that the King would not support the plotters, the coup disintegrated, but the crisis had briefly been serious.

The PSOE soundly beat the Alianza Popular in the 1982 general elections and remained in power for the next 13 years. Fraga resigned in 1986 and Antonio Hernández Mancha took over, to be replaced by José María Aznar, who nudged the party towards the centre. In the 1996 general elections, following a number of scandals, the PSOE government of Felipe González was defeated, but Aznar's party could only form a government with the help of various regional parties. Aznar promised to take a firm line on Gibraltar, but it seemed doubtful whether Andalucía would benefit from the new government in the same way that it did from its predecessor. González resigned leadership of the PSOE in 1997 and Joaquín Almunia took over, but he lost the contest for presidential candidate for the 2000 elections to José Borrell.

In the 2000 general elections, Aznar and his party were re-elected by an elector - ate seemingly satisfied with the last four-year term, widely perceived to be the most stable in more than 20 years of democratic government. The PSOE continued as the main opposition party, but the United Left trailed behind, losing considerable ground due to the ill health of their leader, Julio Anguita.

Politics in Although the Constitution emphasizes the 'indissoluble unity of the Spanish nation',
Andalucía it also guarantees the right of autonomy of the nationalities and regions. Andalucía became autonomous in 1982, one of the 17 autonomous communities with its own assembly elected for a four-year term and its own government (the Junta de Andalucía) with powers over local functions including town planning, housing and tourism. Andalucía comprises eight administrative provinces – Almería, Cádiz, Córdoba, Granada, Huelva, Jaén, Málaga and Sevilla, each with a capital city of the same name. These in turn are divided into city, town and village *municipios*, or

municipalities, headed by an elected council and mayor. The council has a certain amount of power locally and control over its own budget, even in small villages. Andalucía benefited financially from the policies of the PSOE, leading to an improved standard of living and a fall in rural poverty. The party´s present and former leaders, Manuel Chaves and Felipe González respectively, and several other leading figures in the national government are from Andalucía, a PSOE stronghold with the party con - trolling the Junta de Andalucía and the larger towns.

Under González's leadership, Spain joined the EU and NATO and enjoyed rapid economic growth accompanied by infrastructure improvements and large scale for - eign investment. In Andalucía, spending on the highly successful Expo in Sevilla in 1992 resulted in the modernization of the region´s infrastructure, particularly of the road and rail network (like the AVE high speed rail link between Madrid and Sevilla) and the major airports.

Tight control of government spending brought down inflation at the cost of increased unemployment and the hostility of the PSOE 's former allies in the unions. Unemployment in Andalucía, however, remained high at around 28%, compared with 18% for Spain as a whole, with many of the jobless agricultural labourers. Whilst landowners benefited from EU grants and modernized their farms, opportunities for day labourers fell due to increased mechanization.

In the 2000 regional elections, the PSOE and its leader, Manuel Chavez, won again with a large majority of the votes, promising major rail improvements and investment for Andalucía, including a a new station for the high-speed AVE train in Málaga. He beat the Popular Party´s candidate, Teófila Martínez, whose campaign pledge centred on fighting Andalucía´s high unemployment through increased training programmes. Also running was the extreme right independent candidate, Jesús Gil.

Government

The Kingdom of Spain, according to the 1978 Constitution, is 'parliamentary monar-chy' in which 'sovereignty resides in the people'. Parliament contains two chambers, the Congress of Deputies with 350 members elected by proportional representation and the Senate with 208 elected members (four from each province) and 49 appointed members. The main political parties are the the the ruling conservative Partido Popular, or Popular Party, the opposition socialist PSOE, and the left-wing United Left.

Gibraltar is a democratically self-governing colony of the UK though its territory is claimed by Spain, for which the dispute over the Rock is long-running and bitterly contested. Border controls continue to exist between Spain and Gibraltar.

Economy

Agriculture

Despite the advent of mass tourism and a degree of industrialization in the cities of the region, farming is still the economic backbone of Andalucía. The variety and mildness of the climate combined with generally reliable rainfall and generous surface water flows provide a considerable, albeit increasingly overstretched, irri-gation potential. Irrigated lands provide a series of world famous products - Sevilla's oranges, lemons, grapes for wine and sherry from Jerez, the olive crop which is the largest in the world - in addition to a wide range of vegetables, cotton and fruits.

Away from the lowlands, farming is hard and until recent years the mainly self sufficient cultivators and herders of the sierras were very poor, eking a living from poor soils. The higher, marginal environments have now been abandoned as fami-lies move to employment in the towns and tourist complexes. Livestock is impor-tant, Andalucía producing cattle in great numbers for meat and milk as well as

Background

specimens for bullfighting. Most farms keep sheep and despite conservation laws, flocks of goats still graze (and often overgraze) the hillsides. There are approximately 800,000 cattle, four million sheep and 2.25 million pigs in Andalucía.

The most flourishing sector of farming is that of the private estates or *latifundios*, generally in large holdings. Average farm sizes of commercial enterprises on the lowlands are in the region of 1,000 ha and on the uplands more than 5,000 ha with a large range of sizes in both areas. In the Mediterranean coastlands the farms are small and intensively cultivated on the Huerta model, inherited from a Moorish tradition, in which horticultural techniques are used to produce high quality and high value crops for the local markets and for export. The citrus, vine and olive districts use similar techniques but for virtual monocultures over fairly wide areas. There are new plantings of orange and lemon groves, developing the specialisms introduced by the Moors centuries ago. Olive cultivation is tending to decline slightly as a result of competition from cheaper producers in North Africa. Spain has the world's third largest grape harvest. Although Andalucía is well-known for table grapes, it has few remarkable wines and vintages, except for those of Jerez where the bulk are converted into sherry, much for export. A fall in the popularity of sherry in the UK has adversely affected the prosperity of the Jerez farming region, despite the fact that fino is a hugely popular Andalucían drink.

The main national crops in which Andalucía has an approximate 20% share are barley (9.4 million tonnes), grapes (6½ million tonnes) and olives (2.2 million tonnes).

The most remarkable agricultural development in recent years has been the growth of *plasticultura* - fruit and vegetables grown in plastic greenhouses - mainly in the province of Almería. Grown with the aid of drip feed irrigation, the produce is transported by refrigerated lorries to destinations throughout northern Europe (see box, page 402).

Energy & petroleum Spain is able to produce little of her energy requirements. It has some poor quality coal available in Asturias (but none in Andalucía) providing some 36 million tonnes a year, but is otherwise import-dependent. Imports of crude oil run at 50 million tonnes a year against a domestic output of seven million tonnes. An active subsidized oil refining industry is located at Algeciras, exporting oil products as well as supplying the domestic market. A major experiment in the use of wind-generated electricity can be seen on the heights immediately inland from the Straits of Gibraltar. Many propeller type generators have been installed to catch the strong wind funnelling in from the Atlantic. A small amount of hydroelectric power is produced in the mountains north of Málaga.

Economic plans Regional development plans exist as master plans for each of the subdistricts within Andalucía. They are mainly indicative land use plans for urban areas provided to act as guidelines for the control of building permissions. There is great variation in the scope and level of the provisions of the local plans. In very recent years, local authorities have become more conscious of the need to improve and protect the environment to prevent the complete destruction of the coast through the over building of hotels and tourist sites. The controls are belated and much of the coast is already severely blighted by ill considered property development, much of it incomplete, and by the crowding of properties onto the beaches. National laws *(leyes de la costa)* protecting beaches are gradually taking hold and might save some residual areas from encroachment but local authorities seem to have little resolve in enforcing the laws.

Industry Industry is an important element of the economy in Andalucía. The major centre is Sevilla, where there is a highly diversified industrial manufacturing base including food processing, brewing, textiles, light engineering and energy related plants.

Elsewhere in the urban centres of the Guadalquivir - Cádiz, Chiclana, San Fernando and to a lesser extent, Córdoba - there are food processing and packing plants and other smaller industries which service the thriving agricultural sector. In Málaga there are breweries and consumer goods industries together with plants making items for the tourist sector. The tourist industry is large and Andalucía earned approximately 10% of Spain's total income in this sector. Gibraltar is gradually developing an economy based on international financial services.

After joining the EU in 1986, Spain had one of Europe's fastest growing economies with growth averaging 4.1% over the following five years. Andalucía mirrored this national trend, experiencing a boom in land prices, wages and employment until 1991. Large flows of foreign finance, particularly from the EU, came to Spain and much of it was invested in projects and properties on the Mediterranean coast, especially in Andalucía. There was a slump in the tourist trade and building industry between 1991 and 1994, but by 1995, recovery was underway. Today, Spain's economy is the fifth largest in Europe and the trend in growth in Andalucía has also been upward again, with some areas of Andalucía seeing a property boom. Tourism is the biggest growth sector, while agriculture is in decline. The advent of the Euro could be partly responsible for this, with many black market pesetas in circulation necessitating cash purchases of property, as well as goods and services. **Economic trends**

Unemployment remains higher than the national average, at 22.5 % in Andalucía, compared to 12.8% for Spain. The introduction of the Euro on 1 January 2002 went smoothly.

Culture

People

Considering the vast number of settlers and invaders who have come to the region during historical times, it is not surprising that in appearance it is hard to describe a 'typical' Andalucían. Although predominantly dark haired and olive skinned, fair haired people are not uncommon, particularly in Cádiz province.

The family is still the strongest influence on everyday life, with the mother the dominant figure, but the Catholic church is less authoritative than in the past. The home is a private place and strangers are rarely invited in. Even friends are met on the street or in a bar or restaurant. Noise is an everyday fact of lifeChildren are often over-indulged, while the elderly and the handicapped are well cared for and respected.

Above all the Andalucíans love their leisure. Extended weekends and holidays are enjoyed with intensity. So-called religious events such as *fiestas* and *romerías* are times for eating, drinking, fireworks and dancing. The highlight of all the festivities comes at *Semana Santa* or Holy Week, with its eerie processions. Each small town will have its *feria* or fair, which although originally agricultural, has now lost this purpose. The Feria de Abril in Sevilla is the best known of these jamborees, lasting for a full week during the second half of April.

Andalucían society has changed rapidly over the past 20 years, particularly in the urban areas. For the wealthy landowners and aristocracy little has altered, but for many ordinary people the opportunity for upward social mobility is there and the new-found affluence is clear to see.

Flamenco

To the outside world flamenco is synonymous with Spain as a whole, particularly the colourful dance and sanitized song styles that were promoted during the Franco dic - tatorship. Whilst attractive to the influx of tourists to the country in the post-war era, these politically uncontentious forms threatened to damage the art form perma - nently. Although flamenco dance, particularly *sevillanas* (from Sevilla), remains the most popular element, it was thanks to gypsy singers such as Antonio Mairena that some of the older forms of flamenco have been rediscovered.

Flamenco is, in fact, primarily from Andalucía. Jerez de la Frontera is often called the *cuna* or cradle of flamenco, but it really developed within the triangle bounded by Cádiz, Córdoba and Sevilla, particularly in their gypsy barrios like Sevilla´s Triana. As the region was the last to be retaken in the Reconquest, it´s unsurprising that there should be Moorish elements. But flamenco is a hybrid art with diverse influ - ences and its exact roots have attracted much discussion and research. What seems certain is that its origins are from minority groups at the time of the Christian Reconquest; as well as the Moors, the Jews and gypsies were also important, as well as Indian and other European influences.

Although there is some suggestion that the gypsies arrived with the Arab armies in the eighth century, there was mass migration in the 14th and 15th cen- turies. Gypsies arrived in Europe after a long journey that started in Hindustan, bringing with them non-western chord structures and progressions that devel- oped into the distinctive Phrygian mode, the sound associated with flamenco today. The 12-beat *compás* cycles of flamenco and the hand movements of dance are thought to derive from Indian ragas and dance respectively. In addition to this, the sound of the songs is possibly reminiscent of Jewish religious song.

The word itself possibly emerged when the Jews migrated to Flanders where they were able to live and sing freely. When they came to Spain they were known as 'Fleming-goes'. (Other researchers suggest that the name has Arab origins.) There they were able to practise their religion and sing openly, and these became known as flamenco songs to their poor relations in Spain. Later, however, the term was used to refer to anything scandalous and in bad taste.

As outsiders, anything the gypsies did was frowned upon. Although Carlos III officially gave them equal rights in the 18th century, they remained on the borders of society. There was a degree of improvement for them, however, and some were able to afford guitars, giving a new style to their music. Much like North American blues, flamenco song was an expression of poverty, hardship, oppression, grief and a voice of protest. Until the 18th century the music was not a public display, but confined to social gatherings of gypsy friends and family as an impromptu art form. Gradually, though, they were hired by the rich to sing at parties or *juergas*, and this eventually led to the opening of *cafés cantantes* or music cafés in the sec- ond half of the 19th century. Dance and guitar continued to gain popularity and flamenco's first professional star performers were born, including El Planeta, El Fillo and El Loco Mateo.

Although the composer Manuel de Falla organized a contest in Granada in 1922 to promote authentic *cante jondo*, between the 1920s and 1950s real flamenco fell into decline and the glossy stage shows emerged. It was only due to artists such as Antonio Mairena, Manuel Torre, Tomás Pavón and Manolo Caracol performing at private gypsy gatherings that the older forms survived. During the flamenco renaissance in the post-Franco era outstanding dancers moved to the stages of large theatres and concert halls, flamenco festivals emerged and other stars, such as guitarist Paco de Lucía and the late singer-songwriter Camarón de la Isla, went on the international circuit.

Born in Algeciras, Paco de Lucía is a non-gypsy who started out by accompanying singers such as Fosforito and La Niña de los Peines, as well as having a partnership with Camarón. But gradually de Lucía began to play solo and it was his 1974 recording *Entre dos Aguas* that brought him worldwide fame. This was a result of mixing various forms of *cantes chicos* with Latin American influences, including rumbas, colombianas and milongas. Since then he has collaborated with musicians such as Chick Corea, John McCloughlin and Al di Meola, combining flamenco with rock and jazz. Camarón also developed an eclectic modernised sound and from the 1980s was mainly accompanied by José Fernández, more popularly known as Tomatito. Camerón died of cancer in 1992 but left a legacy of recordings that are still massively popular today.

Flamenco theatre has become increasingly popular, with performers often trained in ballet and music schools. The latest sensation is Joaquín Cortés, who although a gypsy, has graduated from ballet school and scandalized the flamenco purists by dancing bare-chested. Nevertheless, his flamenco stage show, *Pasión Gitana*, which has as its theme the gypsy culture, plays to full houses wherever it goes.

Flamenco has become linked with rock, salsa and Latin American music and introduced new instruments such as the flute and saxophone. Flamenco rock groups such as Ketama and Pata Negra, developed in the 1990s what has become known as 'flamenco nueva'.

Other artists to look out for include the male singers Enrique Morente, El terremoto de Jerez, Manolo Caracol, El Agujetas, José Menese, Fosforito, El Chocolate and Arcangel and female singers Carmen Linares, La Perla de Cádiz, Estrella Morente and Mayte Martín, and guitarists Ramón Montoya and Manolo de Huelva. Also check out Antonio Gades' flamenco dance troupe, particularly in the film *Carmen* directed by Carlos Saura, as well as Joaquín Cortés, Isabel Bayón, Ana Mari Bueno, Mercho Esmeralda, Milagros Mengíbar, the Carmen Cortés dance company, El Farruquito, El Güito and Manuela Carrasco. A good source of music is www.flamenco-world.com

There are three elements of flamenco. Firstly, there is el cante or the song, often performed in an agonized, melancholic, way full of despair and lamentations on the lot of the discriminated minorities. Secondly, there is el toque or the guitar, which is a much lighter instrument than the classical guitar, to accompany the singer and establish a rapport with listeners. During the 20th century, guitar playing developed as a solo form of flamenco. Lastly, there is el baile or the dance, performed by an individual or a pair. Since the second half of the 20th century, group flamenco folk dances have developed such as the Sevillanas and the Malagueñas and flamenco dancing has moved into the theatre with the advent of flamenco ballet.

Flamenco forms

In addition, there is el jaleo, involving percussion sounds produced by shouts, finger snapping, clapping and footwork. Castañets, incidentally, are not part of the traditional jaleo.

Within these forms, flamenco can be divided into four basic types: tonás, siguiriyas, soleá and tangos, which are characterised by their *compás* or form, rhythm and accentuation, and are either *cante jondo* (emotionally deep)/*cante grande* (big) or *cante ligero* (lighter)/*cante chico* (small). Tonás is the most primitive form of flamenco and includes deblas, martinetes and carceleras, which are all sung *a palo seco* (unaccompanied) and, being about unhappiness, are *cante jondo*. Siguiriyas developed in part from deblas and so are also sad songs (about death of loved ones), relying on a rough or *rajao* voice. Soleás and its evolved forms of alegrías, bulerías, caracoles, romeras and serranas, deal with unhappy love, and the tangos (tanguillos and tientos) have a lilting *compás*. Although these still exist, today there are many fandangos, with influences from the rest of Spain, and which all vary regionally - mineras, tarantos, granainas, malagueñas, cartageneras.

Architecture

Domestic architecture Although the majority of Andalucíans live in high or low rise apartments in the suburbs of towns or cities, a significant minority still live in the older parts of urban areas or in country towns and villages, where a distinct style of architecture still remains and indeed has been adapted for some of the better modern *urbanizaciones* in the tourist areas.

The style owes much to the Moors, but is also influenced by the climate, which leads to subtle differences within Andalucía. Villages have narrow, winding alleyways more suited to the donkey than the car, which often lead to small squares or *plazuelas*, sometimes with a fountain or communal washing areas. Houses are small and whitewashed to reflect the sun, with only small openings on the outside. Within the house, there is often an inner courtyard or *patio*, around which family life centres. Many patios will have a small fountain playing, while the walls are hung with pot plants, particularly geraniums, and are often partly covered in decorated ceramic tiles or *azulejos*. Roofs are either flat or gently sloping and pantiled. The flat roof of one house may be the terrace of another, where fruit and washing can be dried. Windows are usually covered with iron grilles or *rejas*, allowing security, but at the same time letting air circulate. Ground floor rooms with high ceilings are often used as bedrooms in the summer, while sunny top floor rooms are warmer in the winter - the continuance of an old Moorish tradition.

The influence of climate is obvious everywhere. In the drier areas, such as Almería, flat roofs predominate. In the southeast of Granada province, many still live in caves, with their constant temperatures throughout the year. In wetter, mountainous regions, tiled roofs are the norm, while stonework tends to replace whitewashed plaster and chimneys put in an appearance. One of the most distinctive forms of domestic architecture is to be found in the Alpujarras on the southern slopes of the Sierra Nevada. Here, despite the high rainfall and snow, roofs are flat. They are composed of thin stone slabs covered with shards of slate. The circular chimneys with their mushroom-like cappings reflect the need for fires for much of the year.

In the more prosperous rural areas, particularly in the west of Andalucía, are large agricultural estates known as *latifundios*, dating back to Roman times and carried on by the Moors. At the centre of the estate is a large farmstead, known as a *cortijo,* in the corn growing areas and a *hacienda* in the olive and wine growing regions. They are often quite palatial, with a central courtyard surrounded by accommodation. There were, additionally, living quarters for seasonal workers, stables, stores, oil mills and wine cellars. The main entry to the *cortijo* was often impressive, with a large studded doorway topped with a bell tower. The specially planted palm trees add a note of distinction as well as shade.

Cathedrals Each Andalucían provincial capital city has a cathedral and while Sevilla is undoubted the most stunning, they are all worth an inspection. For British or French visitors, however, a first glance at an Andalucían cathedral gives an impression of disorientation. In Britain the design of a cathedral concentrated on length order to give the observer a vista. In France, it was height which provided the vista. Well known patterns of window tracery, columns and arches place the building into clear architectural styles, such as Norman, Early English, Decorated and Perpendicular. The windows make the interiors well lit with natural light, showing stained glass off to good effect, while the Dissolution of the Monasteries meant that much of the internal ornamentation and statuary were removed leaving an essential simplicity.

Andalucían cathedrals, on the other hand, are nearly always square in shape and as a result do not attain great height. Pillars and arches abound and some buildings may have as many as five parallel naves. This shape is explained by the fact that they were usually built on the site of a mosque, occupying its rectangular ground plan.

Furthermore, the High Altar and the choir, or *coro*, are centrally placed and even walled in, forming the *capilla mayor*, so that the general impression is of one building contained within another. This does not give any sort of vista, so that the size of the building is rarely appreciated. Sevilla cathedral, for example, is the largest cathedral in the world (according to the Guinness Book of Records), but you don´t get that impression when standing in the interior. Around English cathedrals, there is usually an open space - the 'Cathedral Close'. Andalucían cathedrals, however, are invariably hemmed in by houses and other buildings.

Another strong immediate feeling is one of gloom, due to the lack of natural light. Windows tend to be few and small. In coastal cathedrals, such as Almería, this was because they had a defensive function, as the inhabitants fled to the cathedral when raiding Berbers approached the city. This also explains the paucity of good quality stained glass. The lack of windows also makes the identification of architectural styles more tricky. Most cathedrals have some **Mudéjar** elements, which were passed on by the Moorish craftsmen who stayed to work for the Christians. The latter introduced the **Gothic** style, which in Spain was subdivided into **Fernandine** and **Isabelline** after the Catholic Monarchs. During Renaissance times the **Plateresque** style, which covered surfaces in richly decorated stonework, was predominant in Andalucía. It gained its name from its resemblance to the work of silversmiths. A much plainer type of Renaissance work was known as **Herreran**, after the architect who designed the Escorial in Madrid. Finally, there was the **Baroque**, flourishing in the 17th and 18th centuries and perhaps the dominating style in Andalucían cathe - drals. **Churrigueresque**, named after José Churriguera who was its main exponent, was a particularly flamboyant form of Baroque.

It´s hard not to be impressed by the ornamentation of the cathedral interiors. They are full of statuary, silverwork, and decorated iron grills or *rejas*, plus rich art work and imposing tombs (which is indeed a feature of the smallest church). The central feature is always the *retablo*, the altarpiece behind the High Altar, which is invariably rich in carving and dripping with gold leaf. Look too, for the effigies, such as the Virgen, which are carried on the *pasos* on the Easter processions.

Land and environment

Andalucía is some 87,000 sq km in area, occupying 17% of Spain and being the larg - est of Spain´s so-called autonomous communities. It is larger than countries such as Austria or Ireland. Its northern boundary is formed by a range of mountains, known as the Sierra Morena in the west and their eastward extension of the Sierra Madrona and the Sierra Aguila. The one major pass through these mountains to the interior of Spain is the Despeñaperros Pass, which is followed by both road and railway routes. To the west, Andalucía borders with the Portuguese Algarve and the Atlantic. The southern boundary provided by the Mediterranean is interrupted only by the small peninsula of Gibraltar.

Background

Geography

Andalucía falls neatly into four zones:

Dominated by the Sierra Morena, this region rises to rugged hills topping in places 1,000 m. This region is the one most rarely visited by tourists and has suffered con - siderable depopulation during the present century.

The northern mountains

☞ Who´s who in wildlife conservation

The **organizations** involved in conservation are the following:

ICONA This is the National Institute for Nature Conservation, a branch of the Ministerio de Agricultura, Pesca y Alimentación (the Ministry of Agriculture, Fisheries and Food), based in Madrid. Many Spanish environmentalists consider the title to be a misnomer, as the organization is dominated by engineers, rather than nature conservationists. Fortunately, it only controls national parks and in Andalucía there are only two.

AMA This is the Agencia de Medio Ambiente, the environmental agency of the Junta de Andalucía, or the autonomous regional government, and it has done a marvellous job in giving some kind of protected status to all key wildlife sites of the area. Its educational efforts in making Andalucíans more environmentally aware are under recognized. Contacted AMA at Avenida Eritaña 1, 41071 Sevilla, T954627202.

SEO The Sociedad Española de Ornitología is the Spanish birdwatching equivalent of Britain's RSPB or the US AOU. Based in Madrid, it has branches in Andalucía and has recently opened a splendid new hide and interpretation centre overlooking the marshes at El Rocio, in the Parque Nacional Coto Doñana in Huelva province. It can be contacted at the Facultad de Biología, University of Madrid, 28040, Madrid, T915493554.

The types of **reserves** are the following:

Reserva Natural (Natural Reserve) Equivalent to the British SSSI (Sites of Special Scientific Interest), these are small scale affairs such as lagoons or small patches of woodland. Activities which threaten the survival of the ecosystem are banned.

Paraje Natural (Natural Locality) Similar to the above, but generally protecting a wider area of scenic or ecological interest.

Parque Natural (Natural Park) Covers a large area of, say, mountains or coastline and prevents unsuitable development, while allowing traditional activities, such as charcoal burning or cork cutting, to continue. Recreational and educational facilities are provided, with interpretation centres, hides and wardens. Examples include the Odiel marshlands in Huelva province, El Torcal limestone complex in Málaga province and the Cabo de Gata coastal headland in Almería province.

Parque Nacional (National Park) The top of the conservation ladder, with only nine national parks in the whole of Spain, and two in Andalucía – the incomparable Coto Doñana in Huelva province and the Sierra Nevada in Granada. These are areas of international importance with restricted access and strong control of human activities and are administered by central government.

The Guadalquivir Valley Derived from the Arabic *Wad Al-Kebir*, the valley and its delta form flatlands, rich in alluvial soils and with abundant water for irrigation. The river itself is the fifth longest in Spain, rising in the mountains of Jaén province and flowing for 657 km through Córdoba and Sevilla to enter the Atlantic via the marshlands of the Coto Doñana in Huelva province. In Roman times, when the river was known as Betis, it was navigable as far as Córdoba, but now ships can only reach as far inland as Sevilla. The valley was extensively farmed in Roman times, while the Moors introduced complex irrigation systems. It remains today the hub of Andalucía's agricultural production of cereals and fruit. The delta itself has only comparatively recently been reclaimed from marshes to permanent agriculture and water taken for farming has seriously lowered levels in the Parque Nacional Coto Doñana, one of Europe's foremost wetland nature reserves.

The southern sierras These may divided into the **Sistema Subbetico**, which rises to its highest point of 3,398 m in the Parque Natural de Cazorla in northeast Andalucía, and the **Sistema**

Penibético in the south, with Spain's highest mainland mountain, Mulhacén at 3,482 m, in Europe's most southerly mainland skiing resort in the Sierra Nevada range. The lower slopes in the northern sierras are dotted with olive groves, particu - larly in Jaén and Córdoba provinces, while the spectacular higher slopes have a high concentration of protected areas.

Although narrow and discontinuous, the coastal plain has the highest density of population in Andalucía, due to the growth of the tourist industry. From Málaga westwards to Gibraltar, the Costa del Sol has developed into a linear conurbation, swollen by tourists throughout the year and providing employment for Andalucíans, thereby depopulating the interior. West of Gibraltar to the Portuguese border, the Costa de la Luz is less developed due its distance from a major international airport (although the expansion of Jerez airport may change this in future) and its fierce *levante* wind – this, however, also accounts for it being one of the world's top three windsurf spots. In Almería province, the coastal plain is wider and is extensively used for the production of fruit and vegetables grown under plastic and transported all over northern Europe. The Granada stretch of the coast, the Costa Tropical, is moun - tainous and, like the Costa de la Luz, its distance from a major airport has meant that tourism is relatively underdeveloped.

The coastal plain

The Guadalquivir has a large number of tributaries, from the mountains both to the north and to the south. It is the dominant river system of Andalucía, draining the entire region, with the exception of the generally short south flowing rivers which descend rapidly to the Mediterranean. The region's large number of reservoirs mean that with normal winter rainfall, precipitation is usually sufficient to cope with the demands of the dry Andalucían summer. During the period 1990-1995, however, the winter rains failed. In addition, Expo 92 in Sevilla, caused severe strains on water sup - plies, so that water rationing became common. But since 1996, winter rains have

Rivers & water supply

Wildlife sites in Andalucía

1 River Odiel Marshes
2 Cota Doñana
3 Sierra Morena
4 Bay of Cádiz
5 Barbate Cliffs / Cape Trafalgar
6 Sierra de la Plata
7 Playa de los Lances
8 Tarira / Gibraltar migration points

9 Laguna de Medina
10 Los Alcornocales
11 Serranía de Ronda
12 El Torcal
13 Laguna de Fuente de Piedra
14 Lagunas del sur de Córdoba
15 Sierra Nevada
16 Alpujarras

17 Sierra de Cazorla
18 Sierra Mágina
19 Albufera de Adra
20 Salinas de Roquetas
21 Desierto de Tabernas
22 Cabo de Gata
23 Gibraltar Upper Rock

been normal. Mindful of the effect that this situation could have on the tourist industry, many towns on the Costa del Sol are considering the construction of desalinization plants. This is not a recent problem - the remains of both Roman and Moorish
water channels and aqueducts can be seen in many parts of Andalucía even today.

Land tenure   Andalucía is a region of large farms and estates, especially away from the Mediterranean coast. The system derives from the Reconquest when land was redistrib-
uted in huge plots or *latifundia*. The often absent landlords of these estates
created appalling conditions for the farm workers or *jornaleros*, who were often
hired on a daily basis - a situation which has only marginally improved today. Elsewhere there are middle-ranking private farms or *fincas*. On the poorer land, farms
are often no more than small holdings used for self sufficiency and some small
scale commercial cropping.

Climate

In an area which extends 400 km from west to east and an average of 225 km from
north to south and with altitudes varying from sea level to 3,482 m in the Sierra
Nevada, it is hardly surprising that there are wide variations in climate. In fact,
Andalucía is home to both the wettest place in Spain, the Sierra de Grazalema, and
the driest place, the Cabo de Gata area of Almería province.

Andalucía has, in general, what is known as a Mediterranean climate: hot, dry
summers and mild wet winters, with high sunshine totals. The wind pattern is generally westerly in winter and easterly in summer. The coastal areas, particularly the
Costa del Sol, have the most agreeable climate on mainland Europe, which explains
the high number of northern Europeans who settle here. West of Gibraltar, the
levante wind from the east can blow fiercely for days on end. Such is the persistence
and power of the *levante* that suicide rates are said to increase when the wind blows,
while courts are reputedly more lenient in dealing with crimes committed at this
time. In summer, the strong, hot *sirocco* blows up from North Africa, bringing air-
borne sand, high temperatures and low humidity, usually for shorter periods.

While the summer temperatures on the coast are moderated by sea breezes,
inland the heat can be searing. Ejica, in Sevilla province, is known as the *sartenilla de
Andalucía* (the frying pan of Andalucía), and temperatures of over 40°C in summer
are not uncommon. In the east, the province of Almería is noted for its aridity. The
city of Almería itself may have only several days of rain a year, while the interior is
semi-desert. Western Andalucía is wetter than the east, as the prevailing winds come
off the Atlantic Ocean.

Inland, the height of the sierras leads to an increase in precipitation during the
winter months. Apart from the aforementioned Sierra de Grazalema, snowfall on the
Sierra Nevada supports a thriving winter sports industry.

Vegetation and wildlife

The wide diversity of wildlife found in Andalucía is truly amazing. Because of the
geographical isolation of the Iberian peninsula and in particular Andalucía, cut off to
the north by high ranges, the area is rich in endemic species - found nowhere else in
the world.

There are a number of reasons for the region's unique and abundant wildlife.
Andalucía is located at the geographical crossroads where Europe meets Africa and
where the Atlantic connects to the Mediterranean. There is a wide range of habitat
within Andalucía, varying from semi desert in the east to wetlands in the west, from
broad river valleys to high mountain ranges. The coastline, too, provides contrasts,

with dunes, cliffs and salt marshes. The almost landlocked Mediterranean is virtually tideless, but west of Gibraltar the tidal estuaries and beaches provide yet another environment. The original Mediterranean forests were destroyed in prehistoric times and these have been replaced by cork oaks, pines and *maquis*. Farmland, in contrast with northern Europe, also provides a rich habitat, as methods of production are often, while mechanized, still traditional. Furthermore, large areas of Andalucía remain wild and undeveloped. The Andalucían government has enthusiastically promoted the cause of nature conservation. There are over 80 protected areas covering nearly 15,000 sq km, 17% of Andalucía. Both Andalucía and Spain in general used to have a particularly bad reputation for cruelty to animals, indiscriminate shooting and the liming and trapping of birds. This has begun to change in recent years. There is now a network of natural parks and nature reserves, an increasing number equipped with hides, wardens, nature trails and information and interpretation centres.

Plants & trees

There are more than 5,000 species of flowering plant found in Andalucía, a total which includes over 150 which are endemic, mainly found in the Sierra Nevada and the Cazorla range. A favoured spot for botanists is the 'painted fields' area between Vejer and Tarifa, where meadows which have never known pesticides are a riot of colour in spring, with mallows, convolvulus, lupins, irises and squills in abundance. There are, however, flowers to be seen in all seasons, with roadside verges covered with Bermuda buttercups and narcissi as early as January. Even in the aridity of August, coastal dunes can produce surprising numbers of sea daffodils. Alpine plants are found in the Sierra Nevada, where by early to mid summer the snow is melting from the upper slopes. In the *maquis* areas, cistus, rock roses and aromatic herbs, like lavender, rosemary, thyme and oregano, are abundant. A wide range of orchids can be found in all the habitats, but particularly on the limestone soils.

The rare and ancient Spanish fir, the pinsapo, is becoming more common in the Parque Natural de Grazalema, thanks to conservation efforts. Woodlands of encina, or holm oak, sweet chestnut and cork trees are also widespread in certain areas; see boxes on page and 197.

Mammals

There is a wide variety of mammals in Andalucía, although it must be said that many of the species are either very scarce or nocturnal and therefore highly unlikely to be seen. Of the three North African species, the mongoose and genet are quite common, while Barbary macaques have been introduced to Gibraltar. Of the more endangered species, the wolf hangs on in small numbers in the Sierra Morena, while the pardel lynx (of which Andalucía has 60% of the surviving world population) can occasionally be spotted in the Parque Nacional Coto Doñana. Otters, on the other hand, whilst rarely seen are still common. Of the herbivores, both red and fallow deer appear in a number of locations, as do wild boar. The Spanish ibex seems to be increasing its numbers and can be easily seen in the Sierra Nevada, Cazorla, and the Serranía de Ronda, while mouflon – a type of wild sheep - have been introduced in some areas like Cazorla as a game species.

Common hedgehogs are joined along the Costa del Sol by the Algerian variety. Rabbits and hares are common, despite widespread hunting. The garden dormouse is often found in trees close to houses, where it is often persecuted in mistake for a tree rat. There are numerous varieties of bats. Most are of the small pipistrelle type, which will often fly during the day. Indeed, they have frequently been seen hunted by kestrels. The larger noctules are also common. Daubenton 's bats can often be seen taking water and insects from swimming pools.

Both common and bottle nosed dolphins can always be seen in the Straits of Gibraltar, where there are also regular sightings of pilot whales and occasionally orcas.

Background

Butterflies With over 130 species of butterfly, including more than 30 types of blue alone, Andalucía is a lepidopterist's nirvana. Many of the butterflies seen in northern Europe have in fact bred in Andalucía, such as clouded yellows, while others migrate to the area from north Africa, like painted Ladies. There are also a small number of endemics, including Nevada blues and Nevada graylings. Amongst the more spec-tacular and common butterflies are two varieties of swallowtails, Spanish festoons, Cleopatras, the ubiquitous speckled wood and the Moroccan orange tip. Most strik-ing of all is the huge two tailed pasha, which you could easily mistake for a small bird when it is in flight. On occasions, large numbers of American vagrants turn up, including the monarch. There are also a number of day flying moths, of which great peacock moths and hummingbird moths are most likely to be noticed.

Reptiles, amphibians & insects There are some 17 species of amphibian, including a variety of frogs, toads and newts. Of these, the noisy marsh frog and the delightful little green tree frog are notable, while salamanders can often be seen.

Reptiles are widespread, particularly lizards, which vary from the iguana-like ocellated lizard, which can grow up to 1 m in length down to common wall lizards and geckoes. The latter can often be observed at night hunting insects close to elec-tric lights on the side of houses. Also common are the spiny footed lizards found in dunes and other dry habitats, the young being very noticeable with their bright red tails. At waterside margins, two varieties of terrapin can be seen, European pond ter-rapins and striped neck terrapins. Both terrapins and the land based spur thighed tortoise seem to survive hunting for the pet trade. Finally, in the southern coastal fringes of Andalucía, the highly protected chameleon may still be seen in a few places if you´re lucky.

Of the eight species of snake, only one, the latastes viper, is venomous, while the largest is the Montpellier snake, which can grow up to 2 m. Most common are the familiar grass snake and the southern smooth snake.

Amongst the insects the most fascinating is the praying mantis, which may be brown or green. Noisy cicadas, crickets and grasshoppers are heard everywhere dur-ing the summer months. Dung beetles make fascinating watching. The plethora of ants and flies are less welcome.

Birds While Andalucía is attractive for many forms of wildlife, it is the wide selection of birds which is a magnet for naturalists from far afield. There are over 400 birds on the systematic list and nearly half of these breed. It is the only place in Europe where you will find, for example, white-headed ducks, marbled ducks, black shouldered kites, Spanish imperial eagles, purple gallinules, black-bellied sand grouses, red-necked nightjars, Dupont's larks, black wheatears, azure-winged magpies, spotless starlings and trumpeter finches. This is enough to wet the appetite of all keen birdwatchers, let alone the most fanatical 'twitchers'.

The reasons for the wide range of birds are twofold. Firstly, the strategic location of Andalucía at the meeting point of bird migration routes, and secondly the wide variety of available habitats. The assemblage of birds varies according to the season. There are **resident** birds which are present all the year round, which includes many typical Mediterranean species, such as crested larks, crag martins, blue rock thrushes, fan-tailed warblers, short-toed treecreepers and serin. **Winter visitors** include a range of wildfowl and gulls, plus passerines such as meadow pipits, white wagtails, blackcaps and chiffchaffs. **Summer visitors** include such spectacular species as little bitterns, purple herons, black storks, white storks, short-toed eagles, booted eagles, collared pratincoles, bee eaters, rollers and golden orioles. Other birds simply pass through Andalucía on their way north and south - these are called **passage migrants** and include a whole range of warblers, terns, waders and raptors.

All habitats have their attractions, even man-made environments. Hordes of pallid swifts can be seen screaming around unfinished apartment blocks, while golf courses, with their well-watered greens, are particularly appealing to hoopoes, many of which now remain in coastal Andalucía throughout the year. In the west of the region, especially in Cádiz province, church towers and railway pylons are favourite nesting spots for white storks. Nearly all the cathedrals of Andalucía have colonies of lesser kestrels. Even the well tended gardens of villas along the Costa del Sol provide suitable territory for blackbirds and, in the winter, robins and chiffchaffs.

It is the wetlands, however, which attract most birds and birdwatchers. The incomparable Parque Nacional Coto Doñana at the mouth of the Río Guadalquivir is arguably Europe's best wetland reserve. Apart from over 300,000 wintering wildfowl, its breeding species include cattle and little egrets, grey, night and purple herons, spoonbills and white storks. Raptors include black and red kites, short-toed eagles and marsh harriers, while there are some 15 pairs of the rare Spanish imperial eagle within the park boundary. Among other coastal wetlands are the Odiel marshes west of Huelva city and the Cabo de Gata-Níjar in Almería province. There are also a number of inland wetlands, such as the group of freshwater lakes south of Córdoba and the Laguna de Medina east of Cádiz. The salt lake of Fuente de Piedra in Málaga province can have as many as 40,000 breeding flamingoes when conditions are right.

The mountain areas have their own bird communities, which will include raptors such as golden eagles, griffon vultures and Bonelli's eagles. Blue rock thrushes and black wheatears are typical of rocky slopes, while at the highest levels ravens, choughs, Alpine accenters and rock buntings are the specialities.

There are still many roads in Andalucía with telephone wires and these make excellent vantage points and song posts for corn buntings, stonechats, rollers, bee eaters and shrikes, while in the adjacent farmland with its extensive methods of production are great and little bustards, red-legged partridges and Montagu's harriers. The forests, olive groves and *maquis* are also rich in bird life.

Observing the migration   The soaring birds, such as raptors and storks, which migrate to Africa for their winter quarters, face the problem of crossing the Mediterranean Sea. They are obliged to head for the narrowest point, which is the Straits of Gibraltar. Here they gain height in thermals over the land and then attempt to glide over the water (where thermals are usually lacking) to the other side. Observing this movement when conditions are right and numbers are high can be an unforgettable sight. For more details and advice, see box, page .

For a list of recommended wildlife sites, see the map . For full descriptions and details of access, see the regional sections.

Books

Travelogues

There are an abundance of these on Andalucía, many by British writers on the theme of the trials and tribulations of buying a farm and grappling with the local customs and culture.

Baird, David, *Inside Andalusia*, Lookout. A collection from the perceptive monthly travel articles that the author has written for the *Lookout* magazine.
Boyd, Alastair, *The Sierras of the South* (1992), Flamingo. Interesting for its glimpse of pre-package tour Franco's Spain, in and around Ronda with much philosophising by the author about the disappearance of the Andalucían 'arcadia'.
Ford, Richard, *A Handbook for Travellers in Spain* One of the world's great classic travel guides. Written in the mid-19th century, it is full of typically English humour,

condescension and wry observation.

Irving, Washington, *Tales of the Alhambra*. Published in 1832, Irving's romantic account of his residence in the then rundown Alhambra as well as stories of its inhabitants. The book drew attention to what had been a somewhat neglected part of Spain's heritage and the Alhambra was designated a national monument soon after Irving's work was published.

Jacobs, Michael, *Andalucía* (1998), Pallas Athene. The best introduction to the region, this book is a great mix of the erudite and irreverent and an indispensible reference to all things Andalucían. By the same author is *Between Hopes and Memories: A Spanish Journey* (1994) Picador, an entertaining account of the writer's travels through Spain just before the Fifth Centenary celebrations of 1992, including a visit to pre-Expo Sevilla.

Lee, Laurie, *As I Walked Out One Midsummer Morning*, Penguin. Beautifully written classic story of the author's journey at 19 on foot from his home in Wiltshire to Andalucía on the eve of the Spanish Civil War. Also by the same author is A Rose for Winter, in which Laurie Lee returns to his beloved Andalucía after a 15-year gap and finds it as enticingly romantic as before.

Luard, Nicholas, *Andalucía – A Portrait of Southern Spain*, Century. Luard took his family to live in a remote valley between Algeciras and Tarifa and wrote this account of their life there, which is interesting for its historic setting in the change from the Franco period to democracy in the 1960s and 1970s, as well as commentary on this area of Andalucía.

Stewart, Chris, *Driving over lemons*, (1999) Vintage. Popular and candid account of the move of the ex-Genesis guitarist and his family to a farm in the Alpujarras.

Fiction, literary criticism & biography

Brenan, Gerald, *South from Granada*, (1998) Kodansha Globe. This is a perceptive insight into everyday life in an Andalucían *pueblo* in the 1920s, when the English writer Brenan lived in Yegen in the Alpujarras. It is now regarded as a sociological masterpiece. For a fascinating account of Brenan's life, see:

Gathorne-Hardy, Johnathan, *The Interior Castle: A life of Gerald Brenan*.

García Lorca, Federico, *Bodas de Sangre*, (Blood Wedding), *Yerma* and *La Casa de Bernarda Alba*. Lorca's best plays, published between 1933 and 1936, which dealt with the passions and emotions of rural people. Also see his *Lament for the Death of a Bullfighter and other poems*, his most famous series of poems, which emphasized the nobility of the gypsies.

Gibson, Ian, *Lorca's Granada*, Faber and Faber. *Federico García Lorca* Penguin *The Assassination of Federico García Lorca* Pantheon. This trilogy covers walks around places in Granada relating to Lorca; his life; and a reconstruction of his assassination by Franco's men.

Hemingway, Ernest, *Death in the Afternoon* (1996), Touchstone Books. Written in 1932, this is actually a non-fictional book, a classic account of bullfighting, which for Hemingway was an art form and not merely a sport. *For Whom the Bell Tolls* is his famous fictionalised account of the Civil War.

Wildlife

Palmer, Michael, *A Bird Watching Guide to Southern Spain*, Arlequin.

Blum, Joachim, *European Reptiles and Amphibians*, Foulis Spectrum.

Corbett and Overton, *The Mammals of Britain and Europe*, Prion.

Finlayson, Clive, *A Birdwatchers Guide to Southern Spain and Gibraltar*, Collins.

García, Ernest and Patterson, Andrew, *Where to Watch Birds in Southern Spain*, Helm.

Heinsel, Fitter and Parslow, *Guide to the Birds of Britain and Europe* Collins. Along with Peterson et al below, this is one of the best field guides.

Higgins and Hargreaves, *Butterflies of Britain and Europe*, Collins.

Innes, Clive, *Wild Flowers of Spain*, Cockatrice.
Molesworth Allen, Betty, *Wildflowers of Southern Spain*, Mirador Books.
Peterson, Mountford and Hollom, *Field Guide to the Birds of Britain and Europe*, Collins.
Phillips, Roger, *Mediterranean Wild Flowers* Elm Tree Books.
Polunin, Oleg and Huxley, Anthony, *Flowers of the Mediterranean*, Chatto and Windus.
Whallas, Paul, *Pocket Guide to Butterflies*, Mitchell Beazley.

Brenan, Gerald, *The Spanish Labyrinth*, Cambridge University Press. Historic and sometimes personal account of the social and political context leading up to the Civil War.
Elms, Robert, *Spain – A Portrait After the General* (1994). A quasi-sociological and highly idiosyncractic look at Spain in the post Franco years by a former editor of *The Face*.
Fletcher, Richard, *Moorish Spain*, Weidenfeld and Nicholson. Arguably the best account of the history of the Moorish occupation of Southern Spain.
Lalaguna, Juan, *A Traveller's History of Spain*, Windrush. Concise guide from the Moors to the present.
Sultana, Donald, *Benjamin Disraeli in Spain, Malta and Albania 1830-32*, (1976) Tamesis Books.

History

Barrucand, Marianne and **Bednoz, Achim**, *Moorish Architecture*, Taschen. The classic guide to Moorish monuments.
Bevan, Bernard, *History of Spanish Architecture*, Batsford. Marvellous account of the post Moorish development of Spanish architecture. Now out-of-print, but can be found in some second-hand bookshops.
Goodwin, Godfrey, *Islamic Spain* (1990), Penguin. A scholarly guide to Moorish Spain for serious architecture buffs.

Architecture

Gudiol, José, *The Arts of Spain*, Thames and Hudson. Comprehensive account of Spanish art from prehistoric times to the present.

Art

Hunter-Watts, Guy, *Walking in Andalucía* (2000), Santana. Details of specific walks, background information and accommodation.
Craggs, Chris, *Andalusian Rock Climbs*, Cicerone Press. Description of all the major climbs in the area.
Walmsley, Andy, *Walking in the Sierra Nevada*, Cicerone Press. Nearly 50 walks of differing severity are described in one of Andalucía's most popular hiking areas.

Walking guides

Carrick, Bob, *Ventas*, Santana. Details of some of the better *ventas* within easy reach of resorts along the Costa del Sol. Written by an American resident in Andalucía who has tried out more than 70 *ventas* and describes some of their recommended specialities.
Casas, Penelope, *The Foods and Wines of Spain* (1982), Knopf. Considered by many as the definitive book on Spanish cooking, the author is married to a Madrileño and covers regional cuisine as well as tapas and traditional desserts, other than the ubiquitous *flan*.
Luard, Elizabeth, *The La Ina Book of Tapas*, Simon and Schuster. Essential reading for all tapas buffs.
Mendel, Janet, *Cooking in Spain* (1996), Santana. Comprehensive cookbook detailing a wide variety of Spanish regional dishes (including Andalucía), with a useful guide on forages into food markets and shops, extensive glossary and tips on what to buy when.

Food & drink

Background

Millon, Mark and Kim, *Wine Roads of Spain*, HarperCollins. A comprehensive guide to Spanish wines and sherries, their production and location.

Living in Spain **Hampshire, David**, *Living and Working in Spain* (2000), Survival Books. Comprehensive source of information about everyday life in Spain, written with humour and an impressive attention to detail.

Searl, David, *You and the Law in Spain* (2001), Santana. An up-to-date guide to the baffling Spanish bureaucratic procedures, covering everything from starting a business to making a will.

Footnotes

12

Footnotes

Basic Spanish for travellers

Spanish has been described as an easy language to learn. Certainly it is spoken more or less as it appears and travellers who have fluency in other Latin-based languages such as French or Italian should not find it difficult. Bear in mind that in *castellano* or standard Spanish, *z*, and *c* before *e* and *i* are a soft *th*. Other points to remember are that *ll* approximates to the English y, the *h* is invariably silent, while *j* and *g* are pronounced like an *h* when they are at the start of a word. *R's*, and especially double *r's* are rolled, often to excess. When *ñ* has an accent or *tilde* above it, the pronounciation is similar to the English *ny*. When consulting a dictionary, remember that *LL*, *CH* and *Ñ* are considered as separate letters in Spanish.

Emphasis is routine, with stress on the penultimate syllable unless there is an accent. Exceptions are when a word ends in *d*, *l*, *r* or *z*, when emphasis is on the final syllable.

The main problem for visitors to the south of Spain is the Andalucían dialect (or *Andalu'* as it is popularly known). Spoken at bullet-like speed, consonants, and indeed whole syllables, are frequently omitted, particularly at the end of a word. In addition (as in South American) *ci* and *ce* are pronounced with an *s* rather than the castellano lisp, so that *cerveza* (beer) becomes 'sairvaisa' rather than the Madrid 'thairvaitha'. Andalucíans treat all attempts to speak their language with patience and good humour, so that the effort is well worth while.

Numbers

0	*cero*	16	*dieciséis*
1	*uno (m) una (f)*	17	*diecisiete*
2	*dos*	18	*dieciocho*
3	*tres*	19	*diecinueve*
4	*cuatro*	20	*veinte*
5	*cinco*	30	*treinta*
6	*seis*	40	*cuarenta*
7	*siete*	50	*cíncuenta*
8	*ocho*	60	*sesenta*
9	*nueve*	70	*setenta*
10	*diez*	80	*ochenta*
11	*once*	90	*noventa.*
12	*doce*	100	*cien*
13	*trece*	200	*doscientos*
14	*catorce*	300	*trescientos*
15	*quince*	1000	*mil*

Days and months

Sunday	*domingo*	Friday	*viernes*
Monday	*lunes*	Saturday	*sábado*
Tuesday	*martes*	January	*enero*
Wednesday	*miércoles*	February	*febrero*
Thursday	*jueves*	March	*marzo*

April *abril*
May *mayo*
June *junio*
July *julio*
August *agosto*

September *septiembre*
October *octubre*
November *noviembre*
December *dicembre*

Seasons

Spring *la primavera*
Summer *el verano*

Autumn *el otoño*
Winter *el invierno*

Greetings

Hello/Goodbye *Hola/Adiós*
Good morning *Buenos días*
Good afternoon *Buenos tardes*
Good evening *Buenos noches*
See you later *Hasta luego*
How are you? *¿cómo esta?*
Sorry *Perdón/lo siento*
Yes/no *Si/no*
Thank you *Muchas gracias*
OK *Vale*
Excuse me *Con permiso*

It's nothing/you're welcome *De nada*
Do you speak English? *¿Habla Inglés?*
Go away! *¡Márchese!*
I don't understand *No entiendo*
Merry Christmas *¡Feliz Navidad!*
Happy New Year! *¡Feliz Año Nuevo!*
Happy Birthday *¡Feliz cumpleaños!*
Congratulations *¡Enhorabuena!*
Good luck *¡Buena suerte!*
Have a nice trip *¡Buen viaje!*

Other common words

after *después*
afternoon *tarde (f)*
and *y*
before *antes de*
big *grande*
cheap *barato*
chemist *farmacia (f)*
church *iglesia (f)*
closed *cerrado*
cold/hot *frío/caliente*
day/night *día (m)/noche (f)*
doctor *médico/a*
enough *bastante*
evening *tarde (f)*
expensive (too) *caro (demasiado)*
film *pelicula (f)*
forbidden *prohibido*
full *lleno*
good (very good) *bien (muy bien)*
house *casa (f)*
how much? *¿cuánto es?*
is there/are there? *¿hay un ..?*
key *llave (f)*
later *más tarde*
little *pequeño*

market *mercado (m)*
more/less *más/menos*
morning *mañana (f)*
near *cerca*
newspaper *periódico (m)*
new *nuevo*
now *ahora*
open *abierto*
police *policía (f)*
post office *correos (m)*
price *precio (m)*
shop *tienda (f)*
shower *ducha (f)*
small *pequeño*
square *plaza (f)*
stamp *sello (m)*
today *hoy*
toilet *servicio (m)*
tomorrow *mañana*
what? *¿qué?*
when? *¿cuándo?*
where (is)? *¿dónde (esta)?*
why *¿por qué?*
yesterday *ayer*

Geography

Beach *playa (f)*
Castle *castillo (m)*
Cathedral *catedral (f)*
Countryside *campo (m)*
England *Inglaterra (f)*
Europe *Europa (f)*
Fertile plain *vega (f)*
France *Francia (f)*
Forest *bosque (m)*
Germany *Alemania (f)*
Lake *lago (m)*
Morocco *Marruecos (m)*

Port *puerto (m)*
Portugal *Portugal (m)*
Reservoir *Embalso (f)*
River *Río (m)*
Road *carretera (f)*
Sea *mar (f)*
Spain *España (f)*
Street *Calle (f)*
Town/city *ciudad (f)*
United States *Estados Unidos (m)*
Village *pueblo (m)*

Accommodation

Air conditioning *aire acondicionado*
Apartment *apartamento (m)*
Bathroom (with) *(con) baño*
Bed/double bed *cama (f)/cama matrimonial*
Bill *cuenta (f)*
Credit cards *tarjetas de crédito*
Change *cambio (m)*
Country/Inn *albergue (m)*
Heating *calefacción (f)*
Hotel *hotel (m)*
Hostel *hostal (m)*

How much? *¿cuánto es?*
Laundry *lavandería (f)*
Money *dinero (m)*
Receptionist *recepcionista (f)*
Room *habitación (m)*
Shower *ducha (f)*
State run hotel *parador (m)*
Telephone *teléfono (m)*
Toilet *servicio (m)*
View *vista (f)*
Waiter *camarero (m)*
Water (hot) *agua (caliente)*

Travel

airport *aeropuerto (m)*
arrival *llegada (f)*
bus *autobus (m)*
bus station *estación de autobuses (f)*
car *coche (m)*
car hire *alquilar de coches*
customs *aduana (f)*
departure *salida (f)*
duty free *libre de impuestos*
fare *precio del billete (m)*
ferry (boat) *barca (f)*
garage *taller (m)*
left luggage *consigna (f)*
map *mapa (m)*
oil (engine) *aceite (m)*

papers (documents) *documentación (f)*
parking *aparcamiento (m)*
passport *pasaporte (m)*
petrol *gasolina (f)*
puncture *pinchazo (m)*
railway *ferrocarril (m)*
taxi *taxi (m)*
taxi rank *parada de taxis (f)*
ticket (single/return) *billete (m) (de ida/devuelta)*
ticket (return) *billete de ida y vuelta (m)*
what time is it? *¿qué hora es?*
train station *estación de trenes (f)*
train *tren (m)*
tyre *neumá tico (m)*

Food glossary

Essential food

aceite (de olivo) (olive) oil
arroz rice
azúcar sugar
bollo bread roll
huevo egg
miel honey

pimienta black pepper
pan bread
pan integral wholemeal bread
sal salt
vinagre vinegar

Common terms

a la brasa charcoal grilled
a la plancha grilled on a hotplate
adobo marinade
al horno baked
al vapor steamed
albondigas meatballs
aliño dressing or marinade
alioli garlic mayonnaise
asado/a roasted
bocadillo sandwich
caldereta stew
caldo meat and/or vegetable broth
caliente hot
casero/a homemade
cazuela casserole
chuleta chop (eg pork or lamb)
cocido stew of meat, pulses and
vegetables, or cooke
d/boiled
congelado a frozen
costilla rib
crema cream, as in cream of tomato
soup
crudo raw
croquetas croquettes
duro hard boiled
empanada pie
empanado/a fried in breadcrumbs
encebollado/a cooked with onions
ensalada salad
escabeche marinade

estofado stew
fiambre paté
filete steak (meat); fillet (fish)
frito/a fried
fritura mixta de pescados selection of
fried fish
fresco/a fresh
frío/a cold
guiso stew
jamón ham
manteca lard
migas fried breadcrumbs with garlic
olla cooking pot
paella rice cooked with saffron, meat,
fish or shellfish
picante spicy hot
pisto vegetable stew
plato combinado dish of two or more
items, such as pork and chips
potaje thick soup or stew
ración a larger portion than a tapas
amount
rebozado/a fried in batter
relleno/a stuffed
revuelta scrambled eggs dish
salado/a salted
salsa sauce
sopa soup
surtido assortment
tortilla omelette
tostado/a toasted/toast

Fish *pescado* and seafood *mariscos*

almejas clams
anchoa anchovies (usually tinned)
atún tuna
bacalao dried salt codfish
boquerones fresh anchovies

caballa mackerel
calamares squid
camarones small prawns
cangrejo crab
cazón dogfish

chiporones baby squid
choco cuttlefish
dorada sea bass
gambas prawns
huevas fish roe
langostino large prawns
lenguado sole
lubina sea bass

mariscos seafood
mejillones mussels
melva a type of tuna, usually tinned
merluza hake
mero grouper sea bass
pescadilla whiting
pez espada swordfish

Meat *carne* and poultry *ave*

caña de lomo cured pork loin sausage
caracoles snails
caza game
cerdo pork
chacina cured meat
chorizo spicy cured pork sausage
conejo rabbit
cordero lamb
embutidos sausages
hígado liver
jamón (serrano) (cured) ham
lengua tongue
lomo loin (usually pork)

morcilla black pudding
rabo de toro oxtail
pata negra cured ham from Iberian pigs
pato duck
pavo turkey
pechuga breast (poultry)
pinchito skewered kebab
pollo chicken
riñones kidneys
salchicha sausage
salchichón salami sausage
solomillo sirloin (usually pork)
tocino bacon

Dairy products

desnatada skimmed
leche (entera) (whole) milk
mantequilla butter

nata fresh cream
queso cheese
yogurt yoghurt

Vegetables *legumbres*

aceitunas olives
aguacate avocado
ajo garlic
albahaca basil
alcaparras capers
alcaparrones large capers
almendras almonds
berenjena aubergine
cebolla onion
champiñones cultivated mushrooms
cilantro coriander
col cabbage
coliflor cauliflower
espárrrgos asparagus

espinacas spinach
garbanzos chick peas
guisantes peas
habas broad beans
laurel bay leaf
lechuga lettuce
lentejas lentils
patatas potatoes
pepino cucumber
perejil parsley
Remolacha beetroot
setas wild mushrooms
tomate tomato
zanahoria carrot

Footnotes

Fruit *fruta*

caqui persimmon
cereza cherry
chirimoya custard apple
ciruela plum
datiles dates
fresa strawberry
granada pomegranate
higo fig
limón lemon
manzana apple
melocotón peach

membrillo quince
naranja orange
nectarina nectarine
pasas raisins
pera pear
piña pineapple
plátano banana
sandía watermelon
uvas grapes
zarzamora blackberry

Dessert/sweets *postre/dulces*

bizcocho sponge cake
galleta biscuit
helado ice-cream
pastel pie or cake

rosco doughnut
turrón nougat
yema sweet made of egg yolks

A tapas taster

Atún a la plancha fresh tuna
Patatas fritas in a restaurant means chips, but in a bar it could mean crisps. You may be asked if you want them *de bolsa* (in a bag) or *de la cocina* (literally, from the kitchen); crisps or chips, respectively.
albóndigas homemade meatballs
boquerones fresh anchovies
caña de lomo cured pork loin sausage
caracoles snails
cazón en adobo chunks of dogfish that has been marinated then deepfried
champiñones con jamón mushrooms with ham
chipirónes a la plancha grilled baby squid
choco frito fried cuttlefish
croquetas caseras homemade croquettes
ensaladilla Rusa Russian salad

espinaca con garbanzos spinach with chickpeas
gambas al ajillo shrimps cooked in garlic and oil (and sometimes chilli)
gazpacho chilled tomato and garlic soup
jamón serrano cured ham
lomo a la plancha grilled pork loin
manitas de cerdo pig's trotters
montadito de melva toasted sandwich of a type of tinned tuna
patatas alioli potatoes in garlic mayonnaise
pimientos asados roasted red peppers in oil
queso de oveja/cabra sheep/goat's cheese
serranito bread roll with ham, pork, grilled green pepper and fried egg
tortilla Española typical Spanish potato omelette

Drinks *bebidas*

a tiempo at room temperature
agua (de grifo) (tap) water
agua mineral con gas fizzy mineral water
agua mineral sin gas still mineral water
botella bottle
café con leche white coffee
café solo espresso coffee
cerveza beer
cava a type of Spanish champagne
chocolate hot chocolate
coñac brandy
descafeinado decaffinated
fino sherry
frio a cold
gaseosa fizzy drink

(con/sin) hielo (with/without) ice
horchata tiger nut or almond drink
infusión (de Manzanilla) herbal (camomile) tea
limonada lemonade
naranjada orangeade
refresco soft drink
ron rum
sangría red wine punch
sidra cider
té tea
tinto de verano red wine and lemonade
vino blanco/dulce/tinto white/sweet /red wine
zumo fruit juice

Eating out

camarero/a waiter/waitress
cuchara spoon
almuerzo lunch
carta menu
cena dinner
copa cup
cuchillo knife
cuenta bill
desayuno breakfast
menú del día set menu
merienda morning/afternoon snack
mesa table
plato course, dish or plate
serviettas napkins
silla chair
silla alta high chair
taza cup
tenador fork
vaso glass

Quiero reservar una mesa I would like to reserve a table
¿Tiene usted una mesa para dos personas? Do you have a table for two?
¿Podría ver la carta/la lista de vino? Could I see the menu/wine list?
¿Qué recomendería usted? What do you recommend?
Soy vegetariano/a I'm vegetarian
Puedo tener otro… Can I have another…
La cuenta, por favor Could I have the bill, please?
¿Está incluido la IVA/ el servicio? Is IVA/service included?

Index

Shorts

Special interest pieces on or about Andalucía

Map Index

Footnotes

Advert Index

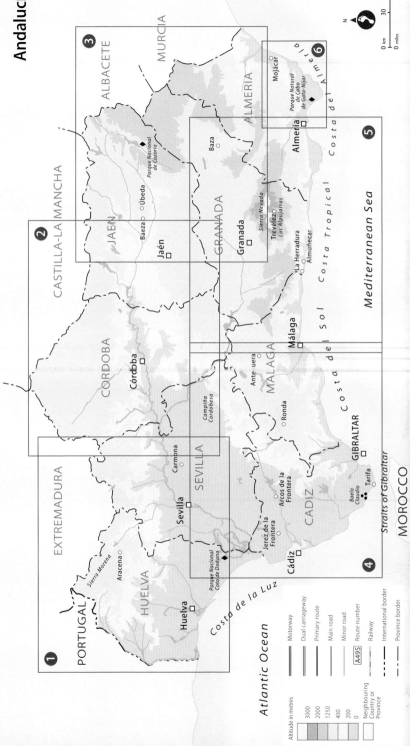

Andalucía

EXTREMADURA

Embalse de Aracena

Rivera de Huelva

Guadalcanal

Alanís

Embalse del Pintado

Real de la Jara

Santa Olalla del Cala

M

o

r

e

n

a

Cazalla de la Sierra

◆ *Parque Natural Sierra Norte*

Higuera de la Sierra

Zufre

Almadén de la Plata

A461

N630

El Pedroso

Constantina

N433

Embalse de Cala

Embalse de Minilla

Ronquillo

A432

A455

Castillo de las Guardas

El Garrobo

Cantillana

A431

Lora del Rio

Embalse del Agrio

Embalse del Gérgal

Valliverde del Rio

Río Guadalquivir

Gerena

Guillena

Brenes

Aznalcóllar

Alcalá del Rio

N630

SEVILLA

Italica

Santiponce

A472

Sanlúcar La Mayor

A49

NIV

Carmona

A455

Map 4

C

inojos

Pilas

Sevilla ✈

A92

A460

Aznalcázar

Alcalá de Guadaira

Coria del Rio

Río Guadalquivir

Map 2

Marchena

Villafranco del Guadalquivir

Isla Menor

Dos Hermanas

A4

A443

4

NIV

5

6

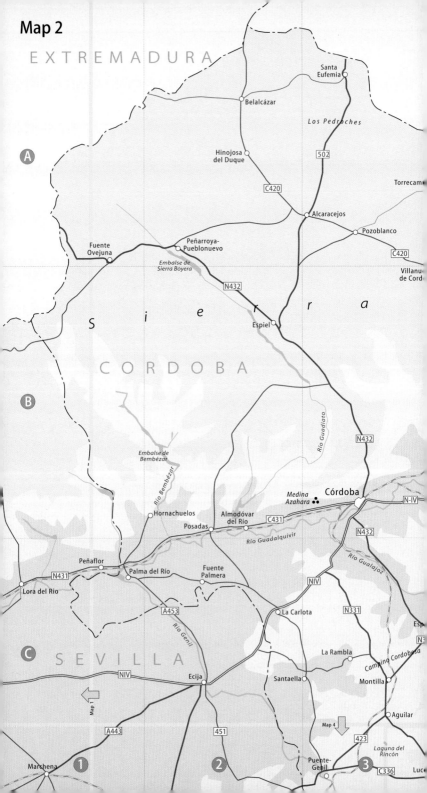

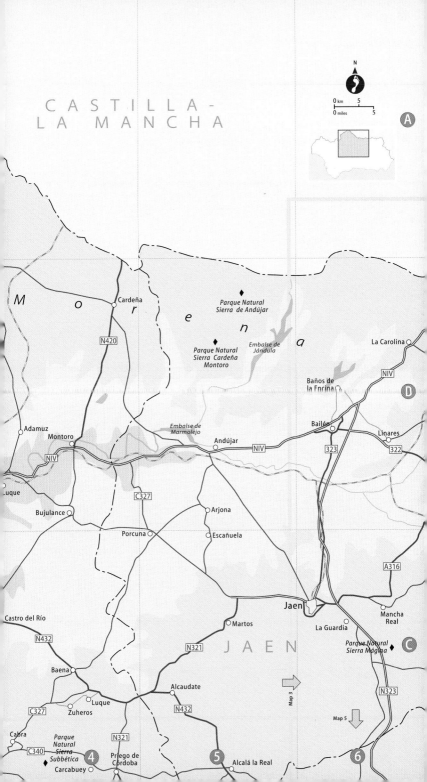

CASTILLA-
LA MANCHA

N

0 km   5
0 miles   5

A

M   o   r   e   n   a

Cardeña

N420

Parque Natural
Sierra de Andújar

Parque Natural
Sierra Cardeña
Montoro

Embalse de
Jándula

La Carolina

Baños de
la Encina

NIV

D

Adamuz

Montoro

NIV

Luque

Embalse de
Marmolejo

Andújar   NIV

Bailén

Linares

323

322

Bujulance

C327

Arjona

Porcuna

Escañuela

A316

Castro del Río

N432

Baena

Martos

N321

J   A   E   N

Jaen

La Guardia

Mancha
Real

Parque Natural
Sierra Mágina

C

Map 3

Alcaudate

N432

N323

Luque

C327

Zuheros

Cabra

C340

Parque
Natural
Sierra
Subbética

N321

Carcabuey

4

Priego de
Cordoba

5

Alcalá la Real

Map 5

6

Map 3

CASTILLA-LA MANCHA

Despeñaperros Pass

Parque Natural Despeñaperros

Río Guadalén

Embalse d Guadalme

A

La Carolina

A401

Embalse de Panzacola

Santisteban del Puerto

Baños de la Encina

NIV

Embalse de Guadalén

Arquillos

Sorihuela de Guadalimar

Beas de Segura

Villanueva del Arzobispo

Bailén

323

Linares

Río Guadalimit

Iznatorof

Río Guadalén

N322

Villacarrillo

N322

Baeza

Torreperogil

Río Guadalquivir

Coto Rí Torre del Vinagre

Úbeda

J A E N

Puerto de las Palomas (1,290m)

Parque Natur Sierras de Cazorla, Segur Las Villas

316

A401

La Iruela

Peal de Becerro

Cazorla

Jimena

Jódar

Parador el Adelantado

Sierra de Cazorla

Jaén

Mancha Real

Map 2

Quesada

B

La Guardia

Parque Natural Sierra Mágina

Los Rosales

A324

Huesa

Parque Natura Sierra d Castril

N323

Huelma

Hinejares

A401

Pozo Alcón

Map 5

Guadahortuna

Embalse de Negratín

Torre-Cardela

Zújar

Freila

Ba

A92N

Iznalloz

G R A N A D A

Baul

C

N323

A92

Gor

Parque Natural Sierra de Baza

Parque Natural Sierra de Huétor

Purullena

Guadix

Granada

A92

N323

1

Parque Natural Sierra Nevada

2

Ferreira

3

A92

N

0 km 5
0 miles 5

Ⓐ

N322

Génave

ente de
énave

Siles

a Puerta
e Segura

Orcera

Segura
de la Sierra

Parque Natural
Sierras de
◆ Cazorla, Segura y
Las Villas

Hornos de
Segura
anco

nbalse del
nco de Beas

Sierra de Almorchón

M U R C I A

Puebla de
Don Fadrique

Ⓑ

Huéscar

A330

Parque Natural
Sierra de María
◆

María
(2,406m) ▲

Vélez
Blanco

Sierra de María

Vélez
Rubio

342

Cúllar Baza

A92N

Sierra de las Estancias

Ⓒ

Pulpí

Tíjola Purchena Olula

A334

Huércal-Overa

Cantoria

Cantoria

Río Almanzora

A L M E R I A

Albánchez

N340

Cuevas de
Almanzora

Sierra de los Filabres

Puerto de la Virgen
(1,070m)

C3325

④

⑤

Uleila

Vera

⑥

Palomares

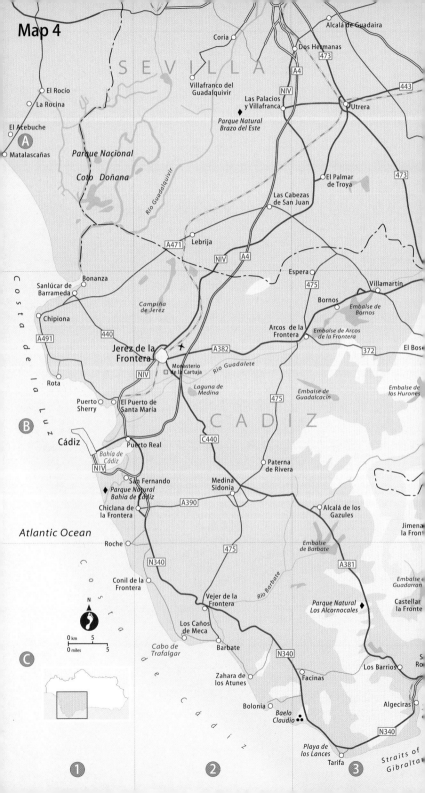

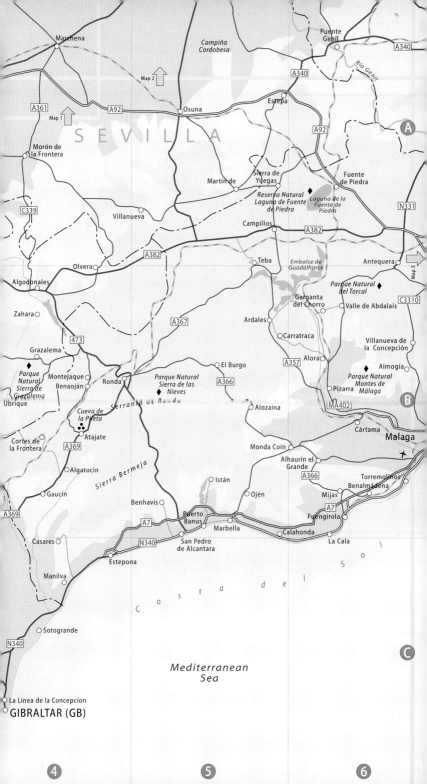

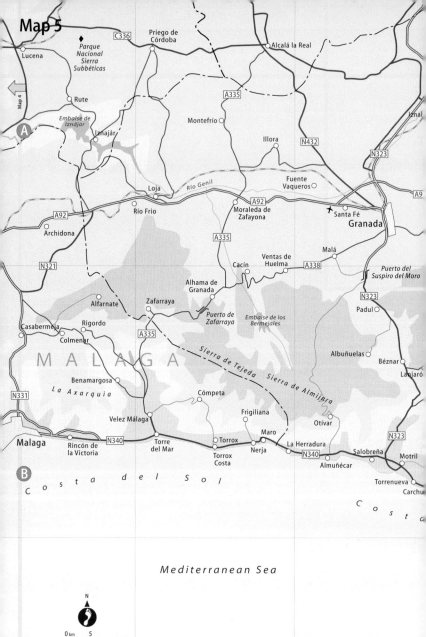

Map 5

Lucena

C336

Priego de Córdoba

Alcalá la Real

◆ *Parque Nacional Sierra Subbéticas*

Rute

A335

Iznal

A

Embalse de Iznájar

Iznájar

Montefrío

Illora

N432

N323

Loja

Río Genil

Fuente Vaqueros

Santa Fé

A9

A92

Río Frio

Moraleda de Zafayona

A92

Granada

Archidona

A335

Malá

N321

Cacín

Ventas de Huelma

A338

Puerto del Suspiro del Moro

Alhama de Granada

N323

Alfarnate

Zafarraya

Padul

Casabermeja

Rigordo

A335

Puerto de Zafarraya

Embalse de los Bermejales

Albuñuelas

Béznar

Colmenar

M A L A G A

Sierra de Tejeda

Sierra de Almijara

Lanjaró

Benamargosa

La Axarquia

Cómpeta

N331

Frigiliana

Otívar

Velez Málaga

Maro

N323

Malaga

Rincón de la Victoria

N340

Torre del Mar

Torrox

Torrox Costa

Nerja

La Herradura

N340

Salobreña

Motril

Almuñécar

B

C o s t a   d e l   S o l

Torrenueva

Carchu

C o s t a

C

Mediterranean Sea

N

0 km 5

0 miles 5

①   **②**   **③**

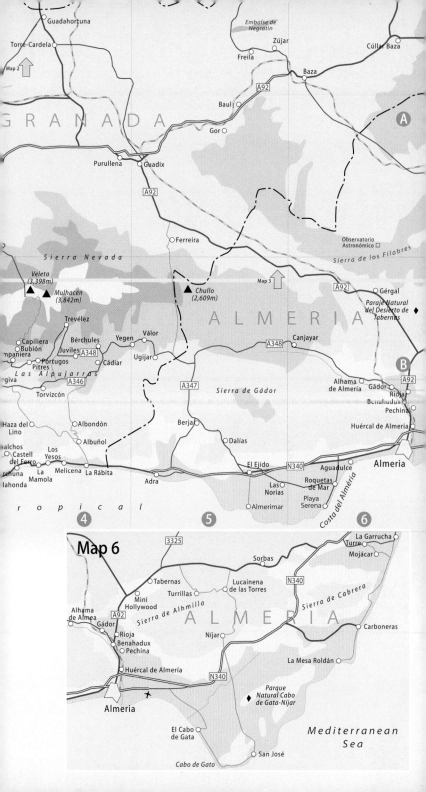

Footprint travel list

Footprint publish travel guides to over 120 countries worldwide. Each guide is packed with practical, concise and colourful information for everybody from first-time travellers to travel aficionados . The list is growing fast and current titles are noted below. For further information check out the website **www.footprintbooks.com**

Andalucía Handbook
Argentina Handbook
Bali & the Eastern Isles Hbk
Bangkok & the Beaches Hbk
Barcelona Handbook
Bolivia Handbook
Brazil Handbook
Cambodia Handbook
Caribbean Islands Handbook
Central America & Mexico Hbk
Chile Handbook
Colombia Handbook
Costa Rica Handbook
Cuba Handbook
Cusco & the Sacred Valley Hbk
Dominican Republic Handbook
Dublin Handbook
East Africa Handbook
Ecuador & Galápagos Handbook
Edinburgh Handbook
Egypt Handbook
Goa Handbook
Guatemala Handbook
India Handbook
Indian Himalaya Handbook
Indonesia Handbook
Ireland Handbook
Israel Handbook
Jordan Handbook
Laos Handbook
Libya Handbook
London Handbook
Malaysia Handbook
Marrakech & the High Atlas Hbk
Myanmar Handbook
Mexico Handbook
Morocco Handbook

Namibia Handbook
Nepal Handbook
New Zealand Handbook
Nicaragua Handbook
Pakistan Handbook
Peru Handbook
Rajasthan & Gujarat Handbook
Rio de Janeiro Handbook
Scotland Handbook
Scotland Highlands & Islands Hbk
Singapore Handbook
South Africa Handbook
South American Handbook
South India Handbook
Sri Lanka Handbook
Sumatra Handbook
Syria & Lebanon Handbook
Thailand Handbook
Tibet Handbook
Tunisia Handbook
Turkey Handbook
Venezuela Handbook
Vietnam Handbook

Also available from Footprint
Traveller's Handbook
Traveller's Healthbook
Traveller's Internet Guide

Available at all good bookshops

What the papers say

"I carried the South American Handbook from Cape Horn to Cartagena and consulted it every night for two and a half months. I wouldn't do that for anything else except my hip flask."
Michael Palin, BBC Full Circle

"The titles in the Footprint Handbooks series are about as comprehensive as travel guides get."
Travel Reference Library

"If 'the essence of real travel' is what you have been secretly yearning for all these years, then Footprint are the guides for you."
Under 26 magazine

"Excellent, best buy whether travelling independently or with a tour operator."
Adventure Travel

"Footprint can be depended on for accurate travel information and for imparting a deep sense of respect for the lands and people they cover."
World News

"Footprint Handbooks, the best of the best."
Le Monde, Paris

Mail order
Available worldwide in bookshops and on-line. Footprint travel guides can also be ordered directly from us in Bath, via our website **www.footprintbooks.com** or from the address on the imprint page of this book.

www.footprintbooks.com
A new place to visit

Acknowledgements

The author wishes to thank the many readers of the previous editions, too numerous to mention here, who have made suggestions and updates. The information contained in this edition is, as far as possible, correct at the time of going to print. However, details change, inflation rears its ugly head and restaurants change hands and decline (or improve). For this reason, all these letters and emails are gratefully received.

Thanks also to countless friends and acquaintances in Andalucía, who all contributed, often unwittingly, to this Handbook. Finally my gratitude goes to my wife for her patience and help in situations which often went beyond the call of duty.

The publishers wish to thank Josephine Hodgson for her contributions to the cities of Granada, Córdoba and Málaga; Jo Williams for her thorough update of the Sevilla chapter, Essentials and the Sierra de Aracena; and Sarah Thorowgood for her continued contribution to the Handbook, this time for updating the Cádiz chapter. Most of the walks in this guide are taken from *Walking in Andalucía* by Guy Hunter-Watts, published by Santana Books. Finally thanks to Louise Pole-Baker for her piece on flamenco and Jack Fortune for his useful comments.

Rowlead Mead

Rowland first went to Spain in the late 1960s with a minisail on the roof of his car and binoculars around his neck. He has been hooked ever since on Andalucía's variety of culture, landscape, wildlife and food.

He has a house in Andalucía and lives there for three or four months of the year. The area satisfies all of his main interests; church architecture, wildlife, geology, beach sociology, food and wine and all at a suitably leisurely Andalucía pace. Rowland also reguarly contributes articles to magazines on wildlife and travel.

Map symbols

Administration
International border
Regional border
Regional capital
Other town

Roads and travel
Urban
Main through route
Main street
Minor street
Pedestrianized street
One way street
Regional
National highway
Main road
Other road
Jeepable road/track
Footpath
Railway with station

Sights and services
Sleeping
Eating
Sight
Building
Parking
Steps
Park, garden, stadium
Fortified wall
Airport
Bus station
Hospital
Market
Museum
Cathedral, church
Mosque

Synagogue
Petrol station
Police station
Bank
Post office
Telephone office
Internet
Tourist office
Guided route
Bridge
Archaeological site
Vineyard, bodega
Golf course
Viewing point
National park, wildlife
    sanctuary
Camp site
Palm trees
Detail map

Water features
River
Lake, reservoir tank
Sand bank, beach
Seasonal marshland
Ocean
Waterfall
Ferry

Topographical features
Contours (approx),
    rock outcrop
Mountain
Mountain pass
Gorge
Escarpment

Weights and measures

Weight
1 kilogram = 2.205 pounds
1 pound = 0.454 kilograms

Capacity
1 litre = 0.220 gallons
1 gallon = 4.546 litres
1 pint = 0.863 litres

Length
1 metre = 1.094 yards
1 yard = 0.914 metres

1 kilometre = 0.621 miles
1 mile = 1.609 kilometres

See inside front cover for hotel price guide, exchange rates, useful dialling codes and credit card websites.

"Who should pack Footprint guides – people who want to escape the crowd."
The Observer

As one of the sunniest parts of Europe, Andalucía is for those who like it hot, as well as those who have a passion for the fiery things in life. More tranquil types could treat themselves to tapas and meander around a medieval church, before sleeping off the excitement in a siesta.

★ Places to sleep and eat from paradores to paella stalls

★ Details for those who want to climb a rock face or take a stroll in the sierras

★ Dip into Andalucía's rich history, from Roman baths to Moorish mezquitas

www.footprintbooks.com

Andalucía Handbook
UK & worldwide £11.99   USA $19.95
ISBN 1 900949 83 0

90000

9 781900 949835

Distribution: UK and worldwide by Footprint; USA by Publishers Group West